FROMMER'S

COMPREHENSIVE TRAVEL GUIDE

NEW YORK STATE

4TH EDITION

by John Foreman

PRENTICE HALL TRAVEL

NEW YORK • LONDON • TORONTO • SYDNEY • TOKYO • SINGAPORE

FROMMER BOOKS

Published by Prentice Hall General Reference
A division of Simon & Schuster Inc.
15 Columbus Circle
New York, NY 10023

ISBN 0-671-86657-5
ISSN 1044-2308

Text design by Levavi & Levavi, Inc.

FROMMER'S EDITORIAL STAFF
Editorial Director: Marilyn Wood
Editorial Manager/Senior Editor: Alice Fellows
Senior Editors: Sara Hinsey Raveret, Lisa Renaud
Editors: Charlotte Allstrom, Thomas F. Hirsch, Peter Katucki, Theodore Stavrou
Assistant Editors: Margaret Bowen, Christopher Hollander, Alice Thompson, Ian Wilker
Editorial Assistants: Gretchen Henderson, Bethany Jewett
Managing Editor: Leanne Coupe

Special Sales
Bulk purchases (10+ copies) of Frommer's Travel Guides are available to corporations at special discounts. The Special Sales Department can produce custom editions to be used as premiums and/or for sales promotion to suit individual needs. Existing editions can be produced with custom cover imprints such as a corporate logo. For more information write to: Special Sales, Prentice Hall Travel, 15 Columbus Circle, New York, NY 10023.

Manufactured in the United States of America

CONTENTS

MAPS

ACKNOWLEDGMENTS

The author wishes to thank Jean Marie Echementia-Marcogliese and Robbe and Susan Stimson for their professional research and editorial assistance in the preparation of this edition of *Frommer's New York State*.

Invitation to the Readers

In researching this book, I have come across many wonderful establishments, the best of which I have included here. I am sure that many of you will also come across appealing hotels, inns, restaurants, guest houses, shops, and attractions. Please don't keep them to yourself. Share your experiences, especially if you want to comment on places that have been included in this edition that have changed for the worse. You can address your letters to:

John Foreman
Frommer's New York State 4th Edition
c/o Prentice Hall Travel
15 Columbus Circle
New York, NY 10023

A Disclaimer

Readers are advised that prices fluctuate in the course of time and travel information changes under the impact of the varied and volatile factors that affect the travel industry. Neither the author nor the publisher can be held responsible for the experiences of readers while traveling. Readers are invited to write to the publisher with ideas, comments, and suggestions for future editions.

Safety Advisory

Whenever you're traveling in an unfamiliar city or country, stay alert. Be aware of your immediate surroundings. Wear a moneybelt and keep a close eye on your possessions. Be particularly careful with cameras, purses, and wallets, all favorite targets of thieves and pickpockets.

INTRODUCING NEW YORK STATE

I'll bet you have opinions about New York already, even if you've never been here. Most people do, and most of these opinions conflict. Well, it's hard to achieve a consensus on a subject so vast and diverse. Over 500 miles of highway stretch from Niagara Falls to Montauk Point. And between those two watery locales lies everything from the largest wilderness park in America to the most sophisticated urban center in the world. New Yorkers as a group don't have all that much in common. How, then, did this place ever come to be?

1. A Brief History of New York State

Before Europeans arrived, Algonquian Indians lived in the Hudson River area and on Long Island, and Iroquoian Indians inhabited central and western New York State. In the late 16th century, the latter formed the great Iroquois Confederation, which was symbolized by an eternal flame that burned as late as the 1870s, a reminder to any who cared to notice that organized society in New York State predated the Dutch and the English by a considerable amount of time. The confederation, while strong, was never exactly placid. Resentments and jealousies among the constituent groups, such as the Cayuga, Mohawk, Oneida, and Seneca, were a constant leitmotif. The very first thing the early European arrivals did was to foment and aggravate these differences to the maximum degree possible.

EARLY TRADING MORALS
The French were perhaps the most perfidious. Or at least they perfected the tactics earliest. The first of them were traders out to make a buck without much care or respect for their Native American counterparts. The easiest and most profitable of the early trades was in fur. French traders made a practice of promising rights to one tribe, then delivering them to another. Unhappy Onondaga would arrive at a trading post with canoes full of hides, only to find the traders gone, having already consummated a deal with competing Cayuga. The result was one local war after another, wherein Indians fought one another bitterly in order to secure deals with the elusive white men.
To be fair, it wasn't just the French who engaged in commercial double cross-

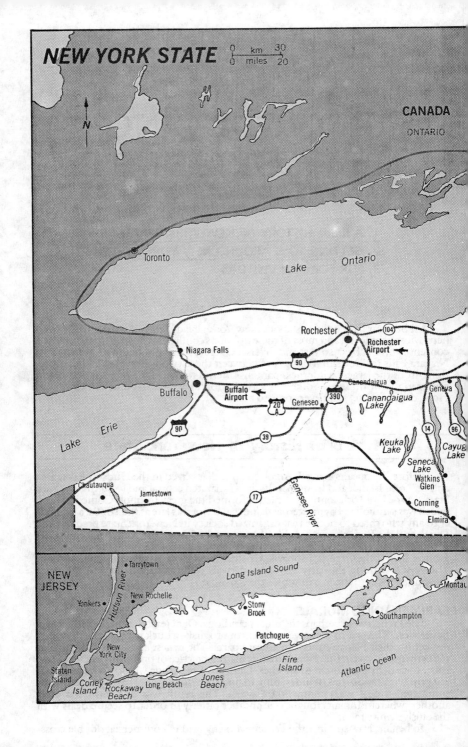

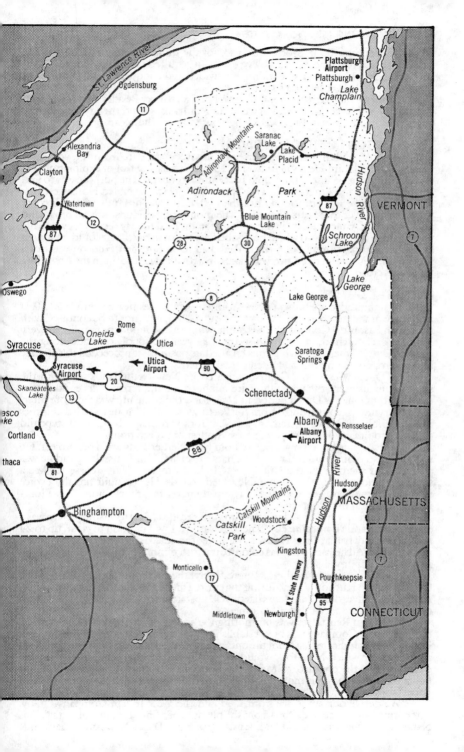

ing. All Europeans did it. Worse luck, too, for the Indians, since they had become
fatally susceptible to these tactics by virtue of an acquired taste for whisky and fire-
arms. They found themselves continually divided and conquered, and the old Iroquois order no longer seemed to work.

Of course, the Native Americans never had a chance. Besides newly acquired
tastes, they had to contend with newly acquired diseases. And then there were the
never-ending numbers of Europeans who poured across the ocean.

THE "HUDSON" OF HUDSON RIVER

New York traditionally considers its "discovery" to date from the voyage of
Hendrik (we call him Henry) Hudson in 1609. This daring feat of exploration was
undertaken at the behest of the Dutch East India Company. The purpose was to find
a passage across the Americas into the spice-rich Pacific, the fabled Northwest Passage. The passage was not found until the 19th century, but Hudson did discover
the beautiful river that bears his name. The mouth of the Hudson is so broad and
salty that, for a while at least, he must have thought he'd hit pay dirt. But eventually
the splendid waterway into which he'd sailed grew so narrow that it could no longer
be mistaken for anything but a river. Well, bad luck. But then Hudson was not a
lucky man. His career ended two years later, in a rowboat cast adrift in the Arctic by a
mutinous crew.

ENTER THE DUTCH

The significance of Hudson's New York adventure became clearer in 1621. This
is the date of the charter of the Dutch West India Company (not to be confused with
the Dutch East India Company). This outfit, whose name should be familiar to every
New York schoolchild, managed to secure a 24-year monopoly on trade along the
coast of Dutch America. Having thus ensured its position, it proceeded to colonize
its new property along typical Dutch feudal patterns.

The Dutch West India Company treated its New Netherlands turf with the
same vague disinterest that a millionaire might treat a not terribly clever poor relation. Throughout the Dutch period in New York, the company was far more interested in trying to capture Brazil from the Portuguese and cultivate its richer colonies
in the Caribbean. New Amsterdam, as New York was then called, was a stepchild
that never quite lived up even to the most modest of expectations.

There was one man, however, to whom New Netherlands was a pet project. He
was an Amsterdam diamond merchant named Kiliaen Van Rensselaer, and he was
also a board member of the Dutch West India Company. Van Rensselaer was a
tireless promoter of colonization in New Netherlands. He was quite literally a voice
in the wilderness, however, since the company never had much more than a luke-
warm interest in the property.

Undaunted, Van Rensselaer came up with the idea of patroonships. Here was a
concept with scale if nothing else. The idea was to allow a patroon to claim up to 24
miles along any bank of the Hudson, or along the seacoast if he so desired, and it
would be his. All he had to do was colonize it with a minimum of 50 settlers within a
maximum of four years.

Sounds like a good deal, no? Interestingly, the total number of patroonships
founded in the Hudson Valley during the entire Dutch period came to a measly five.
And of those five, only Van Rensselaerwyck, upstate, ever succeeded for any length
of time. But more about that in a moment.

While Van Rensselaer was promoting the spread of Dutch feudalism upstate,
the West India Company was busy establishing its trading post at New Amsterdam.
Early accounts indicate that from the outset New Amsterdam demonstrated personality traits for which New York would eventually become famous. In 1644, it was
estimated that the populace of Manhattan spoke in 18 different languages. A Jesuit
father named Jogues was moved to observe that the place had all the "arrogance of
Babel" as well.

"We derive our authority from God and the West Indian Company," Gov.
Peter Stuyvesant once said, "not from the pleasure of a few ignorant subjects." This
blatant tone belies the live-and-let-live quality of life in Dutch New Amsterdam. Side

by side with the rowdy elements that offended Father Jogues was a prosperous and placid middle class whose nature was singularly Dutch. New Amsterdam looked like a miniature Holland, complete with step-roofed gables, winding canals, fat burghers, cows browsing in the streets, and immaculate gardens. Life was certainly milder here than in nearby New England. The Dutch never went in for the hellfire and brimstone of the English Puritans. To the contrary, they tolerated other people's religions, celebrated Christmas with Santa Claus and stockings full of presents (unheard of in the Puritan north), drank a lot of beer, told a lot of jokes, and were generally a warm-blooded lot.

At least such was the case down in New Amsterdam. Up north in patroon country nobody seemed to be cooperating. Native Americans kept raiding, settlers were almost impossible to obtain, and the Dutch West India Company was barely interested in what happened upriver, even when it affected the fur trade. And on top of it all, 17th-century Holland was, quite simply, a much more wonderful place to live. It was rich, tolerant, and stable. Few wanted to leave.

ENTER THE ENGLISH

The Dutch era in New York trundled along with its unique blend of cantankerousness and surface calm until 1664. In that year the king of England, Charles II, decided simply to expropriate Holland's possessions in North America. Highhanded, no? Well, Dutch New Netherlands lay inconveniently between English New England and English Virginia. The king's government was vexed by the problems this created in the uniform administration of English trade and navigation acts. One supposes that the day finally arrived when some minister wondered aloud why His Majesty didn't just kick the Dutch out. And that's exactly what he did.

Stuyvesant wanted to fight. The citizenry, however, would have none of it. Faced with a refusal by the populace to do anything that might jeopardize their property, the Dutch governor accepted the inevitable and handed power over to the English. The terms of surrender were exceedingly generous. Property rights were fully confirmed. Religious freedom continued. Court decisions reached during the Dutch period were all confirmed. Even the apparatus of local government was left intact. Instead of the West India Company, the populace found itself under the ultimate power and authority of the king's brother, James, Duke of York. Day-to-day life barely missed a beat.

If the English had continued to govern as benignly as they started, there might never have been an American Revolution. The duke of York was a concerned and tolerant proprietor. Alas, his new possession netted him no better return than it had his Dutch predecessors. New York simply was not a good investment. It cost a fortune to defend and its inhabitants loathed paying taxes. It was prosperous enough as little towns in the boondocks went, but it wasn't making anyone in England rich.

A string of English governors administered New York. Some were better than others. One celebrated case (Lord Cornbury) conducted his administration wearing women's dresses. But the needs and wants of England grew increasingly at variance with those of its colonies. On the eve of the American Revolution the English considered the colonists, with some justification, to be a bunch of ingrates. After all they'd done for us, we'd never come close to paying them back.

THE REVOLUTION

And so the deluge broke. For New York City, it really was a deluge. It's hard to imagine the barbarism that took place in the city during those years. While major battles were fought all along the Hudson Valley, notably at Saratoga, the city itself suffered a different fate. It was occupied by the British from the start of the war until its very end. The first thing that happened was a mysterious fire that transformed half the town into a pile of ashes. Then came long years during which houses were plundered; women were raped; husbands and fathers were beaten and branded; and the pleasant countryside of Manhattan, Long Island, and lower Westchester became an armed no-man's-land where law resided in the barrel of a gun.

Upstate, things were only slightly better. The Native Americans allied themselves with the British, putting every country settlement in jeopardy. Probably, the

Iroquois Confederation saw in the Revolution its last chance to reassert ancient prerogatives. Ultimately, Native American raids in the Finger Lakes district led to a devastating American retaliation led by John Sullivan and James Clinton in 1779. This dealt the Iroquois Confederation a blow from which it never recovered.

POSTWAR PROSPERITY

New York City revived after the Revolution with amazing speed. Trade in the port of New York on the eve of the British surrender equaled a big goose egg. But by 1791, the combined value of New York's imports and exports had already reached an amazing $8 million. By 1831, that figure had risen to $82 million. This kind of geometric increase in everything continued right through the 19th century.

What set New York apart from other developing areas, and as a consequence accounted for its tremendous growth, was an unsurpassed natural system of transportation. It's difficult to imagine, in this era of interstate highways, airports, and railroads, the degree to which our nation once depended on rivers. Many of the streams we hardly even notice in today's metropolitan area were at one time part of a major network of natural trade and communication routes that connected the city with the rural interior.

And then, as if all those rivers weren't enough, along came the Erie Canal. Here was a navigable waterway that allowed a boat to go all the way from Manhattan to Buffalo. When the canal was opened in October 1825, the entire state went a little nuts. A grand salute was contrived involving a battery of guns that stretched across 500 miles of countryside. At the culmination of a statewide celebration Gov. DeWitt Clinton ceremoniously poured a keg of Lake Erie water into the choppy Atlantic. And history, as they say, was made.

THE FATE OF THE UPSTATE ARISTOCRACY

But what of the upstate patroons? Well, some of them went bust. Others, like the Philipses of Philipsburg Manor, had the bad luck or bad judgment to be on the wrong side in the Revolution, so their property was confiscated. But the Van Rensselaers displayed the sort of staying power that would have warmed old Kiliaen's heart. Over two centuries had passed, bringing with them war, revolution, and sweeping change. But the Van Rensselaers still presided in feudal splendor at the headwaters of the Hudson, still lords of hundreds of thousands of acres and thousands upon thousands of tenants.

In 1839, Stephen Van Rensselaer died—after which his heirs, accustomed to acting in whatever manner they chose, made a serious tactical mistake. Stephen had been a lax landlord. So lax, in fact, that he had neglected to collect rent from many of his tenants for quite a number of years. His heirs were further dismayed to discover that he had left behind debts to the tune of $400,000, a staggering sum in those days. What did they do? They attempted to collect back rent.

Of course, one of the reasons Stephen had been so lax had to do with the extreme poverty of his tenants. The efforts of his heirs created panic across vast portions of upstate New York. Faced with a demand for accumulated rent they could never hope to pay, the tenant farmers formed farmers' committees to try to reason with the landlord. Stephen Van Rensselaer, Junior, would have none of them. Instead, he embarked on a campaign of wholesale evictions. Local marshals were asked to evict entire townships. By 1844, Delaware County was in a state of open insurrection. Antirenters plagued rural landlords everywhere with physical violence. Finally, a concentrated antilandlord campaign in the state legislature resulted in an 1846 law that forbade future leases of agricultural land for periods in excess of 12 years. And with that, feudalism in New York State came to an end.

THE AGE OF VANDERBILT

By that time, New York's old-style feudal aristocracy was on the wane anyway. Nipping at its heels were the steam age and the barons of industry. The model of the New Man of the New Age was Cornelius Vanderbilt—not just in New York but across the country. Vanderbilt started out rowing passengers across the bay to New York from his native Staten Island. By the time he was 24, he had become captain of his own steamboat. By 1828, at the age of 34, Vanderbilt had established his own network of steamboat routes. Over the next 30 years he extended these routes to New Jersey, Long Island Sound, up the Hudson, down to Panama and Nicaragua, and even back and forth across the Atlantic. This is why he was known as Commodore Vanderbilt. By 1864, having already amassed a fortune of $20 million, he turned to railroads. And then he really got rich!

It was railroads that set the stage for New York's next leap in wealth and influence. The pull of New York City's urban market became even more irresistible by virtue of its once again increased accessibility. At the same time, upstate farmers discovered that they could make the most money by selling dairy products to New York. Given the new competition from the soil-rich midwestern plains states, the switch to dairying was both profitable and prudent. To this day dairying remains the king of rural New York.

WAR WITH THE SOUTH

In 1861, New York gubernatorial candidate Edward Morgan came out strongly for Lincoln. He won by a landslide. Unfortunately, the pro-Union, antislavery sentiments that this victory suggested were largely illusory. New York business interests resented the interference with trade occasioned by the war with the South. The New Yorker in the street—and it must be noted that there was a vast homeless underclass in the city at that time—was something less than unprejudiced when it came to black people. The low ebb in race relations came in 1863. The war was taking longer than anticipated and was devouring young men in alarming quantities. A draft lottery was established in New York to supply fresh conscripts. What it supplied instead was a full-scale insurrection since the wealthy could buy "substitutes" for $300 and the less well off were forced to risk their lives.

Not many Americans realize the extent of that insurrection. During the Draft Riot of 1863, huge mobs roamed the streets of New York, murdering and mutilating any black they encountered. Even the black orphan asylum, then located on Fifth Avenue in the 50s, was besieged by a bloodthirsty mob determined to lynch the children within. Fortunately, they escaped out the back in time and were spirited to safe hiding places. For three horrifying days there was no law in New York City at all. The mobs trained cannon down the streets. Houses were looted and burned. The populace was stricken with terror. It took the army to reassert order.

THE GILDED AGE

After the Civil War came the giddiest period of all in New York's history. A great prosperity was afoot in the country. And in New York a perfect saturnalia of greed and corruption burst upon an unsuspecting populace. The man whose name became most closely identified with the times was one William Marcy ("Boss") Tweed. Tweed was originally an alderman on the New York City Board of Supervisors. Through skillful political machinations he subsequently became school commissioner, deputy street commissioner, deputy commissioner of public works, even a state senator. All sounds on the up and up, doesn't it? However, during his tenure in these various posts Tweed managed to construct a system of patronage that enabled him to assert total personal control over the entire city government.

Between 1869 and 1871, the so-called Tweed Ring managed to steal the amazing sum of $30 million or more from the City of New York. How did they do it? Well, first they had a good front man. He was the mayor, A. Oakey Hall. Hall and Tweed had another stalwart in the person of City Chamberlain Peter B. Sweeney. And in their collective pocket (so to speak) was the last heavyweight of the ring, City Comptroller Richard B. ("Slippery Dick") Connolly.

These men were common thieves, even if they did do it in a big way. They kept themselves in office through blatant vote fraud. Corrupt judges routinely naturalized thousands of illegal immigrants whenever votes were needed. It was the era of the "Black Horse Cavalry," those Albany legislators who sold their votes to the highest bidder. "Plunderbunds" was a term of the time, applied equally to both major parties. Victory at the polls meant one thing: a chance to rob and steal.

A tale that truly captures the flavor of post–Civil War New York is that of Commodore Vanderbilt's battle with the railroad barons Jay Gould, Jim Fisk, and Dan Drew. Vanderbilt had started buying Erie Railroad stock in 1867, in an attempt to stamp out a rate war. Gould, Fisk, and Drew controlled Erie at the time. As soon as Vanderbilt began buying, Erie's treasurer, Drew, began issuing new stock certificates. Vanderbilt purchased $7-million worth of Erie stock in 1867 but never managed to obtain a majority interest. "If this printing press don't break down," observed Drew, "I'll be damned if I don't give the old hog all he wants of Erie."

When Drew's comment was reported to Vanderbilt, the enraged commodore proceeded to obtain a warrant in the New York courts for the arrest of all three of them. The charge: illegal issuance of stock certificates. But he was too late. Hearing of the warrant, Drew, Gould, and Fisk immediately decamped to Jersey City, where they bribed a judge to set the warrant aside. Gould then left for Albany with suitcases full of cash. The plan was to bribe the Black Horse Cavalry to change the New York laws governing the issuance of stock, thereby legitimizing their maneuvers at Erie.

But since two could play this game, Vanderbilt left for Albany himself with the intention of buying Gould's men off. Some legislators began to expect millions. The collective level of greed was such that even Gould and Vanderbilt were brought up short. In fact, they decided it would be cheaper to call the whole thing off. And that's what they did. Vanderbilt abandoned the Erie Railroad to Gould, Fisk, and Drew, who stripped it of every asset, after which it entered into New York folklore as the archetypical corporate victim of a "robber baron."

REFORM

New York wasn't the only corrupt state during the latter part of the 19th century. But we certainly hit some dollar highs. The constant refrain of whichever Plunderbund was out of office was "Throw the rascals out!" And finally, to everyone's amazement, that's exactly what happened. As the century drew to a close, a new generation of honest politicians took office in New York. National figures like Samuel J. Tilden, Grover Cleveland, Theodore Roosevelt, and Al Smith all got their start in reform politics in the State of New York. They and others like them began a tradition of corruption-free government based on merit and efficiency that was to have sweeping implications both for New York State and for the nation as a whole.

Which brings us to the present. Despite all the changes of the tumultuous past, New York State remains eerily recognizable. "Sodom-on-the-Hudson" is richer and more polyglot than ever. And it still presents the same contrasts to the bucolic upstate dairylands that it has for centuries. The patroons are gone, but the banks of the Hudson are still, in many places, lined with riverfront estates occupied by a squireocracy that has been in place for generations. Albany, a city that possessed only 19 bathrooms in the year 1860, is today a sophisticated state capital. And yet it's still a provincial outpost in the minds of those who live in Manhattan. As for the rest of the state, the world of the Native Americans is largely gone but the rural vastness remains. And in places like the Adirondacks, the wilderness itself still exists as it did at the dawn of time.

It is, in short, a marvelous state to explore, full of contrasts and content, rich in history and contradiction. It would take a lifetime to know even a small part of it. So on the assumption that you have only a few weeks, let's begin.

2. Getting To & Around New York State

BY AIR

For most people, the gateway to New York State will be one of the three New York City metropolitan area airports: **John F. Kennedy International Airport**, on Jamaica Bay in southern Queens; **LaGuardia Airport**, on Long Island Sound in northern Queens; or **Newark International Airport**, across New York Harbor in neighboring New Jersey. Of the three, LaGuardia is the most accessible to Midtown Manhattan. There are other major airports in New York State, notably serving Newburgh, Albany, and Buffalo, but they don't handle jumbo jets.

It used to be the practice in guidebooks such as this to quote established fares from various points of origin. Well, in today's era of deregulated airfares and airline price wars, there are no more established fares. One day it costs $199 to fly from Los Angeles to New York. A month later it's twice that. Then a day after that it's down to $159.

Virtually every major carrier in the country flies into the New York City area. You can either take the phone book and start calling them in alphabetical order or call a travel agent instead. The latter course is much the more sensible of the two. Travel agents cost you nothing. They receive a percentage of the fare from the carrier. And in the present age of deregulation, nobody else will be able to quote all the fares that you'll want to know.

A well-developed network of small (sometimes not-so-small) feeder airlines services many areas in upstate New York. These carriers include USAir Express, American Eagle, Business Express, United Express, Mall, and others. Again, for travel arrangements upstate, you really should go to a travel agent. They're all connected with the airlines by computer these days. So wherever you live your local agent will be as informed as those right here in New York.

Here are some toll-free airline telephone numbers that might be helpful: **American Airlines,** 800/433-7300; **Continental,** 800/525-0280; **Delta Air Lines,** 800/221-1212; **Northwest Orient,** 800/225-2525; **Trans World Airlines,** 800/221-2000; **United Airlines,** 800/241-6522; **USAir,** 800/428-4322.

BY BUS

Greyhound/Trailways services nearly every city of any size in New York. It's fortunate that travel by bus is cheap, since, frankly, it's a little, shall we say, "tiring." Even its low-budget status is occasionally imperiled by those incredible airline fare wars. (Always check with the airlines to see if they are offering special fares at the time you'll be traveling.)

The bus companies also offer special passes and excursion fares. An example is Greyhound's "Ameripass," which entitles you to unlimited travel anywhere in the country and portions of Canada for the flat rate of $450. Other fares and packages are always coming and going. If this sounds interesting, call your local Greyhound/Trailways office and see what its got when you plan to go.

BY RAIL

Also big with special fares is **Amtrak** (tel. toll free 800/872-7245), whose nonrefundable "All Aboard Fare," for example, costs only $179 round trip, Miami to Manhattan. Admittedly, this is cheaper than the cheapest airfare so far advertised. However, not all of Amtrak's routes are so reasonable. Indeed, cross-country rates are downright expensive ($223 for the fare; $357 for three nights in a sleeping compartment) one way, New York to L.A., with no stopovers. On top of this, the trip is *long*. Even in the case of the aforementioned Miami run, the train takes 24 hours instead of 3 on a plane.

Travel agents don't handle buses, but they do make Amtrak reservations. If the extra travel time doesn't bother you, ask your agent to inquire. A train trip might take a long time, but it usually provides excellent scenery, as well as departures and arrivals from the heart of whatever towns you're visiting. Not to mention the chance to get up and move around when your legs go to sleep.

BY CAR

No doubt the most American way to travel is by car, and this is by far the best way to savor the pleasures of upstate New York. If you plan to tour with a rented car, try to rent it outside the New York metropolitan area. Hertz, Avis, Budget, Econo-Car, and all the rest of them offer the same cars at their various locations. But the prices are different.

In New York City, for example, Avis's compact Chevy Cavalier might cost $79 a day, with free unlimited miles. But in Poughkeepsie, a city on the Hudson halfway to Albany, the same car from the same company might be only $40 a day, also with unlimited miles. Even though prices and specials are constantly changing, this general law holds true for all rental-car agencies, and in fact for purveyors of all manner of goods and services. If you're planning to drive a rented car upstate, rent it as far from Manhattan as you can.

For that matter, if you plan to rent a car for use in New York City, do so as far from the airport as possible. In Manhattan, as well as in most upstate cities of any size, you'll find hot competition among the cut-rate rental-car trade. It's a rule of thumb that the cheapest outfits don't maintain offices at the airports. All of them, cheap and not so cheap, are listed in the *local* Yellow Pages. In fact, the New York metropolitan area has dozens of possibilities. Quite a few also advertise in those airline magazines they tuck into the seatbacks underneath your tray. Budget is one of my personal favorites—it's unpretentious and it offers a great corporate discount. Those who care to shop around will always find that there is life after Hertz and Avis.

The big companies, however, are the ones with the most offices. Here are some toll-free telephone numbers: **Avis**, 800/331-1212; **Budget**, 800/527-0700; **Hertz**, 800/654-3131; **National**, 800/227-7368.

---

3. For Foreign Visitors

PREPARING FOR YOUR TRIP

Necessary Documents

Most foreigners entering the United States must carry two documents: (1) a valid **passport**, expiring not fewer than six months prior to the scheduled end of the visit to the United States, and (2) a **tourist visa**, which can be obtained without charge at any American consulate.

Exceptions are Canadian nationals, who must merely carry proof of residence, and British, French, Spanish, Italian, German, and Japanese nationals, who require a passport but no visa.

To obtain a visa you merely complete a form and submit a passport-size photo. At most consulates, it's an overnight process, though it can take longer during busy June, July, and August. Those who apply by mail should enclose a large self-addressed stamped envelope and expect a response in about two weeks. In addition to consulates, visa application forms can be obtained from airline offices and leading travel agencies.

In theory, a tourist visa (Visa B) is valid for single or multiple entries for a period of one year. In practice, the consulate that issues the visa uses its discretion in granting length of stay. Applicants of good appearance, who can supply the address of a relative, friend, or business acquaintance in the United States, are most likely to be granted longer stays. (American resident contacts are also useful in passing through Customs quickly and for numerous other details.) For further information, the Immigration number is 212/206-6500.

Medical Requirements

New arrivals in the United States do not need any inoculations unless they are coming from, or have stopped over in, an area known to be suffering from an epidemic, particularly cholera or yellow fever.

Anyone applying for an immigrant's visa must undergo a screening test for the AIDS-associated HIV virus, under a law passed in 1987. This test does not apply to tourists.

Any visitor with a medical condition that requires treatment with narcotics or other drugs, or with paraphernalia such as syringes, must carry a valid, signed prescription from a physician. This allays suspicions of drug smuggling.

Traveler's Insurance

All such insurance is optional in the United States. Medical care is very costly, however, and every traveler is strongly advised to secure full insurance coverage before starting a trip.

For a relatively low premium, numerous specialized insurance companies will cover (1) loss or theft of baggage, (2) costs of trip cancellation, (3) guaranteed bail in the event of a suit or other legal difficulties, (4) the cost of medical assistance—including surgery and hospitalization—in the event of sickness or injury, and (5) the cost of an accident, death, or repatriation. Travel agencies, automobile clubs, and banks are among those selling travel insurance packages at attractive rates.

GETTING TO & AROUND THE UNITED STATES

Nearly all major airlines, including those of the United States, Europe, Asia, Australia, and New Zealand, offer **APEX (advance purchase excursion) fares** that significantly reduce the cost of transoceanic air travel. This enables travelers to pick their dates and ports, but requires that they prepurchase their ticket, and meet minimum- and maximum-stay requirements—often 15 to 90 days. Season of travel and individual airline discounts also affect fares, but this is the most widely acknowledged means of cheap, flexible travel.

Some large airlines, including Delta, Continental, American, Northwest, TWA, and United, offer foreign travelers special add-on discount fares under the names **Visit USA** and **Stand-by Airpass.** These tickets (which can be purchased overseas only) allow unlimited travel between U.S. destinations at minimum rates for specified time periods, such as 21, 30, or 60 days. Short of bus or train travel, which can be inconvenient and time-consuming, this is the best way of traveling around the country at low cost.

Amtrak, the American rail system, offers a **USA Railpass** to non-U.S. citizens. Available only overseas, it allows unlimited stopovers during a 15-, 30-, or 45-day period of validity. Fares vary according to the size of the region being traveled.

Foreign students can obtain the **International Ameripass** for unlimited bus travel on Greyhound/Trailways throughout the United States and Canada. Available for 7 to 30 days, it can be purchased with a student ID and a passport in New York, Orlando, Miami, San Francisco, and Los Angeles.

Foreign visitors who plan to rent a car can visit an **American Automobile Association** (AAA) office to obtain a "touring permit," which validates foreign driver's licenses. The Manhattan office of AAA is at Broadway and 62nd Street (tel. 212/157-2000 or 586-1166).

FAST FACTS FOR THE FOREIGN TRAVELER

CURRENCY & EXCHANGE: In the American decimal monetary system, 100 cents (¢) are equal to one dollar ($1).

Foreign visitors used to paper money of varied colors should look carefully at the U.S. "greenbacks"—all bills are mostly green, and all are the same size regardless of value. Aside from the numbers, Americans often differentiate them by the portrait they bear: The $1 bill ("a buck") depicts George Washington; the seldom-seen $2, Thomas Jefferson; the $5, Abraham Lincoln; the $10, Alexander Hamilton; the $20, Andrew Jackson. Larger bills, including the $50 (Ulysses S. Grant) and the $100 (William McKinley), are not welcome in payment for small purchases.

There are six coins, four of them widely used: 1¢ ("penny") is copper color; 5¢ ("nickel"); 10¢ ("dime"); and 25¢ ("quarter"). The 50¢ piece ("half dollar") is less widely circulated, and $1 coins—including the older, large silver dollar and the newer, small Susan B. Anthony coin—are rare.

Traveler's checks in *U.S. dollars* are easily cashed in payment for goods or services at most hotels, motels, restaurants, and large stores. The best rates, however, are given at banks; a major bank is also the only place where you can confidently cash traveler's checks in any currency *but* U.S. dollars. In fact, don't plan on changing any foreign currency here; the foreign-exchange bureaus common in other countries are largely absent from U.S. cities. If you find it necessary to exchange currency, see "Currency Exchange" under "ABCs of New York City" in Chapter II.

Credit cards are the most widely used method of payment by travelers in the United States. In New York, VISA (BarclayCard in Britain, Chargex in Canada) and MasterCard (EuroCard in Europe, Access in Britain, Diamond in Japan) are accepted almost everywhere; American Express, by most establishments; Diners Club and Carte Blanche, by a small number; Discover and Japan's JCB, by an increasing number.

Use of this "plastic money" reduces the necessity to carry large sums of cash or traveler's checks. It is accepted almost everywhere, except in stores selling liquor. Credit cards can be recorded as a deposit for car rental, as proof of identity (often preferred to a passport) when cashing a check, or as a "cash card" for withdrawing money from banks and automatic-teller machines that accept them.

CUSTOMS & IMMIGRATION: U.S. Customs allow each adult visitor to import the following, duty free: (1) one liter of wine or hard liquor; (2) 1,000 cigarettes or 100 cigars (*not* from Cuba) or three pounds of smoking tobacco; and (3) $400 worth of gifts. The only restrictions are that the visitor must spend at least 72 hours in the United States and must not have claimed them within the preceding six months. Food and plants are forbidden from import.

Foreign tourists may import or export up to $5,000 in U.S. or foreign currency, with no formalities. Larger amounts of money must be declared to Customs.

Visitors arriving by air, no matter what the port of entry, are advised to be exceedingly patient and resigned to a wait in the Customs and immigration line. At busy times, especially when several overseas flights arrive within a few minutes of one another, it can take two or three hours just to get a passport stamped for arrival. Allot *plenty* of time for connections between international and domestic flights! Border formalities by road or rail from Canada are relatively quick and easy.

EMBASSIES & CONSULATES: Embassies in the U.S. include: **Australian Embassy,** 1601 Massachusetts Ave. NW, Washington, DC 20036 (tel. 202/797-3000); **Canadian Embassy,** 501 Pennsylvania Ave. NW, Washington, DC 20001 (tel. 202/682-1740); **Irish Embassy,** 2234 Massachusetts Ave. NW, Washington, DC 20008 (tel. 202/462-3939); **New Zealand Embassy,** 37 Observatory Circle NW, Washington, DC 20008 (tel. 202/328-4800); **U.K. Embassy,** 3100 Massachusetts Ave. NW, Washington, DC 20008 (tel. 202/462-1340). In addition, most countries maintain **UN missions** in New York City, and many have **consulates** there.

EMERGENCIES: A single emergency telephone number, **911,** will put you in touch with police, ambulance, or fire department in New York City.

LEGAL AID: Those accused of serious offenses are advised to say and do nothing before consulting a lawyer. Under U.S. law, an arrested person is allowed one telephone call to a party of his or her choice: call your embassy. If you are pulled up for a minor infraction, such as a traffic offense, *never* attempt to pay the fine directly to a police officer. You may wind up arrested on the much more serious charge of attempted bribery. Pay fines by mail or directly into the hands of the clerk of a court.

NEWSPAPERS & MAGAZINES: New York City is the leading American publishing center. *The New York Times* is the country's most influential daily paper, and *The New Yorker* is a noted weekly magazine. Many other newspapers and magazines are published throughout the state. New Yorkers have access to numerous foreign newspapers and magazines through **Hotalings,** 142 W. 42nd St., between Sixth Avenue and Broadway (tel. 840-1868), which carries over 200 papers from around the world.

RADIO & TELEVISION: There are many radio broadcasters, on both AM and FM, offering a wide variety of music, information, and discussion programs. Television, with five coast-to-coast networks, ABC, CBS, Fox, NBC, and the Public Broadcasting System (PBS), plays a major part in American life. In addition, there are numerous cable networks, such as CNN and MTV. Few accommodations in New York do not include a TV as a standard furnishing.

TAXES: In the United States, there is no VAT (value-added tax) or other indirect taxes at a national level. New York State levies a 7% sales tax on gross receipts (and New York City adds an additional 1¼%), including hotel checks and shop purchases. There is also a 5% tax for hotel bills over $100, plus a $2-per-night surcharge, in New York City.

TELEPHONE & FAX: Public telephone booths are easily spotted in cities like New York and Albany but may be more difficult to find outside urban areas. Stores and gas stations are your best bet. Hotels often add a per-call surcharge to your room bill. Local calls are 25¢. For area codes in New York City and various parts of New York State, see "ABCs of New York City" in Chapter II. For direct overseas calls, dial 011, followed by the country code (Australia, 61; France, 33; Italy, 39; United Kingdom, 44), then by the city code and the number of the person you are calling. For Canada and long-distance calls in the United States, dial 1 followed by the area code and the number you want. For reversed-charge or collect calls and for person-to-person calls, dial 0 (zero) instead of 1, then follow the same procedure as above, and an operator will come on the line. For long-distance directory assistance, dial 1, the area code you need, then 555-1212. Fax service (for instant facsimile transmission) can be provided by major hotels at a nominal charge or by business service centers in most towns and cities.

TIME: The United States is divided into six time zones. From east to west, they are eastern time (ET), central (CT), mountain (MT), Pacific (PT), Alaska (AT), and Hawaii (HT). Keep time zones in mind when traveling or telephoning long distances in the U.S. For example, noon in New York City (ET) is 11am in Chicago (CT), 10am in Salt Lake City (MT), 9am in San Francisco (PT), 8am in Anchorage (AT), and 7am in Honolulu (HT). Daylight saving time is in effect from the last Sunday in April through the last Saturday in October; this alters the clock so that sunrise and sunset are an hour later.

TOILETS: Some foreign visitors complain that public toilets are hard to find in the States. There are none on the streets, but most hotels, restaurants, bars, department stores, gasoline stations, and museums and other tourist attractions make them available.

WHITE PAGES & YELLOW PAGES: There are two kinds of telephone directory. The general directory is called the **White Pages** and includes individuals and businesses alphabetically by name. The second directory, called the **Yellow Pages,** lists local services, businesses, and industries alphabetically by category, with an index in the back. Listings include not only the obvious, such as automobile repair and drugstores (pharmacies), but also restaurants by cuisine and location, places of worship by religious denomination, and other information that a tourist might not otherwise readily find. The Yellow Pages also include city plans or detailed area maps and often show postal ZIP codes and public transportation routes.

SAFETY

While tourist areas are usually safe, crime is on the increase everywhere, and U.S. urban areas tend to be less safe than those in Europe or Japan. Visitors should always be alert. This is particularly true in large U.S. cities. It is wise to ask the city or area's tourist office if you are in doubt about which neighborhoods are safe. Avoid deserted areas, especially at night. Don't go into a city park at night unless there is an occasion that attracts crowds—for example, New York City's concerts in the parks. Generally speaking, you can feel safe in areas where there are many people and many open establishments.

Avoid carrying valuables with you on the street and don't display expensive cameras or electronic equipment. Hold on to your pocketbook and place your billfold in an inside pocket. In restaurants, theaters, and other public places, keep your possessions in sight.

Remember also that hotels are open to the public, and in a large hotel, security may not be able to screen everyone entering. Always lock your room door; don't assume that once inside your hotel you are automatically safe and need no longer be aware of your surroundings.

Driving

Safety while driving is particularly important. Question your rental agency about personal safety or ask for a brochure of traveler safety tips when you pick up your car. Obtain written directions, or a map with the route marked in red, from the agency showing how to reach your destination. And, if possible, arrive and depart during daylight hours.

Recently more and more crime has involved cars and drivers. If you drive off a highway into a neighborhood that seems threatening, leave the area as quickly as possible. If you have an accident, even on the highway, stay in your car with the doors locked until you assess the situation or until the police arrive. If you are bumped from behind on the street or are involved in a minor accident with no injuries and the situation appears suspicious, motion to the other driver to follow you. *Never* get out of your car in such situations. You can also keep a premade sign in your car reading, "PLEASE FOLLOW THIS VEHICLE TO REPORT THE ACCIDENT." Show the sign to the other driver and go directly to the nearest police precinct, well-lighted service station, or open store.

If you see someone on the road who indicates a need for help, do not stop. Take note of the location, drive on to a well-lighted area, and telephone the police by dialing 911.

Park in well-lighted, well-traveled areas if possible. Always keep your car doors locked, whether the car is attended or unattended. Look around you before you get out of your car and never leave any packages or valuables in sight. If someone attempts to rob you or steal your car, do not try to resist and report the incident to the police immediately.

The Crime Prevention Division of the New York City Police Department publishes a "Safety Tips for Visitors" brochure. It is translated into French, Spanish, Hebrew, German, Japanese, Dutch, Italian, Russian, Chinese, Portuguese, and Swedish and contains general safety information. For a copy, write to the **Crime Prevention Division Office of D.C.C.A.,** 80-45 Winchester Blvd., Queens Village, NY 11427.

"BIG APPLE" ORIENTATION

It's not easy to pinpoint what makes New York so "New Yorkish." That it has a decided character, there can be no doubt. Yet it's a city so infinite in its effects on residents and visitors alike that its essence remains elusive. To begin with the obvious, it's big. Indeed, it's the biggest city in North America (population within the city limits: approximately 7.3 million). According to the Convention and Visitors Bureau, there were almost 25 *million* additional souls who came to New York in a recent year, just to visit. That's more people than live in many countries.

Such statistics boggle the mind. But the visitor soon learns to accept the mind boggling as one of New York City's municipal traits. Astounding statistics abound. For example, all those aforementioned visitors spent the staggering sum of about $10 *billion* while here in the Big Apple. Can't you just hear all that cash jingling into New York City cash registers? And that's just what came from the tourists; it doesn't even count what the locals spent.

"Spending" is probably another trait associated with New York City. We get it, and then, boy, do we spend it. How many other cities contain some 17,000 eating places? Or 97,000 hotel rooms? Or 12,000 licensed taxis? Not many.

Of course, people are drawn to New York City by more than a compulsion to spend for spending's sake. This place has the real goods, more so perhaps than any other spot on the globe. It is where you can buy couture clothing, high technology, pork bellies, space-age weaponry, oil tankers, and superlative pastrami. New York's great libraries and seats of learning are the places to research rare manuscripts; its 400 galleries and almost 200 museums display art of the highest caliber; its 40 legitimate theaters present every manner of drama, and what they don't present you can still see in over 200 Off- or Off-Off-Broadway theaters. In fact, you can see anything in New York, and not necessarily on a stage either. New York is a place in which to become famous, to learn, to indulge one's highest aspirations, or to gratify one's lowest urges. It is a place in which to vanish into the healing anonymity of a crowd. It is the place in which to succeed. Or, for that matter, to fail.

It is, quite simply, a city with everything. Yes, I will say it categorically: There is *nothing* one cannot find in New York.

Many people will protest, however, that New York City does lack one very important quality—tranquility. They will call this city the very definition of the "madding crowd" from which people must retreat from time to time for sanity's sake. Usually these people live upstate or out of state (this amounts to the same thing for most New Yorkers).

And yet anyone who has gazed upon the lighted skyline of Manhattan from, say, the heights of Weehawken, NJ, or a window high in the World Trade Center, has known, if only for an instant, the serenity of true awe. This is a sight the likes of which does not exist elsewhere on earth. To see those same towers rising pale in the dawn above the green mists of Central Park is to feel the stillness that always lies at the core of man's greatest works. Even in this mightiest of cities there is breathless beauty and peace for whomever takes the moment to look for them.

---

1. Getting To & From Manhattan

Visitors pour in and out of Manhattan on various forms of transportation. Here is some information on how it is done.

BY CAR

Though it is not recommended that you bring a car into Manhattan (street parking is a nightmare, and private garage parking is expensive), if you must, you should know that Manhattan is an island connected to the surrounding land masses by a number of bridges and tunnels. From the north, to get to the East Side, take the **Governor Thomas E. Dewey Thruway** (also known as the New York Thruway or I-87) or I-95 and watch for signs for the **Triboro Bridge** that will put you (if you stay to your left off the bridge) onto the southbound lanes of the **Franklin D. Roosevelt Drive** (also known as the East River Drive). Or to get to the West Side from the north, take the **Saw Mill River Parkway** to the **Henry Hudson Parkway** over the **Henry Hudson Bridge**. From New Jersey, I-95 has signs directing you to both the **Holland** and **Lincoln Tunnels** (to lower Manhattan). From further north in New Jersey, I-80, I-95, and Route 4 lead to the **George Washington Bridge,** which will take you to the southbound Henry Hudson Parkway (a.k.a. West Side Highway) down the West Side. From Long Island, in the east, the **Long Island Expressway** (I-495) leads to Manhattan via the **Queensboro Bridge** or the **Queens-Midtown Tunnel.**

BY BUS OR TRAIN

Trains arrive at either **Pennsylvania Station** (34th Street and Seventh Avenue) or **Grand Central Terminal** (42nd Street and Park Avenue). Buses arrive at the **Port Authority Bus Terminal** (41st Street and Eighth Avenue).

BY PLANE

There are three major airports serving New York City—**John F. Kennedy International Airport** and **LaGuardia Airport,** both in Queens, and **Newark International Airport** in New Jersey. Buses, subway trains, and taxis connect with them.

Carey Airport Express (tel. 718/632-0500) runs frequent **bus** service to and from Kennedy and LaGuardia airports with five separate Manhattan stops: at 125 Park Ave., between 41st and 42nd Streets; at the "Airport Transportation Center" in the Port Authority Bus Terminal on West 42nd Street between Eighth and Ninth Avenues; at the New York Hilton Hotel on Sixth Avenue between 53rd and 54th Streets; at the Sheraton City Squire Hotel on Seventh Avenue between 51st and 52nd Streets; and at the Marriott Marquis Hotel on Broadway between 45th and 46th Streets. Departures are at least every half hour. The one-way fare to Kennedy and LaGuardia from Grand Central Station or Pennsylvania Station is $11; from hotels the price is $12.50. Please be sure to call and confirm these schedules and fares as they are subject to change.

Newark International Airport service is by New Jersey Transit and Olympia Airport Express bus companies. **New Jersey Transit** (tel. 201/762-5100, or 212/

564-8484) runs buses every 15 minutes to and from the Port Authority Bus Terminal from 6am to midnight. The one-way fare is $7. **Olympia Airport Express** (tel. 212/964-6233) runs buses to and from both the World Trade Center downtown every 20 minutes from 5:15am to 11:15pm. A Grand Central Station stop at 41st Street and Park Avenue is every 20 minutes from 5am to 11pm. The one-way fare, which you pay the driver, is $7.

The New York City Transit Authority operates a free shuttle bus between Kennedy Airport and the Howard Beach **subway** stop on the A train. Transport to and from the airport in this manner can be accomplished at a fraction of the cost of a taxi or even of the airport bus, but it's time consuming and somewhat of a trudge. Call the **New York City Transit Authority** (tel. 718/858-7272) for more detailed instructions and information.

At the airports, look for the **taxi** stands at each terminal. There will often be a line of people feeding in an orderly fashion into each taxi as it pulls up, and you may find someone to share a ride if you are both going to Manhattan. From JFK and LaGuardia airports, you pay whatever is on the meter (plus tip), which will be around $45 to Midtown from JFK and about $30 from LaGuardia. If you land at Newark Airport (across the Hudson River in New Jersey), you will notice there's a taxi booth outside the terminal. You tell your destination to the clerk inside and he or she will tell you the price of the trip (about $40 to Midtown) and will hand the taxi driver a slip of paper in confirmation.

To return to the airports from Manhattan, just flag a cab and tell the driver which one you want to go to. For JFK and LaGuardia, pay the amount on the meter. For Newark, the fare on the meter can be doubled once you cross the state line.

If traffic is slow the fare will be higher, since waiting time adds to the meter rate. Remember that you are responsible for all bridge or tunnel tolls, in addition to the meter charges.

2. The Geography of the "Big Apple"

Why in the world is New York called the "Big Apple"? The term started out among jazz musicians some 70 years ago. The "big" apple, as opposed to all the other apples, meant the big-time gig in New York. The perception was then, as it is now, that if you had "made" it in New York, you had therefore "made" it everywhere. Slang terminology like this often moves from people in the arts into the common parlance. It should be noted that during the early 1970s, when New York was suffering from a combined fiscal crisis and bad overall image, a number of people in business, the arts, and government got together to change America's perception of the place. The result was a media blitz consisting of promotional themes, television spots, musical jingles, and the like. All this municipal boosterism resulted, among other things, in a campaign to promote the city under the theme of "The Big Apple." It has been the endless repetition of this theme that has probably most solidified the term in the public mind.

MANHATTAN & THE BOROUGHS

The Apple is big, but the first-time visitor will be pleased to know that it's easy to find one's way around. The city consists of five boroughs, each of which is a separate county within the State of New York. These boroughs are New York County, which occupies the island of Manhattan; Kings County, which is otherwise known as Brooklyn; the Bronx, which has no other name; Queens County, which is also called just Queens; and Richmond County, also known as Staten Island. Of course, few people think of them as separate counties. They are just the boroughs—Brooklyn, Queens, the Bronx, and Staten Island. Some Staten Islanders would like their borough to secede from the city, however.

Manhattan is a borough too. But it's so preeminently the prima donna borough

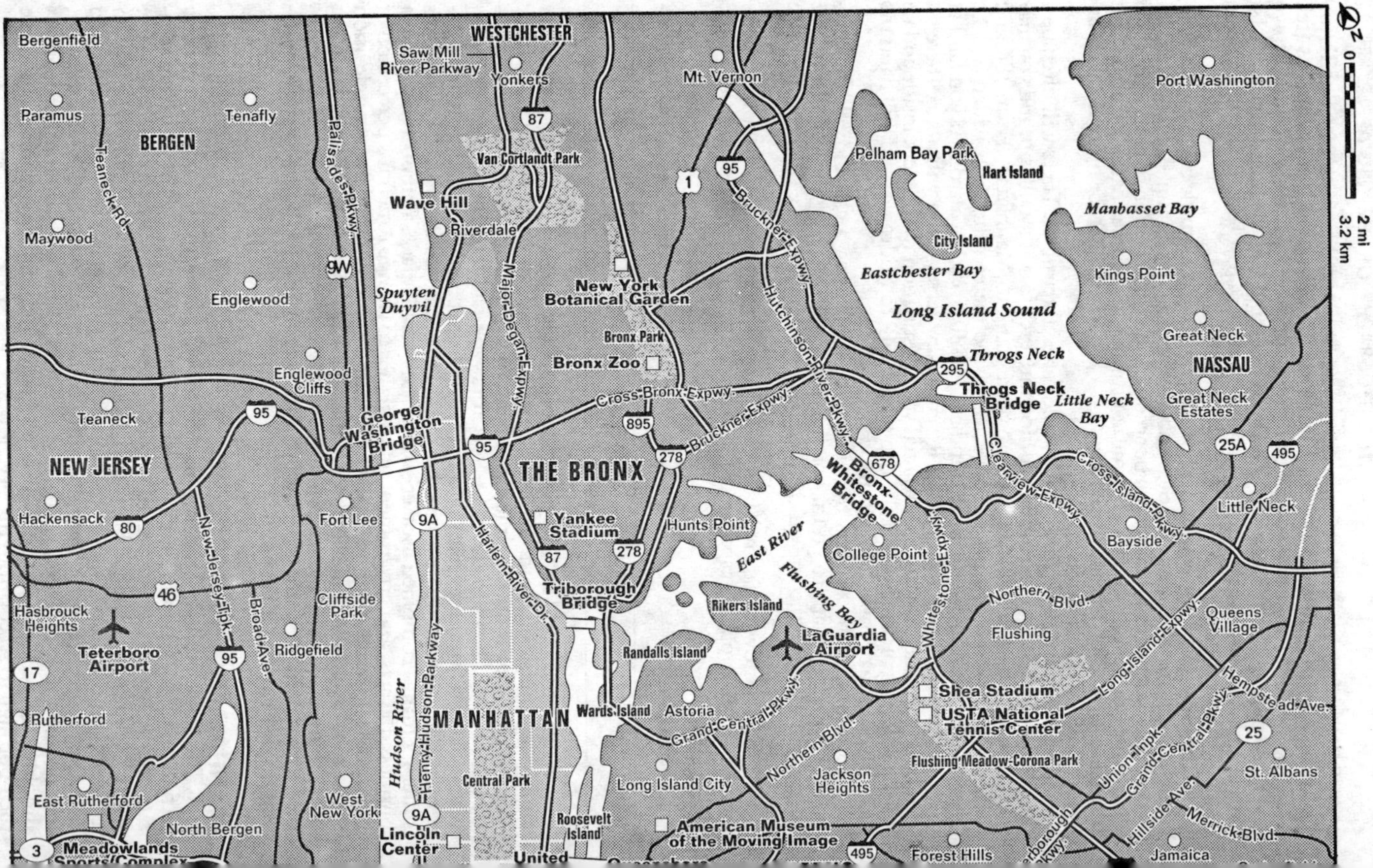
0
2 mi
3.2 km
N
WESTCHESTER
Saw Mill River Parkway
Yonkers
Mt. Vernon
Port Washington
Bergenfield
Paramus
Tenafly
BERGEN
Teaneck Rd.
Palisades Pkwy.
9W
87
Van Cortlandt Park
Wave Hill
Riverdale
95
1
Bruckner Expwy.
Pelham Bay Park
Hart Island
Manbasset Bay
City Island
Eastchester Bay
Kings Point
Maywood
Englewood
Spuyten Duyvil
Major Degan Expwy.
New York Botanical Garden
Hutchinson River Pkwy.
Long Island Sound
Great Neck
Bronx Park
Bronx Zoo
Throgs Neck
295
NASSAU
Englewood Cliffs
Cross Bronx Expwy.
Throgs Neck Bridge
Little Neck Bay
Great Neck Estates
Teaneck
George Washington Bridge
895
Bruckner Expwy.
25A
495
NEW JERSEY
THE BRONX
278
678
Bronx-Whitestone Bridge
Clearview Expwy.
Cross Island Pkwy.
Little Neck
Hackensack
80
Fort Lee
9A
Yankee Stadium
Hunts Point
East River
College Point
Bayside
Harlem River Dr.
Whitestone Expwy.
46
New Jersey Tpk.
Broad Ave.
Cliffside Park
Triborough Bridge
Rikers Island
Flushing Bay
Northern Blvd.
Queens Village
Hasbrouck Heights
Teterboro Airport
Ridgefield
LaGuardia Airport
Flushing
Long Island Expwy.
17
Randalls Island
Hempstead Ave.
Shea Stadium
Hudson River
Henry Hudson Parkway
MANHATTAN
Wards Island
Astoria
Grand Central Pkwy.
USTA National Tennis Center
25
Rutherford
Northern Blvd.
Flushing Meadow-Corona Park
Union Tnpk.
Grand Central Pkwy.
Central Park
Long Island City
Jackson Heights
St. Albans
East Rutherford
West New York
Roosevelt Island
Hillside Ave.
Merrick Blvd.
North Bergen
American Museum of the Moving Image
3
Meadowlands
Lincoln Center
495
Forest Hills
Jamaica

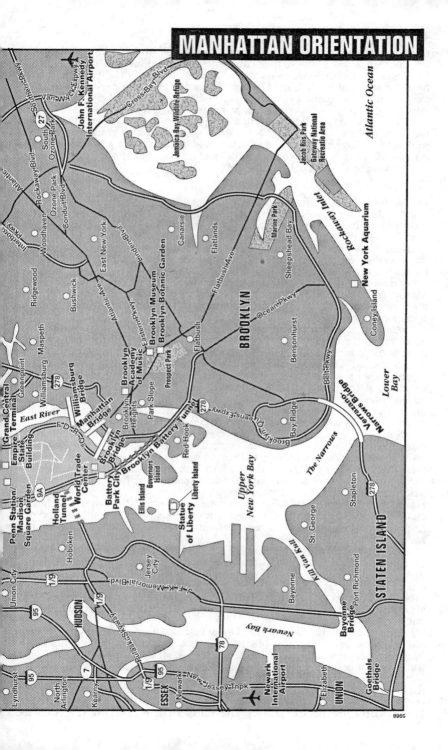

MANHATTAN ORIENTATION

John F. Kennedy
International Airport

Cross Bay Blvd.

Jamaica Bay Wildlife Refuge

Atlantic Ocean

Jacob Riis Park

Gateway National
Recreatio Area

Southern-Pkwy.

Van Wyck Expwy.

27

South
Ozone Park

Ozone Park

Rockaway Blvd.

Woodhaven

Conduit Blvd.

Interboro Pkwy.

Atlantic

Belt-Pkwy.

East New York

New York Aquarium

Rockaway Inlet

Marine Park

Ridgewood

Bushwick

Canarsie

Flatlands

Sheepshead Bay

Coney Island

Maspeth

Atlantic-Ave.

Brooklyn Museum

Brooklyn Botanic Garden

Flatbush Ave.

BROOKLYN

Ocean Pkwy.

Bensonhurst

Greenpoint

Williamsburg

278

Brooklyn
Academy
of Music

Eastern Pkwy.

Flatbush

Lower
Bay

Grand Central
Terminal

Empire
State
Building

East River

Williamsburg
Bridge

Park Slope

Prospect Park

Manhattan
Bridge

Brooklyn
Heights

Brooklyn
Bridge

278

Brooklyn-Queens Expwy.

Bay Ridge

Verrazano-
Narrows Bridge

F.D.R.

Battery
Park City

Brooklyn Battery Tunnel

Red Hook

The Narrows

Penn Station/
Madison
Square Garden

9A

World Trade
Center

Holland
Tunnel

Governors
Island

Ellis Island

Liberty Island

Statue
of Liberty

Upper
New York Bay

Stapleton

278

Hoboken

Jersey
City

St. George

STATEN ISLAND

Union City

9

Kill Van Kull

Bayonne

Port Richmond

Bayonne
Bridge

J.F.K. Memorial Blvd.

95

HUDSON

1/9

Newark Bay

Goethals
Bridge

Lyndhurst

North
Arlington

95

7

Pulaski Skwy.

1/9

78

Newark
International
Airport

Elizabeth

UNION

Kearny

95

Newark

New Jersey Tnpk.

ESSEX

8965

that New Yorkers set it apart from the other four. People in Queens and Brooklyn tell one another they're going to the "city" when they head for Manhattan. Snobbish Manhattan rock club doormen condemn the untrendy as "BBQs" (meaning people from the Bronx, Brooklyn, and Queens) if they don't blend with the cream of fashion within. Manhattan is probably as yearned for and sought after—as well as reviled and dismissed—in Brooklyn or Staten Island as it is in Nebraska.

New York is so easy for the visitor to navigate primarily because it's unlikely that the average visitor will ever leave Manhattan. Guidebook after guidebook implores readers to explore the other boroughs, which in truth have many attractions. If you do leave Manhattan, except for transit back and forth to the airport, congratulations. You took the advice that nobody else did.

MANHATTAN GEOGRAPHY

Manhattan is a slender island, some 13 miles long, which forms the eastern shore of the Hudson River at its entrance to Upper New York Bay. It runs roughly north and south, and so do its **avenues.** These avenues are numbered from one to twelve, First Avenue lying far to the east and Twelfth Avenue skirting the Hudson River on the west. The shoreline of Manhattan, despite centuries of landfilling, still bulges in and out in many places, and whenever this happens those straight avenues either disappear off the map or are augmented by additions. Hence, the Lower East Side sports Avenues A, B, C, and D, all east of First Avenue, while north of 155th Street in Washington Heights there is nothing at all east of Tenth Avenue (which up there is called Amsterdam).

Running in an irregular diagonal from Manhattan's northernmost tip all the way down to the Battery (a park located at the southern tip of the island) is famous **Broadway.** Where Broadway intersects one of the north-south avenues, a square is usually created. Of course, they aren't really square at all, but the intersection of broad roadways at acute angles creates open spaces that cry out for some kind of name. So at the point where Broadway crosses Seventh Avenue we have Times Square; where it crosses Sixth Avenue we have Herald Square; Madison Square is at the intersection of Broadway and Fifth; Union Square marks Broadway's transit of Fourth Avenue (now grandly called Park Avenue South); and so forth.

Some avenues acquired names over the years, usually as part of an effort to upgrade the image of surrounding real estate. Patrician Park Avenue, for example, is really a continuation of schlumpy old Fourth Avenue (sorry, it's Park Avenue South these days, save the short stretch from 8th to 14th Streets). Its predominant feature used to be an open railway cut that carried the tracks of the New York Central Railroad. The tracks were covered in the early part of this century, and *voilà!*—sooty old Fourth Avenue above Grand Central became swanky new Park Avenue. Other real estate booms also led to rechristenings. For example, Ninth, Tenth, and Eleventh Avenues on the Upper West Side reemerged in the 1880s as Columbus, Amsterdam, and West End Avenues, respectively.

The case of Sixth Avenue is unique. Up in Harlem, it was renamed Lenox a century ago. But down in the Midtown district the name Sixth Avenue remained. Then in the 1930s, Mayor Fiorello La Guardia saddled it with the designation "Avenue of the Americas." No New Yorker in over 60 years has called it that, except to explain to a baffled tourist where Sixth Avenue is. I am glad to note that the city has at last remounted street signs that say "Sixth Avenue" beneath those that read "Avenue of the Americas."

In the heart of the Midtown and Upper East Side districts you're going to come across another pair of avenues, Madison and Lexington. These thoroughfares confuse many people searching for East Side addresses. It will help to know that Madison Avenue is between Fifth and Park and Lexington is between Park and Third.

The numerical progression of the **east-west streets** starts a little irregularly in the lower part of town. Above 14th Street, however, the progression becomes steady and remarkably regular almost all the way to Spuyten Duyvil (pronounced SPY-ten DIE-vull), the ancient creek that separates northern Manhattan from the mainland

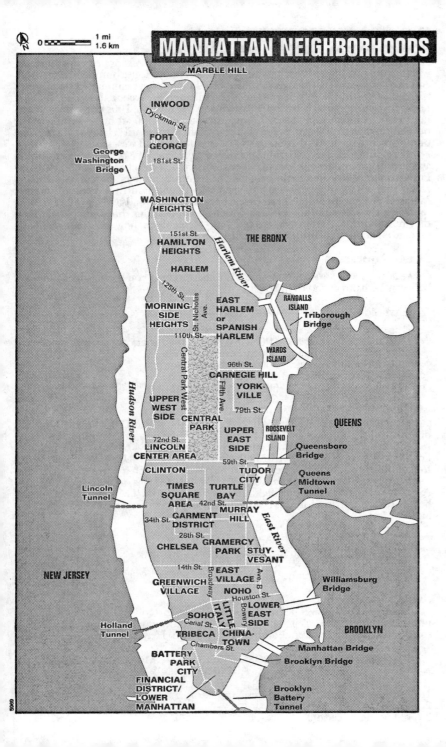

MANHATTAN NEIGHBORHOODS

1 mi
0
1.6 km

MARBLE HILL

INWOOD
Dyckman St.

FORT
GEORGE

George
Washington
Bridge

181st St.

WASHINGTON
HEIGHTS

151st St.

THE BRONX

HAMILTON
HEIGHTS

HARLEM

Harlem River

125th St.

MORNING-
SIDE
HEIGHTS

EAST
HARLEM
or
SPANISH
HARLEM

RANDALLS
ISLAND

Triborough
Bridge

110th St.

St. Nicholas Ave.

WARDS
ISLAND

96th St.

CARNEGIE HILL

Central Park West

YORK-
VILLE

UPPER
WEST
SIDE

Hudson River

CENTRAL
PARK

Fifth Ave.

79th St.

QUEENS

Roosevelt
Island

72nd St.

LINCOLN
CENTER AREA

UPPER
EAST
SIDE

Queensboro
Bridge

CLINTON

59th St.

TUDOR
CITY

Queens
Midtown
Tunnel

Lincoln
Tunnel

TIMES
SQUARE
AREA

TURTLE
BAY

42nd St.

MURRAY
HILL

34th St.

GARMENT
DISTRICT

East River

28th St.

CHELSEA

GRAMERCY
PARK

STUY-
VESANT

NEW JERSEY

14th St.

GREENWICH
VILLAGE

EAST
VILLAGE

Broadway

NOHO

Ave. B

Houston St.

Williamsburg
Bridge

Holland
Tunnel

SOHO

Canal St.

LITTLE ITALY

Bowery

LOWER
EAST
SIDE

TRIBECA

Chambers St.

CHINA-
TOWN

BROOKLYN

Manhattan Bridge

BATTERY
PARK
CITY

Brooklyn Bridge

FINANCIAL
DISTRICT/
LOWER
MANHATTAN

Brooklyn
Battery
Tunnel

HOW TO FIND AN ADDRESS IN MANHATTAN

Addresses on the side streets are designated as either *east* or *west* depending on whether they are located east or west of **Fifth Avenue.** House numbers start with 1 and run consecutively (unless combined building lots have eliminated them) until the end of the block. When you cross the intervening avenue, however, the first number you'll come to is 100, after which you'll stay in the 100s until the next avenue, when numbers jump to 200. Then they jump to 300 at the beginning of the next block, then to 400 at the start of the block after that, until at last you'll reach one or the other of the rivers that bracket Manhattan's east and west sides.

East Side addresses are complicated by the presence of Madison and Lexington avenues. For example, one would expect 59 E. 62nd St. to be on the first block off Fifth Avenue. According to the original 1811 Commissioners' Plan, it is—which is to say that it's located between the original Fifth and Fourth Avenues. But since Madison Avenue now interposes itself between those roads, 59 E. 62nd will be found on the second block off Fifth. Similar complications throw people off when they're looking for addresses around Lex. Remember, however, that the basic scheme is simple and fairly consistent.

Street Addresses

BETWEEN 14TH AND 59TH STREETS Here is a chart to help you locate street addresses between 14th Street and 59th Street.

East Side	West Side
1 at Fifth Avenue	1 at Fifth Avenue
100 at Park Avenue	100 at Avenue of the Americas (Sixth Avenue)
200 at Third Avenue	200 at Seventh Avenue
300 at Second Avenue	300 at Eighth Avenue
400 at First Avenue	400 at Ninth Avenue
500 at York Avenue	500 at Tenth Avenue
	600 at Eleventh Avenue

59TH TO 110TH STREETS Above 59th Street and all the way to 110th Street, things are different on the Upper West Side *only.* This is the region of **Central Park,** whose magnificent rectangle of planned rusticity has eliminated what would have been the first three West Side blocks of 51 Manhattan streets. On the Upper West Side, therefore, numbers on the streets begin at Eighth Avenue, which in this once-again fashionable quarter is called Central Park West. Number 100 is on the corner of Ninth Avenue, which up here is called Columbus, and so forth. The following chart will help you locate street addresses between 59th and 110th Streets on the Upper West Side.

1 at Central Park West (Eighth Avenue)
100 at Columbus Avenue (Ninth Avenue)
200 at Amsterdam Avenue (Tenth Avenue)
300 at West End Avenue (Eleventh Avenue)

Avenue Addresses

Addresses on the avenues might seem to follow no consistent order save that of numerical progression. But there's a method of locating the nearest intersecting street to virtually every avenue address on the island. Here is that magical method.

TO FIND THE NEAREST CROSS STREET TO A MANHATTAN AVENUE ADDRESS

1. Drop the last digit of the address number.
2. Divide by 2.
3. Follow the directions.

street	directions
Avenue A, B, C, or D	add 3
First Avenue	add 3
Second Avenue	add 3
Third Avenue	add 10
Lexington Avenue	add 22
Fourth Avenue (Park Ave. South)	add 8
Park Avenue	add 34 or 35
Madison Avenue	add 26
Fifth Avenue	
up to 200	add 13
201 to 400	add 16
401 to 600	add 18
601 to 775	add 20
776 to 1286	skip step 2 and substract 18
1287 to 1500	add 45
Avenue of the Americas (Sixth Avenue)	subtract 12
Seventh Avenue	
1 to 1800	add 12
1801 and above	add 20
Eighth Avenue	add 9 or 10
Central Park West	divide house number by 10 and add 60
Ninth Avenue	add 13
Columbus Avenue	add 59 or 60
Tenth Avenue	add 14
Amsterdam Avenue	add 59 or 60
Eleventh Avenue	add 15
West End Avenue	add 59 or 60
Riverside Drive	divide house number by 10 and add 72 (to number 567) or 78 (number 568 and above)
Broadway	
up to 754	all below 8th Street
755 to 858	subtract 29
859 to 958	subtract 25
above 1000	subtract 31

NEIGHBORHOODS

Whereas most great cities have one major downtown area, Manhattan has two. When viewed from afar they rise like the twin humps on a camel, two glittering glass-and-stone mountains towering above the city that surrounds them.

DOWNTOWN Downtown is another name for the **Financial District,** a region of big financial institutions at the southern tip of Manhattan. The famous World Trade Center and the adjacent World Financial Center are located downtown. So are City Hall, Police Headquarters, and all the courthouses. Not only are Financial District skyscrapers immensely high, but also many are arranged along former winding cowpaths with quaint names like Maiden Lane, Beaver Street, Old Slip, and so forth. Some of the canyons formed by 70- and 80-story buildings ranged along 20-foot-wide streets are something to behold.

MIDTOWN This is Manhattan's other major skyscraper district, the heart of which is Fifth Avenue in the 50s. The Empire State Building, down at Fifth Avenue and 34th Street, is about as far south as you can get and still consider yourself in Midtown (even then it's a stretch). Midtown is the heart of big-time corporate New York. It consists primarily of office buildings, restaurants, department stores, lots of shops, good clubs, and plush hotels. The most impressive of the Midtown modern sky-scraper avenues are Third, Park, to a certain extent Fifth, and Sixth. Of course you'll find huge glass buildings on other avenues. But these in particular are lined with them, sometimes uninterruptedly for 20-block stretches in the 40s and 50s.

CENTRAL PARK New York's most famous park forms the northern boundary of Midtown. It is also the divider between two of Manhattan's famous residential districts, the **Upper East Side** and the **Upper West Side.**

UPPER EAST SIDE This is the swankiest part of New York, a fact about which there can be no discussion. It is bracketed by Central Park and the East River, between the 60s and 96th Street. The part of it bounded by Fifth and Lexington Avenues, extending between the low 60s and 86th Street, contains an abundance of real palaces, dripping with gilt and marble, many of which are still private houses. And inside some of those dignified if anonymous-looking old apartment buildings along Fifth and Park are 15-, 20-, 30-, sometimes even 40-room apartments. Of course, not everybody on the Upper East Side lives in such splendor. But a lot of people do. Their presence here has created a shopping district along Madison in the 60s and 70s that is unequaled in sumptuousness anywhere in the country, with the *possible* exception of Rodeo Drive in Beverly Hills.

UPPER WEST SIDE The Upper West Side is sandwiched between the Hudson River and Central Park and extends roughly from the low 60s to the upper 90s. It was developed in the closing years of the 19th century as a stronghold of the haute bourgeoisie. Block after block after block of big, ornate, and gloomy brownstones were built, usually on speculation, for the professional class of the day. After World War II the Upper West Side really hit the skids. In the 1980s, it became fashionable again with a young and prosperous crowd. Today it's sometimes called, not too originally, the Yupper West Side. Whatever one's political views on gentrification, the fact remains that the old brownstones are looking pretty swell again.

HARLEM The whole world seems fascinated by Harlem, located on a plain to the north of Central Park. Having been at various times a select suburb, a neighborhood of city "swells," the capital of black America, and a nearly desperate slum, Harlem has in recent years seen considerable improvement. The hot Manhattan real estate market of the 1980s forced some redevelopment attention even on long-neglected Harlem. The neighborhood is very feisty, very alive, filled with astonishing contrasts as well as historic and architectural treasures. Parts of it are poor to the point of being burnt out, but 125th Street, which is the main thoroughfare, is safe enough during the day. Generally the other big avenues are too. It's not recommended that out-of-towners venture into this neighborhood, especially at night, except with a guided tour.

OTHER MANHATTAN AREAS

There are far too many Manhattan neighborhoods to list every one. But a few other notable ones about which you'll want to know include the following.

SOHO The name is an acronym for *So*uth of *Ho*uston Street (pronounced HOUSE-ton). It's located between Houston and Canal Streets in the middle of the island, a little below where the numbered streets begin. SoHo is full of historic 19th-century cast-iron buildings. Formerly a factory and warehouse district, it now brims with ultrachic lofts, trendy restaurants, and galleries, galleries, galleries.

TRIBECA A somewhat tortured acronym, standing for *Tri*angle *Be*low *Ca*nal, TriBeCa is located on the west side of the island just north of the Financial District. It has more trendy lofts, more distinguished 19th-century commercial buildings, and more galleries and boutiques. It exists because SoHo got too expensive.

GARMENT DISTRICT Located in the West 30s, mostly between Sixth and Seventh Avenues, it's a major manufacturing area for women's clothing and often has incredible traffic jams.

DIAMOND DISTRICT West 47th Street between Fifth and Sixth Avenues is lined with diamond merchants. I'll bet you've never seen so many jewelry stores on one block in your life.

BROADWAY/TIMES SQUARE For decades this was an unacknowledged porno district, an entity which flourished on West 42nd Street between Sixth and Eighth and then up Eighth into the mid-40s. It's not completely gone yet, but already legitimate theaters are replacing grind houses on 42nd Street and porno shops are moving farther west. The whole Times Square area is undergoing a multibillion-dollar redevelopment. Of course, city administrations have been trying to clean up 42nd Street for longer than I, for one, have been alive. However, this time they've built a multimillion-dollar hotel, the Marriott Marquis, right in the middle of Times Square itself. So they seem to be really doing it this time.

THEATER DISTRICT Most legitimate theaters are in the West 40s, generally between Broadway and Eighth. Many a midblock is lined with glittering theaters (where tickets cost $60 to $100 a shot), the streets crammed at curtain time with long black limousines, the sidewalks clogged with excited and well-dressed theatergoers from all over the world. And at the end of the same block is a flophouse and a gaggle of prostitutes. While it is perfectly safe, especially at theater time, it is best to be alert, to notice your immediate surroundings, and keep a close eye on your possessions. Be particularly careful with cameras, purses, necklaces, and wallets, all favorite targets of thieves.

---

3. Getting Around Town

WALKING

This is the most rewarding means of transit. Remember that a mile equals about 20 short north-south blocks and 6 to 10 long east-west blocks. The city streets teem with every human and architectural type. Walking is a feast for the senses and a lot of fun.

BUSES

Public buses cost $1.25 a ride and require exact change or a token. They're kind of fun, too, except when overcrowded during rush hour. Almost every major avenue has a bus route going whichever direction that avenue goes. The stops are clearly marked at curbside, but not every bus stops at every bus stop. Sometimes there are little route maps mounted on steel posts anchored in the sidewalk. If you can't understand the maps, you can ask the driver if the bus is going where you're headed.

Many buses go crosstown as well, which is to say east and west on the side streets instead of north and south on the avenues.

Streets with crosstown buses include 8th (M13—eastbound only), 9th (M13—westbound only), 14th, 23rd, 34th, 42nd, 49th (westbound only), 50th (eastbound only), 57th, 59th (called Central Park South between Fifth and Eighth Avenues), 66th (westbound only), 67th (eastbound only), 72nd (this route detours down to 57th Street between Fifth and Eighth Avenues), 79th, 86th, 96th, 116th, 125th, 145th, and 155th.

Transfers from one route to another are free. You must ask for the transfer when you board the bus.

Bus maps are hard to come by. The best idea is to request one in advance. Write to Customer Service, New York City Transit Authority, 370 Jay St., Room 875, Brooklyn, NY 11201. They're free, as long as you include a self-addressed stamped envelope. If you need immediate help, call 718/330-1234 between 6am and 9pm.

SUBWAYS

New York's underground trains (sometimes elevated above ground) provide the fastest transportation over long distances. If you're going, say, from Midtown to the World Trade Center, it'll take 15 minutes by subway as opposed to maybe an hour (or maybe two hours if traffic is bad) by bus. Many New Yorkers won't set foot in a subway. For years, they've had the (justified) reputation of being noisy, dangerous, and incredibly dirty. Fortunately, in recent years the subways have been greatly improved. Even the grafitti is gone, at least in Manhattan.

The New York City subway system is also rather magnificent. It's certainly larger than any other. Just how large is illustrated by the fact that it's possible to take a single subway train (the "A") for 32.29 miles. If you change trains just once, the longest run is an amazing 38.31 miles (from White Plains Road in the Bronx to Far Rockaway in Queens, changing at Fulton Street in downtown Manhattan).

Over a *billion* subway tokens are sold each year, at the glass-enclosed booths located at every stop. On an average day, almost $3½ million are slipped under the cashiers' windows and a corresponding number of tokens (at $1.25 each) are slipped back out. These tokens are then deposited into turnstiles for access to train platforms.

On weekdays between about 7 and 10am and again between about 4 and 7pm, the subways are packed. The rest of the day it's easier to get a seat. Trains run every couple of minutes during peak hours. In the middle of the night, however, you might wait up to half an hour. Unlike those in other cities, New York's subways run 24 hours a day.

Finding your way around the subways is not too difficult—*if* you have a map. Therein, however, lies the rub. **Subway maps** are usually available at every change booth, and they should be posted in each car. However, there are four relatively dependable sources of subway maps. The first is the Transit Authority, to which you can write in care of Customer Service, New York City Transit Authority, 370 Jay St., Room 875, Brooklyn, NY 11201. Enclose a self-addressed stamped envelope. They'll send you one free of charge. Alternatively, you can go to the Convention and Visitors Bureau on the ground floor of 2 Columbus Circle (that's at Eighth Avenue and 59th Street, at the southwest corner of Central Park). They'll give you one for free too. Or go to the information booth on the main concourse of Grand Central Station (Park Avenue and 42nd Street) or to the information booth at Pennsylvania Station over on Seventh Avenue and 33rd Street. Also, see the subway map on pages 28–29 of this guide.

Subway maps superimpose various **numbered and lettered train routes** over a stylized map of the city. They take a bit of studying, but anyone with reasonable intelligence can determine which train goes closest to his or her destination. Anyway, it's not a good idea to get on a train unless you know in advance where it's going.

You'll often hear New Yorkers refer to the "Lexington Avenue" or the "Broadway IRT" or the "Eighth Avenue IND" and so forth. When you look at a subway map, however, these terms are nowhere to be seen. What you're hearing are the old names of various subway lines that operated independently of one another in the days when most were privately owned. Nowadays the city operates the entire system. And it differentiates only between individual train routes and no longer between former lines.

Final notes: The subways get a little lonely (read *scary*) at night. Go with friends and avoid empty cars. And stand in the middle of the platform where it's most lit while waiting at night. At all times of the day or night, stand within the specially demarcated waiting area on the platform and do not go too close to the platform edge.

TAXIS

There are three kinds of taxi. The ones you hail on the street are painted yellow, bear a city-issued medallion riveted to the hood, and have the words *NYC Taxi* on the door and a little superstructure attached to the roof over the windshield. If that thingamajig on the roof is lighted, the cab is looking for a fare. If it's not lighted, then someone is inside the cab already or the driver is on radio call. If the off-duty lights (also located on the roof) are lighted, then that cab won't stop for you even if you get down on your knees.

The meter in a cab starts at $1.50, then increases 25¢ for every ⅕ of a mile. "Waiting time" racks up another 25¢ for every 75 seconds while you are in slow traffic or stopped. There is an extra 50¢ charge per trip between 8pm and 6am. Tipping is customary. (See Section 4, "ABCs of New York City," below.) This sounds a bit more horrible than it really is. Most cab rides cost less than $6, including the tip.

Sharing a cab is perfectly legal, and there is nothing that says you have to pay anything extra if one of you gets off at one address and another stays on to a second address or even to a third. Bridge and tunnel tolls, however, are your responsibility. Hand the money to the driver when needed.

Taxis, like subways and buses, are crowded during rush hours. In Midtown, as a matter of fact, it's almost impossible to hail one. Don't get locked into a schedule that requires catching a cab on Fifth Avenue and 48th Street at quarter to five. If you do, you'll be late.

Many visitors are uncertain how, exactly, to hail a cab. Good cab-flagging form requires, above all, confidence. Don't look timid; look determined. Remember to flag only cabs with lighted roof devices. Keep the chin down, the feet firmly planted on the ground, and the right arm raised in a commanding manner. One might even mutter a little "sieg heil" under one's breath. Keep the raised arm almost rigid and the eyes steely and alert for the advance of a likely cab. Be prepared to sprint if you see one. The competition will give no quarter, nor expect it in return. And remember to keep your dignity. Points are earned for a masklike face even when some creep darts across moving traffic to grab the cab that's veered all the way across an avenue just for you.

There are also nonyellow "gypsy cabs" on the prowl in New York. Gypsies are actually car services that mostly originate outside Manhattan. They are not licensed to pick up people who don't telephone and make a reservation first. As a practical matter, they do a little illicit cruising anyway. "Illicit" is decidedly the buzzword on the gypsies. They not only look slightly disreputable but have a pesky reputation for taking the unsuspecting on wild goose chases. Avoid them.

"Car services" are not all like the seediest of the gypsies. Many sport late-model Lincolns or other perfectly clean and nice cars. They provide transportation to and from vast areas of town that yellow cabs don't frequent. If during your stay in New York you find yourself in some hinterland late at night, ask your hosts to recommend a car service or look one up in the Yellow Pages under "Car Services." Nail down the rate before you make the reservation.

PRIVATE CARS

It's difficult to drive in New York City, with so much auto and pedestrian traffic. It's not just a coincidence that if you look around, you'll mostly see professionals, such as taxis and rented or private limos. Those that don't look like they know where they're going usually will have out-of-state plates—thus the term "Jersey driver."

---

4. ABCs of New York City

AREA CODES New York City has been telephonically Balkanized. Manhattan now has the area code that used to cover the whole city, **212,** all to itself. Brooklyn, Queens, the Bronx, and Staten Island, although a part of the same municipality,

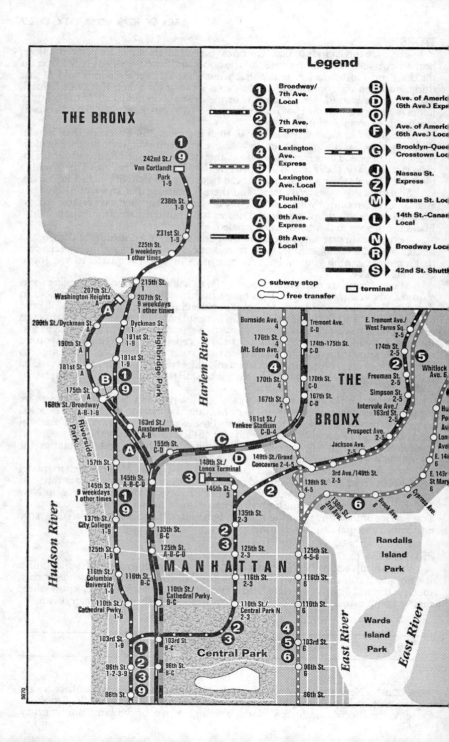

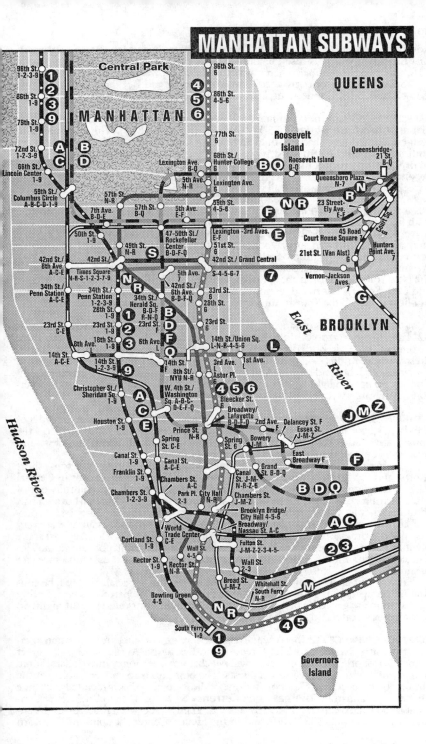

MANHATTAN SUBWAYS

now have a separate area code, **718.** That means if you're in Manhattan and want to dial Brooklyn, you must use the long-distance prefix 1, followed by the area code 718, and then the number. There's no extra charge, however.

Suburban area codes are as follows: Westchester and Rockland counties, **914;** Long Island, **516;** Connecticut, **203;** and New Jersey, **201** and **908.**

BABYSITTERS   Oftentimes your hotel will be able to set you up. But if it can't, try the **Gilbert Child Care Agency,** 25 W. 39th St. (tel. 921-4848). This reputable and well-established firm charges $6.25 an hour for kids over 9 months, plus $1.00 per additional sibling. Infants cost more. There's a four-hour minimum, plus sitters' transportation charges of $4 before 8pm and $8 after 8pm. The **Robin Kellner Agency,** 221 W. 57th St. (tel. 247-4141), offers longer-term nanny service—from a weekend to a few months or all year. Advance notice is required.

BUS & SUBWAY INFORMATION   As of this writing, bus and subway cost $1.25 per ride, with free transfers at intersecting lines. Subway token booths make change, but bus drivers don't. To board a bus you'll need either the exact fare (no paper money) or a subway token. Bus and subway maps are hard to come by. The most dependable sources are the information booths at Grand Central Terminal, 42nd Street at Park Avenue, and Pennsylvania Station, Seventh Avenue at 32nd Street, or at the office of the New York Convention and Visitors Bureau, 2 Columbus Circle (Eighth Avenue and 59th Street). For free directions on how to get from Point A to Point B using public transit, call the Transit Authority at 718/330-1234 between 6am and 9pm.

CLIMATE   In the depths of January, New York City's average daytime temperature is 32° Fahrenheit; in tropical July the average high is 86°. As a practical matter, these extremes vary 10° in both directions. Visitors during the winter months had better dress warmly. Bring boots too—slushy winter streets get pretty sloppy. Summer in the city is often hot and humid. Add to this the extra hazard of deep-freeze air conditioning. So bring a light jacket or wrap. Spring and fall, however, are crisp and perfect during the day, only mildly cool in the evening.

CLOTHING   In a city where rubber dresses and purple Mohawks are, if not the order of the day, at least nothing unusual, it's ironic that dressing still tends to be on the conservative side. Perhaps that's because Manhattan is all about business, and businesspeople wear suits and ties.

During the day you can sightsee in jeans and casual shirts. Tank tops, short shorts, and flip-flops, however, are inappropriate in Manhattan, except in Central Park. When 6pm rolls around, things get more formal. You'll feel painfully out of place wearing jeans in the lobby of a first-class hotel after six. Or in a Midtown bar, assuming they let you in. Athletic shoes, however comfortable they may be for touring, are a definite no-no at night. Many very nice neighborhood restaurants are very casual about dress. But the better places are going to require, if not a tie, at least some obvious effort at dressing up. First-class restaurants and nightspots are rigid: Ties and jackets are a must for men. All women need, however, is a dress with a nice pair of shoes.

If you visit New York in winter, bring warm clothes, especially if you'll be continuing on upstate. If you're coming in the summer, be prepared to sweat. Spring and autumn are generally pleasant during the daylight hours but chilly at night. So take along a sweater and/or a light jacket.

CURRENCY EXCHANGE   **Citibank** will exchange foreign currency in Manhattan at either the Fifth Avenue and 51st Street or the Lexington Avenue and 54th Street branch. Most other banks, however, will *not* change your money into dollars. Some hotels will, but only for registered guests. The best idea is to convert money at the airport. If you need more later on, try one of the following recommended exchange bureaus in Manhattan: **Thomas Cook Currency Services, Inc.,** in Rockefeller Center at 630 Fifth Ave. (tel. 757-6915), at 41 E. 42nd St., between Madison and Vanderbilt Avenues (tel. 883-0400), and in the Herald Center shopping mall at 33rd

Street and Sixth Avenue (tel. 736-9790); **New York Foreign Exchange, Inc.**, 61 Broadway between Rector Street and Exchange Place (tel. 248-4700); and **Cheque Point,** 1568 Broadway, at 47th St. in the Embassy Hotel (tel. 869-6281), at 551 Madison Ave., at 55th Street (tel. 980-6443), and at 22 Central Park South off Fifth Avenue (tel. 750-2400).

DOCTOR Doctors on Call (tel. 718/745-5900), a private health care service, provides house calls. Alternatively, almost every big hospital in town maintains a 24-hour emergency room.

DRINKING The legal minimum age for drinking in New York State is 21, so have proof of age handy if you look younger. Bars in New York are permitted to stay open till 4am, but this is not to say that all of them do. If you're on a roll and they start to close the place down at 2am, know that someplace else is bound to be open. Actually, a whole category of unlicensed and at times unsavory (if exciting) establishments don't even start until 4am. These are the notorious "after-hours clubs," whose special delights lie beyond the scope of this work.

DRUGSTORES The popular chain **Duane Reed** (tel. 421-4880) has various locations throughout the city. **Windsor Pharmacy,** open every day from 8am to midnight, is on Sixth Avenue between 57th and 58th Streets (tel. 247-1538), and **Kaufman's,** open 24 hours, is at Lexington Avenue and 50th Street (tel. 755-2266).

EMERGENCY To call the **police,** dial 911—but only in an emergency. For normal police inquiries, call 374-5000. For an **ambulance** or to report a **fire,** also dial 911.

EVENTS New York City is either the scene and/or the host of a very considerable number of events and activities. For a daily listing of free city-sponsored activities, call 360-1333. The **New York Convention and Visitors Bureau,** 2 Columbus Circle (tel. 397-8222), publishes a quarterly calendar of events, covering everything from parades on Fifth Avenue to jogging marathons to the Japanese Cherry Blossom Festival in Brooklyn. Call or drop by for a copy.

OUT-OF-TOWN NEWSPAPERS A famous outfit called **Hotalings,** 142 W. 42nd St., between Sixth Avenue and Broadway (tel. 840-1868), carries over 200 papers from all over the world.

PARKING Everybody will tell you that parking is impossible in Manhattan. This is only partly true. There are **privately owned parking garages** all over the place, but they're extremely dear. Just how dear is illustrated by the following rates, copied recently off the wall of a typical Midtown garage located in the basement of a skyscraper near 59th and Fifth: Up to 1 hour is $14.50; up to 2 hours is $16.75; up to 3 hours is $18.75; up to 10 hours is $22.50; and up to 12 hours is $24.50. Also added is an extra 18¼% New York City Parking Tax.

A sobering set of rates, no? Actually, if this had been a 24-hour garage the maximum rate wouldn't have been too bad. Most Manhattan hotels, when they do offer parking, usually offer it for $25 to $40 per 24 hours.

The farther you are from the fashionable core of Midtown or downtown, the lower the rates. But with the exception of the occasional "early bird special," which might lure parkers in before 10am and out before 6pm for $10, $11, or $12, there are few bargains among Manhattan's lots and garages.

Kinney Systems (tel. 889-4444), which is one of the big parking operators in town, runs a few cut-rate **municipal garages** for the city. But be advised that the municipal garages are not particularly cheap if you want to park for days or weeks. Nor are they very conveniently located. The one in Midtown, a park-and-lock at Eighth Avenue between 53rd and 54th Streets, is the most accessible. It charges $3 per hour and is open 24 hours a day, with a maximum daytime charge of $13.50 and a maximum overnight charge from 8pm to 8am of $10.50. The other municipals— under Police Headquarters way down at 103 Park Row; on Leonard Street between

Lafayette and Centre Streets; and, remotest of all, at 113 Essex St. near Delancey—are about as convenient as parking in Pennsylvania.

A possible longer-term parking idea for visitors is an outfit in Brooklyn called **Auto Baby Sitters,** 827 Sterling Place (between Nostrand and Rogers; tel. 718/493-9800). You can store your car here for $50 a week or $93 for two weeks to a month. Don't forget the 10.25% tax. Auto Baby Sitters requires an appointment in advance, and charges more for vans. If the thought of searching Brooklyn for Sterling Place intimidates you, they will pick up (for $15) or drop off (for $20) your car for you in Manhattan or elsewhere in the boroughs. Call between 9am and 4:30pm during the week, and 9am to noon on Saturday (closed Sunday).

Free street parking in Manhattan is possible, but it's subject to regulations known as "alternate side of the street parking laws." You'll mostly find alternate-side parking in residential neighborhoods. A typical sign, say, on West 74th Street between Columbus and Central Park West, will read "No Parking 11am to 2pm, Mon, Wed, Fri." Signs on the opposite side have the same restrictions, except that they're in effect on "Tues, Thurs, and Sat." Sunday is a free day. Therefore, if you arrive on West 74th Street at 1:30pm, as so many do, you can pull up to a gradually filling curb, sit in your car until 2pm, then get out and leave it in place until 11am two days hence. Get it?

On many East Side streets Wednesday is a free day too. A typical sign, say, on East 77th Street between Park and Madison, might read "No Parking 8am to 11am, Tues and Fri." Arrive at 10:30am on Friday and you've got a legal spot for the whole weekend—in fact until Tuesday morning.

If you don't catch the alternate hours, you'll find yourself in the pack of piranhas, and at a disadvantage since you won't know the lay of the land. Whatever happens, do *not* park illegally. To be towed in Manhattan means a $150 towing charge, plus the cost of the ticket (usually around $60), plus the cost of a cab to get you to one of the city parking pounds, which are not exactly on the beaten track. If it happens to you, the **Parking Violations Bureau** (tel. 788-7800) has all the bad news.

As for **metered parking,** it exists, but not in great profusion. A quarter usually buys you 20 minutes on Broadway or Madison or Third. What's the best advice? Leave your car at home.

POST OFFICE The main post office, an enormous edifice, is at 33rd Street and Eighth Avenue (tel. 967-8585). It's open from 8am to 6pm and operates a 24-hour emergency window for certified and express mail. Numerous branch post offices are located throughout the city.

RAILROAD INFORMATION Commuter rail lines to the northern suburbs are operated by **Metro North** (tel. 532-4900). Trains for the whole of Long Island are run by the **Long Island Rail Road** (tel. 718/217-5477). The toll-free number for **Amtrak** trains to other destinations is 800/USA-RAIL.

SAFETY On the subject of **general safety,** be advised that New York is no more dangerous than most big cities. But wherever you go, keep your wits about you. Don't let a fat wallet bulge out of your back pocket or somebody may pick it. Beware of people who jostle or crowd in front or back of you. Don't leave your purse on the seat beside you, or worse, under the table at a restaurant, or somebody will relieve you of it. Don't wear expensive jewelry on a subway or somebody may snatch it. These are just facts of city life.

As for getting mugged, which is local parlance for street robbery, it won't happen to you unless you stray into some lonely area, usually at night. Wherever you go, don't dawdle on the streets. Muggers go for the slow and easy marks. Keep moving, keep with the crowds, stay alert, and you'll be quite safe. However, if you are accosted, give them what they want as they may be armed.

Bicycles are thought by some New Yorkers to be the perfect solution to traffic-crowded streets. Most cyclists are the politest of souls, but many among them take a high-handed attitude toward pedestrians. You will see bicycles streaking down one-way streets the wrong way, ignoring red lights, expecting you to hear the faint slish of skinny tires on asphalt above the roar of Midtown traffic. If you get hit, your as-sailant is not going to stop unless his or her precious ten-speed is rendered inopera-ble by the collision. *Always* look both ways when stepping off a curb. With all the one-way streets in New York, people often forget to do this. And people have actually been killed by bikes. At the least you're in jeopardy of having your clothes ripped and your composure severely disrupted.

Although the ranks of card sharps are thinning, it is still possible on street cor-ners in this town, even in the most fashionable districts, to see a card game called **three-card monte.** A player with a slick patter stands behind a cardboard box on which he or she deals out three cards face down. Passersby are invited to bet on the identity of these cards. Lots of money flashes back and forth and people seem to be winning. Don't get involved. This is strictly a sucker ploy. You'll lose.

TELEPHONES   Local calls cost 25¢ at pay phones, more from your hotel room (how much more depends on the hotel). See also "Area Codes," above.

TIPPING   There's an old story about the girl who came to New York in August and caught pneumonia. You see, she couldn't turn off the air conditioner in her hotel room, and she was too embarrassed to call a bellman because she didn't know how much to tip. So here's how much to tip:
Restaurants: Everybody says 15% to 20%, but most New Yorkers tip closer to the 20% end. In ritzy establishments the presence of a captain inevitably raises ques-tions. Do you have to tip this tuxedo-clad model of Manhattan urbanity simply be-cause he led you to a table and handed you a menu? No, you don't. Stick with the regular 20% to the waiter. But what if Monsieur Marc (or whatever the name) con-trives to get you some favorite dish even though it isn't on the menu, undertakes a successful search for your favorite wine, or arranges on the sly to surprise your spouse with a little cake for his or her birthday? Then you tip him. How much? Not a fortune; usually around 5% of the bill.
Taxis: Again, people will tell you to tip between 15% and 20% of whatever's on the meter. But something a bit on the shady side of 20% is more customary. Never give a cabby less than 50¢, unless you want to part company as avowed enemies.
Bellhops: They expect a buck per bag, unless it's a tiny little thing they can tuck under an arm. In the really elegant hotels it's more like $2 for a single bag, $3 for two bags, etc. Anytime they walk in the door, to bring something in or take it away again, plan on pressing a couple of bucks into the outstretched palm. (Don't forget, these people live on tips.)
At the airport: If you engage a porter either to carry your things or to load them onto a trolley or to take care of your bags at curb-side-checking, plan on paying him 50¢ for each small bag and $1 for each big one.
At the theater: Ushers in American theaters do not expect tips.

TOURIST INFORMATION   The **New York Convention and Visitors Bureau** is located near the southwest corner of Central Park, at 2 Columbus Circle, New York, NY 10019 (tel. 397-8222). Helpful people at the desk will answer all manner of ques-tions, provide maps, and give useful advice. The C&V also publishes a free calendar of events and it would be clever of you to write in advance for this publication. New York is always hosting something or other, be it an antiques show, a dog show, an auto show, a street festival, fireworks displays, or a major parade. The calendar of events tells you everything that's scheduled for each season.

TRAVELER'S AID   This organization provides emergency assistance to people stranded in New York. It might be in the form of aid in reaching family or friends, transportation, or possibly even temporary shelter. There are two offices—one in the International Arrivals Building at JFK Airport (tel. 718/656-4870) and the oth-er at 1481 Broadway, between 42nd and 43rd Streets (tel. 944-0013).

III

NEW YORK CITY HOTELS

1. GRAND ARMY PLAZA–FIFTH AVENUE
2. EAST MIDTOWN
3. WEST MIDTOWN
4. UPPER EAST SIDE
5. UPPER WEST SIDE
6. DOWNTOWN
7. BED & BREAKFASTS

For the purposes of hotel recommendations, I've divided Manhattan into six areas: Grand Army Plaza–Fifth Avenue, East Midtown, West Midtown, Upper East Side, Upper West Side, and Downtown. Each area has a distinct flavor, reflected in its accommodations.

A WORD ABOUT "PACKAGES"

New York City hotels are thronged during the week but rather empty on weekends. Demand for hotel rooms is overwhelming in November but lackluster in March. In order to lessen the impact of these rhythms of room occupancy, the hotel industry has created the "package."

I'm not talking about tour packages here, of the sort that include airfare, rental cars, and guided tours, but about minipackages concocted by individual hotels in hopes of attracting warm bodies to otherwise empty rooms. If you're making your own hotel reservations, *be sure to ask* if there's a package rate in effect during your proposed stay. It can save you lots of money, sometimes as much as half the room rate.

The typical hotel package is often aimed squarely at the libido of the New York–area suburbanite. Packages bear names like "Romance in New York," "The Suite Weekend," "Japanese Fantasy in New York," "S'Glamorous," "Weekend in the Sky," "Posh and Pampered," and so on. Even though special packages are advertised all over the local press, reservation clerks won't tell you about them unless you ask. The rates quoted in the descriptions below are permanent rates in effect at press time. Packages are temporary special deals.

Prepare yourself, before we start, for some of these prices. It is a sad truth that a decent Manhattan hotel room for under $100 is virtually unknown. And a double in the hotel you may have dreamed of staying at might well cost well over $300.

Remember to always ask for "specials" or corporate discounts. *And to every price quoted, you must add 8¼% sales tax, plus 6% New York City Hotel tax, plus 5% New York State tax on all hotel rooms over $100 (we're already up to 19¼%) plus another $2 per night New York City hotel occupancy tax.*

Note: In New York City you can assume all major credit cards are accepted, unless stated otherwise.

1. Grand Army Plaza—Fifth Avenue

Grand Army Plaza is an elegant small square bounded by Fifth Avenue, 58th and 59th Streets, and the east wall of the famous Plaza Hotel. The nearby area is the very heart of fashionable Manhattan, full of expensive hotels, many of which overlook Central Park. To stay here is to be surrounded by glittering shops and skyscrapers, posh clubs, streets crowded with taxis, and sidewalks thronged with the well-heeled.

Just south of Grand Army Plaza is the glorious, newly restored **St. Regis,** 2 E. 55th St. (at Fifth Avenue), New York, NY 10019 (tel. 212/753-4500). The lobby is abundant with rare marble, soaring columns, and gilt frills. Hand-painted cupids float between the seven lobby chandeliers. The staff members are concerned about making your stay the best ever in any hotel in the world, and they offer to unpack and press your clothing and provide bottled water, fax service in your room, and free unlimited local phone calls!

The rooms are reminiscent of those when the stock market was soaring and the rich were getting richer quicker than ever. Opulent tapestries and overstuffed pillows along with luxurious Egyptian cotton sheets adorn the beds. The walls are silk covered, the inlaid mahogany night tables stand on tiny gilt feet, the high ceilings are accented with molding, and the closets are spacious enough for long stays and big purchases. The ultradeluxe marble baths feature gold fixtures fit for a king, and kings have made the St. Regis home in the past. Don't worry about your chilly feet on marble floors, as the chambermaid will make sure you have a new pair of terry slippers to match your plush terry robe supplied daily.

Of course, all this is at a price, which some consider the highest in the city. Rooms at the St. Regis range from $350 for superior to $450 for grand luxe. Suites start at $550 and soar to $3,000 per night for the nine-room Presidential. Downstairs is the King Cole Bar, just off the lobby, where the Bloody Mary was invented in the 1930s. It boasts a famous mural by Maxfield Parrish, telling just why King Cole was a merry old soul. Tea and light fare can be had at the Astor Court, and the hotel restaurant, Lespinasse, offers French gourmet dining with an Oriental flair. A great, almost secret place is the Cognac Room, between the reception area and the court. It's an intimate mahogany-paneled room where tea can be sipped and a newspaper read in peace and elegance for just $3, not including tip.

Across the street from the St. Regis is **The Peninsula, New York,** 700 Fifth Ave. at 55th Street, New York, NY 10019 (tel. 212/247-2200). This is also a grand old New York building, but it was recently redone in the grand 1980s style of mahogany and green marble.

When you enter, the sweeping stair takes you past a restaurant, a café, and a bar that's almost always lively with Sunday brunchers or business lunchers. The staff provides every amenity for a luxurious stay. The executivelike rooms are art nouveau with fine cherrywood furniture, curved ceilings, and etched-crystal sconces; each features a safe spacious enough to fit a laptop computer and a briefcase. The baths are peach marble, and many rooms have Jacuzzis with separate stall showers and double sinks. The lights, TVs, room temperature, and radios are controlled by the bedside computer phones, which also give you the time anywhere around the world and "speak" six languages. But the best part is high above the bustle of Fifth Avenue on the 21st, 22nd, and 23rd floors: an oasis called The Peninsula Spa. This is not your everyday hotel workout room with two Stairmasters and one attendant to hand out overused towels—it is the most plush private-membership spa in the city. Although membership prices aren't discussed over the phone, they are rumored to be $1,500 per year, plus monthly dues of $300. The spa boasts mahogany locker rooms with marble vanities and showers and even provides plush towels, robes, spa sandals, and workout clothing. All you need is your own athletic shoes and the desire to be pampered. After your workout with the free weights or Cybex, LifeStep/Cycle, Stairmaster, or Gravitron, you can take advantage of the resident Swedish masseur or indulge in a seaweed purifying wrap. You can then meander over to the whirlpool for further relaxation or swim in the Olympic-size pool with some of the best views of the city. The glass slides away in the summer for the ritualistic sun seekers, and light fare is also served poolside. Then, to round the day out, you may want to enjoy a steam bath in the eucalyptus room or simply purify your body in the sauna. You can hide away in this paradise for hours. And the absolutely best part about this spa is that hotel guests have unlimited free access during their stay.

After the spa is closed, you can still enjoy the view high atop everything from yet another New York secret: the rooftop bar. With only eight tables, this is a great place to enjoy the serene Fifth Avenue view at night without the hustle and bustle below.

Rates range from $295 to $395 for a superior room to $495 to $595 for a junior or an executive suite. A deluxe, which is a one- or two-bedroom suite, costs $950 to $1,250. The corner suites are truly splendid, with views up Fifth to Central Park.

Back to the plaza and over to Central Park South, and there stands the **Helmsley Park Lane Hotel,** 36 Central Park South (between Fifth and Sixth Avenues), New York, NY 10019 (tel. 212/371-4000, or toll free 800/221-4982), a 46-story glass-and-limestone high-rise built in 1971. It is deluxe and contemporary and patronized by movie people from the West Coast.

Everything about this place reflects the Helmsley chain's attention to detail. The lobby is chandelier city, a great vault of polished marble, crimson carpets, a sweeping staircase, and an eye-boggling display of dangling crystal. Every marble console in sight carries a spectacular spray of fresh flowers.

Care and pride are clearly in evidence upstairs in the guest rooms too. No moldings or old-mansion airs up here. Instead, the rooms have a lush contemporary suburban look. There are plenty of comfortable chairs, lots of handsome brass table lamps, a refrigerator and a phone in the bathroom, full-length mirrors on the closet doors, a thermos, a clock radio, three movie channels on the color TV, even an ironing board and a hairdryer. The rooms aren't huge but are extremely appealing and comfortable. The furniture is Louis-Louis, and the views, even when you don't face the park, are sensational. (If a view is important, tell them you want a room above the 20th floor.)

Room rates range between $235 and $255. One-bedroom suites are $550 to $675. Top-rate rooms face Central Park; minimum-rate rooms are just as nice but without the park view (in my opinion many of these city views are every bit as interesting as those overlooking the park).

On the hotel's second floor, at the top of the sweeping staircase, is the Park Room Restaurant, a lofty chamber that provides diners with treetop views of Central Park. Cuisine is classic French-continental, and dinner will cost a good $50 per person. Adjacent to the restaurant is an appealing wood-paneled bar with a piano-chanteuse in the evening. In the basement garage your car can snooze, for $35 a night, in the splendorous company of Bentleys and Mercedeses. Room service is, of course, available 24 hours a day.

The Ritz-Carlton, 112 Central Park South (between Sixth and Seventh Avenues), New York, NY 10019 (tel. 212/757-1900, or toll free 800/241-3333), is a horse of a different color. To be more specific, it's a hotel that aspires to be the horsey set's home away from the country estate. The dignified limestone building with its bright-blue awning started life in the 1920s as an apartment house. A few years back it was gutted and rebuilt, then decorated by New York society decorator Mrs. Henry ("Sister") Parrish. The result is lots of pickled pine, lacquered walls, gilt-framed pictures of dogs, Chippendale-style sofas, Chinese vases made over into lamps, and a discreet but pervasive air of unpretentious luxury.

With only 228 rooms and suites, the place is not big. But, of course, "bigness" is just what management is trying to avoid. It has the air of an English country house, where elegant informality reigns. The lobby is small and discreet—no Helmsley glitz at the Ritz. No profusion of public rooms either. Upstairs, rooms are smallish but exceedingly well tailored. They have thick dark rugs; nice wood furniture; not one but two telephone lines; and marble-topped vanities bearing the usual little bottles of deluxe shampoo, hair conditioner, and so forth. There are hunt prints on the walls and free copies of *The New York Times* at doorways in the morning. Room service, as well as a concierge who is part magician, is available 24 hours. And there is a fitness room available to all guests.

Rates run all the way from $200 to $350 for singles, $220 to $380 for doubles; expect a standard double to cost around $280 nightly. Suites are $500 to $750, depending on view. The ground-floor Jockey Club Restaurant has more expanses of pickled pine, including a long pine bar over which hangs a handsome painting of a hunting hound. For those who don't like flash but do like quality, this is an excellent choice. (P.S.: Don't forget to ask about holiday and weekend packages.)

The Plaza Hotel, Fifth Avenue at 59th Street, New York, NY 10019 (tel. 212/759-3000, or toll free 800/228-3000), is a magnificent Edwardian pile dating from 1907. Its opulent gilt-and-marble lobbies were once the definition of New York luxury. Today its palatial ballrooms remain favorites for charity balls and society dances.

The heart of The Plaza is the Palm Court, which ripples with violin music and the tinkle of laughter each afternoon and evening. The hotel's other restaurants include the famous Edwardian Room, the somberly elegant Oak Room, the Oyster Bar, and the Tahitian excesses of Trader Vic's. Mirrored and marbled corridors meander this way and that, lined with shops that sell everything from exquisite jewels to aspirin.

Since The Plaza was bought by real estate mogul Donald Trump, every one of the 815 rooms has been upgraded and redecorated. All have pretty chintz flowered bedspreads and matching wallpaper. At their best they are big, handsomely proportioned, and graced with marvelous green views of Central Park.

Although at times overcrowded with ogling tourists in the lobby, the place has a glamour uniquely its own. Singles at The Plaza cost from $215 for an interior room to $450 for a deluxe room with a park view. Most singles are priced between $260 and $475 nightly. Double rooms start at $260 and range to $485, the latter price being for rooms facing the park. Many rooms facing Fifth Avenue or 58th Street are just as nice and more reasonably priced. Avoid the interior rooms. For another $35 nightly you can store your car in the hotel's garage.

Unquestionably the best value for the money in Midtown, and perhaps anywhere in town, is the **Wyndham,** 42 W. 58th St. (between Fifth and Sixth Avenues), New York, NY 10019 (tel. 212/753-3500). The building looks like a typical apartment house dating from sometime after World War I. Inside is a slightly cluttered and rather pretty little lobby furnished with painted screens, a profusion of potted plants, Chinese rugs, gilt mirrors, and sofas. It looks like someone's living room. Which is what it is. The owners of the Wyndham, Mr. and Mrs. John Mados, live upstairs. Mr. Mados runs the business, and Mrs. Mados decorates the rooms. The employees, many of whom have been here for years, are like an extended family. The Madoses' personal touch attracts Broadway and Hollywood celebrities and savvy world travelers, as do the rooms, which are unbelievably luxurious for the price.

The suites are simply huge, carpeted with thick pastel-colored rugs and decorated with botanical prints in gilded frames, comfortable sofas, Chinese throw rugs, and even the occasional marble fireplace. Every piece of fabric and furniture is immaculate. All suites have little kitchenettes; some even have dressing rooms adjacent to the bedrooms. They look like classy little New York apartments. The truth is that they are absolutely the equal of suites in the very best hotels in town. The standard rooms are just as nice. And big!

What's most amazing about the Wyndham is the price. Half the 212 units are suites, priced between $175 and $205 a night. The rest, from the ninth floor down, are standard rooms, renting for $115 to $125 for a single and $130 to $140 for a double. The main-floor restaurant is called Jonathan's. If you've brought a car, you'll have to take care of your own parking, but that's easy enough at nearby garages.

2. East Midtown

The hotels that follow are in the East 40s and 50s between Fifth Avenue and the East River.

First choice in the area is the **Waldorf-Astoria,** Park Avenue at 50th Street, New York, NY 10022 (tel. 212/355-3000). This double-towered 47-story Hilton-owned limestone behemoth (1,400 rooms) is the epitome of the ultralavish hotel of the art deco period. Everything is vast and satisfyingly opulent. The lobby is in the middle of a block-long progression of sumptuously carpeted and chandeliered interiors. There are soaring ceilings, glittering mosaics, precious marbles, priceless furniture, and a labyrinth of corridors lined with chic boutiques and restaurants. If you stroll down Peacock Alley during the day, you're liable to hear the music of a harp; at night it'll be Cole Porter's own piano, moved from his suite to the lobby when he died in 1964. It's the glamorous lobby life of the Waldorf that, quite frankly, is one of the major reasons for staying here.

Presidents, movie stars, and the social and business elite from every continent stay at the Waldorf. Guest rooms are reached via corridors so long they seem to vanish into distant pinpoints. The suites (famous for art deco marble bathrooms) and "special executive accommodations" are roomy and sumptuous. The standard rooms tend to be on the small side, but they've all been beautifully redecorated with flowered wallpapers, heavy traditional furniture, minibars, marble bathrooms, and plenty of light. And after all, it's a Hilton, so everything really is first class.

The rate structure at the Waldorf is as labyrinthine as the floor plan. Supposedly, there are rooms that go for as little as $175 single and $240 double per night. As a practical matter, you'll find most singles in the $235 to $265 range, with most doubles priced between $270 and $315. Special rates and weekend packages abound, however, so call in advance for those rates. The suites are quite opulent but also quite expensive. Occupying a part of the building and managed as a separate entity is the Waldorf Towers, where rooms and suites are even more elaborate and expensive.

The hotel has a garage (for around $30 a night storage) as well as hot and cold running restaurants. There is the Bull and Bear for steaks and chops, Sir Harry's, Peacock Alley, Inagiku for Japanese food, the Cocktail Terrace, and Oscar's Coffee Shop. Besides newsstands and ticket brokers you'll find a florist, an antiques shop, several jewelers, leather goods, and clothiers tucked along the hotel's many gold-leafed passageways. How big is the Waldorf? Some 690,000 paying guests in a recent year.

The **New York Palace,** 456 Madison Ave. (between 50th and 51st Streets), New York, NY 10022 (tel. 212/888-7000, or toll free 800/221-4982), gets its name from a landmark complex of 19th-century town houses that forms its Madison Avenue streetfront. When originally built, the Villard Houses, as they are called, gave the appearance of a single Italian Renaissance palace. To a great extent they still do, even though a monolithic glass box of hotel rooms now rises behind them.

Inside the old mansions is a series of palatial restored rooms that serve as lounges, restaurants, and a bar. The vaulted and gilded music room is now the Gold Room, where for $20 per person you can have afternoon tea to the strains of a harpist between 2 and 5pm. The Hunt Bar, formerly a dining room, has sumptuous dark-stained paneling plus little sofa and table groupings. The Madison Room, once a drawing room, is now a lounge with crystal chandeliers, French furniture, marble columns, and an air of St. Petersburg before the Revolution.

Most of the Palace is located in the new structure. The block-through lobby is huge and opulently decorated with damask-covered walls, crimson-velvet poufs, urns on pedestals, and mirrored wall cases filled with expensive watches and jewels. A chandelier as big as a compact car hangs above the grand stairway. The nearly 1,000 guest rooms have marble-topped Louis-esque furniture, hilariously monarchical gilded headboards, a soft pastel color palette, curtains bracketed by paneled valances, and rugs thick enough to wade through. For all the "traditional" details, rooms still have a distinctly contemporary air. And, boy, are they comfortable. And big. And filled with touches like satin hangers in the closet, piles of oversize fluffy towels, scales, bathroom telephones, state-of-the-art color TVs, and little amenity trays filled with complimentary toiletries.

Basic singles range from $195 to $280 nightly; doubles run from $205 to $310. Above the 41st floor is something they call the "tower," even though it's in no way structurally articulated from the rest of the building. Rooms up here are reached by private elevators, have a little private lobby in the sky, and cost $250 for a single, $275 for a double. Up here is where the suites are, including the famous triplex penthouses that rent for $3,000 a night. As a practical matter, the minimum-price rooms in the Palace offer the best value. The hotel restaurant, Le Trianon, serves breakfast, lunch, dinner, and a late-night supper until quarter past midnight. Expect parking to run another $48 a night.

One of the city's newest luxury hotels is the **Four Seasons Hotel, New York,** 57 E. 57th St. (between Madison and Park Avenues), New York, NY 10022 (tel. 212/758-5700). Architect I. M. Pei has tapped Eastern influences that tranlate into an updated, streamlined Moderne look, complete with larger-than-usual windows that actually open and a lot of fresh flowers. The standard rooms are the largest in the city, each with a sitting and desk area, minibar, and separate dressing area off the extra-large marble bath. Rates run from $295 to $420 for a standard or deluxe, depending on the view. A great deal is the $225 rate for a room on a higher floor with only a shower stall in the bathroom. The suites start at $525 and soar to $3,000 for the two-bedroom Presidential. Remember to ask about packages and specials.

Not many tourists know about the ultramodern **U.N. Plaza–Park Hyatt,** One United Nations Plaza (that's East 44th Street between First and Second Avenues), New York, NY 10017 (tel. 212/758-1234, or toll free 800/228-9000). The location is a bit far east, but nearby 42nd Street provides easy access to the rest of town. And there is a sheltering restfulness to this hotel that's extremely appealing. Not to mention the knockout views from almost every room, and the high-floor pool complete with skyline panorama.

The building is a dramatically angular affair, sheathed in tinted glass and brushed aluminum and entered from a covered drive (the hotel entrance is the closest to First Avenue). The 21st-century lobby is a multilevel fantasy of smoked mirrors and geometric green-and-white marble floors. There are so many clever turns and reflective surfaces that one might well walk into a mirrored wall. Museum-quality tapestries are framed and hung throughout the hotel.

All 428 guest rooms are located between the 28th and the 38th floors (U.N. offices and the like fill the rest of the building), which means superb views from every window. Accommodations have a tailored, futuristic look. There are low ceilings, mirrored tabletops, tub chairs, and remote-control TVs with HBO. The huge beds are equipped with polished brass reading lamps and solid oak headboards. The bathrooms have indirect lighting, marble tiles, and stacks of rose-colored towels. Deluxe rooms on the corners have double views.

Singles run between $240 and $260; doubles cost $260 to $280. Parking is available for $24 nightly, and room service operates 24 hours a day. At lobby level is the Ambassador Grill, which serves breakfast and offers a great three-course prix-fixe lunch ($20) and dinner ($25). There's a bar attached, with a piano player in the evening, plus a little lounge area full of crimson plush tub chairs. On the 27th floor is a complete health club, including the aforementioned pool, and there's even an indoor tennis court. During the week, the U.N. Plaza is basically a corporate hotel for upper-bracket traveling execs and CEOs. On the weekends it gets a lot of suburbanites in on the package deals. But for some reason it doesn't have nearly the amount of tourist traffic it would seem to merit.

The **Lyden House,** 320 E. 53rd St. (between First and Second Avenues), New York, NY 10022 (tel. 212/888-6070, or toll free 800/637-8483), far from looking like a hotel, seems instead to be an unassuming little apartment house. The diminutive green-marble lobby has no bar, no concierge, no bustle of bellmen or murmur of Muzak. It's just a pleasant entrance with a tiny desk. But upstairs are 45 transient units of superlative comfort and quality, ranging from single rooms to small suites.

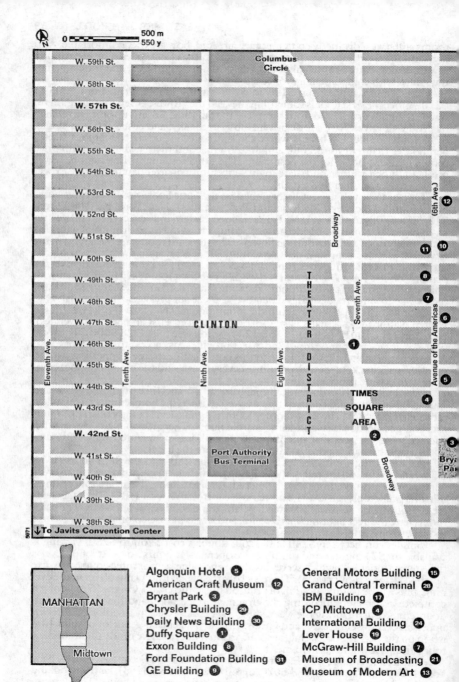

0 — 500 m / 550 y

W. 59th St.
W. 58th St.
W. 57th St.
W. 56th St.
W. 55th St.
W. 54th St.
W. 53rd St.
W. 52nd St.
W. 51st St.
W. 50th St.
W. 49th St.
W. 48th St.
W. 47th St.
W. 46th St.
W. 45th St.
W. 44th St.
W. 43rd St.
W. 42nd St.
W. 41st St.
W. 40th St.
W. 39th St.
W. 38th St.

Columbus Circle

Broadway

Seventh Ave.

(6th Ave.)

Avenue of the Americas

THEATER DISTRICT

TIMES SQUARE AREA

CLINTON

Eleventh Ave.
Tenth Ave.
Ninth Ave.
Eighth Ave.

Port Authority Bus Terminal

Broadway

Bryant Park

↓To Javits Convention Center

MANHATTAN

Midtown

Algonquin Hotel ⑤
American Craft Museum ⑫
Bryant Park ③
Chrysler Building ㉙
Daily News Building ㉚
Duffy Square ①
Exxon Building ⑧
Ford Foundation Building ㉛
GE Building ⑨

General Motors Building ⑮
Grand Central Terminal ㉘
IBM Building ⑰
ICP Midtown ④
International Building ㉔
Lever House ⑲
McGraw-Hill Building ⑦
Museum of Broadcasting ㉑
Museum of Modern Art ⑬

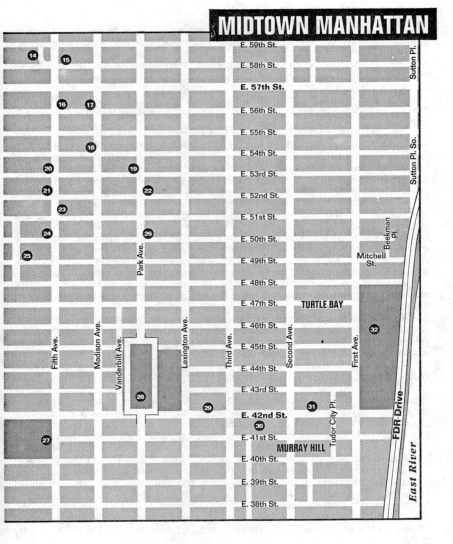

New York Public Library 27
The Plaza 14
Radio City Music Hall 10
Rockefeller Center 25
St. Bartholomew's Church 26
St. Patrick's Cathedral 23
St. Thomas Church 20
Seagram Building 22
Simon & Schuster Building 6

Sony Building 18
Time-Life Building 11
Times Square 2
Trump Tower 16
United Nations Headquarters 32

The Lyden is one of nine properties belonging to a local outfit called Manhattan East Suite Hotels. The rooms here are stylishly decorated in tones of buff, rose, and beige. They have thick rugs, matching floral spreads and curtains, very nice traditional furniture, and immaculate white-tiled bathrooms with real tubs and showers. The one-bedroom suites are handsomely decorated, roomy, and immaculately clean, with eat-in kitchens.

Best part of all is the price: Studio suites start at $185 for a single, $205 for a double. One-bedroom suites start at $205 per night for two, plus $20 per additional person.

The **Helmsley Middletowne,** 148 E. 48th St. (between Lexington and Third Avenues), New York, NY 10017 (tel. 212/755-3000, or toll free 800/221-4982), is an old tapestry brick building, 17 stories tall, with 194 rooms. It also has no restaurant, no bar, no concierge, and no parking (although a lot down the street charges about $24 for 24 hours). In many ways it's just a bigger, more centrally located version of the Lyden. Except for one major difference: the Helmsley touch.

That touch is apparent the minute you set foot in the cozy little gray-marble lobby. Fully half of the ceiling is covered with a crystal chandelier. Upstairs, the halls have nice striped wallpaper and more chandeliers. Each room features a little kitchenette, which many times is the first thing you walk into. Never mind, because the quality of everything is so good. There are thick pile rugs, handsome-looking chairs, desks, plenty of lamps, lots of closets, marble tops on the bureaus, and gleaming white-tiled bathrooms. And then there are the many personal touches, like the shaving mirror, the oversize towels, and the tray of complimentary toiletries. Plus, every morning, complimentary tea and coffee can be sipped in the lobby or brought up to your room.

Room decor is neither old-fashioned nor modern; it looks somehow "traditional" and yet not in any recognizable historical context. The prices for these cheerful and extremely comfortable accommodations range between $135 and $145 for singles, $145 and $155 for doubles, and $195 to $380 for suites.

People don't expect many family-run hotels in Midtown Manhattan, but the **Hotel Beverly,** Lexington Avenue at 50th Street, New York, NY 10022 (tel. 212/753-2700, or toll free 800/223-0945), is yet another. It is a slender brick tower dating from the 1920s, ornamented with stone gargoyles and protruding air conditioners and radiating an unpretentious aura of comfort. The redecorated lobby is elegant with its new mirrored columns, leather sofas, potted palms, and dignified woodwork. There's even a uniformed concierge, unusual for a modest hotel.

Of the 200 units, 175 are either one-bedroom suites or junior suites, which are oversize rooms with separate seating areas and kitchenettes. These suites are enormously appealing. They have lots of windows and unusual floor plans, big rooms, wall-to-wall carpeting, moiré-covered walls, modern tile baths, and matching curtains and spreads; the kitchens usually have new appliances. Suites on even floors from the 16th up have terraces too. They're all bright, clean, and comfortable and often have great views of the surrounding skyscrapers. Even the standard rooms have little refrigerators, comfy blond furniture, framed prints, and huge beds.

Standard rooms cost $139 to $149 for a single, $149 to $159 for a double; junior suites are between $149 and $169; the one-bedroom suites cost between $180 and $255 nightly, single or double. The higher prices apply to the higher floors. Additional persons pay $10 apiece per night, with a maximum of four persons per suite. Kenny's Steak and Seafood Restaurant, located off the lobby, provides breakfast, lunch, and dinner in a family atmosphere. Valet parking is available for about $23 a night.

---

3. West Midtown

This section describes hotels in the West 40s and 50s. Most of the streets hereabouts are not quite so glamorous as their East Side counterparts. And yet here's

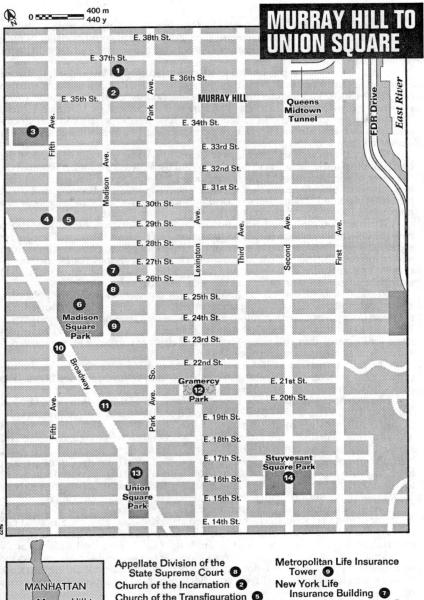

0 — 400 m
440 y

E. 38th St.

E. 37th St.

E. 36th St.

E. 35th St.

MURRAY HILL

Queens Midtown Tunnel

E. 34th St.

E. 33rd St.

E. 32nd St.

E. 31st St.

E. 30th St.

E. 29th St.

E. 28th St.

E. 27th St.

E. 26th St.

E. 25th St.

E. 24th St.

E. 23rd St.

E. 22nd St.

E. 21st St.

E. 20th St.

E. 19th St.

E. 18th St.

E. 17th St.

E. 16th St.

E. 15th St.

E. 14th St.

Madison Square Park

Gramercy Park

Stuyvesant Square Park

Union Square Park

East River

FDR Drive

Fifth Ave.

Madison Ave.

Park Ave.

Lexington Ave.

Third Ave.

Second Ave.

First Ave.

Broadway

Park Ave. So.

5/72

MANHATTAN

Murray Hill to Union Square

Appellate Division of the State Supreme Court ⑧
Church of the Incarnation ②
Church of the Transfiguration ⑤
Empire State Building ③
Flatiron Building ⑩
Gramercy Park ⑫
Madison Square Park ⑥
Marble Collegiate Church ④

Metropolitan Life Insurance Tower ⑨
New York Life Insurance Building ⑦
Pierpont Morgan Library ①
Stuyvesant Square Park ⑭
Theodore Roosevelt Birthplace ⑪
Union Square Park ⑬

where you'll find cultural attractions like Carnegie Hall, business meccas like the awesome glass canyons of Sixth Avenue, the art deco beauties of Rockefeller Center, as well as New York's famous Theater District and the legendary bright lights of Times Square.

First choice in the area is **Le Parker Meridien Hotel**, 118 W. 57th St. (between Sixth and Seventh Avenues), New York, NY 10019 (tel. 212/245-5000, or toll free 800/543-4300). This architecturally spectacular (at least on the inside) new tower is owned by American industrialist Jack Parker and operated by Meridien Hotels. The lobby signs are in French and English, the restaurants specialize in French cuisine, and an international atmosphere permeates the place from basement health club to rooftop pool.

The location on 57th Street is near Central Park and adjacent to some of the best shopping and sightseeing in New York. And then there's the lobby: Featured on the cover of the December 1981 issue of *Interior Design,* it combines 65-foot ceilings, classical columns and arches, gleaming sweeps of marble flooring, and a soft palette of roses and creams. It's so glorious as to put to rest permanently those old mutterings about how "they don't make them like they used to."

There are 600 rooms and 100 suites in the Parker Meridien. Accommodations have the low ceilings typical of new construction, but the furnishings and textiles are stylish and very handsome. There are plush carpets; big beds; plenty of light from wide windows; and marble bathrooms complete with telephones, scales, and amenity trays. Deluxe rooms are L-shaped and have handsome wood shelf units that divide sitting areas from sleeping areas, making them like little suites.

In the basement is Club La Raquette with piped-in rock and roll, Nautilus equipment, squash courts, and plenty of mirrors in which to admire yourself. On the 42nd floor is a pool with fabulous city views, as well as an outdoor jogging track. Down at lobby level are Maurice, the elegant main restaurant, and Bar Montparnasse for informal (but still pricey) buffets and drinks. There is 24-hour room service, as well as valet parking for about $28 nightly.

The price is $215 to $235 for a single, $245 to $265 for a double. Minimum-price rooms are every bit as nice as the others—they're just on lower floors. Top prices are for junior suites, meaning those with the clever divider units.

The **Marriott Marquis**, 1535 Broadway (between 45th and 46th Streets), New York, NY 10036 (tel. 212/704-8700, or toll free 800/228-9290), represents one of the critical first steps in the plan to revitalize Times Square. Designed by Atlanta architect John Portman, it's a new 50-story behemoth of poured concrete and smoked glass bulging out over Times Square. The Marriott contains 1,876 guest rooms arranged along balconies overlooking a 37-story atrium that, quite frankly, looks like something that landed from Mars. This is primarily a convention hotel, and as such it features things like a 28,800-square-foot ballroom, easy access to New York's Javits Convention Center, and special deals for corporate customers.

Everything about the Marriott is huge. You must make your way to the eighth floor just to find the lobby. Rooms are reached via vertiginous glass elevators that rise through the middle of the atrium (those with weak stomachs had better keep their eyes tightly closed). The rooms are big and bright, nicely furnished with curiously traditional-looking pieces. Each features a king-size or two double beds and is done in a subdued peach or plum color scheme. There are comfortable sitting and desk areas, even a video checkout wherein your bill is presented for approval on the screen of your TV set.

Prices at the Marriott are steep: $265 for a single and $300 for a double. Package deals can soften the blow somewhat. And staying here is certainly an exciting experience that will appeal to many. There is an exercise room with a whirlpool and sauna, plus various restaurants on the premises, among them the Encore and the Atrium Café, as well as a great field of sofas and chairs in the atrium through which attractive young servers circulate taking drink orders. Up on the roof is a three-level revolving restaurant called the View. Room service is available around the clock, and you can stash your car in the basement garage for about $30 a night.

The **Paramount,** 235 W. 46th St. (between Broadway and Eighth Avenue),

New York, NY 10036 (tel. 212/764-5500), is a great big old hotel (610 rooms) in the heart of the Theater District and has recently undergone a creative renovation with designs by the talented Philippe Starck. Starck, who did the nearby Royalton for the same owners (the Morgan Hotel Group), has created a new-wave budget hotel. The double-height lobby is furnished with plush sofas and chairs and dominated by a startling geometric staircase at the top of which is the dimly lit Mezzanine Restaurant. The look is youthful, exciting, and altogether comfortable.

The rooms upstairs are diminutive but enormously stylish. They have oversized beds piled with European square pillows; high-tech armoires concealing color TVs and VCRs; trendy bathrooms with small black-and-white tiles and stainless-steel sinks; and those unique Starck touches—the bowl of apples under the pencil spot, the projection lamp that casts squiggle patterns on the ceiling, the headboard that re-creates Vermeer's *Lacemaker* in plush. It is so wonderful.

A coffeeshop on the mezzanine, run by Dean and Deluca, adjoins the lobby, serves breakfast and lunch, and has a takeout menu. For quick stops, there is also an espresso bar, and the new Brasserie des Théâtres off the main lobby serves bistro-type fare with an exotic Mediterranean twist until 1am daily. Rates are $99 to $220 for singles, $155 to $240 for doubles; rates for deluxe rooms, suites, and weekend packages are available upon request.

So much has been written about the celebrated **Algonquin Hotel,** 59 W. 44th St. (between Fifth and Sixth Avenues), New York, NY 10036 (tel. 212/840-6800, or toll free 800/548-0345), that one is almost intimidated to write more. In a nutshell, it's a small Edwardian hotel in the heart of Midtown, greatly celebrated in the world of letters as the site of the Round Table. It was here during the 1920s that a group of witty young writers met for lunch almost every day, among them Dorothy Parker, Ring Lardner, Robert Benchley, Heywood Broun, and Edna Ferber. Their bequest to the Algonquin is its continued identification with the world of wit and literature. It is a much-beloved New York institution, with enormous atmosphere and a devoted clientele.

It is a sign of the times that the long-time family owners of the Algonquin have recently sold it to the Aoki Corporation of Tokyo. The highly decorated brick-and-stone façade; the marvelous old lobby with its dark woodwork, heavy moldings, and lofty ceiling; and the 165 rooms aloft were all subsequently restored to pristine Edwardian condition.

The charm of the Algonquin lies in its lobby and its famous (and pricey) restaurants. The former is filled with plush sofas and comfy wing chairs grouped around little oak tables whose attached bells enable you to summon a waiter for drinks. The place is filled with low laughter and the murmur of conversation from people sitting over cocktails, as well as from those in the restaurants that open directly onto the lobby. The Rose Room and the Oak Room do a thriving lunch and dinner business. Many a fashionable literary lunch still takes place in the former. In the evening the latter is a stronghold of ultrasophisticated cabaret.

The rooms upstairs aren't small, they're snug. They are decorated with antique reproductions; paisley spreads and curtains; and glazed or freshly papered walls hung with original drawings, watercolors, and prints. Each room has an immaculate little bathroom, a color TV, and a complimentary copy of *The New Yorker,* the magazine made famous by the members of the Round Table.

The Algonquin attracts many people in the arts, plus a goodly share of youthful travelers who simply like places with atmosphere. Room rates are still reasonable for Manhattan: $175 to $185 for a single, $185 to $195 for a double. One-bedroom suites cost between $340 and $370.

I loved **The Royalton,** 44 W. 44th St., New York, NY 10036 (tel. 212/869-4400, or toll free 800/635-9013), which is unlike anything I've ever seen in my life. Interior designer Philippe Starck (who decorated the aforementioned Paramount) has created a luxury hotel for the Jetsons, via the 1950s, within the shell of a vintage Midtown hotel building. Everything is sleek, sculpted, frosted, glazed, and custom made.

The multilevel lobby with its enormous mirrors aspires to be a living room for

New York's new wave *beau monde*. The main floor features avant-garde seating areas; a circular bar; fish tanks; living art; horn-shaped Daum crystal wall fixtures and vases; and 44, a trendy restaurant run by Jeffrey Choderow of the China Grill.

Upstairs are 171 rooms decorated with more sophistication and wit than you are likely to find in any other hotel in town. Every single item in these rooms— stainless-steel postcard stands, slate floors, arched slate fireplaces (in 40 rooms)— has been custom-designed by Philippe Starck. The overall effect is something like the streamlined luxury of a 1930s first-class cruise ship.

Singles cost between $210 and $325; doubles run between $235 and $350. Weekend rates are great: $160 single or double; $240 for a suite.

The **Salisbury Hotel,** 123 W. 57th St. (between Sixth and Seventh Avenues), New York, NY 10019 (tel. 212/246-1300), has a great location—practically across the street from Carnegie Hall and but two short blocks from Central Park. It's a sedate former apartment house, dating probably from the 1920s. The postage stamp–size lobby is quiet and distinguished, decorated with handsome dark paneling, crystal chandeliers, and an ornate plaster ceiling. Although there's nothing deluxe about the Salisbury, it does have a decided air of refinement.

The 185 rooms are rather spacious and nicely furnished with attractive chenille spreads, pictures in gilded bamboo frames, and muted color schemes. Most rooms also have small serving pantries with miniature sinks and refrigerators. Room rates are very attractive: $144 for a single, $154 for a double, $164 for a one-bedroom suite, plus $15 per additional person in a roll-away bed. The Terrace Café adjoining the lobby, which a local newspaper has aptly termed the "closest thing to the Twin Peaks diner in New York," serves breakfast, lunch, and dinner. There is an abundance of other restaurants in the immediate area.

There are two very excellent budget hotels, both operated by the same management and each providing amazingly nice accommodations at rock-bottom rates. The first is the **Portland Square Hotel,** 132 W. 47th St., New York, NY 10036 (tel. 212/382-0600, or toll free 800/388-8988), located adjacent to Times Square and the Theater District and offering clean, simply decorated rooms with private baths, color TVs, and phones at $60 for a single, $75 for a double, and $85 for a double with two beds. There are even rooms with shared bathrooms that rent for as low as $40 a night single. This clean and decent renovation of a nice old building is a boon to budget travelers. The **Herald Square Hotel,** 19 W. 31st St., New York, NY 10001 (tel. 212/279-4017, or toll free 800/727-1888), offers similar prices and amenities in a location that is just steps from Macy's and the exciting new shopping district below 23rd Street along Fifth Avenue.

---

4. Upper East Side

This is Manhattan's premier residential district. The side streets are lined with houses, not office buildings. And while the avenues have shops, they are often of a rarefied nature ($2,000 dresses, $100,000 rugs). If you want to sample New York elegance, this is the part of town in which to stay.

Perhaps the hotel most associated with the stylish East Side is the **Lowell,** 28 E. 63rd St. (between Madison and Park Avenues), New York, NY 10021 (tel. 212/ 838-1400, or toll free 800/221-4444). In an enviable location just steps from Midtown business offices to the south and the elegant Madison Avenue shops and art galleries to the north, it is surrounded by fine private mansions on a quiet residential block. There are only 61 rooms here, housed in a 1928 mid-rise with glazed rose and beige tiles decorating the first floor.

The lobby is a small tour de force of updated classicism. It has a marble floor, gilded pilasters, Empire furniture covered in sumptuous yellow satin, and a small but rather dramatic black-marble reception desk. The impression is one of luxury, intimacy, and money. Only 8 of the 61 units are what they call studios, which are large deluxe rooms with sitting areas and full kitchens. All the rooms, regardless of

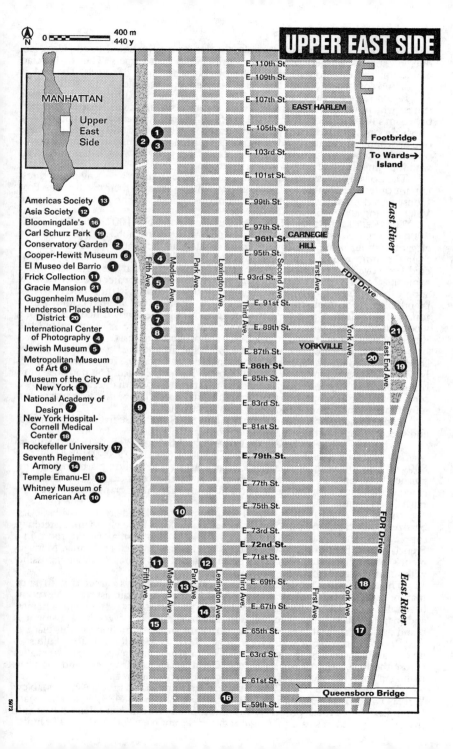

UPPER EAST SIDE

0 ___ 400 m
___ 440 y
N

MANHATTAN

Upper
East
Side

Americas Society 13
Asia Society 12
Bloomingdale's 16
Carl Schurz Park 19
Conservatory Garden 2
Cooper-Hewitt Museum 6
El Museo del Barrio 1
Frick Collection 11
Gracie Mansion 21
Guggenheim Museum 8
Henderson Place Historic
    District 20
International Center
    of Photography 4
Jewish Museum 5
Metropolitan Museum
    of Art 9
Museum of the City of
    New York 3
National Academy of
    Design 7
New York Hospital-
    Cornell Medical
    Center 18
Rockefeller University 17
Seventh Regiment
    Armory 14
Temple Emanu-El 15
Whitney Museum of
    American Art 10

E. 110th St.
E. 109th St.
E. 107th St.   EAST HARLEM
E. 105th St.
E. 103rd St.
E. 101st St.
E. 99th St.
E. 97th St.
E. 96th St.   CARNEGIE
E. 95th St.   HILL
E. 93rd St.
E. 91st St.
E. 89th St.
E. 87th St.   YORKVILLE
E. 86th St.
E. 85th St.
E. 83rd St.
E. 81st St.
E. 79th St.
E. 77th St.
E. 75th St.
E. 73rd St.
E. 72nd St.
E. 71st St.
E. 69th St.
E. 67th St.
E. 65th St.
E. 63rd St.
E. 61st St.
E. 59th St.

Fifth Ave.
Madison Ave.
Park Ave.
Lexington Ave.
Third Ave.
Second Ave.
First Ave.
York Ave.
East End Ave.

FDR Drive

East River

Footbridge

To Wards→
Island

Queensboro Bridge

5973

size, are roomy and beautifully furnished with high-quality upholstered pieces, lacquered cabinets, framed 18th-century prints, and lush carpets. The marble-clad bathrooms are ultramodern, with gold towel bars and tons of towels. The look is one of "no cost spared," and the level of taste is irreproachable.

Room rates for the studios are $260 for a single, $320 for a double; junior suites, which are overscale studios with separate seating areas, cost $420; one-bedroom suites are priced from $520 to $680. The newly opened "Gym Suite"—a one-bedroom suite with a private gym—can be reserved for $680 per night. All the one-bedroom suites have wonderful city views, immaculate full kitchens, real books on the bookshelves, luxuriant potted plants and fresh flowers, oftentimes even woodburning fireplaces or landscaped terraces.

The Lowell serves breakfast, lunch, and afternoon tea in a creamy paneled restaurant called the Pembroke Room; guests can also sign for their meals at the Post House next door or have room service from this famous steakhouse until 10:30pm. Valet parking is available for $25 nightly.

The **Westbury Hotel**, 15 E. 69th St., New York, NY 10021 (tel. 212/535-2000, or toll free 800/225-5843), is owned by the Forte hotel group. Extremely elegant without being overdone, it has an understated elegance—very English—from the sunny rooms done in pale hues of light yellow or powder blue, with flowered bed coverings to match, to the small concierge desk at the entrance, where someone always is ready to take all your bags, help you find theater tickets, or simply supply that day's *New York Times*. There are clustered seatings in the lobby, two large grandfather clocks that truly are grand, and a wood-carved vaulted ceiling with a touch of gold leaf. A popular bar/dining room off the lobby called The Polo, a wood-paneled room with hunter green accents, is great for breakfast, lunch, or a full dinner or simply for a drink to soak in the atmosphere and relax.

Upstairs, the hallways are done in a soft beige silk and the heavy oak doors have solid brass handles. The spacious rooms include seating areas, bathroom amenities by Caswell-Massey, plush towels, and phones all over the place. The staff is eager to bring you extra soap and towels to make your stay most pleasurable, and turn-down service is always prompt. Fully stocked minibars provide for late-night snacks and refreshments, though room service is always available.

Rates for deluxe rooms are from $245 to $265; suites are from $350 to $550; and specialty suites with formal dining rooms and libraries are $1,000.

Paris marries the East Side in the **Hotel Plaza Athénée**, 37 E. 64th St. (between Madison and Park Avenues), New York, NY 10021 (tel. 212/734-9100, or toll free 800/447-8800), with predictably glittery results. The building's been a distinguished hotel since 1927. But it's been the Plaza Athénée since only 1984, when it emerged dripping with marble and ormolu from a Cinderella transformation by the Forte hotel group.

Inside the smallish lobby you'll see gleaming black-and-cream marble floors, bronze cupids clutching ormolu torchières, Louis XVI–style chairs upholstered in supple green leather, and a check-in area that looks like a small sitting room in a French palace. Everything in this hotel is bright, small, quiet, and shiny. Management's clearly delineated policy is to provide as much service as is humanly possible without at the same time being intrusive.

The 160 rooms are arranged along fabulous hallways carpeted with faux-marbre rugs, prints in gold-leaf frames, and Chinese porcelain ashtrays. All rooms have safes, tie bars, hairdryers, scales, lit mirrors, bathrobes, pastel color schemes, and marble-walled baths. The building may be oldish, but everything inside it is brand new. Stylish as it may be, there is no feeling of age or tradition in this place.

Rooms cost $275 to $355 for a single, $310 to $390 for a double. Suites go up . . . and up. Le Régence serves meals in an atmosphere evocative of Versailles before the Revolution; a small bar replete with green-leopard poufs and Brazilian mahogany provides alcoholic refreshment for thirsty plutocrats.

The **Surrey Hotel**, 20 E. 76th St. (between Fifth and Madison Avenues), New York, NY 10021 (tel. 212/288-3700, or toll free 800/637-8483), is another Manhattan East Suite Hotels property, this time located on a block of splendid East Side mansions. Indeed, it's hard to imagine a more elegant New York address. The building was a dignified prewar residential hotel whose small marble lobby is brightened with huge bouquets of flowers, Louis XVI–style chairs, a grandfather clock, and crystal chandeliers. It's quiet, refined, and serene, another of those places that do not at all seem like hotels.

Upstairs, the rather opulent halls with their cream moiré wallcoverings, white paneled doors, and thick rugs lead to a mere 130 units. Studios and suites are surprisingly big and beautifully furnished with upholstered sofas and chairs, thick carpets, enormous beds, crystal lamps with pleated shades, and attractive framed prints on the walls. Virtually every unit has walk-in closets and a kitchenette. The marble baths are plush, with every amenity, and also have full-length mirrors and tubs in which you can actually take a bath. Many New Yorkers would kill to live in apartments like these.

To accommodate their guests further, a small fitness center was added. It is equipped with various machines, free weights, a TV, and a kitchen stocked with refreshments and fruit. After a stiff workout, it's time to let loose just one more time to savor some of Daniel Boloud's French fare in the hotel's restaurant that bears his name (Daniel used to be head chef at tony Le Cirque).

Prices for these attractive accommodations have risen since the last edition; however, the Surrey does offer discounted rates for extended stays. Singles in studio units pay $210 to $230 a night. For doubles the rates rise to $230 to $250. One-bedroom suites are priced from $300 to $355; two-bedroom suites run from $505 to a top end of $585.

The **Hotel Wales,** 1295 Madison Avenue (between 92nd and 93rd Streets), New York, NY 10128 (tel. 212/876-6000), has been in operation since 1901. This old painted-brick building has a new owner and has undergone a $5-million renovation. The lobby sports painted marble walls, plush carpeting, elegant striped wallpaper, a grand marble fireplace, and a reception desk at the far end. The entire building boasts the owner's keen attention to aesthetic detail. The 10 floors of rooms have wonderfully restored woodwork, deep-pile carpeting, reproduction mahogany furniture, oil paintings, and old-world charm.

Single or double rooms, as of this writing, are a very excellent buy at $135 to $145. Suites, which usually consist of two rooms and often a vintage fireplace, cost between $185 and $225. All rates include a complimentary continental breakfast in the Pied Piper Room or in Sarabeth's Kitchen, under separate management, which is open for breakfast, lunch, and dinner in cheerful rooms adjacent to the lobby.

---

5. Upper West Side

The gentrification of the West Side is already aging. The trendsetters have come and gone, but the neighborhood remains a district of handsome renovated brownstones, fine old apartment buildings, and a good (if rapidly changing) collection of boutiques and cafés. It lies to the west of Central Park, just north of the Midtown business district. Transportation to the rest of town is quite convenient as there are lots of subway and bus lines. West Side hotels are modest. Although not luxurious, they offer a lot of value in a good location.

When the **Radisson Empire Hotel,** Broadway at 63rd Street, New York, NY 10023 (tel. 212/265-7400, or toll free 800/333-3333), opened its 500 rooms in 1929, the West Side was a select neighborhood of private townhouses. But the years that followed saw storms of neighborhood change. Today the neighborhood is fashionable again, and so is the Empire.

The old brick building now has modern smoked-glass windows, a location across the street from the world-famous performing arts complex known as Lincoln Center, and trendy restaurants and shops for neighbors. The lobby is sumptuous with rose-colored carpets, double-height ceilings with big chandeliers, a concierge desk, and an overall traditional look. Adjacent to the lobby is a smart café called the Empire Grill and Bar, which serves breakfast, lunch, and dinner.

The newly redecorated rooms are small but luxurious. They are furnished with dark-wood traditional pieces, chintz spreads, floral curtains, and all-white baths with amenity trays. Standard rooms cost $130 for a single, $200 for a double, which is a reasonable price for this level of quality and location. Suites go up to $250 for a one-bedroom and $540 for a two-bedroom. Valet parking is available for $25 nightly.

The **Mayflower Hotel,** overlooking Central Park at 15 Central Park West (at 61st Street), New York, NY 10023 (tel. 212/265-0060; fax 212/265-5098), has big comfortable rooms, a wonderful location between Lincoln Center and Midtown, and a clientele heavy on movie and traveling international types. This family-owned and -operated establishment was built in 1925 as a residential hotel, which accounts for the spaciousness of the standard rooms. It has been upgraded and improved on a more or less continuous basis ever since. The lobby has plush brown rugs, white-and-gold ceilings, Chippendale-style side tables, and a smiling staff in burgundy uniforms. The spacious rooms have color TVs, comfortable furnishings, and clean old-fashioned bathrooms with full amenity trays and the sort of tub in which you can really take a bath. Downstairs is a restaurant called the Conservatory, which serves excellent food and whose busy and convivial bar has piano music and free hors d'oeuvres every Thursday, Friday, and Saturday from 5 to 7pm. The basic double room costs between $160 and $180; suites range from $200 to $260. Very good package deals abound, so be sure to ask in advance.

The **Hotel Olcott,** 27 W. 72nd St. (between Central Park West and Columbus Avenue), New York, NY 10023 (tel. 212/877-4200), is one of the best hotel values in New York. The Olcott is part of a fairly massive palisade of buildings that lines this side of 72nd Street. At the foot of its brick-and-limestone facade is a modern anodized-aluminum awning sheltering automatic doors that slide apart automatically as you approach. Inside is a surprisingly elegant old lobby with gilded moldings on the ceiling, black-marble pilasters, broad expanses of soft brick-colored carpeting, antique carved chairs along the walls, and a couple of fabulously ornate brass elevators. Next to the small marble reception desk is a copy of a 1925 magazine ad that announced the Olcott's opening as a select residential hotel.

The Olcott has pleasant, modest studios (standard rooms) with tiled baths, old moldings on the walls, motel modern furniture, and small cooking pantries; it has many more one-bedroom suites, also simply and pleasantly decorated and equipped with full kitchenettes. About 75% of the place is rented full time; the rest has a 1% vacancy rate—because of the prices: $85 a night for singles or doubles in a studio room, $115 for two in a suite that will sleep four (add $15 nightly per extra person). Weekly rates are even better: studios are $495 for a single and $550 for a double, and the suites are $670 plus $70 weekly for additional persons beyond two. A cable color TV is included. No credit cards accepted.

Needless to say, rates like this make the Olcott an item in much demand. The sooner you make reservations the better. Single-night stays are discouraged, but it is possible to catch an unexpected vacancy at the last minute. No harm trying. Your fellow guests are visiting parents and children, United Nations auditors, Japanese and Israeli educators, lots of opera and ballet people (Lincoln Center is nearby), as well as Tiny Tim. A great cheap restaurant, Dallas BBQ, is located off the lobby (see separate listing in Chapter IV).

Nine blocks to the north, directly across the street from the Museum of Natural History, is the **Excelsior Hotel,** 45 W. 81st St. (between Central Park West and Columbus Avenue), New York, NY 10024 (tel. 212/362-9200, or toll free 800/368-4575). The neighborhood is sedate and residential, convenient to Central Park, Columbus Avenue shopping, and transportation to the rest of town. The Excelsior is some 60-odd years old and features an attractive traditional lobby with wood paneling and an elaborate molded ceiling. About half the lobby has been partitioned off for a coffeeshop, popular with neighborhood people and serving breakfast, lunch, and dinner. Eight clocks beside the reception desk tell the time everywhere from Tokyo to Tel Aviv. A sign on the desk informs visitors that the hotel meets criteria established by the United States Travel Service for providing basic services in English, Spanish, French, and German.

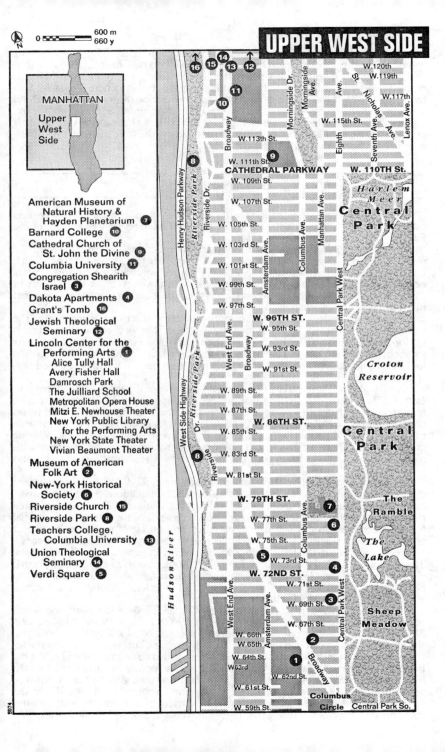

UPPER WEST SIDE

MANHATTAN

Upper
West
Side

American Museum of
 Natural History &
 Hayden Planetarium ⑦
Barnard College ⑩
Cathedral Church of
 St. John the Divine ⑨
Columbia University ⑪
Congregation Shearith
 Israel ③
Dakota Apartments ④
Grant's Tomb ⑯
Jewish Theological
 Seminary ⑫
Lincoln Center for the
 Performing Arts ①
  Alice Tully Hall
  Avery Fisher Hall
  Damrosch Park
  The Juilliard School
  Metropolitan Opera House
  Mitzi E. Newhouse Theater
  New York Public Library
   for the Performing Arts
  New York State Theater
  Vivian Beaumont Theater
Museum of American
 Folk Art ②
New-York Historical
 Society ⑥
Riverside Church ⑮
Riverside Park ⑧
Teachers College,
 Columbia University ⑬
Union Theological
 Seminary ⑭
Verdi Square ⑤

0 600 m
   660 y

W.120th
W.119th
W.117th
St. Nicholas Ave.
Seventh Ave.
Eighth Ave.
Lenox Ave.
Morningside Dr.
Morningside Ave.
W. 115th St.
W.113th St.
Broadway
W. 111th St.
CATHEDRAL PARKWAY
W. 109th St.
W. 110TH St.
*Harlem
Meer*
**Central
Park**
W. 107th St.
Henry Hudson Parkway
Riverside Park
Riverside Dr.
W. 105th St.
W. 103rd St.
Amsterdam Ave.
Columbus Ave.
Manhattan Ave.
Central Park West
W. 101st St.
W. 99th St.
W. 97th St.
W. 96TH ST.
W. 95th St.
West End Ave.
Broadway
W. 93rd St.
W. 91st St.
*Croton
Reservoir*
W. 89th St.
W. 87th St.
W. 86TH ST.
W. 85th St.
**Central
Park**
W. 83rd St.
Riverside Dr.
West Side Highway
W. 81st St.
W. 79TH ST.
W. 77th St.
Columbus Ave.
*The
Ramble*
W. 75th St.
W. 73rd St.
W. 72ND ST.
*The
Lake*
W. 71st St.
W. 69th St.
W. 67th St.
Hudson River
West End Ave.
Amsterdam Ave.
W. 66th
W.65th
W. 64th St.
W63rd
W. 62nd St.
Broadway
Central Park West
*Sheep
Meadow*
W. 61st St.
**Columbus
Circle**
W. 59th St.
Central Park So.

5974

This hotel is particularly popular with foreign tourists. The 175 transient rooms (125 others are occupied by permanent residents) are clean; carpeted wall to wall; and equipped with TVs, kitchenettes (in the suites), and old-fashioned modernized baths with colored towels. No frills or undue aesthetics here. Prices are $65 for a single, $75 for a double. Suites with one separate bedroom cost $99 nightly. There are two-bedroom suites as well, going up to a top end of $160 a night for six. Some of the higher-floor rooms facing 81st Street have skyline views or pleasant prospects of the park surrounding the museum across the street. There is no difference in rates between rooms facing the street or facing the back.

6. Downtown

My first two recommendations really are in the part of town that New Yorkers call "Downtown." The other three are in Murray Hill, a residential enclave in the East 30s, just to the south of Midtown.

Staying at the **New York Vista,** 3 World Trade Center (the entrance is on the west side of the Trade Center complex, on West Street just above Liberty Street), New York, NY 10048 (tel. 212/938-9100), is a novel way to visit New York. This is because most New Yorkers, unless they work here, never even get to this part of town. Which is too bad, since downtown is the oldest and in many ways the most interesting part of Manhattan.

The Vista is a sleek brushed-aluminum-and-glass structure pressed against the knees of the stupendous World Trade Center towers. The view across West Street is no longer much of a vista, however, as the new World Financial Center now sits smack between the Vista and its former unobstructed view of the river. But there is a lot of exciting modern architecture to look at around here, as well as the fabled skyscraper Gothic canyons of the 1920s.

The Vista was damaged by the terrorist bombing of the World Trade Center in early 1993. It was closed, with a planned reopening in April 1994, after extensive remodeling. (The details in this description are basically accurate but should be rechecked after the hotel opens again.) The 821 rooms are operated by Hilton International, so quality is predictably high. Guest rooms are smallish but have a handsome tailored look. There are thick rugs, blond modern furniture, brass lamps with pleated shades, big windows, bathrooms with marble sinktops, lots of light, and piles of towels.

Rates are about $215 to $265 for a standard single, $240 to $290 for a standard double, the higher-priced rooms being those on the higher floors. As a practical matter, minimum-rate rooms are just as appealing. The 20th and 21st floors are titled the "Executive Floors." Here, as in many hotels these days, the rooms have a special lounge/reception area, a few more amenities, and an air of privilege. They cost about $280 for a single, $305 for a double. A marvelous restaurant called American Harvest is located off the second-floor lobby and draws people from all over town. There are also the Tall Ships Bar and the Vista Lounge, as well as a more informal restaurant called the Greenhouse. The Vista also has a beautiful enclosed rooftop pool (kept at a constant 80 degrees), a quarter-mile indoor jogging track, a sauna, and the Executive Fitness Center.

The **New York Marriott Financial Center Hotel,** 85 West St. (two blocks south of the World Trade Center), New York, NY 10006 (tel. 212/385-4900; fax 212/385-9174), is a towering 38-story modern structure, overlooking the harbor and the Financial District. It is essentially a businessperson's hotel with luxurious facilities, including an indoor pool, an exercise room, a lush restaurant called JW's, a big bar called the Liberty Lounge, and 504 sleek guest rooms, the majority of which have fantastic water views. The lobby is grand, too, with double-height ceilings, sweeping staircases, chandeliers, and reproduction antique furnishings. Room decor is Euro-modern, with wooden headboards, framed prints on the walls, paisley curtains, minibars, not one but two telephone lines, remote-controlled color TVs, video check-out, and functional modern baths with amenity trays. Not a great deal of character, perhaps, but it's certainly sleek and comfortable, and the views and location are superb. There are a host of weekend packages that will enable two of you to stay here any Saturday night for $99; the rest of the week, expect standard rooms to cost from $225 to $245 nightly, unless you're a corporate traveler or a member of one of the numerous other organizations that have special deals with Marriott. Suites run from $350 to $1,500.

Why do they call it **Morgans, 237** Madison Ave. (between 37th and 38th Streets), New York, NY 10016 (tel. 212/686-0300, or toll free 800/334-3408)? Because J. P. Morgan once lived down the block in a big brownstone still standing at 37th and Madison. Morgans has a good pseudo-Midtown location and a trendy postmodern look that's very 1990s. Everything in this place seems to be black, white, or gray—from the diamond-patterned rug in the coolly elegant little lobby (where flower arrangements consist of three twigs and two blossoms) to the fashionable uniforms on the doormen. These fellows must be actors, they're so good looking. But then again, so is everybody else. The entire staff is friendly, intelligent, and apparently overqualified.

Morgans is a property of the Morgan Hotel Group, founded by Ian Schrager and the late Steve Rubell of Studio 54 fame. They've created an upmarket little hotel aimed at younger businesspeople, young jet-setters, and young Hollywood types. They're luring them with extra service (fresh flowers in the baths, Christmas cards to everyone who's ever registered) and rooms with sophisticated decor.

The 113 transient units are a bit small but so Milano deluxe it hardly matters. They have gray-green carpets, built-in furniture, AM/FM stereo cassettes, VCRs, color TVs, unusual gray-stained bird's-eye maple wall panels, refrigerators, handy reading lights, and telephones in the baths. Those bathrooms have an intriguing 1930s retro look that's the result of black and white tiles, stainless-steel sinks with a slightly surgical air, flowers, and glass-doored showers. Everything is gray and terribly fashionable. Some rooms are high-tech fantasies, like the cathedral-ceilinged room with the bathtub next to the bed or the penthouse duplex with its spiral staircase and huge potted plants.

Singles cost $180 to $210; doubles are $205 to $235; one-bedroom suites cost $275 to $400. Weekend rates are available upon request. There is tea service on the fourth floor during the week between 4 and 7pm, plus a two-level restaurant with the dining room below and a grill on the mezzanine. Bring money and be chic.

Also in Murray Hill is the **Shelburne Murray Hill,** 303 Lexington Ave. (between 37th and 38th Streets), New York, NY 10016 (tel. 212/689-5200). This is another of the Manhattan East Suite Hotels, several of which have been recommended already. The Shelburne is a very nice small hotel with a dignified facade, located close to Midtown. It has an awning on Lexington Avenue and little trees in white pots. Inside is a smallish but elegant lobby, very much in the established style of the owners. It has French-looking furniture sprinkled with a few genuine antiques, opulent multiarm wall sconces with pleated shades, marble floors, handsome patterned wallpaper, and crystal chandeliers.

There are 258 units available, either nightly or for extended periods. The typical guest room is very nicely decorated with textured wallcoverings, matching spread and curtains, good-quality traditional-style wood furniture, Chinese lamps, gold-framed prints, new bath, and fully equipped modern kitchenette. Everything is immaculately clean and of a very high quality. Some of the rooms look like luxurious living rooms with queen-size beds in the corner.

These accommodations are an excellent value too. Singles cost $190 to $210; doubles run $210 to $230; one-bedroom suites are $210 to $250; two-bedroom suites go for $400 to $440 nightly. Secret Harbor Bistro, located off the lobby, serves reasonably priced meals in a bright, casual atmosphere.

Last but not least is the **Washington Square Hotel,** 103 Waverly Place, New York, NY 10011 (tel. 212/777-9515, or toll free 800/222-0418; fax 212/979-8373). This is a super-budget hotel operated by the same people who manage the previously recommended Herald Square and Portland Square hotels. It is an old

N

0 |■■■■■■| 100 m
         110 y

LOWER EAST SIDE

Manhattan Bridge ↗

Market St.

Madison St.

Henry St.

Catherine St.

Oliver St.

Pell St.

Mott St.

CHINATOWN

Bayard St.

Columbus Park

Mulberry St.

Worth St.

Hogan Pl.

Baxter St.

23

Centre St.

Lafayette St.

22

21

Federal Plaza

Duane St.

Reade St.

Broadway

19

18

Chambers St.

Church St.

Worth St.

Leonard St.

Thomas St.

Duane St.

West Broadway

Warren St.

Murray St.

Park Pl.

Barclay St.

17

City Hall Park

Theatre St.

Park Row

14

Fulton St.

20

Police Plaza

St. James Place

Gov. Alfred E. Smith Houses

Brooklyn Bridge

To Brooklyn →

FDR Drive

Dover St.

Water St.

Front St.

Peck St.

16

SOUTH STREET SEAPORT HISTORICAL DISTRICT

Burling Slip

Fulton Fish Market

Pier 18

15

Frankfort St.

Cliff St.

Ferry St.

Fulton St.

Pearl St.

Spruce St.

Beekman St.

Gold St.

John St.

Ann St.

John St.

Dutch St.

Maiden Lane

11

Nassau St.

ams

Broadway

Dey St.

Cortlandt St.

Church St.

Liberty St.

Cedar St.

WORLD TRADE CENTER

13

Vesey St.

West St.

West Side Highway

West St.

BATTERY PARK CITY

West St.

TRIBECA

Varick St.

N. Moore St.

Franklin St.

Hudson St.

Jay St.

Harrison St.

Greenwich St.

Reade St.

Chambers St.

12

Path Tubes

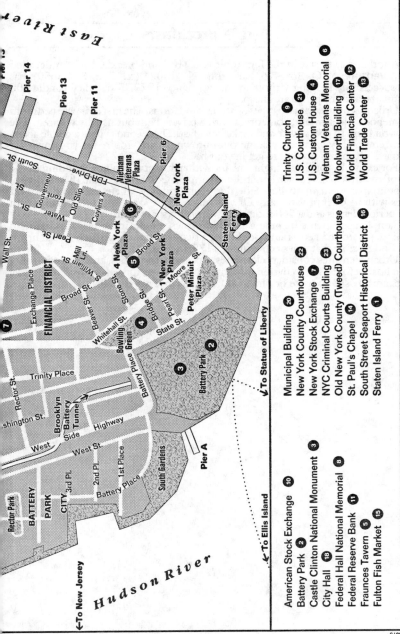

LOWER MANHATTAN

American Stock Exchange ❿
Battery Park ❷
Castle Clinton National Monument ❸
City Hall ⓲
Federal Hall National Memorial ❽
Federal Reserve Bank ⓫
Fraunces Tavern ❺
Fulton Fish Market ⓯

Municipal Building ⓴
New York County Courthouse ㉒
New York Stock Exchange ❼
NYC Criminal Courts Building ㉓
Old New York County (Tweed) Courthouse ⓳
St. Paul's Chapel ⓮
South Street Seaport Historical District ⓰
Staten Island Ferry ❶

Trinity Church ❾
U.S. Courthouse ㉑
U.S. Custom House ❹
Vietnam Veterans Memorial ❻
Woolworth Building ⓱
World Financial Center ⓬
World Trade Center ⓭

5875

building with very simple yet clean and comfortable rooms, all of which have phones and color TVs. Singles cost about $65 to $75; doubles are priced at $95 to $115. A very good value in an excellent Greenwich Village location.

---

7. Bed & Breakfasts

Another way to stay in the Big Apple is at a bed-and-breakfast. An outfit called **Urban Ventures,** P.O. Box 426, New York, NY 10024 (tel. 212/594-5650), has been successfully lodging visitors in this way since 1979. Today they handle 700 apartments, and the prices are cheap.

Urban Ventures has two types of accommodations. The first is a spare bedroom in somebody's apartment, sometimes with a private bath but usually without. The host is on hand to give advice and make breakfast. The second type is a whole apartment, temporarily vacated by some out-of-town owner. You're on your own for breakfast, but there's no host to get in your hair.

For example, for $70 a night one individual can stay in a new building in the East 60s with a planted garden and a doorman. For $85 a night there's a two-bedroom apartment in an East Side doorman building where the room for rent comes with its own private bath. Or you might like a West Side brownstone with great period details and a $68 room for two, with a shared bath.

Sample apartments include a large Midtown studio in an elegant doorman building, priced at $120 a night double; or a two-bedroom/two-bath spread up on West End Avenue that will sleep four for $175 nightly.

Urban Ventures considers cleanliness, location, aesthetics, and the personality of the host before listing anything. Many applicants are turned down. Prospective guests are advised to write or phone as far in advance as possible.

IV

NEW YORK CITY RESTAURANTS

1. MIDTOWN EAST & WEST (INCLUDING THEATER DISTRICT)

2. UPPER EAST SIDE

3. UPPER WEST SIDE

4. SOHO & GREENWICH VILLAGE

5. SPECIAL EXCURSIONS

Let me spare you the typical guidebook gush about New York City, the Fabulous Gastronomic Capital. Suffice it to say that it is. After all, a city with some 17,000 eating places is by definition a city that caters to a lot of demanding eaters.

The recommendations that follow are divided into five sections:

The first three sections correspond approximately to geographic areas in the hotel chapter. It seemed to me that after a busy day sightseeing you'd want to know first which restaurants are within easy walking distance of your hotel. The fourth section contains recommendations in parts of town you're likely to be visiting. The fifth section contains recommended special excursions to selected citadels of haute cuisine, plus a potpourri of places that for one reason or another are worth a special trip, including Chinatown.

Every section contains cuisines of all sorts and is basically organized in descending order of price. As for credit cards, unless noted otherwise you can assume that all major cards will be honored. Now then, let's get something to eat.

1. Midtown East & West (Including Theater District)

The **Russian Tea Room,** 150 W. 57th St., between Sixth and Seventh Avenues (tel. 265-0947), is the place for shashlik, Stroganoff, caviar, and blinis. Located next door to Carnegie Hall in its own little town house, RTR is a longtime favorite with theater types and showbiz celebrities. Beyond its etched-glass doors is a dazzling interior done in crimson and highlighted with gleaming brass. Lunch runs the gamut from red caviar omelets to chicken Kiev. Figure $30 per person, plus drinks. Dinner might be something like pan-roasted breast of duck with lingonberry sauce, eggplant à la Russe, or salmon pojarsky with red caviar. Typically, dinner runs $32 to $47 per person, plus drinks, tip, and tax. RTR is bright and lively and open every day of the year from about 11:30am to 11:30pm. The Sunday and Monday night cabaret shows upstairs are especially festive and feature top performers at 8:30 and 10:30pm.

The **Palm,** 837 Second Ave., between 44th and 45th Streets (tel. 687-2953), is a luxury-price steakhouse with a purposely funky decor. Places like this raise unpretentiousness to the level of fine art. The Palm is located in an old tenement building and comes complete with sawdust on the floor, a scuffed little bar tucked away in the corner, and cartoon caricatures painted on the walls. People are loyal to the Palm like you wouldn't believe. Taste the food and you'll believe it. Steak, filet mignon, roast beef, lamb chops, and so on are the order of the day, with à la carte selections priced at $24 or so per plate. The huge 4-pound lobsters are $60 but well worth it! Open Monday through Friday from noon to 11:30pm, Saturday from 5pm. Reservations accepted only for groups of four or more.

    Smith & Wollensky, 201 E. 49th St., at Third Avenue (tel. 753-1530), is a big (seating capacity: 400), old-fashioned green-and-white wooden building in the heart of Third Avenue skyscraperland. The masculine-looking renovated interior includes a marble bar, framed prints, bare wooden floors, stamped-tin walls, and an airy big-city feeling. Most people come for the steaks, among them the double chateaubriand for two, sliced steak Wollensky, and filet mignon. There are also things like scallops, veal dishes, and lamb chops on the menu, plus the usual satisfying desserts. A dinner of, for example, S&W Famous Pea Soup, prime ribs, two glasses of wine, a piece of cheesecake, and a cup of coffee will run about $50, plus tip. Skip wine and dessert and you'll save $10.

    Go around the corner to **Wollensky's Grill,** in the same building but with an entrance on 49th Street (tel. 753-0444), and you can enjoy a lighter menu at lesser cost. Sliced filet mignon, roast beef hash, and lemon pepper chicken, for example, usually cost between $14 and $19. The room is much smaller but every bit as handsome and open every day until 2am. The main restaurant hours are noon to midnight Monday through Friday and 5pm to midnight Saturday and Sunday. Reservations suggested.

    Hatsuhana, 17 E. 48th St., between Fifth and Madison Avenues (tel. 355-3345), is the largest single customer of the Fulton Fish Market, contains the largest sushi bar in Manhattan (48 seats), and has the largest American Express account of any restaurant in the five boroughs. This is a great place to eat. Bright, modern, paneled in light oak, and carpeted in deep purple, it contains butcher-block tables sufficient to seat 128. Full dinners of the teriyaki, tempura, sushi, or sashimi variety cost between $18 and $25. Most à la carte menu items are priced from about $8 to $17. The lunch menu is not quite as extensive as that at dinner, but it costs a couple of dollars less. Open Monday through Friday for lunch from 11:45am to 2:30pm and for dinner from 5:30 to 10pm. Open Saturday and Sunday for dinner only, from 5 to 9:30pm.

    Shun Lee Palace, 155 E. 55th St., between Lexington and Third Avenues (tel. 371-8844), has been serving top-flight Hunan and Szechuan cuisine to a loyal clientele for over 15 years. It's very sleek and glossy inside, with gold fans on the walls, mirrored columns, multiple levels, and a chrome-railed bar up front. Best-selling dishes are Peking duck and orange beef, but the large and inventive menu contains many other suggestions, such as moo shu pork, Wang's amazing chicken, crispy duckling with vegetables, and Peking pork omelet. Everything is à la carte and most main dishes are in the $20 range. Shun Lee is open seven days a week ("If there were eight days in a week, we would be open then too") from noon to 11pm. Reservations suggested.

    The **Brasserie,** 100 E. 53rd St., in the Seagram Building between Park and Lexington Avenues (tel. 751-4840), resonates with the aesthetics of the 1960s. It also serves meals at all hours of the day or night. In fact, the Brasserie has never once closed in over 30 years. It's a high-ceilinged modern room with a stone floor, soft lighting, and a large counter area, plus flocks of rattan café chairs grouped around crisply clothed tables. Cuisine is Alsatian, which means among other things that the menu's half in French. You can have anything from steak tartare to salade niçoise to fettucine to one of "les hamburgers de la maison" to entrecôte. Most menu items are priced between $10 and $15, while a full meal can be had for around $20. It's an ideal place to meet someone or have an omelet at 3am. Open 24 hours daily.

    The **Oyster Bar,** located on the Lower Level of Grand Central Terminal, Vanderbilt Avenue and 42nd Street (tel. 490-6650), is a vast old room with buff-colored brick arches and a tiled floor. To one side is a big counter with comfortable white chairs; on the other is a sea of tables with red-checked cloths. The specialty of the house, of course, is ultrafresh oysters, which come in 55 varieties and cost between $1.25 and $2.25 apiece. The very large menu also offers all manner of cold buffet plates, delicious fresh fish, as well as a wide selection of homemade desserts. The average à la carte main dish costs somewhere between $9 and $25, meaning that a full dinner with tip will probably run about $35 per person. The wine list is impressive, with a wide range of American wine. Open only on weekdays from 11:30am to 9:30pm.

Clarke's, 915 Third Ave., at 55th Street (tel. 759-1650), also called **P. J. Clarke's,** is an original Third Avenue Irish saloon that has miraculously survived in near-original condition. There they are, the old tiles and the sawdust on the floor, the ornate Victorian bar stained almost black with time and tobacco smoke, the beveled mirrors, the stained glass, and the ebullient atmosphere. The big carved bar is up front, with a few tables beyond it for the burgers and fries listed on a chalkboard menu. In the back is a large dim dining room with the blue-checked cloths, yellow shaded lamps, walls full of Victorian framed stuff, and sometimes live music. Clarke's is the place for drinks and burgers, and occasionally chicken, spaghetti, or steak if the spirit moves you. It's loud, congenial, informal, packed after work, and cheap. Few menu items cost over $10. If you do run up a bill it's because you drank a lot. Open daily from about noon until the wee hours.

Siam Inn, 916 Eighth Ave., near 55th Street (tel. 489-5237), is an intimate little place with a bar up front and a cluster of little pink-clothed tables to the rear. Thai cuisine is notable for dishes like chicken Masamen, prepared with avocado, coconut milk, peanuts, spices, and chili; or pla lad prig, a deep-fried fish with a spicy Thai sauce; or salmon broiled with green curry, ground shrimp, coconut milk, chili, and spices. The food at Siam Inn is exotic, very reasonably priced, and absolutely delicious. People come regularly from all parts of town. The average dinner, exclusive of tip and tax, will run about $20 per person, including a drink. Lunch with a drink will probably cost around $10. Open seven days a week for dinner, from 5 to about 11:30pm; lunch is served only on weekdays, from noon to 3pm.

Hard Rock Café, 221 W. 57th St., between Seventh Avenue and Broadway (tel. 459-9320), is a clone of the London establishment of the same name. The rear end of a 1960 Cadillac is embedded in the building wall over the shiny brass doors, its backup lights aglitter. But if the car's in reverse, the café is not. They line up on the sidewalk to get inside here—not to dance either, but simply to enjoy burgers, ribs, and sandwiches to the accompaniment of taped rock and roll in an atmosphere that really is fun. The room is huge and consists of various levels decorated, well, with just about any old thing. Religious statues stand cheek by jowl with neon signs proclaiming "Victims Wanted." An immense black horseshoe hangs on a wall decorated with every whatnot you can imagine. There's an $18 steak, but the menu emphasis is on things like the "pig" sandwich (that's smoked pork), barbecued chicken, chiliburgers, veggie sandwich, ribs, and the like, none of which costs over $10. All manner of soda-fountain desserts and sundaes are available as well. They have the same menu at both lunch and dinner, and meals are served between 11:30am and 2am daily. Handsome personnel behind a 40-foot Fender Stratocaster guitar–shaped bar pour drinks for a youthful clientele until 4am on weekends.

Now for a few delis, starting with **The New York Delicatessen,** 104 W. 57th St., between Sixth and Seventh Avenues (tel. 541-8320). The vintage building looks like an enormous jukebox with windows full of hanging salamis. Behind the bowed glass walls overlooking 57th Street is a huge multilevel room dominated by a gilded statue of a woman who holds aloft a globe of light. Judging from her figure she hasn't been eating at the New York Deli, where stupendous portions are the order of the day. Salad platters, overstuffed sandwiches, half-pound burgers, omelets, hot open sandwiches, blintzes, and more run in the neighborhood of $6 to $10. Full meals like chicken-in-the-pot, pastrami or corned beef platters, and the "top of the line fish platter" are usually between $14 and $16. Open 24 hours a day.

The **Carnegie Delicatessen,** 854 Seventh Ave., between 54th and 55th Streets (tel. 757-2245), has a flashing neon sign outside and more hanging salamis in the window. Up front they make sandwiches, in the back the crowds sit, talking, laughing, and eating and eating and eating. The menu is one long gag: "Bacon Whoopee" (get it?) is a chicken salad club, "The Mouth That Roared" is a roast beef sandwich with sliced onion. Actually, the food is of legendary quality, and almost everything is priced between $9 and $15. Seems like a lot, but one sandwich can feed two people. Open "22 out of every 24 hours," seven days a week.

Sarge's Deli, 548 Third Ave., between 36th and 37th Streets (tel. 679-0442), is a neighborhood favorite that's slightly out of the way but worth the trip. There's plenty of comfortable seating in two brightly lit rooms. Patrons are mostly individuals and families from the area, though many make longer trips to shop in the attached gourmet shop. Sarge's has nobly proportioned sandwiches of every imaginable type priced around $8 to $9. Generous full dinners like goulash, filet of sole, London broil, and fried shrimp run from around $13 to $18. Often these are featured as "Complete Family Dinners" including salad, soup, main course, beverage, and even dessert. Open 24 hours daily.

TWO IN THE THEATER DISTRICT

Restaurants all over the place serve pre- and post-theater suppers. But it's convenient to know a place that's only steps from the theater itself. The following are personal favorites, heavy on atmosphere and value and not particularly expensive.

Café Un Deux Trois, 123 W. 44th St., between Sixth and Seventh Avenues (tel. 354-4148), serves hearty bistro fare to an eclectic crowd of businesspeople and theatergoers. It's in a large old-fashioned room with quite a fantastical decor. The columns holding up the lofty ceiling have been voluptuously painted to resemble veined marble. Large murals of clouds surround flocks of white-clothed tables and comfortable red banquettes. The menu lists à la carte items like onion soup, country pâté, escargots, steak tartare, roast chicken, steak au poivre, lamb curry, and omelets of choice, all at reasonable prices. A typical lunch with appetizer, main course, and a glass of wine will run close to $25, plus tip and tax. If you skip the appetizer and have just an omelet, it'll be closer to $15. The dinner menu offers similar fare for slightly higher prices. Open daily from 11:45am to midnight.

My own particular favorite in the Theater District, for creative northern Italian cuisine and high-style Manhattan ambiance, is **Orso,** 322 W. 46th St., between Eighth and Ninth Avenues (tel. 489-7212). There's a small pink-marble bar right at the front door, parquet floors, framed pictures of movie stars on the walls, and tables set with hand-painted dishes filling the long narrow dining room. The innovative menu includes appetizers like grilled bread with tomato and basil and grilled eggplant with goat cheese and sun-dried tomatoes, priced mostly from $7 to $8, plus small pizzas for $9 and main dishes like grilled chicken with leeks, oregano, radicchio, and plum tomatoes or grilled shrimp with white beans and thyme, both priced between $18 and $21. Open daily from noon to midnight; reservations a must.

DON'T FORGET THE HOTEL RESTAURANTS

Many of the big Midtown hotels have luxury restaurants that are famous in their own right. Particularly worth remembering, if you're looking for an elegant dinner spot, are the **Edwardian Room** and the **Oak Room** at the Plaza, the **Café Pierre** or **The Rotunda** at the Pierre, the **Café Carlyle** at the Carlyle Hotel, **La Régence** at the Hotel Plaza Athénée, and the **Rose Room** at the Algonquin Hotel. Also terrific and very stylish in that particular Manhattan idiom are **44**, the restaurant in the Hotel Royalton, and the **Mezzanine Restaurant** in the Paramount Hotel.

2. Upper East Side

The **Post House,** 28 E. 63rd St., off Madison Avenue (tel. 935-2888), is an old New York standard. Great steaks, chops, and seafood are served in a handsome clubby atmosphere. The dining room with oak wainscoting is situated on different levels, so everyone can be seen but not heard, and there are also nooks that one can request if one wishes not to be seen. Regulars have name plates over their usual seats, but the staff will treat you as warmly as an old-timer even if you're a newcomer. To start, the Caesar salad is done tableside to your liking. More exotic is the seafood sausage or a mainstay such as the tremendous shrimp cocktail. Fresh oysters or clams are their forté. Excellent chops and steaks are done in a variety of styles, such as au poivre, grilled, broiled, or black and blue. Appetizers range from $6 to $13. The oversize main dishes are between $18 and $33. Open Monday through Friday from noon to 11pm and Saturday and Sunday from 5:30pm to midnight. Reservations suggested.

Coco Pazzo, 23 E. 74th St., between Fifth and Madison (tel. 794-0205), is the hot Italian spot of the moment. The bar gets lively with people anxious for a table; if you don't reserve, you'll usually have to wait. The barside tables are great for having a small bite and people-watching. On one night, I saw Woody Allen, Robert DeNiro, Joe Pesci, and Bruce Springsteen. The crowd is a mix of area old money and Hollywood people out wheeling and dealing. In the main dining room, with its Florentine beige-stucco walls and fabric-swathed ceiling, the atmosphere is relaxing and pleasant. You may want to start with *pulpo grigliata,* grilled octopus, or the more tame assorted antipasto, which can be chosen with the waiter's help at the antipasto bar. As a main course, the mixed grill, a platter of assorted meats, is a favorite. The risotto with white truffles, when in season, will take you to Italy without the jet lag. Appetizers are pricey, starting at $7 and going to $14, but the plentiful main dishes are fairly priced from $15 to $25. A multitude of pasta and game are always available, and all can be had "family style" on the weekends. Open daily for lunch from noon to 2:30pm and for dinner from 6pm to midnight. Reservations suggested.

Ferrier, 29 E. 65th St., between Madison and Park (tel. 772-9000), is known for its great location in the heart of the Historic District, its unbelievably authentic and generous French fare, and its 6-foot-tall bombshell hostesses. A small bar gets a mellow crowd just after work, but by 9pm the place is filled with a mix of the area's beautiful people and Wall Street go-getters. If a scene isn't your scene, struggle past the short bar into the cozy, dimly lit dining room. Done in mahoghany with frosted-glass wall lamps, this is perhaps a more elegant bistro than found on a small Paris street. The food is the best, from the couscous—typical peasant stew with a variety of meats and sausage—to the steak frites (with fries), to the cassoulet, a mix of lamb and duck confit. As an appetizer, you might want to try the mussels marinated in white wine or the escargot served in a pastry puff. A wide range of pasta, poultry, game, and fresh fish are available for both lunch and dinner, and a three-course prix-fixe ($20) meal from an extensive menu is offered from 4:30 to 6pm daily—the best value in the city! Appetizers run from $5 to $8, main dishes from $15 to $22—and the atmosphere is free! Open for lunch from 11am to 3:30pm and for dinner from 4:30pm to 1am.

Calcutta, 1708 Second Ave., between 88th and 89th Streets (tel. 996-8037), is a small neighborhood Indian place where both service and food are good and generous. The decor is sleek and Westernized, and the tables are spaced just far enough so that the conversation at the next table cannot be overheard. The inexpensive appetizers range from onion bhasia ($2), a plate of onion fritters, to mixed samosa ($3), a combination plate of deep-fried little pockets of potato or beef, and to larger combo platters ($6). Chicken tandoori, a deep-grilled method of cooking; fish tikka, also cooked tandoori style; or a vegetarian plate can be had as a main course from $8 to $16. Lots of sauces, Indian-spiced crackers, and puff bread are served complementary during the meal. Open daily from noon to midnight.

EJ's Luncheonette, 1271 Third Ave., at 73rd Street (tel. 472-0600) and 433 Amsterdam Ave., at 81st Street (tel. 873-3444), are perfect for a hearty brunch or diner-type food for lunch or dinner. Specialties are buckwheat flapjacks with real maple syrup, French toast made with challah bread 3 inches thick, and fruit-topped pancakes and waffles—all served in a retro-50s setting. The blue-vinyl booths and the chromed open grill make this place casual and fun. EJ's also has great burgers, shakes, salads, sandwiches on challah, and overloaded blue-plate specials. Prices range from $4 for eggs and other breakfast items to $10 for a main dish at night.

Open daily from 8am to midnight; breakfast is served all day; lunch/dinner starts at 11am.

Hosteria Fiorella, 1081 Third Ave., at 64th Street (tel. 838-7570), is my favorite restaurant when I want a light satisfying meal in the busy Midtown shopping district. Fresh pasta, seafood, and lightly grilled vegetables are superb and provide just enough energy to tackle nearby Bloomingdale's. Appetizers, from antipasto misto, to the best fried calamari in the city with two sauces, to *insalata d'aragosta,* to lobster-and-arugula salad with shiitake-and-truffle olive oil, are large enough for a complete lunch. For something even larger, you may want to try *linguine pescatore,* a delicious combination of fresh shrimp, clams, calamari, and mussels over linguine, or penne zampognara, pasta tubes under a veal bolognese sauce with wild mushrooms. The dinner menu is much more extensive and features such Italian specialties as *aragosta fra diavolo,* half a lobster over black linguine, veal chop with grilled vegetables, and a variety of pizzas for those who want to keep it light. Appetizers range from $4.50 to $13, with dinner main dishes, from $14 to $22. Lunch is a few dollars cheaper, but what's great about this place is the true Italian belief that a meal should be lingered over, no matter how much is ordered. A great value is the $12.50 brunch on the weekend from 11am to 3pm, which also includes a glass of champagne or other drink, a basket of fresh-baked sweet breads and homemade jams, and coffee or tea. Open daily from 11:30am to 3pm for lunch and 5pm to midnight for dinner.

J. G. Melon, 1291 Third Ave., at 74th Street (tel. 744-0585) is an old-fashioned Irish bar with a veneer of East Side chic. It's full of dark woodwork, the obligatory carved Victorian bar, lots of little tables covered with blue-checked tablecloths, a jukebox with rock and roll, walls covered with framed pictures of melons, and plenty of neighborhood patrons who come for the convivial surroundings and cheap eats. The chalkboard menu lists hamburgers, chili, club sandwiches, chef's salad, turkey sandwich, and a few more filling items from $6 to $13. Open daily from about 11:30am until 4am.

---

3. Upper West Side

Tavern on the Green, inside Central Park, adjacent to the intersection of Central Park West and 67th Street (tel. 212/873-3200), is a local institution as popular with New Yorkers as it is with tourists. Built in the 19th century as a sheepfold, it's currently decorated with ankle-deep carpets, acres of gleaming brass, and an abundance of chandeliers. The big restaurant has a complex plan: The Chestnut Room has massive green-plush chairs, a beamed ceiling, and huge chandeliers; the Park Room has a 52-foot mural depicting Central Park at the turn of the century; the Crystal Room is surrounded with walls of glass, contains more chandeliers than a maharaja's palace, and is the room where everyone wants to sit. Indeed, sitting in the dazzle of the Crystal Room and gazing at the trees outside, their limbs lined with tens of thousands of tiny lights, is an experience not soon forgotten. The extensive à la carte menu is the same wherever you sit. At lunch it features things like broiled halibut steak with five greens, smoked chicken crêpes with mushrooms, and veal blanquette, mostly priced between $10 and $20. You can always get a hamburger or the Tavern's Classic Club Sandwich for about $10. Many of the same items appear on the dinner menu, priced $3 or $4 higher. A huge and varied à la carte brunch is served on Saturday and Sunday. Open daily for lunch from noon to 3:30pm and for dinner from 5:30pm to midnight. Reservations are a must.

What could be more romantic than dinner (or lunch) at **Café des Artistes,** 1 W. 67th St., off Central Park West (tel. 877-3500)? This intimate Edwardian-era room was muraled in 1933 by the famous Howard Chandler Christy. Today his rosy naked nymphs and satyrs are as much a draw as owners George and Jenifer Lang's continental cuisine. One enters through the paneled and marbled lobby of the residential Hotel des Artistes. Inside the café are deep-green rugs, small booths and tables covered with pristine white cloths, and appealing images of gilded youths cavorting with their clothes off. The luncheon menu includes a wide selection of à la carte appetizers and main courses, like sliced fresh peppered duck liver, snails sautéed with onions, swordfish paillard with mustard sauce, and fabulous desserts. Main courses at lunch cost between about $14 and $23. Dinner might be red snapper in orange crust, steak au poivre, pot-au-feu, duck with raisins in pear brandy, or any number of other things, priced mostly between $20 and $25. The house also serves a prix-fixe lunch and dinner, priced as of this writing at about $20 and $33, respectively. Lunch is served Monday through Saturday from noon to 3pm; brunch is served Sunday from 10am to 4pm; dinner hours are 5:30pm to 12:30am Monday through Saturday and 5 to 11pm on Sunday.

La Mirabelle, 333 W. 86th St., between West End Avenue and Riverside Drive (tel. 496-0458), is a real neighborhood find. Cuisine is classic French, and reservations are a must. There are three small pink-and-white dining rooms with modern chairs and mirrors on the walls; everything is crisp and immaculate. Only dinner is served, between 6 and 10pm nightly. It might consist of roasted duck in Mirabelle (plum) sauce, veal with light mustard sauce, shell steak with green-peppercorn sauce, or lamb chops with fresh herbs. A la carte main courses range from $13 to $21.

Isabella's, 359 Columbus Ave., at 77th Street (tel. 724-2100), is a great sidewalk café. Located near the Museum of Natural History and across the street from the Green Flea, this large, airy restaurant takes on a quaint feel when packed (which is most of the time). In the warmer months, the tables pour onto the sidewalk, and a lazy lunch is welcomed. The food can range from the exotic, like fettucine with duck in Madeira sauce, to the usual, like a hamburger with Jack cheese. Appetizers are from $4 to $7, and some salads are big enough for a light lunch. Main dishes run from $8 to $15. Open Monday to Thursday from 11:30am to 12:30am, until 1am on Friday and Saturday; Sunday brunch is served from 11am. Reservations are suggested, although the bar is pleasant for people-watching if you must wait.

Across the street, The Museum Café, 366 Columbus Ave., at 77th Street (tel. 799-0150), has an enclosed porch with French windows overlooking Columbus Avenue and the Museum of Natural History. This busy convivial neighborhood spot, with its long antique bar, dark floors, and flocks of little tables with crisp white cloths, features a very large menu. Appetizers, like the three lentil salad, are priced between $5 and $7. Main courses—such as angel-hair pasta primavera with fresh vegetable sauce; grilled Caribbean chicken cutlets served with beans and rice, fried plaintains, and pineapple salsa; daily fish specials; or one of the pasta selections (which come in oversize bowls)—are priced between $9 and $17. There are also lots of good sandwiches at lunchtime. Open Monday through Friday from noon until midnight, from 11am on Saturday and Sunday.

Yarben, 285 Columbus Ave., between 73rd and 74th Streets (tel. 721-5333), is a tiny establishment serving authentic Middle Eastern cuisine. The soups are homemade, and you can see the daily selection of appetizers, like rolled grape leaves, stuffed peppers, or fresh Israeli vegetable salad, displayed in a glass case when you walk in the door. I particularly like the "Maza," a combination plate that includes falafel, hummus, tahini, baba ganoush, and tabouli, priced either at $6 or $10, depending on the size of the portion. Grilled Israeli and Yemeni items, served either in pita or on a plate, range from $7 to $10. Open daily from noon to midnight, this is a good place for a low-priced, exotic meal.

Perretti Italian Café (or just "Perretti's"), 270 Columbus Ave., between 72nd and 73rd Streets (tel. 362-3939), is located at the spiritual epicenter of the West Side. It has red-checked tablecloths covered with paper sheets, a (very) small counter (only four seats), modern industrial hanging lamps, fake black tiles on the walls, and neighborhood families and singles who like the unpretentious style and solid food. Meals include fresh pasta in every style from bolognese to primavera; frittati made of eggs, sausage, eggplant, peppers, onions, or any combination thereof; veal; lasagne; ziti; pizza; and so on. Almost everything costs between $8 and $12. Open Sunday to Thursday from noon to midnight, to 1am on Friday and Saturday.

Not far away is Café La Fortuna, 69 W. 71st St., between Columbus Avenue and Central Park West (tel. 724-5846), a real Italian café/bakery that's been in the neighborhood for a long time. You walk down a few stairs, past the sign that says

"Children welcome, no strollers please," into a long room that goes all the way to the back of the building where it opens onto an outdoor café. The old-time decor includes green-lace curtains, framed pictures of Italian opera singers, a photo tribute to John Lennon (who lived in the neighborhood), and a big display case full of wonderful desserts. There's a good selection of sweets, like homemade cannoli, Sachertorte, strawberry shortcake, and tray after tray of biscotti—Italian cookies. At La Fortuna you can have a cup of cappuccino or iced cappuccino, with Italian ice and a plate of biscotti, for about $7. It's a great place to take a break from a day of shopping on the West Side. It's open Tuesday to Sunday from noon to 2am.

Dallas BBQ, 27 W. 72nd St., between Central Park West and Columbus Avenue (tel. 873-2004), used to be the catering hall of the recommended Hotel Olcott. It's a cavernous old room with a Western decor installed sometime in the late 1980s. There are Navajo blankets and longhorn steer skulls on the walls; comfortable upholstered chairs; and a bar that serves "Colossal" frozen margaritas, regular ($4.25) or Texas size ($6.50). This is the place for half a chicken with cornbread and french fries, a fresh-fruit main course with a mountain of frozen yogurt, hamburgers, ribs, or a loaf of onion rings. What does it matter if the menu is limited when a Texas-size portion of ribs with all the fixin's costs $8.95? Open daily from noon: Sunday through Thursday until midnight; Friday and Saturday until 1am. Three new locations are: 1265 Third Ave., at 73rd Street (tel. 772-9393); 132 Second Ave., at 8th Street (tel. 777-5574); and 21 University Place (tel. 674-4450).

4. SoHo & Greenwich Village

SOHO

The name of this famous district of art galleries and boutiques is a contraction of "*So*uth of *Ho*uston." It's not a very big area, being bounded by Houston Street on the north and Canal Street on the south. The main drag is called West Broadway, and one of our walking tours will take you through it. Herewith, a few recommended restaurants for those in SoHo at mealtime.

For serious haute cuisine, try **Zoe,** at 90 Prince St. between Broadway and Mercer (tel. 966-6722), one of the most innovative new restaurants in the city. The place has a Santa Fe feel, with buff-colored walls, a lofty ceiling, wide open space, and an exposed grill in the rear. The food is undeniably gourmet. To start, the crispy noodles wrapped around jumbo shrimp with sesame dressing is a specialty; or be more adventurous and try the barbecued quail with fois-gras brioche. For a main course, sample the yellowfin tuna served over jasmine rice in Chinese chili sauce; angus rib-eye steak; or assorted game, poultry, and pasta dishes. Appetizers are from $7 to $11, and main dishes are from $16 to $25; considering the food's quality and presentation, the great service, and the wonderful ambience, this place is a great find by New York standards. Open Tuesday through Sunday from noon to 3pm for lunch and 6 to 11pm for dinner. Reservations suggested.

I Tre Merli, 463 W. Broadway, between Houston and Prince (tel. 254-8699), has been packed since it first opened in SoHo years ago. A favorite with the young and stylish, this bilevel hangout brings them in with its oversize bar and scrumptious northern Italian cuisine. To start, the marinated seafood salad is great, and the fried calamari are crisp and wonderful. For a main course, a good choice is the scallopine Milanese or a pasta specialty, such as the penne with artichoke and grilled shrimp. Open Sunday to Thursday from noon to 1am, until 2am on Friday and Saturday. Appetizers start at $3.50 for focaccia and go to $12. Main courses are $13 to $20.

The intersection of West Broadway and Grand Street offers five stylish establishments—**Felix, Jour et Nuit, Toad Hall, La Jumelle,** and **Lucky Strike.** Each is frequented weekends by a combination of in-the-know uptowners and the downtown art crowd. The best for ambience *and* cuisine is **Toad Hall,** 57 Grand St. (tel. 431-8145). The place looks like a regular pub, with oak flooring, exposed brick, and a long oak bar at the entrance. What makes this different, however, is the funky Motown music played and the attitude concerning the food, which is to satisfy without going wild on the price. As an appetizer, you may want to try the roasted whole head of garlic with goat cheese, olives, and bruschetta or the specialty, fried lamb nuggets with lemon yogurt. The baby greens salad with marinated vegetables is large enough for a light meal. For a main course, you'll find a variety of sandwiches, such as a tuna steak club done to your liking, cheddar-cheeseburgers on English muffins, or a more exotic combo of grilled eggplant and red pepper; also there are pasta, free range chicken, fish, and sautéed filet mignon with wild mushrooms. Everything is fresh and abundant. Prices are reasonable, with appetizers between $3.50 and $7 and main courses starting at $5 and going to $11 for steak. Open daily from noon to 2am, with the bar open until 4am.

An old SoHo standard is **The Cupping Room Café**, 359 West Broadway, at Broome Street (tel. 925-2898). This is a congenial neighborhood bar/restaurant filled with a boisterous crowd. It has a long bar, high ceilings, lots of plants, exposed-brick walls, antique lighting fixtures, and plenty of atmosphere. There are lots of sandwiches at lunchtime, like blackened chicken breast with pesto mayonnaise or smoked turkey and brie with apple chutney, both on a baguette, plus all manner of burgers and omelets (mostly from $7 to $10). Dinner main courses and special desserts are also priced moderately. The kitchen is open daily from 11am to 1am.

GREENWICH VILLAGE

Greenwich Village was a rural hamlet until engulfed by urban sprawl in the 1830s (there's nothing new about urban sprawl). What people today call the "West Village" contains the site of the original town. What people call "The Village," however, is usually meant to be the region around Washington Square, from 14th Street to Houston Street.

Presiding for the last 44 years over a Village street off Washington Square is **The Coach House**, 110 Waverly Place, which would be 7th Street if it had a number, between Washington Square West and Sixth Avenue (tel. 777-0303). Once the carriage house for a nearby mansion, it's now a spacious, comfortable restaurant serving big American meals. The decor is airy, handsome, and traditional, with high ceilings, modernistic chandeliers, a collection of framed oil paintings on the walls, red-leatherette chairs, white-clothed tables, and a rear mezzanine reached by a flight of crimson-carpeted stairs. Only dinner is served, and the menu focuses on just those things they do with superlative skill. House specialties like American chicken pie, rack of lamb, and boneless sirloin cost from about $20 to $27. Additional à la carte dishes such as prime rib, baby lobster tails, roasted red snapper, and poached striped bass cost from $24 all the way up to about $38 for complete dinners. Appetizers like fresh oysters, prosciutto and melon, or baked clams will run another $5 to $10 apiece. People come from around the world to eat at this restaurant, so reservations are suggested. Open Tuesday to Saturday from 5:30 to 10:30pm, Sunday from 4:30pm; closed in August.

Il Mulino, 86 W. 3rd St., between Thompson and Sullivan Streets (tel. 673-3783), is the classic little Village restaurant that people love to brag about finding. Rock singers, grandmothers, movie stars, sports personalities, and people from all over town beat a regular path to its discreet gray-and-white awning. Inside is a not-very-large dining room with a bar up front, a profusion of healthy potted plants, lush Muzak in the air, and a flock of white-clothed tables in the back. The à la carte menu is the same at lunch and dinner. It lists things like sautéed veal in cream and champagne, veal in lemon and butter, pastas from spaghettini to tortellini, morsels of chicken braised in wine and artichokes, and breast of chicken in cream and Calvados —all priced from around $15 to $30, with most selections falling somewhere in the middle. This is the place for a rich, classic Italian meal where calories don't count, finished off with one of their many grappas. Open Monday to Saturday except holidays, from noon to 2:30pm for lunch and 5 to 11:30pm for dinner. Reservations required.

Café Raffaela, 137 Seventh Ave. South, between West 10th and Charles

MANHATTAN

SoHo, TriBeCa, Little Italy & Chinatown

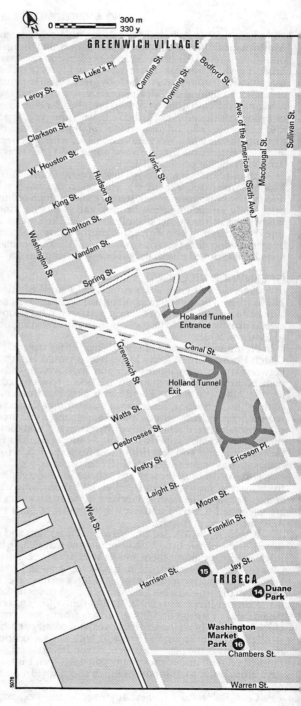

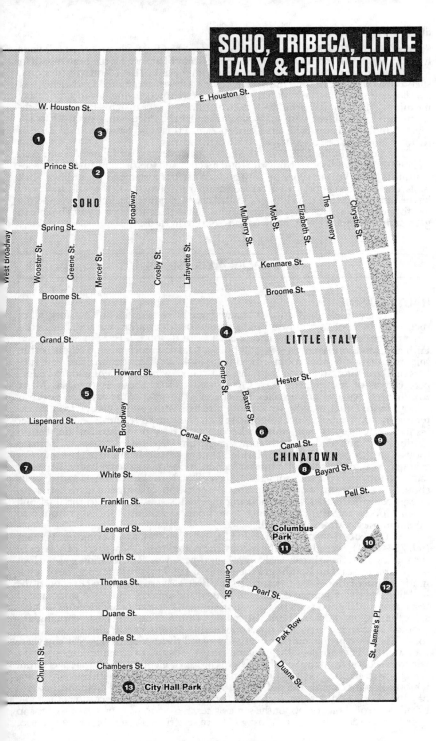

SOHO, TRIBECA, LITTLE ITALY & CHINATOWN

W. Houston St.

E. Houston St.

1

3

Prince St.

2

SOHO

Broadway

Spring St.

Mulberry St.

Mott St.

Elizabeth St.

The Bowery

Chrystie St.

west broadway

Wooster St.

Greene St.

Mercer St.

Crosby St.

Lafayette St.

Kenmare St.

Broome St.

Broome St.

Grand St.

4

LITTLE ITALY

Howard St.

Centre St.

Hester St.

5

Broadway

Lispenard St.

Canal St.

Baxter St.

6

Canal St.

9

Walker St.

CHINATOWN

White St.

8 Bayard St.

7

Pell St.

Franklin St.

Leonard St.

Columbus Park

Worth St.

11

10

Thomas St.

Centre St.

Pearl St.

12

Duane St.

Park Row

St. James's Pl.

Reade St.

Church St.

Chambers St.

Duane St.

13 **City Hall Park**

Streets (tel. 929-7247), is the kind of place you stumble upon and then tell your friends about. This is a tiny restaurant, reminiscent of a place off the beaten path in Venice, where you can stop for just an espresso or for one of the 20 amazing desserts, such as the mud cake of solid fudge. The café also serves overstuffed sandwiches and overflowing salads and always has plenty of newspapers laying around for a lazy morning. The decor is charming—no two chairs or tables match—and has a 15th-century monastical feel, with many small chandeliers. Prices range from $3 to $8. Open Sunday to Thursday from 11am to 2am, Friday and Saturday until 3am. If there's a line, don't be discouraged: It's worth the wait.

The **Corner Bistro,** 331 W. 4th St., at Jane Street just off Eighth Avenue (tel. 242-9502), is an old corner bar with a loud jukebox and lots of youthful (and not-so-youthful) West Village types on low budgets. It has a stamped-tin ceiling; brick walls; dark wooden booths; a big carved bar up front; a menu on the wall; and a tiny kitchen that cranks out tasty burgers, grilled cheese sandwiches, french fries, and the like for under $6 a plate. Very unpretentious, but at peak hours you won't be able to get a table. Open daily from noon to 4am. No credit cards.

---

5. Special Excursions

HAUTE CUISINE

There are at least half a dozen "haute French" restaurants in New York, all of them with an air of "grand luxe" and a reputation for exquisite cuisine. But since I must choose among them, my choice is **La Côte Basque,** 5 E. 55th St., between Fifth and Madison Avenues (tel. 688-6525). Classic French cuisine reigns within this spacious and famous room tricked up to look like a seaside inn. There are timbers on the ceiling, stucco on the walls, and "faux" windows opening onto "faux" perspectives of the French coast. Of course, it looks about as rustic as Marie Antoinette's "village" at Versailles. But charm is the order of the day here, as well as famous food. Lunch and dinner are both prix fixe, with courses chosen from an extensive menu. A sample lunch might start with pheasant en croûte or perhaps lobster bisque, move on to something like poached bass or "cassoulet du Patron Toulousain," and end up with something from the dessert "chariot," perhaps mousse au chocolat with Grand Marnier. Dinner is basically more of the same: For example, you might start with lobster terrine, move on to a main course like roast rack of lamb, and end with something incredible from the "chariot." Lunch costs about $28 per person; at dinner the tab is closer to $60. Many menu items have separate prices in parentheses and choosing these adds substantially to the final bill. Open Monday to Saturday for lunch from noon to 2:30pm, for dinner from 6 to 10:30pm. Reservations suggested.

At **The Four Seasons,** 99 E. 52nd St., between Park and Lexington Avenues (tel. 754-9494), everything—the menus, the potted trees, the waiters' jackets, even the matches and the ashtrays—changes four times a year. The location is at the foot of the famous Seagram Building. When built in 1959 this was the epitome of ultra-modern, international-style swank. Today, over a quarter century later, both the building and the restaurant remain unchanged and are now registered landmarks, a testament to the good parts of a now-unfashionable school of architecture. But besides the shallow stairs and immense ceilings, shimmering gold-chain curtains, 10-foot-tall Picasso tapestry, and travertine-marble floors, there is also the matter of food. The same people eat here every day—and these people could eat anywhere they wanted. They are the captains of industry, the barons of communications, and a fair cross section from the Social Register. The lunch menu contains appetizers from Beluga caviar to pheasant consomme; main courses like shrimp with mustard fruits, lemon sole with crayfish and dill, sirloin steak, omelets prepared tableside, or a trio of lamb chops; and desserts such as pear poached in port. Dinner offers the same broad range of choices at about the same prices. Expect to pay upward of $14 for an appetizer and $32 and up for most à la carte selections. Vegetables are extra too, albeit exquisite. At both lunch and dinner you have the option of "spa cuisine" (dishes from $32 to $42), which consists of main courses with ultralow calorie counts. Above the bar in the Grill Room is an amazing hanging sculpture composed of thousands of slender rods of burnished bronze. In the Pool Room is a startlingly large and tranquil reflecting pond. Reservations are imperative; try to get the Pool Room for a romantic dinner. The Grill Room offers a prix-fixe dinner from $29 to $37, depending on the main course. Open Monday to Saturday for lunch from noon to 2:30pm, for dinner from 5 to 11:30pm. A must try for wine lovers, this has the most extensive wine cellar in the city.

Barbetta, 321 W. 46th St., between Eighth and Ninth Avenues (tel. 246-9171), celebrated its 80th anniversary in 1986. It's located in a pair of old brownstones that look, on the inside, not unlike a small palace. From the street, you pass through a progression of intimate wood-paneled rooms filled with old paintings, needlepoint chairs, little chandeliers, and an air of European elegance. In the back is a fine large dining room with Venetian curtains on the arched windows, a splendid chandelier, old giltwood wall sconces, and French doors opening onto one of the most delicious formal outdoor dining patios in New York. The cuisine is northern Italian—Piedmontese. Lunch might be wild hare in civet, pheasant of the day (!), *tagliarini verdi alla bolognese* with wild porcini mushrooms, broiled fresh sole, or veal chop in parsley sauce. Everything, of course, is à la carte. Most main lunch courses cost between $25 and $30. Dinner selections are pretty much in the same price range and include beef braised in red wine, *bolliti misti piemontesi* (a mixture of beef, chicken, and vegetables), or *veal tonné* (thin-sliced veal with tuna and caper sauce, a summertime special). Open Monday to Saturday for lunch from noon to 2pm, for dinner from 5pm to midnight. Reservations are required; and if you come in the summer, reserve a table in that garden.

ATMOSPHERIC CUISINE

A number of city skyscrapers have restaurants on top, and the most famous of them all is **Windows on the World,** 107th floor, One World Trade Center (tel. 938-1111). Get ready for your ears to pop on the way up to this one. But once you're there, the view is truly awesome, especially looking south across the harbor and out into the Atlantic. The Statue of Liberty looks like a toy. To the north the towers of Manhattan appear to be intricate scale models wrought by a race of watchmakers run amok. The 107th floor has a number of separate eating areas, each with its own name and menu. Only dinner is served in the Restaurant, whose cool champagne color scheme and multiple-level seating set the view off quite nicely. The room—big and hushed and golden—offers several table d'hôte dinners, as well as à la carte items like grilled scallops with white basil butter, roast veal tenderloin, sautéed fresh venison, salmon steak, filet mignon, and fricassee of lobster and crayfish. Appetizers include fresh salmon marinated in dill, *pesto agnolotti* in cream, and mussel bisque. **Note:** As a result of a bomb explosion at the World Trade Center in early 1993, Windows on the World was closed. It was expected to reopen by early 1994. The Cellar in the Sky features a prix-fixe haute cuisine dinner for a maximum of 36 people. This room has no view; one supposes patrons are too busy with the food. The Hors D'Oeuvrerie is the best deal in the place. No reservations are needed, there are piano music and dancing every evening (cover is a mere $3 or so per person), and the menu consists of all manner of light appetizer-type fare at relatively low prices. Examples are deep-fried mozzarella, crab fritters, and Korean short ribs of beef. The full Sunday brunch features things like cold barbecued chicken breast, baked seafood pot pie, and grilled baby chicken with ratatouille. Hours for the dinner-only Restaurant are 5 to 10pm Monday through Saturday; the Hors D'Oeuvrerie opens at 3pm and closes at 1am (on weekends open at noon). On Sunday the Hors D'Oeuvrerie serves only brunch.

Across the street from the Twin Towers of the World Trade Center, flanking either side of the architecturally exciting rotunda of the World Financial Center, is a pair of excellent new restaurants that warrant special trips. **Le Pactole,** 2 World Financial Center (tel. 945-9444), serves classic French cuisine in a spare and serenely elegant modern dining room overlooking the yacht basin and the Hudson River beyond. Beautifully prepared and presented luncheons like grilled tuna on sweet peppers with capers, chicken sautéed in curry, and black angus steak with french fries cost between $12 and $23. At dinner expect to pay between $25 and $35 for classic dishes like Dover sole grilled with wild mushrooms and shallots, coquilles St. Jacques in beurre rouge, red snapper with fennel and butter sauce, or paillard of beef. Everything is done beautifully, and the service by the tuxedo-clad staff is faultless. Open daily: lunch, at which reservations are required, is served Monday through Friday only from noon to 3pm; dinner, which is not as crowded, is available Monday through Saturday from 5:30 to 11pm; the $27 prix-fixe Sunday brunch is available from noon to 5:30pm.

Classic American cuisine with a Hudson River accent is available on the other side of the rotunda in the wood-paneled and multileveled **Hudson River Club, 4** World Financial Center (tel. 786-1500). This restaurant has a warm clubby atmosphere and the same fine views as Le Pactole. Typical dinner choices include roasted pheasant with Finger Lake Riesling, rabbit pot pie, and bacon-wrapped swordfish, priced generally from $27 to $34. Open for lunch Monday through Friday from 11:30am to 2:30pm, and for dinner Monday to Saturday from 5 to 9:30pm (from noon to 6pm only on Sunday).

The **River Café,** 1 Water St. in the borough of Brooklyn (tel. 718/522-5200), is situated on a barge moored practically underneath the Brooklyn Bridge. The view across the glittering surface of the East River toward the downtown skyline is something never to be forgotten. The lacy spans of the Brooklyn Bridge loom overhead, all manner of shipping from yachts to barges passes majestically back and forth, and the city from this angle looks like Oz. It's quite a wonderful place for either lunch or dinner. Cuisine here is "New American," which means things are lightly basted, "deep-frying" is a dirty term, and nothing is too heavy. Lunch might start with the black and white bean soup with smoked shrimp and Jack cheese quesadilla or fresh duck foie gras with warm apple brioche, then move on to fruitwood-grilled pork tenderloin with apples or swordfish steak with grilled shrimp. Figure $30 to $35 per person for a luncheon appetizer and a main course. The prix-fixe $55 (at this writing) dinner might start with eggplant-and-pesto terrine or select oysters, move on to sautéed Maine lobster or pan-fried red snapper, and end with a ginger-pecan flan or warm strudel with two cheeses. The smallish dining room, reached by a cute enclosed gangplank, contains a bar, a grand piano, pencil spotlights trained on dramatic flower arrangements, and a wall of windows overlooking the river. There are excellent views from every seat. Lunch is served Monday through Friday from noon to 2:30pm; Saturday and Sunday brunch (basically the lunch menu with a few egg dishes) also runs from noon to 2:30pm. Dinner is served from 6:00 to 11pm Monday through Saturday, from 6:30 to 11pm on Sunday. Management is a stickler about reservations, which they advise you to make two weeks in advance and then reconfirm (on pain of cancellation) by 3pm on the afternoon of your proposed visit. Last-minute reservations can sometimes be gotten, however, during the week. Parking is free, and most taxis know where the place is. For the trip back to your hotel, management will call you a cab.

Jezebel, 630 Ninth Ave., at 45th Street (tel. 582-1045), serves high-class soul food in a lofty room filled with hanging beaded dresses, lace tablecloths, art deco chandeliers, potted palms, fringed lampshades, and an attractive urban crowd of people in the arts and theater. Only a small metal plaque marks the door, which is easy to miss. A la carte main courses, such as spicy honey chicken with yams, hot-and-spicy shrimp, hamhocks with rice and greens, and smothered chicken, cost mostly between $17 and $26. A bowl of Jezebel's cowpea soup or a piece of sweet-potato pie will add another $5 to $7. The food is authentic and delicious. The atmosphere is a suave combination of down-hominess and big-city sophistication, very much an "only in New York" combination. The patroness is usually on hand. Open daily only for dinner from 5:30pm to 12:30am; the bar stays open to 1am. Reservations required.

For a meal in the heart of Rockefeller Center, I'd recommend the **American Festival Café,** 20 W. 50th St. (tel. 246-6699), which overlooks the famous skating rink at the foot of 30 Rockefeller Plaza. This place is that happy blend of a restaurant in a touristy area that actually serves good food. The contemporary dining room is broad and airy, and almost every table has a view of skaters on the rink outside or, in summer, of a garden restaurant with fountains and umbrella tables. The menu includes lots of lunchtime burgers and sandwiches, and there are dinner choices such as roast Long Island duckling, charred salmon filet, or certified angus steak. Expect typical à la carte dinner selections to cost between $18 and $22; an excellent prix-fixe dinner is priced at $25; the wintertime "Skate-a-Date," a full dinner and skating special, is $24 for adults and $15 for children. Open daily until 11pm.

Positano, 250 Park Ave. South, at 20th Street (tel. 777-6211), is one of those sleek high-tech places so popular with successful young professionals from the worlds of publishing, advertising, and business. It has a very imposing entrance on the corner of an old limestone office building. Inside, everything is ultranew and white, from the walls and floors to the curtains on the plate-glass windows. Seating is on several levels arranged above and below a central bar. Accompanying the soothing jazz in the air is the modulated murmur of prosperous patrons enjoying the Italian cuisine. The antipasti include such dishes as eggplant with pomodoro and provolone cheese and sliced mozzarella with grilled mushrooms and fresh basil, priced around $8 each. Pasta dishes like risotto with seafood or farfalle alla calabra (bow-tie pasta with broccoli) run around $11 to $15. Meat and seafood dishes, such as boneless rabbit with celery and onions, Italian broccoli simmered with sweet sausage, or butter-fried whiting, cost from around $15 to $22. Open for lunch Monday through Friday from noon to 3pm; dinner is served Monday through Saturday from 5:30 to 11:30pm. Reservations suggested.

Indochine, 430 Lafayette St., south of Astor Place, which in turn is quite close to East 8th Street (tel. 505-5111), serves French-Vietnamese cuisine in tropical Saigonish surroundings. There are murals of banana palms on the walls, lazy fans rotating on the ceilings, potted trees, soft lighting, a few pieces of vintage rattan, and fresh flowers on the tables. Dinner only is served in one not terribly large room. It might be a salad of fresh pineapple and shrimp, squid with fresh mint and tamarind, steamed whole fish with ginger, spicy frog legs with fried leeks, or spareribs with lemon grass, to name but a few—all priced from about $8 to $16. Open daily from 5:30pm to 12:30am; a prix-fixe menu is $19.50 from 5:30 to 7pm. Reservations suggested.

"TriBeCa" is the name given to a neighborhood of trendy loft conversions, as well as chic shops and restaurants, spawned by the prohibitively high prices in nearby SoHo. The word stands for "*Triangle Below Canal*" Street. And whatever your opinion on the issue of gentrification, the fact remains that several excellent restaurants have accompanied the phenomenon around here.

Most famous, perhaps, is **TriBeCa Grill,** 375 Greenwich St. at the corner of Franklin Street (tel. 941-3900). It's a massive place, with steam pipes and brick walls exposed to give a rough quality to the room. Owner Robert DeNiro, however, made sure that those were the only rough spots, because both the food and the crowd are right on time all the time. Original oil paintings by DeNiro's father warm the room, and a huge horseshoe-shaped oak bar is an anchor to those wanting to enjoy the atmosphere without sitting for a full meal. If you decide to sit and enjoy, to start you may want to try the crisp fried oysters with garlic aioli or the rare seared tuna with sesame noodles. As a main course, the grilled rib-eye steak with potato-and-leak cake is a specialty, or, for something light, try the excellent penne pasta with plum tomatoes, broccoli rabe, and eggplant served with sausage-cheese bread. Appetizers range from $8 to $12; main courses are from $18 to $24. Open for lunch Monday through Friday from noon to 3pm and for dinner Monday through Saturday from 5:30 to 11pm; open on Sunday from noon until 10pm for brunch and dinner. Reservations suggested.

CHINATOWN

A decidedly foreign air pervades the short blocks on either side of Mott Street between Canal Street and Chatham Square. This is the heart of New York's famous Chinatown, a compact district where the phone booths have pagoda roofs, the street signs have subtitles, and the crowded sidewalks could just as well be in Shanghai.

The visitor senses immediately that this is another world, one that he or she is unlikely to get to know in any depth. Mott Street, although it has an Asian ring to it, is actually named after an old New York family. It's crooked and narrow, and lined with elderly walk-up tenement houses whose ground floors are filled with Chinese grocery stores, souvenir shops, and one restaurant after another. New Yorkers rarely come to Chinatown for any reason other than to eat. The atmosphere on the streets provides an exotic counterpoint to the food.

It's pretty hard to get a bad meal in Chinatown, but here now are several particularly good recommendations, each of which is open daily. The first advertises its address in its name: **20 Mott Street,** near Pell Street (tel. 964-0380). It's a three-story mirrored palace with brightly lit rooms and marbled walls. The menu provides a choice of everything from lo mein to foo young to chop suey to very tasty roast duck and many seafood specialties.

Also good is **Bo Ky Pho,** 80 Bayard St. (tel. 406-2292), at whose crowded, communal-style tables you can get a very good meal for about $12 a person, including tax and tip.

Nice Restaurant, 35 East Broadway (tel. 406-9510), is famous for its dim sum as well as its enormous Cantonese menu, on which practically nothing exceeds $10.

Finally, there's the **Silver Palace,** 52 Bowery, just south of Canal Street (tel. 964-1204), which occupies a vast second-floor room accessible via a mirrored escalator. It too offers all manner of dim sum (for instance, steamed dumplings, crabmeat delight, chicken bundle, and Chinese popcorn), plus a huge selection of traditional Cantonese dishes. At any of these places, it's going to take an effort to spend more than $10 a head per meal.

SIGHTSEEING IN NEW YORK CITY

1. FAMOUS SIGHTS
2. DO-IT-YOURSELF WALKING TOURS
3. MUSEUMS & GALLERIES

New York City possesses an abundance of famous sightseeing attractions. The first section of this chapter contains what I consider the most important, listed in order of my preference and profiled briefly to give you a sense of each at a glance. After reading this section you should have a pretty good idea which will interest you and which won't.

The second section contains walking tours that will enable you to explore New York's most fascinating neighborhoods at your own speed. Walking is the best way to see the city. Again, glance through them and pick those you think will be the most fun.

Many people come to New York City for the sole purpose of enjoying its famous museums and galleries. The third section of this chapter is a descriptive list of these and of the sorts of things you're likely to see in them.

A GOOD NUMBER TO KNOW

The **New York Department of Parks and Recreation** (tel. 360-1333) sponsors a considerable agenda of concerts, special events, and regular programs in all the boroughs and at all times of the year. Dial the above number and you'll get a recording of a hale and hearty individual whose accent could come from only one city in the world. You'll learn of swimming programs in city-owned pools, ice skating on city-owned ponds or rinks, concerts in churches, bands in the parks, movies at the many branches of the New York Public Library, and more. All events are sp by the city, many are specifically designed for children, and most are f

NEW YORK CONVENTION AND VISITORS BUREAU

This helpful and highly professional organization dispenses ment, brochures, and subway and bus maps from a street-level lot Circle, where Broadway crosses Eighth Avenue at Central Park 8222). Have a travel-related problem? Call or drop by; they'll answ help make your visit more pleasant.

ORGANIZED TOURS

It's quite possible, of course, to see New York via one of the many standard bus tours run by sightseeing companies. **American Sightseeing/Short Line Tours,** 166 W. 46th St., at Seventh Avenue (tel. 354-5122), has city tours that last from two to eight hours and will take you to different parts of town. No advance reservations are needed; just show up at the terminal. Another major bus tour operator is **Gray Line of New York,** 900 Eighth Ave., at 54th Street (tel. 397-2590). Again, no advance reservations are necessary, but it's wise to call ahead for the day's schedule. Expect prices to start at about $17 per person, at either Gray Line or Short Line, for a basic two-hour-plus city tour.

---

1. Famous Sights

EMPIRE STATE BUILDING

This famous building is a tour de force of art deco design and decoration. Wait till you see this lobby with its matching imported marbles and angular decorative motifs. Happily, the building's present owners are fully aware of its quality and historic importance, so maintenance is first-rate and alterations have been handled sensitively.

The Empire State Building was conceived in the frenzied days of the late 1920s. The site at Fifth Avenue and 34th Street was originally that of Mrs. William B. Astor's New York town house and later that of the original Waldorf-Astoria hotel. When the Empire State opened in 1931, it was the tallest building in the world, a distinction it maintained for almost two generations (the World Trade Center, downtown, and the Sears Tower in Chicago are both taller, albeit not by a lot).

All sorts of things have happened here. King Kong blazoned it into the national consciousness in the 1930s; a plane crashed into it in the 1940s; the top 30 floors were illuminated in color beginning in the 1970s; the New York Road Runners began staging footraces up the stairwells in the 1980s. The slender and elegant mast that forms the building's very pinnacle was intended as an aerial mooring in the days when transatlantic dirigibles seemed the coming thing. Of course, it's so windy up there no dirigible was ever able to tie up. One try was made, but a sudden updraft stood the thing on end, terrifying everybody. The captain only managed to dump the water ballast before abandoning 34th Street for New Jersey, in the process drenching scores of unsuspecting pedestrians below.

The views from both the 86th- and 102nd-floor observation decks are truly awesome. Management estimates that over two million people come up here every year to have a look. If the weather's clear it's possible to see Massachusetts and Pennsylvania. But the vistas of the city itself are the most fascinating. Both observation decks have just been redone. You can go outside on the 86th floor; the enclosed area on the 102nd floor resembles the interior of a spaceship.

The Empire State Building is located at Fifth Avenue and 34th Street (tel. 736-3100). The observation decks are open daily from 9:30am to 11:30pm (they close early on Christmas Eve, Christmas Day, and New Year's Day). Admission is $3.75 for adults, $1.75 for seniors and children under 12.

WORLD TRADE CENTER & WORLD FINANCIAL CENTER

The Empire State Plaza in Albany and the World Trade Center at the tip of Manhattan embody New York State's style of big government and big public works as it was in the 1960s. Already the era is beginning to seem (dare I say it?) antique. The WTC, which opened in 1970, is also very much in New York City's own tradition of being/having the "biggest." What it is, by the way, is an immense office complex (10 million square feet!) that belongs to a quasi-public organization called the Authority of New York and New Jersey. It occupies 16 acres at the edge of the Financial District, and it has not one but two 110-story buildings, numerous other smaller but stylistically unified high-rises (one of which is a first-class hotel), a plaza the size of four football fields, an underground shopping mall, dozens of restaurants and banks, and a major terminus for trans-Hudson commuter travel via a subway called the PATH (short for Port Authority Trans-Hudson) Tube. It's tenanted by a roster of firms, mostly engaged in international trade, that employs almost 50,000 people. It also houses the New York Commodities Exchange and an observation deck. Explosives detonated by terrorists badly damaged the World Trade Center in early 1993, but most offices there were reoccupied by mid-1993. The noted Windows on the World restaurant was expected to reopen only in late 1993, however, and the New York Vista hotel was closed until 1994.

It is the "Deck at the World Trade Center" that draws most visitors to New York (about a million and a half a year). You buy your tickets on the mezzanine level of Two World Trade Center (that's the southernmost of the twin towers), then take a special elevator (1,377 feet in 58 seconds) to the 107th floor. The view is entirely different from the one uptown at 34th Street. There's a much greater sense of port activities and industrial vastness, less of a sense of Manhattan. On the 110th floor is the open-air promenade, the "highest in the world" (even if the building isn't).

The World Trade Center is located at the southern end of Manhattan, not far from City Hall Park, on a site bounded by Church, Vesey, West, and Liberty Streets. Observation facilities (tel. 212/435-7377) are open every day from 9:30am to 9:30pm. Admission is $3.50 for adults, $1.75 for seniors and children under 12, free for kids under 6.

Directly across West Street from the Twin Towers is the **World Financial Center,** built mainly in the 1980s, an extremely large and architecturally dramatic complex of offices, shops, and restaurants whose centerpiece is the enormous glass-enclosed Winter Garden, filled with towering palm trees. The arcades adjoining the Winter Garden contain about 50 stores and restaurants. Outside is a wonderfully landscaped esplanade overlooking a yacht basin. You'll find outposts of such important Manhattan retailers as Barneys New York, Mark Cross, Rizzoli, and The Gap, plus restaurants that serve everything from haute French cuisine to Chinese to Italian fast food. In addition to the dining and shopping possibilities, there is a busy schedule of free public entertainment in the Winter Garden. This could be anything from dance theater to chamber music to ballroom dancing to exhibitions of cartoon art. To find out what's doing at the time of your visit call 945-0505. You can also request an arts and events program and a guide to shops and restaurants by writing to the World Financial Center, 200 Liberty St., 18th floor, New York, NY 10281.

ROCKEFELLER CENTER

In the late 1920s, megamillionaire John D. Rockefeller planned to build a great opera house on a Midtown site he'd acquired adjacent to Fifth Avenue. Then the stock market collapsed and the deal went sour. Rockefeller, however, was determined to build. Instead of an opera house, New York got Rockefeller Center, one of the first (and grandest) multiple-use urban developments in the nation.

Rockefeller Center is both beautiful and photogenic. It's a collection of stone-clad skyscrapers in high-1930s drag, augmented in recent years by a string of lordly glass boxes along Sixth Avenue. The original structures are embellished everywhere with almost Maya-looking art in the form of statuary, murals, and monumental reliefs. At the heart of it all is a landscaped pedestrian mall whose plantings change with the seasons. Called the **Promenade,** it creates a sort of triumphal approach to 30 Rockefeller Plaza, a soaring office tower straight out of Flash Gordon. A famous sunken plaza with a gilded statue of Prometheus stands at its foot. In winter filled with ice skaters; in summer, gaily colored umbrellas shelter tables door diners.

Rockefeller Center is also the home of the world-famous R (for details on programming and prices, refer to "Music & Danc Chapter VI, "New York City After Dark"). You can see its fascina fantastically opulent auditorium and lobbies on a tour for $7 (whic the cost of a ticket). Call 632-4041 for information. Besides the M feller Center contains the radio and television broadcast studios of 30 Rockefeller Plaza. Regular tours run through the sets of the "Today

day Night Live," and local news shows. Call 664-7174 between 9am and 5pm week-days for details or drop by the lobby ticket desk. Tickets are sold on a first-come, first-served basis.

The Promenade at Rockefeller Center is located at Fifth Avenue between 49th and 50th Streets. An interesting and informative brochure titled "Walking Tour of Rockefeller Center" is available at the information desk just inside the main entrance to 30 Rockefeller Plaza.

STATUE OF LIBERTY

These days the statue looks marvelous thanks to a zillion-dollar restoration scheme financed entirely by private contributions. The statue itself sits atop Liberty Island, a former sandbar located a short ferry ride from the southern tip of Manhattan. Designed by French sculptor Frédéric Auguste Bartholdi, it is made of copper mounted on an iron frame by Gustave Eiffel, the man who did that famous tower in Paris. Skin and framework were assembled in Paris and presented to the people of America at a ceremony in France on July 4, 1884. The statue and supporting frame were then disassembled, shipped across the Atlantic, reassembled in New York Harbor, and dedicated by President Grover Cleveland on October 28, 1886. As with today's restoration funds, the cost of design, construction, shipment, and reassembling were borne entirely by generous individuals.

Few structures in America evoke the same emotional response as the Statue of Liberty. It's beautiful, and the setting certainly is dramatic. But its symbolic message —that there is a welcoming haven on this continent where people can live without fear—has the sort of universal import that touches every one of our lives. Symbolism aside, it's a great excursion. You'll probably take a subway either to the South Ferry or Bowling Green station (depending what line you take), then find your way the short distance to the Circle Line pier (tel. 269-5755) at the southern end of Battery Park. Boats for Liberty Island leave every half hour between 9:30am and 3:30pm on weekends and every 45 minutes on weekdays. Round-trip fare is $6 for adults and $3 for children.

ELLIS ISLAND

Accessible by the same ferry that takes you to the Statue of Liberty, Ellis Island was the gateway to America for more than 17 million immigrants. Between 1892 and 1954, this handsome beaux arts architectural complex hummed with activity. Closed in the mid-1950s, it was left to decay for the better part of two generations. Today it has undergone what is described as the most expensive restoration in U.S. history, a project costing almost $350 million. Besides the magnificent buildings, you can see the fascinating and at times quite moving exhibits that show just what it was like to have been an American immigrant. Ellis Island is open all year; ferries depart for it and for the Statue of Liberty every half hour from 9am to 3pm from the Circle Line pier (tel. 269-5755) at the southern end of Battery Park. Fares are $6 for adults and $3 for kids. You can call Ellis Island directly at 363-3200 for further information.

UNITED NATIONS

U.N. Headquarters occupies an 18-acre site on First Avenue between 42nd and 48th Streets. People's perceptions of the U.N. have changed considerably since it was founded in 1945. A signature air of dedicated idealism clings to the place, and it remains an ever-hopeful symbol of the possibility of a better world.

As a sightseeing attraction, it has a lot to offer. Physically, it's quite impressive, with its sweeping lawns and soaring marble-and-glass buildings in the high modern style of the late 1940s. Its interior meeting rooms are stupendous. The meetings where issues of peace, justice, and human well-being are discussed by representatives of some 179 member states are occasionally open to the public. Free tickets are issued on a first-come, first-served basis. Call 963-1234 for schedules (no kids under permitted).

Hour-long guided tours of U.N. buildings and activities leave about every 15 from the General Assembly Building. They cost $6.50 for adults, $4.50 for senior citizens and students, and $3.50 for children grades 1 through 8 (no kids under 5). The tour information number is 963-7713. You can, if you wish, stroll around the grounds for free.

CIRCLE LINE

"America's Favorite Boat Ride" has been operating since 1945. It's a 3-hour, 35-mile cruise around Manhattan Island, passing under 20 famous bridges and over 4 tunnels and 73 transit tubes. The Circle Line fleet includes 8 snackbar-equipped sightseeing yachts, each of which holds between 400 and 600 people. Interestingly, most of these boats were built for the U.S. Navy as LCIs (Landing Craft Infantry) and destined for the beaches of Normandy and Okinawa. One ship, as it happens, was the first American craft to return to Corregidor.

Few views compare to that of Manhattan's Financial District on a sunny day, rising from the sparkling waters of the harbor. Other parts of the cruise are just as interesting, especially up in the region of sheer cliffs known as the Palisades above the George Washington Bridge.

The Circle Line is located at Pier 83, at the foot of West 42nd Street. If you drive, on-site parking is available for $10. The three-hour cruise costs $18 for adults and $9 for children under 12. Call 563-3200 for current sailing schedules. Between May and October the Harbor Lights Cruise leaves every night at 7pm and returns at 9pm. The price is the same as the daytime cruise.

NEW YORK STOCK EXCHANGE

This gorgeous Roman temple, designed in 1903 by George B. Post, contains an immense interior trading floor and overhanging galleries that can be toured for free. A visit to the Stock Exchange is actually quite interesting. You'll learn how stock is traded, how brokers communicate, and how prices are set, plus other seemingly logical and orderly processes that hardly seem possible in the cacophonous roar below you. The atmosphere of financial might—this is, after all, one of the most important financial centers on earth—is worth experiencing.

Visually, the trading floor is a wild combination of beaux arts magnificence and state-of-the-art communications equipment populated by hordes of people in a frenzy of activity. Up in the NYSE Visitors' Center are multi-image slide shows and tricky technological displays that explain what's really afoot downstairs.

The NYSE Visitors Center is located at 20 Broad St., between Wall Street and Exchange Place (tel. 656-5167). Tours can be had from 9:15am to 4pm Monday through Friday. A limited number of free admission tickets are distributed daily starting at 9am. This is a good site to include on the Financial District walking tour (see the next section, "Do-It-Yourself Walking Tours").

SOUTH STREET SEAPORT

There's so much going on down here that it's a tough place to comprehend. Basically, the seaport is a restored fragment, encircled by glass towers, of what was once the heart of Manhattan's waterfront in sailing-ship days. Half is operated by the South Street Seaport Museum as a sort of mini-Williamsburg; the other half is run, with considerable flash and efficiency, as a sort of theme park–cum–shopping mall by the Rouse Organization.

The seaport's centerpiece is the old Fulton Fish Market, now a multilevel complex of gourmet food stalls and restaurants. Surrounding this are restored historical buildings (almost embarrassingly perfect and clean), several fantastic old sailing ships that you can walk around on, and an enormous new pier (Pier 17) that is essentially a large enclosed shopping mall. Some condemn the seaport as the new "mesquite coast," an allusion to the trendy cookery served in its many restaurants. But in fairness, much has been saved hereabouts that would otherwise have been lost. And the theme-park atmosphere, while hardly an authentic re-creation of the rowdy past, happens to be enormously appealing.

It's possible just to browse around the seaport for free, peeking in the windows and strolling through the Fulton Market or Pier 17. A much better idea is to buy a ticket at one of the many clearly marked booths: $6 for adults, $5 for seniors, and $4 for kids entitles you to any (or all) of three basic guided tours, plus admission to the Seaport Museum's exhibition halls, print shop, photo galleries, film events, and restored sailing ships. These ships, and the stories surrounding them, are perhaps the most intriguing part of a visit here. The tour guide's tales of New York's sailing past are definitely worth the cost of a ticket.

For one price you can tailor your day to include as much guided tour and free exploration as you like. As if there weren't enough to see, the Rouse Organization keeps the cobbled streets full of jugglers, concerts, fashion shows, strolling musicians, and whatever else they can think of. To find out what special events Rouse has cooking, call 669-9424.

The South Street Seaport is located downtown at the eastern end of Fulton Street, an easy walk from Wall Street or City Hall Park. The nearest subway stops are at Fulton Street. There are plenty of places to eat; fast, economical meals in a wide range of cuisines can be had on the top level of Pier 17. Carry your tray to the terrace overlooking the river; it's hard to think of a finer place for a sandwich.

LINCOLN CENTER

America's first performing arts center certainly is grandiose. The complex was erected in the 1960s and includes the New York State Theater, home of the New York City Ballet and New York City Opera; Avery Fisher Hall, home of the New York Philharmonic; the Metropolitan Opera House; the Vivian Beaumont Theater; the famous Juilliard School of Music; an outdoor bandshell; the New York Public Library for the Performing Arts; plus assorted smaller halls and theaters. The heart of the complex is a broad travertine-marble plaza graced with a large fountain and surrounded by 1960s-vintage performance halls.

Lincoln Center is a busy place, and its performance schedule is a full one. For current information, call 875-5400. Even if you don't attend a performance you can tour the buildings and perhaps catch a glimpse of rehearsals in progress. The interiors of the various theaters, particularly the Metropolitan Opera House with its Chagall murals, are sumptuous in the modern manner. Tours operate daily from 10am to 5pm and cost $7.75 for adults, $6.75 for students and seniors, and $4.50 for children. Reservations are advisable, since groups are kept purposely small; call 875-5350.

Lincoln Center is on the Upper West Side, north of Midtown. It occupies the blocks from 62nd to 66th Streets between Columbus and Amsterdam Avenues.

CENTRAL PARK

It may seem odd to recommend a park as a sightseeing attraction, but in the case of Central Park, an exception is in order. It's both a highly calculated piece of rural-seeming art and a consummate example of 19th-century engineering. It is the ancestor of every picturesque park in America and a great gift to the common person. Central Park was designed so that the beauty and restorative effects of unsullied nature would be within the reach of all. Its purpose is to nurture the soul, which it has been doing since the 1850s.

The park design was the result of a competition won by Calvert Vaux and Frederick Law Olmsted. The "Greensward Plan," as it was called, combined pastoral vistas of woodlands, meadows, rocky outcrops, and tranquil lakes with an ingenious traffic plan. This latter feature allowed elaborate systems of walkways, roadways, bridle paths, and sunken transverse roads (connecting the East and West Sides of Manhattan) to coexist without once getting clumsily in one another's way. The 20 years of blasting; grading; planting; and constructing picturesque bridges, fountains, pavilions, and lakes, transformed a blighted wasteland into a dream of rural perfection. When the park was first built, the low-rise city was invisible behind the trees, a fact that added greatly to the intended effect. But even today, with the looming city skyline so often visible, the effect of tranquility remains.

Central Park is worth leisurely exploration and is quite safe during the day, at least in heavily trafficked areas. Be sure to visit **Central Park Zoo** at Fifth Avenue and

CENTRAL PARK

MANHATTAN

Central Park

American Museum of
  Natural History ⑩
Belvedere Castle ⑦
Belvedere Lake ⑧
Bethesda Fountain ⑭
Bow Bridge ⑫
Carousel ㉕
Central Park Zoo ㉚
Cherry Hill Fountain ⑲
Chess and Checkers
  House ㉖
Children's Zoo ㉘
Conservatory Water ⑯
Dairy (information) ㉗
Delacorte Music Clock ㉙
Delacorte Theater ④
Frick Museum ⑰
Hayden Planetarium ⑨
Heckscher
  Playground ㉞
Information Booth ㉛
Loeb Boathouse ⑮
The Mall ㉒
Metropolitan Museum
  of Art ②
Mineral Springs
  Pavilion ㉑
Naumburg
  Bandshell ⑱
New-York
  Historical Society ⑪
Obelisk (Cleopatra's
  Needle) ③
The Pond ㉜
The Ramble ⑬
The Reservoir ①
Shakespeare
  Garden ⑥
Sheep Meadow ㉓
Strawberry Fields ⑳
Swedish Cottage ⑤
Tavern on the Green ㉔
Wollman Rink ㉝

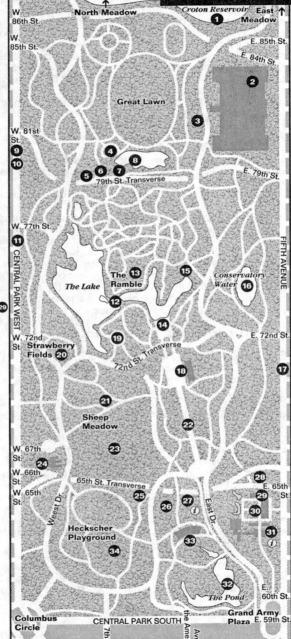

64th Street, newly restored in an unzoolike manner, with penguins swimming in the "North Pole" and toucans perched in the "Rainforest"—a wonderful destination for a leisurely afternoon. Be sure to visit **Bethesda Fountain** and its romantic lakefront plaza. You'll find it in the middle of the park, about on the line of 72nd Street. Immediately to the south of it is the **Mall**, a fine Victorian promenade lined with multiple alleys of stately trees and brooding statues of literary figures. Between the Mall and Tavern on the Green (over by 67th Street and Central Park West) is the **Sheep Meadow.** This vast lawn, a favorite spot for Frisbee-throwing and sunbathing, provides spectacular views of the Midtown skyline. The park also contains a formal garden (the **Conservatory Garden,** at Fifth Avenue in the low 100s) and a large, toy boat pond (at Fifth Avenue north of the 72nd Street entrance), to name but a few of its many additional attractions.

ST. PATRICK'S CATHEDRAL

This magnificent limestone cathedral was the brainchild of the Right Reverend John Hughes, a highly motivated Irish immigrant who became the first Catholic archbishop of New York. In 1850, Hughes announced his intention to build a church that would be a credit both to Roman Catholicism and to the City of New York. These were brave sentiments at the time, as Irish Catholics then constituted the city's most impoverished, uneducated, and despised underclass.

Despite 19th-century New York's anti-Catholic prejudices, St. Patrick's was duly erected in what was to become the most elite residential section of town. The structure was designed by James Renwick, Jr., in an eclectic Gothic Revival style. Begun in 1858, it was dedicated in 1879 and had its twin towers completed in 1888. Architectural experts may get a few grins out of St. Patrick's, since it's not a very scholarly essay on European Gothic. However, the rest of us can only marvel at its immense scale and gorgeous decoration. It also forms a nice contrast to the art deco of Rockefeller Center across Fifth Avenue.

St. Patrick's occupies the entire block between Fifth and Madison Avenues and 50th and 51st Streets. Be sure to go inside; the silence and majesty are memorable.

U.S.S. *INTREPID* SEA-AIR-SPACE MUSEUM

This is a real navy aircraft carrier. What's more, it's historic. Construction started on the *Intrepid* a mere six days before the bombing of Pearl Harbor. Between August 1943 and the end of World War II it saw almost continuous duty in the Pacific. It survived three direct hits by suicide kamikazes and played a major role in the Battle of Leyte Gulf, a forerunner to the liberation of the Philippines.

After total modernization in the early 1950s, the *Intrepid* continued active duty. This was the ship that plucked returning astronauts Scott Carpenter, Gus Grissom, and John Young from the choppy Atlantic in the mid-1960s. A few years later it was in the Gulf of Tonkin off the coast of North Vietnam. It wasn't until 1974, after a stint of antisubmarine duty with the Sixth Fleet, that it was finally decommissioned.

Today the *Intrepid* is a floating museum containing one huge military exhibit hall after another. These contain audiovisual presentations, special films (repeated every 20 or so minutes), artifacts of war and aviation, galleries devoted to aircraft design and space exploration, as well as a considerable number of parked aircraft, all of which can be examined at your own speed.

The *Intrepid* is tied up in the Hudson at Pier 86, located at the foot of West 46th Street (tel. 212/245-0072). Admission is $7 for adults, $6 for seniors, and $4 for children. From Memorial Day to Labor Day, it's open daily from 10am to 5pm; the rest of the year, it's open Wednesday to Sunday from 10am to 5pm. Last admission is at 4pm.

CHINATOWN

New York's Chinatown section has been drawing ethnic Chinese since the 1850s. For the visitor, it's an undeniably colorful quarter, characterized by tiny shops filled with esoteric goods and foodstuffs, dozens upon dozens of restaurants, phone booths and the occasional building topped with a brightly painted pagoda roof, narrow crooked streets, and sidewalks teeming with Chinese. For the people who live here it's an overcrowded ghetto, reeling from recent waves of moneyless immigrants, high rents, and substandard housing.

But it certainly is picturesque, as well as being a superior place for delicious inexpensive meals (see "Special Excursions" in Chapter IV, "New York City Restaurants"). The busiest day in Chinatown is Sunday, when everything's open and former residents from all over town come back to stock up on things Chinese. Also memorable is Chinese New Year, celebrated with fireworks and dancing dragons on the first full moon after January 21.

The heart of Chinatown is Mott Street between Canal Street and the Bowery. In recent years the Bowery itself, between Chatham Square and Canal Street, has become a full-fledged part of the neighborhood instead of just its eastern boundary. There's no architectural grandeur hereabouts, nor is the area particularly large. But it is special.

2. Do-It-Yourself Walking Tours

The following itineraries contain easy-to-follow directions, ample descriptions of what there is to see, and the approximate time it takes to walk each from start to finish at a leisurely pace.

TOUR 1: MIDTOWN–FIFTH AVENUE

Start: Grand Army Plaza, Fifth Avenue and 59th Street. *Finish:* Seventh Avenue and Central Park South. *Time required:* Approximately 1½ hours.

Grand Army Plaza, or simply "the Plaza," is one of New York's most handsome outdoor spaces. Its centerpiece is a fountain atop stacked reflecting pools, donated to the city in 1916 by publishing baron Joseph Pulitzer. At its summit is a graceful statue of *Pomona,* Roman goddess of bounteous gardens. Some of the finest private mansions in New York once overlooked this square, notably the 138-room château of Cornelius Vanderbilt II, grandson of the original Commodore Vanderbilt. This lamentably long-demolished house once occupied the entire Fifth Avenue blockfront from 57th to 58th Streets. The site has been occupied since 1928 by **Bergdorf Goodman.** Bergdorf's is one of the most deluxe stores in New York, and the facial expressions and body language of its display mannequins are a ready barometer of fashionable attitudes. Also overlooking the Plaza is the august **Metropolitan Club,** designed in 1893 by McKim, Mead, and White and located on the corner of 60th Street and Fifth Avenue. This club was initially organized by J. P. Morgan to accommodate a friend who couldn't get into the old Union Club.

If you're interested in magnificence, you should take a quick look at the gilt-and-marble lobbies of **The Plaza Hotel,** on the western boundary of the Plaza between 58th Street and Central Park South. Designed by Henry Hardenbergh in 1907, it is quite magnificent. Also worth a look inside is the **General Motors Building,** which is the white-marble tower directly across Fifth from the Plaza Hotel. The G.M. Building was finished in 1968, and its ground floor houses **FAO Schwarz,** the famous luxury toy store. You may not have realized that toys could be so opulent.

The Plaza is a divider between business districts to the south and swank residential areas to the north. Northward from this spot Fifth Avenue was once called "Millionaires' Mile." It was literally lined with the ornate châteaux and brownstone palaces of the merchant elite. Today, most are gone (others like them survive along the side streets), replaced by luxurious apartment houses. But I'm saving the uppercrust East Side until later. For now you will head south down Fifth Avenue.

The corner of 57th Street and Fifth Avenue is perhaps the best retailing address in Manhattan. Three of New York's world-class jewelers, **Tiffany & Co., Bulgari,** and **Van Cleef & Arpels,** overlook this intersection and provide nuclear-proof-looking windows full of heart-stoppingly amazing gems. Glance up at the Crown Building above Bulgari on the southwest corner of 57th and Fifth. All that glittery yellow stuff on the stonework is real gold leaf.

Stay on the Tiffany side of Fifth for another half a block. About midway between 56th and 57th Streets is the entrance to **Trump Tower**. This glitzy mixed-use cooperative has commercial tenants on the lower floors and million-dollar-plus apartments upstairs. This was one of the trophy properties of real estate developer Donald Trump, who was New York's "Wunderkind" of the 1980s. Push the huge gold Ts mounted on the doors and you'll enter a posh shopping atrium with an 80-foot waterfall and more pink marble than you would have supposed was in all of Italy. Shops here sell antiques, Paris fashions, jewels, and all sorts of other good stuff. After a few exhilarating breaths of Mr. Trump's world, follow the sign to the left of the escalator that says "To IBM Plaza and Madison Avenue." You'll cross through a little bit of **Galeries Lafayette**, a French-based department store adjoining Trump Tower, before emerging in yet another dramatic enclosed atrium.

IBM Plaza, where you are now, is nothing less than a glass-enclosed bamboo forest. It's a great place to sit and have a light snack from the refreshment kiosk (crowded, however, at lunchtime). There are tables and chairs, aromatic floral plantings that change with the seasons, and an impressive sense of space. If you're fortunate there may even be a little concert (chamber music or some such) in progress beneath the bamboos. IBM deserves high marks for this one.

Leave IBM Plaza by the 57th Street door, then cross Madison Avenue. That good-looking art deco office tower on the northeast corner of Madison and 57th is the **Fuller Building**, built in 1929. If you stand at the foot of the Fuller Building and look south down Madison, you'll get a fine view of the **Sony** (formerly the AT&T) **Building**. It's the big granite number that looks like a Queen Anne highboy standing on the east side of Madison between 55th and 56th.

Continue walking on **57th Street** now, eastbound in the direction of Park Avenue. This is one of the most splendid and cosmopolitan shopping districts on earth. The shop windows are filled with museum-quality antiques, precious crystal and jewels, and the latest fashions.

When you reach Park Avenue, pause for a moment. That slender and elegant building across the avenue on the northeast corner of Park and 57th is the **Ritz Tower**. Built in 1925, it is best known as the former home of Le Pavillon, once the most famous French restaurant in New York. Now look to the south down Park Avenue. Straddling the roadway is the gilded **Helmsley Building**, formerly the New York Central Building. Its famous silhouette was severely injured in 1963 by the construction of the egg-crate-like **MetLife** (formerly Pan Am) **Building** right behind it.

Stroll down the west side of Park to 56th Street, then glance down 56th toward Madison Avenue. The new **Park Avenue Tower**, which isn't on Park Avenue at all but rather on the south side of 56th Street, gives the appearance of twisting at the strangest angle. Now continue down Park to 55th and cross to the east side of the street. The green-roofed tower down the road, by the way, belongs to the **Waldorf-Astoria Hotel** at Park and 50th Street.

Continue eastbound on 55th Street for one block to the corner of Lexington Avenue. The block from Park to Lex, with its dignified town houses, will give you a good idea of what this neighborhood looked like before the era of the mighty glass office building. The onion-domed structure at the southwest corner of Lex and 55th looks like a little bit of old Moscow. Actually it's the **Central Synagogue**, the oldest synagogue building in continuous use in New York City. The structure was designed by Henry Fernbach, New York's first practicing Jewish architect. It was erected in 1871.

Continue south one block on Lex to 54th Street. That huge complex on the east side of Lex between 53rd and 54th is the **Citicorp Building**. Inside is yet another atrium, this one called the Market. It contains the obligatory incredible interior space, plus lots and lots of places (many quite reasonable) to eat. Most sell food that you can carry to one of the many tables and chairs beneath a very lofty skylight. If you're temporarily full of atriums, turn right (west) on 54th Street back in the direction of Park Avenue.

At Park Avenue and 54th Street, look downtown at that low building on the west side of Park between 52nd and 53rd Streets. This is the **Racquet and Tennis Club**, a patrician stronghold containing one of the handful of court tennis courts in the country. (Court tennis, by the way, is more difficult and complicated than regular tennis and was played by Henry VIII at Hampton Court Palace on a 90- by 30-foot court still in use there.) Several years ago the Racquet Club assured its future finances by selling valuable air rights to the developer of the glass office tower that now looms behind it.

Stay on 54th Street, cross Park Avenue and continue one block west to Madison Avenue. Now cross to the west side of Madison Avenue and go one block south to 53rd Street. You might do a bit of window-shopping while you're here in the chic shops at the foot of the angular **Continental Illinois Building.**

Turn right on 53rd Street and head west one block toward Fifth Avenue. The East 50s were once New York's most exclusive and opulent mansion district. A survivor is **12 E. 53rd St.,** no longer a residence but still complete with battlements, balconies, and leaded windows. On the north (right-hand) side of this block, just before Fifth Avenue, is **Paley Park,** a delectable little cobbled enclave furnished with lacy locust trees, climbing ivy, metal chairs and tables, and a wall of falling water at its far end. Built in 1967 on the site of the famous Stork Club, it's a wonderful place to sit and meditate on life or maybe have a sandwich.

Leave Paley Park and go to the corner of Fifth Avenue. To your right, up at the northwest corner of Fifth and 54th Street, is the lordly **University Club,** McKim, Mead, and White's 1899 homage to the Italian Renaissance. You're going the other direction, however, one block south to 52nd Street. Note **Cartier,** housed in a former private palace on the southeast corner of Fifth and 52nd. A now-forgotten millionaire named Morton Plant was induced by the Vanderbilt family to build this house in 1904. The Vanderbilts, many of whom had houses on Fifth in the 50s, were trying desperately to keep the area residential. They failed, and all their houses are gone. Mr. Plant's remains, however, and has been occupied by the jewelry firm of Cartier since 1917.

Continue south on Fifth Avenue for another block to 51st Street. The big brown-glass tower on the northeast corner of Fifth and 51st is **Olympic Tower,** another fashionable multiple-use building. **St. Patrick's Cathedral** occupies the east side of Fifth between 51st and 50th. It rates a separate discussion (see the previous section, "Famous Sights"). The towers were topped off in 1888, and the inside is well worth a look.

Continue south to 50th Street and cross Fifth Avenue. Now you're in the region of **Rockefeller Center** (also described under "Famous Sights"). Facing the famous Promenade, which leads off Fifth, and occupying the entire eastern blockfront from 49th to 50th Streets is **Saks Fifth Avenue,** one of New York's great department stores. Save Saks for a later browse and turn right (west) into the Promenade, located midway between 49th and 50th Streets.

Rockefeller Center is one of the most handsome urban complexes in New York, perhaps in the nation. As you turn off Fifth into the Promenade, you'll see the slender tower of the **GE** (formerly RCA) **Building** (known also as 30 Rockefeller Plaza), looking like something out of H. G. Wells. At Christmastime, the Rockefeller Center tree stands before it. Stroll down the Promenade, admire the beautiful plantings, and have a look at the sunken plaza. In good weather, meals can be had under brightly colored umbrella tables; in winter, you can rent ice skates (about $5 for the skates; under $10 for admission to the rink).

Walk around the sunken plaza and have a look inside 30 Rockefeller Plaza. The lobby is the epitome of high style à la 1933 (the building's completion date). Above the black-marble floors and walls are monumental sepia-toned murals depicting the unending labors of Michelangelo-esque men and women. They were painted by José Maria Sert. Originally, a highly political mural by Diego Rivera faced the building's front door. Rather than remove images of Lenin and venereal germs hovering over a tableau of rich people playing cards, Rivera insisted the mural be destroyed. The Rockefellers willingly obliged.

Walk all the way down the lobby of the GE Building to the exit onto **Sixth Avenue.** Now turn right (north) and start walking back uptown. There used to be an elevated train on Sixth Avenue, which for most of the neighborhood's history exercised a fairly depressing influence. A building boom in the 1960s and 1970s transformed the dreary blockfronts into an astonishing canyon of 50-story glass sky-scrapers. Although this is just another Manhattan business district and the buildings individually aren't of great note, taken together they form an urban environment of considerable grandeur.

At 56th Street, turn left (west) toward Seventh Avenue and go a few steps to the entrance to **Le Parker Meridien Hotel,** located on the north side of the street. Enter the lobby doors and walk straight across the reception area toward the big hanging tapestry on the wall ahead. Bear to the right into the atrium court. This is a public area, not restricted to guests. And the atrium, with its columns and balustrades and palette of pale peach, coral, and cream, is quite beautiful. Exit the atrium via the door marked "57e Rue" (which means "57th Street" in French). You'll pass through another spectacular interior space with marble floors and an immensely high poly-chrome ceiling. Its sole purpose is to serve as a passageway to 57th Street.

Outside on 57th, turn left (west) toward Seventh Avenue. At the end of the block, on the southeast corner of 57th and Seventh, is **Carnegie Hall,** New York's most famous recital hall, built in 1891 and saved from demolition by a hairsbreadth in the early 1960s. It recently underwent total restoration.

Now cross 57th Street and continue north (uptown) on **Seventh Avenue.** This neighborhood is really an extension of the apartment-house district along Central Park South. Most of the buildings hereabouts are anonymous enough, with the blinding exception of **Alwyn Court.** Built in 1909 on the southeast corner of Seventh and 58th Street, it boasts a facade that is a frenzied tour de force in terra-cotta ornamentation. Descriptions cannot do it justice; it must be seen to be believed.

The next block of Seventh, between 58th and Central Park South, contains the **New York Athletic Club,** famous for its prosperous ambience. And the corner ahead, that of Seventh Avenue and Central Park South, marks the end of your tour.

TOUR 2: GREENWICH VILLAGE

Start: "West 4th Street, Washington Square" subway station, whose entrances are at Sixth Avenue and West 3rd Street and at Sixth Avenue and Waverly Place. *Finish:* Same as start. *Time required:* Approximately 1¼ hours.

It's erroneously believed, even by many New Yorkers, that Greenwich Village centers around Washington Square and two honky-tonk strips on Bleecker and West 3rd Street between Sixth Avenue and LaGuardia Place. This is not at all the case.

The original Greenwich Village, the separate town that once lay beyond the boundaries of New York, is located someplace else. Today people sometimes refer to that area as the "West Village," and it occupies the region between Greenwich Avenue and the Hudson River, bounded on the south by West Houston Street. Greenwich Village was one of the earliest settlements on Manhattan. It remained a bucolic hamlet during and after the Revolution, then experienced explosive growth in the 1820s. Its sudden prosperity was largely a function of the poor quality of the drinking water in the neighboring city of New York. In those days epidemics of typhoid and smallpox were almost annual affairs. As soon as the new season's plague struck New York, everyone who could afford to decamped immediately to healthful semi-rural and nearby Greenwich.

Greenwich possessed its own network of built-up streets well before burgeoning New York City engulfed it. They still exist, radiating at bewildering angles from the grid plan that dominates the rest of Manhattan. The old Village surveyors must have been a little weak when it came to right angles. Original Village blocks are al-most, but not quite, square. Many are parallelograms. The block plan is further com-plicated by subsequent swaths slashed through it for the construction of Seventh and Eighth Avenues. On top of all this, some of the old named streets have been given numbers supposedly corresponding to adjacent numbered streets. The results are baffling intersections, such as that point where West 4th Street, West 12th Street, and Eighth Avenue all converge. Even native New Yorkers get lost in the Village, at least without a map.

Your tour starts at **Sixth Avenue and Waverly Place,** an intersection one block

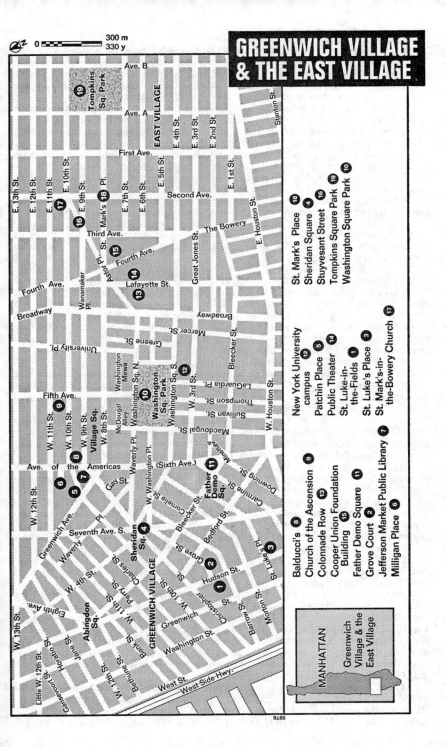

GREENWICH VILLAGE & THE EAST VILLAGE

0 — 300 m
330 y

EAST VILLAGE

Ave. B
Ave. A
First Ave.
Second Ave.
Third Ave.
Fourth Ave.
Broadway
Fifth Ave.
Ave. of the Americas (Sixth Ave.)
Seventh Ave. S.
Eighth Ave.
Greenwich Ave.
University Pl.
Fourth Ave.
Lafayette St.
The Bowery
Great Jones St.
E. Houston St.
Stanton St.
Bleecker St.
Broadway
Mercer St.
Greene St.
W. 3rd St.
LaGuardia Pl.
Thompson St.
Sullivan St.
Macdougal St.
W. Houston St.
Minetta St.
Carmine St.
Downing St.
Bedford St.
Grove St.
Barrow St.
Morton St.
Christopher St.
West-Side Hwy.
West St.
Washington St.
Greenwich St.
Hudson St.
W. 10th St.
W. 4th St.
Charles St.
Perry St.
W. 11th St.
Bank St.
Bethune St.
W. 12th St.
Jane St.
Horatio St.
Gansevoort St.
Little W. 12th St.
W. 13th St.
Washington Sq. N.
Washington Sq. S.
Washington Sq. W.
Washington Sq. E.
Washington Mews
McDougal Alley
Village Sq.
W. 8th St.
W. 9th St.
W. 10th St.
W. 11th St.
W. 12th St.
Gay St.
Waverly Pl.
Waverly
Wanamaker Pl.
Astor Pl.
St. Mark's Pl.
E. 10th St.
E. 9th St.
E. 11th St.
E. 12th St.
E. 13th St.
E. 1st St.
E. 2nd St.
E. 3rd St.
E. 4th St.
E. 5th St.
E. 6th St.
E. 7th St.
Cornelia St.
Tompkins Sq. Park **19**

Washington Sq. Park **10**
Washington Sq. Park
Father Demo Sq. **11**
Sheridan Sq. **4**
Abingdon Sq.

GREENWICH VILLAGE

1 St. Luke-in-the-Fields
2 Grove Court
3 St. Luke's Place
4 Sheridan Square
5 Patchin Place
6 Milligan Place
7 Jefferson Market Public Library
8 Balducci's
9 Church of the Ascension
10 Washington Square Park
11 Father Demo Square
12 New York University campus
13 Colonnade Row
14 Public Theater
15 Cooper Union Foundation Building
16 Stuyvesant Street
17 St. Mark's-in-the-Bowery Church
18 St. Mark's Place
19 Tompkins Square Park

MANHATTAN

Greenwich Village & the East Village

5976

south of 8th Street, near the uptown exits from the Washington Square–West 4th Street subway stop. Proceed east from Sixth Avenue toward Washington Square Park. Waverly Place is a typical Village street lined with well-used brick town houses from the early 19th century, as well as buildings of more recent vintage. After one block you arrive at Macdougal Street and **Washington Square Park.**

In 1789, the park was a pauper's burial ground. It was an unprepossessing patch of land then, not terribly close to New York, not wanted by anyone else. But by 1826, fashion was on the march. The paupers were unceremoniously removed, and the former graveyard became a parade ground. Soon fine Greek Revival houses began to appear along the southern boundary. All have disappeared, victims of time and the encroaching building programs of New York University's campus.

The brick houses that still stand on the park's northern boundary, however, give a vivid idea of what the whole square once looked like. Known collectively as **The Row,** they enjoyed their day (in the 1830s) as the home of New York's elite. Like good neighborhoods everywhere, they were eventually abandoned for palmier addresses, this time farther up Fifth Avenue. Henry James and Edith Wharton, incidentally, both lived and worked at 1 Washington Square North. Today many of these old mansions are only facades masking new apartments inside. But a few have survived almost intact.

Now make a short detour. Turn to your left (north) and head away from Washington Square Park up Macdougal Street. After a few steps you'll see **Macdougal Alley** on your right. This little street, lined with former carriage houses, is typical of the sort of small enclave that makes the Village such an appealing place to live. You might stroll up to the end of Macdougal Street (the Alley is private) and have a look at **West 8th Street** while you're here. It's a wilderness of shoe stores, clothing stores, poster shops, and copy centers. It's hard to believe that its mutilated buildings were ever aristocratic private houses.

Now return to Washington Square, turn left (east) and walk along the Row toward Fifth Avenue. Note the double house at no. 20, built in 1828 as a freestanding suburban mansion for one George P. Rogers. The very air on this block is redolent with the gentility of the past. One can almost imagine the clip-clop of horses' hooves and the creak of carriage springs as the ladies climbed out to make their calls.

At Fifth Avenue, turn left (uptown). On the east side you'll see **Washington Mews,** another alley lined with former carriage houses now converted to residences. Although the original town houses along this stretch of Fifth were long ago replaced with apartment houses, the street preserves a dignified residential air.

Three blocks north of Washington Square at 10th Street is the **Church of the Ascension,** a pleasant old place set back from the street behind an antique iron fence. It's been here since 1841, although the interior dates from a renovation in the 1880s by the celebrated McKim, Mead, and White. Turn left off Fifth Avenue onto **West 10th Street.** This is one of the nicest blocks in the Village, lined with fine city houses. Note no. 12, a particularly capacious old manse once owned by Bruce Price, the architect of Tuxedo Park and the father of etiquette expert Emily Post. The row of once identical "English-front" (meaning no high stoop) town houses between no. 20 and no. 38 tells the whole sorry history of brownstone "modernization." No. 38 has been shamefully stripped of ornamentation; no. 26 is in perfect original condition. There's no debate as to which is the better looking.

At the end of the block you'll reach the corner of Sixth Avenue. Here you'll have a fine view of the **Jefferson Market Courthouse,** located across Sixth and now a branch of the New York Public Library. This exuberant Victorian castle, dating from the 1870s, was once considered one of the half dozen most beautiful buildings in the United States. Subsequent generations considered it a horror. Concerned Villagers saved it from demolition in the late 1960s after it had stood vacant for over 20 years. When built, it was part of an innovative multiple-use complex that included a jail, a market, a courthouse, and a prison.

Cross Sixth Avenue for a closer look at it. Note how 10th Street now angles off to the south, following old Village road lines. The lovely garden (except for a perfectly awful chain-link fence that surrounds it) occupying the rest of the courthouse block replaces a 1931 House of Detention for Women. Until its demolition in 1974, evenings on this block were characterized by husbands and boyfriends down on the street howling up to their womenfolk behind bars.

Across 10th Street from the Jefferson Courthouse is another little enclave of the sort that typifies Greenwich Village. Called **Patchin Place,** it contains ten modest brick houses facing one another across a leafy cul-de-sac. Theodore Dreiser, Jane Bowles, and e. e. cummings were among Patchin Place's illustrious residents in the days when the Village was America's "bohemia."

Now continue walking west on 10th Street away from Sixth Avenue. The corner ahead is **Greenwich Avenue,** a busy local shopping street. Originally it was called Monument Lane after a pre-Revolutionary obelisk that stood at its northern terminus. Note the bathroom-brick behemoth at 33 Greenwich Ave. This is the sort of building that won't be built anymore in landmark Greenwich Village. Cross Greenwich Avenue and keep walking west on 10th Street. The modest-looking tenements that line the street contain apartments as pricey as those on the elegant block between Fifth and Sixth. Why? Because they're on West 10th Street, a premium New York address.

Continue straight across the intersection of 10th Street and Waverly Place. After one more short block you'll come to **Seventh Avenue South,** slashing brutally through the venerable Village blocks. Seventh Avenue used to stop up at 11th Street. It was extended south about the time of the World War I, over the protests of the entire Village. Before you move on, glance downtown (to your left) to see the gleaming twin towers of the World Trade Center down on Vesey Street.

Crossing Seventh Avenue is something of a hazard. You want to get over to where West 10th Street picks up on the other side. When you regain West 10th, go just a few steps to the intersection of West 10th and West 4th Streets, one of those conceptually bizarre intersections for which the Village is famous. Now turn right and start walking northwest up West 4th. Now we're getting into the real Village, or "West" Village as it's called. The next couple of intersecting streets—Charles, Perry, West 11th, and Bank—are filled with old brick houses, shady trees, a smattering of better shops and galleries, and a great feeling of calm. Note the brick house at the corner of West 11th and West 4th. It must have looked just as it does now for over 100 years, which is no mean feat in New York.

When you reach **Bank Street,** turn left (west). During a particularly virulent smallpox epidemic in the 1820s, so many New York banking institutions set up temporary offices on this street that the Village of Greenwich named it after them. Note the ancient wisteria growing on no. 60. This is the sort of tenement house that invaded the Village as it became less fashionable in the latter part of the 19th century. Today even the tenements have an appealing patina of age. Many fine old Greek Revival houses remain on this block of Bank, making it one of the Village's nicest.

At the end of the block, Bank intersects **Bleecker Street** adjacent to Abingdon Square. Turn left (south) and continue down Bleecker. This is a street of antiques shops whose windows display Dutch chests and French chandeliers. There are occasional boutiques, interesting bookstores, cracked sidewalks, and blowsy-looking modernish buildings. The narrow tree-lined side streets, however, are absolutely delightful. Continue south on Bleecker for five blocks to **Christopher Street** and turn right (west toward the Hudson). Ahead in the distance you can see New Jersey across the river. On the street around you, you'll see gay New York in full flower, as Christopher Street is more or less its spiritual center.

Stay on Christopher for one short block to **Bedford Street** and turn left (south). At the end of the block, on the corner of Grove Street, is a nest of particularly picturesque wooden houses. No. 17 Grove St., on the corner of Bedford and Grove, was built by a Village sashmaker in the 1820s. It sags wonderfully and evokes the past vividly. No. 100 Bedford St., located midblock between Grove and Christopher, is a Grimm's fairy-tale concoction of stucco, timbers, and crazy angles. This individualistic renovation was paid for in 1925 by financier Otto Kahn. Called **Twin Peaks,** it is the design of Clifford Daily, who thought the Village was becoming too dull architecturally for the proper stimulation of its artistic population. During a wild housewarming party in 1926, Princess Anna Troubetzsky climbed atop one peak to make an offering of burnt acorns to the gods, while screen star Mabel

Normand climbed atop the other and smashed a bottle of champagne on the ridge-pole. Kahn's daughter lived in the house for many years, hence her father's willing-ness to foot the bill.

Make a right on Grove Street in the direction of the Hudson. The road makes a dogleg turn just a few steps from Bedford. Right at the angle of the turn you'll see a little gate set into a brick wall. Although it's private beyond, you can step up to the gate and look over it into **Grove Court**. Built for blue-collar tenants about 1830 and originally called Mixed Ale Alley, this tree-shaded enclave of little brick houses is the sort of Village spot many New Yorkers would kill to live in.

After you've admired the Federal houses in Grove Court, continue another half block to the end of Grove at **Hudson Street**. The old church across Hudson is **St. Luke's in the Fields,** built in the 1820s when so much of this part of the Village was going up. The original St. Luke's was destroyed by fire, but the restoration preserves its rural look, despite the Victorian-era warehouses looming behind it.

As you leave Grove Street, turn left (south) on Hudson for one block to **Barrow Street** and turn left again. The first corner you'll come to is called **Commerce Street**. The intersection sports an interesting pair of identical houses, no. 39 and no. 41 Commerce St., which were built in the 1830s and "modernized" in the 1870s with matching mansard roofs. Turn right off Barrow into tiny Commerce Street. This crooked little thoroughfare used to be called Cherry Lane until the big smallpox scare of 1822 sent so many businesses up here from New York that the name was changed. When you reach the end of the block, you'll be back on Bedford Street. Turn right (south) again, then look to your right for 75½ Bedford St. This 9½-foot-wide house holds the distinction of being the narrowest in Greenwich Village, as well as the one-time residence of poet Edna St. Vincent Millay.

Keep walking south on Bedford. In another block you'll come to one of the violent intersections wrought so many years ago by the extension of Seventh Avenue. Immediately on your right is Morton Street. Don't turn here, but continue another block south on Seventh Avenue to **St. Luke's Place**. Now turn right. Although the south side of St. Luke's Place is occupied by a modern playground, the north side preserves a terrific old row of houses from the 1850s. No. 6 St. Luke's Place was the residence of a former mayor of New York, the popular James J. ("Gentleman Jimmy") Walker. Although a crook and a scoundrel, Walker managed to epitomize the glamour of the 1920s. Incredibly, he is remembered fondly to this day.

After you've admired Jimmy Walker's digs, return to Seventh Avenue and continue straight across it on the line of St. Luke's Place. Once across Seventh you'll note that St. Luke's becomes **Leroy Street**. Stay on Leroy, past the continuation of Bedford Street for one block to the corner of Bleecker Street. Just before this intersection, note 7 Leroy St., a nearly perfect 1810 house, complete with alley entrance and original dormers.

When you get to Bleecker, you'll find a local shopping area with enterprises such as Rocco's Pastry Shop, the Bleecker Street Fish Market ("If It Swims, We Have It"), and assorted souvenir shops. Turn left on Bleecker for two very short blocks to **Jones Street**. Turn right onto Jones and take a quick look at no. 17 to see what usually happens to old houses like the one at no. 7 Leroy. A pity, no? At the end of the block, you'll be back on West 4th Street. Turn right for another short block and you are back on Sixth Avenue, a mere two blocks south of Waverly Place where your tour began.

TOUR 3: DOWNTOWN–FINANCIAL DISTRICT

Start: Broadway and Chambers Street (half the subways in Manhattan must stop within a block or so of this intersection). *Finish:* Bowling Green (adjacent to the Lexington Avenue IRT station). *Time required:* About 1¼ hours.

Broadway and Chambers Street is at the upper corner of **City Hall Park,** a 250-year-old greensward surrounded by landmark buildings. Before you go anywhere, look east on Chambers Street toward the **Municipal Building**. It's that slightly Stalinesque wedding cake straddling Chambers Street on the other side of the park. This is really the best vantage point for admiring McKim, Mead, and White's monumental city office complex built in 1914. It cleverly utilizes an awkward site and combines functionalism with beauty in a manner too often forgotten by modern architects. The statue at the very pinnacle of the thing represents *Civic Fame,* whatever that might be. Certainly the statue is high enough to overlook the corruption that has historically plagued this region of Manhattan.

Those interested in beaux arts architecture should walk east on Chambers to the end of the block. At 31 Chambers St., at the corner of Park Row and across from the Municipal Building, is a 1911 Frenchified palace that's New York's **Surrogate's Court.** The stupendous marble lobby is worth a look. Here is a public building built to impress, not merely to drag along with the drab duties of civic life.

Now turn around and retrace your steps along Chambers Street in the direction of Broadway. That dull-gray and capacious 1872 Italianate building just inside City Hall Park on your left is the famous **Tweed Courthouse.** Actually, it is officially called the New York City Courthouse. But William Marcy ("Boss") Tweed, during whose tenure on the Board of Supervisors it was built, stole so much of its construction funds that it has evermore borne his name. When the cornerstone was laid in 1861, the city had budgeted $250,000 for its construction. By the time it was finished 10 years later, the total cost had approached $14 *million.* Tweed and his cronies (described in Chapter I) induced every subcontractor to present padded bills. For example, one Andrew Garvey, subsequently known in the press as the "Prince of Plasterers," was paid $45,966.89 by the city for a single day's work. An estimated $10 million went into the pockets of Tweed and his pals. The ensuing scandal eventually ended Tweed's career. He died in prison four years later, penniless.

When you reach Broadway again, turn left and continue south for two blocks to Murray Street. Now you're going to enter City Hall Park and head for the front door of **City Hall,** which faces the parking area in the middle of the park, about on the line of Murray Street. In what historian T. A. Janvier termed a "shrewd thrust of prophetic sarcasm," New York City originally housed both convicted felons and city officials in the same building down on Wall Street. The present City Hall is a rather fragile-looking gem, considering the hardball that's been played here since 1811. The design is clearly 18th century, an amalgam of French and British antecedents cooked up as part of a city-sponsored contest. The winning architects were Joseph Mangin, a Frenchman who had worked in Paris on the Place de la Concorde, and a Scot by the name of John McComb. When completed in 1811, this was practically the northernmost structure in town. As a result the rear wall was faced with brownstone (cheaper than the limestone used on the rest of the place) on the theory that hardly anybody would see it, so why not save the money? In subsequent years the brownstone was replaced. Parts of City Hall are open to the public on weekdays from 10am to 4pm. It's a beautiful place, but one constantly wonders how such a big city can be managed from such a small city hall.

Before leaving City Hall, stop for a moment on the steps to admire the **Brooklyn Bridge,** looming impressively in the east. Completed in 1883, it was the world's first steel-wire suspension bridge. It's possible, if you are so inclined, to walk all the way across it to Brooklyn. The walkway is free, and the views are truly superb. However, leave this for another day's excursion and continue with your tour.

Return now to Broadway at Murray Street, noting Frederick MacMonnies' **statue of Nathan Hale,** located just inside the park opposite Murray. Noble, isn't it? (Guess who designed the base? Stanford White.) Turn left on Broadway and continue south for one block to Park Place. On the west side of Broadway, occupying the block between Park Place and Barclay Street, is the **Woolworth Building.** Five-and-dime tycoon Frank W. Woolworth ponied up $13 million in *cash* back in 1913 to pay for his new headquarters. During the opening ceremonies President Woodrow Wilson himself pressed a button in Washington that illuminated 80,000 bulbs in the tower. The Rev. S. Parkes Cadman, witnessing the scene, declared the building to be a "Cathedral of Commerce," the sight of which provoked "feelings too deep even for tears." For 17 years this architectural marriage of Gothic Europe and the American skyscraper was the tallest building in the world. It still ranks as one of New York's handsomest. By all means, go inside the lobby. With its marble walls and domed ceiling it's certainly as ornate as most cathedrals.

Leave the Woolworth Building and pause for a moment on the sidewalk outside. The other side of City Hall Park is bounded by a street called **Park Row** which, in the early years of this century, contained the offices of 12 New York City newspapers. In those days the area now containing the approaches to the Brooklyn Bridge was known as Printing House Square. Today the entire industry has scattered to various other parts of town.

Go another block down Broadway from the Woolworth Building, past Barclay Street, to Vesey Street. On your right, occupying the western blockfront of Broadway between Vesey and Fulton Streets, is **St. Paul's Chapel.** This delicious Georgian church dates from 1766, although the steeple wasn't added until after the Revolution in 1794. George Washington worshiped here; Pierre L'Enfant, the planner of Washington, D.C., designed the gilded sunburst above the altar; the graveyard outside contains the picturesque tombs of now-forgotten city squires and ladies. The building is an incredible contrast to the huge towers of the World Trade Center scraping the sky behind it. You're free to wander inside for a look. And if the interior layout seems confusing, bear in mind that St. Paul's was originally designed to face the river. That's the side with the steeple. But as Broadway grew to become the town's most important thoroughfare, it was decided to erect a new portico here instead of on the original front.

Leave St. Paul's, turn right, and continue south again on Broadway. Across Fulton Street on the next block, occupying a site that extends from Fulton south to Dey Street, is no. 195 Broadway, the original **AT&T Building.** If you're in the mood for another taste of the majesty of capitalism, have a look at the lobby. It's a perfect forest of immense columns. Indeed, the exterior of this building has more columns than any other stone structure in the world. Built in 1917, it was eventually abandoned by AT&T for new headquarters uptown.

When you've marveled sufficiently at what long-distance rates hath wrought, exit 195 Broadway and turn right (south) to the corner of Dey and Broadway. Turn right again onto Dey Street and continue west to the corner of Church Street. Before you is the $700-million **World Trade Center** (described in detail earlier in this chapter under "Famous Sights"). If you wish, you can detour to the Observation Deck on the 110th floor of Two World Trade Center, the tower to your left as you face the complex from the other side of Church Street. Alternatively you can just take a spin around the immense plaza at the foot of the twin towers, save the deck for later, and continue with your tour.

After you've checked out the Trade Center, retrace your steps back up Dey Street to Broadway. Now cross Broadway and continue east on **John Street** (which is just Dey Street with its name changed). This canyonlike thoroughfare is so narrow that it's closed to traffic at lunch hour. Note the modern skyscraper castle, complete with crenelated turrets, at the corner of John and Nassau.

Cross Nassau, keeping on John, and continue east. The simple steeple-less church at 44 John St. (in the shadow of the huge new tower) is the **John Street Methodist Church.** The present building was erected in 1841, but the congregation has owned and worshiped at this address since 1768, making it the oldest Methodist society in America.

Keep going east on John Street for 4½ more blocks. It's a short walk, down an 18th-century street lined with towering 20th-century buildings. On the last of these blocks, between Pearl and Water Streets, is **127 John St.,** a 1969 office building with a street-level concourse filled with 1960s nonsense. There are an astonishingly complicated digital clock, blue neon-lined tubes leading to the elevators, and all manner of whimsical constructs for seating and shelter. Not beautiful, but very evocative of the 1960s. (Pearl Street, by the way, was originally called Mother-of-Pearl Street, because it was once the beach that ran along the shore of the East River. Water Street, a block farther east, was built on landfill, as was everything beyond it.)

Turn left off John onto Water Street, skirting the perimeter of 127 John, and continue north for one block to Fulton Street. The corner of Fulton and Water marks the entrance to the **South Street Seaport** (also described separately under "Famous Sights"). From this point to the East River Fulton Street has been transformed into a cobbled pedestrian mall. Between Water Street and South Street it's lined with restored buildings, Seaport Museum galleries, pricey shops, and "intriguing" restaurants. The seaport is definitely worth a day unto itself. For now, you might stroll the two short blocks down Fulton to South and admire the sailing ships at berth in the river. You might get a snack at one of the restaurants or food stalls in Pier 17, then return one block up Fulton to Front Street and turn left (south).

Keep south on **Front Street** for six short blocks. Until recently this area was filled with ancient brick buildings similar to those in the seaport. Their sudden disappearance and replacement by the modern behemoths that line the street today were a principal factor leading to the founding of the Seaport Museum.

The sixth intersection you'll come to is that of Front Street and **Wall Street,** and here you'll turn right. As you may already have heard, Wall Street follows the line of a crude palisade erected in the 17th century by the Dutch to deter Native American attacks. It was never put to a test, even though the Indians did almost as much mischief as the Dutch in other regions of Manhattan. Start walking west on Wall Street, past Water and Pearl Streets. Ahead you'll see the slender spire of **Trinity Church,** located at Broadway and Wall. It's hard to believe that this tiny antique, cringing at the bottom of a Grand Canyon of concrete, was once the tallest structure on Manhattan, a landmark visible from far out in the harbor.

On the left side of the next block, just past Hanover Street, is the entrance to **55 Wall St.** This was the site of a Merchants' Exchange destroyed in the great New York fire of 1835. The exchange was rebuilt in 1836, and the first three floors of it still exist right here in 55 Wall. In 1907 the place was remodeled for the National City Bank, and its size was doubled in the process. The building now belongs to Citibank, and its banking floor is well worth a look. This interior resembles nothing so much as an imperial Roman bath. Beneath the soaring marble walls and columns are perfectly ridiculous-looking modern banking islands. We should be glad, however, that nobody has tried to tear the place down.

Exit 55 Wall, turn left (west), and continue in the direction you've been heading. Stay on Wall past the intersection of William Street until you see on your right the statue of George Washington standing above the steps to **Federal Hall National Memorial.** This museum, located at the corner of Wall and Nassau Streets, occupies a very fine Greek Revival building erected in 1842. New York's City Hall, before being relocated to the present City Hall Park, stood at this site. In 1789, the father of our country took the oath of office on the balcony of the old building, which at that point had been remodeled by Major L'Enfant and rechristened Federal Hall. There's a free museum inside the present Federal Hall, with exhibits pertaining to the building, the Revolution, and Washington.

Federal Hall stands at the head of **Broad Street,** down which you're now going to turn. Just south of Wall, on the right (west) side of Broad Street, is the gratifyingly magnificent columned facade of the **New York Stock Exchange,** at 3 Broad St. There's been a stock exchange in New York since 1792, when a group of brokers started meeting under a buttonwood tree near Wall and William Streets. The initial purpose of the exchange was to sell government bonds to pay off the debt left over from the Revolutionary War. The market grew in power and importance throughout the 19th century. In 1903, it moved to the present building, which can be visited for free (refer to "Famous Sights" earlier in this chapter for details).

The next intersection to the south is that of Broad and **Exchange Place.** Turn left (east) onto Exchange and behold the popular image of "Wall Street" before your very eyes. This street is so narrow you want to turn sideways to walk down it. And the buildings along its sides are so tall that direct sunlight probably hasn't hit the pavement since 1917. Continue to the end of the block and cross William Street. Then continue on Exchange to the end of the next block (these are very short blocks by the way) and turn right onto **Hanover Street.** It's only about 30 feet to the corner of **Beaver Street,** where you'll turn right again for another 30 or 40 feet until you arrive at the corner of **William Street.** And here, with Delmonico's Restaurant facing you across the street, you'll turn left onto William for another 50-odd feet until you arrive at **Hanover Square.**

This is quite a historic corner of old New York. Like so many other districts, Hanover Square had its day in the sun as an elite residential enclave. The premier householder was none other than Captain Kidd, a notorious pirate abroad (the English caught him and hanged him in 1701) but a respected citizen of New York City and a contributor to Trinity Church. The first newspaper in town, the *New-York Gazette,* was also printed in Hanover Square, in 1725 by William Bradford. The great Fire of 1835 started with a gas explosion in Hanover Square. The ensuing conflagration engulfed 20 acres and destroyed 650 buildings, including everything that had survived until then from the Dutch period. **India House,** that charming old brownstone building on the south side of William at the corner of Pearl, was built in 1854 as the Hanover Bank. It is today a private club.

Now turn around and go back on William Street to Delmonico's. When you reach the corner of William and Beaver, take a sharp left onto **South William Street.** The wall of Delmonico's will be on your right as you walk down South William. There are wonderful opportunities hereabouts for pictures of twisting narrow streets and huge soaring skyscrapers. South William continues for one block only, until it joins Broad Street. When you get to the corner, turn left (south) onto Broad for two blocks to **Bridge Street** and pause for a moment on the corner.

That old brick building just ahead of you down at Broad and Pearl is **Fraunces Tavern.** Samuel Fraunces was a black man whose "Queen's Head Tavern," as the place was originally called, figured in several passages of American history. The New York Chamber of Commerce was founded here in 1768. In 1783, the tavern was the scene of DeWitt Clinton's gala celebration of the British evacuation of occupied New York. It was here, also in 1783, that George Washington (Fraunces was his chief steward) bade farewell to his officers and announced his retirement to Mount Vernon. The building had fallen pretty low by the end of the 19th century. In 1904, it was lovingly restored by the Sons of the Revolution, although the authenticity of its present appearance is questionable. Today it is again a restaurant, with a small museum attached.

Turn right off Broad Street onto Bridge Street and walk one block to the corner of Whitehall Street. Cross Whitehall and continue another short block to **State Street,** where you'll turn right. The huge building to your right was until 1973 the **U.S. Custom House.** It's a shame Custom moved to the World Trade Center. Nothing could match the magnificence of this 1907 beaux arts masterpiece, which has stood vacant ever since.

The main entrance to the Customs House is at the head of State Street facing **Bowling Green.** This little park was once a Dutch cattle market, then a green for bowls. The iron fence around it has been there since 1771 and was erected originally to protect an equestrian statue of King George III. On July 9, 1776, a rowdy crowd, excited by a reading of the Declaration of Independence, descended upon Bowling Green, tore the statue down, and broke it into pieces. Legend has it the lead was melted into bullets that subsequently felled 400 British soldiers.

The greensward that faces the side wall of the Customs House on the other side of State Street is **Battery Park,** named after a gun emplacement that once stood along the line of present State Street. Usually just called the Battery, this very pleasant park is constructed entirely on landfill. It's an ideal place for strolling and admiring unobstructed views of New York Harbor.

At the northern end of the Battery, located directly on the waterfront, is **Castle Clinton.** This old fortress started life in 1807 as another gun emplacement. Before the waterfront was filled in, it sat about 300 feet offshore on a pile of rocks. In the 1820s, the federal government ceded it to the city, which converted it to a civic reception hall. Lafayette, President Jackson, and Edward, Prince of Wales, were all officially greeted here by the City of New York. By 1850, it was called Castle Garden and operated as a concert hall. This is where P. T. Barnum first presented Jenny Lind, "The Swedish Nightingale," to an adoring American audience. Five years after that the building was converted to the Immigrant Landing Depot. Almost eight million future Americans were processed at Castle Garden before Ellis Island was completed in 1892. After its immigrant era it became the New York Aquarium, which it remained until that institution moved to Coney Island in 1941. Vacant and threatened with demolition in the years thereafter, it was eventually rescued and restored in 1976 by the National Park Service to its present somewhat dry appearance.

TOUR 4: SOHO GALLERIES & THE CAST-IRON DISTRICT

Start: West Broadway and Houston Street. *Finish:* Sixth Avenue and Houston Street. *Time required:* About 1½ hours.

Until the late 1840s, what we now call SoHo (an acronym for *South of Houston Street*) was a quiet residential quarter of the northern edge of town. Starting in about 1850, a commercial building boom (petering out finally in the 1890s) totally transformed the place into a neighborhood of pricey retail stores and loft buildings for light manufacturing. All this activity coincided with the development of cast iron as a building material. Columns, arches, pediments, brackets, keystones, and everything else that once had to be carved in stone could now be mass produced at lower cost in iron. The result was a commercial building spree that gave free rein to the opulent architectural styles of the day.

But after the spree came long generations of neglect. By the late 1960s, the area was dismissed as too dismal for words. And for that precise reason it began attracting impoverished artists. Back then you could rent huge spaces in SoHo's former sweatshops (considerable exploitation went on behind these handsome facades) for next to nothing. But restless fashion was not about to ignore a developing new brew of art and historic architecture. By the early 1970s, the land boom was on. Today West Broadway is literally lined with rarefied boutiques, avant-garde galleries, and trendy restaurants. SoHo lofts now appear in the pages of *Architectural Digest,* and they're more likely to be inhabited by art patrons than artists.

Yet one cannot dismiss SoHo as a travesty of art sold out to commerce. Its concentration of galleries soon made it a major force in world art markets, and as such a major force in the very shape of today's art. The intellectual and artistic ferment in SoHo had strong parallels to what was happening in Paris and Berlin between the wars or in Greenwich Village at the turn of the century. The rediscovery of the old buildings is somewhat ironic (no pun intended) as they are about as spiritually distant from modern art as it is possible for buildings to be.

Admittedly, SoHo doesn't look too promising from the departure point at Houston and West Broadway. Back in the 1920s, Houston was widened as part of the construction of the IND subway line. It seems somehow never to have healed.

Proceed south from Houston down **West Broadway** in the direction of the World Trade Center towers that loom so picturesquely in the distance. Although this street is the center of the gallery world and SoHo's most famous thoroughfare, it does not by a long shot contain the best cast-iron buildings. Top honors in that category probably belong to Broome Street, which you'll visit farther on.

What makes West Broadway so famous, besides lots of places to shop for chic clothes, is its concentration of galleries. You don't need an appointment to go in and look. And what you'll see could be anything from the highly representational to the intensely personal, from neo-impressionist landscapes to sculpture to constructions that challenge your entire definition of art. In between galleries bearing names like Boone, Castelli, Cowles, Hirschl & Adler, and Sonnabend are shops like If, Pour Toi, Dapy, Victoria Falls, and Rizzoli, selling everything from books to clothing designed in Milan. Although art as big business has faltered a bit of late, West Broadway's streetside atmosphere remains exciting and cosmopolitan.

When you reach the end of the fourth block south of Houston Street, you'll be at the intersection of West Broadway and **Grand Street.** Turn left on Grand and head east. Now you're really getting into cast-iron country. Note the renovated building at the end of this block, on the corner of Grand and Wooster Streets. This marvelous Victorian facade is typical of what's been rediscovered down here. Structurally speaking, cast-iron buildings were not particularly innovative. They were usually supported by the same brick walls and timber floors as the buildings they replaced. The cast iron was merely mounted on the facades as a substitute for carved stone. Nor did it necessarily cover an entire facade.

But it did have a definite "look." And the next block of Grand, between **Wooster and Greene Streets,** shows this look to best advantage. Iron pillars seem to line the street into infinity. A century ago these sidewalks were crowded with shoppers. The ground floors of the buildings contained all manner of dry-goods emporia, while the upper levels were jammed with immigrants crouched over sewing machines for 12 hours a day. The building at the southwest corner of Greene and Grand (the one that says 1873 on top) sums up the commercial aesthetic of those times. It is a real iron palace, lifted direct from the Italian Renaissance as interpreted by some 19th-century architect. The cast-iron building at the southeast corner of the same intersection sums up the SoHo of today: innovative, visually arresting, and expensive looking. Before we move on, glance up Greene Street for more cast-iron vistas. *Historical footnote:* During the cast-iron heyday of SoHo, Greene Street was one of New York's premier red-light districts. Continue another block east on Grand to the corner of **Mercer Street.** The old Empire Safe Company Building on the south side of the street shows how cast iron was combined with other building materials. In this case, it's been confined to the first floor façade, which doesn't look as if it's changed one bit in the last century.

Turn right and continue one block south to the corner of Mercer and **Howard Street.** Proceed east on Howard Street (it's the only direction you can go, since Howard begins at Mercer Street) and go one block to the corner of Broadway. Note the extravagant **Dittenhofer Building** (built in 1870) on your right at the near corner of Howard and Broadway. These are the sorts of buildings we 20th-century Americans have traditionally been trained to ignore. And what a pleasure it is to rediscover them under our very noses.

Turn left on Broadway and walk uptown for one block to Grand Street. That wonderful old building on the corner of Grand and Broadway shows the heavy hand of modernization on its first floor. (Who could have really thought the modernish mess they've made of the street level was better than what was there in the first place?)

Continue north up Broadway for another block to **Broome Street.** At 488 Broadway, on the northeast corner of Broadway and Broome, is the many-pillared **Haughwout Building.** Among other things this building is noted for its original 1857 Otis elevator, still in service. The street-level showrooms of 488 Broadway were once filled with the silver, chandeliers, and crystal goods of one Eder Haughwout. While the original cream-colored paint job is a distant memory, the structure remains essentially unaltered, an evocative reminder of Broadway's former commercial glory.

Turn left onto Broome Street and continue two blocks west to the intersection of Broome and Greene Streets. Much of SoHo, as you can see, remains pretty gritty and industrial notwithstanding its historic buildings and trendy new art culture. And yet a critical mass has definitely been achieved. Today the dirtiest SoHo Street corner manages somehow to look "fashionable," at least in the eyes of a downtown New Yorker.

Turn right onto Greene Street and proceed two blocks north to the corner of Prince Street. Before you reach Prince you'll see examples of just about everything that's happening in SoHo these days. There are cast-iron buildings—some gloriously renovated, some still grotty—another clutch of galleries, a new condominium (in a renovated iron building at 97 Greene that's clearly not being marketed to starving artists), plus various unglamorous old-time tool and rag businesses.

Pause for a moment at Prince and Greene and look up at the eastern wall of **114 Prince St.,** also called the SoHo Center. This cleverly painted blank brick wall recreates the cast-iron street facade, complete to the painted cat in the painted open window. Turn left off Greene onto Prince Street and walk west for two blocks to West Broadway. Chic shops and restaurants proliferate the closer you draw to that celebrated thoroughfare. Cross West Broadway, keeping on Prince, and continue for another block to **Thompson Street.** The cast-iron district is behind you now; this is tenement country. The next street you'll cross is Sullivan Street, shortly after which you'll see **203 Prince St.** on your right. This perfectly beautiful restored Federal house holds out hope for every mutilated building in town. If they can be brought back to this, then no damage is beyond repair. The next street that crosses Prince is Macdougal, and a few steps farther is the great swath of widened Sixth Avenue hurtling south from Greenwich Village.

Directly across Sixth Avenue, angling a little to the south of the course of Spring Street, is **Charlton Street.** That's where you want to go, although crossing Sixth Avenue can be daunting. Charlton Street is the center of a small historic district notable for its concentration of intact Federal-period houses. The site was originally a country estate located midway between New York and Greenwich. The mansion, built in 1767 and named Richmond Hill, surveyed the surrounding countryside from the top of a sizable hill, leveled in 1817, when John Jacob Astor developed the property into building lots. Illustrious inhabitants of Richmond Hill have included Vice President John Adams, whose wife, Abigail, described the view south to New York as "delicious," and Aaron Burr, who lived here at the time of his fateful duel with Alexander Hamilton.

After its hilltop was sliced from beneath it, the Richmond Hill mansion was moved to a new site on the southeast corner of Varick and Charlton. It became a theater, then was a tavern, and was finally torn down in 1849. Despite the towering loft buildings standing in the background, the block of Charlton between Sixth Avenue and Varick Street retains much of the flavor of early 19th-century New York. It gives you a good idea, too, of what SoHo looked like before the cast-iron invasion.

When you reach Varick Street, turn right for one block to **King Street** and turn right again. King Street is less intact than Charlton, but it still contains its share of old houses. Nos. 32 and 34 King St., on the south side of the block near Sixth Avenue, tell interesting stories for the student of architecture. No. 34 King St. is in near original condition; 32 King St. obviously started life as a Federal house and was then "modernized" in the 1860s or 1870s. It now sports a Second Empire mansard roof and Italianate door and window hoods.

At the end of King Street you'll be back on Sixth Avenue (a major uptown bus route), one block south of Houston Street.

---

3. Museums & Galleries

Here, in alphabetical order, is a list of some of the city's most important or unusual museums, each with a brief description of the sort of exhibits presented.

AMERICAN CRAFT MUSEUM

This handsome museum, at 40 W. 53rd St. (tel. 956-3535), offers exhibits of American contemporary crafts: glass, wood, fiber, and ceramics. Admission is $4.50 for adults and $2 for students and seniors; children under 12 are free. It is open Tuesday from 10am to 8pm and Wednesday through Sunday from 10am to 5pm.

AMERICAN MUSEUM OF NATURAL HISTORY

Known to every kid in New York as the museum with the dinosaurs, this noble institution has been in existence for well over a century. It's immense, containing within its four-square-block campus over 36 million specimens and artifacts arranged artfully and dramatically. The 40 separate exhibition spaces, bearing names like the Hall of Ocean Life, the Hall of African Peoples, the Hall of Oceanic Birds, and the Hall of Minerals, contain everything from lifelike dioramas to enormous reconstructed dinosaur skeletons to the fabulous Star of India sapphire. Adjoining the museum is the Hayden Planetarium, which presents computer-automated sky shows projected on a domed ceiling.

The museum's main entrance is at Central Park West and West 79th Street. Doors are open Sunday to Thursday from 10am to 5:45pm and Friday and Saturday until 8:45pm. On school days nobody under 18 is admitted unless accompanied by an adult (presumably as an antitruancy measure). Admission is $5 for adults and $2.50 for children. The Planetarium show costs another $5 for adults and $2.50 for kids. For further information and Planetarium schedules, call 769-5100.

COOPER-HEWITT MUSEUM OF DESIGN AND DECORATIVE ARTS

Three granddaughters of local philanthropist Peter Cooper founded this museum in 1897 to provide visual information for the study of design. What that means is that they collected examples of decorative art—drawings, prints, silverware, glass, fabrics, furniture, metalwork, jewelry, and so on—so as to preserve them for future study. Since 1968, this venerable New York institution has been a part of the Smithsonian. In 1976, the collection was installed in the former Andrew Carnegie mansion on Fifth Avenue and 91st Street, a fitting display case for decorative arts if ever there was one. Scheduled for February 1994 is "Packaging the New: Design and the American Consumer." Recent exhibitions have included "Collecting A to Z" and "Czech Cubism: Architecture and Design." The Cooper-Hewitt additionally runs lectures, workshops, and tours. It's worth a visit just to see the Carnegie mansion.

The museum is located on the corner of Fifth Avenue and 91st Street (tel. 860-6868). Hours are Tuesday from 10am to 9pm, Wednesday through Saturday from 10am to 5pm, and Sunday from noon to 5pm; closed major holidays. Admission is $3 for adults and $1.50 for seniors and students over 12.

THE CLOISTERS

This museum of medieval art is located in northern Manhattan in the middle of Fort Tryon Park. It's quite a place up there on its hilltop, surveying the Hudson and the Palisades. Both the museum and the park were given to the city in 1938 by John D. Rockefeller. The museum building, which looks like a medieval monastery, contains rare tapestries (particularly a famous series called the *Unicorn Tapestries*), 13th-century stained glass, 12th-century wooden religious statuary, paintings, precious small objects, and tomb ornaments. A cloister is a covered walkway, usually surrounding an open courtyard. Several ancient European cloisters were moved here and incorporated into the present structure, hence the museum's name. All in all it's a grand place, its inherent erudition counterbalanced by a dramatic location and the imposing scale of many of its exhibits.

The Cloisters is actually an adjunct of the Metropolitan Museum of Art (see below). Its location in Fort Tryon Park and is accessible either by the IND Eighth Avenue A train to 190th Street and Overlook Terrace (from which you walk through the park to the museum), or by the Madison Avenue M4 bus, which will take you to the door. Open Tuesday to Sunday from 9:30am to 5:15pm in March to September, until 4:45pm in November to February. Admission is by contribution, the amount suggested being $6 for adults, $3 for students and senior citizens. Kids under 12 are admitted free. For information, call 923-3700.

FORBES MAGAZINE GALLERY

This is not a terribly large gallery, but its collection reflects the panache of *Forbes* magazine and the family that owns it. Perhaps most exciting are the precious objects and bibelots made of gold, enamel, silver, and rare gems. Forbes owns 12 Fabergé Easter Eggs originally made for the Russian imperial family, plus cases of exquisite Fabergé objets d'art (music boxes to decanter stoppers), constituting the largest private collection of it in the world. Also on display are rare letters from American presidents, 12,000 toy soldiers, models of *Forbes* magazine yachts, and a collection of trophies commemorating forgotten events.

The *Forbes* Gallery is located at 62 Fifth Ave., between 12th and 13th Streets (tel. 206-5548), and it's open Tuesday, Wednesday, Friday, and Saturday from 10am to 4pm. Admission is free.

FRICK COLLECTION

When industrialist Henry Clay Frick died in 1919, his will stipulated that his Fifth Avenue house be eventually opened to the public "for the study of art and kindred subjects." In 1935, after certain alterations, this wish was carried out. The Frick contains painting by Renoir, Boucher, Holbein, El Greco, Vermeer, Rembrandt, and Gainsborough, among others, plus sculpture by Houdon, furniture by Boulle, and painted 16th-century enamels from Limoges. Much of the Frick family's original furniture remains. The Fragonard Room, decorated with a series of painted canvases entitled *The Progress of Love*, is the apotheosis of a New York society, pre–World War I, French-style reception room. Also part of the permanent collection is a fine display of blue-and-white Chinese porcelains. This museum is a place of great elegance and beauty, a visit to which will be a memorable event.

The location is 1 E. 70th St., at the corner of Fifth Avenue (tel. 288-0700). The hours are 10am to 6pm Tuesday through Saturday, and 1 to 6pm on Sunday; closed assorted major holidays. Admission is $3 for adults and $1.50 for students and senior citizens. Children under 10 not admitted.

GUGGENHEIM MUSEUM

Designed by Frank Lloyd Wright (his only building in New York City), the controversial Guggenheim houses a famous collection of modern masterpieces. French impressionists and postimpressionists like Manet, Bonnard, Cézanne, Gauguin, and Seurat dominate the permanent collection, which also includes Picassos, Modiglianis, and other recognizable names. The principal gallery occupies one side of a long winding ramp that hugs the interior of a snail-shaped stucco structure plopped down in the midst of dignified Fifth Avenue. The constantly changing roster of temporary exhibits concentrates exclusively on 20th-century artists.

The Guggenheim is located at 1071 Fifth Ave., between 88th and 89th Streets (tel. 423-3500). Hours are Friday to Wednesday from 10am to 8pm. Admission is $7 for adults and $4 for students and seniors with valid ID.

JEWISH MUSEUM

Housed since 1947 in the Fifth Avenue French Gothic–style mansion of financier Felix Warburg, the museum contains one of the three largest collections of Judaica in the world. The permanent collection contains over 14,000 objects inspired by the Jewish experience, spanning over 4000 years, among them paintings, graphics, sculpture, and religious artifacts. Every year the museum mounts two or three major exhibitions, plus four or five smaller ones. Shows include "The Art of Memory: Holocaust Memorials in History" and "In This House: A History of the Jewish Museum."

Located at Fifth Avenue and 92nd Street, the Jewish Museum (tel. 423-3200) has just undergone a two-year renovation and expansion project. Open Sunday, Monday, Wednesday, and Thursday from 11am to 5:45pm; Tuesday open until 8pm. Admission is $6 for adults and $4 for students and seniors; kids under 12 are admitted free.

METROPOLITAN MUSEUM OF ART

The "Met" is one of the great cultural resources of New York City. It also happens to be the largest art museum in the Western Hemisphere. The permanent collection consists of over three million works of art representing almost every epoch in the history of humans. There are treasures from ancient Egypt, classical Rome, the Islamic Empire, the Far East, and particularly Europe from medieval times to the 20th century. Besides its famous collections of sculpture, painting, period rooms, and bronzes, as well as the Costume Institute, the Met mounts continuous changing exhibits. A few scheduled for 1994 include, "Degas Landscapes," "Picasso and The Weeping Woman," "Origins of Impressionism," and "Dalí in the Twenties." With 1½ million square feet of space to play around with and an annual budget of $78 million, you can imagine the scope and quality of these exhibits.

The entrance to the Met is on Fifth Avenue and 82nd Street (tel. 535-7710). Hours are Tuesday to Thursday and Sunday from 9:30am to 5:15pm, Friday and Saturday until 8:45pm. Admission is by contribution, the suggested amounts being $6 for adults and $3 for students and seniors; kids under 12 are admitted free.

MUSEUM OF AMERICAN FOLK ART

Devoted exclusively to American folk art, this museum displays a charming array of paintings, sculpture, textiles, and decorative art objects from the 18th through the 20th centuries. To see everything from stunning old weather vanes to the primitive paintings of Grandma Moses, go to 2 Lincoln Square (tel. 595-9533) opposite Lincoln Center on Tuesday through Sunday from 11:30am to 7:30pm.

MUSEUM OF THE CITY OF NEW YORK

This place has been collecting artifacts and memorabilia connected with New York City since 1923. In those days it was located over in Gracie Mansion, before that pleasant old house became the residence of New York City's mayor. The present building was erected in 1932 and contains everything from antique fire engines, Tiffany silver, Duncan Phyfe furniture, and historical portraits to entire historic rooms (notably John D. Rockefeller's bedroom rescued from his demolished town house on West 54th Street), hundreds of antique toys, and some truly incredible antique dollhouses. There are many old pictures as well, chronicling the march of time across the City of New York.

The museum, located at Fifth Avenue and 103rd Street (tel. 534-1672), is open Wednesday through Saturday from 10am to 5pm and Sunday and holidays from 1 to 5pm. Admission is $5 for adults and $3 for children and seniors.

MUSEUM OF MODERN ART

MoMA's collection of modern art spans the period from the 1880s to the present and includes the masterpieces of Van Gogh and Cézanne as well as more recent works by Rauschenberg and Stella. There are over 30 galleries in the recently renovated building, as well as a quite lovely sculpture court (decorated with the works of Picasso, Rodin, and Lachaise), a theater showing film classics, two museum stores, and two restaurants. The permanent collection includes architectural drawings by people like Mies van der Rohe and Le Corbusier; photographs taken by people like Stieglitz, Man Ray, Steichen, and Walker Evans; paintings by Matisse, Pollock, and Miró; engravings and etchings of artists like Dubuffet, Klee, and Munch. Some exhibitions in 1994 will include a retrospective of the works of Robert Ryman, a Joan Miró show, and "Frank Lloyd Wright—Architect," to name but a few.

You'll find MoMA at 11 W. 53rd St., between Fifth and Sixth Avenues (tel. 708-9480). Hours are Friday to Tuesday from 11am to 6pm, Thursday until 9pm. Admission is $7.50 for adults, $4.50 for seniors and students with current ID. Films are free with museum admission. On Thursday nights, pay what you wish. For film schedules, call 708-9490.

OLD MERCHANT'S HOUSE

This little gem of a house was built in 1832 on what is now a seedy downtown industrial block. But back then East 4th Street was a select and aristocratic quarter. In 1835, the lot was purchased by Seabury Tredwell, and it wasn't until a century later that his youngest daughter finally died. Throughout all those years Miss Tredwell kept her father's house virtually unchanged. When she died in 1933, a rich cousin bought the place and endowed it, and it's been open to the public ever since. Actually, not many people visit this part of town. It's not dangerous, but it's ugly and out of the way. As a matter of fact, the neighborhood was pretty well shot by the 1870s, three generations before Miss Tredwell finally died. One imagines her all alone down here in her father's house, watching the world pass her by from behind hand-blown window panes. This is an unusual opportunity to view intact an upper-middle-class New York domestic decor (the place was redecorated in the late 1860s, two years before "papa" died. Even Miss Tredwell's clothes are still in the closets.

The Old Merchant's House is located at 29 E. 4th St., between Lafayette Street and the Bowery (tel. 777-1089), and is open Sunday through Thursday from 1 to 4pm. Admission is $3 for adults and $2 for students and seniors; free to children under 12.

STUDIO MUSEUM IN HARLEM

The Studio Museum's handsome Harlem gallery is devoted to the collection and documentation of the art of black America and the African Diaspora. The institution is young, a mere 23 years having passed since it was founded. But it's ambitious, heartfelt, and professional. Its growing collection includes painting, sculpture, drawing, prints, posters, photographs, artifacts, etc. The Studio Museum is a concerned member of the Harlem community too, sponsoring artist-in-residence programs, conducting seminars for aspiring collectors, exposing school-children to art, presenting lectures, and mounting a changing series of exhibits. It has been described as the foremost center for the study of African-American art in America.

The museum, located at 144 W. 125th St., between Lenox Avenue and Adam Clayton Powell Boulevard, as Sixth and Seventh Avenues are called uptown (tel. 864-4500), is open Wednesday through Friday from 10am to 5pm, Saturday and Sunday from 1 to 6pm. Admission is $5 for adults, $3 for seniors and students, and $1 for children.

WHITNEY MUSEUM OF AMERICAN ART

Gertrude Vanderbilt Whitney, herself a sculptor, was the leading patron of American art from 1907 until her death in 1942. By the late 1920s, she had acquired so many works of art that she attempted to give them to the Metropolitan Museum, but the Met turned her down. So in 1930, she founded the Whitney Museum of American Art and a year later installed her collection in an old house on West 8th Street. Today's Whitney, housed in a startling-looking stone building built on the Upper East Side in 1966, presents the full range of American art from colonial times to the present. The overwhelming emphasis, however, is on the work of living art-ists. The permanent collection includes names like Ralston Crawford, George Sugarman, Alexander Calder, and Eric Fischl. Typical exhibits are challenging, to say the least. Yet for those passionate about modern American art, this is a museum that cannot be missed.

The Whitney is at 945 Madison Ave., between 74th and 75th Streets (tel. 570-3676). It's open Wednesday from 11am to 6pm, Thursday from 1 to 8pm, and Fri-day to Sunday from 11am to 6pm. Admission is $6 for adults and $4 for students and seniors; children are free (everyone is free on Thursday between 6 and 8pm).

NEW YORK CITY AFTER DARK

My daughter, at the age of 4, once explained to me why there are such big crowds on the streets of New York at night. She said that since all the houses were filled up, there was no place else for the people to go. Perhaps she was right, which would also explain why New York has so much nightlife.

Here are some suggested after-dark activities, from the sedate to the devil-may-care.

1. Movies

To find out what's playing where, do one of the following: buy *The New York Times* or the New York *Daily News* and look at the ads on the inside pages for current first-run features. Both papers also carry a smattering of advertising for less mainstream stuff. The "Arts and Leisure" section of the Sunday *New York Times* is an excellent guide to the overall entertainment scene, including movies.

The New Yorker is a glossy international publication that also has a sophisticated local entertainment guide. *The New Yorker* provides capsule reviews for a selective list of films it deems of special interest. Manhattan movie houses and museums show many fascinating films you're not liable to see elsewhere, and *The New Yorker* is a good way to track them down.

The above publications are all available at the sort of well-stocked newsstand you'll find at major street corners, big subway stops, and large hotel lobbies. Also available (at least in the subways and on the streets) is the *Village Voice,* a thick liberal weekly paper, which also covers the entertainment scene but specializes in its downtown area and includes many of the more off-beat presentations that might not make it into the uptown press. It hits the stands on Wednesdays.

Manhattan has a couple of movie-house concentrations, but none really qualifies as the center of local moviedom. Third Avenue in the low 60s has a bunch of first-run houses; and Loew's 84th Street, up on Broadway and West 84th, has six theaters under one roof. The majority of Manhattan's movies, be they first-run or revival houses, are mainly scattered around the residential districts.

Every autumn since 1963 the Film Society of Lincoln Center, at Broadway and 65th Street, has sponsored the **New York Film Festival.** This is one of the most important annual film events in the United States. The Film Society does not run a theater all year long, but at festival time it sponsors an intensive series of screenings featuring films from around the world. Most screenings are open to the public, although tickets are limited. If it's autumn and you're interested, call the society at 875-5610 for program information.

The **Museum of Modern Art,** 11 W. 53rd St., between Fifth and Sixth Avenues, runs a variegated film program all year. Museum admission includes the cost of a ticket, but if it's a popular show they're liable to run out of seats early. The program may consist of a fabulous old comedy classic from the museum's archives or videomakers discussing and showing their work; or it may be a part of a series of films from India, Cuba, Italy, or wherever. Call 708-9490 to find out what's on.

---

2. Theaters

There are about 40 big-time legitimate Broadway theaters in New York. Added to that are another 300 or so Off-Broadway theaters, many offering shows that are at least as exciting as (occasionally more so) anything on the Great White Way. The same papers and magazines that list the movies (described above) also list and describe shows at the theaters. Box office prices ain't cheap; expect to pay $50 or more per ticket on Broadway. Prices are considerably less by the time you get to Off-Off-Broadway, which might be a theater in a loft, a church, somebody's basement, a storefront, or anyplace else the rent is cheap. Ticket brokers can often supply otherwise-impossible-to-obtain tickets to hot shows, either on or Off-Broadway. If you use one, expect to pay a service charge.

Alternatively, you might try to get day-of-performance, discount tickets from the Times Square Ticket Center, called simply **TKTS** (tel. 768-1818) and located on the traffic island between Broadway and Seventh Avenue at 47th Street. Every day from 3pm to curtain time, and from 10am to 2pm on matinee days, TKTS sells surplus tickets to that evening's performances. Everything is first-come, first-served, and there's usually a line (though it moves quickly). If your heart is set on a particular show, come early.

---

3. Music & Dance Performances

Various halls around town specialize in music and dance, but none is as well known as **Carnegie Hall,** at the corner of Seventh Avenue and 57th Street. Built a century ago by industrialist Andrew Carnegie, this lovely old landmark is blessed with perfect acoustics. It presents world-famous virtuosos of keyboard and string, symphony orchestras, great singers in recital, competition winners, chamber music, even the occasional benefit performance. Call 247-7800 for program and ticket information.

Lincoln Center, at Broadway and 65th Street, possesses three of the city's foremost halls, arranged around a broad plaza with a big fountain in the center. The **New York State Theater,** whose stage was partly designed by George Ballanchine, is the home of the New York City Ballet and the New York City Opera. To find out the current program, call the box office at 870-5570. The **Metropolitan Opera House** is home to a company that's over 110 years old. The box office number is 362-6000. **Avery Fisher Hall,** the third in the fountain plaza triumvirate, bears the name of a stereo-equipment manufacturer who paid for its renovation some years back. It's the home of the New York Philharmonic, and the location of all manner of music concerts from symphonic to rock. Call 875-5000 to find out what (if anything) will be on during your visit. For plays, Lincoln Center has the **Vivian Beaumont Theater** and the smaller **Mitzi Newhouse Theater** (tel. 239-6200), located behind the plaza between Avery Fisher Hall and the Met. Across 65th Street is **Alice Tully Hall,** a concert hall whose programs range from chamber music to experimental theater to screenings of the New York Film Festival. The box office number is 875-5050.

The **Brooklyn Academy of Music** (often abbreviated BAM), at 30 Lafayette Ave., near Atlantic Avenue in Brooklyn, is a bit of a trip by subway or bus. But BAM's presentations of dance, theater, and music are always ambitious and usually first rate. This landmark hall began to acquire its experimental reputation in the early part of the century when people like Isadora Duncan and Sergei Rachmaninoff appeared between engagements of the New York Philharmonic and the Metropolitan Opera. Today's programs range from Pina Bausch and Robert Wilson to the annual Next Wave Festival that runs from October through December every year. Some performances are in the newly restored **Majestic Theater** nearby. Call the box office at 718/636-4100 for program information (and directions).

Radio City Music Hall, 1260 Sixth Ave., at 50th Street, was the last of the Manhattan movie palaces presenting a full stage show and a new Hollywood movie. It's a gloriously glitzy art deco palace of awe-inspiring proportions, a mere glimpse of whose golden interior is worth the price of admission. Threatened with demolition in the late 1970s, it was rescued, landmarked, and reopened with what management calls a "multifaceted entertainment policy." That means they don't show movies anymore. The stage shows are now ultralavish productions, twice as long as they used to be. They bear names like *Manhattan Showboat, Gotta Getaway!,* and *America* and still feature the famous 32-woman precision dance team known as the Rockettes. Big-name entertainers frequently give concerts at the Music Hall these days: Ray Charles, Liza Minnelli, Diana Ross, and Tina Turner have all appeared here in recent years. The holiday shows, particularly the "Magnificent Christmas Spectacular," really are fun. For prices and program information, call the Radio City information line at 247-4777. For information on backstage tours, call 632-4041.

The New York Times and the *Village Voice* both carry considerable advertising for music and dance events. There is also a day-of-performance, half-price ticket booth, the **Bryant Park Music and Dance Half-Price Ticket Booth.** You'll find it at the 42nd Street and Sixth Avenue corner of Bryant Park. It carries tickets for performances at Lincoln Center, Carnegie Hall, and the **City Center** (a famous hall on 55th Street between Sixth and Seventh Avenues), among other places, and is open Tuesday through Sunday from noon to 2pm and 3 to 7pm. For information call Artsline at 382-2323.

Woodpeckers Tap Dance Center & InterArts Space, 170 Mercer St. in SoHo (tel. 219-8284), is the home of the American Tap Dance Orchestra, which bills itself (with justification) as "a totally new concept in contemporary tap." Choreographer Brenda Bufalino creates a passionate and sophisticated orchestration of movement and sound, and her ATDO repertory includes works by everybody from Duke Ellington to George Gershwin, from Glenn Miller to Hoagy Carmichael. It really is a fun and unusual show—*and* it's cheap. In addition to tap, jazz, and cabaret performances, Woodpeckers also offers a full schedule of tap dance classes. Call the number above for showtimes and further information.

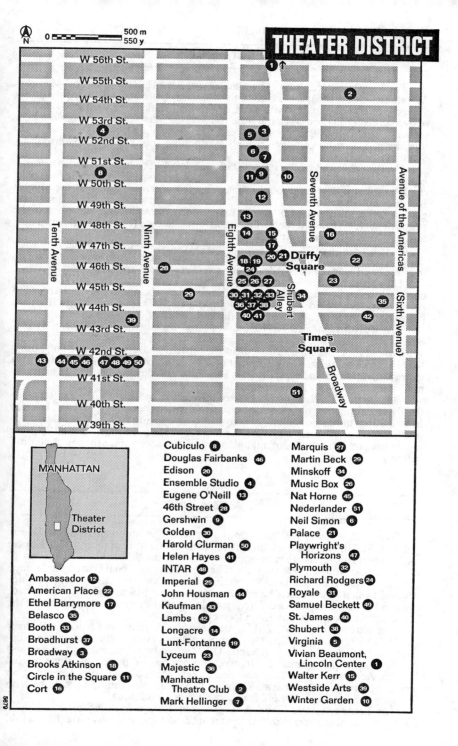

THEATER DISTRICT

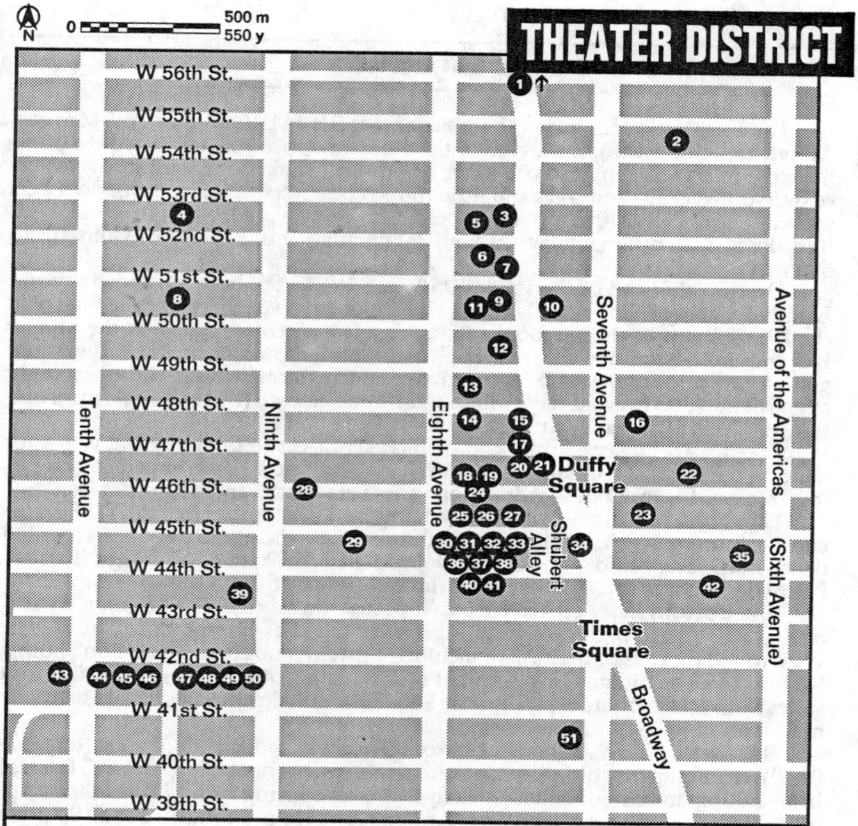
N
0
500 m
550 y
W 56th St.
W 55th St.
W 54th St.
W 53rd St.
W 52nd St.
W 51st St.
W 50th St.
W 49th St.
W 48th St.
W 47th St.
W 46th St.
W 45th St.
W 44th St.
W 43rd St.
W 42nd St.
W 41st St.
W 40th St.
W 39th St.
Tenth Avenue
Ninth Avenue
Eighth Avenue
Seventh Avenue
Avenue of the Americas (Sixth Avenue)
Broadway
Duffy Square
Shubert Alley
Times Square
1 2 3 4 5 6 7 8 9 10 11 12 13 14 15 16 17 18 19 20 21 22 23 24 25 26 27 28 29 30 31 32 33 34 35 36 37 38 39 40 41 42 43 44 45 46 47 48 49 50 51

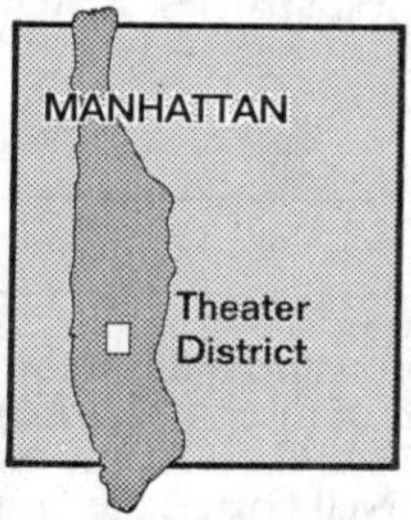
MANHATTAN
Theater District

- Ambassador 12
- American Place 22
- Ethel Barrymore 17
- Belasco 35
- Booth 33
- Broadhurst 37
- Broadway 3
- Brooks Atkinson 18
- Circle in the Square 11
- Cort 16
- Cubiculo 8
- Douglas Fairbanks 46
- Edison 20
- Ensemble Studio 4
- Eugene O'Neill 13
- 46th Street 28
- Gershwin 9
- Golden 30
- Harold Clurman 50
- Helen Hayes 41
- INTAR 48
- Imperial 25
- John Housman 44
- Kaufman 43
- Lambs 42
- Longacre 14
- Lunt-Fontanne 19
- Lyceum 23
- Majestic 36
- Manhattan Theatre Club 2
- Mark Hellinger 7
- Marquis 27
- Martin Beck 29
- Minskoff 34
- Music Box 26
- Nat Horne 45
- Nederlander 51
- Neil Simon 6
- Palace 21
- Playwright's Horizons 47
- Plymouth 32
- Richard Rodgers 24
- Royale 31
- Samuel Beckett 49
- St. James 40
- Shubert 38
- Virginia 5
- Vivian Beaumont, Lincoln Center 1
- Walter Kerr 15
- Westside Arts 39
- Winter Garden 10

4. Nightclubs

For a sophisticated, intimate ambience, **Au Bar,** 41 E. 58th St., off Madison Avenue (tel. 308-9455), is the club of the moment. Once you get passed the doormen, the plush red steps lead you down to a dimly lit oak room, with small clusters of overstuffed chairs and sofas and little round cocktail tables. The dance floor gets packed toward 2am with European types. Open every night from 9pm to 4am. Admission is $10 from Sunday through Wednesday and $15 from Thursday to Saturday.

On the other end of the scale is **USA,** 218 W. 47 St., between Broadway and Eighth Avenue (tel. 869-6001). This is a huge club, the type that everyone tired of in the 1980s, but it has been reborn to include a few anterooms, such as the Mugler Bar, and enough technomusic to keep all awake until the wee hours. The dance floor gets packed, and although USA is open Wednesday through Sunday, the best night to go is Thursday, to avoid the "bridge-and-tunnel" crowd (that is, people from outside Manhattan). Open from 10pm to 4am; admission is $15.

CBGB, 315 Bowery, at the end of Bleecker Street (tel. 982-4052), is not for dancing but for seeing ultranew bands. What's been "new" lately? Helmet, Screaming Trees, and Lemonheads. Admission varies between $3 and $10.

Limelight, 660 Sixth Ave., between 20th and 21st Streets (tel. 807-7850), occupies a former church. If this isn't titillating enough, there's very hot new recorded dance music every Friday and Saturday night for a $15 admission charge. This is a place you've got to see. Open Tuesday through Sunday from 10am to 4am.

The Bottom Line, 15 W. 4th St., at Mercer Street (tel. 228-7880), is a long-established Village nightspot featuring a wide range of entertainment from New Wave to old rock. Recent acts have included Buster Poindexter, Bob Geldof, Sonny Rollins, and The Indigo Girls. Again, it's for watching, not for dancing. Admission varies from act to act and typically runs $15. Food and drink are available; there's no minimum.

Roseland, 239 W. 52nd St., between Broadway and Eighth Avenue (tel. 247-0200), is an immense old place that caters to a wide variety of types. On Thursday from 2:30pm until midnight it's strictly ballroom dancing with a DJ and tapes. Admission is $6. On Sunday night they have an orchestra and admission is $10. Other nights have other sorts of dancing, plus special acts and private parties. Better call before you come.

5. Jazz Clubs

The **Village Gate,** 160 Bleecker St., between Thompson and Sullivan Streets (tel. 475-5120), is a New York landmark. It actually consists of three separate clubs: the Top of the Gate, the Terrace, and Downstairs at the Village Gate. At any one of these locations you can hear the likes of Branford Marsalis, Nell Carter, the Lounge Lizards, or Ruben Blades. The Downstairs is really a cabaret theater, except on Monday night when "Salsa Meets Jazz" (Latin dancing for $15 admission). The Terrace features a pleasant bar with a different jazz duo every other week. Admission for the bigger acts can be as much as $25. Open every night.

The **Blue Note,** 131 W. 3rd St., between Sixth Avenue and Macdougal Street (tel. 475-8592), usually offers two complete shows every night of the week. Top-name entertainers like Dizzy Gillespie, The Modern Jazz Quartet, Ray Charles, and Nancy Wilson play regularly. On weekend afternoons there's usually a special brunch. Admission is typically somewhere between $20 and $40, depending on who's appearing. Add to that a $5 food and/or drink minimum. A jazz brunch on Saturday and Sunday is $14.50, for a show, brunch, and drink.

Fat Tuesday's, 190 Third Ave., between 17th and 18th Streets (tel. 533-7900), is an intimate jazz club. Management books top-name talent like the Les Paul

Trio on Monday nights, Ahmed Jamal, and Scott Hamilton. The music charge ranges from $15 to $25, and there's a $10 per-person minimum for food and/or drink.

Sweet Basil, 88 Seventh Ave. South, near Bleecker Street (tel. 242-1785), is also open every day of the week and presents two and sometimes three separate shows. People like Nat Adderley, McCoy Tyner, and Doc Cheatham perform regularly. The music charge is $15, to which you add a $6 drink minimum. Reservations are required.

---

6. Country & Western Clubs

The **Lone Star Roadhouse,** 240 W. 52nd St. (tel. 212/245-2950), with a facade that resembles a bus, is probably the best place in New York City to hear live country music. Their lineup includes bands like NRBQ, Donald Fagen, Marshal Tucker, Dan Hicks, and even the Kentucky Headhunters. There's a bar up front, while in the back is the stage with a big dance floor and lots of tables where you can enjoy dinner and the show. The Lone Star Roadhouse is open for happy hour and dinner, when the menu includes home-style favorites like chicken fried steak with gravy ($10.50), burgers served with cole slaw and fries ($7), and Cajun popcorn, which is spicy "crawfish" tails deep-fried and served with spicy hot sauce ($5.50). The music charge is $5 to $20 depending on the group. Open 5pm to 3am daily. Reservations advised; credit cards accepted.

O'Lunney's, 12 W. 44th St. (tel. 840-6688), is a laid-back spot featuring country acts like Ricky Vacca and Vicki Russel on Monday to Saturday. No cover and no minimum.

---

7. Cabaret & Supper Clubs

What has been fully restored to 1934 splendor, is two stories high, and has dozens of floor-to-ceiling windows overlooking one of the most magnificent skyline views in Manhattan? Answer: The **Rainbow Room,** 30 Rockefeller Plaza, 65th floor (tel. 632-5000). Dining here is quite literally a theatrical experience—waiters in pastel tails; a 32-foot revolving dance floor; terraced seating on three levels; a 12-piece orchestra; aubergine silk walls; oodles of 1930s glamour. Even the food is good. Full dinners, with main courses like steak with béarnaise sauce, lobster thermidor, or rack of lamb for two, are apt to cost $100 per person, including the $15-per-person cover charge. There's also a prix-fixe, pretheater dinner for about $40 a head. Besides dinner, one can also enjoy dancing Tuesday through Saturday and/or a cabaret called Rainbow and Stars ($35 cover). The Rainbow Room is open until 1am Tuesday through Saturday, and until midnight on Sunday. Closed Monday. Reservations a must.

The Ballroom, 253 W. 28th St., between Seventh and Eighth Avenues (tel. 244-3005), is part established restaurant, part cabaret presenting noted vocal and instrumental acts in a separate room. Peggy Lee, Martha Raye, Blossom Dearie, and Eartha Kitt are typical of the acts that have played here. Admission to the cabaret runs $20 (occasionally higher). Add to that a two-drink minimum, which can, however, be spent on *tapas* (small, Spanish-style appetizers). There are two shows a night, Tuesday through Saturday.

The **Oak Room** at the Algonquin Hotel, 59 W. 44th St., between Fifth and Sixth Avenues (tel. 840-6800), is the nighttime home of Julie Wilson, stylist and cabaret singer extraordinaire. Her material is very sophisticated stuff—Kurt Weill, Noël Coward—presented in elegant surroundings. She does have a marvelous touch. The music charge is $25, to which you add a $15-per-person minimum. Shows are Tuesday through Saturday.

The **Café Carlyle** in the Hotel Carlyle, entrance on Madison Avenue between

76th and 77th Streets (tel. 570-7189), is smallish and elite and usually presents the famous Bobby Short or someone of similar stature at the piano. Cover charge is $35 for Bobby Short Tuesday through Saturday, to which you'll usually add the cost of a deluxe dinner. Right across the hall is **Bemelmans Bar,** with more of the same Upper East Side atmosphere, plus a jazz pianist and a modest $5 cover Monday through Saturday. The café is closed on Sunday and Monday nights.

Last, but certainly not least, is **Chippendale's,** 1110 First Ave., near 61st Street (tel. 212/935-6060), whose "For Ladies Only" show has been packing 'em in since 1983. Chippendale's amusing print ads ("New York, where some men still take off their hats for a lady") tell only part of the story. These men take off a good deal more than their hats. Open from 6:30pm Wednesday through Saturday. Admission is $25, seating is on a first-come, first-served basis. There's an extra charge for ring and rail seating. After 10:30pm men are admitted. But during the show it's ladies only —and they mean it. Reservations required.

8. Comedy Clubs

Improvisation, 358 W. 44th St., between Eighth and Ninth Avenues (tel. 765-8268), is a showcase for new comics who haven't yet made it to the big time. Richard Pryor, Jerry Stiller, Anne Meara, David Brenner, Joe Piscopo, and many others have had their moments on the funky stage of the Improv. Food is available and cheap: Monday through Thursday the cover and minimum are each $9; on Friday, Saturday, and Sunday they're $12 and $9, respectively.

Catch a Rising Star, 1487 First Ave., between 77th and 78th Streets (tel. 794-1906), is a similar concept, with more-established comedians onstage. Open all week with a two-drink minimum and cover charge of $8 Sunday through Thursday and $12 on Friday and Saturday. Reservations must be made a day in advance.

Dangerfield's, 1118 First Ave., between 61st and 62nd Streets (tel. 593-1650), presents comedians from all over the country performing seven nights a week. You may or may not see comic-proprietor Rodney Dangerfield himself. There's a $12.50 cover Sunday through Thursday; $15 cover on Friday and Saturday.

9. Atmospheric Bars

For Edwardian-era plush, dark-wood paneling, and an atmosphere of oldtime big-city grandeur, try the **Oak Bar** in The Plaza Hotel, at Fifth Avenue and Central Park South (tel. 546-5330). One side is a restaurant; the other is a bar with numerous tables and leather chairs. This dimly lit and exceedingly popular watering spot is an appropriate place to linger over drinks and contemplate the majesty of the Big Apple.

The lobby of the **Algonquin Hotel,** 59 W. 44th St., between Fifth and Sixth Avenues (tel. 840-6800), is like a baronial living room in some English country mansion. It's filled with fashionable people in the arts and theater, coming and going. There are comfortable sofas and chairs scattered around, all within easy reach of little tables with attached bells for summoning the drink waiter. A superb place to meet your friends, have a nightcap after the theater, or soak up the sophisticated Manhattan atmosphere.

The **Hunt Bar** (not to be confused with Harry's Bar) upstairs in the New York Palace Hotel, Madison Avenue between 49th and 50th Streets (tel. 888-7000), used to be the wood-paneled dining room in a New York millionaire's mansion. It's small, elegant, and very comfortable. Its little groupings of upholstered furniture and atmosphere of grand luxe invite intimacy.

The **Four Seasons,** at 99 E. 52nd St., between Park and Lexington Avenues, is an enormous deluxe restaurant with a splendorous modern bar. Suspended above it are zillions of gleaming bronze rods that together form a fairly startling piece of modern sculpture. Lots of leather banquettes and chairs for those who don't like to sit on stools. Very sleek and sophisticated.

In the Theater District, a favorite is **Sardi's,** 234 W. 44th St., between Broadway and Eighth Avenue (tel. 221-8440). This elegant restaurant with adjacent bar is practically synonymous with New York theater folk and big-name entertainers.

The **Top of the Tower,** atop the Beekman Tower Hotel, 3 Mitchell Place, at the corner of First Avenue and 48th Street (tel. 355-7300), provides great city vistas from almost every table. It's actually an enclosed terrace surrounding the building's art deco pinnacle. Only open in the evening.

Clarke's (also known as P.J. Clarke's), 915 Third Ave., at the corner of 55th Street (tel. 759-1650), is a boisterous upscale saloon, complete with sawdust on the floor, carved woodwork that's black with age, a loud jukebox, and café tables with blue-checked cloths. Lots of singles here too, seemingly from the professional classes.

The **White Horse Tavern,** 567 Hudson St., at the corner of 11th Street (tel. 243-9260), is an old-time bar with lots of funky atmosphere and considerable Greenwich Village literary associations, notably with Dylan Thomas. It's especially nice if it's warm enough to sit outside at picnic tables and cool off with one of seven different draft beers. Or **McSorley's Old Ale House,** 15 E. 7th St., near the Bowery (tel. 473-9148), whose 19th-century saloon policies were intact to the point of prohibiting women until only a few years ago. And finally **Chumley's,** 86 Bedford St., at Barrow Street (tel. 675-4449), a dark, smoky pub hidden away in a courtyard that attracts oldtime Villagers and young movie stars.

All of these are good spots to hang out and, well, drink.

NEW YORK CITY SHOPPING

Any Western city as rich and populous as New York has got to have good shopping, almost by definition. On top of its wealth and size New York is also a major international port, a gateway to all the other consuming citizens of America. Many people come to New York for the sole purpose of shopping for things that are unavailable elsewhere. Perhaps you're one of these and know precisely where you're going as soon as you get off the plane.

This chapter, however, is for those who don't know much about New York City shopping. As such, it's an abbreviated orientation designed for visiting tourists, not a thorough directory for dedicated shoppers in search of rare or specialized goods.

The first section provides an overview of the famous department stores, in terms of what they've got and to whom they cater. The second section provides block-by-block tours of several of Manhattan's most celebrated shopping avenues. The third section is a guide to discount stores. The fourth section contains recommended antiques shops and flea markets. The fifth and last section is a directory of selected museum shops whose fine reproductions and giftwares make them good shopping destinations in and of themselves.

1. The Big Stores

BLOOMINGDALE'S
It's high-class without being swanky, deluxe without being exclusive, enormously large but still very stylish. Bloomingdale's local reputation rests on its fashionable clothing for men and women. It was the first store to present Ralph Lauren, Perry Ellis, Halston, Calvin Klein, and Yves Saint Laurent in on-site shops of their own. It has pioneered "country promotions," wherein the whole place is periodically inundated with goods from China, Ireland, Japan, India, and so on. The main

floor teems with people hurrying this way and that, especially up the glittering black-and-white marble-floored alley lined with opulent cosmetics counters. Other departments sell home furnishings, Waterford and Lalique crystal, gourmet foods, sportswear, telephone answering machines, and the like. Interpreters are on hand for foreign shoppers. And there are even four restaurants: the deluxe Train Bleu, Forty Carrots for health-food aficionados, the Espresso Bar for light Italian, and the Showtime Café for self-service snacks.

The main entrance to Bloomingdale's is on Lexington Avenue, between 59th and 60th Streets (tel. 705-2000). Open Monday to Wednesday and Friday from 10am to 7pm, Thursday until 9pm, Saturday and Sunday from 11:30am to 6pm.

SAKS FIFTH AVENUE

Saks has got a different atmosphere than Bloomies. It's deeper, more conservative, but somehow more lushly luxurious. Again, it's known primarily for its high-quality clothing for men and women. But unlike Bloomingdale's it has very few departments unrelated to clothing. (You can also buy things like gourmet chocolates, fine crystal, stationery, and a few other odds and ends.) The overwhelming emphasis is on deluxe clothing and accessories, from sportswear, designer clothes, and Vuitton luggage to lingerie, shoes, furs, estate jewelry, and so forth. No matter what it's on, a Saks label is certainly a flattering one to have in one's closet.

Saks' huge and glamorous Manhattan store is located in the middle of Midtown, on Fifth Avenue, between 49th and 50th Streets (tel. 753-4000). Open Monday to Wednesday and Friday and Saturday from 10am to 6:30pm, Thursday until 8pm, and Sunday from noon to 6pm.

MACY'S

This is the largest store in the world, each of whose nine floors contains three *acres* of retailing space. Not too many years ago Macy's reputation had sunk to that of a borderline bargain basement. But it has been substantially revamped and upgraded in recent years. Nowadays it has some departments that are as upscale as anything in Bloomingdale's.

And, boy, do they have a lot of stuff! You can buy gourmet cheeses; antiques; a fur coat; a home computer; toys; cosmetics; housewares; linens; shoes; luggage; sporting goods; rugs; and clothes for men, women, and children. This doesn't even begin to suggest the exceptional range of merchandise. One good measure of Macy's size is the fact that it contains six separate restaurants.

The main entrance is on Broadway between 34th and 35th Streets (tel. 695-4400). The store is open Sunday from 11am to 6pm; Tuesday, Wednesday, and Saturday until 7pm; and Monday, Thursday, and Friday until 8:30pm.

LORD & TAYLOR

There are now something like 46 Lord & Taylors across the country. But they all take their inspiration from the landmark store on New York's Fifth Avenue. This is the home of what management calls the "American Look," which is their way of describing prosperous conservatism. The majority of the merchandise consists of high-quality clothing for women, even though there are departments for men and children. You can buy outfits for posh country weekends, all manner of accessories, and of course, cosmetics. If you arrive at 9:30am, you'll be treated to a preshopping complimentary cup of coffee. At 10 o'clock sharp, the "Star-Spangled Banner" is played over the loudspeaker, everyone stands at attention, and only when the music is over does the shopping begin.

Lord & Taylor is on Fifth Avenue between 38th and 39th Streets (tel. 391-3344). It's open Tuesday, Wednesday, and Friday to Sunday from 10am to 6:45pm; Monday and Thursday until 8:30pm.

BERGDORF GOODMAN

Bergdorf's, the *ne plus ultra* of New York department stores, is not the sort of place to bother with branch locations. It's a perfectly gorgeous establishment filled with the most extravagant clothing and accessories money can buy. It's the only place in New York where, for example, you can purchase Turnbull & Asser shirts, Angela Cummings jewelry, or Galanos gowns. Also available are the clothing designs of Giorgio Armani, Calvin Klein, Donna Karan, and Christian Lacroix, each housed in a little boutique of its own. Bergdorf's has something for every rich person that he or she finds impossible to live without.

The main entrance to Bergdorf Goodman is on Fifth Avenue between 57th and 58th Streets (tel. 753-7300). Store hours are Monday to Wednesday and Friday and Saturday from 10am to 6pm, Thursday until 8pm. Across Fifth Avenue is Bergdorf Goodman Men, among whose amenities are portable telephones, a barbershop, and high-style fashions by the likes of Ralph Lauren, Luciano Barbera, and Giorgio Armani.

HENRI BENDEL

This elegant store in the landmark Coty Building intends to be everything to one customer, rather than a little bit of something to a lot of customers. That one customer, in the words of Bendel's former president Geraldine Stutz, is a "hip, big-city woman." She is also small (only sizes 2 to 10 are carried in the store), adventurous, and pretty rich. Bendel's (pronounced BEN-dels) was the first store to bring Chloë, Sonia Rykiel, and Dorothee Bis designs to New York. It has a reputation for deluxe avant-garde merchandise, most of which is women's clothing. Also in stock are gloves, bags, tableware, jewelry, linens, scarves, and stationery. It's a very inventive and exciting store.

Bendel's address is 712 Fifth Ave. at 56th Street (tel. 247-1100). Open Monday to Wednesday and Friday and Saturday from 10am to 6pm, Thursday until 8pm, and Sunday from noon to 6pm.

BARNEYS NEW YORK

This is a very big, very stylish, and very attractive department store that has been family run for a very long time. Barneys carries men's, women's, and children's designer clothes representing every American and international designer you can think of—Hermès, Ralph Lauren, Gianfranco Ferre, Giorgio Armani, and so on. This store has traditionally been a great place to buy a men's suit, and now they have just about anything else you can think of too. Even their own parking lot across the street, at their downtown location.

Barneys downtown is located at 106 Seventh Ave., between 16th and 17th Streets (tel. 929-9000), and uptown on Madison Avenue at 61st Street.

The new uptown location is the largest specialty store to open in New York City since 1929 and features nine floors of clothing, with half of the store devoted to menswear—plus a restaurant, café, and beauty salon. Hours for both locations are Monday through Thursday from 10am to 9pm, Friday and Saturday from 10am to 8pm, and Sunday from noon to 6pm.

---

2. Famous Shopping Avenues

MADISON AVENUE

From about 59th Street to about 80th Street, Madison Avenue offers the sort of shopping associated with world-class cities. It is primarily a street of exclusive designer clothing, antiques, and art, and the stores hereabouts obviously cater to the carriage trade. But even if you're not in the luxury league, a stroll up Madison will provide unsurpassed window-shopping opportunities. In fact, with the possible exception of the much shorter Rodeo Drive in Beverly Hills, there is no other street like this in the United States. Dedicated shoppers won't want to miss it. Besides, great buys are always to be had at sales, one or more of which may well be under way at the time of your visit.

We'll start our walk at Madison Avenue and the southwest corner of 58th Street

with **Eddie Bauer,** the adventure clothier. Across the street going toward 59th
Street is **Lederer,** for fine leather handbags and luggage; **Baccarat,** the famed French
crystal house; **Wolford,** for women's hosiery; and the rear entrance to **FAO Schwarz**
toy store, the savvy way to shop when the line is too long on Fifth.

Continuing north, to where the glass skyscrapers of Midtown give way to the
low-rise mansions of the East Side Historic District, you'll find **Bottega Veneta,** for
woven Italian leather goods, just before 60th Street. The big new **Barneys New
York** anchors 61st. **Jewelbox** is a tiny find, specializing in individual service for their
Greco-Roman-inspired 22-karat gold pieces. The international flair in this neighborhood is evident with **Bodum,** selling gourmet coffee; **Sherry-Lehman,** with the
most extensive wine selection in the city; **Le Bistro de Maxim's,** for a quick gourmet
bite, and **Maxim's Fleurs,** for flower arrangements with French flair; **Royal Copen-
hagen,** for fine china, crystal and silver; and **Robert Talbott,** a neckwear showcase.

Going toward 63rd, you may want to stop at **Baratti & Milano** for an espresso; **Nello**
for a light Italian lunch; **Floris** for the finest in English fragrance; **Daum** for crystal
with a twist of nature; **Stéphane Kelian** for the latest in French footwear; or **Tim-
berland** for rugged wear and hiking boots.

Just above 63rd Street, **Laura Ashley Home** is filled with chintz prints for
walls, floors, beds, sofas, and accent items. **E. Braun,** across the street, caters to those
who will sleep only on linen or silk. **M. J. Knoud** sells saddlery and apparel for the
horsey set, while **Sprei Frères** offers fur coats in winter and wraps in summer. **Pilar
Rossi** is the suitier of the ladies that lunch. Up the avenue, facing each other, is the
ultrahot jeweler **Demner,** with estate and new creations, and Greek **Lalaounis,** with
signature special pieces. **Manfredi** sells gems with an Italian flair. For fine French
linens and towels, stop by the **Leron** salon.

At 65th, a crop of new antiques and jewelry shops has sprung up, and between
them is a French clothing store for toddlers, **Lapin Lapin. Spectra** is a high-tech
electronic/spy shop. The all-weather leather line of **Dooney-Bourke** has its flagship
store here. **LS Collection** specializes in ultramodern home furnishings and
silverwear by top designers, such as Philippe Starck. **Charles Jourdan** and its smaller
Bis sell French-styled ladies' and men's shoes. **JF Lazartique** offers every tonic, po-
tion, and treatment for keeping hair, scalp, and skin as beautiful as possible.

Continuing past 66th Street, you'll find **North Beach Leather,** selling high-
styled leather clothing. **Fred Leighton** jewelers features bigger and more exquisite
baubles than you've ever seen. Luxury sportswear with a California look is at **Henry
Lehr.** Classic French knits are sold at **Sonia Rykiel.**

Haute couture designers are clustered on 72nd Street, with **Krizia, Valentino,
Ungaro, Giorgio Armani,** and **Gianni Versace** between 66th and 68th Streets.
Missoni, the Italian knitwear store, and **Pratesi,** Italian makers of bedding for royal-
ty, are both at 69th Street. At 70th Street, **Saint Laurent Rive Gauche** is almost a
block long and features men's and women's couture and sportswear. **Gianfranco
Ferre,** with pink-marble walls and silver accents, caters to those who must have
something but can't wait to go to Italy to get it. **Pierre Deux** sells French country
home furnishings, and the whole south end of 72nd Street is taken by **Ralph
Lauren's** mansion (formerly the Rhinelander) on the right and **Ralph Lauren Polo**
on the left.

Almost the entire western blockfront between 72nd and 73rd Streets is taken
up by **Sharper Image,** purveyors of high-tech, high-priced grownup toys.

Cross 74th Street and you'll come to the area known more for antiques and art
than for clothing. **Stair & Co.** and **Devenish** specialize in furniture for palaces. The
block from 74th to 75th Streets, besides being home to the famous Whitney Museum of American Art, contains **Antiquarium** (filled with fine ancient art) and **Len &
Gerry Trent** (a source of art nouveau objets and Tiffany lamps).

On the next block, **Givenchy's** showcase boutique takes up the southwest corner; **Delorenzo** has extravagant early 20th-century furniture; **Florian Papp** is known
for its fine English antiques; **Time Will Tell** is a shop full of antique wristwatches;
Vito Giallo is more of a unique gift shop, again with emphasis on antiques; and **Ari-
adne Galleries** sells rare sculptures.

That big modernish building between 76th and 77th Streets, opposite the Carlyle Hotel, used to be Parke Bernet. Now both it and the ground floor of the Carlyle contain exclusive art galleries. **Larry Gagosian's** base is here. The **Davlyn Gallery** (modern art), **Michael Weisbrod** (Chinese porcelain), and the **Pace Collection** (things deco) are only some of the establishments on this single block. **Vera Wang** showcases her couture wedding gowns here as well.

Other galleries of interest as you head northward from 77th Street are **Weintraub** (specializing in Botero and Calder), **Perls Galleries** (painting and sculpture), **Jacob Frères** (more furniture for palaces), **Kenneth Lux** (fine European paintings), and **E. & J. Frankel** (Chinese and Oriental fine arts). For reproduction pieces at great prices, **The Bombay Company** is a gem.

After 79th Street, Madison sombers somewhat. **Ann Taylor** and **Betsy Johnson** are outposts at 80th Street, and after these the glitter subsides. As the avenue continues north through Carnegie Hill (89th to 96th) there are many interesting small boutiques and neighborhood restaurants. This is actually a wonderful Manhattan neighborhood, much favored by prosperous families. But the world-class shopping definitely lies to the south.

COLUMBUS AVENUE

From 67th Street (across from Lincoln Center) to 80th Street, shopping on Columbus Avenue is an afternoon trip in itself. A range of small privately owned boutiques has sprung up, and with the mix of the shops that sell their own well-known labels, you can almost find anything here without parting with your life savings. On the weekend in warm weather, the sidewalks from 66th to 70th Streets jam with street vendors selling lots of stuff for $5—sunglasses, silver jewelry, neck beads, and braided ties. At 70th Street, **Nautica** features its brand of clothing, **Banana Republic** specializes in safari wear, and **Gap Kids** sells fashion for the little ones. **Dapy**, the fun neon-electronic store, is on the next block. Continuing to 72nd Street, you'll find **McNulty's** of Greenwich Village, which grinds gourmet coffee; **Swatch** sells its fun watches; **Betsy Johnson** offers the latest in Lycra chic; and **Charivari** features designs on the cutting edge for men and women.

An explosion of designer clothing starts at 72nd Street. First, stop at **The Silver Palate** for gourmet goodies. On the next block, shoes can be bought at **Wild Pair** for the funky or **Sacha of London** for the funkier. Menswear is at **Tommy Hilfiger.** Continuing north, **Faust** for women's clothing with European flair is at 75th Street. **Kenar, French Connection,** and **Oaktree** all have fashions of their own brand. **Variazioni** has womenswear with city savvy. On the next block, **The Gap** offers its staples. **Goodebodies** sells potions for skin and hair that are ecologically correct. **Eileen Fisher** offers California-style womenswear, and **Kenneth Cole** has shoes for both men and women. At 78th Street, **Alice Underground** is an old and famous post for true thrift-shop fashions, à la grunge. Right above 79th is **Laura Ashley,** for flowers on cotton everywhere. Although there are little shops to the north, the big labels stop here.

MIDTOWN FIFTH AVENUE

The very name is synonymous with luxury clothing and jewelry. But over the last 20 years most of the fashionable shops have moved to Madison Avenue. Great stores still remain on Fifth, but only on a relatively short stretch from the Plaza at 59th Street down to the region of Rockefeller Center at 49th Street.

We'll start at the top and work our way downtown. Between 60th and 59th Streets, on the ground floor of the Sherry Netherland Hotel, is **Geoffrey Beene's** couture salon as well as **A la Vieille Russie,** for malachite urns, satinwood marquetry commodes, and Fabergé eggs. Just looking in the windows is a treat if you're partial to exquisite small objects. Cross 59th Street heading south. The block from 58th to 59th on the east side of the street is occupied by the huge white-marble General Motors Building. The sunken plaza out front never quite developed into the exclusive plaza G.M. no doubt envisioned, but it does contain outposts of **Christine Valmy** (the skin-care specialists), **Vidal Sassoon** (of haircutting fame), plus assorted purveyors of jewelry and airline tickets. **FAO Schwarz,** the luxury toy store famous for its displays, occupies the south side of the G.M. Building's main level.

Between 58th and 57th Streets, Fifth Avenue is at its best. The east side of the block is the home of **Bergdorf's Men;** just next door is stiff competition from swanky **Ermenegildo Zegna;** that elegant building across Fifth Avenue on this same block is **Bergdorf Goodman,** perhaps the most posh specialty store in New York (see the previous section, "The Big Stores"). On the corner of 57th Street, at the southern end of the Bergdorf building, is **Van Cleef & Arpels,** a famous jewelry store whose windows are also worth a look.

Speaking of windows, across 57th Street is **Tiffany & Co.,** the world-famous jeweler whose small (and seemingly nuclear-proof) windows hold the sort of jewels worn by the haute monde, displayed with the most artistic elegance. Also on the block between 57th and 56th are **Salvatore Ferragamo** (designer clothes for men), **Doubleday** (a huge and fascinating bookstore), **Bulgari** (famous jewelry), **Fendi** (Italian leather shop), **Buccellati** (more jewels), **Charles Jourdan** (shoes that cost as much as jewels), **Asprey** (jewel-encrusted collectibles), and last but not least, **Trump Tower.** This latter structure contains an immense and glittery atrium filled with luxury shops.

Between 56th and 55th Streets is, first of all, the wonderful **Henri Bendel,** occupying landmark Fifth Avenue buildings, one of which contains a wall of Lalique glass windows. Across the street is another **Salvatore Ferragamo,** this one catering to women, in the **Steuben Glass** Building, which has an interesting gallery of glass objects. You're free to go in and browse around. Also on this block are **Harry Winston** (jewels for plutocrafts; can't just browse around in here), **Bally** (chic and sporty clothes and accessories for men and women), and finally **Nat Sherman,** tobacconist.

The block from 55th to 54th sports more than a few merchandising heavyweights. **Christian Dior** sells haute couture; **Godiva** sells the sorts of chocolates Marie Antoinette might have tried giving to the mob; **Bijan** is a men's boutique so exclusive that you must phone ahead for an appointment; **Wempe** is the place to buy a $10,000 Rolex watch; **Gucci** is, well, the prince of luxury leather goods (closed during lunch hour, since all its regular patrons are busy at swanky restaurants); and **Takashimaya,** is a Japanese department store and art gallery.

Between 54th and 53rd Streets, next to **Gucci,** is the big **Fortunoff** store selling everything from silver to jewelry to fabulous gifts. Fortunoff calls itself "the source," and for good gifts and durable luxuries at better prices, it's exactly that.

Books are the order of the day at **B. Dalton,** at 666 Fifth Ave. between 53rd and 52nd Streets. There aren't too many bookstores in the world that are quite this huge. Across 52nd Street is the limestone palace built for Morton Plant but occupied for 70 years by the fine jeweler **Cartier.** In an adjoining building on 52nd Street, between Fifth and Madison, is **Les Maisons de Cartier,** selling little things you *must* have (silver picture frames, bits of jewelry, little trays, amusing boxes, lighters). If you've detoured over to Les Maisons, you might as well duck into the pedestrian passage of the brown-glass Olympic Tower. This enclosed walkway, complete with potted palms, a splashing waterfall, benches, a florist, a Japanese restaurant, and a snack bar, connects 52nd and 51st Streets. It's a good place to stop and rest and perhaps contemplate the commercial glories around you.

Between 51st and 50th Streets are St. Patrick's Cathedral on one side of Fifth and a section of Rockefeller Center on the other. The shopping picks up again on the block between 50th and 49th, where you'll find **Saks Fifth Avenue** (see "The Big Stores), facing a row of specialty shops across the street in Rockefeller Center.

The corner of 49th Street is really the termination of ultrafashionable Fifth Avenue, at least as far as shopping is concerned. Great stores like **Lord & Taylor** do, of course, exist south of here. But the street lacks the intensity of those blocks in the 50s through which you've just strolled.

Before leaving Fifth Avenue, book lovers should have a look at **Barnes & Noble,** between 49th and 48th Streets. It's really a huge supermarket for books. Besides cutrate bestsellers, this is a good place to pick up remainders of lavish coffeetable books for a fraction of the cover prices. Across the street is the splendid old Scribner's bookstore, still selling books, but now called **Brentano's.**

South of 48th Street, Fifth Avenue begins literally to get "shiny patches" like a too-old suit. These are in the form of too brightly lit discount houses, often with banners proclaiming a "Going Out of Business" sale. The curious thing is that this type of establishment never actually seems to close permanently. Instead it continues "Going Out of Business" indefinitely. There are interesting stores below 48th, however, especially on Lower Fifth Avenue (see below).

At the corner of Fifth and 47th Street is the **International Jewelers Exchange,** which forms the portal to 47th Street, New York's fabled **Diamond District.** Extending only from Fifth Avenue to Sixth Avenue, this block contains hundreds upon hundreds of individual dealers whose sole business is buying and selling diamonds, gold, and silver. Picturesque Hasidic Jews, in beaver hats, long coats, and flowing beards, bustle back and forth across the crowded pavements. One could easily spend hours going to all the kiosks and trying on or just browsing. Unobtrusive plainclothes police will swoop out of nowhere if a known criminal has the bad judgment to set foot on this block.

57TH STREET

From Third Avenue to Sixth Avenue, 57th Street offers some of New York's most sophisticated shopping for clothes, precious antiques, and gifts. There is definitely a "57th Street Style"—the "real" thing is the only thing you'll find on 57th Street. The rents are too high for anything else.

On the north side of the block between Third and Lexington Avenues is **Hammacher Schlemmer,** source of things like James Bondian adult toys, poolside elves, luxe sporting goods, and lawn chairs. With a few exceptions, like **Neslé** for chandeliers and other cut-glass objets d'art, the rest of the block is not so interesting.

Between Lexington and Park Avenues, is **Places des Antiquaires,** a mall filled with fine art and antiques, and **Gazebo,** a home furnishings store with lots of pastel quilts, handmade dolls, and wicker. **Peal** sells cashmere; **Dempsey and Carroll** has been a custom stationer since 1878; **S. J. Shrubsole** has a window full of antique English silver that's almost beyond imagination, and **David Webb** has animal-inspired jewelry.

The block between Park and Madison Avenues is the epicenter of fashionable 57th Street shopping. Right in the middle of all this is the new **Four Seasons Hotel** designed by I. M. Pei, with the largest "standard" rooms in the city. **Sherle Wagner** deals in fantasy bathroom fixtures; **Orrefors** is a gallery of crystal; **Alfred Dunhill** is the British haberdasher transplanted here to New York; the silversmith **Buccellati** might have a life-size boxer dog made of sterling; **Guy Laroche** has sports couture for women; **Louis Vuitton** is headquarters for top-of-the-line luggage; **Victoria's Secret** is famous for luxury lingerie; **Ghurka** has high-styled, sturdy luggage; **Diego della Valle** has shoes and exquisite accessories; **Prada** features Italian fashions for women plus matching footwear; **Celine** has handbags and accessories heavy on ornamentation; and **Sheridan** (on the northeast corner of 57th Street) has a big selection of designer linens, quilts, and bedspreads.

After a block like that it's hard to summon the energy to continue. Yet 57th between Madison and Fifth is still quite fabulous. A few of the highlights would include **Laura Ashley** for clothing and accessories with her English country accent; **James Robinson** for more extraordinary English silver and table settings; **Hermès** with its famous leather goods; the properly elegant furnishings for men and women at **Burberry's; Chanel** for Lagerfeld's latest; plus designer clothes for women at **Escada** and **Ann Taylor;** not to mention **Tiffany & Co.,** a New York City institution that also happens to be on this block.

Fifth Avenue and 57th Street is no longer the geographical heart of Manhattan's elite retail district, whose center of gravity has shifted northward up Madison. But it remains a mighty glittering intersection, with Tiffany's and Bergdorf's commanding its opposite corners.

Now then, on to the block between Fifth and Sixth Avenues. The stores closest to Fifth are much like their counterparts on the Madison-Fifth block. **Van Cleef & Arpels** (in the Bergdorf building) sells incredible jewels; **Bulgari** (on the southwest corner) sells even bigger rocks; **Sharper Image** is next door; **Charivari** sells the trendiest clothes; **Susan Bennis Warren Edwards** sells 57th Street–type shoes; and **Rizzoli** is the famous and beautiful international bookstore, open every day of the week.

Sixth Avenue marks the western boundary of the fashionable shopping district on 57th Street. But worth a look, since you've gone this far, is the **Ritz Thrift Shop,** just a few steps off Sixth Avenue. The sign says it all: "Slightly Used Furs at a Fraction of Their Original Cost." It's doubtful anyone could tell the difference.

LOWER FIFTH AVENUE

The stretch of Fifth between 23rd and 14th Streets has undergone a remarkable renaissance. Suddenly (and unexpectedly) it has become an interesting place to shop. It is still filled with the fine bookstores, but now there is a new infusion of ultrafashionable clothing stores and amusing theme and accessory shops. The area is compact, contains establishments selling things in all price ranges, and best of all it's *unusual*. In fact, I doubt you'll find another retailing area outside New York with so much unpretentious style.

The district begins at 23rd Street in the base of the Flatiron Building. Built in 1902, this much-loved landmark is noted for its triangular shape, an architectural adaptation to the plot of land upon which it stands. On the main floor is **C.P. & Company,** typical of the new retailers in the area, selling sporty safari-type and casual clothes for men and women. Part of the charm of lower Fifth is that so much of the ungentrified past remains; delis, discount houses, and a place called **Scuba Network** (for underwater types) still remain on this block.

Between 22nd and 21st are all manner of unusual shopping opportunities: **Medici** specializes in "au courant" fashion and shoes for men and women; **BFO** and **Moe Ginzburg** have discounted men's clothing; and **Elor de Mexico** has exotic cigars.

Between the travel agencies and pharmacies on the 21st to 20th block are stylish new arrivals: **Matsuda,** whose mannequins (male and female) wear intimidatingly chic outfits; **Laise Adzer,** for Arabesque womenswear; and **Otto Tootsi Plohound,** for the latest in avant-garde shoes. The 20th to 19th block is mostly full of things like computer stores and copy centers. But there's also a very smart women's clothier called **Barami Studio.**

The 19th to 18th block begins to get literary, which is what the district used to be known for prior to the onset of the new fashionability. The **Librarie de France** and **Libreria Hispanica** occupy the same premises, which is full of maps and books in French and Spanish. Also on this block is one of those innovative New York–type retailers called **Daffy's,** which in this case sells "clothing bargains for millionaires." There's a huge sales floor and browsing is lots of fun.

Eighteenth Street is the center of the literary district hereabouts. **Barnes & Noble,** the "world's largest bookstore," occupies the southeast corner of 18th and Fifth, and the Barnes & Noble **Sale Annex** is directly across Fifth—both great for browsing. Farther down the block toward 17th Street is another chic clothing emporium called **Eileen Fisher,** an outpost of **The Gap,** and an entire store devoted to computer software called (not surprisingly) **Software, Etc.**

Worth knowing about in this vicinity is the **Book Friends Café,** 16 W. 18th St. (tel. 255-7407), which specializes in belle epoque literature and biography, and serves high tea, low-priced lunches, and interesting wines in a charming café adjacent to the bookshelves. This is an excellent place to soak up literary atmosphere and get a bite to eat at the same time. All manner of unusual programs are offered as well, such as talks by authors, tea dances, etc. The block on which it is located also contains a number of other interesting bookstores.

Returning to Fifth Avenue, and the block between 17th and 16th Streets, you'll find **Kenneth Cole** (new-age shoes), the huge and terribly handsome **Emporio Armani** (Italian designer clothing by Giorgio Armani), **Banana Republic** (safari clothing), plus a famous New York institution for party favors and novelties called **B. Shackman.**

The 16th to 15th block, in between Blimpies fast food and banks from the old days, also contains **Paul Smith,** purveyor of clothes for the fashionable downtown man, and **Joan and David,** shoes for the elite of both sexes. **Vidal Sassoon** is on the block between 15th and 14th Streets, but by the time you reach this point, the show is pretty much over. If you're any kind of shopper, however, you must have at least one bagful of goodies.

---

3. Discounts

CENTURY 21

Century, as city-dwellers call it, is jammed with designer clothing for men and women with all the labels intact. Coming here will make you never want to shop retail again. For women, on any given day, there will be racks loaded with top designers like Lacroix, Montana, Ferre, Moschino, Mugler, and even Chanel cashmere! I'm talking merchandise from the main collection too, not the "second line." A suit that would cost $2,100 retail could cost as low as $150 here. The men's department also features hot designers of the moment, such as Gaultier, Moschino, and Dolce & Gabbana. For those who aren't into high fashion, they have everything from discount perfumes; to toiletries; underwear; socks; tennis clothing; white T-shirts; well-known mainstream labels like Levi's, Liz Claiborne, Izod Lacoste, Fila, and Tahari; plus brands from Europe you've probably never heard of. This is a must for the bargain hunter! Century has two locations, in Manhattan at 22 Cortlandt St., between Broadway and Church (tel. 227-9092), and in Bay Ridge, Brooklyn, at 472 86th St. (tel. 718/748-3266). Hours in Manhattan are Monday to Friday from 8am to 7pm and Saturday from 10am to 6pm. In Bay Ridge, hours are Monday to Friday from 8am to 7pm, Saturday from 10am to 9pm, and Sunday from 10am to 6pm. The Manhattan store, by the way, is larger and has a wider selection. Have fun!

LOEHMANN'S

The Bronx flagship store of this famous nationwide chain has recently moved from Fordham Road to Riverdale. It's a bit of a trek from Midtown, but worth the trip. Loehmann's is a fabulous source of bargains, filled with high-fashion designer clothes for women, some minus the labels, and priced at a fraction of their original cost. Knowledgeable shoppers will be in heaven. The store is located at 5740 Broadway at the corner of West 236th Street in Riverdale. You can take the no. 1 train to the West 238th Street stop (or take a fairly pricey taxicab). The hours are Monday through Saturday from 10am to 9pm, on Sunday from 11am to 6pm. VISA, MasterCard, and Discover cards accepted.

RICHARDS ARMY-NAVY & AQUALUNG CENTER

This place stocks military-surplus stuff like regulation pea jackets, "military-chic" items like flight jackets and camouflage fatigues, as well as jeans, fashion swimsuits, and footwear. Richards is the largest supplier of scuba-diving equipment in the United States.

The store is at 233 W. 42nd St., between Seventh and Eighth Avenues (tel. 947-5018), and the hours are Monday through Wednesday from 9:15am to 7pm, Thursday through Saturday to 7:30pm.

CANAL JEAN

Besides tons of discounted jeans, this place has sportswear, T-shirts, hiking boots, vintage sunglasses, beach towels, knit sweaters, and more. It's at 504 Broadway, between Spring and Broome Streets (tel. 226-1130), and the hours are 10am to 8pm daily.

ORCHARD STREET

Every Sunday, half a dozen blocks of Orchard Street (located on the Lower East Side, parallel to and five blocks east of the Bowery, between Houston and Grand streets) are closed to traffic. The street is lined with little discount clothing shops on the ground floors of old tenement buildings, and on Sunday the goods spill right out onto the sidewalk, creating an open-air bargain bazaar. Every conceivable item of clothing, from jeans to exotic designer dresses, and even specialty fabrics, appears to be available. The crowds are huge, the competition stiff, and the haggling intense. The stores are open on other days as well. But a visit on Sunday will be as much a sightseeing experience as an excursion for bargains.

---

4. Antiques & Flea Markets

MANHATTAN ART & ANTIQUE CENTER

Most Manhattan antiques stores are scattered around the city in no particular district. This center brings together 120 dealers, each occupying his or her own shop on the main floor and two concourse levels of a Midtown high-rise. There is everything here from rare paintings to antique jewelry, from bronze sculpture to quilts, from Tiffany glass to Oriental rugs. Prices range from $10 to $300,000. At the very least it's a good browse.

The center is located at 1050 Second Ave., at 56th Street (tel. 355-4400). It's open Monday to Saturday from 10:30am to 6pm, Sunday from noon to 6pm.

BLEECKER STREET

The six blocks of Greenwich Village's Bleecker Street between Abingdon Square and Seventh Avenue South contain a fair collection of antiques shops. Some are not too expensive. Starting at Abingdon Square, **Hamilton Hyre Ltd.** (413 Bleecker) sports windows full of faux bamboo desks, Empire chandeliers, and unusual bibelots; **Treasures and Trifles** (409 Bleecker) has lots of crystal chandeliers, Louis XVI bergères, and bronze and crystal objects; **Susan Parrish** (390 Bleecker) has antique American quilts, folk art, and American Indian art; **American Folk Art** (374 Bleecker) displays Americana, old signs, and quilts; **Pierre Deux** (369 Bleecker), home of the French country look, has scrubbed pine chests and long country tables, Provençal fabrics, and home accessories; **Niall Smith** (344 Bleecker) offers busts, statues, urns, and bronzes; **Dorothy's Closet** (335 Bleecker) is full of vintage clothes and 1950s dining-table accessories; **The Antique Buff** (321½ Bleecker) has tons of "smalls," from cases full of antique jewelry to crystal perfume bottles to little things made out of silver and glass and porcelain; and **Tim McKoy** (318 Bleecker) sells statues, gargoyles, and other dramatic architectural elements in wood and stone. There are plenty of other stores as well, but this should give an idea of the area's flavor.

THE ANNEX

This unlikely name attaches itself to an outdoor flea market and adjacent antiques bazaar. Both are held every Saturday and Sunday, year-round, from 9am to 5pm in a parking lot on the corner of Sixth Avenue and 25th Street (tel. 243-5343). Dealers from all over the place come with furniture, Oriental rugs, antique dolls, bric-a-brac, bronzes, silver, jewelry, you name it. A small entrance fee is charged to the antiques fair, mostly to discourage marauding kids.

GREEN FLEA

At Columbus Avenue, between 76th and 77th Streets, every Sunday from 10am to 5pm, (tel. 721-0900, Monday through Wednesday from 10am to noon only), this is one of the best flea markets around, especially if you love to browse. There are about 300 or so vendors, many of them regulars, with a wide variety of antique "stuff." One dealer specializes in watches from the 1920s, '30s, and '40s. There are lots of large collections of old jewelry—Victorian earrings, huge '40s brooches and necklaces, lots of Bakelite jewelry, and radios too. Another dealer has Amish quilts, country quilts, quilt tops, antique tablecloths, linens, lace pillows, and on and on. The variety is wide and the prices go anywhere from $5 to $5,000.

5. Museum Shops

Almost every big museum in town has a lobby gift shop stocked with reproductions of items in the collections, plus posters, prints, books, and so forth. One of the finest and largest is that of the **Metropolitan Museum of Art,** Fifth Avenue at 82nd Street (tel. 879-5500). This place has perfectly beautiful things, plus an especially inventive collection of children's books. The **Museum of Modern Art,** 11 W. 53rd St., between Fifth and Sixth Avenues (tel. 708-9700), has a shop that's pretty extensive. This is a great place for beautiful art publications relating to "MoMA" collection and for household items made with form and function in mind. Also intriguing is the shop at the **Cooper-Hewitt Museum,** Fifth Avenue at 91st Street (tel. 860-6878), whose merchandise reflects the museum's commitment to preserve and disseminate fine designs.

It's a good idea to explore the museum shop at every museum you visit. They're all interesting, if only for postcards. These three are worth special trips.

SUBURBAN LONG ISLAND: NASSAU & WESTERN SUFFOLK COUNTIES

1. WHAT TO SEE & DO
2. SELECTED SUBURBAN ATTRACTIONS
3. WHERE TO STAY & EAT

I love Long Island: It is historic, congested, luxurious, educational, occasionally exasperating, and possessed of enough attractions to gratify everyone from aesthete to sybarite. There's one thing about the Island for which you'd better be prepared from the outset—the traffic. There are wonderful expressways all over the place, but they typically bottle up at least twice a day at rush hour and sometimes come to a complete halt at more unexpected hours as well. How can there possibly be a traffic jam at three in the morning, you may ask yourself as you sit stock still in a line of cars on the Long Island Expressway. Answer: I don't know, but sometimes it happens.

Explosive population growth has a lot to do with it. When poet Walt Whitman lived here and called the island by its Indian name, "Paumanok," it was a vast farming area with a population of only a little over 100,000 souls. There are 118 miles of plains and rolling woodlands between the East River and Montauk Point. Even though it's never more than 20 miles wide, nobody was very crowded. Then came the rapid urban growth and suburban sprawl of the early 20th century. The economic engine of Manhattan directed much of this out onto the island, and by 1950 the population had topped 670,000. Then, in a boom unprecedented in history, the population doubled by 1960. And then it doubled *again* by 1980. There are now more than 2.7 million people living on old Paumanok.

How amazing it is to discover that Suffolk County still remains the largest agricultural producer, based on the wholesale value of its farm products, in the state of New York. Or that grape growing and vineyards are currently a Long Island growth industry. Or that numerous spacious and luxurious country estates (some private, some open to the public) still survive within 20 miles of Queens.

Between Jericho Turnpike (Route 25) and the shore of Long Island Sound, there is more open woodland than you might suspect. It belongs to various nature conservancies, county parks, and a fair number of remaining private estate owners.

Notwithstanding these anomalies, however, the bulk of suburban Long Island, especially the area south of Jericho Turnpike, is very densely developed. The tractless former potato fields around towns with names like Farmingdale and Hicksville have long ago sprouted a permanent crop of split levels.

Any Long Island–bound traveler who plans ahead, for business or for pleasure, will want to know about the very helpful **Long Island Convention and Visitors Bureau.** It has all manner of printed material about Long Island, including brochures, a Long Island travel guide, and an especially useful quarterly calendar of events. They'll gladly send it to you, free of charge, if you call 516/794-4222, or toll free at 800/441-4601, or write The Long Island Convention and Visitors Bureau, Nassau Coliseum, 1255 Hempstead Turnpike, Uniondale, NY 11553. From about Memorial Day to Labor Day, the bureau also maintains two information centers. Each is located on a major parkway, staffed by helpful attendants, and stocked with all manner of interesting brochures and pamphlets. One is at Exit 13 on the eastbound lanes of the Southern State Parkway in Valley Stream; the other is between Exits 52 and 53 on the Long Island Expressway in Commack. Hours are somewhat flexible, but you can usually count on someone being on hand most summer days from late morning until the close of business.

---

1. What to See & Do

One end of Long Island actually faces Manhattan across the East River. However, over in Brooklyn and Queens people never think of themselves as being on Long Island. No, one must first travel approximately 14 miles to the Nassau County line; cross over it on parkway (the local name for restricted-access highway), path, or foot; and only then will one have arrived on Long Island. Even though the island technically contains four counties (Brooklyn, Queens, Nassau, and Suffolk), only two (Nassau and Suffolk) are considered by the locals to be on Long Island. Curious, but that's the way it is.

So what is there to do out here? Well, first of all there are the beaches, some of which actually lie within the borders of New York City. It comes as a surprise to many out-of-towners to learn that broad expanses of sand and Atlantic surf are readily accessible by public transit. Even though a day at the beach isn't on your typical New York City itinerary, you can have it if you wish. Details follow below.

After the beaches I'd have to say that the so-called Gold Coast along the North Shore of Nassau County qualifies as the next-greatest attraction. This region, to use a recognizable term, is "Gatsby country." Of course, F. Scott Fitzgerald's Gatsby was a poor boy turned gangster who tried to woo a rich girl by throwing big parties in a showy house. Most of the real people who built estates on the North Shore were more substantial individuals. It is accepted doctrine that all the great houses of the era between the turn of the century and the 1929 Crash have been either razed or turned into schools. Not true. More than you think are still in private hands. And many others are open to the public as house-and-garden museums that provide vivid glimpses of the Gilded Age.

Then there are the museums, more than one could possibly hope to see. It would take an avid historian indeed to plow through all of them. Some are quite unusual. One, for example, is an entirely preserved farming village where costumed "inhabitants" trudge around hauling butter churns or spinning thread or shoeing horses. You'd never know it, standing in the middle of this place, that beyond the crests of the nearby sandy hills lie Levittown and Massapequa, places not noted for their rural associations. Other museums contain artifacts from Long Island's daredevil whaling days; another contains a millionaire natural historian's cache of marine life specimens housed in his former baronial home; yet another was the former summer White House in the days of Teddy Roosevelt.

An area as rich and populous as suburban Long Island also supports major classical and pop cultural events, shopping on a grand scale, and sports facilities catering to a huge, sophisticated market. I've included suggestions on some of these below.

2. Selected Suburban Attractions

BEACHES

As mentioned earlier, a number of beaches are actually within New York City limits. In fact, every borough but Manhattan has at least a couple. They vary widely in desirability, however. Of the bunch, my favorites are Rockaway Beach and Riis Park, both located in Queens on a slender, sandy finger of land that forms the southern border of Jamaica Bay.

Perhaps the most appealing—and on weekends the busiest—is that part of **Rockaway Beach** that adjoins the neighborhoods of Belle Harbor and Seaside, between about Beach 88th and Beach 118th Streets. These are comfortable middle-class areas that don't look a lot different from many inland tracts in Queens. You can take a subway practically to the line of the surf; the A train goes right to Beach 116th Street. And there are plenty of facilities for snacks and seaside diversions.

About a mile and a half to the west is **Riis Park,** now part of Gateway National Recreation Area. Gateway is operated by the federal government, is patrolled by park rangers in Smokey the Bear hats, and comprises a hodgepodge of rescued undeveloped tracts situated at or near the entrance to New York Harbor. Riis Park was a public beach long before Gateway was established. Indeed, it includes a noble (if tattered) bathhouse in high-1930s style. The beach is broad and sandy, and instead of adjacent bedroom communities there's parking for 9,000 cars. The western fringe of Riis Park, close to Fort Tilden, is what the local press calls the "land of the total tan," in case that's of interest. You can reach Riis Park by car via the Belt Parkway, which follows the bulge of the Brooklyn shoreline, to the Riis Park–Marine Parkway Bridge exit. If you take the A train to Beach 116th Street in Rockaway, you'll have to transfer to a Q35 bus for the mile-or-so trip to Riis.

But beaches on the Rockaway Peninsula, albeit close and nice, are mere antipasti to New York's big beach experience: That's **Jones Beach,** located about 25 miles from Midtown as the crow flies, in the southeastern corner of Nassau County. Jones Beach is a state park surrounded by sand dunes instead of housing projects. It's open all year, but lifeguards are on duty only from May 24 to September 1. It's a huge place, with six parking fields holding a total of 23,000 cars, eight Atlantic beaches, two Olympic-size pools, snackbars, a restaurant, a cocktail lounge, ball fields, pitch 'n putt golf, lockers, showers, and so on. There's even the **Jones Beach Theater,** which throws rock and pop concerts during the summer. Recent acts have included Bonnie Raitt, the B-52's, Paula Abdul, and Rush. Call 516/221-1000 for current program information.

Fortunately, the beach is magnificent enough not to be overpowered by all this. If you want easy access to hot dogs and the boardwalk, park in field 4 or 5. The crowds are thinnest over by field 6 at the eastern end of the beach. A half mile past field 6 is, unless people complain, the local no-swimsuit land. Wherever you settle, the sand is gorgeous and white, and the surf is at times pretty big.

Two major parkways, the Wantagh State and the Meadowbrook State, connect Jones Beach State Park to two of Long Island's major east-west arteries, namely, the Southern State and the Northern State Parkways. The drive would be short and simple were it not for the traffic. How long does it take to drive 25 or so miles across Queens and Nassau Counties on a sunny Saturday in July? That's a question with no answer. If you drive during the week, at least the beach won't be crowded.

Alternately, you can take advantage of the Long Island Rail Road's summertime Jones Beach excursion fare. Round trip from Penn Station (32nd Street and Seventh Avenue) costs about $11 for adults and $4 for kids under 11. Actually, you just take the regular train to Freeport, a former fishing village engulfed by postwar suburbia, where you pick up a shuttlebus to the beach. During July and August trains leave almost every half hour, at least on weekends. The trip takes something under an hour and a half each way. There's no charge to use Jones Beach once you get there, but it does cost 50¢ to swim in the pools. For exact train times, call either of

Amagansett ③	Jones Beach ㉔
Beach Hampton ②	Jones Beach Theater
Bridgehampton ⑨	Levittown ㉒
Centerport ⑮	Lloyd Harbor ⑱
The Vanderbilt Museum	The Lloyd Manor Houses
Cold Spring Harbor ⑰	Montauk ①
Whaling Museum	Montauk Point State Park
East Hampton ⑤	Old Bethpage Village ㉓
Clinton Academy	Old Westbury ㉑
"Home Sweet Home" Museum	Oyster Bay ⑲
Fire Island ⑬	Planting Fields Arboretum
Fire Island National Seashore	Raynham Hall
Robert Moses State Park	Sagamore Hill National
Sunken Forest	Historic Site
Greenport ⑧	Sag Harbor ⑥
Huntington Station ⑯	The Custom House
Walt Whitman House	Sag Harbor Whaling
	and Historical Museum

the Long Island Rail Road's 24-hour information numbers: 516/822-5477 or 718/217-5477.

If you've come by car, a few other (and at times less crowded) beaches can be found just to the east of Jones Beach down Ocean Parkway. **Gilgo Beach** is a surfer haven in a Town of Babylon beach. Unfortunately, nonresident parking fees are high. If you hanker for the full state park complement of bathhouse/snackbar/ ballpark and so forth, you might also check out **Robert Moses State Park,** about 6 miles east of Gilgo. Like Jones, Moses is open daily all year, has lifeguards between May 24 and September 1, and charges $4 per car. It's located on the westernmost tip

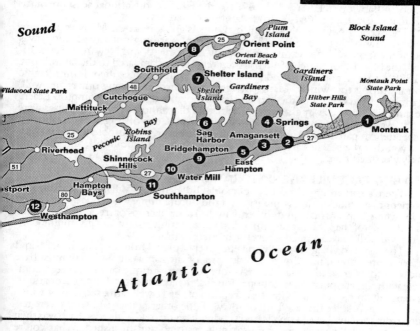

of auto-free Fire Island, and its parking lots are about the only place on that island where cars are permitted.

Two further items before we leave the subject of beaches: The first concerns Robert Moses State Park, which contains a vintage lighthouse in addition to the fine white sands. The **Fire Island Lighthouse** was constructed in 1858, at a time when Fire Island was about the wildest, most remote locale that one could imagine. Today, it and the former keeper's quarters have been restored and transformed into a fascinating museum—definitely something to vary the day's routine at the beach. Admission is free (although donations are welcome), and the hours are five days a week from 9:30am to 5pm. You can call either the Fire Island Lighthouse Preservation Society in Babylon (tel. 516/321-7028) or the Fire Island National Seashore office in Patchogue (tel. 516/661-4876) to confirm closed days.

The second point applies to all of Long Island's beaches. Many readers are doubtless aware that the 1992–93 winter (global warming notwithstanding) was one of the most severe, weather-wise, of any in the history of New York State. Indeed, the blizzard of March 1993 has been repeatedly compared to the famous one of 1888, and with good cause. Long Island's beautiful beaches suffered considerable erosion during this winter. Many emerged unscathed, but many others are, well, "narrower." On certain of the barrier islands, notably that at Westhampton Beach, the sand was washed away altogether. We're told that almost a hundred houses were lost at Westhampton. As of this writing, the Army Corp of Engineers is laboring desperately to patch the island back together. However, the purpose of this is to assure you that the beaches are still there (or mostly so), still beautiful, and still definitely worth visiting.

OLD BETHPAGE VILLAGE RESTORATION

There's something almost eerie about Old Bethpage Village Restoration. A moment may come during your visit, as it did during mine, when no tourists are in sight, when there are no sounds other than the rustle of crops or trees, and when not a single trace of the 20th century intrudes. For a fleeting instant you just might wonder if you really have stepped across the barriers of time.

The restored village is wisely and effectively isolated from its parking fields and visitor center. You tramp down a sandy road, of the sort Walt Whitman must have known and loved, and presto: There before you is an antique farming village, complete with rural population in antique clothing engaged in typical rural occupations, depending on the season. With the exception of the Powell farm, sections of which have been here since the late 18th century, all the other houses and stores were rescued from the clutches of Long Island subdividers and road wideners. Each was then moved to Old Bethpage and painstakingly restored and furnished. What you're looking at is a pretty thorough reconstruction of a pre–Civil War village, although strictly speaking no such village ever really stood here.

All sorts of things are going on in Old Bethpage Village, and you'll want to allot about three hours to do the place properly. If you come in May, you'll see a Union Army training center beside the village; in June, there's a Spring Festival with an historical horticultural show; during August, competing teams play baseball according to 1860 rules; October means the Long Island Fair, done à la 1860. The village is open all year, and something different happens every month. Incidentally, this is not a privately owned theme park but rather a property of the Nassau County Museum Division. There's a total absence of Disney glitz—this is all the real stuff.

Old Bethpage Village Restoration is located on the eastern border of Nassau County, on Round Swamp Road, just south of exit 48 on the Long Island Expressway. From June until the end of August, it is open Wednesday to Sunday from 10am to 5pm; during the rest of the year, hours are the same days from 10am to 4pm. Admission is $5 for adults, $3 for children and seniors. The telephone number is 516/572-8400.

OLD WESTBURY GARDENS

Less than 10 miles from the border of Queens is one of the most fabulous estates ever developed on Long Island's North Shore. It has survived virtually in its entirety and is now open to the public.

Originally called Westbury House, this was the Long Island residence of John S. Phipps (1874–1958) and his wife, Margarita Grace Phipps (1876–1957). He was the son of Carnegie partner Henry Phipps; she was one of the Graces of shipping-line fame. The house they built in 1906 is about the most sumptuous Georgian Revival mansion one can imagine. It still has all its original gilt-framed oils, English antiques, brocaded curtains, crystal chandeliers, and overscale chintz-covered furniture. But more incredible than this truly palatial house are the magnificent grounds that complement its formal architecture. There are a two-acre walled garden complete with ornamental pools and statues, a boxwood garden, a temple of love, a woodland walk, a cottage garden with a little girl's thatched cottage, and even a ghost walk complete with bronze peacocks with topiary tails. The view from the rear of the house across a huge lawn and down an allee of linden trees is the sort of vista one associates with Versailles.

The above description does not at all do justice to Westbury House. It's an extraordinary place, filled with good backdrops for pictures. Besides the house and grounds, there's a busy schedule of lectures, workshops, and concerts held pretty much throughout the year. The estate is open from 10am to 5pm Wednesday through Monday from early April through mid-December. Admission to the gardens is $5 for adults and $1.50 for children 6 to 12. To tour the inside of the house you'll pay an additional $3 for adults and $1.50 for kids 6 to 12. There are two shops, a snackbar, and picnic areas on the grounds.

Old Westbury Gardens is located on Old Westbury Road, just south of the Long Island Expressway. Get off the expressway at exit 39 and continue for about a mile on the eastbound service road. You'll see Old Westbury Road on your right. For information about the estate or the concerts, call 516/333-0048.

SAGAMORE HILL

This rambling stone-and-shingle Victorian mansion was the summer home of Theodore Roosevelt, former assistant secretary of the navy, lieutenant colonel of the Rough Riders, governor of New York State, president of the United States, and lifelong proponent of the "strenuous life." Here Roosevelt, his wife, and their six children spent the summers hiking, swimming, shooting, riding horseback, and entertaining important personages of the day.

The house, museum, and 89 acres are administered by the National Park Service and have been open to the public since the early 1960s. The newly restored interior boasts dramatic rooms paneled in swamp cypress, mahogany, and black walnut and furnished with big-game trophies and Victorian antiques. It's an eminently livable house, most evocative of the dynamic and patrician American family that built it and loved it for so many years.

Sagamore Hill is located at 20 Sagamore Hill Road, just outside the village of Oyster Bay. Take the Long Island Expressway to exit 41 North, then follow Rte. 106 north to Oyster Bay. At the third traffic light, turn right and follow the signs to Sagamore Hill (tel. 516/922-4447). The estate is open daily from 9:30am to 5pm all year long; entrance fee is $2.

Oyster Bay retains a slightly ramshackle country look in spite of all the postwar development on Long Island. It's still surrounded by fine country estates tucked away behind impressive walls and magnificent gates. The forests hereabouts are lush and mature, and the roads narrow and canopied with green.

Right in the middle of Oyster Bay, at 20 W. Main St. (a stone's throw from the intersection of South Street, which is also N.Y. 106), is **Raynham Hall**. At the time of the Revolution this house was owned by one Samuel Townsend, a suspected Tory whose son was later revealed (although not until 1939) to be General Washington's personal spy, known only as "Culper Jr." In spite of its owner's supposedly royalist sentiments, Raynham Hall was expropriated during the Revolution by the occupying British Lieutenant Colonel John Simcoe and used as the headquarters of the Queen's Rangers.

Townsend's daughter Sally stayed behind, however, and charmed the British with her wit and grace. She kept her ear to the door too, for it was Sally Townsend who overheard Major John André and Colonel Simcoe discussing Benedict Arnold's planned betrayal of West Point. She conveyed the message to her brother, and the treachery was thwarted. Such is Raynham Hall's claim to fame. (Another variation of the story credits Samuel's son instead of his sister with the discovery of the plot.) The house was considerably altered over the years to suit Victorian tastes, then restored to a late 18th-century appearance in 1951. It's not a big museum, but if the Revolutionary period interests you and you're already in Oyster Bay, you should stop in for a look. The hours are 1 to 5pm Tuesday through Sunday. Admission is $2 for adults, $1 for students and seniors, and free for kids under 6. The phone number is 516/922-6808.

PLANTING FIELDS ARBORETUM

The unpretentious Native American name of Planting Fields was given by one William Robertson Coe to his spectacular Long Island estate located just west of Oyster Bay. Coe was an English immigrant who became a prominent insurance executive. It was his marriage to a daughter of H. H. Rogers of Standard Oil fame, however, that put him in the financial big leagues. The 409-acre Coe estate, developed between the end of World War I and its owner's death in 1955, has the aesthetic clout of an English country house.

Driving around the neighborhood hereabouts would seem to disprove the notion that the Gold Coast is dead. Judging from the succession of stupendous estates still lining the roads, it certainly seems intact. The original main gate to the Coe property, a grand affair of imported 18th-century English wrought iron complete with formal gatehouse, is located on a country lane with the amusing name of Chicken Valley Road. Alas, the public isn't allowed to enter through this gate, which is a shame since the drive to the house from here was very much part of the property's intended aesthetic effect. Instead, you'll have to detour around to a side entrance that leads to an anonymous-looking parking lot.

This is a small price to pay, however, for the opportunity to see one of the North Shore's most grandiose and beautifully maintained estates. Mr. Coe did everything in a handsome manner. When advised to start a collection of camellias, he built a pavilion for them the size of a small railroad station. Recently restored, it is a fairyland at any time of year. Beneath its glass roof in February and March is a breathtaking profusion of red, white, rose, and lavender camellias hanging from immaculate old bushes bordered by velvety beds of baby's tears. The smell is delicious, and the only sounds that break the almost otherworldly silence come from a pair of macaws, one of whom is over 10 years older than I am.

Besides the camellia house are extraordinary formal gardens, impressive greenhouses, and the Tudor Revival mansion itself. Now called Coe Hall, it was designed by the firm of Walker and Gillette and completed in 1921. It is an immense stone house, furnished with many original pieces, which have been returned in recent years by interested Coe family members. If you liked Old Westbury, you'll be just as excited about Planting Fields. Despite architectural differences, they are both cut from the same deluxe-quality cloth.

The entrance to Planting Fields Arboretum is located on Planting Fields Road outside the village of Oyster Bay. To get there, take the Long Island Expressway to Exit 39 North (Glen Cove Road). Go north on Glen Cove Road to N.Y. 25A; turn right (east) and continue to Wolver Hollow Road (the Old Brookville Police Station is on the corner of 25A and Wolver Hollow). Turn left on Wolver Hollow and continue to Chicken Valley Road; then turn right, admire those gorgeous if no-longer-operable gates, and follow the signs to the arboretum entrance. The arboretum grounds are open daily all year from 10am to 5pm. There's a $3-per-car admission charge. Hours for the Camellia House are 10am to 4pm daily. The mansion is also open daily, but only between April and September. Guided tours run from 12:30 to 3:30pm. Adults must pay an extra $2, kids and seniors another $1 to take the mansion tour. For further information, call 516/922-9200.

WHALING MUSEUM AT COLD SPRING HARBOR

This charming little colonial village still retains a rural air, abetted by lovely views of green hills, blue water, and bobbing boats from Harbor Road. Between 1836 and 1862, Cold Spring supported no fewer than nine whaling vessels, each engaged in the business of bringing back whale oil for pre-petroleum era illumination and lubrication. Whaling expeditions could last up to five years, and the adventure and bravery associated with whaling are part of American folklore.

Cold Spring's Whaling Museum started in 1936 with the modest donation of a 19th-century whaleboat and a collection of whaling implements. Today the collection includes 10,000 whaling artifacts; thousands of journals, letters, and logs; and

700 pieces of scrimshaw, which is the name given to the carvings on whalebone or whale ivory made by patient seamen on the trail of the great whales. Some 50,000 visitors explored the whaling museum in a recent year, a statistic quoted with considerable pride by the staff. It's not a big place physically, occupying a smallish but picturesque one-story building on Main Street with a whale atop the cupola. But it's a treasured community resource. Besides permanent exhibits like the miniature replica of Cold Spring in the 1840s and "Mark Well the Whale," there are constantly changing displays that tell the story of whaling. Walking tours, scrimshaw workshops, and lectures and films pertaining to whaling are offered throughout the summer, usually on Sunday at 3pm.

The whaling museum is located just across the Suffolk County line, at 25 Main St. in the middle of the village of Cold Spring Harbor. The best way to get here from town is via the Long Island Expressway again to exit 41 North. Take N.Y. 106 north to N.Y. 25A, then 25A east to Cold Spring Harbor. Museum hours are Tuesday through Sunday from 11am to 5pm; open Monday as well on holiday weekends and during the months of June through August. Admission is $2 for adults, $1.50 for seniors, and $1 for children over 6 (5 and under are free). The telephone number is 516/367-3418.

SANDS POINT PRESERVE

This was the Guggenheim estate, developed over a number of years and possessing several formidable mansions that belonged to various Guggenheim family members. Actually, railroad heir Howard Gould did the original planning. In 1902, he erected a perfectly enormous crenellated stone parade stable known today as **Castlegould.** This is currently a visitors' center with changing exhibits. The main residence, called **Hempstead House,** went up in 1910 to the designs of Hunt and Hunt. During the war this immense stone mansion suffered serious depredation at the hands of the U.S. Naval Special Devises Training Center. It has been partly patched up in recent years but is closed to the public except on special occasions. You can walk around the outside, however, and marvel that something so big could be the private house of a man whose grandfather came to America as a peddler.

Daniel Guggenheim bought Hempstead House and the surrounding 200-or-so acre estate in 1917. His son, Capt. Harry Guggenheim, subsequently built a house of his own on the property in 1923. Captain Guggenheim and his wife, Alicia Patterson, were the founders of *Newsday*. His Norman-style château, called **La Falaise,** is considerably smaller than Hempstead House but, still and all, imposing atop its cliff overlooking Long Island Sound. La Falaise is in original condition, chock-a-block with European antiques and carved moldings, and open to the public. The guides and brochures here make much of Captain Guggenheim's friendship with Charles Lindbergh, who wrote a book called *We* while staying here in 1927. Lindbergh's later flirtation with the Nazis is conspicuously ignored by the present-day guardians of his Jewish host's estate. Yet another family house on the property, a suave French affair called **Mille Fleures,** is, like Hempstead House, closed and unfurnished.

The entrance to the Sands Point Preserve is on Middleneck Road, which is the extension of N.Y. 101 or Port Washington Boulevard. Take exit 36 from the Long Island Expressway and proceed north on Searingtown Road, which runs directly into Port Washington Boulevard. The estate, which was willed to Nassau County by Captain Guggenheim in 1971, comprises about a mile of shoreline on Long Island Sound, plus atmospheric estate buildings, woods, fields, and a wonderful old iron fence along Middleneck Road. There's a $4 fee for the tour of La Falaise, which is open for guided tours May through October on Wednesday through Sunday from noon to 3:30pm (no kids under 10). The grounds are open for a little longer season, from March until late November. The telephone number is 516/883-1612.

THE VANDERBILT MUSEUM

William K. Vanderbilt II, great-grandson of the famous Commodore Vanderbilt, developed this 43-acre North Shore estate between 1908 and 1934. An avid natural historian, Vanderbilt designed special private museum wings for his Spanish baroque mansion and filled them with wildlife dioramas and artifacts picked up in the course of family travels all over the world. In the high tide of his enthusiasm he even had a separate **Marine Museum** constructed on the Little Neck Road border of the property. Done up with the same florid architectural flourishes as the main house, it contains everything from an antique deep-sea diving suit to an Egyptian mummy.

When Mr. Vanderbilt died in 1944, he willed **The Eagles Nest,** as the estate is called, to the people of Suffolk County, "for the education and enjoyment of the public." In 1971, a planetarium was built on the site of the former tennis courts, a logical extension of Vanderbilt's lifelong curiosity about the natural world.

The Eagles Nest is another sumptuous Long Island estate, designed this time by Whitney Warren, architect of Grand Central Terminal and the New York Yacht Club. The house is a rambling, romantic concoction, over half of which is and always was a museum. It's massed around a central courtyard entered via a bridge through a belltower. The effect is rather like a set from a 1926 production of *Zorro.* Original Vanderbilt furniture remains throughout, as do the marble and wood fireplaces, elaborate ceilings, and 1918 Aeolian Duo-Art pipe organ. Besides the main house and the Marine Museum, visitors can explore a romantic **boathouse** down on Northport Harbor, as well as lovely lawns and gardens, all still maintained quite beautifully. The **Planetarium** is one of the most sophisticated in the country and presents sky shows throughout the year.

The Vanderbilt Museum is located on Little Neck Road in Centerport, on the North Shore of Long Island not quite 40 miles from Midtown. You can tour the main house Tuesday to Sunday from noon to 4pm. Admission is $5 for adults, $3 for students and seniors, and $1 for kids under 12. Call 516/262-7800 for further information. The Planetarium also charges $3 (no children under 6 admitted to the sky shows). The phone number for program information is 516/262-STAR.

WALT WHITMAN BIRTHPLACE STATE HISTORIC SITE

Whitman's father built this charming shingled farmhouse, but the future author of *Leaves of Grass* left it when he was only four and the family moved to Brooklyn. Although he didn't live here very long, his birthplace is an eloquent symbol of Long Island's rural past, a tangible link to one of its most famous native sons.

It is a rustic, sunny little house whose hand-hewn architecture and period furnishings are evocative testaments of preindustrial America. A helpful museum guide will tell you about the Whitmans, the furniture, the construction of the house, and describe how meals were produced in the amazingly basic kitchen. Your guide will also invite you upstairs to see a short movie, consisting of images of the poet's life and loves, accompanied by passages from *Leaves of Grass.* It is actually quite moving. One could spend hours pouring over the old exhibits in cases and on the walls. Over 14,000 people a year do.

The Whitman Birthplace was part of a working farm until the time of World War I. After that it was a weekend retreat for a New York couple, then a tearoom. It came on the market again in 1949, on the eve of Long Island's greatest suburban expansion. The Walt Whitman Birthplace Association was then formed to buy and preserve it. It purchased an option without difficulty, but then couldn't come up with the cash. In September 1951, with only a month left on the option and country estates and potato farms in every direction being bulldozed into subdivision lots, *Newsday* adopted the cause and challenged Long Islanders to raise the money. It was the island's schoolchildren who—in an incredible outpouring of pennies, nickels, and dimes plus $100 won on the game show "Strike It Rich" by Valley Stream Central Junior High students—came up with it at the eleventh hour.

The Walt Whitman Birthplace today stands on a small lot located on a spur of Route 110, which, a mile to the south, is a corporate corridor lined with sleek hotels and glass office campuses. The poet's birthplace is but a stone's throw from the Walt Whitman Mall. This massive structure, surrounded by acres of paved parking lots, would have prompted a new canto or two from the author of *Leaves of Grass,* had he lived to see it (or even to dream of it). The wooded hills immediately to the west contain some remarkably similar houses, also built by Whitman's father, and still in private hands.

The Whitman House is open all year, Wednesday through Friday from 1pm to 4pm and Saturday and Sunday from 10am to 4pm. It is closed on holidays. Admission is free, but donations are welcome. The exact address is 246 Old Walt Whitman Rd., Huntington Station, NY 11746 (tel. 516/427-5240).

LEVITTOWN

Levittown was one of America's great social experiments, a mid-20th-century attempt to provide "affordable housing" for the masses. Its thousands of acres of little houses have thus taken on new importance in recent years after a generation of disparagement as "rows of boxes made of ticky tacky."

There are Levittowns elsewhere, but the original is on Long Island. The geographical heart of it is the intersection of Hempstead Turnpike (Route 24) and Jerusalem Avenue, between Plainedge and East Meadow. The names of these two former farming villages give a good idea of what the place looked like when builder William Levitt arrived at the end of World War II. Aided by mass production–type construction techniques and federal legislation that made it easy for returning GIs to borrow the $3,000 to $5,000 it took to buy a house back then, Levitt transformed the potato fields of central Nassau County into Everyman's suburbia on a scale never before seen.

He did it in stages, reflected today less by the differences in architectural design (there never was much of that) as by the different street names. Mallard, Swan, Windmill, Sheep, and Market strike a bucolic note in one section; Jupiter, Comet, Satellite, Meridian, and Universe are forward looking and cosmic in another; Eagle, Squirrel, Furrow, and Bucket bespeak an interest in nature in yet another.

Originally, all the houses in Levittown were identical 30-foot squares topped with steep pitched roofs. In the intervening years since construction, virtually every one has sprouted some combination of dormers and wings, and/or has assumed some manner of new siding, from shingles, to aluminum, to pseudo-Tudor half timbering. In fact, everything possible seems to have been tried on these houses to increase living space without overlapping the tiny lots. Some have become quite bourgeois in the process; others have grown frankly shabby. In some places the trees lining the streets have become so mature that they are dying off.

Levitt grew rich from his enormous construction projects and lived in a mansion on the North Shore, at least until he went bankrupt. His Levittowns, however, continue to provide decent housing to the middle class. The visual ordinariness of this part of Long Island doesn't make it less of a social phenomenon.

AN AUTO TOUR OF THE GOLD COAST

Maybe if you hear the word "Gatsby" one more time, you'll scream. But if your visits to Planting Fields and Old Westbury Gardens (see above) have only whetted your appetite or if you've read Nelson DeMille's hilarious *The Gold Coast* or Dominick Dunne's juicy *The Two Mrs. Grenvilles* and want to see the scenes of the crimes yourself, then I know you're going to enjoy the following insider's itinerary. It will take you along the most interesting roads, past the niftiest estates, and through the most charming villages. The trip is 35 miles long and will take about an hour and a half to drive at a slow cruise.

Starting Point: Coming from New York City, take either the Long Island Expressway to exit 39 South (Glen Cove Road) or the Northern State Parkway to exit 30 (I.U. Willets Road). Your tour begins at the traffic light on the corner of Glen Cove and I.U. Willets Roads, on the border of the Village of Old Westbury.

Turn east onto **I.U. Willets Road** and everything will become amazingly woodsy. Cedarpole fences conceal spacious properties with gracious houses. Some are traditional colonials; others are "new" mansions with angular gray-stained walls and 10,000 to 12,000 square feet. In about a mile, just before the intersection with **Old Westbury Road,** you'll see along I.U. Willets Road houses that are nothing short of captivating, assuming you like suburban places with 10-acre front lawns and full stables. At this point you'll be less than 10 miles from Queens.

Turn left (north) onto **Old Westbury Road.** Immediately on your right you'll see the brick walls, limestone piers, and ornate ironwork that mark the entrance to

Old Westbury Gardens, described separately above. Note Mr. Phipps's initials, "JSP," wrought in iron above a slightly Maya looking gilded bronze mask, as well as the splendid allee of trees lining the driveway. **Old Westbury Gardens** has been open to the public for over 30 years, but everything else around here is still private.

Continue for about half a mile north on Old Westbury Road until you come to the Long Island Expressway (I-495). The local gentry fought the violent intrusion of this superhighway with all their might. They were no match for Robert Moses, however, which is a whole other story. When you come to the expressway turn right (east) onto **Store Hill Road,** which has become the east-bound service road to I-495. Admire all that luscious open pasture land on your right, lament the 24-hour roar of traffic that defiles it today, and wonder who in the world can afford to pay Long Island's legendarily high taxes on it.

Take your first right off Store Hill Road onto **Post Road.** This country lane winds around an enchanting duck pond bordered by woods and a few noble old houses. Inside your car, you won't hear the expressway, and it might seem as if you have been transported deep into the country. But it is a highly idealized sort of country, as is soon obvious from the procession of imposing formal gates, some complete with feudal-looking gatehouses, that lead to country mansions hidden in deep woods above Post Road.

Then suddenly in less than two miles, you'll be at **Jericho Turnpike,** across which lies the village of Westbury. In the past, this was the border between estates to the north and farmland to the south. Today that farmland is solidly built up with subdivision houses, corporate parks, and shopping centers, all the way to Jamaica Bay. The population density is incredible, as is the contrast between Westbury and Old Westbury. Turn left (east) onto six-lane Jericho Turnpike and continue to the first traffic light. Now turn left again onto **Hitchcock Lane,** and you'll immediately note that the world changes again. Like magic, you'll be back in the "country," in this case a deliciously contrived landscape of rolling open meadows, rambling antique mansions, and dark untouched-looking woods. It's hard not to be astonished at the sight of all this open land so close to Jericho Turnpike.

In another mile you'll be back at the duck pond by Post Road. Turn right onto Post heading north and go under the I-495 viaduct. The Gold Coast has taken a few body blows hereabouts, in the form of new construction and subdivision. But quite a lot of it remains. Be sure to admire the imposing gates to **Knole,** which come up quite soon on your left. This is one of the great houses of the Gilded Age, still in private hands and appropriately invisible from the road.

Right after Knole, Post Road is joined on the left by **Wheatley Road.** At this point the name Post mysteriously disappears, and, without making any turns, you'll find yourself on Wheatley Road. Keep heading north, between the very fine alley of trees. Mature alleys like this are a hallmark of the North Shore. Too bad the people who planted them couldn't have seen them in their mature glory.

The long, low, somewhat modernized Tudor building on the hillside that soon appears on the left side of Wheatley Road is the **Old Westbury Golf and Tennis Club.** When built at the turn of the century, it was used to house the racing stable of millionaire William C. Whitney. During the 1920s, Whitney's son, Harry Payne Whitney, kept over 200 horses here, and the legendary Whitney Stables were winners in 270 races. The club's property today includes a Whitney mansion (not the original), beyond which is the studio that was used by Harry's wife, the sculptress Gertrude Vanderbilt Whitney. This beautiful building, still deep in unspoilt woods, remains a private residence.

There are some new houses along Wheatley Road, but it still preserves a unique North Shore Long Island atmosphere. Bear right at the stop sign at **Whitney Lane,** staying on Wheatley Road. The lovely rural feeling hereabouts is totally bogus but nonetheless pleasant. Soon you'll cross into the village of **Brookville.** The boundaries of these little North Shore villages meander all over the place, and you'll be constantly crossing back and forth between them.

Continue on Wheatley Road through the traffic light at **Route 107 (Cedar Swamp Road),** and just before the classic facade of the gleaming white **Brookville Reformed Church,** you'll cross into the village of **Muttontown.** Turn left at the church onto Brookville Road, then make a quick right at the traffic light onto **Route 25A (North Hempstead Turnpike).**

Route 25A is the main east-west drag through the countrified North Shore. As you continue eastbound you'll pass a string of very large estates, all of which no doubt are in dire jeopardy of being subdivided and turned into housing developments. One particularly fine pillared specimen already has a new "mansion" plopped right by its tree-lined drive.

Shortly after the **Muttontown Club,** a former estate on your left whose important clubhouse was designed by society architect Horace Trumbauer, is the little village of **East Norwich.** On the western edge of the village, just before 25A widens into four lanes, is a stucco gatehouse on the right with a sign that reads, "Chelsea Center—Nassau County Office of Cultural Development." **Chelsea** is a marvelous old French provincial mansion owned today by the county. The house isn't open regularly for tours, but you can roam the grounds and admire the mansion's exterior and the woodland stillness of the adjoining Muttontown Preserve.

Road widening has robbed East Norwich of a considerable amount of its original charm. (Old Bethpage Village, incidentally, is said to resemble East Norwich a century ago.) At the intersection of 25A and Route 107, note the very excellent **Rothmann's Restaurant** (recommended below), behind which is the equally excellent **East Norwich Inn** (also described below). When the light changes, continue straight (east) on 25A for about a mile and a half to **Berry Hill Road** and make a very acute left turn onto Berry Hill. There's a quantity of suburban construction hereabouts. An I-495 type road, intended as an extension of the Seaford–Oyster Bay Expressway, was to have blasted right through this area along the line of Berry Hill Road. Fortunately, the plan is now dead.

In about half a mile, you'll want to bear right onto **Sandy Hill Road.** The land bordering Berry Hill north of this intersection was once part of the Ann and William Woodward, Jr., estate, whose tangled true-life history was the origin for Dominick Dunne's marvelous potboiler (and TV miniseries).

Sandy Hill Road, from this point until it dips down into the village of Oyster Bay, very much retains the look of the North Shore during its peak in the 1920s. For most of its length this little country lane is flanked on both sides by the manicured lands (and get a load of that stable complex) of the baronial Schiff estate. By some accounts there were once over 1,000 estates of this caliber on the North Shore, of which perhaps 15% remain. This one certainly gives a good sense of the flavor of times past. The mansion itself is hidden by woods.

At the end of Sandy Hill Road, turn left (west) onto **East Main Street.** You're now on the eastern edge of the village of **Oyster Bay.** (Teddy Roosevelt's Sagamore Hill, described separately above, is just a couple of miles to the right.) Oyster Bay is pleasant without being overly quaint. In a few blocks you'll be in the very heart of it. Turn left (south) at the first traffic light onto **South Street;** then turn right (west) at the next light onto **West Main Street.** You'll pass **Raynham Hall** (described above under "Sagamore Hill") on your right, and in another half dozen blocks you'll be passing out of the village and back into the surrounding countryside. West Main Street at this point changes its name to **Shore Road.**

Momentarily you'll cross another boundary line and enter the exclusive village of **Mill Neck.** There are lovely views to the right of Shore Road across the glittering waters of Oyster Bay Harbor to Centre Island, home of the oh-so-social **Sewanhaka Corinthian Yacht Club.** At the first light, turn left off Shore Road onto **Cleft Road.** This climbs a hill dotted with geometric modern mansions on one side and a Long Island showplace called **Oak Knoll** on the other. Oak Knoll is still private; only the gates with their huge lead eagles on limestone piers hint at what's on the hilltop.

Cleft Road meanders through a rural-suburban wonderland of very long tree-lined driveways, vast lawns, stone walls, and clipped shrubs. When you come to **Frost Mill Road,** turn left. More pretty properties abound here, including the spectacular Mill Neck Manor, which hunkers on a hilltop just before the railroad viaduct.

You'll have a bit of road-rally work before you now, so pay attention. Shortly after the viaduct, Frost Mill Road forks; you bear right over a little bridge with a "No Trucks" sign. In about a quarter mile, you'll come to a stop sign at **Oyster Bay**

Road. At this point, by the way, you're very close to Planting Fields, described separately above. Turn right (north) onto Oyster Bay Road in the direction of **Locust Valley,** home of the amusing WASPy dialect known as Locust Valley lockjaw. You aren't going all the way into the village, however. After an interesting three-story white house on the right with a very unusual set of gates, followed by another railroad viaduct, you will turn right off Oyster Bay Road onto **Bayville Road.**

Bayville Road climbs a hill, and immediately over the crest is a blinker light. You'll see the Locust Valley School on your left. Turn left here onto **Ryefield Road,** named after a wonderful old mansion with a columned portico, which will shortly appear on your left. Happily, it is very visible from the road. Stay on Ryefield Road to the blinker at **Birch Hill Road,** take a quick right, and then make a quick left onto **Horse Hollow Road.** Now we're in **Lattingtown,** home of some of Long Island's most wonderful driveways. One of the best is that of the elite **Creek Club,** just ahead, at the corner of **Horse Hollow** and **Lattingtown Roads.**

You will turn right off of Horse Hollow onto Lattingtown Road and wend your way westward toward **Glen Cove.** Well, things begin to get a little more democratic now. This area was once dominated by the Pratt family of Standard Oil fame. They maintained 20 contiguous country estates between here and downtown Glen Cove, known collectively as **Dosoris Park.** Almost all of these are now in institutional hands and/or surrounded by modern suburban development.

At the corner of Lattingtown and **Dosoris Lane,** turn left. One of the Pratt houses, now a conference center, is on your left just before Old Tappan Road. Another, belonging today to the Russian mission to the United Nations, is hidden in the woods across Dosoris Lane. Stay on this road until the traffic light at **School Street.** Then turn right onto the four-lane artery that bypasses the center of built-up Glen Cove. Soon you'll come to a traffic light at the foot of a hill and a sign for I-495 to the left. Turn left onto **Glen Cove Road,** which for a short distance is also Route 107.

If you stay on four-lane Glen Cove Road for another 6 miles, you'll arrive back at your starting place, exit 39 of the Long Island Expressway. Or, you could make a final sightseeing dogleg about 1½ miles outside Glen Cove, where 107 bears left off the main highway onto picturesque **Cedar Swamp Road.** In about 2 miles Cedar Swamp intersects with Route 25A in a district of institutionalized country estates. These properties may well represent the fate that lies in store for all the good things we've seen in the last 90 minutes.

Turn right (west) onto 25A, and in about 3 miles you'll be back at Glen Cove Road. It's a big intersection with a swanky shopping mall called **The Wheatley Center** (home of one of the excellent **Ben's Delis,** recommended below) on the left corner. Turn left (south) onto Glen Cove Road; the expressway is 2 miles south.

SHOPPING

Suburban Long Island is a shopper's lotus land, which may not be the best way to put it, but at least conveys a sense of luxuriously unlimited choice. It's beyond the scope of this book to rigorously profile so mercurial a phenomenon as "good shopping." However, some of the established shopping boulevards, as well as a few of the enclosed malls, are worthy of note.

The **Miracle Mile** actually stretches for about 2 miles along Route 25A (Northern Boulevard) between Whitney Pond Park in Manhasset and Port Washington Boulevard (Route 101) in Munsey Park. Here you'll find outposts of some of the best department stores in New York (like Filene's, Lane Bryant, and Lord & Taylor) plus minimalls crammed with exclusive specialty shops and posh restaurants. This is deluxe territory, memorialized in the Billy Joel song "It's Still Rock 'n Roll to Me," and no place for bargain hunters. A similar upscale retailing environment (Bloomie's, Saks, another Lord & Taylor) can be found along **Franklin Avenue** in Garden City, north of Stewart Avenue.

If enclosed megamalls are your kind of thing, you might want to check out **Roosevelt Field** (tel. 516/742-8000) at exit M2 of the Meadowbrook Parkway in Garden City. There are (gasp!) almost 160 stores here, including 4 major anchors (Macy's, Stern's, Penney's, and A&S). Only slightly less enormous is the **Walt Whit-**

man Mall, (tel. 516/271-1741), on Route 110 in Huntington, just south of Jericho Turnpike (Route 25). A&S and Macy's are the anchors here, with over 100 smaller shops in between.

A little farther out, on the South Shore of Suffolk County in Bellport, is a new outdoor center with about 30 outlet stores. **Bellport Outlet Center** is located at Exit 56 on Sunrise Highway (Route 27) and sells everything from designer clothing to luggage to cosmetics to shoes, at prices ranging from 40% to 75% below retail. At this writing, well-known manufacturers such as Jones NY Sport, Adolfo II, Van Heusen, Jordache, Nike, Geoffrey Beene, and American Tourister were a few of the many represented here. Call toll free 800/969-3767 if you need more information.

There are plenty of other suburban malls, especially farther out in Suffolk. But the above will give you a representative taste.

---

3. Where to Stay & Eat

HOTELS

Nassau County as yet imposes no hotel room tax; Suffolk charges ¾ percent. All the rates quoted below will be subject also to the 8% sales tax, plus the additional 5% New York State tax on hotel rooms costing over $100. That's a 13% bite (13¾% in Suffolk), which you had better figure as a part of your budget calculations.

The following list represents less than a third of the total number of places I reviewed. In every case I looked for style, solid value, and a certain indefinable quality that would somehow enhance the experience of staying on Long Island. I believe the establishments recommended below do all of this better than any others on the island, certainly better than others I saw.

The grandest hotel of all (and this includes those in the later resort chapters) is the **Garden City Hotel**, 45 7th St., Garden City, NY 11530 (tel. 516/747-3000, or toll free 800/547-0400 outside New York; fax 516/747-1414). This large (280 rooms) contemporary structure with its landmark cupola/clocktower is the third hotel on the site to bear this name. It is a marriage of Miami Beach glamour and North Shore dignity, in the center of a historic planned community only 5 miles from the border of Queens. Garden City's broad leafy boulevards, upscale shopping, and abundance of gracious late 19th- and early 20th-century houses on large leafy lots have made it synonymous with Long Island suburban luxury.

Garden City is also the home of a handsome Episcopal cathedral, started in 1877. There's a story about that cathedral, about which more in a moment.

The entrances of the Garden City Hotel are flanked with enormous golden urns holding artificial ficus trees. Inside is a dazzling contemporary lobby with multiple levels, acres of shiny marble, and lots of smiling attendants in discreet gray uniforms. Each of the big luxurious rooms upstairs is furnished with thick rugs, lush fabrics, much-better-than-usual hotel furniture, big color TVs, two phone lines (with voice mailbox), glistening white-tile baths with stacks of plump white towels, hairdryers, luxurious amenities, and (in the suites) even tiny bathroom TVs. It aims for Manhattan luxury, and I'd say the hotel hit the mark pretty squarely.

Along various corridors radiating from the glittering lobby are a shopping arcade, a piano lounge, a nightclub, a good continental-American restaurant called the Polo Grill (à la carte dinner selections from $16 to $28), and, on a lower level, an excellent health spa. This latter facility contains top-quality workout equipment plus an indoor pool, the ceiling of which is decorated with painted clouds lit by fetching pink lights.

Rack rates for single occupancy range from $185 to $235 nightly, $210 to $260 for doubles, and $400 to $900 for suites. Reduced-rate weekend packages abound (usually some combination of meals and lodging), so if you're planning a stay, be sure to inquire in advance. All major credit cards accepted.

About that cathedral story: The land beneath Garden City was once part of a huge tract of wasteland called the Hempstead Plain. Merchandizing magnate A. T. Stewart shocked New York when he bought 7,000 acres of it in 1869 and announced his new planned community. He died before the work had progressed very far. And in a bizarre chapter from New York social history, his body was robbed from its Manhattan grave and held for ransom. How much the widow paid to get it back is not recorded. But the magnate's next (and final) resting place was in a crypt beneath the tower of the new Garden City Cathedral, supposedly rigged with a device that would ring the cathedral's bell should anyone attempt to steal it in the future.

The **East Norwich Inn,** 6321 Northern Blvd. at Route 106, East Norwich, NY 11732 (tel. 516/922-1500, or toll free 800/334-4798; fax 516/922-1089), is an attractive Tudor Revival building dating from the 1970s. It is nestled amidst a tree-lined parking lot behind old Rothmann's Restaurant. East Norwich, by the way, is in the middle of the North Shore Gold Coast, and the hotel is only a few miles from Old Westbury Gardens, Planting Fields Arboretum, Sagamore Hill, and the patrician environs of Oyster Bay Village.

The inn is composed of five separate stucco-and-timber-covered two-story buildings, connected by attractive corridors. Although it rambles a bit (there are 72 rooms), it has the air of a hideaway. Accommodations are furnished in motor inn colonial style. They are spacious; quiet; and have nice thick carpets, cut-glass table lamps with pleated shades, new TVs, big beds, and bathrooms with amenity trays and piles of fluffy beige towels. Every morning a complimentary continental breakfast is laid out in the diminutive dark-green lobby with its wing chairs and hunting prints. Monday through Thursday evening, in that same lobby, management will treat you to a complimentary glass of wine.

Room rates are quite reasonable: $95 for a single and $115 for a double. There are a Ping Pong table, a treadmill, a rowing machine, Stairmaster, a couple of stationary bikes, and a Universal machine in a mirrored exercise room in the basement, plus a cozy and attractive outdoor pool. All major credit cards accepted.

Just east of the Nassau-Suffolk border, a bit south of the Long Island Expressway, is the glamorous **Huntington Hilton,** 598 Broad Hollow Rd. (Route 110), Melville, NY 11747 (tel. 516/845-1000; fax 516/845-1223). Route 110 is a major corporate corridor, lined with big hotels and office complexes, some of which are architecturally distinctive. The Hilton certainly is: It has lots of swoopy brick curves, acres of greenish tinted glass, and a look of 1990s luxury. Inside is a vast rose-marble lobby—containing a multilevel, plant-filled restaurant called **Watercolors**—and overlooking a sensational glass-roofed, amoeba-shaped indoor pool, complete with a waterfall.

The 306 rooms are extremely nice, in the current corporate high-tech conventional mode. They have pale blue, blond, and beige color schemes; remote-control TVs; brass-pole lamps; padded headboards; upholstered chairs; and luxurious modern baths with lots of Hilton-type amenities. Also on the premises are an excellent work-out facility with 10 stations, 3 treadmills, bikes, and rowing machines; a very big outdoor pool that could use a little landscaping; a piano bar called **Lusty's** overlooking the lobby; and a busy disco called **The Savoy,** which caters to those 25 to 35 and has a sign by the door forbidding men with hats(?).

The Hilton consciously caters to business travelers but does so with such panache that any sort of visitor will enjoy a stay here. Single-room rates range from $125 to $179 nightly; add $20 for each additional person. Remember that at all Hilton hotels children of any age stay free in the same room with their parents. Don't forget to ask about weekend packages; the Hilton "Bounce-Back," for example, was priced at $99 for a double as of this writing, thereby evading the 5% state tax for rooms over $100. It includes a deluxe room on the "concierge floor" (really only marginally nicer than the standard room), plus continental breakfast and late checkout. All major credit cards accepted.

It seems like everybody in central Nassau knows how to get to the **Island Inn,** Old Country Road (corner of Zeckendorf Boulevard), Westbury, NY 11590 (tel. 516/228-9500). That's because it's the home of an excellent steak and seafood restaurant called **John Peel** (recommended below), whose sign is as big as that of the inn. It's also a very appealing low-rise hotel whose 204 rooms embrace a lovely central courtyard filled with sculpted bushes, blooming trees, and a beautiful big pool. The Island Inn was one of the early invaders of the potato fields hereabouts (in 1960). The area is densely developed today. Indeed, **Fortunoff's**, one of the island's largest and most interesting department stores, is just a few doors down on what, in spite of the massive retail and office development of the last thirty years, is still called Old Country Road.

The recently renovated facade of the inn sports a geometric, postmodern look with a slight chinoiserie spin. The big lobby has an air of efficient luxury: a free-standing fireplace with gas logs that never burn down; a complete lack of messy-looking ashtrays; mirrored walls in alternating smoky shades; and one of those hanging 1960s staircases that is bound to become a period piece if it's not eliminated in the next redecoration scheme.

About half the rooms have been renovated as of this writing. The older ones have dark paneling, blond furniture, vertical blinds, new TVs, and nice colored baths from the 1960s. The newer models (typically those facing the pool) have pale wallcoverings, rich green carpeting, quilted floral spreads, and quasi-colonial furnishings. None of the rooms is very big, but they're all very nice, especially those with the courtyard view. Singles range from $125 to $160 nightly, depending on location; doubles run between $145 and $175. There is no exercise room, but the hotel has an arrangement with a nearby Jack LaLanne Spa that makes the spa's facilities available to guests free of charge. Weekend packages come in various sizes and shapes and start at $89 nightly double. All major credit cards accepted.

About 10 miles to the east is the **Marriott Residence Inn,** 9 Gerhard Rd., Plainview, NY 11803 (tel. 516/433-6200, or toll free 800/331-3131; fax 516/433-2569). You'll never find Gerhard Road without directions. It intersects Old Country Road one block east of the Seaford–Oyster Bay Expressway. Turn south on Gerhard and the hotel is immediately on your right.

The Marriott Residence Inn contains fully equipped apartments that range in size from 350 to 1,050 square feet. Originally built in 1988 as a condominium, it has an asymmetrical, highly contemporary exterior that looks as if so many beigy-brown boxes were lowered into place by cranes. Inside is a dramatic two-story lobby with lots of green-marble planters, glass, brass railings, and a grand piano.

A large percentage of the guests stay for at least a week. They include families visiting from Florida, business execs on special assignment, and people building houses on the island. Mindful of the specific needs of this assortment of people, management shows movies, gives barbecue parties, organizes wine-and-cheese soirees, and arranges food shopping—all in the name of making an extended stay in unfamiliar surroundings as pleasant and homelike as possible.

The rooms and suites have fully equipped kitchenettes and spacious layouts and are outfitted with pale-blue carpets, attractive pine furniture, remote-control color TVs, brass lamps, and modern baths.

The smallest unit is a roomy bargain at $115 per night, single or double. For $155, the 560-square-foot one-bedroom suite is even more of a deal. And for $240 nightly, you can rent a deluxe suite with 2 bedrooms, 2½ baths (with a Jacuzzi in the master), a full separate kitchen, and a big living room with a balcony. There are significant discounts for stays of over seven days and even bigger discounts if you stay for a month. Continental breakfast is included in every rate.

Also on the premises are separate saunas and needle showers for men and women, an exercise room with multiuse weight machines, a great indoor lap pool, and a very large and handsome outdoor pool screened from the expressway by a dense row of pines. Definitely a good value. All major credit cards accepted.

Most hotels in the Long Island suburbs are located in the middle of the island. The **Freeport Motor Inn and Boatel,** 445 South Main St., Freeport, NY 11520 (tel. 516/623-9100) is an exception, sitting quite literally *on* the South Shore and overlooking docks full of moored yachts on Freeport Creek. The current owner's father built this traditional double-decker motel for the 1964 World's Fair, held in Flushing Meadow. It has been immaculately maintained and periodically upgraded ever since and offers one of the best overnight values on the island.

Shamrock-green doors open off exterior walkways into the spacious rooms equipped with remote-control color TVs and phones and decorated with weldwood paneling, quilted bedspreads, vinyl-covered armchairs, and sailboat prints. Everything is pleasant and neat as a pin. The prices are great: $57 to $62 for a single, $75 to $80 for a double, $5 for each additional adult. There are six municipal tennis courts down the block, a nearby jogging track overlooking the bay, and the facilities of the municipal Freeport Recreation Center (pool, workout equipment) are available to guests free of charge. Complimentary coffee and poundcake are set out every morning in the postage stamp–sized lobby. People have been coming back to this place for 15 to 20 years. Reason: a lot of value for the price, and a nice atmosphere to boot. Management provides free cable TVs, and you can rent a movie in your room for a nominal price. All major credit cards accepted.

RESTAURANTS

I've divided my recommendations into three categories: North Shore Restaurants; Mid-Island Restaurants; and South Shore Restaurants. In general, upscale eating establishments head each list, while cheaper and faster luncheon places (including several terrific Irish pubs) are toward the end. My seafood restaurant recommendations are all on the North Shore.

North Shore Restaurants

Bryant & Cooper Steak House (tel. 516/783-2700), a popular steakhouse on Middle Neck Road at the intersection of Northern Boulevard (Route 25A), about a mile west of the village of Roslyn, is a handsome-looking place, with polished-wood and marble wainscoting, crisp white tablecloths, tucked banquettes, and an air of established suburban luxury. The lunch menu features the expected filet mignon, steak au poivre, and 16-oz. sirloin, plus assorted chicken, veal, pasta, and seafood dishes. During lunch the price of an à la carte main course will run from about $8 to $12.50. At dinner, various filets, sirloins, porterhouse, plus lighter fare like lemon pepper chicken, Norwegian salmon, and swordfish, are priced from about $14 to $26. Lunch is served Monday through Friday from noon to 3:30pm; dinner is from 5 to 10pm Monday through Thursday, to 11pm on Friday, until midnight on Saturday, and from 3 until 10pm on Sunday. Dress is "neat casual" and reservations are a good idea. All major credit cards accepted.

Over on the Miracle Mile, amidst a string of smart shops just west of Port Washington Boulevard (Route 101), is **Millie's Place,** 2014 Northern Blvd. (Route 25A), in Munsey Park (tel. 516/365-4344). The small shopping center that contains this restaurant is on the south side of Northern Boulevard; the entrance to it is beside the sign for "The Americana of Manhasset." Even from the parking lot, Millie's is a little hard to spot; its suave stone exterior and elegant gilded oval sign are so discreet as to be practically unnoticeable. The long string of lofty rooms inside is light and spring-like, with huge vases of flowers, vines crawling over the high ceilings, and a bar with a big green-marble fireplace up front. This is the place for a light lunch after heavy shopping; say, seafood salad, poached salmon, stirfry swordfish with lo mein, spinach linguini with shrimp, grilled steak Japanese, chicken pot pie, or an artistic sandwich. Expect your lunch selection to cost between $8 and $20. Equally original dinner items include pecan-crusted chicken breast, Cajun swordfish, salmon Mediterranean, and the same range of cold salads served at lunch. Dinner selections cost between $14 and $20. Open daily for lunch from 11:30am to 4pm, and for dinner from 4pm to 11pm. AE, MC, and V accepted.

You won't find better seafood anywhere on Long Island than at **Steve's Pier 1,** a galleon-style restaurant on the beach overlooking Long Island Sound, 33 Bayville Ave. (tel. 516/628-2153). This location is on the western fringe of the village of Bayville, which lies across Oyster Bay Harbor from Oyster Bay. Steve's has big white-painted anchors out front and a lobster pool inside the front door; for a time (in 1976) this tank contained the largest lobster in the world (44 lbs., 200 years old, and named Charlie). The spacious dining rooms are filled with pink-clothed tables, decorated with lots of shiny woodwork and ships' wheels, and overlook Long Island Sound through sheets of plate glass. Steve's is an institution and justly famous, particularly for Alaska king crab and lobster. At lunch all manner of additional fresh seafood—soft shell crab, bluefish, red snapper, sole, salmon, halibut, brook trout, bouillabaisse, and lobster in every style—plus a few nonfish items like sliced steak and broiled chicken, are priced from about $14 to $16 à la carte. The typical dinner selection, chosen from a similarly extensive menu, will cost between about $17 and $19. Lunch is served Monday through Friday from noon to 2:30pm; dinner hours are 2:30 to 10pm Monday through Friday, to 11:30pm on Saturday, and from 1 to 9:30pm on Sunday and holidays. No reservations accepted. All major credit cards accepted.

The Jolly Fisherman, 25 Main St., Roslyn (tel. 516/621-0055), is another seafood and steakhouse that has been in this location for 35 years. It is a low, modern brick building located just down the street from the clock tower in the middle of Roslyn. There's a friendly bar up front, plus several trim and fresh dining rooms with pewter chandeliers, crisp white tablecloths, and wood walls. Most people like the back room, which overlooks the duck pond. A typical lunch selection—such as broiled bluefish filet; broiled L.I. flounder; deep-sea scallops; rainbow trout almondine; jumbo fried shrimp; or nonfish dishes like the chef's salad, broiled calves' liver, or filet mignon—costs between $10 and $22. The much-larger dinner menu offers a similar range of dependably good fare with à la carte selection prices ranging from $14 to $25. Open Sunday to Tuesday to Thursday and Sunday for lunch from noon to 2:30pm, for dinner from 3 to 9:30pm (to 11pm on Friday and Saturday). All major credit cards accepted.

The **Roslyn Café** is a terrific neighborhood Italian-American restaurant located a stone's throw from the Long Island Expressway at 235 Rosyln Rd. (an extension of Main Street) in Roslyn (tel. 516/621-2398). This is the sort of solid value, family-style tavern/restaurant that people dream about having in their own neighborhoods. Beyond the long bar with its TV and red-vinyl booths is a spacious dining room decorated with stained-glass windows, lots of plants, and a big mural of Rosyln Harbor. At lunch excellent sandwiches, burgers, pasta main dishes, and seafood platters are priced between $6 and $9. The dinner menu runs the gamut from romanos, scaloppines, and parmigianas, to a full range of pasta and seafood dishes. There is even a children's menu. Most à la carte dinner selections cost between $11 and $17. Lunch is served daily from 11:30am to 3pm; dinner is from 3 to 11:30pm (to 12:30am on Friday and Saturday). Dress is informal; reservations are a must on weekends. All major credit cards accepted.

For something a bit more exotic, you might like to try the dependably good **Shish-Kebab Restaurant,** at 283 Main St., Port Washington (tel. 516/883-9309), which is located just before the intersection with Shore Road. There are Middle Eastern motifs on a series of miniature awnings outside, and twangy music is played in the series of cheerful dining rooms inside. Decor consists of green-and-pink plastic tablecloths, black-vinyl chairs, and a profusion of hanging plants and Middle Eastern prints. Lunch specials really are a good deal: souvlaki, gyros, falafel, burgers in pita bread, artichoke pizza, and broiled flounder with spinach and feta—all costing between $5 and $7. At dinner, you'll pay anywhere from about $6 to $12 for a dish like salmon Marmaris (baked in tomato-garlic-dill sauce), a Greek dinner salad, spinach fish, beef shish-kebab, or various Middle Eastern mixed grill platters. If you're a fan of baklava, be sure to have some here. Open for lunch and dinner, Monday through Thursday from 11am to 10pm, Friday and Saturday to 11pm, and Sunday from 11:30am to 10pm. AE, MC, and V are accepted.

For Chinese food, I recommend **Lily Pond**, 1073 Northern Blvd. (tel. 516/626-3930), located about a mile west of the village of Roslyn. This is a glamorous-looking place, with colored lights and glowering Chinese lions outside and pale-burgundy carpeting, crisp white linens, and smoked mirrors on the walls inside. Prices are moderate, however, and the cuisine is excellent. The extensive menu includes chicken, pork, vegetables, and seafood prepared in every (Chinese) manner imaginable. The chef additionally offers a "Lite Menu" as well as a list of "new creations," such as snow shrimp with Grand Marnier, tinking bells with 10 ingredients (a combination of crispy sizzling beef, chicken, shrimp, and lobster), and bird's nest delicacies (assorted seafood and vegetables in a secret sauce). At lunch, expect the typical dish to run between $8 and $14; prices are a bit higher at dinner with a few items costing up to $17. Open Sunday to Thursday from noon until 10pm, until 11pm on Friday and Saturday. All major credit cards accepted.

The Homestead, in the center of the village of Oyster Bay at 107 South St. (tel. 516/624-7410), is an upscale pub complete with leaded-glass dividers, exposed-brick walls, a long bar with a TV mounted above it, rock and roll music at a discreet volume level, and flocks of little tables covered with green-checked cloths and fresh white paper. At lunchtime, The Homestead serves dependable sandwiches and burgers from $6 to $8, plus seafood dishes like sea scallops, crab cakes, and steamed clams for around $9 to $11. Dinner features similar fare, plus steak au poivre, various types of pan-blackened fish, and a big marinated steak, for à la carte prices that run about $13 to $20. Everything comes with salad and vegetables, and the atmosphere is inviting. Open daily for lunch from 11:30am to 4:30pm; for dinner from 5 to 10pm (until 11pm on weekends).

Finally, in Greenvale, which is a crossroads on Northern Boulevard (Route 25A) at Glen Cove Road, there's **Ben's Kosher Delicatessen** (tel. 516/621-3340), right on the corner of the Wheatley Plaza Shopping Center overlooking the intersection. This is the kind of place with unbelieveably good pickles and coleslaw already sitting on every table. The decor is bright and modern, with multiple levels, butcher-block tables, a deli counter up front with display cases packed with mouth-watering food, and an air of New York City efficiency. I don't think you could go wrong choosing anything from the enormous menu. There are mountainous sandwiches —both hot and cold—burgers, omelets of every description, platters of Roumanian steak, broiled liver, roast turkey, chicken fricassee, plus wonderful cold chicken salad, egg salad, and more. Bear in mind it's kosher, which means no milk with the tea, among other things. This doesn't seem to bother the crowds who swear by the place. Open Sunday to Thursday from 9am to 9pm, to 10pm on Friday, and to 11pm on Saturday. There are actually *five* Ben's on Long Island, the others being located at 95 Old Country Rd. (tel. 516/742-3354), in Carle Place (between Mineola and Garden City); 437 N. Broadway (tel. 516/939-2367), in Jericho (about 4 miles south of East Norwich); 933 Atlantic Ave. (tel. 516/868-2072), in Baldwin (immediately west of Freeport); and 135 Alexander Ave. (tel. 516/979-8770), way out in Lake Grove, which is south of Stony Brook (see Chapter XI).

Mid-Island Restaurants

John Peel (tel. 516/228-8430), is a steak-and-seafood palace located in the Island Inn on Old Country Road in Westbury, a stone's throw from Fortunoff's. It is a big, handsome, comfortable place with thick rugs; brass chandeliers; a pub with paneled walls and a fireplace; and a dining room with brick arches, leather chairs, soothingly dim lighting, and an air of settled establishment. Lunch specials include things like pan-seared salmon, chicken-and-shrimp stirfry, and black fettuccine with shrimp, plus satisfying burgers, sandwiches, and specialties such as sautéed scallops and shrimp fried in ale batter. The typical lunch selection will cost between $8 to $10. At dinner, à la carte selections like prime rib, American lamb chops, Cajun swordfish steak, plus the obligatory 16-oz. sirloin and filet mignon, are priced generally between $18 and $28. There is a four-piece combo Tuesday through Saturday. If you come on Friday, try the Fisherman's Feast, a special complete dinner, one of whose main course options is a two-lb. lobster for $22.95. Open daily for breakfast from 7am to 11am, lunch from noon to 4pm, and dinner from 5 to 11pm. Reserve on weekends. All major credit cards accepted.

Maine Maid Inn (tel. 516/935-6400) is a little piece of Long Island's Quaker past located adjacent to the intersection of Routes 106 and 107 and Jericho Turnpike (Route 25). It's a pretty white farmhouse with a gabled roof and black-and-white awnings. Inside are two floors of picturesque old-fashioned rooms with names like Hicks, Garden, Tiffany, and Island. They are filled with a charming clutter of early Americana, a few working fireplaces, lots of pine paneling, floral-print wallpaper, portraits on the walls, and prosperous parental types at the tables. This is definitely the sort of place to which your maiden aunt would take you. For lunch, you might choose something like the club sandwich, chef's salad, capon ambassador (topped with mushrooms and artichokes), veal marsala, or pasta primavera, priced mostly between $9 and $12. The dinner menu features selections such as Long Island duckling, veal francese, prime rib, and lamb chops, either à la carte (mostly for between $16 and $22) or on a complete dinner (for $5 more). On the cover of the menu is a very interesting description of little Jericho's recent past. Open for lunch from 11:45am to 4pm Monday through Saturday, and for dinner on the same days from 4:15 to 10pm (to 11pm on Friday and Saturday); a buffet brunch is served on Sunday from noon until 3pm; dinner afterward is served until 8. All major credit cards accepted.

Within sight of the Northern State Parkway in Mineola (near Garden City) is the very stylish **Caffè Spuntino, 348** E. Jericho Tpke. (tel. 516/747-8111). This really is a great-looking place, in the high-tech modern Italian fashion. Good-looking waiters in pink shirts glide between the various levels. A neon sign that says "wine by the glass" hangs on a wall with an orange, green, and gray color scheme. There are purple banquettes, an open kitchen, and jazzy-looking open-back black chairs. The cuisine is northern Italian with a sort of nouvelle Adriatic touch. It features all sorts of fresh pastas and pizza, plus light and original veal, chicken, and fish dishes. Prices are moderate, too; expect to pay $7 to $10 for lunch and about $10 to $16 for nonpasta à la carte dinner selection. Open Sunday to Thursday from 11:30am to 10:30pm (to 11:30pm on Friday and Saturday). All major credit cards accepted.

If you like authentic Irish pubs, there's a swell one called **B. K. Sweeney's Pub,** at 55 New Hyde Park Rd. (tel. 516/328-8326), on the extreme western edge of Garden City, half a mile south of Stewart Avenue. There's a pinball machine up front, a tin ceiling, two bars filled with neighborhood families complete with kids, a few cozy booths, a dim jolly atmosphere, and great cheap pub food. Things like jumbo club or hot pastrami sandwiches, chef's salad, burgers (a specialty of the house), fried shrimp platter, plus weekday specials and the 16-oz. charbroiled shell steak, are priced from $5 to $13. The $9 Sunday brunch is a particularly good deal. Lunch is served daily from noon to 5pm, dinner from 5pm to 2am. All major credit cards accepted.

If you're near Old Bethpage Village at mealtime, you might want to try another of the island's great neighborhood Irish cafés. It's called **Kenny's Café,** 729 South Oyster Bay Rd., Bethpage (tel. 516/433-3338), a few blocks south of Old Country Road. Kenny's is a modest suburban pub, family run, not too big, and located in a solid middle-class neighborhood of firefighters, cops, and their wives and families. The food is always good; café steak, Irish barley soup, calves' liver, tuna salad plate, a multitude of sandwiches, and changing daily specials mostly cost $6 to $10 all day long. There are a garden room up front, a bar in the middle, and a main dining room behind. The kitchen is open Monday to Friday until midnight, and until 2am on weekends. AE accepted.

Finally, don't forget the branches of **Ben's Delicatessen** (described above under North Shore Restaurants) in Carle Place and Jericho.

South Shore Restaurants

When you bought this guidebook you probably wanted to learn about places like **McCluskey's Steak House,** 157 West Sunrise Hwy. (Route 27), in Bellmore (tel. 516/785-9711). In operation for over 55 years, this South Shore landmark, with the big red neon sign on the roof, is located almost directly opposite the Bellmore station of the Long Island Rail Road, a bit west of the Wantagh State Parkway. The large, indirectly lit dining room is bisected by a very long bar. There are butcher-block tables, paper napkins that say "Famous For Steaks," a dark-blue, blown acoustical ceiling, long vinyl banquettes, and a very comfortable and unpretentious tavern atmosphere. The food is fantastic. Some of it is also incredibly cheap, like the bar menu that offers an entire range of grilled sandwiches and burgers for under $3. Regular burger platters are $6 and under; the 21-oz. steak, 28-oz. porterhouse, filet mignon for one, 16-oz. steak sandwich, plus assorted ham, shrimp, chicken, and salad selections cost between $8 and $27. You won't go hungry no matter what you order. My waitress informed me McCluskey's was "notorious for potatoes," and she was absolutely right; they come in nine different varieties, and a single $2 order is more than enough for two. Open Monday to Thursday from noon until 11pm, until midnight on Friday and Saturday, and until 10pm on Sunday. All major credit cards accepted.

About 6 miles west of McCluskey's on Sunrise Highway (Route 27), is another longtime landmark in this part of the world: **Raay-Nor's Cabin,** 550 Sunrise Hwy., a block west of Grand Avenue in Baldwin (tel. 516/223-4886 or 223-4841). I love places like this. Raay-Nor's has history and character and has been serving fried chicken in this log cabin in the pines more or less without interruption since 1932. The interior sports log walls, low ceilings, wooden tables, red-leatherette booths, a small bar up front, and cut-out lamps in the shape of chickens. A really enormous (and delicious) fried chicken dinner, including yams and corn fritters, costs less than $9. If you want your chicken Maryland style (with sliced bacon), sautéed, or barbecued (wings only), they can arrange that too, for approximately the same price. Also on the menu are broiled and fried seafood dishes, barbecued ribs, and a few steak, lamb, and ham platters as well, priced between $10 and $15. Fried chicken, however, is definitely the order of the day. Open for dinner only, Monday through Friday from 5 to 9:30pm, from 4 to 10pm on Saturday, and from 1 to 9pm on Sunday. No credit cards accepted.

LONG ISLAND RESORTS: THE SOUTH SHORE

The South Shore is composed of a great many worlds: Between the union men in Massapequa, the working stiffs in Brentwood, the gay vacationers in Cherry Grove, the socialites in Bellport, the arrivistes in Southampton, and the bluebloods in East Hampton, there's not a great deal of common ground. Yet this entire crew has gravitated to the flatter, ocean side of the island, where the views are longer and the variety of special pleasures is broader.

1. What to See & Do

Southern Long Island's greatest natural asset is its beaches. Resort towns up and down the coast each cater to the divergent tastes of their respective summer populations. For example, the Hamptons (a generic term encompassing half a dozen adjacent villages) combine beautiful beaches with fashionable inns and restaurants, fast-track nightlife, streets full of fancy cars and socialites (real and aspirant), exclusive clubs, and elaborate mansions. Southampton has been a society resort for a long time. It's beautiful—and it knows it. Other villages in the Hamptons don't have the same hard glitter. It's possible, for instance, to be quietly elegant and relaxed in East Hampton or plain relaxed in Amagansett. Like it or not, wherever you go in this most easterly part of the island, the genie of fashion will always be nearby. Of course, that may be the point of your travels, in which case you will have come to the right spot.

It's also possible to have a quiet "inn" experience in this part of the world.

Quogue, for example, is a patrician little beach resort with very little going on, a gorgeous village beach, and big nifty old shingled houses. Sag Harbor is a handsome old whaling tow   aling restored hotel. Ev

Other type   ; strip of
barrier beach tha   National Seashore stati   munities
here, reachable   sphere in
each little town   ther (and
occasionally at   cast flirta-
tious looks at   e working
families alterna   ow-profile
WASPs enjoy s   O Woods;
and so it goes.   h is both a
function and   nfront the
daytripper. Th   ons are divided about e

Though   in relation to
the beach, oth   York to Southampton at his   don't, the non-
stop trip to th   can take less than
two and a half hours. If everything goes   eeping bumper to
bumper all the way to Smithtown, it still takes only four hours.

Alternately, you might postpone the Hamptons indefinitely, as many people do, stash your car in Patchogue, and take one of the ferries to Fire Island.

2. Fire Island

There are over 20 separate summer communities on the island, yet all 32 miles of it are now designated as a National Seashore. Most people are only dimly aware of this fact. Indeed, Fire Island is (quite unintentionally) one of the best-kept secrets in the National Park System. National Park Service personnel, complete with Smokey-the-Bear uniforms, administer a number of magnificent beaches on the island, each complete with concession stands; bathhouses; interpretive centers; snack bars; and, in one case, a campground.

NATIONAL PARK SERVICE BEACHES

Two of these beaches are accessible only by water. Whereas many people arrive on private boats, the great majority of visitors to these unspoilt and uncrowded strands of clean white sands are middle-class families who've crossed the Great South Bay via public ferry for a day at the beach. It is a day, I might add, that is far more civilized than what one often encounters at big public beaches elsewhere.

The great storms that lashed the eastern seaboard during the 1993 winter washed 34 houses, as well as the beach upon which they stood, completely off Fire Island's western extremity. There are still beaches down there, but certain small municipalities are having to do some rearranging. These same storms added greatly to the width of the island's easternmost beaches, especially some of those administered by the Park Service. From Sailor's Haven to Smith Point, as of this writing, the beach is enormous, far wider than it's ever been. The dunes are gone, but the beach is huge.

The Park Service installation at **Sailors Haven** is reached via a ferry from Sayville. The atmosphere at this beach is easygoing, unpretentious, and family oriented, and the broad expanses of clean white sand are lifeguarded from Memorial Day to Labor Day. There is a very attractive **snack bar** where you can enjoy genuinely tasty sandwiches, burgers, and ice cream on a shady shingled porch overlooking the ferry dock and the Great South Bay. A gift shop/souvenir stand is adjacent, as are restrooms, picnic tables, and places to buy groceries, cook burgers, and rent umbrellas.

Buried in vegetation at the head of a stairs leading from the ferry dock is the **visitor center** (tel. 516/597-6183). Here you can peruse modest photographic and/or natural history exhibits and sign up for the many interesting free programs offered each summer by the Park Service. These range from "seaside stories and crafts" for children 3 to 10; to the seven-week "junior ranger" program for older kids; to evening "campfire programs" for all ages, when rangers give talks on things like ghosts and legends of Fire Island, famous hurricanes, and star-watching.

The glorious **beach** itself is reached via a twisting boardwalk that crosses diminished dunes and passes a fully equipped bathhouse en route. Everyone who comes to Fire Island is warned constantly about the deer ticks and the poison ivy. The former can cause Lyme disease; the latter is probably one of the most dangerous poisonous plants in the Western Hemisphere. However, if you keep on the boardwalk and the open sand beach and pay attention, your chances of getting either are negligible. In fact, the suburbanites mowing lawns and wrestling with weeds on the other side of the Great South Bay are probably at greater risk. The beach at Sailors Haven is as magnificent as any on the eastern seaboard of the United States, and it's far less crowded than other Long Island beaches accessible by car.

The most unusual part of Sailors Haven, however, is an anomalous hardwood forest that thrives behind a second set of dunes: **Sunken Forest.** This unusual habitat has survived for centuries because of a huge sandbar, ¼ to ½ mile offshore, which has blunted the ocean's force. Park Service rangers conduct tours down the mysteriously silent and sun-dappled boardwalks that thread through this unexpected (on a sand bar, 12 miles from Long Island) woodland. Like all the Park Service programs, the tours are free and very informative. I would never have guessed that some of the holly trees overarching the boardwalk were over 200 years old, that the deer on the island eat the poison ivy, or that parts of the Sunken Forest are actually below sea level. You can explore on your own, of course, but the tours add an extra dimension to the experience. They leave twice daily on weekends, once daily on Wednesday and Thursday. Schedules change frequently in our budget-cutting times, so check at the visitor center.

To get to Sailors Haven, take the ferry from the **Sayville Ferry Service,** 41 River Rd., P.O. Box 626, Sayville, NY 11782 (tel. 516/589-8980). Adults pay $3.75 each way; kids under 12 pay $2.25. The Sayville Ferry also services Cherry Grove and Fire Island Pines, discussed below.

The Park Service operates a larger facility at **Watch Hill,** about 6 miles east of Sailors Haven. There is a far greater feeling of remoteness at Watch Hill, despite more elaborate facilities, due to the presence of an adjacent wilderness area that stretches 6 or 7 miles to the east. Except for the Bellport Village beach, this tract of wilderness dune and unpopulated beach is in virginal condition. It very much retains the lonely look and feel of the barrier beaches of centuries past. It's interesting how few people actually venture out here. There are no boardwalks, of course, so unless you have a compelling desire to be bitten by a tick or contract a raging case of poison ivy, you'd be ill advised to stray off the beach. The mere presence of all that empty space is oddly provocative, however, and sets Watch Hill apart from the Park Service's other public beaches.

Besides a modern snack bar, a visitor center, a nature walk, a grocery store, restrooms, a bathhouse, an umbrella rental, and a yacht basin, all on a larger scale than at Sailors Haven, Watch Hill boasts a full service, dinner-only seafood restaurant called the **Seashore Inn** (tel. 516/597-6655). Here you can enjoy such appetizers as steamed mussels, clams casino, and scallops ceviche for about $6 to $8, plus seafood, pasta, and beef main courses from $16 to $22. You can sit either in a bright modern dining room with lots of windows, pine paneling, and light oak tables and chairs or out on a terrace overlooking the harbor. There are more (and larger) private boats at Watch Hill than at Sailors Haven, many of whose owners make a point to stop at the Seashore for dinner.

Between mid-May and mid-October, it is also possible to rent a **campsite** at Watch Hill or obtain a permit to camp amidst the desolate dunes of the wilderness area. Demand for these campsites and permits far outstrips supply, and reservations are obtained on a first-come, first-served basis. To participate, you must submit an application between January 1 and March 31; after that, you're likely to be out of luck. For more information, write the Watch Hill Campground, Fire Island National Seashore, 120 Laurel St., Patchogue, NY 11772, or call the visitor center at either 516/289-4810 or 516/597-6455. Other than campsites, there are no overnight accommodations at Watch Hill or Sailors Haven.

To get to Watch Hill, take the ferry from Patchogue operated by the **Davis Park Ferry Co.,** Box 814, Patchogue, NY 11772. One-way adult fare is $5; kids under 12 pay $3; for schedule information call 516/475-1665. The Patchogue ferry also runs to Davis Park, discussed below.

You may wonder why ferry rates are quoted one-way only. This is because many people go out to the island on one ferry, walk or take a water taxi to another town, then return to Long Island via another ferry. There are three separate ferry companies connecting various parts of Fire Island to Patchogue, Sayville, and Bayshore, respectively. The companies have no connection with one another, do not offer round-trip discounted fares, and do not honor one another's passes or tickets.

Save for a few Park Service vehicles, there are no cars on Fire Island. If you want to get from one community to another you either walk, hitch a ride with a friend who's a ranger, or take a **water taxi.** Water taxis are small cabin cruisers in the 25- to 30-foot category. One will pick you up upon your telephoned request at any ferry dock. Although not cheap, taking a water taxi is less expensive than taking a ferry back to Long Island, a taxi to the town whose ferry services the community to which you want to go, and then another ferry back to Fire Island. You can call **Island Water Taxi** from the phone booths at any ferry dock. The number for reservations is 516/363-2121 or 516/665-8885. Be advised that the water taxi won't always go where you want it to and that sometimes you'll have to wait a bit for an available boat.

Although you can't drive on Fire Island, there are two places to which you can drive. Both are beaches operated by the National Park Service. The first is **Robert Moses State Park,** a public beach since 1898, which is located at the extreme western end of the island closest to New York City. It is readily accessible from the Long Island Expressway (exit 52), from the Southern State Parkway (exit 40), and via the Ocean Parkway from nearby Jones Beach. It's not exactly isolated—there are parking facilities for over 8,000 cars, beach shops, boat basins, pitch 'n' putt golf, comfort stations, and so on—but it is less crowded than Jones Beach. The same $4-per-car fee charged at Jones is also charged here. It is a beautiful beach? Yes, without question. Is it better to drive here or to take one of the ferries to other parts of Fire Island? That depends: If you want a more adventuresome excursion, take the ferry; if you don't mind big crowds on your beautiful beach, then go to Robert Moses.

Another fine beach partly operated by the Park Service is called **Smith Point West** and is also accessible by private car. It is located about 20 miles east of Robert Moses State Park, at the far end of the wilderness area adjacent to Watch Hill, and is connected to Long Island by the William Floyd Parkway. Parking fees are the same as at Robert Moses; rangers at the **visitor center** (tel. 516/281-3010) also conduct walks on a nature trail. Although the final 6 miles to the eastern tip of Fire Island have not been designated a wilderness area, they contain nothing but deserted beach. Actually, it is amazing that such a long stretch of untouched barrier beach managed to survive to the present day and a lucky thing that the government got hold of it before real estate developers did.

Be advised that the National Park Service prints and distributes an extremely useful **free map of Fire Island.** It is really a brochure describing the various park facilities. Its great virtue, however, is a full-length map of Fire Island that locates all communities, ferry lines, and major parkways and towns on the Long Island side of Great South Bay. There are free stacks of them in every Park Service visitor center and often at ferry terminals as well. You can obtain a copy in advance by writing to the Fire Island National Seashore, 120 Laurel St., Patchogue, NY 11772.

SOME OTHER FIRE ISLAND COMMUNITIES

Now, then, what about all those little summer colonies dotted up and down the island? They happen to be about as different from one another as countries in Eu-

$275 with bathroom

rope. They all share the same beach, however, and that beach is legally open to any member of the public. The merchants and residents of the various beach communities are not of a single mind on the subject of tourism: Some want it; others don't. Some want it in only certain places, others want it in only certain other places, and some don't want any of it anywhere near them.

The ferry companies offer unrestricted public service to the island; you don't have to go only to the National Park Service beaches if you don't want to. However, these beaches do offer precisely what many visitors are looking for—namely, a beautiful beach and convenient facilities for a day trip.

To protect themselves from unwanted daytrippers, many of the island's summer communities have adopted indirect regulations whose purpose is to keep certain types of visitors from ever coming back. For example, in some places you cannot walk around with an open beverage container—*any* open beverage container. If the local police are so inclined, they can give you a ticket for carrying a glass of water! Many villages purposely lack public restrooms or changing facilities. Some require you to wear a shirt on the picturesque boardwalks that substitute for streets. The idea seems to be to intentionally fill the world of the daytripper with unsuspected pitfalls.

To be fair, these municipalities are often small, family-oriented summer colonies that don't want beer-swilling teenagers baying at the moon outside their cottage windows. You can't really blame them, especially when other places exist on Fire Island where moon baying is, if not quite the order of the day, at least nothing about which to get too upset. A number of these latter communities, such as Davis Park, Kismet, or the famous gay resort of Cherry Grove, depend to a great extent on daytrippers. The key to enjoying Fire Island, far more so than many other places, is knowing in advance precisely where you'll want to go.

Here now is a series of thumbnail sketches, moving from west to east, of some of the more important communities, together with useful tourist information on the ones that welcome outsiders. The villages at the westernmost end of the island, closest to Robert Moses State Park—**Saltaire, Dunewood, Atlantique,** (but not **Kismet!**)—fall mostly into that category that would just as well have you visit elsewhere, at least if you're only coming for the day. It is in this vicinity that unsuspecting beachgoers will risk a ticket walking shirtless on the boardwalk.

Things loosen up considerably as you move east. **Kismet, Ocean Beach,** and **Ocean Bay Park** are all reached via the **Bayshore Ferry** (tel. 516/665-2115), which charges a one-way fare of $5 for adults and $3 for children under 12. After stashing your car in the dockside lot at Bayshore ($9 daily), you'll join a throng of holidaymakers on the pier. There are crowds of kids, shouting parents, piles of groceries, boxes full of household goods, and an atmosphere of happy anticipation. Fire Island ferries are essentially metal barges, covered down below, open up top, and at times piloted by surprisingly youthful captains. The trip across the Great South Bay takes a little over half an hour. Sparkling whitecaps break over the prow of the boat and a holiday air prevails.

None of these places is in any way pretentious, architecturally, socially, or in any other manner. They are all long-established, middle-class summer beach resorts, much of whose charm stems from the absence of automobiles. Most of the people here either own or rent one of the many tiny cottages that line the boardwalk lanes.

There is a pleasant hostelry for transients in Ocean Bay Park called the **Fire Island Hotel** (mailing address: 1 East Main St., Suite 213, Bayshore, NY 11706; tel. 516/583-8000). This establishment consists of a collection of converted Coast Guard buildings that were moved to the site at various times since 1930. The 45 rooms are furnished with nice flowered curtains, fresh towels and bathmats folded neatly on the beds, and hotel pieces from the 1920s and 1930s. The rooms are small but bright, some paneled in pine, all with private baths. The hotel is not quite on the beach, but the surf is only a stone's throw away. A clean, modest family air prevails. Weekday rates are $100 for a double; weekend stays have a two-night minimum and cost $350 for a double for two nights. There are additionally all manner of midweek and weekly specials, plus four two-bedroom cabins that sleep six comfortably and cost $700 per weekend or $1,200 by the week.

Immediately east of Ocean Bay Park is **Point 'O Woods,** a private and elegant old-fashioned compound where outsiders are not welcome. After this, moving eastward, are Sailors Haven and the Sunken Forest, both of which are described above.

CHERRY GROVE

Immediately east of Sailors Haven and also serviced by the Sayville Ferry is the little community whose big reputation has somehow (without justification) extended itself over the whole of Fire Island: the gay resort of Cherry Grove.

Fire Island, taken in its entirety, is anything but gay. The Grove, however, is about as gay as you can get. It is much smaller than you might imagine, hardly more than a cluster of appealingly ramshackle buildings built along wooden boardwalks extending from the bay to the ocean beach. The atmosphere is exceedingly cheerful and welcoming, the place is as full of women (albeit gay) as men, and the nightlife is the best on the island.

Where to Stay

The biggest building in town, the focus of activity day and night, is **Cherry Grove Beach Hotel** (mailing address: P.O. Box 537, Sayville, NY 11782; tel. 516/597-6600), whose awninged rampway is within sight of the ferry dock. The hotel's Olympic-size pool (the biggest on Fire Island) is surrounded by sun-drenched chaises. To the west are two floors of diminutive motel-type rooms; to the north is a weight-lifting station where somebody is always pumping or curling; to the east is the terrace of the **Ice Palace,** a cavernous establishment from whose famous "blender bar" come all manner of potent concoctions whipped up by one Johnny Poole. They're pretty great. The place literally throbs at all hours with rock music.

The hotel is open only from the beginning of May until November and posts a dizzying array of rates depending on the time of the season and the day of the week. High summer midweek rates are as low as $60 for a double; weekend rates for two persons can range from $125 to $155 nightly or $175 to $225 for a two-night package. On some holiday weekends management requires a three-night minimum. The best idea is to call them and request a rate for the time you want to visit.

There are numerous guesthouses in the Grove, the most unusual of which is undoubtedly **Belvedere,** Cherry Grove, NY 11782 (tel. 516/597-6448). What a place! The interior is suffused with piped violin music and decorated with fauxpainted surfaces of every description, while the outside positively drips with Corinthian columns, lead statues, cupolas, brackets, balustrades, swags, urns, splashing fountains, and shady bowers of climbing roses intertwined with poison ivy. There are a pool, a hot tub, and 26 small but stylish rooms (most of which share a bath) extending off a vast double-height living room belonging to the resident owners. It is all really fabulous. Midweek double-room rates (nobody seems to quote single rates hereabouts) are as low as $60 nightly, $80 for rooms with private baths; on weekends there's a two-night minimum, and a double for both nights runs from $225 to $275, the latter rate being for a deluxe room or one with its own bath; on holidays there's a three-night minimum and a rate structure that goes all the way to $600 for two, including a cocktail party and breakfast each morning.

Where to Eat

There are many excellent places to eat in Cherry Grove. **Top of the Bay** (tel. 516/597-6699) is a seafood restaurant perched on the second floor of a building overlooking the ferry dock and the bay. It serves excellent seafood dishes such as swordfish, crabcakes, and shrimp Sambucca, priced from $15 to $22 and served in a breezy open-sided dining room with an intimate bar up front. Very friendly and atmospheric. **The Monster** (tel. 516/597-6888) is a branch of the famous gay bar/restaurant with other locations in Key West and New York City. Out here it's located right behind the Cherry Grove Beach Hotel. The Monster contains a bar/disco and a dim and stylish dining room on the main floor, plus a raw bar, a lounge, and another liquor bar on a deck upstairs. Prices are a bit more than those at Top of the Bay, but the food is brilliant. For less expensive fare, try **Dee Marie's** (tel. 516/597-6155), just around the corner from Top of the Bay. This diminutive restaurant and pizzeria has plastic forks, paper plates, and Styrofoam cups, but the inexpensive Italian cuisine is home cooked and absolutely delicious. Plenty of dinners here for under $10. On the other side of Top of the Bay is **Michael's** (tel. 516/597-6555), essentially a neighborhood coffeeshop that serves inexpensive breakfasts, lunches, and dinners, either on an outdoor terrace or at an indoor lunch counter.

FIRE ISLAND PINES
A short stretch of undeveloped dunes to the east (now protected by the Park Service) separates the Grove from **Fire Island Pines**. This community, also serviced by the Sayville ferry, is the newest and most luxurious on the island. The planned dockside village contains a coordinated ensemble of low-key, gray-stained buildings that gaze across a narrow harbor full of yachts to an opposite shore dense with greenery, above which peek the angular tops of elaborate, modern beach houses.

There is a hotel at dockside called the **Fire Island Pines Botel** (tel. 516/597-6500). It is a three-story structure of painted cinderblocks, apparently dating from the 1960s, whose exterior balconies give access to small, simple rooms. Rates are cheap in midweek, even during the July and August high season ($65 for a double; $55 with a shared bath); things get pricier on high season weekends, when you'll pay as much as $350 for two nights in a room with a private bath.

The Pines, it should be noted, is another community that does not really welcome casual visitors. One suspects the Botel exists primarily for the convenience of surplus house guests and visitors who have arrived by yacht. **Pavilion** is a big bar/dancehall that overlooks the small harbor. There's also an excellent upscale restaurant located in the Botel. It's officially called the **Pines and Dunes Yacht Club,** but everyone knows it as John Whyte's, after the owner. Open daily in the season, it's a comfortably stylish venue for seafood, steaks, chops, and burgers, served indoors and/or outdoors. Other than that, there isn't much else in the way of entertainment, certainly nothing on the scale of nearby Cherry Grove.

What there is instead is a collection of extremely lavish beach houses, designed in the contemporary architectural vernacular of sharp edges and dramatic angles. The line-up along the beachfront could as easily be somewhere in the Hamptons as here on Fire Island. Even those not directly on the water are fairly elaborate, far more than the run-of-the-mill in neighboring communities. Although primarily gay, the Pines attracts a considerable number of straight householders, including many entertainment personalities. No doubt this phenomenon is another reason the locals cherish their luxurious anonymity.

East of the Pines is a stretch of largely undeveloped beachfront dotted with little hideaways like **Water Island,** which got ferry service only in the early 1990s! About 4 miles from Fire Island Pines is the singles' haven of **Davis Park,** which really ought to have overnight accommodations but doesn't. What it does have is regular ferry service from Patchogue (via the Davis Park Ferry Co., tel. 516/475-1665), a very informal and unpretentious collection of beach cottages, tenanted in great part each summer by groups of young singles, and the **Leja Beach Casino.** This oceanfront establishment consists of a moderately priced seafood restaurant on one side and an active jukebox bar with dance floor on the other.

Like every place on Fire Island, Davis Park cooks from Friday afternoon to Sunday evening. The rest of the week it's pretty dead. In the winter, like every other community, it shuts down altogether. A few hardy souls stay on the island through January and February, but most towns turn off the water during the winter. And the ferries, with very few exceptions, don't run after November.

The overwhelming majority of Fire Island vacationers either rent entire houses or share houses. Every community has real estate people who are intimately acquainted with what's available locally. No matter what you'd like to rent, my advice is to contact the **Fire Island Tourist Bureau,** P.O. Box 248, Sayville, NY 11782 (tel. 516/563-8448). If ever there was a knowledgeable and conscientious group, this is it. Those at the bureau are as glad to recommend rooming houses as real estate brokers, plus give you all the information on plays, contests, special events, and/or whatever else is happening on the island. Someone is usually by the phone daily from mid-May to mid-September; other times there's a tape machine.

Also good to know about are the local tabloid-size biweeklies, the **Fire Island Tide** and the **Fire Island News**. Of the two, I rather like the *Tide*, which publishes more community news, as well as local ads, ferry schedules, maps, and unusual feature stories.

---

3. The South Shore Route to the Hamptons

From the outset, it should be noted that the *fastest* route to the Hamptons is via the Long Island Expressway to exit 70 at Manorville. Proceed south on N.Y. 111 to the Sunrise Highway Extension (also called N.Y. 27). Take Sunrise Highway eastbound (like the expressway and N.Y. 111 it's a high-speed road) right across the Shinnecock Canal and you'll be within striking distance of Southampton. Sunrise Highway actually runs parallel to the Long Island Expressway all the way from town. But it's a heavily traveled local artery for much of its length, and offsetting its multitude of lanes is a multitude of traffic lights.

Here's another bit of advice: No doubt there are explorers out there who see the old Montauk Highway on their map. Don't be tempted by that tantalizingly snakey route through all the old villages. Montauk Highway is disfigured by commercialism virtually all the way to Southampton. It's the one dependably overbuilt road even in the South Shore's remaining rural regions.

Although the lion's share of Long Island's great country estates went up on the North Shore, there were enclaves of aristocratic country living on the South Shore as well. One of these was around **Oakdale,** a somewhat anonymous area nowadays but one that still provides evocative glimpses of the gilded past. Two that are open to the public include a former millionaire sportsmen's club and the waterfront mansion of a former member of the 400.

William K. Vanderbilt—grandson of the commodore, one-time husband of flamboyant social climber and woman suffragist Alva Vanderbilt, father of William K. Vanderbilt, Jr. (whose Eagle's Nest in Centerport is now the Vanderbilt Museum), and proprietor of Marble House in Newport—was also once a resident of Oakdale. His spectacular residence, **Idle Hour,** still stands on Idle Hour Boulevard just south of Montauk Highway. The grounds have been chopped to pieces for split-levels, and the mansion is now part of Dowling College. But at least it's still standing, and is it immense!

Vanderbilt's one-time neighbor was a fellow named Frederick G. Bourne, whose place immediately to the east of Idle Hour is often called the largest house on Long Island. The walls and gates along Montauk Highway are certainly impressive, if no longer perfectly manicured. The property has been owned for many years by the **LaSalle Military Academy** and is not open to the public.

However, facing Idle Hour across the little Connetquot River is another sumptuous former private estate called Westbrook, which *is* open to the public. It was developed in the 1880s by a railroad baron named William Bayard Cutting (1850–1912). When his 94-year-old widow died in 1949, she left it to the Long Island State Park Commission. Today the mansion, designed by Charles C. Haight, and the grounds, laid out by the famous Frederick Law Olmsted (who designed New York City's Central Park), are called **Bayard Cutting Arboretum,** Box 466, Oakdale, NY 11769 (tel. 516/581-1002). Hours are Wednesday through Sunday from 10am to 5pm year-round. In summer, there's a program of outdoor concerts, Shakespearean drama, and the like; call the number above for current programs. The mansion is open only from mid-April through October. There is a $3-per-car admission charge.

Mr. Cutting's house is a sprawling "shingle-style" mansion with Tudor-timbered gables and a forest of chimneys. It contains wonderful woodwork and fireplaces, plus a handy snack bar that could have been inserted more sensitively. The grounds contain scenic walks and specimen trees and give a good idea of how the millionaires once lived. It was Mrs. Cutting's hope that through her gift the public would gain "a greater appreciation and understanding of the value and importance of informal planting."

Also in Oakdale is the site of a famous millionaire's shooting preserve called the Southside Sportsmen's Club. Today the grounds are preserved as the **Connetquot River State Park Preserve** and open to the public by permit and reservation. The important early Shingle Style clubhouse, designed in the late 1880s by Isaac H. Green, plus an ancient 17th-century gristmill, can be visited by appointment between April and October. Call 516/581-1005 for reservations. The park offers thousands of acres of walking trails and a full schedule of botany and wildlife programs as well. The entrance is on Sunrise Highway.

If you'd like to visit Oakdale, take exit 57 (Veterans Memorial Highway) from the expressway, then Connetquot Road south to Great River Station, at which point you'll be practically in the Cutting Arboretum. Oakdale and Idle Hour are less than 2 miles east on Montauk Highway.

The South Shore of Long Island is very densely built up all the way to Patchogue, a bustling town 6 or 7 miles beyond Oakdale. In fact, except for the state parks and the national seashore, there's hardly a square foot of land south of the expressway that doesn't have somebody's house standing on it. After Patchogue, things begin to open up. The land is mostly pine barrens, still in a primeval state yet perilously close to the cutting edge of suburbia.

Another good detour for those not in such a hurry to get to the Hamptons would be to the fashionable village of **Bellport,** about 4 miles east of Patchogue on N.Y. 36. Bellport has a society feel to it and boasts many fine restored colonial and Edwardian houses. There are picket fences galore, all gleaming under fresh coats of white paint; tall leafy trees; views of the Great South Bay; a pretty village center; and a few good restaurants.

I think you'll like **The Bellport,** 159 South Country Rd. (tel. 516/286-7550), which occupies a blue-trimmed white cottage in the center of the village, across from the fire station. The interior is fresh and summery, with paisley seatcovers, polished oak floors, hand-painted tabletops, and an enclosed porch flooded with afternoon sunlight. The owner/chef specializes in contemporary American-country cooking and changes his menus with dizzying frequency. Luncheon sandwiches (turkey breast, burgers, Bellport club, melted swiss; pizzetta, frittata, or pasta du jour, cost between $7 and $11. The dinner menu might offer selections like North Pacific salmon encrusted with herbs, seared rib-eye steak, rack of lamb with apple chutney, or grilled swordfish, priced between $14 to $18 à la carte. The "Creole Festival" dinner special, available as we went to press, ran the gamut from okra to crabmeat to crayfish to rib-eye dookey chase (the latter being a blackened steak). Also interesting, although it will perhaps be discontinued by the time you read this, was the prix-fixe "Recession Monday" table d'hôte. Lunch hours are daily from noon to 3pm; dinner is from 5:30pm to 10pm on Sunday to Thursday until 11pm on Friday and Saturday. V and MC accepted.

I thought the food was truly terrific at the **Bellport Country Club,** South County Road (near Station Road), Bellport (tel. 516/286-7329). Despite the name, this is a public restaurant located in the community-owned golf club. The large white clubhouse is set behind a parking field. The restaurant has high ceilings, lavender tablecloths, beachy watercolors on the walls, and long views down the fairway to glimpses of glittering waters. The chef, trained at the Culinary Institute of America (see "The East Bank of the Hudson" in Chapter XII) gives creative salads and burger plates unexpected pizzazz. Dinner might be anything from spa chicken, to grilled pork chops with apple chutney, to marinated rib-eye steak, plus a range of changing daily specials. Expect afternoon main courses to cost between $6 and $9; at dinner, the menu broadens and à la carte prices range to $12 to $18. Open Tuesday to Sunday from 11:30am to 3pm for lunch and from 4 to 9pm for dinner. Truly the sort of place you'd never find without a guidebook.

South Country Road (Route 36) from Bellport to **Brookhaven** now begins to pass the occasional working farm. After Brookhaven you have several options. The first is to rejoin Montauk Highway for the short hop to the Sunrise Highway Extension. It's less than 30 miles from here to Southampton. If you're up for another big country estate, this one with notable Revolutionary War connotations, consider detouring around Bellport Bay to Mastic and the **William Floyd Estate.**

William Floyd, a craggy and thin-lipped patriot, judging from old paintings, was one of the signers of the Declaration of Independence. His huge plantation at Mastic was originally run (at least partly) by slaves. Although the original acreage was reduced over the years, an incredible 613 acres of fields, forests, marshlands, historic outbuildings, and a large mansion survived in family hands until the late 1970s. The year before her death in 1977, Cornelia Floyd Nichols transferred the estate to the National Park Service. It's now open to the public as part of the Fire Island National Seashore.

The 25-room mansion started modestly in 1724 as a six-room farmhouse. It was renovated seven times after that, getting bigger and grander each time. The Floyd estate was developed as a working farm, not as a badge of social advancement. Consequently, the house, while large and full of interesting furniture, isn't one of those Long Island showplaces dripping with crystal, gilt, and damask.

The surrounding 613 acres are big enough to convey a sense of a rural place even though the adjacent land is closely developed with tract houses. Besides the main house, 11 outbuildings and a family cemetery are open to visitors. There's no charge for either the guided tours of the house or the self-guided tours of the grounds. The estate is open on weekends only in July and August, from 10am to 4pm (tel. 516/399-2030). The shortest route, either from nearby Brookhaven or from the Long Island Expressway, is via the William Floyd Parkway (exit 68 on the expressway) to Havenwood Drive. Take a left at Havenwood and follow the signs.

Another alternative to the Hampton experience can be found in the aristocratic old seaside resort village of **Quogue.** Even Montauk Highway is attractive in the environs of Quogue. The village itself possesses a sleepy center surrounded by wonderful shingled and Colonial-style mansions on spacious lots shielded from the roads by huge old hedges.

Right in the middle of all this is the **Inn at Quogue,** 47 Quogue St., Box 521, Quogue, NY 11959 (tel. 516/653-6560, or toll free 800/628-6166). The 68 units are contained in 3 locations straddling Quogue Street. The main house is a clapboarded and gabled old rooming house sitting behind a picket fence. It contains a smart restaurant (open all year, but not every day in the winter), and 16 really charming little rooms with chintz spreads, pastel cotton rugs, color TVs, freshly painted old-fashioned wooden furniture, and an air of unpretentious beachy chic. The east house across the road is an old Long Island farmhouse with a porch and black-painted shutters. It contains the modest reception office, plus nine rooms on the upper floors. Behind it, and surrounding an attractive outdoor pool, are what they call "the cottages." These are in fact 1960s-vintage motel units, very attractively furnished with pale blue wall-to-wall carpeting, blond French provincial or summery rattan furniture, brass reading lights, and the occasional kitchenette. The 43 cottage units all have phones and color cable TVs. As with any resort hotel, the room rates are a perfect tangle, and in the high season you are subject to a minimum stay of two to three days. Basically, off-season doubles can be had for around $85 to $185 nightly; midweek high-season doubles run from $105 to $225; weekend peak-of-the-summer rates (and those for winter holidays like Christmas and Thanksgiving) cost the same as midweek, but management requires a three-day minimum stay. It's a charming place with a very hospitable attitude. I suggest that you call and clarify the applicable rate yourself. All credit cards accepted.

If you're making a special trip to Quogue, take exit 64 off the Sunrise Highway Extension (Route 27) and proceed south on Route 104 to Montauk Highway (Route 80); the village is less than a mile to your right.

---

4. Touring the Hamptons

The South Fork of Long Island, site of the famous Hamptons, is an approximately 35-mile-long spear of randomly bulging land stretching from the Shinnecock Canal in the west to Montauk Point in the east. Strictly speaking, there are "Hamptons" on both sides of the canal. The traveler heading east from New York City will, for example, pass **Westhampton, Westhampton Beach,** and **Hampton Bays** (as well as Quogue) before even reaching the bridges at Shinnecock Hills. But it is to the towns beyond the canal that most visitors are heading. And with good reason, since that's where the most Hamptonish attractions lie.

The South Fork is a very old part of New York State. In fact, the town of Southampton claims to be the state's first English settlement (although Southold on the North Fork disputes this claim). Farms and villages were well established here as long ago as the 17th century. A surprising number of old buildings survive from those days, lovingly cared for by the various villages. Actually, you could spend an awful lot of time climbing around picturesque windmills and peering at fully furnished houses that were built in the 1660s. There are enough of them around here to sate the appetite of the most dedicated antiquarian.

The South Fork's agrarian look persists, at least in places, despite a century of fashionable summer visitors and the intense development pressure of the past two decades. Adjoining the summer traffic jams on Montauk Highway (Route 27) are huge fields of potatoes, serenely ablossom under the June sun. Away from the beachfront mansions are sparsely trafficked country lanes twisting through empty-seeming pine barrens and placid abundant farms.

There is also a human current on the South Fork—really more of a riptide—that's as impossible to ignore as the seasons. It flows first east on Friday and Saturday, then west on Sunday and Monday, always back and forth on Montauk Highway. The other roads on the South Fork are barely affected by this lemminglike ebb and flow. But since Montauk Highway is about the only way to go east or west, it's a hard flow to avoid. Longtime residents, including longtime summer people, blame it (rather acidly) on New York City. Weekend people, who are the source of the problem, seem unfazed by four-hour one-way jaunts to or from the city at peak hours. Drivers hereabouts have developed a level of derring-do unmatched in other parts of the state. One needs the bravery and abandon of a kamikaze pilot just to pull onto Montauk Highway on a summer Saturday. If you want to make a left turn, better add to that the patience of Job.

Of course, if this state of affairs ever altered, the local economy would go straight down the drain. Free movement and commerce were once before restricted on this part of Long Island—by the British blockade and occupation at the time of the Revolution. The result was hunger, depopulation, and general misery. Like it or not, the South Fork is married to the tourist industry, despite its occasional agricultural posturing.

SOUTHAMPTON

The closest Hampton past the Shinnecock Canal is Southampton, settled in 1640 by a group of disgruntled pilgrims from Lynn, Massachusetts. They landed at a place called Conscience Point, a region enlivened until recently by a discothèque of the same name, and proceeded to form a small republic. Practically nothing remains of colonial (or Republican) Southampton, a notable exception being the **Halsey Homestead** (tel. 516/283-3527). This delicious little shingled cottage has stood on South Main Street just a few blocks from the center of town since 1648. It hugs the side of the road, oblivious to the tall clipped hedges, broad lawns, and white mansions all around it. The interior is open to the public from mid-June through mid-September, Tuesday to Saturday from 11am to 4:30pm and Sunday from 2 to 4:30pm. Donations are requested.

A few blocks north and half a block east of Main Street is another interesting artifact (or collection of artifacts) from a somewhat later period of history. This is the museum of the **Southampton Historical Society,** 17 Meeting House Lane (an extension of Job's Lane, in the center of the village), Southampton, NY 11968 (tel. 516/283-1612). The museum, housed in a very fine white Greek Revival mansion built by a ship's captain in 1843, is open Tuesday to Sunday from mid-June to late September. It has a classical balustrade, elegant cupola, green shutters, and a velvety lawn out front. Inside are period furnishings and display cases full of decorative and useful odds and ends from the vanished past. Adjacent to the Captain Rogers Homestead, as it is called, is a collection of often tiny weathered wooden buildings grouped around neat brick paths and clipped lawns, with a sign out front proclaiming them "The Village Street 1887." There is a blacksmith shop, Corwith's Drug Store, a carpenter shop, a stable, and so forth, each outfitted with vintage accoutrements and displaying a little plaque commemorating a generous donor. It's certainly interesting, if not quite Old Bethpage Village.

Neither the Halsey Homestead nor the historical museum, however, is representative of Southampton today, or even 100 years ago. Rather, it's the spacious and manicured mansions and grounds radiating on tree-lined roads from the center of town to the beach that capture the true spirit of this town. Sometimes all you can see of these houses are glimpses of chimneys or upper stories at the ends of long drives or above 10-foot-tall privet hedges. Even along the beach, the lawns are vast and rolling and the houses secluded from one another by generous amounts of expensive beachfront. Southampton's summer houses are real showplaces, running the architectural gamut from Shingled Behemoth to Norman Château to Giant Colonial to Victorian Monsteresque—with almost every other architectural stop in between. Head straight down South Main Street and you'll be right in the thick of them.

The center of the village itself is the intersection of Job's Lane and Main Street. This is a sophisticated shopping district with luxurious stores and boutiques, many bearing the names seen on Fifth or Madison Avenue and catering to a similar clientele. It's a nice-looking downtown, not too big, but running a couple of blocks in several directions. The streets are broad; tree shaded; and full of expensive cars, slim women with pulled-back blonde hair, tanned older men in expensive sports clothes, and lots of attractive younger people with blue eyes and tennis racquets.

You're going to find it difficult, probably impossible, to use the beach in any of the Hamptons. Of course, America's beaches are free once you get onto them, and finding a public access even in Southampton isn't too difficult. The problem is what to do with the car. Free legal parking spots do exist, but they're unmarked and pitifully few. Park illegally and you'll be fined and/or towed. People staying in the various villages can usually get low-cost day passes from their hotels. Others pay $16 a day on weekends and $11 on weekdays to park in the town lot at Cooper's Beach, a few miles west of the Southampton Bath and Tennis Club on Dune Road.

Worth a visit in addition to (or possibly in lieu of) the Southampton beach is the **Parrish Art Museum,** 25 Job's Lane (tel. 516/283-2118). Founded in 1898 by a prosperous summer resident who paid for the building and donated his collection, the Parrish has grown into a noted museum of 19th- and 20th-century American art. It's a delightful spot, with a cool garden full of beautiful statuary and sculpture; a busy schedule of special events; and regular summer programs of music in the garden, film, and theater. Even if you're not a museumgoer you'll doubtless find something of interest. Open Monday and Thursday to Saturday from 10am to 5pm, Sunday from 1 to 5pm. From June to September, open Tuesday as well. A donation is suggested.

Southampton also has terrific places to stay (see "Where to Stay & Eat in the Hamptons," below). Let's now continue touring the South Fork.

WATER MILL

Until a little beyond Southampton, twisting two-lane Montauk Highway is designated as N.Y. 27A, while larger roads have borne the larger designation of N.Y. 27. All that ends in the fields east of Southampton. Much of Southampton's semi-suburban sprawl ends too. So that by the time you reach Water Mill, a picture-perfect little hamlet 3 miles from Job's Lane and Main Street, you'll feel truly in the country —except for the insane summer traffic. That big windmill in the center of town isn't the 1644 model that gave the place its name. Today's mill is a relative newcomer, dating only from 1800. Actually, it was built in Sag Harbor, a former whaling center somewhat to the northeast, and moved to Water Mill in 1814. It's now called the **Water Mill Museum,** Old Mill Road (tel. 516/726-4625), and you can check it out and buy freshly ground cornmeal and wheat flour, plus various other items in the mill museum shop. The museum is open Monday and Thursday through Saturday from 10am to 5pm, Sunday from 1 to 5pm. Admission is $1. Water Mill, despite its name, is considered to be one of the Hamptons. As such, it's surrounded by attractive weekend homes, the nicest ones being closest to the beach. Many former potato fields hereabouts have in recent years sprouted dramatic, geometrically shaped houses sheathed in glass and weathered wood. But the potatoes still grow too—at least as of this writing.

BRIDGEHAMPTON

Montauk Highway continues east from Water Mill through farm fields, past country restaurants, antiques stores, farm stands, and the occasional shopping center. After about 5 miles you'll come to Bridgehampton, another attractive town with an established summer colony. Pretty much all the land around here, at least that which lies south of the highway, has been developed for summer and weekend houses. Former farming hamlets like **Sagaponack, Mecox,** and **Wainscott** dot the flat and formerly rural fields, many of which are bordered no longer by trees or fences but by angular modern summer houses. It's a characteristic of much of the South Fork, and the North Fork too, that still-active farmland runs to the very edge of the summer-house lawns and that farm machinery shares narrow back roads with shiny Mercedes Benzes. This peculiar situation is, in large part, the result of Suffolk County's aggressive and ingenious efforts to preserve its open farmland by means of the transfer of development rights. In some places these efforts have come too late. But in others they haven't, and the visual results—like working farms encircled by exclusive summer homes—are often pleasant, if somewhat anomalous.

At Bridgehampton you have the option of continuing east toward Montauk or detouring 4½ miles to the north up N.Y. 79. This picturesque country road is also called the Sag Harbor Turnpike, as it leads directly into the bustling town of Sag Harbor. It's a nice drive and chances are you'll be glad to be off N.Y. 27 for a while.

SAG HARBOR

Sag Harbor styles itself the "Un-Hampton Hampton," which I suppose means that it has the cachet without the congestion. Certainly it's removed from the horrid traffic jams on N.Y. 27, even though unless you live here you'll have to face those eventually. The village is bigger than most of the other Hamptons, except Southampton. While the towns along the Atlantic beaches attracted vacationers throughout the last century, the old whaling port of Sag Harbor up on Shelter Island Sound just languished. Whaling, which began here in the 1760s, peaked in the 1840s. Then came the 1849 California gold rush, followed by the long and inexorable decline of the whaling industry. By the 1870s, Sag Harbor was dead. It remained more or less moribund until the 1980s real estate boom brought it back to life. Even today, its streets crowded, its shop windows full, its charming old buildings restored, the population is only about two-thirds of what it was in 1845.

Sag Harbor is simply a beautiful village, filled with early to late 19th-century houses and huge trees and surrounded by vast tracts of still-active farmland. One of the finest buildings in town is the **Sag Harbor Whaling and Historical Museum,** on Main Street just before the business center (tel. 516/725-0770). This elegant Greek Revival mansion houses memorabilia and artifacts from the days when Sag Harbor was home port to 114 whalers. The museum charges $3 for adults, $1 for kids 6 to 13, and is open Monday to Saturday in mid-May until October from 10am to 5pm (1 to 5pm on Sunday). Across the street is **The Custom House** (tel. 516/725-0250), set far back on a lawn and filled with maps, portraits, and furniture dating from the late 18th century. The house was the home of the custom master when Sag Harbor was a federal port of entry to New York State. It is a serene and elegant little place, open to the public Tuesday to Sunday from 10am to 5pm. Admission is $1.50 for adults and $1 for children; there are guided tours and children's activities.

Lunch and dinner suggestions, plus a description of Sag Harbor's attractive American Hotel, appear below. Besides strolling around, peeking in antiques shops, and soaking up the 19th-century ambience, there's not much else to do. As soon as you're ready, climb back in the car, find N.Y. 114 (it's at the very top of Main Street, within sight of the American Hotel), and head back south for about 7 miles to Montauk Highway and the village of East Hampton.

EAST HAMPTON

East Hampton is without a doubt the most beautiful village in the Hamptons. It's a manicured little world of sweeping elm trees, rambling Colonial mansions, velvety lawns, clipped hedges, picturesque ponds, and occasional pockets of ancient 17th-century buildings. The central business district has fashionable shops and restaurants, even an adjacent windmill. The beach areas sport a collection of Southampton-type summer mansions, many of which are breathtaking. Also here is the exclusive Maidstone Club, whose very name is synonymous with Hampton luxury. The most interesting areas to explore are down Ocean Avenue toward Apaquogue and along Further Lane in the vicinity of the Maidstone.

East Hampton's favorite attraction, as far as the locals are concerned, is the **"Home Sweet Home" Museum,** facing the Village Green at 14 James Lane (tel. 516/324-0713). "Home Sweet Home" rings a bell with almost everybody, but it's the rare individual who knows quite why. It was a song, first performed on the stage of Covent Garden in 1822 but written by an American named John Howard Payne. Payne was an East Hampton native who became a theatrical sensation. By the time of his death, in a typical American bit of overlap between politics and the stage, he had become the American consul at Tunis.

Payne's father settled here in the late 18th century to teach at the **Clinton Academy,** a historic early prep school whose building at 151 Main St. (tel. 516/324-1850) is also open in the summer as a museum. In 1907, a fellow named Gustav Buek and his wife purchased and occupied the Payne house. For the next 20 years, the Bueks painstakingly restored and furnished it with 18th-century antiques. After Buek's death the village of East Hampton bought both house and contents. And since 1928 it has been open year-round as a museum. It's not a big house, nor is it an elaborate one. Built in 1660, it's a shingled saltbox full of country treasures whose look has recently become fashionable. Outside on the lawn is another windmill, also rescued, moved, and restored by Mr. Buek.

Besides historic houses and posh estates, East Hampton offers good shopping for gifts and antiques and a great bar called O'Mally's, which I'll discuss later.

AMAGANSETT & SPRINGS

A few miles east of East Hampton on N.Y. 27 is the next Hampton, a village called Amagansett. This place showed great commercial promise back in the 18th century as a farming and manufacturing center, but it never recovered from the British Revolutionary War blockade. Today's Amagansett looks like a junior version of East Hampton, pretty but neither as plush nor as big. To the north of it lies a hilly, piney area whose spiritual center is a hamlet (really a crossroads) called Springs. No big mansions, posh clubs, magnificent beaches, museums from the 1600s, or any similar Hamptons-type attractions are associated with Springs. Yet, ironically, it's rather a fashionable area. To drive through it, you'd never know. In fact, you'd probably get lost in the spaghetti tangle of narrow roads through dense but low pine forests. There are many lovely little beaches, modest crescents of golden sand lapped by the low waves of Gardiners Bay, all around this area. The problem again is the lack of legal parking. Actually, the parking situation is exactly what preserves the delicate charms of Springs. This woodsy enclave on the crowded South Fork is as appealing as it is precisely because there's no place to park.

Beyond Amagansett the look of the land changes suddenly. Gone are the lush trees and green fields. Gone, too, is pretty much of the land on either side of Montauk Highway. After Beach Hampton, a dot on the map about a mile beyond Amagansett, is an area called Napeague, notable for its open sand dunes upon which is a small cluster of condominium/hotel complexes. The presence of Hither Hills State Park fortunately ensures that the whole beach won't become built up.

MONTAUK

The closer you draw to Montauk Point (it's about 16 miles from the center of Amagansett to the Montauk Lighthouse), the more barren and windswept the landscape. Even on hot days there's a stiff breeze off the ocean and not much onshore to slow it down. The moors around the present village of Montauk were first used by Hampton farmers to pasture cattle in the 1700s. The present lighthouse was constructed in the 1790s on orders from George Washington. In the late 19th century, Stanford White designed a few small but suave shingled cottages for vacationing sportsmen. And Teddy Roosevelt's Rough Riders, 30,000 strong, briefly recuperated hereabouts after the Spanish-American War. Otherwise, not much happened.

But in 1926 things took a bizarre turn. That was the year Carl Fisher, the famous Miami Beach developer, bought up most of Montauk with the intention of developing it into the Miami Beach of the north. He built a village center complete with art deco office tower, shops, and roads; improved the harbor facilities; and erected an enormous Tudor-style luxury resort hotel called Montauk Manor. Shortly after this the Florida land bubble burst, and then in 1929 the stock market collapsed. Fisher went bankrupt, and Montauk entered a long and eerie period of decline. The office tower, never occupied, stood vacant for over 50 years. Montauk Manor remained in operation for quite a while, all things considered, but eventually it went under. A collection of modest beachfront motels developed adjacent to the village, but otherwise the place was pretty still.

Then came the 1980s boom. The existing motels all became "resorts," and new ones were built along the beach. Today there are almost a hundred of them, spread along the ocean and scattered among the low hills. Old Montauk Manor was renovated into a condominium that now rents units on a hotel basis to transients. The bleak office tower was also restyled into a glossy condominium, and the streets and shops and general look of the village itself were upgraded substantially.

The essential charm of Montauk lies in its desolate otherworldliness. This is the edge of the world, or at least that's what it can feel like. Much of the tourist development has smoothed the acute edge off this signature charm. Yet it can be savored still in the large (and largely undeveloped) parks that surround the village.

Hither Hills State Park lies west of the town and borders Napeague Harbor. The great majority of it is accessible only on foot, along paths through the dunes or along narrow stony beaches on Napeague Bay and Napeague Harbor. You can explore the "walking dunes," so called because they slowly shift as a result of the wind, by taking little Napeague Harbor Road, which junctions with Route 27 just east of the Lobster Roll (see below) and deadends at an unmarked parking area by the dunes. You'll need good calves for the sandy paths, but the remoteness of the area and the fine views from the tops of the dunes are worth the effort. There is also a beautiful Atlantic beach in Hither Hills, complete with a bathhouse, campsites, and a diminutive general store. The entrance is on Old Montauk Highway, about half a mile east of the junction with Route 27. The eastern section of Hither Hills can be approached on Navy Road, which skirts Fort Pond Bay north of Montauk village. It's pretty spooky up here, however; there are no signs or parking places, and the old cement roadway simply stops without warning at a chain-link barrier.

On the eastern side of Lake Montauk is another pair of parks. **Montauk County Park** preserves more desolate dunes and scrub-oak forest in generally primeval shape. The north entrance is at the end of East Lake Road, past the little Montauk Airport. Another access point is further east on Montauk Highway (Route 27), by a picnic area and Native American museum at **Third House**. This is a picturesque old structure, parts of which date from 1747. Just beyond Third House is **Deep Hollow Ranch** (tel. 516/668-2744), one of several riding-and-boarding establishments that offer daily beach and trail rides, year-round, into the surrounding thousands of acres of parkland.

Most visitors hurry past Third House, however, en route to **Montauk Point State Park.** This serene ending to the tumult of Long Island is only a little over 5 miles from the center of Montauk village. There are nature trails, a snack bar, unspoilt vistas over rolling hills, and ocean vastnesses. Interestingly, the historic Montauk Lighthouse is not a part of the park. It sits within its own fenced enclave and is supported entirely by donations and admission fees ($2 for adults, $1 for kids) to its interesting little museum.

Montauk Point is liable to be very windy and sometimes crowded with daytrippers. But still, it provides an evocative sense of being at the world's edge and in the presence of forces greater than humans.

GARDINERS ISLAND

Last but not least in this part of the world is Gardiners Island, a private manor that's remained in the hands of the Gardiner family for over three centuries. There is no way out to the island save by boat or plane. And since it's private you'd have to be a guest of the Gardiners to even contemplate the trip.

Yet Gardiners Island is a singularly romantic vestige of the past, complete with a windmill, farm, and manor house. King Charles I of England granted the island, as well as considerable additional tracts in other sections of Long Island, to Lion Gardiner in the early 17th century. Shopping centers, expressways, and tract houses now stand on other Gardiner manors. But the 16th Lord of Gardiner's Island still rules a realm untouched even by 18th-century democracy. The island lies low and mysterious on the horizon, cradled by the curling sandy arm of Montauk. It's like the American class system itself, whose greatest charm lies in the fact that so few people realize it exists.

---

5. Where to Stay & Eat in the Hamptons

Collectively the Hamptons occupy a small region, so if you explore one you'll probably wind up exploring them all (or at least several). Village hopping is an accepted pasttime hereabouts, even among full-time residents. Therefore I have collected all my recommended restaurants and hotels into a single section, divided it by village, and listed the individual villages alphabetically. In this manner you can find a good restaurant wherever in the Hamptons you happen to be and a good hotel in whichever Hampton sounds most to your liking.

AMAGANSETT & NAPEAGUE

Gordon's, on Main Street in Amagansett (tel. 516/267-3010), has operated out of its diminutive white-and-brown building in the center of the village for over 15 years. It looks like a nice small-town restaurant, with a lofty little dining room decorated with hanging plants, wheat-colored tablecloths, and a crystal chandelier hanging from an acoustical ceiling. Actually it enjoys a very stylish patronage from the worlds of film and pop music. The menu is limited, but the food is really good. Lunchtime specialties include broiled sea trout, veal marsala, minute steak, or cannelloni au gratin, priced from about $12 to $19. At dinner you'll pay between $18 and $24 for things like filet mignon, veal piccata, beef bordelaise with wild rice, and Long Island duckling. Everything is à la carte. Lunch is served Tuesday to Sunday from noon to 2pm, dinner from 6 to 10pm; no lunch is served during July and August (everybody's at the beach). The restaurant is closed in January and February. All major credit cards accepted.

Less expensive and more homey is **Stephen Talkhouse,** located on Main

Street, Box 1905, Amagansett (tel. 516/267-3117). This is actually a club featuring music and comedy in an intimate setting (see "Nightlife," below). But during the day it offers a good burger-and-sandwich menu with moderate prices.

Out on Napeague Beach a few miles to the east of Amagansett is the **Lobster Roll,** on Montauk Highway (tel. 516/267-3740), recognizable by its big blue sign that says "Lunch." This is a reasonably priced old-fashioned roadhouse with a family atmosphere and fabulous seafood. It has an outside porch whose plastic screens block the wind, boxes full of geraniums, checked plastic tablecloths, and an adjacent sandy lot crammed with cars bound to or from nearby Montauk. The house specialties are seafood salads made from lobster, crab, shrimp, or combinations thereof. They come either on rolls or platters or in bowls. In addition to these are all manner of burgers, fried clams, fish-and-chips platters, chowders, and special broiled fish. The menu's the same at lunch and dinner, and prices range from $4 to $7 for most lunch items, up to about $10 to $14 for the special seafood platters. Open daily from 11:30am to 10pm from Memorial Day to Labor Day; weekends only in May, September, and October; closed during winter.

BRIDGEHAMPTON & WAINSCOTT

Restaurant

HSF, on Montauk Highway in Bridgehampton (tel. 516/537-0550), besides being one of the most stylish Chinese restaurants I've ever seen, is a cousin of the famous Manhattan HSF in Kips Bay. The place is easy to miss, as the black sign on the south side of Montauk Highway (just before the light at Caldor's west of Bridgehampton) is so low-key and tasteful as to be almost invisible. Inside HSF are tailored black banquettes, linen tablecloths, a polished metal ceiling, and an ultrasleek black bar by the door. Lunch might be black-bean chicken Hong Kong style, barbecued roast duck, prawns and scallops in a love nest, or seafood casserole, drawn from a list of chef's suggestions priced between $7 and $17. The early-bird dinner, called Sunset Special and served from 5 to 6:45pm, includes soup, appetizer, choice of main course, rice, and dessert for only $14. The main à la carte menu contains the usual steamed, roast, and crispy Chinese dishes and runs the gamut from beef and pork to chicken and seafood priced between $10 and $20. People in the Hamptons rave about HSF, which is open daily from noon to 3:30pm for lunch and Sunday to Thursday from 3:30 to 11pm for dinner (until midnight on Friday and Saturday). All major credit cards accepted.

EAST HAMPTON

Restaurants

Down a little alley in the very center of town, directly opposite the traffic light at Main Street and Newtown Lane, is **O'Mally's Saloon,** 11 E. Main St. (tel. 516/324-9757). Actually, this is a pretty gentrified alley, what with its pots of geraniums, umbrella tables, sculpture of giraffes, and chic boutiques. O'Mally's has a hearty Irish-saloon atmosphere and a collection of little rooms decorated with ceiling beams, brass rails, leather-lined booths, and an assortment of decorative junk. There are a bar up front and a garden room with a glass roof and hanging green shades in the back. Every conceivable burger is served here, made with mozzarella cheese, smoked barbecue sauce, western chili, onions, spinach, and mushrooms—you name it. There are even a diet burger and a jogger's burger (topped with carrot, celery sticks, a lemon wedge, and lettuce). They all come with french fries and cost about $6. Also available are a few additional sandwiches, plenty of $7 and $8 special dinners, some great heavy desserts, and a 14-ounce marinated steak served with

Irish potatoes and priced at a reasonable $14. For value, location, and congenial atmosphere, this is a hard place to beat. Open daily from 11am until 3am; the kitchen stays open until 11:30pm; until 1am on weekends. MC and V accepted.

Set amid lawns and ancient trees is the old Huntting Inn (see below), home of a luxurious steak-and-lobster restaurant called **The Palm**, 94 Main St. (tel. 516/324-0411). The Palm has a small bar adjacent to several intimate lounges, one furnished with huge green-plush sofas, the other with brass-railed mezzanines, a piano, and flocks of little tables lit by art-glass lamps. The large dining room has low painted-tin ceilings, crisp white cloths, and an adjacent enclosed porch with additional tables. The Palm is the Hamptons branch of the famous New York City establishment of the same name. Unsurprisingly, the entire place has a big-time New York City atmosphere. Primarily it's a steakhouse, serving dinner only, seven days a week during the season from 5 to 11pm. Filet mignon, prime rib, lamb chops, sirloin, plus a few items like swordfish, veal piccata, and shrimp sauté cost about $18 to $30 per plate, à la carte. Dinner is a very handsome experience, and you certainly won't leave hungry. All major credit cards accepted.

There's an atmosphere midway between that of the last two recommendations at **The Grill**, 29 Newtown Lane (tel. 516/324-6300). The location is in the very center of the village, in a trim painted-brick building whose french doors open onto a flower-girt terrace overlooking bustling Newtown Lane. The sleek green-and-white interior is accented with natural-wood booths, exposed-brick walls, framed pictures of sailboats, and a long busy bar. The service is fast and friendly, and the prices are moderate. Chicken pot pie; barbecue spareribs; generous sandwiches; 8-oz. burgers; 10-, 12-, and 16-oz. steaks—all priced between $7 and $17—are available daily from 10:30am to 4am. I liked it a lot. AE, MC, and V accepted.

Classical Italian dinners in truly generous proportions are offered at **Il Monastero**, 128 N. Main St. (tel. 516/324-8008), at the corner of Cedar across from the East Hampton fire and police station. Inside the small gabled building with its red-and-white awnings is a collection of comfortable carpeted dining rooms, paneled in pine, lighted with subdued hanging fixtures, furnished with small tables covered with clean white linen, and suffused with an upscale family atmosphere. Fettuccine, tortellini, rigatoni, classical spaghetti, and much more are served in all styles and sauces. Generous servings of chicken, shrimp, veal, and flounder are available *al vino bianco*, parmigiana, *francese*—you name it. The food is terrific, and the main-dish prices are quite reasonable, from about $10 to $15. Open daily year-round for dinner only, from 5 until 10pm; closed holidays. The same management also owns Il Capuccino in Sag Harbor, recommended below.

There's an excellent seafood restaurant called **Fresno** at 8 Fresno Place (tel. 516/324-0727), a little street parallel to Race Street, one block to the north. Fresno is still new (1988) and quite popular. It seats 67 diners in a coral-colored dining room decorated with brightly colored fish cutouts designed and executed by the chef himself. There is white wicker furniture by a bar up front, with a relaxed summery air throughout. Cuisine is contemporary American with a Mediterranean flair. Main courses like Ali-Oli grilled salmon, roast dolphin, grilled tuna, assorted pasta dishes, and a filet of beef with roast shallots cost between about $17 and $23 à la carte. Open year-round for dinner only from 6 to 11pm. The seven-day-a-week summer schedule tapers off as the temperature falls; by the depth of winter it's open only four nights a week. AE, MC, and V accepted.

Hotels & Their Restaurants

East Hampton boasts a trio of wonderful old inns, and it's a tossup as to which is the most appealing. The rambling old **Huntting Inn,** 94 Main Street, East Hampton, NY 11937 (tel. 516/324-0410), rents 19 deliciously old-fashioned rooms upstairs from The Palm restaurant (recommended above). They have brass beds, low ceilings, floral wallpaper, phones, no TVs (although they could probably scare one up for you if it really mattered), and lots of intimate charm. Double rooms in the spring and fall cost between $85 and $95 nightly; these rates rise to a peak summer season high of $100 to $195 a night with a three-night minimum on weekends. If the inn is full, they send the overflow to a sort of annex on James Lane, located in a lovely old house called **The Hedges** (tel. 516/324-7100), which overlooks the East Hampton Village Green. The Hedges offers similarly appealing lodgings plus a miniature version of The Palm downstairs. Open May through September only. All major credit cards accepted.

The **1770 House,** 143 Main St., East Hampton, NY 11937 (tel. 516/324-1770), is a roomy old center-hall Colonial with black shutters, shaded by majestic trees, surrounded by other historic houses, and located a stone's throw from East Hampton's lovely Village Green. It's about the nicest looking place one could imagine. The interior is a warren of cozy old rooms, chockablock with wonderful antiques, big leather sofas, a grandfather clock clinging picturesquely to a tiny landing on the stair, beams, old pine paneling, and a delightful profusion of nooks and crannies. Each room has air conditioning, a private bath, antique furnishings, pretty wallpaper, sometimes even a fireplace. Frankly, the Chippendale highboys, canopied beds, and marble-topped vanities in the guest rooms are worth the absence of a pool or a tennis court. Besides, you've got the fantastic East Hampton beach.

During July and August management requires a three-night minimum stay on weekends. Nightly double-occupancy room rates range from $105 to $175 and include a full breakfast. The rest of the year there's a minimum weekend stay as well, but it's only two nights. Rates are the same and include the full breakfast. There are only seven rooms in the inn. Another three are down the street in a fabulous mansion called the Philip Taylor House, belonging to the proprietors. Rooms there have fireplaces, gilt mirrors, four-poster beds, and air conditioning and cost $185 nightly during the off-season, $195 on-season. The perfectly beautiful formal garden behind the Taylor House is a soothing wonder to behold.

The **1770 House Restaurant,** located in the main inn, serves breakfast to guests only, lunch to no one at all, but dinner to any and all comers. It's either a $30 or $35 prix-fixe affair providing appetizer (soup, shrimp casino, Oriental scallop salad), salad, main course (like lobster stuffed with crabmeat, stuffed breast of veal, fresh swordfish), plus vegetable, dessert, and coffee. The special off-season Friday night dinner costs only $19.95. The beamed dining room is filled with antique tables, rose medallion plates, pale-strawberry-colored linen napkins, and an enormous number of antique clocks ticking away on the pink-painted walls. Dinner is served from Thursday to Sunday in summer, but on Saturday night only in winter. AE, MC, and V accepted.

Just down the street is the **Maidstone Arms Inn,** 207 Main St., East Hampton, NY 11937 (tel. 516/324-5006). It is two old white houses joined on the first floor and overlooking Main Street and the tranquil lawny expanses of the Village Green. You walk onto a painted porch with a green-and-white-striped awning, through a handsome front door flanked with sidelights, and into what seems for all the world like an elegant Colonial house. An inn since the 1870s, the Maidstone has a collection of 16 deliciously fresh and summery rooms, suites, and cottages. Everything has been recently redone in seaside tones of pale blue and white. The rooms are furnished with painted wicker, framed botanical prints, white-wool rugs, and antique beds and comforters. Accommodations aren't large, but they're so comfortable it doesn't matter. Each has a TV, a phone, air conditioning, and a private bath. High-season double-occupancy rates range from $160 to $185 a night. One-bedroom suites cost $225 and one-bedroom cottages (complete with romantic fireplaces) out back, $250 and up. There's a minimum three-day stay required on summer weekends; two days in the autumn. There's no minimum at all during the winter, when prices drop by about 15%. AE, MC, and V accepted.

Also on the premises, and worthy of a visit whether or not you're staying at the Inn, is the **Maidstone Arms Restaurant** (tel. 516/324-5006). Located in the rear of the main floor, it has that look of colonial chic one expects in East Hampton. The pale-yellow walls are hung with prints of sailing boats, the tables set with handsome silverware on crisp white linen. At lunch, the imaginative American cuisine includes soufflés, omelets, burgers (beef or tuna), and clever pasta dishes at prices mostly between $8 and $14. During the week, there's a special prix-fixe lunch for $9.50. Things are more elaborate at dinner, when main dishes like grilled tuna with olives, lobster in spinach-and-butter glaze, rosemary-roasted free range chicken, and assorted pastas (fusilli with vegetables and light caper sauce, for example) cost from $15 to $24. Breakfast is served from 8:30 to 10:30am, lunch from noon until 3pm, and dinner from 6 to 10:30pm, seven days a week, year-round. AE, MC, and V accepted.

If you're a fan of bed-and-breakfasts, there's an exceedingly elegant one here called the **Centennial House,** 13 Woods Lane, East Hampton, NY 11937 (tel. 516/324-9414). The location is at the western end of Main Street, at the light where Route 27 makes a right-angle turn. Why is this delectable shingled country farmhouse called the Centennial? Because it was built in 1876, the centennial of the United States, by a local craftsman named Babcock. It is surely more elaborate today than anything Babcock ever dreamed. The parlors—outfitted with Oriental rugs, a grand piano, antique furniture, and precious bibelots—are suffused with a shady air of Victorian splendor. There are five wonderful rooms for rent, all with phones, silver bowls of potpourri, immaculate antique furnishings, and private baths. Each has its own name: The Bay Room, for example, is the biggest and best; the Loft Room is up a steep flight of stairs literally under the eaves; the Lincoln has the sort of solid dark furnishings old Abe would have recognized immediately. Buffet breakfast is served at a Chippendale-style table in the formal dining room. Out back is a wonderful pool surrounded by manicured lawns and fruit trees, overlooked by spacious hardwoods and a three-bedroom cottage, also for rent. Nightly double occupancy ranges from $175 to $275 between May and October; off-season prices go down to $100 to $175. Expect minimum-stay requirements (two to four nights) on high-season weekends. The cottage in the back rents for $2,500 weekly in the high season (because it has a kitchen, breakfast is not included). You could easily accommodate six in the cottage. No smoking is allowed anywhere in this bed-and-breakfast. It's hard to imagine a more charming base for an East Hampton vacation.

MONTAUK

Restaurants

On Main Street just east of the circle in the middle of Montauk village is the **Shagwong** (tel. 516/668-3050), an atmospheric tavern/restaurant whose name recalls an ancient, local, Native American fishing village. One room is a neighborhood bar with pine paneling, stuffed fish mounted on the walls, and lots of vintage-looking framed photos of family and friends (including Mick and Bianca Jagger in happier days, plus Candace Bergen and Lee Radziwill). The dining room has Formica tables, pleated shades on the wall sconces, rope moldings on the walls, a black-painted tin ceiling, and a relaxed efficient atmosphere. The lunch menu offers all manner of hot and cold sandwiches, burgers, salad platters, fish sandwiches, broiled chicken breast, and more, priced between $5 and $8. At dinner, in addition to a very excellent early-bird special (available daily from 4:30pm to 6pm) are à la carte selections like herb-crusted codfish fillets, seafood fettuccine alfredo, smothered sirloin steak, fresh flounder piccata, plus lobsters and hamburgers all ranging from $5 (for the burger) to $18 (for a 20-oz. steak). Open daily from 11am to 11pm. All major credit cards accepted.

Another excellent place, also informal and family oriented but considerably bigger, is **Gosman's,** at the end of Flamingo Road right by the entrance to Lake Montauk (tel. 516/668-5330). Gosman's Dock, where the restaurant is located, is a sort of mini theme shopping center, the accent being on seafood and seafaring. It's an attractive, modern, multilevel complex of gray-sided buildings arranged around odd-shaped courtyards and patios overlooking the water. A constant procession of gleaming-white fishing boats passes back and forth in and out of Montauk Harbor. Whitecaps fleck the surface of the Atlantic, gulls cry, and the wind blows. Gosman's Restaurant is a big airy place with lots of windows, beamed ceilings, and a forest of wooden tables and chairs. Typical menu items include swordfish, cold steamed Montauk lobster, fried clams with coleslaw and fries, and all manner of fresh broiled fish, mostly costing between $10 and $18. Open daily from noon until 10pm from mid-April until mid-October. MC and V accepted.

Also on Montauk Harbor, and also open all year, is **Dave's Grill** (tel. 516/668-9190), a waterfront bistro housed in a little shingled cottage whose awninged terrace overlooks the marina filled with fishing boats. Intimate, clean, and friendly, Dave's offers dinner from a list of à la carte dishes that includes fried coconut shrimp and chicken, swordfish steak, grilled yellowfin tuna, blackened catch of the day, and grilled pepper steak for between $15 and $20. The bread pudding with bourbon sauce might have been the best I've ever tasted. Open April through November on Thursday to Tuesday from 5pm to 10:30pm. There are sometimes long lines, so come early. MC and V accepted.

Hotels

Montauk is a beach resort, and most overnight visitors gravitate to the water. In my mind, however, the most interesting place to stay is at the old **Montauk Manor,** 236 Edgemere St., Montauk, NY 11954 (tel. 516/668-4400; fax 516/668-3335). This Tudor-style stucco-and-timber behemoth sprawls across a hilltop location and is visible from practically everywhere in town. It was built as a resort hotel in the 1920s by Carl Fisher, whose story has already been related above. The building was gut-renovated in the mid-1980s and today contains 140 privately owned modern condominiums, of which 70 are managed by a hotel corporation and rented to visitors. Some units have two levels, others have one. All have kitchenettes and sleek modern furnishings and meet a certain standard of luxury set by the hotel. Downstairs is a very grand lobby with soaring beamed ceilings, potted palms, and Oriental rugs. There's a basement exercise room with seven stations and a couple of bikes, plus an adjacent indoor lap pool and a squash court. There are also a large outdoor heated pool with sweeping views of the surrounding countryside and three tennis courts. No restaurant on the premises as yet, but plenty of them are nearby. Accommodations range from studios to two-bedroom apartments, and the rates are extremely complicated. In low season it's possible for two people to stay overnight in one of the studios for $85 or for four people to take a two-bedroom apartment for $150. On high-season weekends, you'll have to stay for at least two nights and the same units will cost $130 and $250, respectively. Weekly rates are significantly discounted, and there are also package deals about which you should inquire. Open year-round. AE, MC, and V accepted.

Among Montauk's many beachfront hotels, the nicest is the **Surf Club,** Box 1174, S. Essex St., Montauk, NY 11954 (tel. 516/668-3800). This is a cooperatively owned building complex, a portion of whose units are run as a hotel by a management company. The Surf Club is an architecturally interesting, contemporary gray-shingled compound with a central pool located directly on the beach. All the units are duplexes with either one or two bedrooms, galley kitchens, tweed sofabeds, color TVs, gray industrial carpeting, and sliding glass doors to small private terraces. The two-bedroom units have rather dramatic cathedral ceilings as well. There are private men's and women's steambaths, plus two tennis courts, in addition to the large and attractive outdoor heated pool. And, of course, the beach is right at your doorstep. What you'll pay per night (and in high season, you might be required to stay at least four nights) depends on whether your unit is ocean front, ocean view, poolside, or garden view (this latter category being a euphemism for looking at a wooden fence). Low-season spring and fall rates range from $65 to $95 per night per unit; at the peak of the summer those units will cost between $215 and $360 nightly with a four-night minimum. Closed mid-November to mid-April. No credit cards accepted.

There are probably another hundred hotels in Montauk, many of which are located up and down the same beach as the Surf Club. The very helpful **Montauk Chamber of Commerce,** P.O. Box 5029, Montauk, NY (tel. 516/668-2428), located on the circle in the center of the village, keeps tabs on all the hotels in town and can advise you of room availability. If you call or write, it will also be happy to send you all manner of tourist information in advance of your visit. Be advised that it is particularly difficult to get a room in Montauk without reservations during the summer season.

SOUTHAMPTON

Restaurants

There's a terrific restaurant downtown, attached to the Old Post House Inn, called the **Post House,** 136 Main St. (tel. 516/283-9696). The shady slate-floored terrace out front, with its pink and white linen and views of the action on Main Street, is a great spot for a summer meal. Inside, the colonial era meets the 1990s, in decor anyway. There's a big bar, beyond which stretches a largish dining room with pink walls and tablecloths. Lunch, served from noon to 3:30pm daily, might be an omelet, the pasta du jour, broiled flounder, or gourmet sandwiches, priced from $5 to $10. The dinner menu, available from 5 to 10pm weekdays (to 11pm on weekends), features appetizers like chevre baked in puff pastry and main courses like steak au poivre, grilled swordfish, marinated tuna, bay scallops, or the fish du jour; prices are around $16 to $24 per à la carte main course. All major credit cards accepted.

For a fast, inexpensive meal, try the **Sip 'n' Soda,** 40 Hampton Ave. (tel. 516/283-9752), a half block east of Main Street, near the Old Post Inn. "Since 1958," it says on the menu, and indeed it looks as though Lucy Ricardo might come spinning through the door at any moment, shouting for Ricky. This is a place for good luncheonette-style sandwiches, salads, burgers, and homemade ice cream (a house specialty). Expect lunch to cost $7 or less. Popular with the locals, it is open daily from 7:30am to 5pm.

The most venerable, and perhaps venerated, eatery in Southampton is **Silver's,** 15 Main St. (tel. 516/283-6443), which has been owned and operated by the same family for generations. Over those years this airy, Mediterranean-yellow room with the windows on Main Street has changed from a vintage luncheonette with a soda counter up front into a continental/Italian-American restaurant. Nowadays, instead of sodas and newspapers, there's a full bar and summer dining hours until midnight. Main courses include Caesar salad and linguini with fresh clams, plus all manner of steaks and chicken, priced moderately between $8 and $15. Particularly good are the lemon sorbetto and chocolate mousse cake for dessert. Silver's serves breakfast, lunch, and dinner in summer, lunch only on off-season weekdays, and dinner only on off-season weekends.

Hungry for a first-class burger? Try **Fellingham's,** a sports bar half a block east of Main Street at 17 Cameron St. (tel. 516/283-9417). Lots of tavern atmosphere here: rafters loaded with athletic trophies, walls covered with photos of great moments in sport, barn-sided walls, varnished wood tables with blue paper placemats, and a busy bar whose hearty patrons seem hardly to notice the TV perpetually tuned to some contest of physical prowess. Burgers aren't the only thing on the menu, but aside from a few hefty omelets, a hot dog or two, daily specials (such as swordfish, scampi, and ribs, for $11 to $17), and the obligatory heavy desserts, they dominate the field and are reasonably priced at between $5 and $6. Open daily from 11am to 11pm; the bar closes at 4am. AE, MC, and V accepted.

Hotels

My favorite hotel in Southampton is the **Village Latch Inn,** 101 Hill St. (the extension of Job's Lane), Southampton, NY 11968 (tel. 516/283-2160). At first glance it looks like an old mansion pressed into modern-day service as an inn. It has tall hedges, big lawns, a green-shuttered Colonial facade, and aristocratic-looking gates on Hill Street. Actually, it used to be the annex to the Irving Hotel, a famous and now-demolished Southampton hostelry that stood across the street. You enter the building from the rear, at the end of a long, dim hallway adjacent to a tiny office. At the distant end of this hall is a collection of bright public rooms filled with overstuffed furniture, hanging plants, bright pillows in floral prints, and random antiques. There's a cheery breakfast porch, as well as a sun porch filled with white wicker and blue floral fabrics. Everything is atmospheric and rather lush.

The 70 guest rooms are distributed among the inn, a shingled annex in the back, and several former estate buildings rescued and moved to the property by the present owners. All accommodations are quite nice and equipped with thick rugs, stripped-oak furniture, tweed-covered chaises, lazy ceiling fans, private baths, phones, easy chairs, and the occasional fireplace. They look somehow sleeker than the typical "country inn," which is perhaps the inevitable result of being in fashionable Southampton. Unlike so many other inns, the Latch also has a pool (a handsome one), a tennis court, and a former conservatory that now contains a hot tub. Parts of the Latch are open only from Memorial Day to Labor Day; other parts stay open all year. The price of a regular double room ranges between $89 and $125 nightly during the week, between $125 and $160 on weekends, plus a 10% service charge. All rates include a full breakfast; a two-night minimum is required on summer weekends. All major credit cards accepted.

Much smaller (only seven rooms) but just as attractive is **Old Post House Inn,** 136 Main St., Southampton, NY 11968 (tel. 516/283-1717). This is a really charming old building, added to over three centuries, and located adjacent to the hub of Southampton's chic Main Street shopping area. The old wooden structure has three stories, shuttered windows, and a big ivy-clad tree by the front door. Beyond the wicker-filled porch is a small lobby with a beamed ceiling and ladderback rush-seated chairs. The rooms upstairs are small but quite luxurious. Each has a private bath, tastefully papered walls, charming old-fashioned bedroom furniture, and surprisingly thick rugs. There's an indefinable Southampton lushness about this place; it's just somehow extra nice. The room rates rise and fall with the mean monthly temperature. At the height of the season you can expect to pay between $95 and $160 nightly, with a two-night minimum required for weekend stays. Rates are slightly less in spring and fall, about a third less during winter. Continental breakfast, included in the room rates, is served by an ancient fireplace downstairs in a room with a hooked rug, English pine furniture, and low ceiling beams. AE, MC, and V accepted.

Although the location is on busy Route 27, **Southampton Resorts,** County Road 39, Southampton, NY 11968 (tel. 516/283-7600, or toll free 800/321-4969; fax 516/283-4625), offer such solid value, attractive accommodations, and gracious service that you should definitely consider them. There are two locations: One is called **Cold Spring Bay,** located on Route 27 in Shinnecock Hills west of Southampton; the other is the **Bayberry Inn,** also on Route 27, immediately north of Southampton village. Each of these facilities offers extremely attractive motor inn–style rooms with color TVs, phones, pickled-pine furniture, fresh chintz fabrics, pastel wallcoverings, and air conditioning. The Cold Spring has a beautiful outdoor pool and two tennis courts. The Bayberry also has a lovely pool, slightly smaller rooms (although just as nicely decorated), and an adjoining Chinese restaurant. Off-season double-room rates range from $70 to $90 nightly; high-summer doubles cost from $90 to $140; high-summer weekend packages (two-night minimum) cost $350 to $480; one- and two-bedroom suites are more. Reduced-rate packages abound, so be sure to ask. All major credit cards accepted.

Hill Guest House, 535 Hill St., Southampton, NY 11968 (tel. 516/283-9889), occupies a comfy old shingled house painted white and screened from the street by high private hedges. There's a grassy parking lot in the back, between the house and the barn. Scattered on the clipped grass are lawn chairs and plastic chaises. Beyond the wooden-floored porch with its obligatory wicker is a cheerful and modest guesthouse, run for the last nearly 30 summers by Mr. and Mrs. Salerno of Queens, N.Y. The six rooms have window shades, painted furniture, and vintage metal beds and are neat and clean as a pin. It's a great old-fashioned place, and you'll be lucky if you can get in. Weekday rates range from $60 to $70 nightly, double occupancy, the highest rate applying to rooms with private bath. On weekends, when there's a three-night minimum, the rates range from $65 to $75 per night, double occupancy. Continental breakfast is served downstairs in the dining room between 9 and 11am for an additional $1.50. Open during summer only.

SAG HARBOR

Restaurants
There's a wonderful and reasonably priced little Italian place in Sag Harbor, open for dinner only, called **Il Capucino**, on Madison Street (tel. 516/725-2747). It's in a small red building with a hanging picture of a monk outside, located within sight of the commercial center of Sag Harbor just two blocks south of the American Hotel. Inside is a collection of small rooms with hanging chianti bottles, white-washed shingles, unstained pine on the walls, and flocks of little tables with red-and-white-checked cloths. The menu offers antipasti (steamed clams, mussels, calamaretti in bianco) for between $5 and $8, pasta dishes like tortellini al Pistaccio (stuffed with cheese in Alfredo sauce), and veal, chicken, and shrimp dishes sautéed variously in garlic, herbs, and tomatoes, for between $10 and $17. Open daily from 5:30 until 10pm.

Also fun, and reasonably priced, is **Spinnakers**, next to the Municipal Building (the tallest in town, with the cupola) on Main Street (tel. 516/725-9353). Spinnakers has a cheerful yellow awning over the street and shutters with whale cutouts on the second floor. Inside, it is a tavern/restaurant with a new "vintage" look—brown stamped-tin ceiling, carved wood bar, brass gasoliers, dark-wood booths, exposed-brick walls, and hanging ferns in the windows. At lunch it serves club sandwiches, burgers, grilled cheese, and Caesar salad, plus main courses like pan-seared chicken, crabcakes, and grilled sirloin for about $5 to $12. Dinner main courses such as grilled swordfish, poached salmon filet, spiced shrimp with shiitake mushrooms, and surf and turf run from about $15 to $20. A café menu of lighter fare, from $7 to $10, is also available at dinner. Spinnakers is open for lunch weekdays from 11:30am until 5pm; dinner runs from 5 to 10pm (to 11pm on weekends); Sunday brunch is served from 11:30am until 3pm. AE, MC, and V accepted.

Hotels & A Restaurant
You might also consider taking a meal (or staying the night; see below) in the restored Victorian precincts of the **American Hotel**, Main Street, Sag Harbor, NY 11963 (tel. 516/725-3535). This old three-story brick landmark has a lacy white porch tacked onto its front, stone tubs full of flowering rhododendron, antique blue-wicker porch chairs, and people's bikes leaning casually against the walls. The dining areas are divided by a plushy Victorian lobby filled with Oriental rugs, dark carved furniture, and paisley wallpaper. It's small, but plummy. The bar just beyond it has fringed shades on the light fixtures, old dark-wood paneling, a collection of little café tables, and a comfy Victorian clutter. The atmosphere is terrific.

Diners who'd like to smoke can eat in the bar, or in the attractive atrium with skylights and hanging plants. The nonsmokers' dining room, on the opposite side of the bar, is decorated with old-fashioned gilt-framed pictures, patterned wallpaper, crisp white linens, and Victorian chandeliers. Lunch, served daily from noon, might be a sautéed burger, eggs Benedict, chicken club, or a warm duck salad with wild mushrooms, priced from about $5 to $19.50. There's a much larger dinner menu, available from 4pm to 11pm, that includes courses like horseradish-encrusted blackfish with lime vinaigrette, roast Long Island codfish, côte de boeuf bearnaise, veal sweetbreads, brace of grilled quail, even antelope paillard au poivre vert. A la carte prices in the evening range from about $17 to $28.

Upstairs at the American are eight hotel rooms, all with private baths and perfectly restored (reconstructed really). They are furnished with wall-to-wall carpeting, sleigh beds, flowered curtains, gilt-framed pictures, and miscellaneous antiques. They're pretty big too, as "inn" rooms go. Low-season room rates are $130 per night on weekends (two-night minimum; three nights on holidays), $99 per night on weekdays (no minimum), rising to $175 and $125, respectively, in the high season. It's a lovely place, but the physical charm has been known to exceed the hospitality. All major credit cards accepted.

For accommodations of a completely different sort, there's **Baron's Cove,** West Water Street, Sag Harbor, NY 11963 (tel. 516/725-2100). This is an appealing resort motel across the street from a marina that's a stone's throw from the historic center of Sag Harbor. Sixty-six units are housed in a pair of two-story buildings connected by outdoor corridors. Pool and waterview units date from the early 1980s. Each has either a private porch or balcony, overlooking either the large pool or the marina and glittering waters beyond. The farmview units in the older building are similar but lack the private outdoor areas. Every unit has a kitchenette (bring your own pots and pans), a color TV, a modern bathroom, contemporary furniture, and a color scheme of robin's-egg blue and peach. They all have a beachy quality, clearly designed for durability. Besides the pool, there's a fine tennis court out back. Double-occupancy room rates range from a deep-winter weekday low of $69, to a high-season waterview high of $185, with quite a few stops in between. Expect minimum-stay requirements on certain holiday high-season weekends. Water-view loft units, which sleep four, cost from $115 to $130 nightly on the shoulder seasons and $210 nightly in July, August, and September. All major credit cards accepted.

6. Nightlife

Nightclubs and good bars with music come and go at a dizzying rate out here. The very best way to find out what's hot at the time of your visit is to consult *Dan's Papers,* available in stacks at delis, hotels, shops, and restaurants all over the Hamptons. Each issue contains all manner of interesting articles on Hampton topics, plus invaluable lists of good restaurants, stores, and nightspots. It's even free, at least on the east end of the island. You can order a copy at minimal cost by contacting them in advance at 516/537-0500; the editorial offices are located on Main Street, Bridgehampton, NY 11932.

Nightclubs in the Hamptons are dependably open on summer weekends and occasionally on summer weeknights as well. As in the city, they don't get going until late; don't expect much to be happening before 11pm. And be sure there's a designated driver in your party, as random road checks by police are the rule, not the exception.

A good friend and Hampton habituée helped me compile the following list of suggestions that were hot at press time. They are in geographical order, moving from west to east.

There are bands and cabaret acts at **Hampton Square** (tel. 516/288-1877) and all manner of different bands (particularly dixieland and country and western at this writing) at **Montage** (tel. 516/288-2255), both in Westhampton. Several places offer dancing until the proverbial "wee hours." Try **Marakesh** (tel. 516/288-1800) in Westhampton Beach, and/or **Polo Croundo** (tel. 516/728-4200), **Captains Two** (tel. 516/728-5561), and **Boardy Barn** (tel. 516/728-5760), all in Hampton Bays. A good Hampton Bays bar for just plain drinking is **Doran's** (tel. 516/728-9560).

Dance clubs in Southampton include **Element** (tel. 516/283-7700), **Burke's Roadhouse** (tel. 516/283-7228), **Buckley's Irish Pub** (tel. 516/329-0600), and **Hansom House** (tel. 516/283-9772). **Country Club** (tel. 516/283-5550) is more genteel, with good food and dinner dancing.

There are an excellent piano bar called **Bobby Van's** (tel. 516/537-0590) and a late-night dance spot called **Ed's Music Inn** (tel. 516/537-1700), both in Bridgehampton. Up in Sag Harbor are several nightspots worthy of a visit, among them **Corner Bar** (tel. 516/725-9760) and **Johnny's Cove Inn** (tel. 516/725-5777), for all sorts of different music (depending on what's in fashion), plus the great late-night bar at **Sunset Grille** (tel. 516/725-5892), the latter often featuring very cool jazz. Not to forget the bar at the **American Hotel** (tel. 516/725-3535) either, which usually has excellent piano music, and **The Amazon Dock** (tel. 516/725-9000), which has the hottest dance music at the moment in the Sag Harbor area.

East Hampton offers smoother fare at **Jackstraw's Café** (tel. 516/329-0600). A little farther out in Amagansett is the famous **Stephen Talkhouse** (tel. 516/267-3117), featuring a variety of famous music acts, and **Ocean's** (tel. 516/267-6611), with bands, dancing, and a popular bar.

Gurney's (tel. 516/668-2660) is a huge resort in Montauk that always has live music during the season. For something a little more intimate in the same area, try **Tipperary Inn** (tel. 516/668-2010) or **Dave's Grill** (tel. 516/668-9190).

Everything above, of course, is liable to change at any moment. Call before you go. And don't forget to pick up *Dan's Papers!*

LONG ISLAND RESORTS: THE NORTH SHORE

Most visitors to Long Island's North Fork arrive there via the Long Island Expressway from Manhattan or the Shelter Island ferries (see "An Excursion to Shelter Island" at the end of this chapter) from the Hamptons. If you're coming from New York, however, there are good reasons to detour along the way, prime among them being the intriguing region around Stony Brook.

1. Stony Brook

The lovely restored village of **Stony Brook,** located on the North Shore of Suffolk County about 50 miles from Manhattan (exit 62 on the Expressway) bears the indelible mark of a man named Ward Melville, owner of Marshall's and Thom McCann. In 1940, already alert to the aesthetic damage being wrought in other parts of the Island, Melville instigated an ambitious plan to rebuild Stony Brook along 18th-century lines (at his own expense) and to protect the surrounding area with strict zoning. The result, mellowed by half a century of growing trees and careful tending of both new and historic buildings, is a village that is as economically vigorous as it is physically charming.

Stony Brook is one of the nicest places on Long Island. It is the heart of what out here they call the "three villages": **Stony Brook, Setauket,** and **Old Field.** The area possesses rural charm, fascinating Revolutionary War connections, excellent accommodations, great shopping, a major museum with a singularly creative presentation of Americana, and lots of little rural roads and byways to explore, along one of which is the family home (still private) of the famous architect Stanford White.

At the center of Stony Brook is an elliptical row of shops built by Melville in 1941. The Stony Brook Community Fund informs me that this is the nation's first planned shopping center with attached shops and delivery facilities in the rear. Would that every center since had followed a similar model. In the middle of it is Stony Brook's pillared post office, whose pediment contains a noble-looking **mechanical eagle** that flaps its wings on the hour. It looks like the one on the quarter in your pocket, except for one thing: Its head is facing the opposite direction. Ward Melville was an avowed anti–New Dealer. In 1940, he proclaimed his essential conservatism by having Stony Brook's American eagle face the opposite direction as everybody else's.

Mr. Melville's village center was originally a collection of convenience stores (notions, liquor, dry cleaner, delicatessen). It has evolved into something quite different over the years, however, and today houses upscale purveyors of expensive clothing, home furnishings, and gift items. There's still a cleaner and a barber, but these establishments are sandwiched between outposts of Talbots and Laura Ashley.

Stony Brook and adjacent **Setauket** are filled with interesting old houses, churches, even a working grist mill opposite the old Mill Pond. On Wednesday through Sunday during summer you can see a miller actually grinding grain on stone wheels. As of this writing, plans include an adjoining Mill Store to offer local food and gift items for sale. Call the Community Fund at 516/751-2244 for hours and further information.

The Community Fund also publishes package-vacation flyers and a walking-tour brochure that can provide a very pleasant afternoon's excursion. You can pick this up at their office, on the second floor of the Stony Brook Village Center, all the way at the south end of the building, or obtain it in advance by writing: Stony Brook Village Center, P.O. Box 572, Stony Brook, NY 11790 (tel. 516/751-2244). Also available are driving-tour brochures, a local events calendar, and what the helpful staff described to me as "ideas for lovely summer evenings."

Stony Brook and Setauket, among other things, claim to be the cradle of American espionage. The reason Nathan Hale was hanged in 1776 was due to what John LeCarré would call a lack of shopcraft. Washington dispatched Hale on a critical intelligence-gathering mission with neither training, contacts, nor even a cover story. Two years later, desperate for information on what the British were up to on Long Island and in New York, Washington recruited a patriot-major named Tallmadge who, besides having been Hale's roommate at Yale, was a native of Setauket.

Tallmadge proceeded to recruit a spy cell, the first in this nation's history, from trusted friends in the village of his birth. These people were only too happy to assist, as the British occupation of both New York City and Long Island was particularly brutal. One was a housewife named Anna Strong, whose clothesline overlooking the sound became a message center. Another was a local tavern keeper named Austin Roe, the "unsung Paul Revere" of the American Revolution, who rode 1,000 miles with vital secret messages, as opposed to Revere's 16. A third was a rich farmer named Abraham Woodhull, whose frayed nerves led him to recruit the famous Culper, Jr., of Raynham Hall in Oyster Bay. The latter spy's secret intelligence became one of the most valuable weapons in Washington's arsenal.

All these people risked their lives and more to gather and deliver information on British plans and troop movements. Their greatest achievement came in 1780, when a French expeditionary force of seven ships carrying 6,000 troops approached the Long Island shore. The American spies were able to advise Washington of exactly how and where the British intended to respond. Washington then devised a ruse. As British troops left New York to meet the oncoming French, Washington wrote a set of spurious orders detailing an attack on Manhattan, then purposely allowed this document to fall into British hands. The British promptly turned their troops around and marched them back to Manhattan, allowing the French to land unmolested on the shore of Long Island. A year later, those French forces would be just enough to turn the tide of revolution in favor of the American cause.

Woodhull's house survives today, as does the promontory from which Strong hung her clothesline with various combinations of handkerchiefs and petticoats to indicate to which secret drop point her confederates should repair. Those interested in this dramatic period of American history and in the derring-do of three village natives should repair to the **Emma S. Clark Library,** 120 Main St., Setauket (tel. 516/941-4080), and peruse its excellent local history collection. The library is open Monday to Friday from 9:30am to 9pm, from 9am to 5pm on Saturday, and from 1 to 5pm on Sunday during the school year.

Besides having taste, money, and civic-mindedness, Ward Melville was a major collector of antique carriages. His personal collection now constitutes the core of the carriage collection at **The Museums at Stony Brook,** 1208 Rte. 25A (at the corner of Main Street), Stony Brook, NY 11790 (tel. 516/751-0066). The museums are housed in a complex of barn-red buildings surrounding a small green. The carriage house contains 90 horse-drawn vehicles ranging from a 19th-century vis-à-vis to James Beekman's magnificent hand-painted coach, built in 1771. This is the place to learn the difference between a station brougham and a spider phaeton and to marvel at the idea of the world having once moved entirely by horsepower.

The adjacent art museum contains paintings, drawings, and writings of a noted 19th-century genre artist and Stony Brook native named William Sidney Mount. Some of these paintings are marvelously evocative of times past on rural Long Island. If you like art and history, you'll enjoy this part of the exhibition. Also on display are 15 rather incredible, fully furnished miniature rooms, a collection of antique decoys, plus assorted period buildings that have been moved to the little green. Among the latter is a one-room schoolhouse upon whose blackboard, during my last visit, was the following poem: "Who do not any school attend/But trifle as they will/For almost certain in the end/Will come to something ill." Not exactly the Montessori theory, but food for thought.

The museums are open year-round, Wednesday through Saturday and most Monday holidays from 10am to 5pm and Sunday from noon to 5pm. Admission is $6 for adults, $4 for seniors and students, and $3 for kids over 6. Also on the premises is an excellent museum shop.

A little over 2 miles west on 25A is the intersection with Moriches Road. Turn right (north) for half a mile through still unspoilt woodlands until you come to a little clapboard general store on your right at 516 Moriches Rd. This is the **St. James General Store** (tel. 516/862-8333), a National Historic Landmark that has been in continuous operation since 1857. There is a wooden Indian on the porch, a wagon wheel leaning against the wall, and an atmospheric clutter of goods within. No longer is this a rural post office, notions store, and grocery. Today the shelves are filled with stone pears, soap, sachet, postcards, books on Long Island, jams, and homemade baked goods. In short, it's a gift shop, but a historic and atmospheric one. Open daily all year from 10am to 6pm.

Less than a mile north on Moriches Road is a small lane named Cordwood Path that cuts down a steep hill to your right. At this point you're in **Nissequogue.** Set back from the intersection of Moriches and Cordwood, invisible during summer, is **Box Hill,** once the home of architect Stanford White. The property is private and not open to the public. Wintertime glimpses of it from Moriches Road will have to suffice for the devotees of this brilliant American artist.

If you turn right onto Cordwood, you can take the scenic route back to the center of Stony Brook along the edge of picturesque Stony Brook Bay. Cordwood descends into an enchantingly steep wooded hollow. You'll turn sharply right when you reach the water, then proceed along a twisting lane dotted with gracious old houses on expansive grounds enjoying vistas of unspoilt inlets and glittering waters, crying gulls, and leafy woods. Truly this is the Long Island that Stanford White knew. Bear left onto Harbor Road and continue through **Head of the Harbor,** a gracious and comfortable old neighborhood whose waterfront houses enjoy wonderful views of the bay, until you arrive back at the Mill Pond in Stony Brook.

WHERE TO STAY & EAT

After all this sightseeing you must be hungry and probably ready for an interesting place to stay as well. First choice in the area is the **Three Village Inn,** 150 Main St., Stony Brook, NY 11790 (tel. 516/751-0555; fax 516/751-0593), which is both an appealing restaurant and a delightful country inn. It's a leafy, lawny place located right in the middle of orderly and crisply painted Stony Brook. The central building is a rambling, shingled, and dormered farmhouse built in the 18th century by the Hallock family. It sits well back from the road, shaded by immense trees and graced by stone terraces, precisely clipped beds of ivy, and colorful tubs of flowers. The interior looks a bit like the country house of some rich New Yorker. It has paneled walls, elegant colonial-era fireplaces, beamed ceilings, and handsome wing chairs upholstered in dark green and gold. The restaurant serves American and New England specialties and seafood in a collection of attractive, glass-enclosed porches, a flower pattern–papered dining room, and a masculine-looking tap room. Salads, sandwiches, burgers, omelets, and main courses (like fish and chips, grilled salmon, and breast of chicken) cost between $8 and $15 at lunch. A complete dinner, with a main course such as shrimp in ale batter, roast Long Island duckling, double rib lamb chops, and prime rib, are priced between $22 and $30. The restaurant is open daily for breakfast from 7 to 11am, lunch from noon until 4pm, and dinner from 5pm until the last guest leaves. AE, MC, and V accepted.

The inn has a total of 27 rooms, 8 of which are located up tiny stairways and down labyrinthine corridors in the main building, the balance being out back behind ivy-covered trees in half a dozen cottage buildings. They all have air conditioning, phones, TVs, private baths, and sort of a "grandma" look (chenille spreads, spool beds, beamed ceilings, small-patterned wallpaper). I thought they were awfully nice. And the prices—$85 to $100 for a single, $95 to $110 for a double, $125 for the three rooms with working fireplaces and Duraflame logs—are certainly reasonable. AE, MC, and V accepted.

For something more offbeat, you'll doubtlessly enjoy the **Australian Country Inn,** 1036 Ft. Salonga Rd., Route 25A on your road map (tel. 516/754-4400), located 13 miles west of Stony Brook in Northport. This original restaurant is perched on a hillside above the highway, reachable via a steep drive lined with cutouts of kangaroos alternately leaping and holding surfboards. The multilevel interior has an upstairs bar where you can dance to weekend combos as well as a big dining room downstairs. There are stucco walls, heavy beams, and Australian memorabilia everywhere. The menu reflects both the proprietor's sense of humor and her roots "down under." There are steaks "from the outback"; Australian Pacific fish, stuffed shrimp, and the like from the "middle of the tuckerbag"; and jumbucks (lamb chops) "from the sheep station." Most dinner main courses cost between $15 and $25. At lunch, similar semiexotic fare costs about half that. It's really a lot of fun. Open for dinner Sunday to Thursday from 4 to 10:30pm (until midnight on Friday and Saturday). As of this writing, management plans to open for lunch as well; better call first for exact hours. AE, MC, and V accepted.

I have seen the future, of Long Island anyway, and it is in nearby Hauppauge (14 miles south of Stony Brook). That's pronounced HAW-PAWG, with almost equal emphasis on both syllables. It's a 20-minute drive from Stony Brook. Proceed south on Route 97 (Nichols Road) to Route 347; then west on 347 to Route 454 (Veterans Memorial Highway); then east on Vets Highway for less than 2 miles to Vanderbilt Parkway, which is on your left amidst a string of outrageously postmodern office buildings just north of exit 57 on the Long Island Expressway. Turn left (east) and shortly you will arrive at the impressive modern gates to the **Marriott Wind Watch,** 1717 Vanderbilt Pkwy. (exit 57 on the Long Island Expressway), Hauppauge, NY 11788 (tel. 516/232-9800, or toll free 800-228-9290; fax 516/232-9853).

This is some kind of a place, an elegant skyscraper (well, at least 10 floors) perched atop a silent windy hilltop and presiding over a vast panorama of the North Shore of Suffolk County. Marriott has gone all out on the Wind Watch, and truly it has a grand hotel feel to it. There are marble floors by the acre, polished wood columns, severely elegant wall sconces in the shape of classic bowls, and a huge atrium lounge with fat columns and echoey Muzak. Downstairs are broad and silent corridors that drip with crypto-Egyptian grandeur modified somewhat by a contemporary American corporate accent.

The 362 attractive modern rooms are reached by extremely elegant wood, brass, and mirrored elevators. All accommodations have big desks, brass lamps, floral-chintz quilted spreads, digital clocks, gold-framed mirrors or prints of things like Old Westbury Gardens, two phones, color TVs, modern bathrooms with big vanities, full amenities, and an overall air of competent luxury. Most rooms also have balconies, from which you can muse over the curiously empty looking Long Island countryside (where did all that development you passed on the road go?).

Downstairs is an "action lounge" (their term) called Tickets, a very handsome dining room called JW's Sea Grill, a terrific exercise room overlooking what is certainly the most attractive indoor pool I've seen, a huge outdoor pool, plus a separate golf house with snack bar and adjacent 18-hole Joe Lee–designed private course. Predisposed as I am to vintage architecture, I must admit I found this place enormously attractive and ideally situated for an exploration of Stony Brook. The rooms cost $135 to $150 for a single and $155 to $160 for a double depending on location and time of year. As of this writing the weekend "TFB" (that's "two for breakfast") package cost $109 for a double and included a full breakfast. The toll-free number above has Marriott's nationwide specials at any given time. All major credit cards accepted.

About 5 miles east of Stony Brook is the village of Port Jefferson, a bright, beachy former whaling town beyond which the farm fields at last begin to outnumber the housing tracts. Right on the harbor is **Danford's Inn,** 25 E. Broadway, Port Jefferson, NY 11777 (tel. 516/928-5200; fax 516/928-3598). This is an enormous place with endless balconies, brick walls, and boutiques. Although it's completely new, the style is Victorian and the effect isn't bad at all.

The restaurant is really terrific, a big bright room overlooking the harbor, paneled in tongue-and-groove stained wood, lit with faux Tiffany lamps, and graced with a porch perfect for warm-weather dining. The lunch menu lists main courses (fresh sole, sautéed shrimp, shell steak), salad platters, and all manner of hot and cold sandwiches (roast beef, turkey, shrimp salad) for between $8 and $15. The dinner menu features dishes like Long Island duckling Grand Marnier, blackened shell steak, grilled salmon, and chilled seafood salad for about $18 to $27. Open daily from 7am to 11pm.

Also located at Danford's, above all those boutiques (and a lobby with a portrait of Washington labeled "I Never Slept Here"), are 86 particularly nice hotel rooms. All have balconies, 80% of which face the water. The "executive doubles" are really lordly with their Victorian accent pieces, canopied beds, lavish baths, and rattan balcony furniture. But even the standard rooms are pretty terrific. They have wall-to-wall carpeting, very nice framed prints on the walls, color TVs, Queen Anne benches with damask upholstery, and gilt-framed mirrors. Five even have fireplaces. The quality throughout is top-notch. Singles cost $110 to $135 nightly; doubles, $120 to $150. There are suites too, priced from $175 to $300 a night. Rates include breakfast during the week. All major credit cards accepted.

If you're one of those with a penchant for bed-and-breakfasts, there's an appealing one in Port Jefferson, on the west side of town, called the **Compass Rose,** 415 W. Broadway (Route 25A), Port Jefferson, N.Y. 11777 (tel. 516/474-1111, or toll free 800/244-2684; fax 516/928-9326). This is a sweet little blue-shingled cottage with cream trim sitting behind a picket fence. There are four diminutive but attractive rooms, painted in colonial colors, carpeted in thick pink wall-to-wall, and decorated with a mixture of "grandma" and Sears furniture. Prices range from $58 to $88 nightly, the latter being for either of the two rooms with private bath and color cable TV. Breakfast, set out in the morning on the dining room sideboard and taken in an adjoining tiny parlor, consists of bagels, cakes, buns, dry cereal, fruit, tea, and coffee. Everything is immaculately clean, and the ladies who run the place are hospitable. AE, MC, DC, and V accepted.

2. What to See & Do on the North Fork

The North Fork is that complementary spit of land that balances Long Island's South Fork. The tips of their respective tines dandle Gardiners Island between them. A little deeper down their throat lies fashionable Shelter Island. And at the bottom of the split, where both forks originate, lies the little city of Riverhead, seat of Suffolk County.

The North Fork, geography aside, is nothing at all like the South Fork. Besides the glittering waters of Great Peconic Bay, Little Peconic Bay, Shelter Island Sound, and Gardiners Bay, a sort of antipathy has traditionally divided their respective populations. In recent years, the real differences between these two worlds have begun to blur. What's happening is that the North Fork, traditionally rural, agricultural, and unpretentious, is beginning (*just* beginning, mind you) to get a wee bit Hamptonish.

What's the North Fork like now? The most obvious change is that old Long Island bugaboo: heavy traffic. But that's only on summer weekends. During the winter and on rainy summer weekdays, the North Fork looks like any other farming region in rural America. Planted fields stretch away toward the horizon; pretty (albeit slightly ramshackle) villages, each with a nice white church and a single stoplight, cluster around the main road (N.Y. 25) at respectable distances from one another; diner lots and gas stations are full of pickup trucks and battered sedans; there's no suburban sprawl, but there are plenty of modest split-level houses dotted around the countryside. As for flashy mansions and startlingly modern condo complexes of the sort that dominate the South Fork, there is (as yet) hardly a trace.

Oh, but it's coming. At least people seem to think it is. The locals have read the proverbial handwriting on the wall with a curious mixture of outrage and excitement. True, it's getting hard to drive around during the summer. True, that slightly blowsy lot next door that one neglected to pick up 10 years ago for $16,000 was sold to some city people (just before the 1989 crash) for $200,000. On the other hand, there's a curious new prestige associated with the North Fork, something that was never a part of earlier local equations. And most important, the old homestead, especially if it should happen to be a farm with maybe 100 acres, is suddenly worth millions even in a sagging real estate market.

The most interesting recent development on the North Fork is the proliferation of **vineyards** and **wineries.** Visitors can take a leisurely tour of some, sampling the products of each in often quite beautiful surroundings. Since 1983, there has even been a North Fork appellation, limited to wines that contain at least 85% North Fork grapes. There is a Hamptons appellation on the South Fork as well, but it consists of only 2 wineries as opposed to 12 on the North Fork. I am happy to report that some of these Long Island wines are excellent. Certainly the chardonnays and merlots are the equal of any I've drunk.

The vineyards total only about 1,600 North Fork acres, but they have become an increasingly visible part of the rural landscape. As you drive along the main roads you'll see them everywhere, together with green signs proclaiming the near presence of a winery. This new agricultural activity imparts a cultivated aspect to the countryside and represents a very considerable outlay of capital, as well as a dedicated long-term commitment to local winemaking. It takes between five and seven years before there's any output. Nobody does this for a quick profit; planting a vineyard and opening a winery are more of a lifestyle decision than anything else.

There's high art involved in the making of wine. This isn't Lucy stamping around in a vat of grapes with a bunch of women who speak only Italian. Some winemakers demand carte blanche in decisions pertaining to mixture, aging, fermentation, and other matters. Others essentially follow orders. It is a sophisticated field, one that is lending an elegant, unstuffy, and glamourous new atmosphere to agricultural life here. Each winery is actively engaged in a quest to define itself, to perfect its product, and to establish Long Island as a source of high-quality American wine.

What they call the **Wine Trail,** on the North Fork, is an elongated and irregular circle bordered by the following: Route 25, the main east-west drag hereabouts, on the south; Route 105, a divided expressway outside Riverhead, on the west; Sound Avenue and its continuation called Route 48 (or North Road) on the north; and the village of Peconic at the easternmost end. Almost every North Fork winery and vineyard adjoins this circle. You can pick up or leave off pretty much anywhere you choose, stopping at as many or as few wineries as strike your fancy on almost any day typically between about 11am and 5pm. Not all vineyards have wineries attached. Those that do will graciously show you how their wine is made, invite you to taste some (usually, but not always, for free), and then sell you as many bottles as you want. Some have beautiful tasting rooms with views of lush vineyards and distant woods. Others are housed in converted potato barns that may be short on architectural charm even though the wine is good. The wine, it should be stated, varies considerably from one place to the next.

The most westerly of the wineries is also the oldest and arguably the most elaborate. This is **Palmer Winery**, on Sound Avenue in Aquebogue, about a mile east of Route 105 (tel. 516/722-4080). Palmer is very visitor-friendly, and its installation is designed for a short but thorough self-guided tour. You can peer through windows into rooms devoted to the various steps of winemaking and read signs that explain the entire process from grapevine to bottled product—all en route to the tasting room and sales floor at the end.

By far the majority of wineries is on Route 25 in the vicinity of Cutchogue and Peconic. **Gristina Vineyards,** on Main Road (Route 25) in Cutchogue (tel. 516/734-7089), has a beautiful new tasting room that overlooks the winemaking facilities. You can sample the excellent wine and get a tour sitting still. **Peconic Bay Vineyards,** also on Main Road in Cutchogue (tel. 516/734-7361), probably has the most impressive vineyard; it seems to stretch on forever. Cutchogues's **Bedell Cellars** (tel. 516/486-2686) makes what, in the opinion of many, is Long Island's best wine.

Still on Main Road (Route 25), but farther east in Peconic, is **Pindar Vineyards** (tel. 516/734-6200), with a huge tasting room and probably the biggest weekend crowds. Also in Peconic on Route 25 is **Lenz Winery** (tel. 516/734-6010), with very fine wines and perhaps the best-looking winery on the island.

There are others, of course, but this will give you a feel for the area. Expect the typical bottle of Long Island wine to run between $6.50 and $15. High price does not always mean the best taste. Be sure to ask questions; they love answering them. If you're truly a wine fanatic, you're in for a treat.

The North Fork, like its larger and glossier sister to the south, also contains its requisite complement of 17th-century churches and houses. If old colonial stuff is your cup of tea, there's at least one interesting building to look at in almost every village. Out in **Orient**, for instance, there's a small complex of them, administered by the **Oysterponds Historical Society,** on Village Lane (tel. 516/323-2480). An 18th-century house and an adjacent Victorian-style boarding house, both with special exhibits, are just two reasons to visit. The village of Orient itself is really gorgeous too, in a petite, rural, Long Island fashion. Oysterponds is open on weekends from June to mid-September 2 to 5pm (and Wednesday and Thursday too, during July and August). It warrants inclusion in any excursion out to Orient. Admission is $3 for adults and 50¢ for kids.

Greenport, opposite Shelter Island, has several modest attractions, among them the **Stirling Historical Society's restored village house** on Main Street (tel. 516/477-0099). Admission is $1 for adults, children free, and it is open from July 4 until Labor Day, Wednesday, Saturday, and Sunday from 1 to 4pm.

Perhaps more notable in the area is the aptly named **Old House,** on the **Village Green** in Cutchogue, midway between Riverhead and Orient Point. Maintained by the Cutchoque–New Suffolk Historical Council (tel. 516/734-7122), this structure, built in 1649, claims the distinction of being the oldest English house in New York State. Its weathered boards and shingles were restored in 1940, but it still manages to look older than Time itself. Note the rather aristocratic chimney, which would look as comfortable on an East Hampton mansion. The Old House is part of a small complex that includes the Wickham House (the apotheosis of the charming shingled Long Island farmhouse) and a little white schoolhouse complete with circa-1840 desks, blackboard, and maps. Open weekends 2 to 5pm from Memorial Day to Labor Day; Mondays also in July and August; and by appointment in May and October. Admission is $1.50 for adults and 50¢ for kids under 12.

Despite advances in room rates and property prices, plus the recent arrival of horse farms and vineyards, you mustn't think that the North Fork has completely lost its rural, laid-back appeal. Driving through the fields along Sound Avenue or gazing off into the ocean distances from Orient are still soul-soothing experiences. There are a number of charming places to stay and eat, and prices are not as high as they are on the South Fork. The villages are unpretentious but fun to explore. There are abundant farm stands where you can select the freshest imaginable produce right by the side of the field in which it grew. And there are other fields, marked by hand-lettered signs on big pieces of cardboard, where you can still go out and pick your own fresh produce.

It's less than 30 miles from Riverhead all the way to Orient Point, so exploration of the North Fork is not a major undertaking. What with Shelter Island lying where it does, you can easily head out to the end of one fork and return via the other.

Probably the prettiest parts, scenically speaking, of the North Fork are its villages, notably Orient and Greenport, and the seemingly endless farm fields that flank North Road and Sound Avenue parallel to N.Y. 25. The beaches are lovely but much smaller and more tranquil than those facing the Atlantic. The North Fork is going to appeal to people who like beautiful country, calmer pursuits, and are indifferent to the glare of fashion.

---

3. Where to Stay & Eat on the North Fork

The North Fork is smaller and less developed than the South Fork. Accordingly, the range of hotels and restaurants is more limited. Here's a run-down on some of the best deals for your money.

HOTELS

Greenport, the biggest town on the North Fork, isn't very big. It's a fishing village full of old, ungentrified buildings and a harbor crammed with fishing boats and pleasure craft. Greenport is also the terminus of the Shelter Island Ferry, the end of the line for the North Fork branch of the Long Island Rail Road, and the center for overnight accommodations.

The **Townsend Manor Inn,** 714 Main St. (N.Y. 25; between Broad and Webb), Greenport, NY 11944 (tel. 516-477-2000), is a collection of old houses arranged around a very appealing pool and overlooking a marina on Stirling Basin. The main building is a wonderful pillared Greek Revival house dating from 1835. Inside is a collection of wallpapered dining rooms (the inn operates a fairly big, moderately priced restaurant), a cozy parlor with a fireplace, a cocktail lounge, and a small modern paneled office containing the reception desk.

The hotel rooms are located elsewhere, in the Waterfront Cottage, the Gingerbread House, and the Captain's House, respectively. Minimum-rate rooms in the Waterfront Cottage are sparkling clean and have wall-to-wall carpeting, modestly appointed full baths, venetian blinds, curtains on tie-backs, and the vacation smell of a seaside cottage. The Gingerbread House, a neighboring Italianate mansion absorbed by the Townsend complex, has bigger rooms with nonperiod touches like pecky paneling and brightly colored carpeting. The Captain's House contains deluxe rooms fitted out with still-newer decor and little private balconies. High-season double-occupancy rates (early July through late August) range mostly from $75 to $95 during the week and $105 to $130 on weekends. During this same period there's a two-night minimum stay required on weekends. Overnight rates decline gradually on both sides of the peak season to a midwinter low of about $60 nightly. All major credit cards accepted.

The **Sound View Inn,** North Road, Greenport, NY 11944 (tel. 516/477-1910), seems like it's about 10 blocks long. That's because it's only one room wide and every room faces the water across a private sandy beach. The place must be 30-odd years old. Really, it's just a big motel, most of whose units have sliding glass doors to private balconies, two double beds, phones, TVs, and modern motel furnishings. Also on the premises are a blindingly bright pool protected from brisk breezes by glass windbreaks, a quartet of tennis courts across the road, and a popular moderately priced restaurant. Daily peak-season (June 30 to September 6th) double-occupancy rates are about $95 for standard rooms and from $99 to $145 for variously sized suites with cooking facilities. Off-season (October 15 to May 10), double rooms cost about $65 a night. All major credit cards accepted.

The **Silver Sands Motel,** Silvermere Road (which intersects N.Y. 25 on the western edge of Greenport), Greenport, NY 11944 (tel. 516/477-0011), is a small, mint-condition, period-piece 1950s resort motel. It combines the seaside flavor of Greenport before the age of the real estate boom with amenities like a delightful private beach, a tranquil location well away from noisy traffic, and well-maintained rooms. The inner courtyard is flamingo pink; the outer walls below the stylized seahorse "S" are swimming-pool blue; the views across the beach are of Shelter Island and boat traffic on the shining waters. The simple rooms have color TVs, little refrigerators, and coffeemakers. Double-occupancy rates, which include complimentary continental breakfast, range from $80 to $100 nightly (the latter being for a room with kitchenette) during the season (June 20 to September 15) and $70 to $90 in spring and fall. There's a special price of $160 for any consecutive three nights during spring and fall, with complimentary wine and cheese when you check in. Also on the premises are modest but appealing little cottages that sleep six and rent for $800 a week. Closed part of January; sometimes a minimum stay is required in high season. All major credit cards accepted.

Two North Fork bed-and-breakfasts struck me as particularly appealing. The **Bartlett House Inn,** 503 Front St. (N.Y. 25), Greenport, NY 11944 (tel. 516/477-0371), is a roomy shingled house on the corner of 5th Street close to downtown Greenport. Built at the turn of the century by John Bartlett, a former New York State assemblyman, today it's a bed-and-breakfast with 10 rooms. The interior is surprisingly elegant, with its big formal staircase, fluted columns with Corinthian capitals, parquet floors, and brass gasoliers. For a peak-season (June 17 to September 5) double with private bath and continental breakfast you'll pay about $90 a night; for $10 more you can have a fireplace room with a queen-size bed! Rates decline in stages during the rest of the year, hitting a midwinter low of $57. AE, MC, and V accepted.

Alternately you might try the **White Lions,** 433 Main St., Greenport, NY 11944 (tel. 516/477-8819). This is an old mansard-roofed house sandwiched into the middle of a line of commercial buildings in the heart of the village. It has a new wing tacked onto the back and five second-floor rooms (three with private bath) that rent for $55 to $70 in the winter, $70 to $95 in high summer. It's new, and the management is trying hard. MC and V accepted.

RESTAURANTS

Most of my recommended restaurants are either in or near Greenport, including what I consider the two best on the North Fork.

La Gazelle, on Main Road (Route 25) at the eastern edge of Southold (tel. 516/765-2656), is a charming and authentic French restaurant serving classic country cuisine. Inside its little pillared house are intimate dining rooms with low-beamed ceilings, lots of plants, crisp white tablecloths and an air of things "bien fait." The lunch menu offers selections like flounder meunière, moules (mussels) marinières, baby lamb chops, avocado filled with seafood salad, etc., for between $7 and $11. There is a bargain early-bird complete dinner ($14 between 5 and 6:30pm daily), plus regular dinner selections like veau à la francaise, broiled bay scallops, baby lamb chops, filet mignon sautéed with shallots, veal normandie, etc., costing from about $15 to $22. Lunch is served from noon to 3pm; dinner from 5 to 9pm (to 11pm on Friday and Saturday); Sunday brunch from noon until 2pm. AE, MC, and V accepted.

Ross's North Fork, Route 48 (North Road; tel. 516/765-2111), is also in Southold, but on the north side of the village. It has more of a Hamptons air in both decor and reputation than anything else in the area. Cuisine is contemporary American with an emphasis on seafood; there's also a cellar that specializes in excellent local wines. The dining room is pale mauve and white, with immaculate linens, low lights, stylish sprays of flowers, a wall of wine bottles by the front door, and probably more men in tie and jacket (not required, incidentally) than you'll see anywhere else. The menus change regularly. Lunch selections might include warm grilled chicken salad, lobster sandwich, English fish and chips, or a fresh omelet with brie, priced from about $6 to $8. There's also a $12 table d'hôte, which is a scaled-down dinner from soup to nuts. At dinner, beside all manner of inventive appetizers (mesquite smoked duck, puree of watercress, oysters in garlic and Pernod, from $4 to $7) you might see things like baked bluefish with Dijon mustard, grilled salmon with cucumber dill sauce, fried fresh Chincoteague oysters, or a French peppercorn steak flamed in brandy, priced between $18 and $22. Lunch is served Tuesday to Sunday between noon and 2:30pm; dinner is served Tuesday to Saturday from 5 to 9pm (on Sunday from 2pm). Weekend dinner reservations a must. Closed all of January and the first two weeks of February. All major credit cards accepted.

For solid, moderately priced value in the center of Greenport, you can't beat the **Rhumb Line**, 36 Front St. (tel. 516/477-9883). It is a local institution, with the most active bar in town; dining rooms with lots of varnished woodwork, tucked black-leatherette booths, model sailboat hulls, and ship lanterns; and dependably good food. At lunch, besides sandwiches and burgers of all descriptions (and available all day), are things like blackened catfish, fried shrimp, and flounder fillet, priced from $6 to $10. The dinner menu includes a wide range of seafood, plus chicken Cordon Bleu, chargrilled strip steak, and lasagne, costing about $9 to $14. Open daily year-round, for lunch from 11:30am to 3pm and for dinner from 5 to 9pm (to 10:30pm on Saturday and until 10pm on weekdays during the summer). The lunch menu is available all day, and all major credit cards are accepted.

Also reasonably priced, informal, in the center of Greenport, and a favorite with local people, is the **Chowder Pot**, 104 3rd St. (tel. 516/477-9821). This friendly neighborhood bar/tavern occupies a small wooden building with an appealing outdoor terrace overlooking the Shelter Island ferry dock. Lunch is usually a matter of burgers, various sorts of club sandwiches (shrimp, oyster), a fishwich, or one of the daily chalkboard specials priced from $4 to $12. There are also burgers at dinnertime, plus Cajun catfish, fried oysters, charbroiled steak in assorted sizes, and barbecued ribs, costing between $6 and $16 (the latter being for the heftiest steak). Lunch is available from noon to 2:30pm; dinner from 5 to 9pm (to 10pm on Friday and Saturday). Open daily during high summer; closed Monday in spring and fall; and open only Friday through Sunday during the depths of January through March. AE, MC, and V accepted.

Three other recommendations are at the other end of the North Fork, within 5 or 6 miles of Riverhead. My favorite among them is the **Jamesport Country Kitchen**, Main Rd. (Route 25), just east of the stoplight in the center of little Jamesport (tel. 516/722-3537). American café fare is the order of the day here, served in a collection of small bright rooms painted green and white; furnished with café chairs, wooden banquettes, and blond-oak tables under shiny varnish; and suffused with recorded violin music. Chicken niçoise, steak, Caesar salad, homemade pastas, smothered chicken, and fried shrimp and clam combination cost from $5 to $13 at lunch. Dinner might start with appetizers like mozzarella and grilled peppers, sesame wings, or chicken fingers ($4 to $5); move on to seafood pasta (combined with your choice of shrimp or scallops), grilled chicken with spicy onion-ginger sauce, roast Long Island duckling, the fish of the day, or a New York–strip steak ($8 to $14); or simply be something light like chicken Toulouse (basically a club sandwich), burgers, or the aforementioned steak and Caesar salad ($6 to $9). Lunch hours are Wednesday to Monday from 11:30am to 4:30pm; dinner is from 4:30 to 8:30pm (until 9:30pm on summer weekends). AE, MC, and V accepted.

Nearby and rather fun is the **Jamesport Manor Inn**, Long Island's equivalent of the prairie Victorian manse in the movie *Giant*. Located on Manor Lane (which runs between Sound Avenue and N.Y. 25) outside the village of Jamesport (tel. 516/722-3382), it is a highly wrought and heavily mansarded former sea captain's house plopped in the middle of farm fields. The interior has red wallpaper, dark paneling, red rugs, and little tables covered with crisp pink cloths and clustered around atmospheric fireplaces. Lunch dishes like fried flounder, lobster salad Louis, and a club sandwich cost between $6 and $9. A la carte dinner selections, like fried oysters, duck à l'orange, stuffed sole, or a New York–strip sirloin, are priced mostly in the $12 to $20 bracket. Open for lunch from noon to 2pm on Tuesday through Saturday; for dinner from 5 to 9pm on Tuesday through Saturday (until 10pm on Saturday); and on Sunday from 1pm to 9pm. AE accepted.

In nearby Aquebogue, right on N.Y. 25, is a really good family-style diner called the **Modern Snack Bar** (tel. 516/722-3655). You can't miss the big old-fashioned sign that says "Snack Bar" with the swooping neon arrow. People come from all over the North Fork to enjoy seafood plates, "All Time Favorites" (as they call roast turkey, chicken croquettes, meatloaf, fried chicken, and the like around here), and all manner of sandwiches. Particularly good are the seafood salads. This is the place for a $7 lunch or a $12 dinner, in cheery dining rooms attended by bustling young waitresses in white. Open Tuesday through Saturday from 11am to 9pm and Sunday from noon to 9pm.

3. An Excursion to Shelter Island

Much too poised to get mixed up in the hullabaloo down on the South Fork (rather too refined in the opinion of many of its North Fork neighbors), Shelter Island pursues its own handsome and quiet path. This pretty place is graced with 19th-century vacation "cottages" (some of which are quite grand), delightful Victorian villages, heavily wooded hills, quiet beaches, and a luxurious air of upper-middle-class isolation.

The biggest contributor to Shelter Island's air of remove is the ferry—or more correctly, the two ferries. These picturesque little boats steadily plow back and forth from 5am until about midnight. The trips aren't long; in fact, the south ferry is barely more than a puddle jump. But the fares are high. To get your car across the southern arm of Shelter Island Sound, which blocks N.Y. 114 from Sag Harbor to Greenport, costs $6 ($6.50 for a same-day round trip), plus 75¢ per passenger in addition to the driver, on the Shelter Island South Ferry (tel. 516/749-0139). It honestly looks as though a man with a good arm could throw a rock across this same stretch of water. When you reach the village of Shelter Island Heights on the north side of the island, you'll pay the Shelter Island North Ferry (tel. 516/749-1200) the same fares to get over to Greenport. But the result of the high tolls and ferry-line waits is a delightful absence of heavy traffic throughout the island, even at the peak of the summer season.

Shelter Island's history is another version of New England's familiar litany of English pirates, religious settlers, dissenting Quakers, manorial land grants, hard-working farmers, enterprising Prohibition-era bootleggers, and suave vacationers from the city. The lovely summer houses of the latter, some of which have been passed from generation to generation, give the place considerable *ton.* Shelter Island's original manor house, started in the mid-17th century and significantly enlarged in the 18th, still stands. Called **Sylvester Manor,** it's located on the approximate center of the island (gates on N.Y. 114). It remains in private hands, on reduced but still-extensive acreage.

Essentially, Shelter Island is a place where nothing happens, and everybody likes it just that way. The midnight curfew on the ferry does a great deal to keep the lid on things. No wee-hour carryings-on at Southampton watering spots, if you please. That is, not if you expect to get back here for the night. The southeastern portion of the island, occupying about a quarter of its total acreage, is an untouched nature conservancy called the **Mashomack Preserve.** The rest of the place is characterized by country roads, vacant meadows bordered by huge old trees, a handful of delightful Victorian villages with crooked streets and gingerbread cottages, dark forests, and lots of summer houses. There are also a couple of old-fashioned hotels, plus numerous bed-and-breakfasts, nearly all of which are within sight of some body or other of glittering water.

Worth exploration on foot is the village of **Shelter Island Heights,** located adjacent to the Greenport ferry. Lack of sustained traffic, perhaps more than anything else, contributes to the distinct feeling here of other times. The village is like a miniature San Francisco, its twisting roads decorated with little wooden gingerbread wedding cakes, shaded by massive trees. Eastward across a small bay is the village of **Dering Harbor,** a quaint place notable for its tony waterfront houses. Midway along the southwestern coastline is **Nostrand Parkway,** a region of capacious old shingled mansions enjoying delicious sunset views across the bays. Everywhere in between are fresh, rural, and unspoiled vistas, some admittedly getting built up.

WHERE TO STAY & EAT ON SHELTER ISLAND

The mailing address of the **Ram's Head Inn** is Shelter Island Heights, NY 11965 (tel. 516/749-0811). However, it is not in the Heights at all, but out on Big Ram Island. This diminutive sandy hump is connected to the northeast portion of Shelter Island by flat, narrow causeways overlooking Coecles Harbor. The inn is a charming shingled mansion, built actually as an inn on the eve of the 1929 Stock Market Crash, in the Colonial Revival style. It has crisp white trim, shaped juniper trees by the front door, snappy green shutters, and pots of geraniums and climbing roses alongside a crisp gravel circle out front. Inside, all is light, airy, and handsomely done up with floral-print wallpapers and glistening painted trim. There are but 17 rooms, all located on the second floor and furnished with fresh wallpaper, new carpeting, simple wooden furniture, telephones, but no TVs. The look is very 1930s, which is to say that it's not exactly modern, but neither is it old. The inn is open year-round. Prices range from $90 for a double with shared bath to $125 for a double with private bath; there's a two-bedroom suite with an adjoining bathroom for $195 a night. A very excellent deal.

Downstairs is a big restaurant dining room that looks as if it was lifted right out of a good sorority house at a Big 10 school. It has a handsome fireplace, lots of painted woodwork, and french doors overlooking a lawn and distant glimpses of water. It's open only for Sunday brunch and dinner, and the menu lists à la carte selections such as fillet of beef with grilled shrimp, grilled salmon, yellowfin tuna, and loin of lamb for about $19 to $23. The inn additionally provides guests with the use of two sunfish, a 13-foot O'Day sloop, a kayak, a pedalboat, and an on-site tennis court. This was my favorite place on Shelter Island. AE, MC, and V accepted.

There's a very different atmosphere at the **Dering Harbor Inn,** P.O. Box 3028, Shelter Island Heights, NY 11965 (tel. 516/749-0900). This is not an inn at all but a stylish condominium within walking distance of both Dering Harbor and Shelter Island Heights. Besides an excellent central location, there are a saltwater pool and a restaurant off the lobby. What does it look like? A Long Island country club, with a big circa-1962 stone/wood/glass clubhouse looking across the parking lot at a slew of tennis courts. Inside is a two-story lobby with modern furniture and huge picture windows, the aforementioned restaurant, and rice-papered corridors leading back to a complex of newer shingled buildings that contain a total of 30 condominium units. Now each of these units belongs to somebody who's decorated it and furnished it to his own personal taste. Basically, the look is pale wood paneling, wall-to-wall carpeting, color TVs, and nice contemporary furniture. Units all have water views and range in size from a two-bedroom/two-bath waterfront "cottage" to a "studio room," which is essentially a standard hotel room. Of the 30 units, probably about 20 to 23 are available to transients at any given time. The basic high-season double-occupancy rate for the studio is $140 on weekends, $115 on weekdays, and $780 weekly. Rates go up, depending on unit size and view, to a top end of $295 nightly and $1,650 weekly for two people in the cottage described above. Additional persons are charged $20 nightly, and there's a minimum-stay requirement (two nights on weekends, three nights on holidays) between Memorial and Labor Days. The rates decline in stages to an off-season (early spring or late fall) low of $100 to $215 nightly, double occupancy. Closed from November through March.

Shelter Island abounds with bed-and-breakfasts that stay open all year. The **Shelter Island Chamber of Commerce,** Box 598, Shelter Island, NY 11964 (tel. 516/749-0399), has a complete list of them, which they are happy to send to you upon request, together with a useful information booklet that contains a good map of the island.

The bed-and-breakfast that most appealed to me during my most recent field trip is called the **Beach House,** whose mailing address is Box 648, Shelter Island Heights, Shelter Island, NY 11965 (tel. 516/749-0264), but whose location is out in the countryside. This is not an amateur hotel, which is what so many of these places have become. Rather it is the private contemporary home of a woman who truly runs an old-fashioned bed-and-breakfast. The house, built in 1985, sits in a quiet residential district, has sweeping unobstructed views of Shelter Island Sound, a dock, and 200 feet of private sandy beach. Inside are blond-wood floors; walls of glass; bamboo furniture; plants galore; and four spacious, bright, and immaculate modern bedrooms. Only one has a private bath, but all have water views. Friday to Sunday rates are $125 for the room with the bath, $90 nightly for the others; on weekdays and during the off-season, those prices drop to $95 and $70, respectively. There's an additional 15% discount for three-day weekday stays. An extensive continental breakfast is served in the airy common room overlooking the water. No credit cards accepted.

An atmosphere of similar cordiality in vintage architectural surroundings exists at an establishment called the **House on Chase Creek,** 3 Locust Ave., Shelter Island Heights, NY 11965 (tel. 516/749-4379). The village location is within walking distance of the Greenport ferry and the quaint streets and little shops of Shelter Island Heights and Dering Harbor and looks across Locust Avenue (really just a leafy lane) at little Chase Creek. The house itself is a modest early 20th-century family home, clad in beige shingles, with a front porch and a little lawn. The interior is spare, clean, and very bright. The three rooms without private bath are small and cozy; the fourth with the private bath is rather large. All are decorated with white rugs, gauzy curtains, and miscellaneous antiques and suffused with an air of calm. No phone or TV, but lots of old-fashioned charm. High-season weekend rates (May through October) are $90 and $125 nightly, depending on whether or not your room has the private bath, and $60 and $95 during the week. Those prices decline in stages to a mid-winter low of $45 to $65 per night per room. Continental breakfast is served on a pretty glazed porch overlooking the creek. AE accepted.

For a moderately priced meal in a local hangout that's open all year, you might try the **Dory,** also overlooking Chase Creek, on Chase Avenue in Shelter Island Heights (tel. 516/749-8871). This is a tavern with a jukebox, a pool table, a busy bar up front, stuffed fish on the wall, and an outdoor deck for fair weather dining. Nothing fancy here: Burgers, steaks, and seafood cost in the $5 to $8 range at lunch (noon to 4pm) and from $7 to $15 at dinner (5 to 10pm; noon to 6pm on Sunday). Open daily; during the winter, however, you can have dinner only Thursday through Saturday.

WESTCHESTER COUNTY

The lower portion of Westchester County is densely suburban; the rest of it is a sort of faux-rural setpiece where every precious and overtaxed acre is a potential hostage to condo and office park developers. Scattered across the county's rocky and once again densely forested hills are a great number of picturesque and historic sites and many very architecturally interesting environments.

Is Westchester worth exploring? You bet it is, particularly for aficionados of Revolutionary War sites and historic mansions. Are there interesting places to stay and eat? The answer again is an emphatic yes, especially so in recent years. Some of the restaurants in Westchester today equal the best in Manhattan; some of its hotels offer the same amenities you'd find in New York at half the Big Apple price.

What is this place called Westchester really like? Why in the world should a visitor to New York venture into the northern suburbs? I'll get to that, but first, here's a little background.

1. History & Orientation

Westchester used to be a buzz word for baronial country living. More recently it has been identified with platinum-edged corporate headquarters and upscale suburbia. During America's first century, the county was insular, agricultural, and not much different (to the superficial observer) from large stretches of New England.

Westchester struck the country-estate leitmotif early in its history. Its first serious settlers, Jonas Bronck and his wife, Antonia Slagboom, bought most of what is now the southwest Bronx (a part of Westchester until 1874) from the Mohicans in

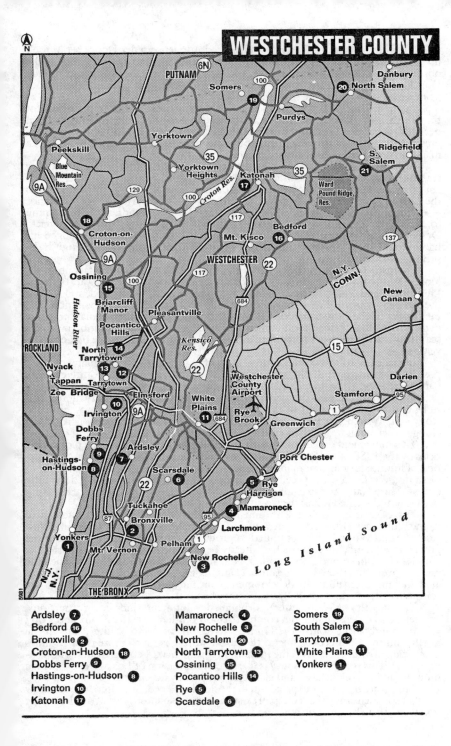

WESTCHESTER COUNTY

Ardsley ⑦	Mamaroneck ④	Somers ⑲
Bedford ⑯	New Rochelle ③	South Salem ㉑
Bronxville ②	North Salem ⑳	Tarrytown ⑫
Croton-on-Hudson ⑱	North Tarrytown ⑬	White Plains ⑪
Dobbs Ferry ⑨	Ossining ⑮	Yonkers ①
Hastings-on-Hudson ⑧	Pocantico Hills ⑭	
Irvington ⑩	Rye ⑤	
Katonah ⑰	Scarsdale ⑥	

1639. Within a decade, a Dutch lawyer named Adriaen van der Donck set himself up as lord of an even-larger estate, stretching from Spuyten Duyvil Creek at the northern end of Manhattan all the way to Tarrytown. It was the prosperous van der Donck who basked in the appellation of "der Jonkeer," or "young gentleman," from which stems the name of the present city of Yonkers.

In 1654, Thomas Pell formed a large estate along the sound from the vicinity of the Hutchinson River in the Bronx all the way to New Rochelle. By English royal decree, Pell became Lord of the Manor of Pelham in 1666. And so it went, one aggressive aspirant lord arriving after another, until most of the county, at least on a map, had been carved into feudal fiefdoms.

Perhaps the grandest of Westchester's manorial lords in the pre-Revolutionary era was Frederick Philipse. This clever immigrant managed to acquire an empire of land that stretched along the eastern Hudson riverfront all the way from Yonkers to the Croton River and then deep into northern Westchester. The lord of the manor —eventually it was two manors, Philipsburg and Van Cortlandt, the latter coming to Philipse as a part of a canny second marriage to Margaret "the Commercial" DeVries—was born in Holland. In a wise public relations move, he changed his name from Vredryk Flypse to Frederick Philipse in 1664, the year the English deprived the Dutch of New Amsterdam.

Philipse's conservative heirs were English royalists to the core, a fact not overlooked by the post-Revolutionary American government. After the war, both the Philipsburg and Van Cortlandt manors were confiscated, subdivided, and sold— the proceeds going toward defrayment of the costs of the American Revolution. The purchasers of the former manor lands were by no means the first small property owners to invade Westchester. But their arrival in force after the revolution marked a sea change in the county's heretofore established pattern of large-scale manorial development.

In the early to mid-19th century, it was the pleasant farms of many of these post-Revolutionary landholders that began to attract rich people from New York City. Gradually, Westchester's agricultural economy began to be augmented by city people who were there for the scenery. As the railroads made the county more accessible, and the development of the Midwest lured farmers steadily away from the stony soil, Westchester began again to assume plutocratic overtones, particularly along the scenic shores of the sound and the Hudson.

This movement gathered strength after the Civil War and reached epic proportions by the 1880s and 1890s. The decades on either side of 1900 saw the construction of hundreds of instant manorial estates. Broadway, from Yonkers all the way to Ossining, was lined with spectacular estates. Vast pseudo-baronies ringed the little city of White Plains and extended down to the Sound. It was all quite breathtaking in its way and seemed for all the world as if it would last forever.

But, of course, it didn't. The same forces that rendered Westchester accessible to the plutocracy also made it attractive to the rising middle class. Cities like New Rochelle and White Plains continued to grow and spread. Even at the peak of the great estate period, speculators had already begun to develop garden suburbs like Park Hill in Yonkers and Beechmont in New Rochelle. After World War I, when the estate movement faltered as a result of changing tastes, rising costs, and the graduated income tax, suburban development continued to flourish throughout the southern districts close to the Bronx County line.

The majority of Westchester's corporate development, sightseeing attractions, and residential density lies in a compact region bordered by the Bronx and Long Island Sound to the South, the Hudson River on the West, White Plains in the north, and the Connecticut line to the east. Nothing is much more than 15 miles away from anything else. And the modern highways make getting around astonishingly easy. This part of the county is like an eastern version of Los Angeles—with a lot more architectural charm and character but equally developed.

Things are much more spread out in the north. Indeed, one often wonders how it is that so much empty land can still exist so close to New York City. Well, let's hope it's all still there by the time you read this.

2. North Along the Hudson

You can't see Westchester without a car, and for the sake of organization, I will assume that the starting point for your motor tour is Manhattan. By all means, plan on leaving town via the West Side Highway and its northern extension, the Henry Hudson Parkway.

With the lower part of the highway under reconstruction, enter above 57th Street. Hope there isn't too much traffic, since cruising at highway speed does a lot for the total effect. To the north in the distance as you head out of town, the graceful span of the George Washington Bridge begins slowly to grow. And beyond it are— what? Wild-looking forested cliffs! This valuable view was preserved back in the 1920s thanks to the efforts of many farsighted people (among them John D. Rockefeller, Jr.) who established a series of interstate parks.

If you're good with maps and want to savor the spot, get off the parkway at Dyckman Street (the last exit in Manhattan) and find your way up to **Fort Tryon Park.** This is a beautifully gardened city park occupying the top of a rocky ridge in what would otherwise be the West 190s. It contains the Metropolitan Museum of Art's medieval collection, housed in a monastic building with a tall square tower. This is the **Cloisters** (see "Museums & Galleries" in Chapter V), to which you can drive right up, climb out of your car (parking spots abound), and admire that view. It certainly does whet the appetite for the road ahead. By the way, that forested hill to the north of Fort Tryon, on the other side of the little valley holding Dyckman Street, is **Inwood Hill Park.** In Victorian days it was a select countrified neighborhood of suburban estates, some of whose foundations remain in the modern-day park. Inwood Hill is about as lonely as you can get on Manhattan. On that equivocal note, you should get back in the car and press northward.

In 1800, it took the famous English tourist John Maude four days to sail from New York to Albany in a sloop with 24 other paying passengers. Four days was pretty good time too. It took the sloop *Sally* a whole day, for instance, just to sail upriver to the vicinity of Tarrytown. When they got there, the captain tossed the anchor overboard and sent a boat to shore to buy provisions for his passengers' dinner, and that's where they all spent the night.

Today it takes 25 minutes to get to the East Side from the Tarrytown Hilton by the fastest, if not the prettiest, route. But since you're going to travel on good-looking roads (or at least try to), my next advice is to leave New York via the **Saw Mill River Parkway.** Besides connecting directly with the Henry Hudson Parkway, the Saw Mill preserves to a certain extent the illusion of woodsy space "out" of the city.

YONKERS

Immediately to the north of the Bronx line is the old river city of Yonkers, an interesting place if not exactly a typical tourist destination. The best route to begin your exploration is to take exit 5 westbound off the Saw Mill River Parkway, follow Yonkers Avenue, then Ashburton Avenue to the center of town.

Yonkers, with a population of about 195,400, is actually the fourth-largest city in the state of New York. Along the Hudson River waterfront, in the vicinity of Broadway, Main Street, and Warburton Avenue, the 19th-century downtown hub retains a fugitive air of architectural distinction despite the present century's urban woes and the municipality's often unaesthetic attempts to correct them.

In the middle of the downtown section, a stone's throw from the river and the railway station, is the venerable **Philipse Manor Hall,** 29 Warburton Ave., at Dock Street (tel. 914/965-4027). This rural stone manor house, today a National Historic Landmark, is the very place in which the upwardly mobile Frederick Philipse, lord of the manors of Philipsburg and Van Cortlandt, resided in rural pomp. Income from tens of thousands of Westchester acres flowed to the master of this house, and the fates of thousands of the Hudson Valley's earliest settlers depended to a large extent on his manorial whim. The original part of the hall, on Dock Street, dates from 1682. Most of what you see today, however, represents the solid provincial Georgian enlargements commissioned by Philipse's heirs in 1725.

Philipse Manor Hall has been a cherished part of Yonkers for three centuries, alternately maintained as a private residence, village hall, and museum. Quite aside from its important historical associations are the fascinating rococo ceilings executed in papier mâché; a famous collection of portraits (of everyone from Washington to Calvin Coolidge) by the likes of Stuart, Sharples, and Sully; and an excellent assortment of vintage furniture.

The Hall is supposedly open from late May to late October on Wednesday through Sunday from noon to 5pm. But you'd better call the number above to check. It's also possible to arrange a tour at other times. Let's hope a drive by and a peer through the windows won't be the only way to glimpse this important relic from our colonial past.

A less tempestuous fate has attended Glenview, the brooding stone Victorian mansion erected in 1876 by John Bond Trevor. Glenview is situated about a dozen blocks north of Philipse Manor Hall at 511 Warburton Ave., Yonkers (tel. 914/963-4550). For generations it has been the home of the **Hudson River Museum**, and its former grounds have done duty as Trevor Park. The museum has long housed a collection of paintings, furniture, books, and ephemera oriented toward the history of the Hudson Valley. In recent years, it has been augmented by an admixture of European and American fine art, plus a new planetarium.

During the 1970s, a huge modern addition was constructed to house the planetarium and provide additional gallery space, a new museum café, and a gift shop. This modernistic cement structure wraps itself around the old Trevor House cutting off the original building from its grounds and many of its original river views. The Hudson River Museum has a laudable sense of mission, an interesting collection, and innovative changing exhibitions and programs and has made dramatic progress in restoring the Trevor mansion's polychromed Victorian interiors. To be honest, however, the new addition will jangle the architectural preservationist's sensibilities.

The museum is open Wednesday, Thursday, and Saturday from 10am until 5pm and Sunday from noon to 5pm. Admission is $3 for adults and $1.50 for seniors and kids under 12. Star shows at the Andrus Planetarium cost $4 for adults and $2 for seniors and kids under 12. Call 914/963-2139 for exhibit information and planetarium schedules.

There are a number of architecturally interesting 19th-century neighborhoods dotted around Yonkers.

Park Hill sits atop a bluff looming over the Ludlow section of south Yonkers. Stupendous views of the river and the Palisades are to be had from some of its steep streets and stylistically varied (to say the least) old mansions. Park Hill lies only about a dozen blocks north of New York City's Van Cortlandt Park and about the same distance south of Yonkers Avenue in Yonkers. Streets worthy of exploration include Undercliff; Park Hill Terrace; Alta Avenue; Park Hill Avenue; and the warren of little intersecting streets like Prospect, Hillside, and Lakeside.

Only a few minutes from Park Hill by car is a much more fascinating place, but it is one to which most visitors would never dream of going. Don't laugh now, but it's **Woodlawn Cemetery**, whose main entrance is located at the intersection of East 233rd St. and Webster Avenue in the Bronx (tel. 212/920-0500).

The idea of visiting a graveyard was introduced to me many years ago in Rome, when friends recommended I have a look at the English Cemetery. I found an enchanted oasis of weeping marble angels, specimen plantings, and a romantic wistful atmosphere. So it is with Woodlawn, a 400-acre preserve in the middle of the north Bronx, an apotheosis of America's rural cemetery movement.

Woodlawn calls itself, with justification, the "Resting Place of the Famous." It prints a free map, available at the main gate, that divides the acreage into quadrants with instructions on how to find important graves. These include people from Jay Gould to Frank Woolworth, from J. C. Penney to George M. Cohan, from Duke Ellington to Herman Melville.

Woodlawn has also been the final destination of choice for much of New York high society. Harrimans, Huntingtons, Colgates, Whitneys, Roosevelts, and

Corbins, for instance, have, over the last century or so, ensconced their ancestors in noble granite and marble mausoleums that in many cases are simply fabulous to behold.

Woodlawn is open daily, year-round, from 9am to 4:30pm. The main gatehouse complex at 233rd Street is located about half a dozen blocks south of the Yonkers–New York City line, adjacent to the Bronx River Parkway.

Back in Yonkers, the same Broadway (or U.S. Route 9)—which skirts the western cliffs of Park Hill, threads northward through the old heart of Yonkers, and peeks over the top of the Hudson River Museum on Warburton Avenue below—will eventually come to a place in the very north of Yonkers called **Untermyer Park.**

Untermyer Park, listed in the National Register of Historic Places, is one of Westchester's most beautiful and important examples of neoclassical revival architecture. It wasn't built as a park at all, but rather as the garden to a preexisting stone behemoth of a house called Greystone, which last belonged to a rich lawyer named Samuel Untermyer. Untermyer's garden was designed in the early 20th century by the famous William Welles Bosworth, whose similarly elaborate garden for the Rockefeller estate in Pocantico Hills remains extant in private hands.

Untermyer's heirs bequeathed Greystone to the city of Yonkers in 1946, after which the house was pulled down and the gardens allowed to fall into such a state of disrepair that they were almost demolished as well. Good thing they weren't, as the restored garden today is an ornament to the city of Yonkers and a fascinating opportunity to glimpse Gilded Era opulence. It is a walled complex with Assyrian gates, octagonal towers, formal reflecting pools, luscious Hudson River vistas, a pair of double Ionic columns topped with stately sphinxes carved by Paul Manship, and, in the good weather, a profusion of beautiful flowers.

Untermyer Park is located on Broadway (Route 9) immediately south of St. John's Riverside Hospital and Odell Avenue. It is open to the public at all times, free of charge.

For a short distance north of Untermyer Park, a palpable aura of the past still clings to Route 9. After the hospital one comes to Alder, the palatial riverfront estate of Col. William Boyce-Thompson. Now the **Elizabeth Seton Campus of Iona College,** 1061 North Broadway, Yonkers (tel. 914/969-4000), Alder was designed in 1912 by Carrère and Hastings, a prominent beaux arts New York architectural firm among whose many other important works are the New York Public Library and the Frick mansion on Fifth Avenue.

Alder remained a private house until the mid-1950s. It is visible today from the road, and for most travelers a fleeting glimpse of its extremely elegant and restrained Renaissance revival facade will be enough.

HASTINGS-ON-HUDSON

Remember that Broadway, known interchangeably as U.S. Route 9, is an extension of the same street that runs the length of Manhattan Island. Things look more and more suburban as you continue north into Hastings. There are lots of houses, old and new, shaded by a suburban forest of considerable age. Hastings is a modest village, rather pretty in an unplanned way. It was home to the famous newspaper publisher Horace Greeley ("Go west, young man!") and of Civil War naval hero Adm. David Farragut. It was also the home in later life of the Hudson River School painter Jasper Francis Cropsey (1823–1900).

Cropsey's yellow-painted rural Gothic cottage in Hastings, called **Ever Rest,** is at 49 Washington Ave., Hastings-on-Hudson, NY 10706 (tel. 914/478-1372). A more delicious place is hard to imagine. Washington Avenue is as steep as any street in San Francisco at this point, and from its hilly slopes Cropsey enjoyed a wonderful view of the Hudson and the Palisades. Although pressed for funds at the time of his residence here, he managed to enlarge this gingerbread cottage—embowered in wisteria and set beneath fine old trees—with a wonderful Victorian studio addition. He designed much of the cottage's rococo revival furniture as well. It's all in there today, virtually as it was when he died.

Cropsey made his name as an artist, but he was also an architect who worked in the complicated eclectic styles of the mid- to late 19th century. Perhaps the best remembered of his architectural works were the exuberant stations for the old Sixth Avenue Elevated Railroad in Manhattan. Painting was always his passion, however. By the age of 24 he had become prosperous and well known. But the fickle public abandoned Cropsey at the floodtide of his powers. As the Hudson River School landscapes became outré, his fame and fortune shriveled. He moved to Hastings in 1885 only because he could no longer afford to maintain the dream house he had built across the river in Orange County.

The Cropsey house exists today as it does—and it really looks as if Cropsey still lives there—because of the painter's granddaughter. She preserved it and established the foundation that oversees it today. The house is open only by reservation and will appeal only to those with a taste for American art and culture; but those people will love seeing the collection here. The otherworldly feel of the 4-acre property is evocative too; time seems literally to have stood still in this little corner of the Hudson Valley. Cropsey's studio, a vast room with a paneled ceiling and furniture from the upstate dream house, is one of the most dramatic and atmospheric Victorian rooms I've ever seen. All in all a very rewarding stop, but only for those with the foresight to make an advance reservation.

Diners take notice: The excellent **Buffet de la Gare,** described in "Where to Stay & Eat" later in this chapter, is just a few blocks from Ever Rest.

As you continue north out of Hastings on Route 9, watch the river side of the road for **Ingleside,** an architecturally important castellated Gothic villa at 71 Broadway. Now part of the St. Christopher's School, Ingleside was designed by the famous Alexander Jackson Davis in 1857 for silk importer Edwin B. Strange.

DOBBS FERRY

Hastings blends seamlessly into the next village, Dobbs Ferry (pop. 10,100). Jeremiah Dobbs was ferrying customers back and forth across the Hudson from here before 1700. During the American Revolution, Benedict Arnold would have betrayed West Point to Major André at Dobbs Ferry had the latter managed to make it to their scheduled tryst.

Comfortably middle class and intensely developed today, Dobbs Ferry was an elite suburban address in the late 19th century. A vivid marker of that era is Estherwood, an enormous châteauesque mansion dating from the mid-1890s and a part of the elite Masters School since 1910. Estherwood is immediately east of Route 9 on Clinton Avenue, overlooking the village from a hilltop site above a modern shopping center. The original owner, James Jennings McComb, had the house constructed around an existing octagonal library, which had been added to an earlier building on the same site. The old house was moved, and the new château was constructed around the library, which still sits in place.

ARDSLEY

Now continue north on Broadway through the traffic lights at Ashford Avenue. Just past Mercy College on your left you will enter the enclave of Ardsley-on-Hudson. Don't blink: You can easily traverse little Ardsley without realizing that you are on hallowed New York society ground.

Cyrus Field, the man responsible for the first transatlantic telegraph cable, once owned an estate here and was responsible for much of Ardsley's early development. Field came a cropper, however, at the hands of his Hudson River neighbor (up stream at Tarrytown), Jay Gould. During the so-called "Manhattan squeeze" on June 24, 1887, Field matched wits with the master manipulator and almost lost his shirt. He did lose his house in Ardsley.

Ultraexclusive New York society didn't hold this against Ardsley, however. In 1896, the select **Ardsley Club** opened its casino-cum-clubhouse, a McKim, Mead and White design, complete with architecturally compatible railroad station, located on the river at the foot of Ardsley Avenue. In the hills to the east of Broadway, the club laid out a still-extant golf course, the third oldest in the United States. Initially, guttapercha balls were used, requiring caddies to carry them around in buckets full of ice lest they become misshapen in the heat.

Society flocked to the Ardsley Club, for its golf and its fashionable entertain ments. During the late 1890s, it was a popular destination for coaching parties from New York, before automobiles forced four-in-hand coaches off the roads. New York Coaching Club member Alfred Vanderbilt, the most handsome and stylish of the old commodore's great-grandchildren, tooled a drag up here every Sunday from the Buckingham Hotel in Manhattan.

The Ardsley Club Casino was replaced forty-odd years ago by a not unattractive apartment building called the Hudson House. But the McKim, Mead, and White railroad station remains, as does the handsome Ardsley Club stable on the north side of Ardsley Avenue, between Hancock and Clifton Places. An upscale residential subdivision, developed after World War I and filled with handsome traditional-style houses, occupies the land between Route 9 and the Hudson House.

IRVINGTON

By the time of World War I, this village and its environs constituted the most opulent and fashionable of the close-in Hudson River suburbs. Despite decades of subdivision and new construction, some surprisingly spacious enclaves still survive, and Broadway continues to be lined with impressive cut-stone walls.

All manner of important people have lived in Irvington (pop. 5,800), among them Chauncey Depew, president of the New York Central Railroad and one-time right-hand man of the Vanderbilts; Albert Bierstadt, the renowned landscape artist; and Madame C. W. Walker. This last-named lady was an African-American millionaire whose fortune stemmed from a patented hair straightener. Her very fine mansion, which she called **Villa Lewaro**, is a neoclassical affair with a semicircular columned portico. It still stands on Broadway, a bit north of the Irvington light at the corner of Fargo Lane. Walker's house was designed in 1917 by Vertner Tandy, the first black member of the American Institute of Architects. A close family friend was Enrico Caruso, who coined the word *Lewaro* from the name of Walker's daughter, Lelia Walker Robinson. The place today is still a private house, clearly visible from the road.

TARRYTOWN

Irvington got its name from a devoted local resident whose famous and historic home is now, by a stroke of zoning irony, located in the adjoining village of Tarrytown (pop. 10,600). I refer of course to Washington Irving, perhaps America's first celebrated man of letters. Your next stop is his delectable Dutch cottage called **Sunnyside,** which is located at the foot of Sunnyside Lane and is open to the public. Actually, the original Dutch house was burned by the British during the Revolution on the orders of Gen. Sir John Vaughan. Pesky patriots had made a hangout of the place, and Vaughan was out to teach them a lesson. Irving bought a cottage on the site in 1835 and converted it into a highly romantic small estate reflecting the romantic architectural tastes of the time, as well as his own interest in the Dutch antecedents of the region.

In Irving's day Sunnyside was the object of pilgrimages by statesmen and literary lions alike. The master of the house was, after all, the famous chronicler of Diedrich Knickerbocker, Rip Van Winkle, and Sleepy Hollow's Headless Horseman. William Makepeace Thackeray, Louis-Napoleon (nephew of Napoleon Bonaparte), and Oliver Wendell Holmes were all guests at Sunnyside. While the house isn't large, it certainly does have charm. Irving's descendants "mansionized" it considerably after his death. But all Victorian accretions have since been systematically demolished, leaving the place exactly (one supposes) as it looked to Irving. Today costumed guides lead visitors through period rooms filled with Irving memorabilia. Outside, you're free to wander around really pretty grounds with great views of the river. Irving himself maintained that nothing in the world compared with the vista from his own front porch.

Sunnyside belongs to an organization called **Historic Hudson Valley,** 150 White Plains Rd., Tarrytown, NY (tel. 914/631-8200), which owns and operates other historic sites on the Hudson, some of which are described below. A single-visit ticket to Sunnyside costs $6 for adults, $5 for seniors, and $3 for children. Sunnyside is open daily from 10am to 5pm, with the last tour starting at 4pm.

Closed Thanksgiving, Christmas, New Year's, and open weekends only in January and February.

The next stop, not even a mile distant, is also a major attraction in the region. It's **Lyndhurst,** the crenellated castle of robber baron Jay Gould, donated in 1961 to the National Trust for Historic Preservation by Gould's daughter, Anna, duchess of Talleyrand-Périgord. What a lot of distance there is between that aristocratic title and Gould's days of manipulating Erie Railroad stock. Literature available at the site takes rather a revisionist position on Gould. But, then again, one doesn't expect to see pamphlets for sale in his own house branding him as a liar and a thief.

The main gate to Lyndhurst is on a stretch of Broadway that's lined with impressive walls and leafy old forests. One of the last estates in private hands hereabouts is immediately south of, and contiguous to, the Lyndhurst property. Called Belvidere, it's the residence of the mysterious Rev. Sun Myung Moon. The fortified gates are impossible to miss.

The National Trust describes Lyndhurst as "the beginning and culmination of residential Gothic Revival architecture in America." Put more simply, it's the be all and end all of authentic American-born castles. Of course, it's a whole lot smaller than a great English country house. But it's still a fabulous-looking place, sufficiently big as American mansions go, and of great historic and architectural significance. The original portion of the house was built in 1838 for one William Paulding in the then new and highly fashionable Gothic style. The architect was Alexander Jackson Davis, and this commission helped establish him as a major new force in American architecture. A fellow named George Merritt bought the place in 1864 and had Davis expand it to its present proportions. It's a neat job, and you'd hardly know the whole house wasn't built of a piece. Gould became the owner in 1880. He cherished Lyndhurst throughout his tenancy, preserving the house and adding only to the outbuildings, which in themselves are fairly fantastic.

Sixty-seven romantically landscaped acres remain around the Gould mansion; the hilly portion of the estate on the inland side of Broadway was sold off by the trust and has become a housing development (albeit not a huge one). Lyndhurst includes, besides the mansion and its original furnishings, a bowling alley, an immense greenhouse (currently under restoration, it must be seen to be believed), various cottages, a stable complex, a noble indoor pool, and views of the Hudson and the Tappan Zee that are, as they say, to "die" for. Lyndhurst is also the scene of numerous events, such as the Antique Auto Show, the Lyndhurst Dog Show, the Craft Show, and the Outdoor Antique Show. The grounds are open between May 2 and October 31 and in December on Tuesday through Sunday from 10am to 5pm. From November through April the estate is only open on weekends, from 10am to 5pm. Admission is $6 for adults, $5 for seniors, and free for kids under 12 and members of the Trust. The entrance is via the original main gatehouse on Broadway. For information about events, the number to call is 914/631-0046.

Just north of Lyndhurst is the center of **Tarrytown,** which has over the years become a village of some size (about 11,000 people). A big General Motors plant (perhaps closed by the time you read this) shares the shoreline with new condominiums and a very pleasant "downtown" area of older low-rise buildings. Steep hills immediately to the east are covered with mature trees and old houses. The view from here is of that great broadening of the Hudson known as the Tappan Zee, bordered in the distance by the cliffs of the Nyack Range. Tarrytown is where, on September 23, 1780, a trio of locals captured Maj. John André, the British spy who conspired with Benedict Arnold to betray West Point. For most of its history it was the eastern terminus of a ferry, rendered obsolete by the huge new Tappan Zee Bridge. Actually, the bridge is not so new anymore, having been opened back in 1955. Its construction was a sore point with Anna, duchess of Talleyrand-Périgord at Lyndhurst, whose view it substantially altered.

Towering on a hilltop overlooking the multilaned approaches to the Tappan Zee Bridge is another picturesque castle. This is **Carrollcliffe,** a local landmark since 1900. Built by Brigadier Gen. Howard Carroll, it has been an office building since 1941. The architecturally incompatible town houses crouching at its feet are relatively new intrusions. Picturesque gatehouses and walls still survive along the original property line, particularly the impressive main gate house on White Plains Road (N.Y. 119).

NORTH TARRYTOWN

About 2 miles north of the New York State Thruway–Tappan Zee Bridge intersection with U.S. 9 is **Philipsburg Manor** (tel. 914/631-3992), a 20-acre compound located just north of the intersection of N.Y. 448 and Broadway/U.S. Route 9 in the village of North Tarrytown. This is a painstaking reconstruction of the 17th-century manor house, mill, dam, kitchen garden, granary, wharf, and mill pond of Frederick Philipse. Today it's a property of the aforementioned Historic Hudson Valley. The Philipse family was a major landholder in pre-Revolutionary New York. This modest-looking manor house was once the nerve center of a 52,500-acre estate, a considerable spread by anyone's standards. Frederick Philipse III made the personally honorable but strategically lamentable decision to side with the Brits during the Revolution. Result: Postwar arrest and confiscation of his property.

Costumed guides will take you around and describe life in colonial times. Historic Hudson's literature aptly describes Philipsburg Manor as the place "where it's never later than 1750 and the Revolution is yet to come." Although luxurious for the wilderness, it is quite simple even in comparison to little Sunnyside. Occupied as a private house until 1940, it was saved by John D. Rockefeller, Jr., and opened in its restored condition in 1969. Daily hours are 10am to 5pm; admission is $6 for adults, $5 for seniors, and $3 for students. Those interested in the Revolutionary period will love the place.

On the inland side of Route 9, almost within sight of Philipsburg Manor, is the famous **Old Dutch Church,** corner of Broadway and Pierson Street (tel. 914/631-1123). It was from the burying ground adjacent to this ancient church that Washington Irving's Headless Horseman, the commander and chief of the spirits and ghosts of the region, set forth to terrorize Ichabod Crane. Actually, there was nothing personal in the event. According to legend, the Horseman was separated from his head by a Revolutionary War cannonball and rode each night only in an attempt to find his noggin. The noise from four lanes of traffic on Route 9 somewhat diminishes but does not entirely dispell the sense of the mystery hereabouts.

The church is a charming antique. It is stone walled, gambrel roofed, perched upon a high knoll, and shaded by mighty trees. It still has neither heat nor electricity, although there are plans to install both. Save for the terror-filled years during the Revolution, when neither British nor Americans completely controlled the area and law resided in the barrel of a bandit's gun, the Old Dutch Church has been in continuous use (except during the winter) since it was built by Frederick Philipse, first lord of the manor, in 1697.

Much of the charm of this spot stems from the interesting old graveyard, many of whose stones bear Dutch inscriptions. Together they constitute a wonderful record of an American community that stretches back three centuries. Andrew Carnegie lies here, as do Washington Irving and a number of the Rockefellers. The Friends of the Old Dutch Burying Ground conduct walking tours of the graveyard most Sundays between late May and late October. If you're interested, call the number above to make a reservation. Alternately, you can tour the premises on your own between 8am and 4:30pm daily. The church is usually locked between services.

Note: At Tarrytown, you may consider crossing to the west bank of the Hudson River via the Tappan Zee Bridge and sampling the pleasures of Nyack and some of the other villages along the western shore. Details are in Chapter XII.

DETOUR TO POCANTICO HILLS

Perhaps you've noticed the name Rockefeller cropping up repeatedly around here. That's because nearby Pocantico Hills, just northeast of Tarrytown, is the Rockefellers' home turf. It's not where the first John D. was born, but it's where he built his great mansion **Kykuit** (still standing, still private) and where considerable numbers of his descendants have, over the years, built a compound of adjoining estates in the midst of a greenbelt of about 3,500 acres. When Gov. Nelson Rockefeller died, he willed his share in Kykuit to the National Trust for Historic Preservation. As yet there are no provisions for the public to see the house. From the air it's stupendous indeed. N.Y. 448 (here known as Bedford Road), which starts at U.S. 9 in North Tarrytown, winds its way through the very heart of the Rockefeller compound. You can't see Kykuit from the road, or much of any of the other houses either. But you can admire the picture-perfect village of **Pocantico Hills,** really a company town for the Rockefeller estates, and savor the undiluted air of privilege that drips from the very trees.

OSSINING

Returning to Scarborough Presbyterian, turn north again onto Route 9, and continue through the village of Ossining (pop. 20,200). They used to call this place Sing Sing, until 1901, when the village fathers tired of jokes connecting them with the riverfront prison of the same name. Sing Sing Prison dates from 1824. In its early years, under the notorious administration of Capt. Elam Lynds, prisoners quarried Sing Sing marble during the day and slept in chains in solitary cells at night. Complaints and/or disobedience were dealt with by whipping, and conversation was forbidden, as were visitors and mail.

Ossining today has a late Victorian look to it, particularly along Main Street in the several blocks immediately west of Broadway (Route 9). Other parts of the village sport interesting Greek Revival and mid- to late Victorian houses. Gentrification has made few inroads. There is not much to hold you here, so head off to the last stop on your north-along-the-Hudson itinerary.

CROTON-ON-HUDSON

On the far side of the Croton River, not quite 3 miles from Main Street in Ossining, is little Croton-on-Hudson (pop. 6,900). This blue-collar village was originally settled in the late 19th century by immigrant laborers working on the Croton Reservoir System. In the early 20th century, an influx of intellectuals, free thinkers, and fellow travelers from Greenwich Village descended on the hills above the village and shocked the original Irish and Italian settlers with their urban ways and attitudes. Edna St. Vincent Millay lived here for a while, as did feminist Doris Stevens, journalist John Reed (whose Russian exploits were dramatized in the movie *Reds*), economist Stuart Chase, and numerous others—all of whom cut quite a swath in their day.

The vicinity was famous long before any of this, however. On the banks of the Croton River at the south end of the village is **Van Cortlandt Manor,** a 17th-century stone-and-wood Dutch manor house that was rescued and restored in the 1940s by John D. Rockefeller, Jr., himself. Like Philipsburg Manor to the south, Van Cortlandt Manor was once the nerve center of an enormous colonial-era estate. Stephanus Van Cortlandt, son of a man who came to America as a soldier in the Dutch West India Company, managed by 1685 to acquire a tract of land that totaled 86,000 acres, stretching from the Croton River to Peekskill and inland as far as the border of Connecticut. In 1697, the king of England chartered these lands as the Royal Manor of Cortlandt. Between 1700 and 1747, nearly every important visitor who sailed up the Hudson paid a call as a matter of course on the lord of Van Cortlandt Manor and his lady, the former Gertrude Schuyler.

The manor house is deceptively modest from the outside. Its restored interior features beautiful woodwork and furniture, and its elaborate grounds are tended in high 18th-century style. After the death of the first lord, the Van Cortlandt family continued to be prominent in local and national affairs. Stephanus's grandson, Pierre, was the first lieutenant governor of New York State. Pierre's son, Philip, served under General Washington. Van Cortlandt family descendants continued to occupy the manor house until 1945, when it was sold and subsequently rescued by the Rockefellers. Open to the public since 1959, it is presently one of the properties of Historic Hudson Valley.

Van Cortlandt Manor is located on a little spur of old Route 9 called South Riverside Avenue, parallel to the new highway crossing over the Croton River. Admission is $6 for adults, $5 for seniors, $3 for students, and free to children under 6. The site is open Wednesday to Monday between 10am and 5pm from March through December. Closed January and February. If you'd like more information, contact Historic Hudson Valley, 150 White Plains Rd., Tarrytown, NY 10591 (tel. 914/631-8200).

---

3. White Plains & Purchase

WHITE PLAINS

White Plains is an appealing small city of about 47,000 that feels much larger than it really is. Although first settled in the early 18th century (there once were extensive iron mines hereabouts), the city today is largely a creature of 19th-century suburban expansion from New York City, only some 12 miles to the south.

Those interested in the history of the American Revolution might want to visit the several **historic revolutionary sites** in town. It was in the courthouse at White Plains—formerly located at South Broadway and Mitchell Place—that New York's provincial congress ratified our new nation's Declaration of Independence. Indeed, that famous document was read aloud for the first time from the courthouse steps on July 11, 1776. This was the official break with Britain and the birth of New York State. A brooding Victorian armory occupies the courthouse site today.

By the autumn of that year, Manhattan was in the hands of the British and Washington was in full retreat. The famous Battle of White Plains, waged in a series of skirmishes during late October 1776, was decisive not so much because the Americans won (they didn't, really) but because the British stopped chasing them, thereby giving Washington the breathing space to continue the fight another day.

One of these skirmishes, between a fairly ragtag collection of American patriots and paid Hessian mercenaries under the command of Lord Howe, took place on Chatterton Hill, or **Battle Hill** as it is also called. This steep bluff is located to the west of downtown White Plains, just on the other side of the Bronx River Parkway (Battle Avenue and Chatterton Parkway join Main Street within sight of the Bronx River Parkway viaduct). The hill today is densely covered with old frame houses. But the steep bluff above Chatterton Parkway hints of the dramatic events that took place there over two centuries ago.

Much of the art of war is knowing when to fight and when to retire. Washington demonstrated his brilliance in the latter case throughout the fall of 1776. Howe routed the Continentals at Battle Hill in White Plains, but that didn't mean Washington was about to surrender. He retired instead to North White Plains and established his headquarters in a tiny cottage owned by a farmer named Miller. The importance of the Miller house is that it marked the end of the long American retreat that had started the previous spring on Long Island. Perhaps it was due to the prospect of the approaching winter, or possibly it was because of the surprising artillery power the American's had been able to muster, or maybe it was due to the mysterious "political reasons" Howe cited four years later to an inquiring Parliament; whatever the cause, his lordship gave up the chase at this point and returned to New York.

The humble Miller house, now known as **Washington's Headquarters Museum,** Virginia Road, North White Plains (tel. 914/949-1236), is one of those incredible survivors from the distant past, huddled in a tiny spot of woods with a factory facing it across Virginia Road and apartment buildings looming over its little roof from a hilltop behind. Washington certainly wouldn't recognize the neighborhood, but the farmhouse itself is absolutely in a time capsule. Built in 1738, listing to starboard because the roots of an enormous ancient tree are literally lifting it on one side, it still contains the actual chair and table that General Washington used while in residence. The low studded room in which he met his generals and plotted strategy at this dramatic moment in history probably looks to us today exactly as it did to him. To stand in the doorway and look at it is fascinating and moving.

One can wander through the farmhouse and peruse the interesting exhibits at one's leisure, although informed assistance is available from a guide on site. Open Wednesday through Sunday from 10am until 4pm; admission is free. Virginia Road begins at North Broadway north of I-287 (Cross Westchester Expressway) five blocks above the White Plains Rural Cemetery. The Miller house is a short distance north of this intersection, on the right.

PURCHASE

This is an unincorporated section in the town of Harrison (pop. 23,000), located immediately east of White Plains and separated from it by the multiple lanes of I-287 (Cross Westchester Expressway). Anderson Hill Road, which junctions with Westchester Avenue in a complicated interchange on top of I-287, leads into the heart of it.

Much of Purchase is in fine condition, to which stretches of Purchase Street, Anderson Hill Road, and Lincoln Avenue eloquently attest. Besides estate dwellers, swank country clubs, and corporations, Purchase is the home of two large college campuses. **State University of New York at Purchase** occupies 500 semirural acres on Anderson Hill Road near the Connecticut border. **Manhattanville College** has a 250-acre campus south of Anderson Hill and Purchase Street intersection.

It is the latter of these two institutions that is of interest, since its centerpiece—one of the grandest mansions ever built in Westchester—is accessible to the public. **Ophir Hall** is an enormous stone castle named after a Western silver mine that once figured in the portfolio of its original builder, a high flyer named Ben Holladay. He made a fortune in frontier days on the Overland Express but lost it all in the panic of 1873. In 1888, his country estate was purchased by Whitelaw Reid, publisher of *The New York Herald-Tribune*. Reid then had it totally renovated by the famous firm of McKim, Mead, and White.

The exterior of Ophir Hall is clad in granite, rises to between three and four stories, and is topped with what look like miles of crenellated battlements. The interior (at least on the main floor) is a paradise of gilded bronze, multicolored marble, Tiffany stained glass, and imported French boiserie salvaged by Reid during his term as U.S. ambassador to France. The western wing of the house, which looks only slightly smaller than Grand Central Terminal, is a 1912 addition, also to the design of McKim, Mead, and White. It was constructed to house the Reid library, which overlooks a series of balustraded terraces that cascades down toward distant dormitories and playing fields.

Manhattanville is private, but the friendly attendant at the gate on Purchase Street, half a mile south of Anderson Hill Road, will usually let respectable-looking persons in. Just tell him you'd like to see the castle and he'll direct you.

4. Near Long Island Sound

Westchester's waterfront along Long Island Sound was well developed by the beginning of the 20th century. The two principal arteries that parallel the sound today—the old Boston Post Road (U.S. 1) and the New England Thruway (I-95)—both traverse more or less unrelieved commercial, residential, and industrial congestion. Neither one is particularly scenic.

The Post Road, which follows Native American trails, forms the spine along which all the Sound villages were originally centered. These villages have long since merged more or less into one long built-up strip. Even though each still retains an individual character, you must get off Route 1 to savor the area's true charms.

The long irregular shoreline, with its many coves and twisting peninsulas, often spacious and quiet, graced with fine old houses and lovely seaside views. However, some of the nicest parts of it—Premium Point in Larchmont, for example, or Manursing Island in Rye—are private communities whose roads are barred by manned gatehouses and restricted to residents and guests.

Having said all this, the dedicated tourist can still find sufficient stops for a interesting afternoon's excursion. Should you be so inclined, my recommendation is to start just west of the border of Connecticut, in the appealing village of Rye.

RYE

Although it looks like a suburban village, Rye is technically a city covering about 6 square miles and housing some 15,100 inhabitants, usually in rather luxurious quarters. The best way to get there is to take either I-95 from the south or I-287 (Cross Westchester Expressway) from White Plains.

If you arrive via the latter, which is the county's principal east-west artery, you can admire the showy architectural endeavors of corporate America that line the so-called **Platinum Mile** outside White Plains. As I-287 nears the sound and crosses the border of Rye Brook, you'll have a good view of the astonishing postmodern **headquarters of General Foods**. It's on the left, just past the exit for Westchester Avenue (Route 120A), a massive white thing with a dome, a private lake, rolling greenswards, and a chic but slightly sinister look to it. (Are there really people inside this place, or only robots?). Built in 1983, it is the work of the New York firm of Kevin Roche, John Dinkeloo & Associates.

Get off I-287 at the Route 1 exit and head west. In just a moment you'll be at the foot of Purchase Street. This is the center of Rye's commercial district, which extends northward along Purchase Street for several pleasant blocks. There are lots of shops (especially antiques shops), shady trees, plenty of street parking, old-fashioned three-story buildings, and a relaxed upscale suburban atmosphere. (Purchase Street, which you have already explored in the estate lands to the north, is a scenic alternative to I-287 for those traveling between Purchase and Rye.)

Opposite the light at Purchase Street and Route 1, on the north side of the intersection, is an ancient-looking gambrel-roofed building facing the Post Road. This is the **Square House Museum,** 1 Purchase St., Rye, NY 10580 (tel. 914/967-7588), originally built as a farmhouse and converted to a tavern in 1760. Back then, this was as far as the stages were able to get in a full day's travel from New York. The building was a famous inn until 1830. For most of those years known as the Widow Haviland's, it hosted almost everybody who traveled between Boston and New York, be they famous or not. Plenty of them were, including John and Samuel Adams, the marquis de Lafayette, and George Washington. In 1903, the building's owners presented it to the village of Rye for use as a municipal hall. So it remained until 1964, when the Rye Historical Society moved in, set up its headquarters, and opened the present interesting historical exhibit. This includes, among other things, a restored 18th-century tavern interior. Open Tuesday to Sunday from 2:30 to 4:30pm; closed holidays; open only on Tuesday and Saturday during winter.

In 1928, shortly before they designed the County Center at White Plains, the architectural firm of Walker and Gillette drew up plans for a fantastical daytripper's seaside resort called **Playland Park,** at the foot of Playland Parkway on the waterfront in Rye (tel. 914/967-2040). Today this wonderful place, with a white sandy beach, a glorious art deco bathhouse, one of the first planned amusement parks in America (complete with Ferris wheel and roller coaster), a music tower, and acres of lovely landscaped parkland, survives in beautifully unmodernized condition. If you swapped the cars in the lot for vintage flivvers you'd be right back in the 1920s.

The huge casino building, which offers ice skating in the winter, is the centerpiece for a complex of arcades that drip with deco period architectural glamor. There are romantic cupolas, towers on the skyline, and a boardwalk with broad views across the beach and Long Island Sound. Even the lampposts are vintage. Playland is fully operational between May 15 and Labor Day, but the grounds are open all year, and there's usually something doing at the casino even in the depths of winter. If nothing else, the architecture is worth a look. (In case you wonder, that trio of distant skyscrapers visible across the sound is North Shore Towers, a condominium complex on the Queens-Nassau border.)

One of the more appealing areas along the Westchester shoreline is directly adjacent to Playland and accessible by public roads. It is **Milton Point,** settled originally by Quakers but long ago evolved into a select residential section of Rye. From the Playland circle, take the first left onto **Forest Avenue.** The real estate becomes successively grander the farther you get from Playland; a few real palazzi front on the Sound here and there. Forest Avenue eventually makes a dogleg turn to the right and deposits you on Stuyvesant Avenue. Turn left and admire the walled mansions, the stately pillared facade of the Coveleigh Club, and the low cabanas of the Shenorock Shore Club. The public way ends just short of Milton Point itself, at the gate to the American Yacht Club. Although you can go no farther, there is a small turnout to park the car and a boulder-strewn beach from which you can admire the wind whipped waters of Milton Harbor and the little sailboats darting back and forth around Hen Island.

Until the 1940s much of the Post Road (Route 1) between Rye and Larchmont was lined with elaborate estates belonging to the likes of Ethel Barrymore, Robert "Believe-It-or-Not" Ripley, and James Montgomery Flagg. Intensive postwar subdivision has changed all that. However, a short stretch remains, complete with a few interesting houses. One of these is **Whitby,** 330 Boston Post Rd., Rye, located about a mile south of Playland Parkway on Route 1. This stone Gothic Revival castle was designed in 1854 by the famous Alexander Jackson Davis. It has for many years been the clubhouse of the Rye Golf Club, a semiprivate organization whose membership is limited to residents of the city of Rye. Whitby has pointed windows, a high crenellated octagonal tower, a porte cochere, and a very asymmetrical silhouette. Although the interior has been altered over the years, the facade facing the Post Road across a rolling lawn remains almost as good an example of the Gothic Revival as Lyndhurst up in Tarrytown.

The estate next door to Whitby has been preserved as the **Marsh Lands Conservancy,** and as a result there is a short stretch of Route 1 that still conjures the faint aura of the rural-suburban past. The property after the conservancy, on the left just before Barlow Lane, is alas in the hands of speculators. Its fine Greek Revival mansion may well be lost by the time you read this. Pity too, since this historic house was the **home of Peter Jay,** brother of the first chief justice of the United States, John Jay. Indeed, John Jay's grave is in a private plot on the property.

MAMARONECK

Shortly after the Jay house, U.S. Route 1 draws close to the water and enters the village of Mamaroneck (pop. 17,600). Like surrounding municipalities, this is a pleasant commuter town with lots of yacht clubs. The nicest areas hereabouts tend to be down on the water and are accessible only by private road.

There survives an 18th-century curiosity adjacent to the center of Mamaroneck, located at 404 West Post Rd. (Route 1), at the corner of Fenimore Road. Today it's a gas station hard by the side of the highway, with a restaurant attached. But when it was built in 1792, it stood at the top of a hill overlooking Mamaroneck Harbor and was known as the **DeLancey Manor House,** residence of Maj. John DeLancey, grandson of the acerbic Caleb Heathcote, first Lord of the Manor of Scarsdale. How the mighty are fallen! In this house in 1811 James Fenimore Cooper took the aristocratic Susan A. DeLancey as his bride. The couple then lived here, in considerable rural splendor, for several years. A century later, the house was sold at auction (supposedly for $11) and ignominiously removed from its hilltop site; in 1924, it was converted into a gas station.

Movie buffs take note: D. W. Griffith's famous Mamaroneck film studio used to be located on **Orienta Avenue,** which intersects Route 1 two blocks south of Fenimore Road. Here, a few blocks off the Post Road, were filmed such silent classics as *Valley Forge* and *Orphans of the Storm,* both with a Mamaroneck backdrop.

NEW ROCHELLE

Only those with an especial interest in Revolutionary-era artifacts need continue the next 2 miles down Route 1. After passing through Larchmont (pop. 6,300), which is a pleasant-enough place, you come to the city of New Rochelle (pop. 70,800), once the home of Norman Rockwell but a place that today has not fared nearly as well as White Plains. Turn right in the middle of town onto North Avenue and proceed for about 2 miles north. You'll cross the New England Thruway (I-95) and then pass a succession of distressed commercial strips and faded 19th-century garden suburbs.

The neighborhood improves, however, by the time you reach the **Thomas Paine Cottage**, 983 North Ave., New Rochelle (tel. 914/632-5376). Paine Cottage is a darling little brown-shingled saltbox with pretty blue shutters, sitting in the middle of a small park beside an embanked brook. When Paine lived here, on a farm granted to him by a grateful legislature in 1784, the house was on top of a nearby hill. Although he owned the property until he died in 1809, he occupied this house only between 1802 and 1806. Paine, as you already know, was the author of the stirring Revolutionary War pamphlet *Common Sense* as well as the Secretary of the Second Continental Congress. His diminutive country cottage has been restored and furnished with 18th-century pieces. The **Thomas Paine Memorial House,** across the street at 983 North Ave., contains additional exhibits relating to Paine and the Revolutionary period. Both the cottage and the house are open from 2 to 5pm on Friday, Saturday, and Sunday only.

If you're like me, always curious to see how people live in different places, you might want to check out **Beechmont.** The northern edge of this gracious, late 19th-century planned suburb is just behind the Paine Cottage. To get the full intended effect of the place, however, I'd return south on North Avenue to Beechmont Drive, which will be on your left as you head southbound, just past Huguenot Lake Park. It's a slightly niftier version of Park Hill; among the more interesting streets are Beechmont, Overlook, and Esplanade.

5. Where to Stay & Eat

The hotels are listed more or less in descending order of price, with my favorites listed first. In the case of the restaurants, I have (with the exception of the rural north) arranged the listings geographically by village or city, then arranged these locations in alphabetical order. The idea is to make it easy to find places that are convenient to the touring routes described above and/or to your hotel at the end of a long and possibly tiring day.

HOTELS

Bear in mind that besides local and state sales taxes, Westchester imposes a 3% tax on all hotel rooms, which is in addition to the regressive New York State 5% surcharge on hotel rooms costing over $100 a night. Notwithstanding, the cost of staying overnight in Westchester County is half of what you'd pay in Manhattan.

Before you make a reservation anywhere, *ask about packages.* The packages mentioned below may or may not be exactly what's offered by the time you arrive. But there's always some promotional special or other, particularly on weekends, when the business travelers are back at home and most hotels are empty. Desk personnel will not tell you about low-cost packages unless you specifically ask. So, don't forget.

Finally, a word about conference centers. Westchester abounds in these facilities; and as the business climate has become more competitive and Westchester has emerged as a hub of corporate activity, conference centers have become increasingly elaborate and luxurious. Only recently have they begun to woo noncorporate customers. This is good news for tourists since these establishments usually offer superlative accommodations and facilities. In fact, my top two recommendations are conference centers.

In my mind there's no question that the very best place is **Doral Arrowwood,** Anderson Hill Road, Rye Brook, NY 10573 (tel. 914/939-5500; fax 914/939-1877). This sprawling (274 rooms), ultramodern, shingle-clad complex was built as a deluxe conference center in 1983. Conferences still constitute the majority of its trade, but an increasing number of pleasure travelers are also discovering it.

The building nestles at the end of a long drive through rolling emerald fairways of the hotel's own 9-hole golf course. The 114-acre site is between Purchase on the west and Greenwich, Connecticut, on the east—which by itself would make it or of my favorite places in the world. Besides location, however, the Arrowwood h spectacular modern architecture, a trio of excellent and highly aesthetic restaurant every big-city hotel convenience you could imagine (vast plush lobbies, a concierg valet parking, helpful uniformed attendants, 24-hour room service), and the mo fantastic and fully equipped hotel sports center in the country. The latter includes a immense indoor pool connected via an underwater tunnel to a heated outdoor po swimmable in the depths of February; a workout room with up-to-the-minu weight machines; a multiplicity of bikes and Stairmasters; a steam room; a saun squash, racquetball, and tennis courts; plus the aforementioned golf course. It is facility on a par with those in Manhattan and, with the exception of the golf cours completely free to registered guests.

Arrowwood's accommodations are located off a maze of lushly carpete branching corridors in which you could easily lose your bearings. Rooms are on t small side, since they were originally designed solely for business travelers. But th are sleek and tailored, each with a big desk area (complete with dictionary, thesauru and built-in chalkboard), woodland views, two phones, a mahogany cabinet with big TV that seems to get every channel on earth, a radio, discreet and streamlin lamps and armchairs, a muted gray-green or coral color scheme, and a bath with suf cient amenities. Not sumptuous, but extremely comfortable.

Meals may be taken in the moderately priced **Pub,** where sandwiches and bur ers costs less than $10; the **Atrium,** which adjoins the lobby, overlooks the go course through another three-story glass wall, and offers excellent continental dish from $16 to $20; or **Provare,** a jazzy trattoria with striking graphics and contemp rary Italian specialties ranging from about $12 to $18.

You'll get the best room deals on winter Friday and Saturday nights, when a b and full American breakfast package costs but $129 a night for two people; that ra rises to $139 in spring and $159 in summer. What they call the "rack rate," which sort of like a car manufacturer's base sticker price, is $149 for a single and $169 fo double, year-round. AE, MC, and V accepted.

Tarrytown House, East Sunnyside Lane, P.O. Box 222, Tarrytown, NY (t 914/591-8200, or toll free 800/553-8118; fax 914/591-7118), is also primaril conference center. This time the property overlooks the Hudson River from a h top site above Washington Irving's Sunnyside. It is surrounded by wooded corp .rate campuses and a few remaining private estates.

Where Arrowwood is sleek and ultramodern, Tarrytown House is magnifice and traditional. Its centerpiece is not one but two terrific old millionaires' mansion Down on Sunnyside Lane are impressive stone gateposts whose bronze plaques st bear the name Linden Court, which was what the old estate was called. Beyond t iron gates, a winding driveway climbs a manicured hillside lawn that's dotted wi sweeping specimen trees and occasional statues and crowned by the enormous ca tellated stone Biddle mansion.

The reception area is located in what they call the carriage house, a tactfully lu urious space with Biedermeier repro furniture, sprays of exotic flowers, and green-marble desk. Uniformed attendants direct you to accommodations housed one of four separate buildings. Three of these—named Rockland, Westchester, a Fairfield after local counties—contain spacious modern rooms, usually decorat in a cool corporate gray palette. They are furnished with attractive Chippenda repro pieces, high-quality bathroom amenities, deluxe TVs, and armoires, sporti a general look of low-key modern luxury.

The fourth building is the other mansion, King House. Only 10 of Tarrytow 148 accommodations are located here, but if you can book one by all means d King House is a white-pillared, early 20th-century Greek Revival manse. It has blac and-white-marble floors and opulent paneling on the main level, with two floors elegant bedrooms above. These are furnished with floral fabrics, antique furnitur beautiful framed prints on the walls, and baths with stacks of fluffy towels a Crabtree & Evelyn amenities. The Hudson River views from these rooms—almo all of which have terraces—are sublime.

There is an exercise center with sufficient stations and an indoor pool, plus extremely attractive outdoor pool. Dinner is available Friday and Saturday in the paneled elegance of King House, and in the Biddle house (named for the former owners) the rest of the week. Breakfast is also served daily on a big covered porch called the Winter Palace. A downstairs pub at Biddle serves burgers and drinks.

Rates for all this style and luxury range from the $99 "Great Estate Weekend" package (double room and continental breakfast), to a $125 "Bed & Breakfast" package (a bigger breakfast, a welcoming bottle of champagne, and a tray of chocolate-dipped strawberries), to a "Wine and Dine" package (breakfast and dinner this time), to the basic room rate (single or double) of $125 a night ($135 in King House). This is a good value, and it's hard to imagine a more beautiful setting. All major credit cards accepted.

On the other side of the county is **Rye Town Hilton,** 699 Westchester Ave., Rye Brook, NY 10573 (tel. 914/939-6300; fax 914/939-5328). Take exit 10 off I-287 and get onto Westchester Avenue in the direction of Port Chester; the hotel driveway faces the corporate headquarters of General Foods (which from this vantage point looks more than ever as though it landed from outer space).

Besides a booming corporate conference and meeting business, the Hilton does a brisk trade among city people fleeing Manhattan for a weekend fling at reduced rates. This can be accomplished in any of 438 rooms, distributed among a complex of modern brick buildings set in a deep forest. There is rather a circuitous route from the gate on Westchester Avenue to the front door. Once you get there, however, it all looks reassuringly Hiltonesque. Big brass doors lead into a spacious lobby, which has thick red-and-green rugs, a mammoth stone fireplace, plush green sofas, and a long green-marble-topped reception desk—all overlooked by a moderate-to-expensive restaurant called Tulip Tree.

Accommodations are very smart, with wood-paneled doors opened by silent key cards, rosewood (or pickled-pine) furniture, attractive seafoam-green or coral color schemes, striped wallpaper, chintz spreads, great TVs, coffeemakers, and Hilton amenities in the baths. These spacious rooms are as nice as any in the county.

Besides Tulip Tree, there is "fine dining" at Penfields (where à la carte dishes range from $19 to $25), or you can settle in for drinks and intimate conversation in The Den. Also indoors are a most attractive indoor pool (usually I find these depressing, but this one is really nice) and an exercise room. Three lighted tennis courts are thoughtfully enclosed in a bubble every winter. The nicest things about this place, however, is the grounds. They plant 20,000 tulip bulbs here every year, and in springtime it is simply gorgeous. The beautiful outdoor pool is precisely the sort of place that would make me want to laze away an entire day.

As of this writing, Rye Town Hilton was offering packages like the "Hilton Bounce-Back" for $99 a night double occupancy, including continental breakfast (available Friday, Saturday, and Sunday), and the "Westchester Weekend" for $135 nightly for two (with a late check-out and a bigger breakfast). The basic single room rate ranges from $105 to $180 nightly; doubles go for between $125 and $200. All major credit cards accepted.

For those who enjoy shopping, stay at the **Holiday Inn Crowne Plaza,** 66 Hale Ave., White Plains, NY 10601 (tel. 914/682-0050, or toll free 800/2-CROWNE; fax 914-682-7404). This 14-story, 401-room full-service hotel is located adjacent to the new Westchester Mall, which features over 150 stores, including Neimann-Marcus, Nordstrom, Ann Taylor and Tiffany. Three blocks away are Bloomingdale's and the Galleria Mall. All the recently renovated rooms at the Crowne Plaza have phones and cable TVs with pay-per-view options; plus there's a pool, a Jacuzzi, and an exercise room. The new restaurant, Fenimore's, features northern Italian cuisine and is open daily for breakfast, lunch, and dinner from 6:30am to 11pm. Room service is available from 6am to midnight. Double-occupancy weekend rates are as low as $85; plan to spend from $120 to $140 for the same accommodations on weekdays. Free parking; all major credit cards accepted.

Tarrytown Hilton Inn, over by the Hudson, immediately south of the Thruway on Route 9 at 455 South Broadway, Tarrytown, NY 10591 (tel. 914/631-5700; fax 914/631-0075), is another amazingly nice place. It's over 30 years old but has been constantly upgraded and redecorated. Fortunately, it also had a good layout to begin with. The pool, instead of being located near the highway, is surrounded by gardens and overlooked by a delightful awninged restaurant. The 236 rooms, instead of being stacked up in a high-rise, are arranged in a trio of tasteful low-rise wings that embraces the vast garden court with the outdoor pool. There are also an indoor pool, a weight room with exercise machines, outdoor tennis courts, a gaggle of attractive restaurants, and an atmospheric bar.

The rooms are tastefully furnished with colonial reproduction furniture, smart wallcoverings, quilted chintz bedspreads, full amenity trays, piles of fluffy towels in the modern baths, and top-quality TVs. The units facing the outdoor pool courtyard have sliding glass doors that lead to the spacious lawn or balconies that overlook same. Rates for single occupancy range from $109 to $135 a night, depending on location; doubles cost between $129 and $155. There are also all manner of weekend packages, among them the "Hilton Bounce-Back Weekend" ($108 for a double, May through September). An excellent place to stay. All major credit cards accepted.

Westchester Marriott, 670 White Plains Rd. (Route 119), Tarrytown, NY 10591 (tel. 914/631-2200, or toll free 800/882-1042; fax 914/631-2832), is an elaborate 10-story concrete structure within sight of the intersection of I-287 (the Cross Westchester Expressway) and I-87 (the New York State Thruway). The hotel's big contemporary porte cochere leads to a lofty lobby filled with thick rugs and lots of seating groups.

Down one corridor is a succession of chandeliered meeting room/ballrooms; down another is a Polynesian restaurant named Kona Kai, a moderately priced pub, and a singles' bar called Gambits; contiguous to the lobby is a small lounge where a player grand piano was tinkling away at a Chopin nocturne when I was there. The most dramatic feature of the hotel's public areas, however, is the five-story atrium with a vaulted glass ceiling (retractable in summer), a pool, and an oversized Jacuzzi. The nearby basement exercise room is just OK.

The rooms, however, are first-rate and modern, each with nice fabrics (a redecoration project underway at this writing will change the palette from 1980s blues and beiges to 1990s greens and pale lavenders), two phones, a clean modern bath, and a color TV with Spectravision. Housekeeping is immaculate.

To get details on Marriott's best weekend packages, call the chain toll free at 800/USA-WKND. Not all hotels participate in the national promotions, but most do. As we went to press, Marriott Westchester was offering an $99 "Two for Breakfast" rate good on Friday, Saturday, and Sunday; sometimes there's a $124 rate for single or double on Friday and Saturday; rack rates are $149 for a single and $169 for a double. All major credit cards accepted.

Smaller (145 rooms) and more modest, but every bit as comfortable, is **Courtyard by Marriott,** over near the Sound about a mile from Playland, at 631 Midland Ave., Rye, NY 10580 (tel. 914/921-1110, or toll free 800/321-2211; fax 914/921-2446). A number of Courtyards have opened in the last few years; indeed, there's another in Westchester at 475 White Plains Rd., Tarrytown, NY (tel. 914/631-1122). They are nearly identical, modular low-rise constructions, half of whose rooms overlook a central landscaped court. It's a formula designed with great care for business travelers.

What they term "upscale basic quality" is a boon for any sort of traveler. At Rye this translates into nice rooms with attractive rugs and window treatments, coordinated coral or green color schemes, bedside clocks, color TVs with pay movies, and modern baths with sufficient amenities—plus a surprisingly good (and inexpensive) lobby restaurant, an indoor pool, and a small mirrored exercise room with a couple of bikes and a Universal machine. The place is efficient and friendly and offers excellent value: $84 for a single or double on Friday or Saturday, $99 for a single and $105 for a double during the week. Members of national groups like the AAA or AARP can get a double room for only $76. Sometimes Marriott runs national promotions that are even cheaper. All major credit cards accepted.

Last but certainly not least (except in price) is the excellent **Days Inn,** a seven-story motel clinging to a steep hillside at 200 Tarrytown Rd. (Route 119), Elmsford, NY 10523 (tel. 914/592-5680, or toll free 800/325-2525, or for national promotions, toll free 800/942-7543). The 147 rooms overlook interstate highways, busy Route 199, and a few wistful castles on nearby mountains. But the place is dazzlingly clean as well as exceedingly comfortable; has rooms with well-kept modern furnishings, color TVs, and immaculate bathrooms; and boasts a very reasonably priced family restaurant called the Greenery just off the lobby. Although there is no exercise room, management has struck a deal with a nearby health club whose facilities are available free to guests. Basic "rack rate" is $84 for a double, dropping to $65 on Friday and Saturday. If you are considering a visit, by all means first call the national promotions toll-free number above and see what deals they're offering. All major credit cards accepted.

RESTAURANTS

The best spots for cheap lunches and budget dinners are in Irvington, Scarsdale, Tarrytown, Bronxville, and Yonkers. The most interesting deluxe restaurants are under Hastings, Tarrytown, and Rye. Scarsdale has the most listings because of its central location. You can be in lots of places in southern Westchester and still be only 10 minutes from Scarsdale.

Bronxville

Lange's Delicatessen, in the center of Bronxville (pop. 6,300), 94 Pondfield Rd., at Park Place (tel. 914/337-3354), is a modest local institution with a deserved reputation for good-tasting food. White-aproned attendants stand behind a huge glass case filled with all manner of mouth-watering salads, specialty foods, freshly baked pot pies, and meats. This is a place for overstuffed sandwiches (smoked ham, Black Forest Delight, smoked turkey and Muenster, Virginia ham and cheese, chicken salad), pot pies, macaroni and cheese, or any sort of salad platter. You order at the counter, then either take it with you or find a seat at one of the several tables overlooking Park Place. It's hard to spend more than $10 for lunch, even with dessert. Open Monday through Saturday from 7am to 7pm, Sunday from 7am to 4pm.

Hastings

Buffet de la Gare, adjacent to the Hastings-on-Hudson railroad station, 155 Southside Ave. (tel. 914/478-1671), is a delightful and authentic French bistro. This place really has charm—from the lace curtains in the front, to the dazzling white linen on the tables, to the painted tin walls and ceilings in the several diminutive dining rooms. Madame is up front at the bar, welcoming guests and making drinks, while Monsieur is back in the kitchen turning out classic French dishes prepared with a Breton accent.

Lunch is served Tuesday through Friday from noon until 2pm. You might start with smoked salmon in puff pastry, move on to an omelet with Swiss cheese and herbs, and finish with crème brûlée à la vanille and coffee. Dinner selections, served Tuesday through Saturday from 6:30 to 9pm, include marinated grilled lamb with Provence herbs, roasted duck in sauce du jour, and Norwegian salmon. Expect to pay between $10 and $17 for à la carte lunch items and around $21 to $28 for those at dinner. There are always daily specials. The atmosphere is lovely, and the presentation of the dishes simply superb. If you don't wear a tie, at least be neat. All major credit cards accepted.

Irvington

Benny's, just south of the Irvington light on U.S. 9 at 6 S. Broadway (tel. 914/591-9811), is a great little local seafood house with an informal atmosphere, moderate prices, and excellent food. There are a bar just inside the door; a small front dining room with captain's chairs and plastic tablecloths; and a larger dining room in the back decorated with murals of fishing boats, white-painted paneling, and harpoons on the walls. Lunch might be something like fried scallops with french fries and coleslaw, fried oysters, hot roast beef sandwich, or chicken salad plate, priced from $6 to $8. At dinner the à la carte selections are mostly from $12 to $20 and include broiled swordfish, bluefish, flounder, veal and pork chops, and steak. Open for lunch daily from 11:30am to 2:30pm and for dinner on Monday to Saturday from 5 to 10pm. Dinner is served on Sunday from 2 to 9pm.

Just north of Benny's, right at the Irvington light, is the utterly unpretentious **Corner Luncheonette,** 2 S. Broadway (tel. 914/591-9815). I confess that I have a fondness for this kind of old-fashioned, unrenovated, neighborhood newspaper stand–cum–lunch counter. The menu on the wall features things like grilled cheese, omelets, burgers, fries, sandwiches, and a few specials such as the pork tenderloin platter. I don't think anything costs over $5, and most of it costs less. There are booths with waitress service as well as the counter. Hardly gentrified, but fast, friendly, tasty, and cheap—which is often what you want. Open Monday to Friday from 5:30am to 5:30pm, to 5pm on Saturday, from 7am to 1pm on Sunday.

Mamaroneck

Charlie Brown's, 181 E. Boston Post Rd., which is also Route 1 (tel. 914/698-6610), is in a little yellow house with red-striped awnings in the middle of Mamaroneck, overlooking the harbor. Although there are other Charlie Browns in the metropolitan area, this one is convenient to know about if you're in this part of the county. There's a friendly bar up front, behind which is a series of small pubby rooms decorated with beams and dark woodwork, stained glass, old clocks, Victorian prints, and cozy burgundy booths. At lunch you might try one of the specialty sandwiches like hot corned beef, sirloin steak, griddled chicken, white breast turkey, or a dish such as London broil, fish and chips, or a nacho platter. Most sandwiches and lunch dishes run between $4 and $7. At dinner, things like filet mignon, prime rib, barbecued ribs, and chicken teriyaki cost between $9 and $17. And you can always have a half-pound burger with steak fries for $7. Open for lunch on Monday through Saturday from 11:30am to 2pm. Dinner is served from 5 to 10pm on Monday through Thursday, until 10:30pm on Friday and Saturday; only dinner is served on Sunday, from 4 to 9pm. All major credit cards accepted.

Rye

Close to Playland and downtown Rye is a superb French restaurant called **La Panetière,** 530 Milton Rd. at the corner of S. Oakland Beach Avenue (tel. 914/967-8140). Inside this Colonial house, painted tan with brown shutters, is an attractive dining room with a beamed ceiling, copper pots full of flowers, immaculate white cloths on the circular tables, and an air of Gallic efficiency and style. Cuisine is contemporary French, and the atmosphere is dressy. Lunch selections, like baked pork morsels with peppercorn sauce, monkfish in red wine, and shellfish and saffron-scented couscous, are priced between $14 to $20. At dinner you'll pay between $21 and $31 for selections like striped bass in rosemary broth, filet of beef in a sauce of juniper berries, or salmon rubbed in cumin seeds. Appetizers and desserts are just as inventive. In addition, there are daily specials that change seasonally and prix-fixe menus priced at either $55 or $70 per person for two. Lunch is served Monday through Friday from noon to 2:30pm; dinner is available Monday through Saturday from 6 to 9:30pm and Sunday from 1 to 8:30pm. All in all, this is a first-class culinary experience. All major credit cards accepted.

Scarsdale

South of Route 22, just above the border between Tuckahoe and Eastchester, is **Pinocchio's,** 309 White Plains Rd., Eastchester (tel. 914/337-0044). The diminutive building contains several simple dining rooms with dark-stained wainscoting and crisp white cloths on the tables. Only dinner is served, from a menu that focuses on classically prepared traditional Italian dishes. Veal chop milanese, filet mignon *castelli* (sautéed with shallots, white wine, and shiitake mushrooms), *pollo martini* (chicken battered in parmesan cheese and sautéed in white wine and lemon), plus pastas like *linguine pescatore, capelli vegetariani,* and spaghetti carbonara are priced between $16 and $25. There are plenty of wines to choose from, and all the desserts are made fresh daily. Dinner hours are Tuesday through Thursday from 5 to 10pm, Friday and Saturday from 5 to 11pm, and Sunday from 5 to 9pm. All major credit cards accepted.

On the other side of Scarsdale, with a Scarsdale address but actually located in an adjacent unincorporated area south of Hartsdale, is a terrific little Thai restaurant called **Siam Orchid,** 750 Central Park Ave. (Route 100), just a few blocks north of Ardsley Road (tel. 914/723-9131). Route 100 is a major commercial thoroughfare in this part of the world, and little Siam Orchid clings to the roadside amidst a line of shops. There are two small dining rooms decorated with liberal amounts of purple paint. A reasonably priced lunch might include an appetizer like Thai fried wonton or Tom Yum Goong (shrimp soup) for $3 or $4, then move on to any number of things "over rice," curried, or fried—all costing under $8. At dinner, the typical selection is from $12 to $18 and includes Ped Choo Chee (Siam duck curry), How Muok Siam (steamed seafood curry), Gai Pad Gra Prow (chicken with basil leaves), and any of a number of other tantalizing tongue twisters. Open for lunch from noon to 3pm on Monday through Saturday; dinner is served daily from 4pm to 10pm. AE, MC, and V accepted.

There are a number of recent Asian immigrants to southern Westchester, so the existence of a superior sushi house is not surprising. **Gyosai,** 30 Garth Rd., Scarsdale (tel. 914/725-3730), is considered by many to be among the best. To find it, head west from downtown Scarsdale on Popham Avenue and cross the tracks; you'll find Garth Road almost immediately on your left. Gyosai is so authentic that most of the signs in the windows are in Japanese. Inside, it is modest, small, and neat as a pin. At lunch, sushi and sashimi platters are priced from $12 to $20; tempura udon, katsu don, and tempura cost between about $7 and $13 Tempura, sushi, and sashimi dinners typically cost from $13 to $18. Lunch is served Tuesday to Sunday from noon until 2pm, dinner from 5:30 to 10pm. AE, MC, and V accepted.

While you're on this side of the tracks, you should know about **Jesperson's,** 40 Garth Rd., Scarsdale (tel. 914/472-0250), which is not a restaurant at all but an old-fashioned bakery. Jesperson's is famous in the area for its cakes, cookies, pastries, muffins, strudels, and cheesecakes. Everything is fresh and fabulous. Open Tuesday to Saturday from 7am to 6pm.

Tarrytown

In the middle of the busy village of Tarrytown, adjacent to Broadway (Route 9), is **Santa Fe,** 5 Main St. (tel. 914/332-4452), an appealing, small Mexican restaurant specializing in fajitas—steak, chicken, shrimp, even shark. Diners sit in a narrow room with painted-brick walls, a cactus or two, chunky oak furniture, and a big plate-glass window overlooking Main Street. The tasty and moderately priced quesadillas, tostadas, enchiladas, combinaciones (of burritos, tacos, tamales), plus burgers and a few sandwiches, all fall somewhere from $5 to $15. Open daily from 11:30am to 11:30pm. All major credit cards accepted.

The **Eldorado Diner,** 55 West Main St. (Route 119, practically opposite the Day's Inn) in nearby Elmsford (tel. 914/592-6197), is a big, bright, modern, moderately priced diner that's conveniently located between Tarrytown and White Plains. Omelets, sandwiches, salad platters, hot dishes, club sandwiches, and the entire vocabulary of diner fare is served up 24 hours a day with the customary faintly Greek culinary accent. There are a long counter, lots of booths, and a full bar; almost everything on the vast menu costs between $5 and $13. All major credit cards accepted.

White Plains (See Also Scarsdale)

Dawat, 230 E. Post Rd. (Route 22), in downtown White Plains (tel. 914/428-4411), though relatively new, has established itself as perhaps the best Indian restaurant in Westchester. The decor—lime-green and lavender walls, red-plush rugs, a black-lacquer bar, and shiny brass planters—is Asian with faint deco overtones. The menu changes daily and features salads, tandoori dishes, vegetarian and nonvegetarian dishes, all sorts of exotic breads, rice, and the like. The $8.95 lunch buffet is a particularly good deal, and even at dinnertime you can expect a bill on the sunny side of $20 per person. Open daily for lunch from noon to 3pm; dinner is served Sunday to Thursday from 5:30 to 10:30pm, until 11pm on Friday and Saturday. All major credit cards accepted.

Also downtown is **Quarropas,** 478 Mamaroneck Ave. (tel. 914/684-0414), which commemorates the Native American name for White Plains (literally "white swamp"). The anthropologist owners have decorated the long narrow room with woven textiles, framed antique packing-crate labels, and a green-tiled bar featuring a bright brass rail. Lunch possibilities include a roast leek, wild mushroom, and mozzarella sandwich plus a seafood stew with roasted garlic and kale, from about $7 to $11. Dinner main courses range from creative pasta dishes to grilled rack of lamb with red-onion-and-rosemary chutney and are about $13 to $20. Lunch is served Tuesday through Saturday from 11am to 2:30pm; dinner is served Tuesday through Friday from 5 to 10pm, until 11pm on Saturday and Sunday. All major credit cards accepted.

Yonkers (See Also Scarsdale)

Hunan Village, 1828 Central Park Ave. (Route 100), a few blocks north of Tuckahoe Road in Yonkers (tel. 914/779-2295 or 914/779-2272), is a truly superior Chinese restaurant. Even the decor is attractive—decorated beams on the ceiling, fresh white tablecloths, black-lacquer chairs, and sprays of fresh flowers. The extensive menu runs the gamut of Chinese cuisine: from glistening scallops to shredded beef with garlic to Hunan lamb, with every sort of noodle, rice, and vegetable dish in between. Most dishes cost between $8 and $14, and even the chef's specialties (like ginger scallop, village prawn, Beijing half duck, and veal Soong) top out at around $17. Open Sunday to Thursday from 11:30am to 11pm, until 1am on Friday and Saturday. AE, MC, V, and CB accepted.

A few minutes north on Route 100 is **Nathan's,** 2290 Central Park Ave., Yonkers (tel. 914/779-1800), which is one of the many suburban spin-offs of the original Nathan's hot-dog stand that started in Coney Island umpteen years ago. This one is located just south of Fort Hill Avenue, which runs into Jackson Avenue en route to Hastings. It is useful to know about if you crave a better quality of fast food. The place is essentially an enormous cafeteria, with separate counters for burgers, franks (which are enormously tasty), deli sandwiches, Ben and Jerry's ice cream, bakery items, and so on. You pick up your order and retreat to one of the hundreds (or so it seems) of little green-topped tables. There are video machines in one direction, howling tots in a kiddie corner in another. Most things cost a couple of bucks; a few of the bigger sandwich items run as much as $4 to $6. Open Sunday to Thursday from 7am to 11pm, until 1am on Friday and Saturday.

---

6. The Rural North

Whether you're in Westchester for a vacation, for a visit, or on business, by all means try to save a sunny day for an excursion to the rural north. The unspoiled countryside is perfectly lovely, there are all sorts of things to see and do, and it'll be an opportunity to enjoy some of the finest and most atmospheric dining in the county. You'll find my recommended restaurants in the "Bedford to North Salem" and "North Salem to Katonah" sections that follow.

For our purposes, the "rural north" encompasses the unsuburbanized northeastern corner of Westchester, from the Kensico Reservoir just north of White Plains as far as the little village of North Salem near the borders of Putnam and Fairfield Counties. From your starting point at White Plains to the outermost limit of the itinerary is about 25 miles as the crow flies. As the twisting colonial-era roadbeds go, it's obviously longer and slower. Even without stops, however, it's only about an hour-long drive from White Plains to North Salem on the back roads.

WHITE PLAINS TO BEDFORD

I-684 slashes rapidly and brutally through the western tier of the rural north. You'll be keeping away from it as much as possible. Route 22, which is Broadway in White Plains, is a far more aesthetic way to go. You can also join 22 by taking the Bronx River Parkway northbound from White Plains to the landscaped traffic circle at the foot of the **Kensico Dam.** The circle is a bit over 2 miles from the Westchester County Center in downtown White Plains.

Kensico holds back a 2,200-acre lake. It is a dwarf compared to, say, Hoover Dam, but in the absence of anything comparable nearby it looks quite large. It also has a wonderful period flavor thanks to massive architectural details executed in weather-darkened granite, as well as an appealing roadway across the top. You might want to drive back and forth over the dam, just for the sake of doing so. You can admire the elegant decorative stonework close up and lament the graffiti.

There are plenty of signs on the circle for Route 22 north, so you won't get lost. For the first few miles, the highway hugs the wooded shore of the Kensico Reservoir. After the reservoir, a short four-lane stretch bypasses the village of Armonk. When you cross under 684, you're halfway to Bedford. The road keeps getting prettier and gradually less and less developed.

Bedford is only 14 miles from the Kensico Circle, but it feels and looks like the heart of New England. The center of the village is a spacious triangular green laid out by Connecticut colonists in 1681. The Bedford Green is still surrounded by utterly charming white-painted 18th- and early 19th-century buildings.

Bypassed by the railroad in the 19th century, Bedford languished without major changes almost until the present. Early in this century, large estates began to be developed on surrounding farmland. These estates survive in great part, and the open tracts of land around them sustain an illusion of rural remoteness. Bedford Village was listed as a historic district on the National Register of Historic Places in 1972. It's not purely a period piece today, as there is a fair degree of suburban commerce in the village and a number of newer buildings adjacent to the green. Still, it is hard to imagine a more picture-perfect early American village.

Some of the buildings on the green are of particular note. That Gothic fantasy in wood on the east side of the triangle is the **Bedford Presbyterian Church,** built in 1872. A lot of ambition and talent went into this building, which is essentially an attempt on the part of the local Presbyterians to create a cathedral out of native materials. The single-room stone building at the base of the green is the **1829 School House,** which has been a local history museum since 1913. The interior looks just as it did for the last school year in 1912. There's a pot-bellied stove, the sort of old-time school desks you've seen in antiques stores, a dunce cap in the corner, and a small collection of interesting photos and early artifacts. The schoolhouse is open Wednesday through Sunday from 2 to 5pm.

Directly across the narrow western point of the green is the serene federal **Bedford Historical Hall,** built in 1806 as a Methodist church. The glory of this building is its vast, open interior. A plaque informs us that the building was moved to the present site in 1837 by a team of 20 oxen. Must have been quite a sight. In 1916, it was almost converted to apartments, a potential aesthetic disaster that prompted the founding of the Bedford Historical Society. The society saved the building, restored it, and still operates it as a community center. Right beside it, beneath a picturesque stony bluff that overhangs the green, is the **Old Burying Ground,** the final resting place for Bedford's own between 1681 and 1885.

At the northern point of the triangular green is the **Bedford Courthouse,** completed in 1787. This was the first building to be reconstructed after the village was destroyed by a fire set by British troops in 1779. The courthouse, with its gambrel roof and handsome cupola, has become the unofficial symbol of Bedford Village. It is a museum today, with a severely elegant reconstruction of the original court chambers on the first floor and exhibits on the floor above. Open Wednesday through Sunday from 2 to 5pm.

If you'd like to see where some of the local gentry live, the following itinerary will take you on a short loop (about 6 miles) around **Guard Hill Road** and **McLean Street.** Anybody who knows anything about this part of the world will recognize those names and nod appreciatively.

Begin at the northern point of the green and continue north on the main street, which is still Route 22. At the end of the village, opposite the junction with Route 121 (which heads off to the right), you'll see little Guard Hill Road immediately on your left. Turn onto Guard Hill, the surface of which, as befits any swanky road with rural pretensions, promptly becomes perfectly horrible. Soon you'll see fine old houses dotted picturesquely here and there. Some are new, most are old, and most are pretty big. As you wind up the slopes of Guard Hill, the properties get progressively more grand. The countryside has a wonderful air of cultivated spaciousness. There are charming guest and employee cottages, elaborate horse barns, huge trees along the narrow dirt road, and imposing mansions (often unseen) at the end of long formal drives.

Just past Succabone Road, I-684 slashes horribly through this idyllic country. Once on the other side you return again into dense woods. At the end of a long downgrade, you'll come to a stop sign at McLean Street. Turn sharply right onto paved McLean Street and head north. There has been a bit of upscale builder activity hereabouts in recent years with mixed results, though many fine and unusual old houses remain. (The busy and largish village of Mt. Kisco, while unseen, is quite close to you at this point.)

McLean Street makes a right-angle turn to the right in about a mile and continues back in the direction of Bedford along a line parallel to Guard Hill Road. The paving ends again after West Patent Road, and McLean Street becomes Broad Brook Road. Note that the worse the surface of the public way, the more imposing the properties that line it. Some of these places are really "to die for," with their columned porticos, formal gardens, and sweeping driveways. Shortly after you cross back over I-684, Broad Brook joins paved Bedford Center Road. Go right at this intersection and continue for a little over a mile to the stone monument marking the junction with Route 22, here called Cantitoe Street.

At this point you have two options: You can return to Bedford (a mile to the south) and continue with your excursion, or you can proceed northward on beautiful Cantitoe Road (Route 22) for a visit to two of Westchester's most appealing attractions.

The first of these is a place for which you should really plan in advance. It is called **Caramoor,** and the main gate to it is located about half a mile east of Cantitoe Street on Girdle Ridge Road. Caramoor is the former Katonah estate of Mr. and Mrs. Walter Tower Rosen. Since 1946, it has been the site of a series of annual summer concerts, begun originally in memory of a son lost in World War II. The **Caramoor Music Festival** has today grown into a world-famous event. The greatest names and finest talents in classical music perform in the Spanish Courtyard and the Venetian Theater (the mansion is Mediterranean in style) every season from late June until mid-August. Concert programming runs the gamut from chamber music to solo recitals, to symphony, to jazz. Says *The New York Times,* "Caramoor is one of the few [outdoor festivals] that makes a persistent effort to present something different from what we have been having indoors all the rest of the year."

The Rosen estate itself is also something to see. Built in the 1930s, it incorporates whole rooms removed from sundry European châteaux and palazzi. The furnishings, all original, are equally sumptuous. And so are the manicured grounds. The admission to the "museum" (the Rosen's house) is $5 for adults and $3 for kids under 12. The 45-minute guided tours start at 11am on Thursday and Saturday, at 1pm on Sunday, and on Wednesday and Friday by appointment only; the last tour on any day begins at 3pm. Concert prices vary depending on who's appearing. A preconcert lecture, held in the Spanish Courtyard, is included in your ticket price and makes a nice transition between a picnic dinner on the lovely lawns and the show itself. For concert information, phone Caramoor at 914/232-5035. Alternately, you can write to Caramoor, P.O. Box R, Katonah, NY 10536, and ask for a current program.

The other site, located on Route 22 about half a mile north of the intersection with Girdle Ridge Road, is the **John Jay Homestead State Historic Site,** P.O. Box AH, Katonah, NY 10536 (tel. 914/232-5651). To refresh your memory, John Jay served as first chief justice of the U.S. Supreme Court, president of the Second Continental Congress, minister to Spain, and two times as governor of New York State. His spacious gambrel-roofed country house was built here in 1797 and occupied by Jay descendants until 1954. Today it's been restored to its appearance in Jay's day and is open to the public free from Memorial Day to Labor Day on Wednesday to Saturday from 10am to 5pm and Sunday from 1 to 5pm. During September and October, hours are cut back to noon to 5pm; in November and December, it's open only on weekends from noon to 5pm; it's closed altogether from January through March. The grounds, however, are open all year.

BEDFORD TO NORTH SALEM

I'm going to recommend two routes to North Salem from the Jay House. The one you take depends on how much you want to drive and how hungry you are.

The first route, via routes 172, 137, 124 and 35, incorporates a detour (part of which must be retraced) through the lush countryside around Pound Ridge as far as the village of South Salem. There are 3 terrific restaurants and about 11 miles of scenic driving from Bedford Village to the farthest point east at South Salem. The second is a direct route, via the equally scenic Route 121, which leads from Bedford directly to North Salem, about 12 miles distant.

Suggested Route 1: Detour to South Salem

Return the approximately 3 miles down Cantitoe Street from the Jay House to Bedford Village. At the center of the village you want to turn east (left) onto Route 172, which is the road that skirts the south side of the Bedford Green. Look for the signs to **Pound Ridge,** about 4 miles distant.

Route 172 is a pleasant road that passes through well-maintained country properties and a smattering of big estates. At the junction with Route 137, turn left. You are now in the middle of Pound Ridge, another picture-postcard village, near to which Native Americans once hunted deer by driving them into a sort of pound against a steep bluff. On the left side of the main street (Route 137), just above its intersection with 172, is one of those places for a great meal.

Inn at Pound Ridge, Route 137 (tel. 914/764-5779), was originally built as a house in 1833. Today's much-enlarged building has been a restaurant for many years, however. Four American presidents—Roosevelt, Truman, Eisenhower, and Kennedy—dined here prior to 1979, when it was known as Emily Shaw's Inn. The new owners took over in 1989, renamed it, remodeled the entire building, and started serving the present new American cuisine. There are two extremely attractive dining rooms. On the main level is a large bright room with beams on the ceiling, French needlepoint chairs, acres of immaculate linen, and the pleasing sounds of recorded chamber music. Downstairs is a slate-floored pub with an atmospheric bar, stone walls, bleached beams and siding, and glass walls overlooking manicured Westchester lawns and gardens. Typical lunch selections include grilled salmon with chianti, pasta with scallops and grilled vegetables, and deviled fish cakes with celery-root remoulade, costing between $7 and $17. At dinner, you might try the roast swordfish with rosemary and fennel, tuna grilled with black pepper and plum glaze, New York–strip steak in red wine, halibut meunière with green and yellow squashes, or any number of similarly creative and delicious alternatives, priced between $14 and $26 à la carte. Open for lunch on Tuesday through Friday from noon until 3pm, for brunch on Sunday, and for dinner daily from 6 until 10pm. Reservations are required on Saturday nights, as are ties and jackets; otherwise, appropriate dress is casual but neat. AE, MC, and V accepted.

The itinerary continues another few hundred yards on Route 137, past the inn, to the first fork in the road, where you will bear right onto Route 124. The road from here to **South Salem** is smooth and sensuously winding. There are attractive houses here and there, both new and old, and lots of deep forest. It is hard to believe that this entire area was denuded of trees by the original settlers and used as crop or pasture land. The mature forest we see today is all second growth. Only the ubiquitous stone walls in the woods, now mostly in picturesque tumbledown condition, attest to the former presence of agriculture.

In about 5 miles you'll come to another fork with a sign directing you to the right toward South Salem. Turn right and proceed to the stop sign at Route 35. The big house set back from the road on your right is the former home of New Deal–era vice president Henry Wallace.

Turn right (east) onto Route 35 and in about 2 miles on your left you'll see the gates to **Le Château,** Route 35 at the junction of Route 123 (tel. 914/533-6631). Perched on a hillside atop a smooth winding driveway is a magnificent stone-and-timber mansion whose handsome wood-paneled rooms command sweeping views of countryside. Built in 1907, the mansion is now a superb restaurant specializing in French continental cuisine. Le Château's combination of gracious service, magnificent surroundings, and fabulous food is pretty hard to beat. Lunch, alas, no longer is served. At dinner, you can expect to pay anywhere from $18 to $28 for a beautifully prepared à la carte main course like rack of lamb in herbs, sautéed shrimp with olives and vegetables, lobster ragôut, or baby pheasant with foie gras and truffles. Dinner is served Tuesday through Friday from 6 to 9pm, until 11pm on Saturday (two seatings, at 6:30 and 9pm), and from 2 to 9pm on Sunday. Jackets are required. All major credit cards accepted.

Another good choice nearby (serving dinner only) is located in the middle of the bucolic hamlet of South Salem. This is the **Horse & Hound** (tel. 914/763-3108), an intimate inn on the corner of Spring and Main Streets (Spring intersects Route 35 immediately east of the point at which you joined it, en route from Pound Ridge). The Horse & Hound occupies an 18th-century building that has alternately done duty as a homestead, a gin mill, a school, a blacksmith shop, and more recently as a sophisticated restaurant. Meals are served in several low-ceilinged, old-fashioned dining rooms. The decor includes an 18th-century paneled fireplace, ladder-back chairs, pink and white table linens, wide-board floors, and heavy beams on the ceiling. Dinner is served daily from 5:30pm until the last guest leaves. You choose from a menu that includes things like fresh tuna steak, duck à l'orange, rack of baby lamb, braised venison, veal roquefort, plus daily specials, priced between $17 and $26 à la carte. Desserts are a specialty of the house, particularly the bread pudding with Wild Turkey bourbon sauce. AE, MC, and V accepted.

If you've had it with rural scenery and fine cuisine, you can leave here by taking Route 35 westbound for about 8 miles to the intersection with I-684 at Katonah. Get on 684 southbound and you'll be back in the White Plains area in about 20 minutes. Alternately, to continue on to North Salem, follow Route 35 westbound for about 3 miles to the intersection with Route 121. Turn right and you'll join the suggested route described below, at a point about 5 miles from the Jay House.

Suggested Route 2: Direct to North Salem

North from the Jay House, Route 22 is called Jay Street. Stay on this pleasant road for a bit over a mile to the intersection of Route 35 and turn right. In a moment you'll see the Cross River Dam, built in 1908 as part of the huge New Croton Water System constructed between 1885 and 1911.

Route 35 follows the scenic shore of the Cross River Reservoir for part of the 3 miles to Cross River itself. The reservoir inundated much of the original village, as other reservoirs hereabouts inundated many another nearby town and hamlet. The woodsy tranquility of the roads today gives no hint of the destruction and upheaval in people's lives (and the attendant bitterness) that dominated this area back when the dams were being built.

Cross River itself is a picturesque crossroads with a general store and, more recently, a discreet small shopping plaza in pseudo-Colonial architectural garb. At the top of the long hill east of the hamlet, turn left at the light onto Route 121.

The next 6½ miles to North Salem is through some of the most beautiful and unspoiled countryside in Westchester County. There are horse farms, lovely old Colonial houses, wooded hills, and a wonderful sense of space. Although the analogy is not exact, this is what much of Long Island's suburban Nassau County looked like as recently as 1950. There is a manicured look to the countryside that, while altogether prepossessing, has nothing whatsoever to do with active agriculture. Which is why, despite all the open spaces, it's not really accurate to call this area "rural."

Just past the intersection of June Road and Hawley Road, you'll glimpse an enormous stone-and-shingle mansion in woods to the left of Route 121. Briefly the summer home of President Ulysses S. Grant, this old mansion was enlarged at the end of the 19th century by McKim, Mead, and White. It contains one of the grandest staircases in Westchester County. A haunted house in my youth, it has been restored in recent years by private owners.

In about 2 more miles, past the point where Route 116 joins Route 121 and just short of **North Salem** itself, you'll pass a local geologic anomaly called (for obvious reasons) **the balancing rock**. Supposedly this is a souvenir from the last glacial period. A modest attraction, perhaps, but then again North Salem isn't noted as a place where much goes on.

It is, however, about as appealing a village as you can possibly imagine. Its lovely old Colonial and 19th-century buildings are surrounded by broad open fields that run into dense forests at the foot of rolling hills. The roads are narrow, and traffic is thin. Ugly new construction is nonexistent. This is land conservancy country—and it looks it. Everybody tries hard to preserve the area's natural and architectural beauty, and they have succeeded to an amazing degree.

On the eastern edge of the village, behind a curious-looking stone arch at the point where Routes 121 and 116 diverge, is **Auberge Maxime**, Route 116 (tel. 914/669-5450). For many years this little stucco cottage was a roadhouse called the Arch. Now it is a superb French country restaurant whose dishes are noted for their classic elegance. There is a lovely terrace with a view of rolling fields for al fresco dining in good weather, plus two intimate dining rooms indoors, decorated with beamed ceilings, striped chairs, and floral-print swagged curtains. Lunch selections like confit de canard, grilled sirloin with cognac and peppercorns, grilled lamb chops, or omelet bonne femme (with mushroom and sausage) are priced between $11 and $19. At dinner, in addition to the à la carte selections—chicken breast with mushrooms, duck à l'orange or roasted with red currents, rack of lamb with garlic and herbs, and grilled salmon in light shallot sauce, priced from $18 to $25—there is a five-course prix-fixe dinner for $49 per person. Lunch hours are Thursday to Tuesday from noon to 3pm; dinner is served on Thursday, Friday, and Sunday to Tuesday from 6 to 9pm. On Saturday there are two evening sittings at 7 and 9pm. Jacket required at dinner. All major credit cards accepted.

NORTH SALEM TO KATONAH

Whether or not you dine at the Auberge, North Salem is definitely worth what my father used to call a "look see." After you've done that, take 121-116 back past the balancing rock to the point at which they diverge on the west side of the village. This time, bear right and follow 116. The next 6 miles traverse more of Westchester's loveliest countryside. Stay on 116 past the intersection of 124, and in less than a mile you'll come to the hamlet of **Salem Center**. On the north side of the highway is a charming 18th-century house that once belonged to the DeLancy family. It is now the home of the local historical society. Note also the elegant small Greek Revival building that houses North Salem's town supervisor and the beautiful dry stone walls that line the road.

West of Salem Center, Route 116 joins the shore of the Titicus Reservoir. The country hereabouts has a distinct Currier-and-Ives look. The combination of the lovely lake, the deep brooding forests, the big Colonial houses, and the wonderful sense of space all conjure a vivid sense of early America, untouched. Actually, this beautiful landscape is entirely a 20th-century creation. When built, those Colonial farmhouses stood amid thousands of acres of open fields, now mostly covered by the Titicus Reservoir. Even the forested hills were in great part devoted to pastureland, as stone walls through today's woodlands clearly show. Not quite every tree was cut down in those days, but if you'd been here in the mid-19th century you would have seen a ratio of woodlands to open fields that is exactly the opposite of today's. Of course, that doesn't mean we can't enjoy this beautiful drive, which all too soon comes to an end at I-684.

From the junction of Routes 116 and 22, a stone's throw from the roaring interstate, you're only about a mile from a terrific Italian restaurant located in the nearby village of Croton Falls. Turn right (north) onto 22, which goes beside and under 684 and soon takes a sharp left into Croton Falls itself.

You can't miss **Mona Trattoria**, Route 22, Croton Falls (tel. 914/277-4580). It is a great big, square, three-story Italianate mansion with red shutters and a cupola, visible from 684. Mona is a relaxed family place specializing in northern Italian cuisine, especially pasta. The same family has run this restaurant for more than a quarter of a century. They serve fettuccine, cannelloni, gnocci, penne, and the like in every conceivable style, plus tempting chicken, veal, beef, and fish dishes prepared with herbs and prosciutto and wine and cheese and everything else that's good. Lunch is served Wednesday through Friday from noon to 2:30pm, with à la carte selections at $11 to $18. Dinner on Wednesday through Saturday is from 6 to 10pm and on Sunday from 3:30 to 9pm; the menu is more extensive in the evening, and à la carte main courses are priced from $15 to $22. Sometimes closed in February. All major credit cards accepted.

You now can either get onto 684 at Croton Falls and return rapidly to the White Plains area (about half an hour's drive south), or, if it's still light out and you'd like to travel farther on the back roads, you can continue to Katonah. If you opt for the latter, follow Route 22 north through Croton Falls to the intersection with Routes 100 and 202. Turn left on 100-202 and head for **Somers,** about 2 miles distant.

In the middle of the little village of Somers is a three-story brick building with the provocative name of **Elephant Hotel.** Now used as the town offices, it was built in 1825 by a Somers native named Hachaliah Bailey, who also erected the statue out front of an elephant perched atop a stone pedestal. The Elephant Hotel and "Old Bet," as the statue is called, hark back to Somers' days as the **birthplace of the American circus.**

In 1815, the entrepreneurial Bailey bought an elephant from a ship captain who'd hauled her over from England. Bailey then began to tour the countryside with Old Bet, as he named her, plus a couple of monkeys and a bear. The show was a success, and Bailey was soon able to lease Old Bet at a profit to a neighbor from Putnam County called "Uncle Nate" Howes. It is this latter gentleman who is credited with introducing the portable canvas "round top" to traveling clown and circus shows. Daniel Drew, a local boy who became one of the 19th century's great financial manipulators, got his start hereabouts as a circus clown.

In those days, no one knew much about animal handling. And Old Bet, despite her name, was neither old nor docile. Indeed, she instilled what amounted to sheer panic in the hearts of many a local villager. Finally a band of Connecticut fanatics crept across the border one night and shot her dead, justifying the deed by claims that she was the Behemoth of Scripture.

Bailey's nephew George later joined forces with Uncle Nate's younger brother, Seth, and a Connecticut storekeeper named Phineas T. Barnum. The eventual result was a famous tour of England by P. T. Barnum's American Museum and Menagerie, and eventually the establishment of the Barnum and Bailey Circus.

Change has definitely invaded this section of Westchester. To be specific, IBM has invaded little Somers. To be sure, much of the resulting development has been as aesthetic as shopping plazas, corporate campuses, and town-house developments can be. But the once empty woods are now about one-third full of houses.

About 5 miles south of Somers on Route 100 is the last stop on tour of the rural north. It is the **Muscoot Farm** located just outside Katonah. This historic 777-acre working farm is owned by the county of Westchester and is a center of year-round activities and programs on everything from barn raising to square dancing, gardening to musical and craft presentations. The barns are full of animals, and the fields are full of crops. Right by the roadside is a great big old farmhouse that was mansionized in 1924 by the Hopkins family, who owned and cherished this place for four generations until the county bought it in 1968.

Muscoot is a wonderful place to stroll around, explore the gardens or the beautiful woodlands, check out the farmyard, maybe even try your hand at milking a cow. The majority of Westchester used to look and smell and sound just like this. Farming was a day to day part of everybody's life. Now we've got I-684 instead. Muscoot is open daily from 10am to 4pm. It's free, but donations are requested. For further information, call 914/232-7118.

The fastest route back to southern Westchester is again via I-684. From Muscoot, go north on Route 100 for a mile to the intersection of Route 35. Turn right (east) onto 35, which junctions with 684 in less than 2 miles.

THE HUDSON RIVER VALLEY

1. WHAT TO SEE & DO
2. THE WEST BANK OF THE HUDSON
3. THE EAST BANK OF THE HUDSON

Three-quarters of the Hudson River Valley—148 miles worth—lies south of Albany. It's an area rife with legend, rich with history, and quite beautiful despite over three centuries of civilization (read pollution, visual and otherwise). Actually, water quality in the Hudson has been steadily improving for well over a decade. These days people actually swim in many parts of it. I have myself on numerous occasions.

Not only swimmers but also fishermen are gradually returning to this most beautiful of American rivers. So what if a few species are too permeated with mercury or PCBs or whatever continues to spew from the pipes of unreconstructed upriver "employers"? The important thing is that fewer fish glow (or whatever polluted fish do) now than in many ages past. A really "clean" river seems eminently possible . . . someday. And whereas one would certainly think twice before taking a dip off, say, West 79th Street in Manhattan, moms and tots frolic in the water as close as Croton-on-Hudson, not 30 miles from Midtown. From Poughkeepsie north to the city of Hudson, save for the immediate environs of a few cement plants, people swim and waterski all the time.

But enough of this aquatic pep talk. The visitor will want to know what else lies in these leafy hills and why one should bother driving up here to have a look.

1. What to See & Do

The Hudson Valley's biggest attraction is probably the scenery. It's a perfectly beautiful place in which to drive around. The visual range—from the sheer and mighty drops of the Palisades to the dramatic chasms of the Hudson Highlands and the startling Catskill vistas north of Hyde Park—is as wide as it is satisfying.

If you're big on historic houses and/or architecturally magnificent old mansions, then that's another reason to explore the Hudson River Valley. It has tons of them, from pre-Revolutionary manors to Edwardian palaces. Happily a great number of these are open to the public. The valley has been a favored locale for country estates for centuries. During the last one, romantic-minded plutocrats graced more than one riverview mountaintop with pinnacled and crenellated castles. Many of these old mansions still stand and are highly scenic, to say the least. They have even provoked frequent characterization of the Hudson as "America's Rhine." This particular notion may be ambitious, but the castles really do look grand.

Antiquing is another pastime (compulsion? vice?) that draws considerable numbers of people up the Hudson. Indeed, the economy of many a village in these parts would seem to rest entirely on its collection of antiques shops. Opportunities for browsing are considerable. I don't know about bargains, but there sure is a lot of old stuff for sale between New York and Albany.

Complementing everything mentioned above is the valley's abundance of sophisticated inns and restaurants. No excursion to a historic mansion, scenic park, or antique district would be complete without a good meal at someplace quaint. This fact of touristic life has not been lost upon the locals, and they have acted accordingly.

Many roads lead up and down the Hudson, some very fast and some very ugly. As much as possible I've suggested routes along scenic roads. Not every city or attraction has been included. For a great deal of additional information contact Hudson River Tourism (tel. toll free 800/232-4782). But I think you'll find the highlights are here, plus an ample selection of places to stay and eat.

2. The West Bank of the Hudson

A great deal of this area can be seen on a day trip. Which is just as well, since there aren't very many interesting hotels in the area. We're dealing here with a bit less than 50 miles of river valley, stretching from New York City in the south to the Hudson Highlands in the north. The Highlands, if you've never been there, are a treat. They're notable for romantically gloomy mountains with very high, cliffhanging, serpentine roads. These roads are cut out of the sheer faces of rock. One bears the wonderful name of **Storm King Highway,** and from its every curve you're confronted alternately with vistas of mountaintops and the spectacle of the Hudson curling along the bottom of a stone chasm. The scenery is almost Swiss, albeit in a gentler Hudson Valley idiom. And, of course, the Highlands are also the site of the famous U.S. Military Academy at West Point, most excellent of day-trip destinations.

NYACK

Flanked by Tarrytown on the east and Nyack on the west, the Tappan Zee is a widening of the Hudson measuring about 2½ by 12 or so miles. The word *Tappan* is an Indian term for "cold spring." *Zee* is Dutch for "sea." *Nyack* possibly means "antiques shoppe" in some obscure Lenni-Lenape tongue.

Nyack (pop. 6,400) can be a day trip all by itself. From New York, a good scenic route would be via the Henry Hudson Parkway to the George Washington Bridge (upper level, if possible). As soon as you cross the bridge into New Jersey, take the first exit onto the **Palisades Interstate Parkway.** The scenic overlooks shortly after you join this parkway are definitely worth a stop. The panorama of Manhattan, the George Washington Bridge, the Hudson, and, on a clear day, even Long Island Sound, is memorable. Continue on the Palisades Parkway to exit 9. Then take the New York State Thruway eastbound to exit 11, "Nyack." Go left at the foot of the exit and you'll be on Main Street.

To get to Nyack from Tarrytown (and if you like antiques shops, you're going to want to go), find the intersection of U.S. 9 and the New York State Thruway. Follow the signs to the Tappan Zee Bridge, which is in sight of the intersection. Crossing the Tappan Zee is visually quite spectacular. Behind you are the scenic

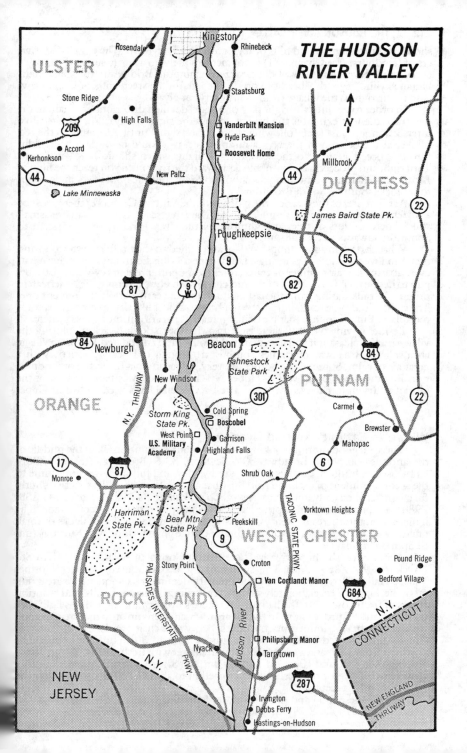

shores and mansion-crested hills of Irvington and Tarrytown. The castellated towers of Lyndhurst (see Chapter XI) loom picturesquely on a lawny slope. If the day's clear, you'll have a fine view of the George Washington Bridge and the spiky Manhattan skyline beyond. Ahead of you on the left are the steep cliffs of Grandview. And to the right is the village (really a little city) of Nyack.

In order to get into the right part of Nyack, detailed directions are again in order. Take the first exit after the bridge, follow the signs to Nyack (a spaghettilike intersection, but just keep following those Nyack signs) until you come to the red blinker at the bottom of the Nyack ramp. You now should be on South Franklin Street. Proceed straight to the second traffic light, which should be Main Street. Turn right and proceed a couple of blocks toward the river until you reach the light at Broadway. There are some antiques shops on Main, but the bulk of them lie about four blocks south on South Broadway.

At the center of the district (the block with the Vintage Car Store) there must be a dozen antiques shops on a single block. The streetscape is Victorian and small scale. There are lots of trees and glimpses of the river. Parking on or adjacent to South Broadway isn't too difficult.

What sort of antiques shops? Well, they're filled to their rafters with wood and metal and rust and lots of paintings. Don't expect Louis Louis or George the Whatever; do expect a fair number of crafts stores (some entrepreneurs evidently have begun to hedge their bets). Most of the merchandise in Nyack seems to be American in origin, the bulk dating from the last century and the early part of the present one. The sight of old ladies exclaiming, "Why, I *gave* one just like that to Mabel!" is commonplace. But, of course, that particular remark is part of antiquing everywhere.

Besides buying old stuff there isn't an awful lot to do in Nyack. Exploring the village itself is pleasant if you like quaint old houses and an updated Victorian village atmosphere. Broadway continues southward through old, leafy districts, with a great air of calm. Some of the houses are very gingerbready. Taken the other direction Broadway will bring you to Upper Nyack, a modest westbank version of the glories of Irvington across the river. The late Helen Hayes used to live in Upper Nyack.

Where to Eat in & Around Nyack

There's a good oldtime-looking bar–cum–burger joint smack in the middle of the antiques on South Broadway. **Old Fashion,** 83 S. Broadway (tel. 914/358-8114), serves burgers, quiches, salads, sandwiches, and full meals at dinnertime to the accompaniment of rock and roll. Busy bar against the side wall; attractive youthful clientele; open daily until 4am. Also good is **Skylark,** 84 Main St. (tel. 914/358-7988), a typical, moderately priced small-town family restaurant/coffeeshop. The lights are bright; there are plenty of seats at the counter, as well as at flocks of small tables; open for breakfast, lunch, and dinner until 8pm on Monday to Saturday (until 5pm on Sunday).

A more-stylish alternative is **The Hudson House of Nyack,** 134 Main St., Nyack (tel. 914/353-1355). This swell-looking place is housed in Nyack's former Village Hall, now renovated and fitted out with demure red banquettes, a great mural of the Tappan Zee, elaborately stamped tin ceilings, mirrored walls, and beautiful sprays of fresh flowers. In the hall upstairs there's live jazz and sometimes light rock on Friday and Saturday night. In the bar area, which opens up onto the street in good weather, are brass-trimmed marble tables, bentwood chairs, and a cappuccino machine. Lunch, served Tuesday through Sunday from 11:30am until 3pm, might be anything from a $5 sandwich to a $9 salmon platter with fresh greens. Dinner, available between 5:30 and 10pm on Tuesday through Saturday (until 9pm on Sunday), costs between $9 for the fresh spinach tortellini to about $16 for a steak au poivre. AE, MC, and V accepted.

For Japanese food and good sushi, try **Ichi Riki,** just a few doors down at 110 Main St. (tel. 914/358-7977). There are shoji screens, large sake barrels, and three traditional Japanese dining rooms. Lunch is served Tuesday through Friday from noon until 2:30pm; luncheon specials are priced from $6 to $9. Dinner—available from 5:30 to 10pm on Tuesday to Thursday, until 11pm on Friday and Saturday, and to 9:30pm on Sunday—might be shabu shabu, yosena cooked at your table, or any number of other dishes priced between $15 and $25. All major credit cards accepted.

Just 5 miles south of Nyack is the charming village of Piermont on the banks of the Hudson. Here you'll find what's probably the most prestigious restaurant in the area, **Xaviar's of Piermont,** 506 Piermont Ave. (tel. 914/359-7007). Owner Peter Kelly also operates the original Xaviar across the river in Garrison (recommended under "The East Bank of the Hudson" later in this chapter. The cuisine at both restaurants is French, and the clientele sophisticated. Dining at the Piermont Xaviar is rather like having dinner in an elegant mansion. Seating is limited to 38 people; the decor includes a crystal chandelier, gleaming silver flatware, and gold-rimmed Haviland china; and there's a tuxedo-clad staff. The $42 prix-fixe dinner menu, which changes daily, is available Wednesday through Sunday from 6 to 9pm; an à la carte lunch with main courses from $10 to $16 is served Wednesday to Friday from noon to 2:30pm; there's also a $23 Sunday brunch available from noon to 2:30pm. Reservations a must. No credit cards accepted.

Xaviar's companion restaurant in Piermont is **Freelance Café and Wine Bar,** also located at 506 Piermont Ave. (tel. 914/365-3250). This smart-looking bistro, with its gray-marble tables, track lighting, and framed architectural prints, provides an opportunity to sample Xaviar's fine cuisine in a casual and less expensive setting. As the name suggests, the wine selection, from both Europe and California, is extensive and available by the glass. The café offers both large and small plate servings and prices that run from $4 for onion soup gratinée to $17 for a steak pommes frites with herb butter. Open Tuesday through Sunday, for lunch from noon to 3pm and for dinner from 5:30 to 10pm. No reservations taken. No credit cards accepted.

WEST POINT

To reach the United States Military Academy at West Point from Nyack or Piermont, you have two choices: You can head directly north on Route 9W, or you can find North Broadway and take the scenic route past the riverside mansions of Upper Nyack. If you choose the latter route you can join Route 9W again just west of Nyack Beach State Park.

The drive up 9W to **Haverstraw,** with the exception of the 1,000-acre Hook Mountain State Park, is frankly unattractive. The only thing flourishing along much of it is uncontrolled commercial strip development. Dyed-in-the-wool architectural historians might want to detour off 9W at the traffic light past the Haverstraw train station, head toward the river, and take a quick look at the intact but tattered riverside village of Haverstraw. This place illustrates an uncomfortable truth—namely, that poverty is often the best tool for historic preservation. Haverstraw still has a surprising number of 18th- and 19th-century buildings in virtually original condition. Perhaps in the decade to come it will undergo a revival similar to that of Nyack. Now head back to unsightly 9W and continue north through West Haverstraw to Stony Point.

STONY POINT

Just north of the village of Stony Point, immediately adjacent to Route 9W, is the **Stony Point Battlefield State Historic Site,** P.O. Box 182, Stony Point, NY 10980 (tel. 914/786-2521). It was on this battlefield that the American Light Infantry, led by Gen. "Mad" Anthony Wayne, defeated a British garrison during a daring midnight assault on July 16, 1779. Asked by Washington whether he felt himself able to take the garrison, Wayne is said to have replied, "I'll storm Hell, sir, if you'll make the plans." Washington's dry response was, "Better try Stony Point first, General." Although seriously wounded during the battle, General Wayne was carried on the shoulders of his men over the rampart to victory.

The rocky bluffs of Stony Point project well into the Hudson River beneath the water line. For navigational safety the federal government erected a lighthouse here in 1826 at 179 feet above sea level (the Hudson River is sea level). It is part of the park today and offers spectacular views of Haverstraw Bay and the lower Hudson valley. The interpretive center is open from late April to the end of October on Wednesday through Sunday from 10am to 5pm. The park itself is open all year.

HUDSON HIGHLANDS & WEST POINT

This is one of the most scenically beautiful stretches of riverfront anywhere in America, and it has been acclaimed as such by travelers for centuries. The Highlands are so called on account of the extremely steep and picturesque mountains that at this point hem the Hudson into a very deep and narrow watercourse. It's not that the mountains are so high, but rather that their slopes are so sheer. Most of the crests of these towering hills are only about 800 or 900 feet above sea level. But their wild and rocky look, plus their dramatic verticality, makes for impressive views and a general air of mystery.

The Highlands stretch from **Dunderberg Mountain** opposite Peekskill on the south to **Storm King Mountain** at the entrance to Newburgh Bay on the north. The distance from one end to the other is about 10 miles. Right in the middle the river makes a hairpin turn around **West Point.** From the military academy atop the cliffs at West Point is an unobstructed view both upstream and downstream. Every ship that passes on the Hudson must do so under the guns of West Point, which rendered the fortifications here so important during the Revolution.

A number of battles were fought in the Highlands during 1776 and 1777 as part of a British effort to dominate the Hudson Valley. The Americans prevented the capture of West Point itself, foiling Benedict Arnold's treason before he was able simply to hand the fort over to the enemy. But elsewhere in the Highlands the British generally managed to get the upper hand. They successfully took forts Clinton and Montgomery in the vicinity of today's Bear Mountain Bridge. By doing so they were able to dismantle a famous "chevaux-de-frise," or iron chain, across the Hudson between Bear Mountain and Anthony's Nose. The Americans had wanted for some time to interdict military transport on the river by means of a chain. The original hope was to install it downriver at Fort Washington in northern Manhattan. However, the Continental Army was forced to abandon Manhattan before anything could be done. The chain at Bear Mountain, installed in 1776, cost the patriots a quarter of a million dollars. The British dismantled it in 1777, took it back to Europe, and used it for many years to protect their harbor at Gibraltar.

Through much of 1777 the British General Burgoyne was surrounded by American forces near the headwaters of the Hudson at Saratoga. In one of the war's major tactical blunders, the British high command never relieved him. Burgoyne was finally forced to surrender, shortly after which the British withdrew from the Highlands and the focus of the war moved south.

The barrenness of Bear Mountain's summit is one of many explanations put forth to explain its name. From what I've read, no one seems seriously to suggest that there were ever many bear in these parts. The Dutch called it by various different names. Why it's come down to us as Bear Mountain is a mystery.

At the foot of the mountain, along the riverfront to the immediate south of the traffic circle on the west side of the Bear Mountain Bridge, is a complex of recreational facilities centered around the old **Bear Mountain Inn** (tel. 914/786-2731). Besides assorted playing fields, there is a roller rink, an ice-skating rink, a pool, a little zoo, the remains of Fort Clinton (conjuring images of a not-very-bright day in the American Revolution), and a shady walk around the verges of **Hessian Lake.** In the last century, this little body of water was owned by the Knickerbocker Ice Company. Huge chutes delivered cut ice down the cliffsides to warehouses on the water's edge. For a century before that it was called Bloody Pond. After the fall of Fort Clinton, the bodies of so many of the dead were thrown into it that the water turned red. The Bear Mountain Inn rents rooms (almost all of which are in modern motel-style satellite buildings) and serves meals. The cafeteria is cheap; the main restaurant is moderately priced and quite grand-looking in an Adirondack-loggy sort of way. Bear Mountain State Park is a great favorite with busloads of city dwellers.

The 1,305-foot summit of **Bear Mountain** can be reached by following U.S. Route 6 westbound about 2½ miles to the Seven Lakes Parkway; then left on Seven Lakes for maybe a mile to Perkins Memorial Drive. The distant views from the summit of Bear Mountain are superb. Considerable wilderness seems to extend in almost every direction. The bulk of it, to the southwest, lies in the Harriman State Forest, an area of some tens of thousands of acres given to the people of New York State by the late Governor Averell Harriman. Originally this land was all part of **Arden,** the Harriman family estate. Arden House, located on a mountaintop above the village of Harriman on N.Y. 17, is now a conference center owned by Columbia University.

Some 5½ miles north of the Bridge Circle (on N.Y. 218 in Highland Falls) is the **United States Military Academy,** better known by the name of the rocky eminence atop which it sits, **West Point.** Although the academy was not formally authorized by Congress until 1802, cadets were attached to a permanent artillery corps here as early as 1794. During the Revolution, West Point was but one, albeit the most strategic, of numerous fortifications in the Highlands. In 1779, well after Burgoyne's surrender at Saratoga and the subsequent waning of the British threat to the Hudson, another chain was stretched across the river, from here to Constitution Island. It was never put to a test. In 1780, the British almost succeeded in playing on the grievances of Benedict Arnold, then commander of West Point. Had British Maj. John André not been captured in Tarrytown with incriminating papers, Arnold might have succeeded in turning over the fort to the British without a fight. Had that happened, yet another chain might have wound up in Gibraltar.

Above West Point is the site of **Fort Putnam,** partly restored around 1910 and now a part of the grounds of the military academy. In 1832, English actress Fanny Kemble took a steamboat up the Hudson. Like today's Day Liners, Miss Kemble's boat stopped at West Point. She and her father climbed to Fort Putnam, which even then was famous for its view. "I was filled with awe," she says in her *Journal of a Residence in America.* "The beauty and wild sublimity of what I beheld seemed almost to crush my faculties. . . . I felt as though I had been carried into the immediate presence of God."

Compared to the secrecy that shrouds military installations in other countries, West Point is astonishingly open. Thayer Road (N.Y. 218) cuts right across the middle of the campus. There are cadets at the various gates waving traffic into and out of the grounds. Once inside, you're free to wander at will. In fact, the best way to see West Point is on a self-guided tour.

Your first stop should be the **visitors center,** located just south of the **Thayer Gate** on N.Y. 218 in Highland Falls. It's well marked; you won't miss it. This sophisticated facility features exhibits, a gift shop, a helpful information desk, even movies on cadet life and the history of the academy. Here also is where you can pick up a visitors guide, which serves as an itinerary for self-conducted tours of the campus. The guide includes a detailed map of the grounds, plus brief details on the academy buildings, historic sites, scenic overlooks, and so on. Also available at the visitors center is the arts-and-entertainment calendar, a listing of theater groups, band concerts, and specialty shows scheduled throughout the year. You can request these publications in advance, and/or inquire as to what events, games, and the like are scheduled during the time of your visit, by writing to the West Point Visitors Center, Building 2107, United States Military Academy, West Point, NY 10996. Alternatively, you can call 914/938-2638.

Presidents Grant and Eisenhower, generals Patton and MacArthur, and astronauts Aldrin and Borman are but a few of West Point's many celebrated graduates— Edgar Allan Poe was a dropout. Currently there are about 4,400 cadets enrolled in a four-year program combining college curricula with intensive military training. The culmination is a Bachelor of Science degree and a stint (usually a career) in the army. Applicants must be between 17 and 22, morally and physically fit, and recommended by a member of Congress.

Also on the grounds of West Point is the **Hotel Thayer,** named after Major Sylvanus Thayer, superintendent of the academy from 1817 to 1833. The Thayer is a good place to eat and to stay. It's described in full below.

After West Point you might want to savor the scenery along the **Storm King Highway.** This cliffhanger of a road (also designated as N.Y. 218) is located immediately north of the academy, and as it's the only route along the river, you can't very well miss it. The scenery is most dramatic, the corners are veritable hairpins, and the pavement is exceedingly narrow. It's a fun couple of miles, at the northern terminus of which is the village of Cornwall-on-Hudson and the end of the Highlands.

Where to Stay & Eat

Among New York State's best-kept secrets are the **rustic cabins and fully equipped cottages** located on state parkland and available for rent on a weekly basis, either from the New York State Department of Environmental Conservation or from the Office of Parks, Recreation and Historic Preservation. There are some charming ones in the vicinity of Bear Mountain State Park, and the cost—from $94 to $250 a week—is certainly reasonable. You must reserve these accommodations at least 90 days in advance. For a list of what's available, call 914/786-2701.

Many people don't realize that the **Hotel Thayer,** just inside the Thayer Gate on the grounds of the U.S. Military Academy, West Point, NY 10996 (tel. 914/446-4731), is open to the public as well as to the military. It's an imposing (almost foreboding) brick edifice dating from 1926, with 210 rooms, a crenellated roofline, and an excellent restaurant. The spacious double-height lobby has marble floors, iron chandeliers, huge ceiling beams (actually made of plaster painted to look like wood), potted palms, leather sofas, and over the fireplace a big portrait of Col. Sylvanus Thayer, the "Father of the Military Academy." Everything is extremely well kept, the location is grand and exciting, and the atmosphere couldn't be friendlier. The rooms are smallish and not elaborate. They have colored tile baths, antique reproduction furniture, TVs, and occasionally a good view. The prices are very reasonable: $64 to $99 for a double, depending on size. Both tennis and swimming at military-academy facilities can be arranged for guests.

The dining room serves breakfast, lunch, and dinner, the latter two meals served from 11:30am until 4pm and 5:30 until 9pm, respectively. It's quite a grand room, with gilded reliefs of parrots and rabbits on its stucco columns, thick rugs, chandeliers, an adjacent terrace room overlooking the Hudson, and beyond that an open-air patio for al fresco dining. Typical full dinners cost under $20. A Sunday champagne brunch, served from 10am until 2:30pm, is priced at about $16. Lunch can be done for under $10 per person. Even if you don't stay at the hotel, it's worth stopping by for a meal. All major credit cards accepted.

NEWBURGH

The culmination of what is sometimes called the "Revolutionary Trail" through this part of the Hudson Valley is at **Washington's Headquarters State Historic Site,** 84 Liberty St., P.O. Box 1783, Newburgh, NY 12551 (tel. 914/562-1195). Having now had a firsthand look at the topography between Stony Point and Newburgh, you can understand how crucial control of the Hudson was in an era that was wholly dependent on water transport. Had the British succeeded in taking West Point, they would have indeed controlled the river, thereby splitting the colonies in half, isolating New England, and establishing uninterrupted supply lines from Canada.

Washington spent 16½ months at **Newburgh** (pop. 23,400) following the British surrender in Yorktown in 1781. Although the war seemed over, the point was to ensure that negotiations in Paris did not break down and to maintain pressure on the 12,000 British troops that were still occupying New York City. Washington's 10,000 troops were encamped several miles southeast at what is now the **New Windsor Cantonment State Historic Site,** Box 207, Vails Gate, NY 12584 (tel. 914/561-1765). His high-ranking officers occupied the now **Knox's Headquar-**

ters State Historic Site on Route 94 in Vails Gate (tel. 914/561-5498). Washington's Headquarters, the New Windsor Cantonment, and Knox's Headquarters are all open to the public from April through October on Wednesday through Saturday from 10am to 5pm and Sunday from 1 to 5pm.

LOCAL WINERIES

There are a dozen wineries in the Newburgh/New Paltz area that specialize in wine made from New York State grapes. Their facilities are often quite interesting and/or aesthetic, and all gladly welcome visitors. You can obtain a free self-tour guide to these establishments, called the *Hudson Valley Winery Tours,* by contacting the **New York Wine and Grape Foundation,** 350 Elm St., Penn Yan, NY 14527 (tel. 315/536-7442).

Perhaps the major highlight of the tour is located southeast of Newburgh, just off Route 208. Called the **Brotherhood Winery,** 35 North St., Washingtonville, NY 10992 (tel. 914/496-9101), it is the site of the largest and oldest underground wine cellars in the United States. It is also a festive place with all manner of seasonal weekend activities, including live entertainment and theme events. Call for schedules and information. Open year-round (except Christmas and New Year's Day); there are daily tours between May and October from 11am to 6pm, weekend tours only the rest of the year, from noon to 5pm. Everyone over 21 pays $4; everyone else is free.

Just south of New Paltz on Route 7 is the **Rivendell Winery** at 714 Albany Post Rd., New Paltz, NY 12561 (tel. 914/255-0892). Rivendell, incidentally, is the house wine at the historic Mohawk Mountain House—a feather in its cap since that august establishment (recommended below) was dry until fairly recently. Rivendell, whose wines have won more awards than any other American vineyard outside California, is open daily for free tours and tastings from 10am to 6pm.

NEW PALTZ

Fifteen miles north of Newburgh and about 8 miles northwest of the Mid-Hudson Bridge, via U.S. 9W and N.Y. 299, is the village of **New Paltz** (pop. 4,900), notable for a branch of the State University of New York, plus **Huguenot Street,** the oldest street in America with its original houses. The latter is quite a remarkable local attraction, encompassing nine restored 17th- and 18th-century buildings distributed among similar compatible structures along an ancient and aesthetic little street adjacent to the heart of New Paltz.

The Huguenots were French Protestants, hounded across Europe by intolerant princes until they immigrated to America. The village of New Paltz is named after "die Pfalz," a temporary refuge in the Rhine-Palatinate that was their last European address. In 1677, 12 Huguenot family heads, known locally as the "Duzine," struck a deal with the local Esopus tribe for about 40,000 acres of land. By 1692, they were sufficiently established to start building stone houses. Incredibly, some of these houses remain today in original condition, right down to the original furnishings.

To drive through New Paltz on N.Y. 299 you'd never dream that Huguenot Street even existed. Most of the village is a fairly typical agglomeration of renovated Victorian-era buildings mixed with modern supermarkets and gas stations. It's not ugly, but neither is it particularly noteworthy. Craft stores, beer bars, and hamburger stands cater to the college population. It's just an average small town with a state college adjacent.

But turn north off N.Y. 299 (Main Street) onto N.Y. 32; find North Front Street; and in a moment you'll enter another world of huge trees, ancient stone buildings, and gentle lawns with glimpses of the Wallkill River. Huguenot Street is an enchanted island unto itself, quite oblivious to the rest of New Paltz.

The Huguenot Historical Society was founded in 1894 to preserve an architectural heritage that was already beginning to disappear. Since then the society has been slowly acquiring properties, improving the ones it owns, and opening them to

Just north of Boscobel is the pretty village of **Cold Spring,** notable for its 19th-century atmosphere, interesting antiques shops, and good inns and restaurants. I'll discuss this further below.

Where to Stay & Eat in Hudson Highlands

This is the land of country inns. At most of the following recommendations you can enjoy a meal, stay overnight, or both. Most are quite small, however, so travelers on summer weekends will need advance reservations.

Hudson House, 2 Main St. (all the way at the foot of the street, on the other side of the railway tracks), Cold Spring, NY 10516 (tel. 914/265-9355), is the second-oldest inn in New York State, although it has been so totally renovated that the interior architectural fabric is no longer antique. It's a two-story frame building with a mansard roof and a tranquil location right at the river's edge. The main floor is a restaurant, divided into several simple, airy rooms, with low ceilings and wonderful river views. There are wide-plank floors, print wallpaper, framed views of the Hudson River, blue-painted chairs, and a little bar across the lobby—the modern "country inn" look par excellence. On a fine day, with the windows open and cooling breezes wafting off the Hudson, you'd be hard-pressed to imagine a nicer spot. Lunch, served daily from 11:30am to 3pm, might be a hamburger, chicken breast, or a surprise omelet. A la carte prices run from about $5 to $10. At dinner, available daily from 5:30 until around 9:30pm, typical main courses include blackened Cajun steak, shellfish assembly, duck and coriander salad, and nesting chicken, costing mostly $15 and $20.

Hudson House has but 15 guest rooms, priced from $80 to $115 for a double. They're small, decorated with wallpaper, bunches of dried flowers, "primitive" wood furniture, and pretty iron beds; all have private baths. Some have terrific river views. But essentially these are modern rooms housed in a building that, from the inside anyway, also looks brand-new. All major credit cards accepted.

A few miles east of Cold Spring on Old Albany Post Road, in a little valley traversed by U.S. 9, is the ultimate hideaway, **Bird & Bottle Inn,** U.S. 9, Garrison, NY 10524 (tel. 914/424-3000). First opened in 1761, Bird & Bottle is an ancient-looking yellow house with a steep shingled roof, brick walls, tall trees, a double porch with square columns, and an air of great seclusion and tranquility. Fortunately, it's a bit off U.S. 9, so the roads around it are all of dirt, and the only sound is the music of a little brook and the whispering of wind in the stately trees. Inside are low ceilings, wide-plank floors, big old fireplaces, and the low gleam of well-maintained early Americana. The first floor is a veritable warren of small, picturesque rooms. You step down into the Drinking Room, which is tiny and dark, with clusters of little tables and a collection of guns mounted over the mantel. The ceilings are beamed; the walls are decorated with framed pictures of ducks.

The French/continental cuisine here is famous. The five-course candlelight dinner includes a selection of dishes like baby rack of lamb, roast pheasant, filet of beef, steak au poivre, duck, chicken, and fresh fish specialties. Dinner is served Wednesday to Friday from 6 to 9pm, Saturday from 6 to 9pm, and Sunday from 4 to 7:30pm. Sunday brunch costs about $17 and is available from noon to 2:30pm.

There are only a few guest rooms at Bird & Bottle, but they're wonderfully atmospheric. Each has its own working fireplace, a canopied bed, hooked rugs, a clock radio, a private bath, old-fashioned framed prints and paintings on the walls, and an abundance of ancient nooks and crannies. They look like guest rooms in the "simple" country house of a rich and sophisticated New Yorker. Overnight rates range from $195 to $215 for two, including dinner and breakfast, the latter price applying to a suite or cottage. To get to the inn, take N.Y. 301 (the extension of Main Street in Cold Spring) east over the hill through Nelsonville to U.S. 9, then turn right (south) for just a few miles.

Back on N.Y. 9D, immediately south of the village of Cold Spring, is the **Plumbush** (tel. 914/265-3904). You'll recognize the place by the long stone wall surmounted by a white picket fence. Beyond the gates is a rambling clapboard Victorian house, painted brown, graced with a wisteria-clad porch, and surrounded by old shade trees. Inside is a warren of rather opulently decorated small dining rooms called variously the Rose Room, the Oak Room, the Lemon Room, and so forth. They have potted palms, heavy swagged curtains, old wood paneling, and wallpaper for which I personally would kill. Lunch might be smoked sausage with sauerkraut, shrimp in beer batter, veal à la Suisse, or Maryland crabcakes, priced mostly from $9 to $14. There's a prix-fixe dinner for about $32, plus an à la carte dinner menu with selections like roast quail, veal chop, tournedos of beef, roast duckling, and steak au poivre, most around $23 to $25. Lunch hours are Wednesday to Sunday from noon to 2:30pm; dinner is served from 5:30 until 9pm or so. Upstairs are three very appealing guest rooms, decorated either with antique Victorian pieces or new wicker furniture, floral wallpaper, and new baths. They cost either $95 or $125 nightly, double occupancy. All major credit cards accepted.

Back in the village of Cold Spring is a terrific bed-and-breakfast with a twist. It's called the **Olde Post Inn,** 43 Main St. (just before the railroad tracks), Cold Spring, NY 10516 (tel. 914/265-2510), and the twist is that it's a combination country inn and jazz tavern. The building is a diminutive 19th-century house, painted yellow and white, with a porch right on the sidewalk. The airy main floor has a little deck, an adjoining breakfast room, and a few comfortable chairs and sofas. Upstairs are five rooms sharing two hall baths. Accommodations are small and immaculately clean, decorated with hooked rugs, antique bureaus, and framed prints. On Friday and Saturday the overnight double-occupancy room rate is about $85; the rest of the week it's $65. The basement tap room has attracted the likes of Junior Mance, Ray Bryant, and Bucky Pizzarelli up from the city to play here ($5 cover). No meals are served, just drinks in the evening. This is a very appealing place. No credit cards accepted.

A good spot in Cold Spring for reasonable lunches and dinners in atmospheric surroundings is the **Depot,** located practically across the street from the Olde Post Inn in Cold Spring's former railway station (tel. 914/265-2305). The tall-ceilinged passenger waiting room has been transformed into an atmospheric bar/restaurant. The menu (full of railroading puns) is the same for lunch and dinner and offers a full range of omelets, burgers, sandwiches, and things-in-the-basket, for about $4 to $8, plus barbecued chicken, filet of flounder, steak, and a seafood combination platter, for around $8 to $12. Open daily from noon to 11pm.

Last but by no means least is **Xaviar,** located in the middle of the golf course in Garrison, just south of the intersection of N.Y. 9D and 403 (tel. 914/424-4228). The Osborn mansion, Castle Rock, is on a mountaintop almost directly overhead, and indeed the elegant little building that houses Xaviar was built originally by the Osborn family as a pavilion for large parties. It's a huge room with tall windows giving onto views of rolling golf links. There is an outdoor terrace under a striped awning, and abundant vases are filled with fresh flowers. Only dinner and Sunday brunch are served. At dinner the à la carte selections include Dublin bay prawns, fresh quail, and Norwegian salmon, costing between $22 and $26. Open for Sunday brunch from noon to 2:30pm for $22.50 and for dinner on Wednesday to Sunday from 6 until 9pm. This is a particular local favorite.

The best advice at this point, for those traveling north, is to return to the Taconic State Parkway. Route 9D north of Cold Spring traverses troubled urban areas. Your next stop is Poughkeepsie.

POUGHKEEPSIE—"QUEEN CITY" OF THE HUDSON

This is the seat of Dutchess County, located on the Hudson about 10 miles from the Taconic Parkway via either Route 44 or 55. The Dutch settled the area in the late 17th century. In 1788, a crucial state convention, attended by Alexander Hamilton and John Jay, was held in Poughkeepsie. The result was a historic vote to accept the nation's new federal Constitution. The railroad came through in 1849, bringing with it a great prosperity that lasted until World War II. However, Poughkeepsie's salad days of manufacturing wealth have been over for a long time. "Urban renewal" has done a considerable amount of damage. The postwar growth of the suburbs, especially the shopping centers south of town along U.S. 9, essentially finished off the job. Yes, Poughkeepsie has been "malled."

To be fair, the "Queen City" of the 19th century is not completely down for the count. It is still the home of **Vassar College,** founded by local magnate Matthew Vassar. The college's reputation for educational excellence is worldwide, and its campus, located on Raymond Avenue south of U.S. 44 and N.Y. 55 near the eastern boundary of town, is quite impressive. The home office of **IBM** is located in (actually just outside) Poughkeepsie too, down among the shopping centers on U.S. 9. This is a very lucky thing, since otherwise the local economy would really be dead.

The city's extremely rich 19th-century architectural heritage is also being belatedly rediscovered, and there are now several "historic" districts in town. The region along the river immediately north of the Mid-Hudson Bridge is in the process of becoming a miniature Georgetown, complete with restored buildings, brick sidewalks, and gas street lamps. Many of the ornate wooden mansions on nearby Academy Street have been restored as well, with fairly spectacular results. Maybe one day even Main Street will be freed from its ersatz, pseudo-modern identity as the desolate and deserted "Main Mall," and turned back into the Victorian street that it was intended to be, complete with life-giving traffic.

In the heart of downtown Poughkeepsie is the **Bardavon 1869 Opera House,** 35 Market St. (tel. 914/473-5288). Rescued from demolition (unlike so many of its worthy neighbors), the Bardavon has been restored to its original splendor and now presents a varied program of theater, music, and dance. If you're staying overnight anywhere near Poughkeepsie, you'd be well advised to call and see what's on. Typical presentations have ranged from the San Francisco Western Opera's *La Bohème,* to Rita Moreno in a one-woman show, to the Vietnam veteran drama *Tracers* mounted by the New York Public Theater, to a festival of Mozart performed by the resident ensemble of Lincoln Center. Poughkeepsie is fortunate to have a resource like the Bardavon, and it deserves support.

Of the assorted historic houses in and around town, the most interesting is probably **Locust Grove,** the Italianate villa of Samuel F. B. Morse, inventor of the telegraph and accomplished portraitist. This great old Victorian mansion overlooks the Hudson from a site on U.S. 9, 2 miles south of the Mid-Hudson Bridge. A family by the name of Young bought it from the Morse estate in 1901, maintained it lovingly until 1975, then endowed it with a trust and opened it to the public. The famous Alexander Jackson Davis collaborated with Morse on the mansion's design. The interior is full of great Victorian stuff, some of it Morse's own. The house is still surrounded by its original 150-acre estate, which contrasts dramatically with the surrounding malls and garden-apartment complexes. The exact address is 370 South Rd., Poughkeepsie (tel. 914/454-4500). Open Memorial Day through September on Wednesday through Sunday from 10am to 4pm. Admission is $4 for adults, $3.50 for seniors, $1 for kids 7 to 16, and free to kids under 7.

Other than that, there's not much reason to tarry in Poughkeepsie. That is, unless like so many others you have business here or you're tired and/or hungry. In which case see below.

Where to Stay & Eat in Poughkeepsie

Poughkeepsie's most stylish accommodation is **Inn at the Falls** on the banks of the Wappingers Creek at 50 Red Oaks Mill Rd., Poughkeepsie, NY 12603 (tel. 914/462-5770; fax 914/462-5943). Tucked away in a woody suburban corner, but still convenient to Vassar, the inn has a more serene environment than those on Route 9 or downtown. The 22 rooms and 14 suites are luxuriously decorated with brass or canopy beds and English or French repro-furnishings. Rates include a "continental plus" breakfast, which can be taken in your own room or the public dining room. There is no restaurant on the premises, but management maintains a service bar adjacent to an inviting living-room area with fireplace. Room rates are $107 for a single or double, $117 for a "minisuite," and $137 to $150 for a full-sized suite. All major credit cards accepted.

Just south of town on Route 9 is the new **Poughkeepsie Courtyard by Marriott,** 408 South Rd., Poughkeepsie, NY 12601 (tel. 914/485-6336, or toll free 800/321-2211; fax 914/485-6514). This is a dependably comfortable and attractive formula motel, designed essentially for traveling businesspeople. Other branches are recommended elsewhere in this guide. Rooms surround a landscaped courtyard, and facilities include an indoor whirlpool, a small indoor swimming pool, an exercise room, and a very good restaurant. The spacious contemporary guest rooms cost between $54 and $115, the latter for a suite. The restaurant is open daily and is also staffed by students of the Culinary Institute of America (see later in this chapter). Prices are very moderate, and the food is great. All major credit cards accepted.

AN EXCURSION TO MILLBROOK

The attractive village of Millbrook (pop. 1,300) sits at the absolute center of Dutchess County, named in honor of the wife of the duke of York. The village is located about 4 miles east of the Taconic Parkway on U.S. 44.

Millbrook has been fashionable since its inception in the late 19th century. The so-called Millbrook Colony once supported a fine resort hotel known as Halcyon Hall. The hotel later became Bennett College for women, and although it has been empty now for many years, the community perpetually hopes that it may again be opened as a hotel. Millbrook remains much as it's always been, the service center of a bucolic area noted for very large estates and horse farms. One of the most magnificent of these is **Thorndale,** whose columned portico is visible just before the Millbrook light. This extremely elaborate and formal estate has been in the Thorne family for well over a century. Numerous equivalent properties are tucked out of sight among the manicured rolling hills that surround the village.

Low-profile Millbrook achieved brief and totally uncharacteristic notoriety during the 1960s. For about 4 years, Timothy Leary operated his League for Spiritual Discovery in a rambling and gloomy Victorian mansion that 50 years before had been a local showplace. Long hair, beads, and curious aromas mixed for a period with the riding boots and streaked hair of the locals. But all that's over now, and in its place Millbrook has become known for antiques. There are three separate antiques malls within a block of one another on Franklin Avenue—the **Millbrook Antiques Mall,** the **Millbrook Antiques Center,** and the **Village Antiques Center**— plus several independent shops. There must be close to 100 individual dealers, every one of whom is constantly bringing in new stuff. There's enough to look at here— from glorified tag-sale junk to decidedly pricey French and English antiques to pre-Revolutionary Americana—to keep you busy for hours.

A few miles west of Millbrook on Tyrrel Road is **Innisfree Gardens** (tel. 914/677-8000), an elaborate Asian "cup garden" that was once the site of an estate belonging to one Walter Beck. The fine Tudor-style house has, alas, been taken down. But the garden, upon which the Becks labored for generations, has been preserved under the auspices of a private trust that opens it to the public between May and October. It's called a "cup" because of its location in a small valley hemmed in by landscaped hills surrounding a jewel-like lake. The original focus of the property was the vanished mansion, which stood on a site across the lake from the parking area. There are abundant manicured lawns, terraces of stone, Oriental gates, ornamental waterfalls, beautiful flowerbeds, and old-fashioned wooden chairs situated to take advantage of carefully thought-out views. This is a great spot for a picnic, especially during the week, when almost nobody is around. Open Wednesday through Friday from 10am to 4pm and Saturday, Sunday, and holidays from 11am to 5pm. There's a $2 admission on weekends. To find Tyrrel Road, look for the Innisfree sign on U.S. 44 just west of the Dutchess Home and Farm Center near N.Y. 44A.

Millbrook Area Wineries

North of Millbrook, at the intersection of Wing Road and the Shunpike (follow the signs from Route 44A) is **Millbrook Vineyards,** Box 167D, Millbrook, NY

12545 (tel. 914/677-8383, or toll free 800/662-WINE). The owner of the vineyard, John Dyson, was once New York State's commissioner of agriculture. In the late 1970s, he was among those who promoted important legislation that encouraged the development of the wine industry in New York. Millbrook Vineyards was established under the guiding hand of Dr. Konstantin Frank, the father of vinifera vines in the new world (much more about this in our section on the Finger Lakes). Dr. Frank was the first to successfully graft and plant classic European grapes in the cold climate of upstate New York. At Millbrook, the experiment is flourishing, and the wine excellent. The 50-acre hillside vineyard and the winery building are beautiful too. Open for free daily tours from noon to 5pm.

Another nearby vineyard, this time with an appealing restaurant attached, is **Cascade Mountain Vineyards & Restaurant,** Flint Hill Road, Amenia, NY 12501 (tel. 914/373-9021). To get there from Millbrook, follow Route 44 east to the traffic light in the middle of Amenia, then turn north onto Route 22 and follow the signs. Cascade's vineyard and restaurant are perched atop a mountain. The views are spectacular—well worth the last trek over the dirt road. The alpine style restaurant serves only lunch, and only on certain days. Between April and December it's open daily from noon to 3pm. The food is exceptionally good and costs $7.50 per selection for things like smoked salmon, red-pepper mousse, or grilled maple chicken salad. Sometimes there's a jazz band outside in the summer. The winery itself is open daily for free, self-guided tours and wine tastings, from 10am to 6pm. There is nothing stuffy about this place. The owners believe that wine tasting should be fun (more power to them!) and will even print up personal labels for customers. AE, MC, and V accepted.

Where to Stay & Eat in Millbrook

If you'd like to picnic at Innisfree, good sandwiches to go can be obtained at the **Millbrook Deli,** on the corner of Church and Franklin Streets in the center of the village (tel. 914/677-9391). Half the people who work in Millbrook seem to line up at the counter here every noontime. Another excellent idea, if like me you have a taste for good small-town sandwich shops, is **Jamos,** a stone's throw from the deli on Church Street (tel. 914/677-5108). This is the spot for inexpensive sandwiches (love that chicken salad), hot dogs, sundaes, ice cream sodas, shakes, and homemade soups. Open only for breakfast and lunch. Just a block away on Franklin Avenue is the **Millbrook Diner** (tel. 914/677-5319), where dependable eggs are served up in vintage stainless-steel-sided surroundings.

There's a horsier atmosphere half a block up Franklin Avenue at **Millbrook Town House** (tel. 914/677-8400). This charming ivy-covered cottage contains several intimate dining rooms decorated with prints of horses and maps of the Millbrook Hunt, plus a small bar that's a favorite haunt of the locals. The lunch menu offers a range of sandwiches from roast beef and Swiss to Monte Cristo, to Reuben, to tuna melt on a croissant, priced mostly between $4 and $7. At dinner there's an extensive à la carte menu listing lamb chops, stuffed shrimp, tenderloin of beef, and liver with onions, plus numerous chicken dishes, costing $12 to $18. The food is great, and the atmosphere very "Millbrook." Open for lunch Tuesday through Saturday from 11:30am to 2:30pm; dinner is served Tuesday through Thursday from 5 to 9:30pm, Friday and Saturday until 10pm. Major credit cards accepted.

The best restaurant in Millbrook, from the standpoints of food and country atmosphere, is **Allyn's,** 4 miles east of the village of Millbrook on U.S. 44 (tel. 914/677-5888). Allyn's has beautifully appointed dining rooms, a beamed café with glass walls overlooking lovely rolling lawns, and a very talented owner/chef. The menu features "cross-cultural cuisine" with ever-changing French, Italian, Oriental, and Spanish dishes. This local favorite is open Wednesday to Monday for lunch from 11:30am to 3pm, dinner is served on Wednesday, Thursday, Sunday, and Monday from 5:30 to 9:30pm (to 10:30pm on Friday and Saturday). Lunch costs between $5 and $8, dinner between $13 and $20. A light café menu is available from 3pm to closing. A champagne Sunday brunch is offered at a fixed rate of $11.95; patio dining is available in summer. All major credit cards accepted.

For an exclusive hideaway retreat, try **Troutbeck,** Leedsville Road, Amenia, NY 12501 (tel. 914/373-9681; fax 914/373-7080). This English country–style estate is secluded amid 450 acres of parklike grounds and woodlands and is graced with such amenities as an indoor pool, a sauna, an exercise room, tennis courts, a large outdoor pool, and a gourmet restaurant. The antiques-filled Tudor-style manor offers 35 rooms, many with fireplaces, and houses a 12,000-volume library. A couple can experience the luxury of Troutbeck—including three meals and an open bar—for between $350 and $475 daily, depending on the room. AE accepted.

Also in the Millbrook area are two excellent bed-and-breakfasts. Just half a mile from the village center of Millbrook is **The Cat in Your Lap,** located at the junction of Old Route 82 and Route 343 at the monument (tel. 914/677-3051). This great 1840s farmhouse offers two double rooms with private baths, as well as two studio apartments. Cost ranges from $55 to $95 a night for double occupancy. Lots of charm for a low cost.

The other B&B is **Mill at Bloomvale Falls,** Route 82, Salt Point, NY 12578 (tel. 914/266-4234), which is a wildly creative alteration of an 18th-century mill, complete with a thundering waterfall, a tranquil mill pond, a dramatic multilevel modern interior, a fountain terrace, and an appealing double-height greenhouse. All four guest rooms share two hall baths. However, the building is so visually interesting and unusual that this doesn't seem to bother anyone. Rates range from $85 to $115, with discounts for extended stays. MC and V accepted.

Recently I visited a country inn that friends had been hounding me to review. To my delight I discovered that the recently revived **Old Drovers Inn,** located west of Millbrook on Old Route 22, Dover Plains, NY 12522 (tel. 914/832-9311), was everything it was cracked up to be. It is a gorgeous early 18th-century building with a crackling fireplace (in winter), handhewn ceiling timbers, elegant table settings, and a collection of tasteful antiques—precisely the ideal image of a New England country inn.

If the architecture and setting weren't enough, I was treated to true American/New England cuisine, complete with popovers just like my grandmother used to make in Vermont. The ceiling in the atmospheric dining room is so low that tall customers had better beware lest they crack their skulls on a historic beam. Possibly this explains the card on our table that read, "It is our normal policy to serve double measures on mixed drinks and cocktails. If you prefer a single measure only, please advise our barman who will be delighted to serve you."

Lunch is available Thursday through Monday from noon until 3pm; à la carte selections start at $11.50. Dinner hours are from 5:30 to 9pm weekdays, 3 to 9:30pm Saturday, and from noon to 8:30pm Sunday and holidays. Dinnertime à la carte selections range from $16.40 to a top end of $31 for double-cut, rack lamb chops with Charlie's tomato chutney.

The four guest rooms at Old Drovers are equally enchanting. All have private baths, and three have their own fireplaces. Decor is late 18th to mid-19th century in flavor, highlighted with fresh flowers in each room. Double occupancy rates range from $100 to $150 midweek and $120 to $170 on weekends. DC, MC, and V accepted.

EAST BANK ROUTE TO ALBANY

Abandon the Taconic Parkway for a while, return to Poughkeepsie on Route 44, and pick up U.S. 9 north. Your next stop, only a few miles upriver, is the historic town of **Hyde Park.**

This aristocratic name was first applied to the locality in 1741, when Peter Fauconnier, private secretary to Edward Hyde, Viscount Cornbury, bought land here. Cornbury was the English governor of New York who perplexed contemporary observers by wearing dresses in public. Hyde Park marks the beginning of the **16-Mile Historic District,** which runs northward along the eastern shore of the river. Listed on the National Register of Historic Places, the district contains a nearly unbroken string of fine riverfront estates, many of which have played important roles in American history.

Perhaps the most important, and certainly the most famous, of these estates is **Springwood, the Home of Franklin D. Roosevelt National Historic Site,** U.S. 9, Hyde Park (tel. 914/229-2501). This formal and elegant country mansion has been preserved just as it was in 1945, when President Roosevelt died. Actually, the place almost burned down in 1982, but it has been so painstakingly restored that you'd never know. The house is typical of the country places maintained by the Dutchess County squirearchy to which the Roosevelts belonged. It sits on a beautiful estate with fine views of the river. FDR was born and raised here, and throughout his life he returned as often as possible. Many famous personages have been guests at Hyde Park, including George VI and his wife on a weekend in 1939 and Winston Churchill upon several occasions during the war.

Springwood was originally a not-too-large clapboard Victorian country house, the outlines of which are still visible on the river facade. But in 1916, FDR and his mother decided to "mansionize" the place in high Georgian Revival style. Now it's got 35 rooms and 9 baths. The interiors reflect the traveled, luxurious life of its privileged owners. But more than that, these lovely rooms preserve a palpable air of FDR himself. He was a remarkable, albeit controversial, man. And he saved America not once but twice: first from the catastrophe of economic collapse, then from the menace of Nazi Germany. FDR looked 80 when he died, even though he was only 63. Greatness takes its toll.

The grounds around the house include architecturally unusual outbuildings, an enchanting rose garden maintained in perfect order and containing the graves of President and Mrs. Roosevelt, a greenhouse dating from 1906, woodland trails, and the **Franklin D. Roosevelt Library Museum.** This latter structure was erected in 1939 to house presidential papers and archives. Today it's a major study and research facility, as well as a museum devoted to the lives of Franklin and Eleanor Roosevelt.

Springwood is open daily in April through October from 9am until 5pm. From November through March, the site is open only Thursday to Monday. Admission is $4 for adults and free to kids under 16 and seniors over 62.

The **Eleanor Roosevelt National Historic Site** is at her former summer and weekend retreat **Val-Kill,** 249 Albany Post Rd. (tel. 914/229-9115). After President Roosevelt's death in 1945, Val-Kill became Eleanor's permanent home. The site, very evocative of its interesting owner, is open daily in April through October from 9am to 5pm; open November, December, and March on weekends only; closed January and February.

While in the area you should also visit the nearby **Vanderbilt Mansion National Historic Site,** U.S. 9, Hyde Park (tel. 914/229-7770). This spectacular beaux arts estate was developed in the 1890s as the country home of Frederick W. Vanderbilt, grandson of the commodore and something of a black sheep (he married an older woman). McKim, Mead, and White designed the house, which was originally the centerpiece of a 700-acre property. The views of the Hudson and the Catskills are superb. The mansion, which contains all its original furniture, is the sort you see in Newport. In other words, it's a palace, from its marble-clad double-height entry hall to its 18th-century French paneled reception room.

The Roosevelts, the Vanderbilts, and the Rogers (whose immense mansion is now in the hands of a religious order) were once quite the princes of little Hyde Park. Nowadays commercialization and the proliferation of tract housing have blurred the feudal configurations of the place somewhat. Yet on the Vanderbilt property the past is quite clearly preserved. Besides the house, there are elaborate formal gardens, an old carriage house (complete with vintage limousines), a pavilion that once served as a guesthouse (it's now the visitors' center), half a mile of riverfront to explore, and, of course, the unbelievably beautiful view. The public owes the late Margaret Van Alen Bruguière a vote of thanks for donating her uncle's house and 212 acres to the U.S. government in 1940. She had tried to sell the place in 1938 and 1939, first for $350,000, finally for $250,000. But there were no takers. In lieu of auction, demolition, and subdivision, she gave it to the public.

The Vanderbilt Mansion is open daily in April through October from 9am to 5pm; from November through March the hours are the same, but the house is open Thursday through Monday. Admission is $2 for adults and free for individuals under 16 and over 62.

Where to Eat in Hyde Park

One of the Hudson Valley's most famous educational institutions—and one of its greatest cultural resources—is the **Culinary Institute of America**, on U.S. 9 about half a mile south of Hyde Park. The CIA, as it's called locally, occupies an imposing former seminary building overlooking the Hudson where 1,850 full-time students attend classes in cooking, baking, and hospitality management. Of particular concern to us are four superb restaurants, operated by CIA students, located on the campus, and open to the public. Eating at the CIA really is fun, and if you can arrange to have a meal here, by all means do so.

The most informal of the restaurants is the **St. Andrew's Café** (tel. 914/471-6608), where $10 or so will buy you a lunch of medallions of pork with red-onion confit, baked salmon filet, or broiled tuna steak, plus dessert and beverage. Dinner is hardly more expensive, sample selections including tenderloin of beef with blue-cheese-and-herb crust, duck ravioli, and pan-smoked breast of chicken. Open Monday through Friday from 11:30am to 1pm for lunch and from 6 to 8pm for dinner. Reservations are suggested. The café is located behind the main building, close to the big parking lot.

The award-winning **American Bounty Restaurant** specializes in American regional cuisine. Specialties include pan-fried crabcakes with smoked-pepper butter sauce served with creamed sweet potatoes and leek soup, roasted pheasant with forest mushrooms and kiln-dried cherry sauce, and grilled black Angus beef tenderloin with roasted-garlic glaze. The American Bounty is open Tuesday through Saturday, with lunch served from 11:30am to 1pm, dinner from 6:30 to 8:30pm. A la carte main courses range from $12 to $15 at lunch and from $16.50 to $21 at dinner. Jackets are required. Reservations are requested and can be made by calling the Institute's Reservations Office at 914/471-6608.

The **Escoffier Restaurant** offers traditional French cuisine served in elegant surroundings overlooking the scenic Hudson. Its à la carte and prix-fixe menus feature such specialties as *salade au confit de canard, consommé au quenelle de beurre, coquilles St-Jacques grillées au romarin,* and *filet de bouef à la moelle gratinée et noix.* Known on campus as the "E-Room," the Escoffier has been awarded four stars by *The Mobil Travel Guide* and three stars by *The New York Times* and also is a recipient of the prestigious Ivy Award from *Restaurants & Institutions Magazine.* Lunch is served Tuesday through Saturday from noon to 1pm, with à la carte selections ranging from $13 to $18 and the prix-fixe costing $23. Dinner is served from 6:30 to 8:30pm and priced from about $16.50 to $25 for à la carte selections and $40 for the prix fixe. Jackets are required. Reservations are requested and can be made by calling the Institute's Reservations Office at 914/471-6608.

Last, but by no means least, is the **Caterina de Medici,** which features regional Italian cuisine. The menu includes *risotto alla Sbirraglia, mille cosedde, osso bucco alla milanese,* and zabaglione. Open Monday through Friday for a single luncheon seating at 11:30am, with one seating for dinner at 6:30pm. The prix-fixe lunch is priced at $16; the prix-fixe dinner is $24. Jackets and reservations are required. For reservations, call 914/471-6608.

Northward to Staatsburg & Rhinebeck

A few miles north of the Vanderbilt Mansion on U.S. 9, you'll see a turnoff to the left opposite the sign for **Staatsburg.** Not much to see in this sleepy little village, save the pleasant stone Episcopal church designed in 1891 by Richard Upjohn. Inside are a pair of 13th-century stained-glass windows from Chartres Cathedral, the gift of Ogden Mills, one of the local riverfront seigneurs.

And it is to the **Mills Mansion State Historic Site,** Old Post Road, in Staatsburg (tel. 914/889-8851), that you are headed next. The house is another McKim, Mead, and White extravaganza dating from 1896. It was built for Ogden and Ruth Livingston Mills and decorated as opulently as the Vanderbilt house to the south. Mills died in 1929, and his daughter donated the property to the State of New York in 1938. The mansion's basement has been the headquarters of the Taconic Region of the New York State Office of Parks Recreation and Historic Preservation ever since.

The Mills house has suffered considerable depredations at the hands of the weather and low state maintenance budgets. Leaking roofs have on occasion caused much of it to be closed. But progress is being made and the ceilings at least no longer drip. Interestingly, the 1896 construction encases a much older house. The views from the lawns are superb, the lawns themselves are immense, and the river is beautiful here. The house is palatial, and if you like this kind of thing you shouldn't miss it. Between April 15 and Labor Day the mansion is open Wednesday through Saturday from 10am to 5pm and Sunday from noon to 5pm. From Labor Day until the last Sunday in October, the hours are noon to 5pm. Admission is free. Closed the rest of the year with the exception of Christmas, even though the beautiful grounds remain open.

The Old Post Road rejoins U.S. 9 about a mile above the Mills house. And from here it's only another 4 or 5 miles to **Rhinebeck** (pop. 2,500), one of the Hudson River Valley's most appealing little towns. Just exactly what makes Rhinebeck so nice? The tree-lined streets? The delightful Victorian buildings? The abundance of excellent restaurants? The fine country properties that surround the village? The interesting shopping? The lovely rural surroundings? All of the above, no doubt, plus proximity to the sights down in Hyde Park and Staatsburg. And the **Old Rhinebeck Aerodrome** (tel. 914/758-8610), located about 3 miles north of town near the neighboring village of Red Hook.

The aerodrome is part museum (three hangars full of antique planes, cars, motorcycles) and part air-show spectacular, and it's open daily from 10am to 5pm, May 15 to October 31. On weekend afternoons, besides the museum exhibits, you can see either the Saturday "History of Flight Show" (World War I and Lindbergh-era planes) or the Sunday "Melodrama" (a staged air battle between the Black Baron and the good guys). Air shows take place every weekend from mid-June to mid-October. Either before or after the show you can also go "barnstorming" in an open-cockpit biplane. Admission is $10 for adults and $5 for kids. Barnstorming costs about $25 per person, takes about 15 minutes, and is on a first-come, first-served basis. Admission on non-air-show days is $5 for adults and $3 for kids (ages 6 to 10).

Where to Stay & Eat in Rhinebeck

Rhinebeck is famous as the home of America's oldest inn, **Beekman Arms,** U.S. 9, Rhinebeck, NY 12572 (tel. 914/876-7077). The Beek's columned facade surveys the very center of the village across a smallish manicured lawn. It's a wonderful old whitewashed building, rambling this way and that, parts of which date to 1766. Beyond the ancient-looking beamed lobby is a popular restaurant with several separate rooms and an air of up-to-date country elegance. Meals can be taken either in an atmospheric tap room complete with dark booths and colonial-era fireplace, in an early American dining room, or amid hanging plants in the "greenhouse." Lunch specialties include seafood pot pie, beef Stroganoff, quiche, and country omelet and usually cost between $6 and $11. At dinner you might settle on prime rib, duck breast, blackened salmon, grilled swordfish, or one of the daily specials, such as braised veal shanks or fresh salmon with béarnaise sauce. Expect to pay between about $16 and $23 for an à la carte selection. The Sunday brunch, a $19.95 buffet extravaganza served between 10am and 2pm, is justly famous. Upstairs in the inn are 13 modest colonial-style rooms with private baths and phones (but no TVs). They cost from $70 to $80 nightly, double occupancy. All major credit cards accepted.

More elaborate overnight accommodations can be had a block to the north at

Delamater 1844 Inn and Conference Center, a rather grand name for the delicious Hudson River Gothic villa located at 44 Montgomery St., Rhinebeck, NY 12572 (tel. 914/876-7080). Built for the founder of the First National Bank of Rhinebeck, it was completely restored/renovated by the Beekman only a few years ago. The rooms are spacious, with tasteful pastel color schemes, antique-reproduction furniture, color TVs, and modern baths. They are extremely handsome and cost but $52 to $85 nightly, double occupancy. The architecturally compatible Delamater Courtyard and Carriage House are located immediately to the rear. Rooms here are even bigger, and most have working fireplaces. Although not located in historic buildings (the courtyard is new, save for one old house in the middle of it), accommodations have the same tasteful traditional interior decor as the Delamater House. Double-occupancy rates back here range from $90 to $110 nightly. As noted above, there are pleasant and less expensive rooms in the inn itself, but value wise, the best and most atmospheric deal is chez Delamater. All major credit cards accepted.

Rhinebeck Village Inn, 6 Route 9 South, Rhinebeck, NY 12572 (tel. 914/876-7000; fax 914/876-4756), is a newer motel with an arts-and-crafts look, located on U.S. 9 at the southern edge of town. For $63 a night double occupancy ($50 on weekdays) you get a very large new room furnished with suave gray carpeting, two queen-size beds, a color TV, individual air conditioning, a very nice bright white bathroom, and even a complimentary continental breakfast. This is an excellent bargain. There are antlers on the walls, stained wooden headboards and desks, and ropes holding the hanger bars. Whatever the owners couldn't make themselves they got at the Rhinebeck Crafts Fair. There are only 16 units. All major credit cards accepted.

Rhinebeck has a disproportionate number of good restaurants for such a small town. Here are four personal favorites.

Around the corner from Beekman Arms is **Le Petit Bistro,** 8 Main St. (tel. 914/876-7400). This small, intimate restaurant with a decor of mirrors and polished wood is a local favorite with those in the know. The menu includes a variety of choices, from veal scallopini with Madeira mushrooms ($15.25) to duck with orange sauce ($16) to the melt-in-your-mouth (at least mine) twin filet mignon with shallots and red wine ($18.25). Both Yvonne, who greets you, and her husband, Jean-Paul Croizer, the chef, combine exceptional food with a commitment to genuine hospitality. Dinner only is available on Thursday through Monday from 5 to 10pm and Sunday from 4 to 9pm. Due to its popularity, I strongly suggest you make reservations. All major credit cards accepted.

Foster's Coach House Tavern, 22 Montgomery St. (tel. 914/876-8052), is a two-story brick Victorian building that once was indeed a coach house. Today there's a strong horse motif running through the decor, from the phone booth (an old coach on springs) to the horseshoe door pulls to the framed prints of horses on the walls. In the backroom thousands of patrons have tucked their business cards between cracks in the barnside paneling. Curious, isn't it?—even though looking them over is interesting. Foster's has great burgers and innumerable sandwiches priced at $3 to $4, plus salad plates, Italian dishes, plus standbys like fried chicken, broiled scallops, open steak sandwich, and red snapper. Most dinner plates cost around $8 or $9. The same menu is available from 11am to 11pm for hot foods and until midnight for cold foods on Tuesday to Sunday. Foster's is so popular there's often a line at the door at peak hours. Don't be discouraged; it moves fast. No credit cards accepted.

Across the street in an old rambling Baptist church is **La Parmigiana,** 37 Montgomery St. (tel. 914/876-3228). The restaurant consists of an 1825 original church later engulfed by a much larger Queen Anne–style addition. The older part of the structure is the principal dining space and also the location of the wood-fired baking ovens. All the pizzas and calzones are baked with wood heat and deliciously flavored with hickory and apple smoke. Creative pizzas, calzones, and a great selection of homemade northern Italian pasta dishes are available for both lunch and dinner. Lunch is served on Wednesday to Sunday from noon to 4pm and costs about $6 to

$9. Dinner selections run from $5 to $15 and are available on the same days from 4 to 11pm. All major credit cards accepted.

For more of a family experience, try **Rolling Rock Café,** located at 46 Route 9, just north of the village and across Route 9 from the county fairgrounds (tel. 914/876-7655). This large American bistro is open Sunday to Thursday from 7:30am to 1am, even later on Friday and Saturday. It consists of three large dining areas decorated with an eclectic mix of Victorian antiques, pop art posters of Marilyn Monroe and James Dean, beamed ceilings, mahogany-and-etched-glass partitions, and stained-glass panels. Taped rock music fills the air. It's big and reasonably priced; the $12.95 surf and turf at dinner is the priciest thing on the menu. This is a good place for sandwiches, burgers, and salads at lunch, when everything's under $9. All major credit cards accepted.

Two Touring Notes

Rhinebeck is a good jumping-off point for an excursion west to the **Catskills.** Just above town on U.S. 9 you'll see signs for N.Y. 9G and the **Kingston-Rhinecliff Bridge.** Chapter XIII describes the Catskills in detail. If you'd like to interrupt your tour of the Hudson Valley, this is a good place to do it.

After Rhinebeck, your east-bank route to Albany will take you eventually to **Clermont,** ancestral home of the legendary Livingstons, then to the old city of Hudson. The most direct road is N.Y. 9G, which you pick up just north of Rhinebeck. A vastly more picturesque route is via the old **River Road,** which winds its way through the 16-Mile Historic District on a route that roughly parallels 9G. You'll pass beneath canopies of old trees, alongside the stone walls and imposing gatehouses of old riverfront estates, past a sleepy village or two, plus some old houses, lots of woods, and the attractive campus of Bard College. There's practically no traffic, and it's a very pretty drive.

To find River Road from the center of Rhinebeck, take Market Street (N.Y. 308) westbound from the light at Beekman Arms toward **Rhinecliff** (a hamlet with an Amtrak station on the water's edge). River Road is just a little over a mile west of the center of Rhinebeck, on the right side of N.Y. 308 as you head toward Rhinecliff.

Road to Red Hook

There are stretches of River Road on which you can easily imagine patriots in tricorn hats galloping this way and that or carriages full of 18th- and 19th-century gentry riding from one estate to another. Many famous people have lived along this stretch of the Hudson, which has not yet lost its rural residential atmosphere.

Soon after turning onto River Road you'll see signs for **Ferncliff,** now the site of a modern nursing home but once the country estate of William B. Astor, Jr. Gore Vidal's novel *1876* has a scene set in Ferncliff during the days of *the* Mrs. Astor. This is Caroline Schermerhorn Astor, the woman whose house on Fifth Avenue and 34th Street contained a ballroom that could accommodate only 400 persons. Her aide de camp, a social-climbing southern lawyer named Ward McAllister, commented at the time that since there were only 400 people worth knowing in New York society, small ballrooms made no difference. Ferncliff is where these exquisite snobs spent parts of each spring and autumn. Portions of the estate, including a fabulous marble "casino" building designed by Stanford White, remain in private hands.

A bit north of the intersection of N.Y. 199 and River Road is **Rokeby,** identified by a historic roadside marker. Built by a Revolutionary War general named Armstrong, Rokeby was for many years the home of William B. Astor, Sr., father of the developer of Ferncliff. Astor Sr.'s granddaughter married a man named Chanler, had eight children, and then, along with her husband, suddenly died. In the late 19th century the so-called Astor Orphans grew up at Rokeby all by themselves (with governesses, servants, and tutors, of course) and went on to become adventurers, noted artists, socialites, and intimates of American presidents. Theirs is a fascinating tale, in which there's much of the flavor of the Hudson River Valley.

At Rokeby, you are in the environs of the little village of **Red Hook** (pop. 1,700), whose center lies a few miles east of the Hudson on Route 199. Red Hook is a modest place with an attractive upstate look about it. Of particular interest is a pair of excellent restaurants, both serving inventive and reasonably priced food, one connected to an original budget motel.

The first, located 10 minutes east of Red Hook on Route 199, bears the curious name of **Another Roadside Attraction,** Route 199, Milan, NY 12571 (tel. 914/758-0535). Actually, the name comes from the Tom Robbins novel, copies of which are to be found in each of the eight little rooms as well as in the reading rack at the restaurant. The restaurant is a pop-1940s country restaurant, complete with a big "Diner" sign, shiny white walls, red-leatherette booths, a long counter, and a wooden Indian out front. It serves possibly the best pancakes, omelets, and monster muffins in the Hudson Valley. The many burgers and sandwiches are just as good, and hardly anything on the menu costs more than $5. Open only for breakfast and lunch (oh, if only they'd extend that to dinner!) from 7am to 3pm daily. The motel rooms are simple but bright, equipped with little black-and-white TVs (when's the last time you saw one of those?), metal furniture, and chenille bedspreads; they cost only $50 a night. No credit cards accepted.

My other recommendation is located a few miles north of Red Hook off Route 9G in the quaint hamlet of Tivoli. **Santa Fe,** 82 Broadway, Tivoli (tel. 914/757-4100), serves what many in this part of the world consider the best Mexican/Southwestern food in the Hudson Valley. It's a busy place with a cosmopolitan atmosphere, lots of patrons up from New York at weekend houses or in for dinner from nearby Bard College. There's a bar up front, an open kitchen in the center, walls painted rich peach and salmon, new-age background music, dramatic lighting, and seemingly always a crowd. Open Tuesday through Sunday from 5pm "til the end" they tell us. The menu runs the gamut from chicken quesadilla at $4.75 to sesame baja shrimp chargrilled with lime and jalapeño butter for $10.95. MC and V accepted.

North to Hudson

Now pick up where you left off on River Road at Rokeby. A little to the north, just before Annandale-on-Hudson, is **Montgomery Place** (tel. 914/758-5461), an estate named in honor of Revolutionary War hero Gen. Richard Montgomery by his widow. The exquisite old house was purchased in 1985, contents intact, by Historic Hudson Valley. The mansion was built from 1804 to 1805 by Janet Livingston Montgomery, widow of the general. The original house, an outstanding example of Federal architecture, was later transformed into a beautiful Classical revival country home by the great 19th-century architect Alexander Jackson Davis. Visitors today can tour restored rooms and roam the more than 400 acres of land at Montgomery Place, savoring the beauty of the woods, streams, and gardens and enjoying the magnificent views of the Hudson River and the Catskill Mountains. In fall, the estate's orchards offer pick-your-own apples. Montgomery Place is open Wednesday to Monday from 10am to 5pm from April through October; open weekends only in November, December, and March from 10am to 5pm; grounds only on Sundays from 10am to 5pm in January and February. Admission is $6 adults, $5 seniors, $3 students, and under 6 free.

The picturesque campus of **Bard College,** a four-year liberal arts institution, straddles River Road north of the hamlet of Annandale. A mile or so beyond Bard, River Road rejoins the highway (N.Y. 9G).

About 5 miles to the north, beyond the turnoff for Tivoli, you'll see a sign on the west side of the highway for **Clermont State Historic Site,** in the town of Clermont (tel. 914/537-4240). Clermont was the home of seven generations of the famous Livingston family. The Clermont mansion stands on a part of the original Manor of Livingston, whose charter was obtained by Robert Livingston in 1686 and which originally encompassed over 160,000 acres. It was built by Robert's son, known rather grandly as Robert of Clermont, in 1730. It was Robert of Clermont's grandson who, during and after the Revolution, was chancellor of New York. He was also a strong advocate of independence, a member of the Second Continental Congress, and one of the five men who drafted the Declaration of Independence.

In 1777, Clermont was burned by the British in retaliation for its owner's political sentiments. But it was rebuilt during the war and flourished along with its distinguished owner's career. Chancellor Livingston went on to become America's first minister of foreign affairs, after which he became minister to France. It was Livingston who negotiated with Napoleon for the Louisiana Purchase. And Livingston's partnership with Robert Fulton led in 1807 to the first successful steamship, known as the *Clermont*.

Livingstons still live all around this area. Indeed, they lived right here until 1962, at which time the state acquired the property. The house is perhaps a bit modest compared to some of its riverfront neighbors. But it literally drips with history, the grounds are quite lovely, and all the furnishings are original. It's open to the public between April 15 and October 31, Wednesday through Sunday from 10am to 5pm. Admission is free. The grounds are open year-round from 8:30am until sunset.

About 10 miles farther north on N.Y. 9G, just before the little city of Hudson, is **Olana** (tel. 518/828-0135). This is the extravagant Persian-style home of Frederic E. Church, famous landscape painter and notable member of the Hudson River School, America's first indigenous art movement. From the threshold of Olana it's easy to see where he got his inspiration. The view from this mountaintop Victorian aerie is absolutely awe-inspiring. "About one hour this side of Albany is the center of the world," wrote Church about his property. "I own it."

The house itself is a curious confection of Moorish arches, towers, loggias, and pinnacles. It's filled with Church family belongings, including canvases by its celebrated owner. Olana is another case of a historic old house being rescued and preserved at the eleventh hour. It certainly deserved to be saved, but whether it's beautiful is a moot point. You can tour it and make up your own mind between April 15 and Labor Day, Wednesday through Saturday from 10am to 5pm and Sunday from noon to 5pm. From Labor Day through October 31 the hours are noon to 5pm Wednesday through Sunday. The charge is $3 for adults and $1 for kids. On weekends you may need reservations. The grounds, open all year from 8am until sunset, are perfect for picnics (no cooking).

The nearby city of **Hudson** (pop. 8,000), a mere 30 miles from Albany, is the seat of Columbia County. Hudson was once a famous boom town. In 1784 it had but one house, but within three short years a mob of settlers (many from Rhode Island) had built over 150 dwellings, plus factories, barns, storehouses, and wharves, and the town supported a population of 1,500. By 1790, Hudson had a 25-ship whaling fleet. But the Erie Canal nipped development in the bud, and the advent of the railroad finished off the job. When Hudson ceased to be a major trade terminus, it entered a long, slow period of decline that has not completely ended.

As in many other places, economic adversity has served to preserve Hudson's remarkable architectural heritage. The length of Warren Street, the main drag running uphill from the river, is an architectural textbook of changing historical styles. There is everything from chaste Greek Revival temples to effulgent early Victorian mansions. There's been a great deal of preservation restoration work. Hudson still has problems, but at least it's nice looking. There are many antiques stores. At the foot of Warren Street is Parade Hill, a public park with a fine view of the river and the mountains beyond. If you like exploring old riverfront towns, you should drive down here for a look. Also interesting is the early Victorian residential district that is bordered on the west by N.Y. 9G and on the north by Warren Street.

Where to Eat

At this point, you might consider detouring across the Rip Van Winkle Bridge to the village of Athens and the wonderful **Stewart House Inn** (tel. 518/945-1357), described under "Kingston & the Catskill Forest Preserve" in Chapter XIII. For family dining about 12 miles distant, take N.Y. 66 eastbound out of Hudson for about 4 miles, until you come to the intersection of N.Y. 9H. Turn left (north) and go about a mile to **Kozel's**, N.Y. 9H, in Ghent (tel. 518/828-3326). This family-style restaurant in the middle of farm country has been a local institution for over 50 years. It's a big, modernized roadhouse with pots of flowers by the door and old New Orleans–type iron posts holding up the porch. Inside is a collection of roomy "modern" dining rooms grouped around a big central bar. Prices are very reasonable and portions are generous. The lunch menu lists all manner of sandwiches, priced mostly from $4 to $5, plus special plates like fried chicken, ham-and-egg plate, turkey with gravy, and a club sandwich, costing about $5 to $7. Dinner selections such as roast sirloin with gravy, brook trout, lobster tails, lamb chops, ham steak Hawaiian, red snapper, and roast turkey are priced mainly from $8 to $20. And these prices include soup, salad, bread, and potato. Kozel's serves lunch from 11am until closing; the dinner menu is available from 5pm onward; the bar stays open late so there's no set closing hour. Open Wednesday to Monday. MC and V accepted.

Only a little farther away from Hudson, about 14 miles east on Route 23, is the elegant **Hostellerie Bressane**, in the center of the hamlet of Hillsdale at the intersection of Routes 22 and 23 (tel. 518/325-3412). This famous restaurant is housed in a federal brick house dating from 1783. Inside is a charming collection of small dining rooms, each tastefully decorated with antiques, floral fabrics, and chintz curtains. Only dinner is served, from 6:30pm on Monday to Friday, from 5:30pm on Saturday, and from 4:30pm on Sunday—until whenever everybody's done. French country fare is the order of the day, with things like Dover sole sautéed with capers and rack of lamb for two, plus all manner of delicious meat and fowl, costing about $16 to $21 à la carte. A particularly good deal is the daily $21.50 prix-fixe dinner (not available on Saturday). Upstairs are six small but delightful rooms, two of which have private baths; for these you'll pay $95 nightly; shared bath rates are $75 a night. No credit cards accepted.

Some Final Attractions Before Albany

Those up to their gills with historic houses may consider themselves excused and proceed directly to Albany. The more determined tourist and historian may want to proceed north on Route 9H to **Lindenwald**, the former country home of Martin Van Buren, president of these United States from 1837 to 1841. The neighboring village of Kinderhook is Van Buren country, and Matty Van is no joke around here. The Martin Van Buren National Historic Site, in Kinderhook (tel. 518/758-9689), was established by another somewhat anonymous president, Gerald Ford, in 1974. This astonishing and much-altered Victorianized mansion is now fully restored. It's a great old house, with a $1 admission fee. You never know when tidbits about Martin Van Buren will come in handy. Open daily from mid-April through October on Wednesday through Sunday during November and to around December 5, from 9am to 5pm. Lindenwald is right on N.Y. 9H about 10 minutes north of Kozel's.

In Kinderhook itself is the graceful and elegant Federal mansion of lawyer James Vanderpoel, known locally as the **House of History,** on U.S. 9 in Kinderhook (tel. 518/758-9265). This is a lovely old place, in need of a bit of paint but full of period furnishings and administered by knowledgeable members of the Columbia County Historical Society. Admission is $3 for adults, $2 for seniors and children over 12, and free to kids under 12. The house is open from Memorial Day to Labor Day, Wednesday through Saturday from 11am to 5pm, Sunday from 1 to 5pm.

Last of all, in nearby Old Chatham (8 miles east of Kinderhook), is the **Shaker Museum and Library,** on Shaker Museum Road (tel. 518/794-9100). The Shakers, officially called the United Society of Believers in Christ's Second Appearing, were a Protestant monastic order that reached a peak about 1850. Even at that date there were only about 6,000 Shakers altogether, living in 18 separate communities (only 2 of which survive today). The Shakers believed in equality of the sexes and celibacy. Their communities were models of industry that produced items notable both for their beauty and their simplicity. The Shaker Museum comprises three buildings that display the sorts of things the Shakers made and the sorts of places in which they made them. Furniture, crafts, textiles, period rooms, plus a café and a gift shop, are among the many exhibits. There is a certain purity and beauty to the things the Shakers made. This museum is dedicated to promoting an understanding of the heritage they bequeathed to us all. The museum is open daily, May through October, from 10am to 5pm. Admission is $6 for adults, $5 for seniors, $3 for students 8 to 17, and free to little ones under 8.

THE CATSKILLS

The wild peaks of New York State's Catskill Mountains have inspired wonder and longing since time began. They aren't very tall—Slide Mountain, the tallest, tops out only at 4,204 feet above sea level—but they possess a lion's share of the picturesque steepness that so typifies the Hudson River Valley. The great names of America's 19th-century landscape movement, the Hudson River School, painted their dense forests, rocky chasms, tumbling streams, and awesome views again and again. Men like Frederic Church, Thomas Cole, George Inness, Asher Durand, and Jasper Cropsey all struggled to capture the exquisite dazzle of light and color on the "divine architecture" of the Catskills. Their great canvases show mists and mountains and colors and sky in ways that can't help but move the imagination.

1. Catskills Orientation

The Indians called them Onteora, or "Land in the Sky." They were closely associated with the magic and legends surrounding the "Great Spirit" who was said to dwell there. Consequently, everybody gave them a wide berth. When the practical Dutch arrived on the scene, they named them the Katsbergs in acknowledgment of the large population of wildcats. Somehow over the centuries this latter name evolved into Catskills, *kill* being the Dutch word for stream.

In the early 19th century the first of the great mountain hotels went up in the Catskills. They bore names like Laurel House, Catskill Mountain House, and Kaaterskill. All of them are gone today, victims of changing tastes and fashions. But there was a time when these opulent pillared palaces were oases of luxury in the very heart of the wilderness. They were originally accessible only by long carriage rides through wild valleys and up the sides of craggy cliffs. The sense of primeval nature contrasted with Victorian engineering must have been exciting indeed. Especially against the inevitable backdrop of a view that might stretch from Albany in the north to the Berkshires in the east to the Hudson Highlands in the south.

The Catskill Mountains are located on the west bank of the Hudson about two-thirds of the way from New York to Albany. The majority of the mountains are contained within the boundaries of **Catskill Forest Preserve**, a New York State–administered wilderness park measuring over 50 miles at its widest point. State land coexists with private property throughout the Catskill Preserve. A light network of high-speed roads and not-very-prosperous villages crisscrosses the area from one end to the other. There is also an elaborate, clearly marked network of hiking and horseback-riding trails, maintained by New York State's Department of Environmental Conservation. To be out on these trails is to savor the wild and romantic atmosphere that drew the first vacationers. To be on the roads is to see a fair amount of junk in the foreground with mysterious peaks sulking in the distance.

Recommended for hikers is the "Catskill Trails" waterproof five-map series for $11.95 from the **New York–New Jersey Trail Conference,** 232 Madison Ave., New York, NY 10116 (tel. 212/685-9699). You can also get map sets for the West Hudson trails ($6.95), Harriman–Bear Mountain ($6.95), South Taconic ($3.50), East Hudson trails ($6.95), and Shawangunk trails ($7.95).

West of the forest preserve, and to a greater extent to the southwest toward Pennsylvania, is a region of resort hotels known colloquially as the **Borscht Belt.** This is the home of enormous establishments like the Concord and Kutsher's. Big hotels in "the mountains" combine Miami Beach high-rise architecture with non-stop activities, including every imaginable daytime sport plus "name" entertainment at night. These places may be in the middle of nowhere, but "solace" and "wilderness" are not part of their mental equation.

Footloose sightseers with a taste for exploration and its attendant change of scenery should probably limit their Catskill excursion to precincts of the forest preserve. The scenery is the best, and there are plenty of interesting things to see and places to stay. Those who like a resort atmosphere where every moment is planned will be happier in the Borscht Belt.

AN EXCURSION TO STONE RIDGE

If you like unspoiled country villages, lush rural scenery, untrafficky roads dotted with an interesting selection of antiques shops, a handsome and luxurious old inn, and a famous country restaurant that rates four stars from *The New York Times,* postpone your trip to the mountains and head instead for **Stone Ridge.** This is a modest 10-mile detour to the southwest of Kingston via N.Y. 209, which intersects N.Y. 28 just west of Thruway exit 19. There's not a great deal to see down here, but the area is just so pretty. Stone Ridge is the sort of hamlet where dogs sleep in the streets. There are a few 18th-century houses, some very big old trees, and clipped lawns and capacious old houses on the outskirts. Absolutely nothing is happening anywhere nearby. But aesthetically speaking, it's an irresistible detour.

The most irresistible part of it is dinner at **DePuy Canal House,** N.Y. 213 in High Falls (tel. 914/687-7700 or 687-7777). This restored landmark building started life in 1797 as a tavern. Today it's a quietly luxurious restaurant with an early American accent. Gourmet dining is the order of the day, conducted in several restored rooms on two floors. Besides Sunday brunch, only dinner is served, Thursday through Sunday, from a prix-fixe menu priced either at $32 for the four-course meal or at $42 for the seven-course alternative. A sample meal might start with brisket beef consommé with tiny spinach leaves and poached quail egg, continue with baked gnocchetti with chicken livers, move on to a main course such as salmon filet in tarragon-lemon egg sauce, and end up with a choice from the dessert tray. There are numerous alternative appetizers, pastas, and main courses, and the menu changes regularly. Open for dinner from 5:30pm on Thursday, Friday, and Saturday and from 3pm on Sunday. Sunday brunch is served between 11:30am and 2:00pm for $13 to $19. Reservations are a must. All major credit cards accepted.

After you've savored the charms of Stone Ridge, take N.Y. 28 west outside Kingston and head for the mountains.

---

2. Kingston & the Catskill Forest Preserve

The natural gateway to the Catskills is the city of **Kingston** (pop. 24,500), on the west bank of the Hudson opposite Rhinebeck. Easy access to Kingston from the east bank is via the **Kingston-Rhinecliff Bridge,** which crosses the river a few miles north of the city limits. For a brief period in 1777, Kingston was the state capital. Driven from New York by the British in 1776, New York's provincial congress fled to White Plains. There it had just enough time to declare itself the Convention of the

Representatives of the State of New York before being forced to flee again, this time to Fishkill. By 1777, the so-called government-on-the-run had retreated to Kingston, where New York's first state constitution was adopted. By October 1777, the British were again at the door. Maj. Gen. John Vaughan landed royal troops at Kingston and set the place on fire. Our representatives saw him coming, fortunately, and decamped to Poughkeepsie in the nick of time.

Kingston is an appealing small city, though there's not much of tourist interest. The center of town is conveniently accessible via a four-lane arterial, marked N.Y. 28, that connects directly with exit 19 on the New York State Thruway. Turn right when you reach the Kingston end of this little spur of divided highway, you'll be right at the edge of a 17th-century district called the Stockade. This was formerly a fortification established by Dutch governor Peter Stuyvesant in 1658. Today the defending walls are gone, but the area is still filled with old stone houses, narrow Colonial-gauge streets, trees, attractive shops and restaurants, and a smattering of historic sites. Among the latter is the stone-walled, gable-roofed **Senate House State Historic Site,** the meeting place of the aforementioned first New York Senate. Located at 312 Fair St., Kingston (tel. 914/338-2786), it's a modest attraction but perhaps of interest to students of the Revolution.

If you've made the detour into the Stockade, a good place to eat is **Anthony's Uptown Restaurant,** 33–35 Crown St., at the corner of John Street (tel. 914/339-2184). The 18th-century stone building was originally built as the Kingston Academy. Today it houses a delightful restaurant justifiably popular with the locals. Chef/owner Tony Fraenkel, a graduate of the Culinary Institute of America, and wife/hostess Debbie have created an atmosphere that is quiet and elegant. Live piano music will accompany your meal on Saturday evening, and classical music is played quietly at other times. There is a bar at the back of the house where conversation seems easy and lively at all hours. The menu is international and creative, the portions are more than generous, and the wine list is well balanced, with both domestic and imported wines on hand. Paintings by local artists adorn the walls and are changed every six weeks. Only dinner is served; selections are mostly from $9 to $17 and might include poached salmon, scallops cappolini, or grilled baby lamb chops. A must for an appetizer (enough for two) is the artichoke-and-jalapeño dip with toasted pita bread. Dinner is from 5 to 10pm on Monday through Saturday; reservations are recommended. All major credit cards accepted.

For lighter fare just a couple blocks away, at 94 North Front St., try **Hoffman House** (tel. 914/338-2626). This 300-year-old stone house serves lunch Monday to Saturday from 11:30am to 5pm ($5 to $7) and dinner until 10:30pm ($9 to $15). All major credit cards accepted.

The most interesting part of Kingston is the southern end of the city, called the Rondout. The historic 19th-century waterfront was known as Kingston Landing until 1828, when the completion of the Delaware and Hudson Canal made the Rondout into a vital terminal port on the Hudson River. By the 1870s, the Rondout had become a congested commercial center with canalboats, steamboats, and trains transporting Pennsylvania coal, Ulster County bluestone, cement, and locally manufactured bricks.

Today this lively and much-restored neighborhood where the Rondout Creek and the Hudson River meet offers a number of interesting activities. Your first stop should be **Hudson River Maritime Center,** Rondout Landing (tel. 914/338-0071). The center is an outdoor and indoor museum featuring tours of the Rondout Lighthouse ($5). It's open daily from 11am to 5pm from May through October, with special educational programs throughout the year. The museum charges $1 for adults, 50¢ for children 6 to 12 (under 6 free), and $1.50 for senior citizens. Across the street is the **Trolley Museum of New York,** 98 East Strand St. (tel. 914/331-3399). This one features trolley rides, a selection of antique trolleys, and a visitors' center, which is open on Friday from June to August, from noon to 5pm, and on weekends from Memorial Day to Columbus Day. Admission is $3 for adults and $1 for kids.

If you want to get out on the Hudson River itself try the *Rip Van Winkle,* a 300-passenger vessel based out of the Rondout. This boat makes a number of excursions, including one to West Point and a Poughkeepsie minicruise, plus various lunch, dinner, and music cruises. Contact **Hudson River Cruises,** P.O. Box 333, Rifton, NY 12471 (tel. 914/255-6515), for schedule and price information.

For riverside dining, try **Mary P's,** 1 Broadway (tel. 914/338-0116). Named after a day steamer out of Kingston to New York, the restaurant features northern Italian cuisine and is open daily for lunch from 11am to 4pm ($4 to $10) and for dinner from 4:30 to 10pm ($9 to $20). Mary P's also offers a summer brunch and seasonal outside patio dining. All major credit cards accepted. Just around the corner you'll find **Armadillo Bar and Grill,** 97 Abeel St. (tel. 914/339-1550). This establishment specializes in southwestern cuisine like fajita steaks and shrimp-stuffed jalapeños served in a sophisticated café atmosphere. The grill is open Tuesday to Sunday for lunch from 11:30am to 3:30pm, for dinner from 4:30 to 11pm. All major credit cards accepted.

On the outskirts of Kingston on N.Y. 28, a stone's throw from Thruway exit 19, is the obligatory **Howard Johnson Motor Lodge** (tel. 914/338-4200) and **Ramada Inn** (tel. 914/339-3900). Hojo's has double-occupancy recession rates ranging from about $35 to $49. Do check the Ramada Super Saver rates of $39 to $69.

Kingston is the point of origin for a logical circular scenic route that swings through the very heart of the Catskills. The road is fast and the total round-trip distance is under 90 miles. Although I'll recommend numerous hotels and restaurants along this route, it's possible to swing right through it all on a day trip.

Of course, to do that is to lose considerable local flavor. What lured people to these mountains in the first place was a peculiar combination of remoteness and otherworldiness. The high-speed roads have changed all that. True, the scenery along these highways is at times absolutely gorgeous—clean serpentine pavements, frowning peaks, pine forests with rivers rushing over rocky shallows. But the real scenic treats lie deeper in the forest. For those you have to get out of the car and walk.

The rub is, how do you know where to walk? How do you find Kaaterskill Falls (a 260-foot drop—quite a sight) or Inspiration Point or Jimmy Dolan Notch or the Pine Orchard? To be honest, you need advance preparation that lies beyond the scope of this book. The New York State Department of Environmental Conservation can provide information. Contact the DEC Catskill Regional Office at 2176 Guilderland Ave., Schenectady, NY 12306 (tel. 518/382-0680). Full-length books exist for that purpose, a good one being *Fifty Hikes in the Hudson Valley* by Barbara McMartin and Peter Kick, published in 1985 by Backcountry Publications, Woodstock, VT 05091. This book will lead you knowledgeably to and around places like Vernooy Kill Falls, Mount Tremper, and Giant Ledge, Black Dome. The typical hike takes four to five hours, and the accompanying text and maps are usually easy to use and informative. These hikes, by the way, require neither pitons nor native guides. Wear good shoes, don't go alone, take matches, and be sure somebody knows where you're going (in case you get lost), and you'll be sufficiently prepared.

WOODSTOCK

This attractive village, located just across the boundary of the Catskill Park about 10 miles from Kingston, is only now reacquiring a New England look. For many years in the wake of the famous 1969 rock festival, Woodstock assumed a sort of tie-dyed disguise. Old wooden porches and gables around town turned purple and lavender while shop windows sprouted displays of unusual art and paraphernalia not often associated with upstate towns.

Woodstock, however, had a bohemian reputation long before anyone ever thought of rock and roll. In 1902, a pair of American artists named Bolton Brown and Hervey White met up with a fellow named Ralph Radcliffe Whitehead, known as the "wealthiest commoner in England." Brown and White brought Whitehead up to Woodstock and sold him on the idea of founding an artists' colony true to the aesthetic of Whitehead's idols, John Ruskin and William Morris. The result was **Byrdcliffe,** a 1,500-acre complex of 30 arts-and-crafts-ish buildings and a mile and a half of roads. By 1903, over 100 artist-types were busy laboring over looms and kilns, taking pictures, carving wood, and throwing pots. Many distinguished people

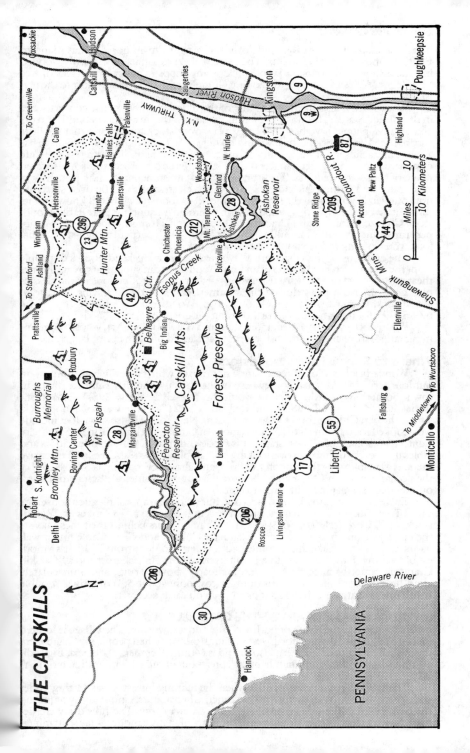

240 □ THE CATSKILLS

have been associated with Byrdcliffe over the years, from author Thomas Mann to FDR's confidant Harry Hopkins. The place still exists, on its now heavily wooded hillside a short drive outside Woodstock. Many shops in town have stacks of free "Byrdcliffe, A Brief History and Walking Guide" brochures, usually next to the register.

Woodstock is also the home of one of the oldest chamber music concert series in the United States. This was a 1916 undertaking of the busy Hervey Smith. Artists and creative people have been homing in on Woodstock for so long that it's little surprise the Woodstock Festival wound up here too. Today, although the village has a new Massachusetts-style serenity (a function of the rekindled interest in white clapboards and dark-green shutters), it is still home to a broad and sophisticated range of shops and galleries. These are quality establishments, dealing primarily in arts, crafts, and fashionable clothing. Girls with electric hair and tie-dyed shirts are not completely gone from the streets, but the new Woodstock is better known for its diminutive but trend-setting emporia with names like Laughing Bear Batik, Woodstock Chimes, White Mare, Crabtree & Evelyn, and Homecoming. Serious shoppers for women's clothes should take note: If you like a particular high-style casual look, you're going to *love* shopping in Woodstock.

The environs of the village are a favorite locale for weekend houses of people from the city, which fact helps explain how Woodstock can support its own summer theater. **River Arts Repertory** features revised original productions of the classics plus new American plays during the summer season at the Bearsville Theatre in Woodstock. Contact them at P.O. Box 1166, Woodstock, NY 12498 (tel. 914/679-5899), for information on forthcoming productions.

Woodstock even has a great radio station, **WDST** (100.1 FM), whose programming ranges from classical to rock, a neat trick carried off with exemplary skill.

Where to Stay & Eat in Woodstock

Woodstock has a lot of restaurants, not one of which is really bad. Burgers on outdoor terraces with a bar somewhere in the back is a familiar summer theme in town. Something a little different would be **The Little Bear,** 295 B Tinker St., Bearsville (tel. 914/679-8899), located on N.Y. 212 a mile west of Woodstock. This is the best Chinese food I've had in upstate New York. House specialties include wok-cooked foods from all the major regions of China—Peking, Hunan, Szechuan, Canton, and Shanghai. The restaurant is rustic and simple, with wooden floors and tables in a porch dining area overlooking the rambling Saw-Kill Creek. An extensive menu is available daily from noon to 10pm, and almost everything is $7 to $15. Try the no-name chicken ("no-name" because it's not on the menu). Reservations recommended. All major credit cards accepted.

There aren't any hotels in Woodstock, but there is an appealing guesthouse. It's called **Twin Gables,** located adjacent to the center of town at 73 Tinker St., Woodstock, NY 12498 (tel. 914/679-9479). "We're 50 years behind the times" boasts the rate sheet, and indeed they are. Claudette Colbert and Clark Gable might well have stayed in a place like this in some madcap Metro comedy from 1936. It's a modest old yellow frame house, with a porch overlooking Tinker Street and a "Catskill Grandma" interior filled with flowery wallpaper, flowery rugs, and immaculately clean little rooms. Share-the-bath doubles cost only about $50 nightly. A double with a private bath costs but $18 more. No credit cards accepted.

SHANDAKEN, THE HEART OF THE CATSKILLS

Shandaken is the name of both a village and a township. The village is located on N.Y. 28 about 30 miles northwest of Kingston. But when people say Shandaken, they usually refer to an area that also includes Mount Tremper, Phoenicia, Big Indian, and several other mountain hamlets spread out along a 20-mile stretch of N.Y. 28.

The township dates from 1804, when the tanning industry was getting under way. There were once seven big leather tanneries hereabouts, cumulatively requiring the bark of 20,000 cords of hemlock trees . . . *every year.* The hillsides were denuded with a ferocity that would warm the heart of many a modern-day strip miner.

So many skinned hemlocks were produced in the course of the first half of the 19th century that a wooden road, complete with toll booths, was laid all the way from Pine Hill to Kingston, a distance of 40 miles. When the last standing hemlock was debarked, the locals, as is so often the case, turned to tourism. There were never any great mountain hotels out here, as there were closer to the Hudson. Instead, there were rooming houses, some of which still stand, in varying states of repair and devoted to varying different uses.

Once in a while even the most jaded traveler stumbles upon an experience that is the more surprising and delightful for being so unexpected. Such is the Shandaken area, often referred to as the **French Catskills.** It is a modern anomaly that spectacular French bourgeois cooking, as good as anything in Paris or Lyons, is available in the middle of the Catskills. The *patrons* seem collectively to have acquired a taste for modern American building materials. Most of their restaurants occupy structures decorated on the outside with textured panels and on the inside with fake wood paneling. But the dining rooms at night are charming withal, and the food is famous.

You could easily spend several days here, hiking in the woods and sampling a different excellent local restaurant every night. Or you could combine a single meal with a day trip from Kingston.

Where to Stay & Eat in Shandaken

My favorite French retreat is **Auberge des 4 Saisons** on N.Y. 42 (½ mile from N.Y. 28), Shandaken, NY (tel. 914/688-2223). During my last visit the modest inn was hosting a birthday party for a chef from one of the other French restaurants. The simple, unpretentious meals might include main courses like filet mignon with sauce béarnaise, veal in Madeira sauce, or rabbit in white wine. They cost about $11 to $18. Dinner is served from 6 to 10pm daily in summer and from 5 to 9:30pm on Friday, Saturday, and Sunday in winter. Not only does the Auberge boast a fine French restaurant, but it also includes a pool and a tennis court, plus facilities for bocce, badminton, volleyball, and croquet—not to mention a variety of lodging options. The renovated Chalet features spacious motel-style rooms with private baths, TVs, and balconies. Cabins with private baths are located near the pool, and additional very simple rooms are available in the inn itself. The entire experience, which includes accommodations, two meals, and all the facilities, costs from $70 to $100 per day per person. All major credit cards accepted.

La Duchesse Anne, 4 Miller Rd., Mount Tremper, NY 12464 (tel. 914/688-5260), occupies an untouched antique rooming house by the side of a river in a woody glen. It's complete with ancient wallpaper, floors that creak and sigh, and wood stoves that still produce heat. The big old-fashioned dining room has low ceilings supported by dark-wood columns, dark-green wallpaper, an elaborate old wood stove, and flocks of tables covered with crisp white cloths. Lunch selections are light, with salads, smoked salmon, and perhaps an omelet costing only $3 to $6. Also available are numerous crêpes and quiches. At dinner, duck flambé, veal scallop normande, or poached trout with white-butter sauce will typically run between $12 and $21. Lunch is served only on weekends, from 10am to 2pm on Saturday and to 4pm on Sunday. Dinner is available from 5:30 until 9:30pm on most weekdays, and until 11pm on Friday, Saturday, and holidays. Closed Tuesday during summer, and Tuesday and Wednesday during winter. Above the dining room are 17 rudimentary guest rooms that share baths (one bath per three rooms). These cost between $35 and $60 per night double occupancy. Children and pets are welcome. All major credit cards accepted.

Yvonne's, on N.Y. 28, Phoenicia, NY 12464 (tel. 914/688-7340), is a wonderful French roadside café. Originally a drive-in offering quiches, roast duck, and the traditional hamburger, Yvonne's has become very popular; it seats up to 60. The waitresses all wear traditional clothing from the Périgord region in France. The food is highly acclaimed and includes such dishes as a venison plate with truffles, wild boar, rabbit, salmon rillettes, and French marinated herring. Dinner is about $15 and can be enjoyed any summer evening (except Tuesday and Wednesday) from 4 to 10pm. During fall and spring, the restaurant is open on weekends only; closed in winter. No credit cards accepted.

Val D'Isère, on N.Y. 28 in Big Indian, NY (tel. 914/254-4646), is located in an old Victorian house that's been Swiss-alpined on the outside. The dining room is bright and cheerful, with acoustic ceilings, faux beams, a mirrored fountain wall on one side, lots of windows on the other, abundant hanging plants, and a capacity of 65. Only dinner is served, year-round, on Wednesday to Monday. Typical selections include grilled salmon, sautéed tournedos of beef with bordelaise sauce, grilled filet of beef with green-peppercorn sauce, and chicken with raspberry vinegar sauce, priced from about $10 to $16. With an appetizer and dessert, neither of which you'll want to skip, dinner will cost about twice that. There are also six guest rooms available with shared baths for $40 a night. All major credit cards accepted.

Rudi's Big Indian, on N.Y. 28 in Big Indian (tel. 914/254-4005), is something completely different. It sits in solitary splendor just outside the two-building town of Big Indian. The restaurant is a modern place with a Frank Lloyd Wright look. Diners have a choice of several appealing places to eat: There are a great outdoor deck with awnings and umbrella tables, a plant-filled "conservatory," and a cathedral-ceilinged main dining room furnished with antique Victorian tables facing walls of glass. The lunch menu offers quiches, burgers, chicken wings, pot pies, omelets, and more, for about $5 to $9. A la carte dinner selections such as hot broccoli salad, turkey scaloppine, broiled sirloin, fresh salmon, and grilled pork chop mostly run from $12 to $20. Open noon to 9:30pm daily from July 4 until Labor Day; closed Tuesday and Wednesday the rest of the year, plus the month of November and part of December. All major credit cards accepted.

Sweet Sue's, on Main Street in Phoenicia (tel. 914/688-7852), is an old-fashioned small-town restaurant whose house specialty is pancakes. Blueberry, peach, whole-wheat, or apple varieties of same cost about $3.50 per stack. Alternatively, you might try Nana's health-bread french toast. There are also sandwiches of turkey, roast beef, and tuna, plus chili and homemade soup, priced at under $4. Only breakfast and lunch are served, in a little room with flowered cloths and white wood chairs. Open daily from 7am to 3pm. No credit cards accepted.

Shandaken Inn, on N.Y. 28 just west of the intersection of N.Y. 42, Shandaken, NY 12480 (tel. 914/688-5100), is a beautiful old vine-clad building nestled amid lawns and gardens just outside the village of Shandaken. This former golf club, built in the 1920s, sports a delightful pool; a tennis court; a rushing brook; lovely stone-flagged terraces furnished with umbrella tables and chairs; and a handsome lodgelike living room complete with fireplaces, wing chairs, pine paneling, and an adjacent bar. The 12 rooms are spotlessly clean, cozy, decorated with random antiques, and looking like the comfortable guest rooms in someone's house. During the week that's exactly what the place is. But on Friday and Saturday two people can rent one of the attractive rooms for between $195 and $225 nightly ($170 if there's no private bath), including breakfast and dinner. Cuisine is French (as is the proprietress), and the Saturday-night meal is like an elegant country-house party. It usually ends up with dancing in the bar. This is the best-looking place in the area. Reservations required; no children. No credit cards accepted.

Right on N.Y. 28 in the steep valley that leads from Mount Tremper to Phoenicia is **Mount Pleasant Lodge,** N.Y. 28, Phoenicia, NY 12464 (tel. 914/688-2278). This is actually a little complex of log-cabin-style buildings that includes a 12-unit motel, 20 duplexes ($120), a bar, even a pool. The well-kept guest rooms are surprisingly big, with shag carpets, natural-log walls, private baths, and color TVs. They're quite good looking. Double-occupancy rates are a reasonable $70 nightly, $15 less during the week. The moderately priced café serves home-cooked breakfast, lunch, and dinner and includes a very congenial bar. On Saturday nights there's even live music. All major credit cards accepted.

My favored non-French restaurant in this neck of the woods is the **Catskill Rose,** on N.Y. 212, Mount Tremper (tel. 914/688-7100). The last time I was there they had a full brass Dixieland band that followed one of the best dinners of smoked duck with plum sauce I've ever had (the only one, but I'd go back for more). The folks here have wonderful vegetarian dishes, as well as their own smoked fish, fowl, and meat. The menu is sort of American eclectic and is served Wednesday through Sunday from 5 to 10:30pm, with a Sunday brunch offered from 10:30am to 3pm.

Dinner will cost between $11 and $16, with brunch about $9 to $11. All major credit cards accepted.

THE ROUTE TO HUNTER

After you've explored the Shandaken area to your satisfaction, find N.Y. 42 (it intersects N.Y. 28 at the village of Shandaken) and head north to Lexington. This is a particularly scenic road with lovely prospects of rushing rivers and craggy mountaintops. The village of **Lexington,** 11 miles from Shandaken, is a nice-looking hamlet with some fabulous old unrenovated Victorian buildings. In the middle of it you'll cross a bridge over the Schoharie Creek, shortly after which you'll arrive at the intersection of N.Y. 23A. Get on 23A eastbound toward Hunter.

Before coming into Hunter, you'll see the **Baptist Ukrainian Church** on the north side of the road. This wooden confection is straight out of a Russian fairy tale. It's also about the last good-looking building you'll see for the next couple of miles. **Hunter,** it would seem, has been infected with a dangerous strain of the "Cutesy Swiss" virus. It's the rare house or store that has escaped a modernization characterized by absurd cut-out eaves, shutters with heart-shaped holes in them, and half-timbering that is all too plainly concocted of one-by-fours tacked onto the facade with roofing nails. The ubiquitous accompaniment to all this seems to be untidy parking lots and dispirited-looking malls.

Things do look better in winter with three feet of snow on the ground and the famous **Hunter Mountain Ski Area** in full swing. Whatever the aesthetic drawbacks of the village of Hunter, there's no doubt that Hunter Mountain has the best skiing in the Catskills. The facilities include 37 trails, a 1,600-foot vertical drop, 17 lifts with a capacity of 17,000 skiers per hour, base and summit lodges, plus rentals, a nursery, and package deals. The entrance to the ski area is smack in the center of the village. For complete information on skiing at Hunter, contact Hunter Mountain, Hunter, NY 12442 (tel. 518/263-4223, or toll free 800/FOR-SNOW). There are other ski areas in the Catskills, information on which can be obtained by writing to Greene County Promotion Dept., P.O. Box 527, Catskill, NY 12414 (tel. 518/943-3223). The *I Love New York Greene County Travel Guide* describes them all.

During summer you can ride up Hunter Mountain on the **Hunter Mountain Skyride,** the longest, highest chair lift in the Catskills. The views are pretty spectacular, and the cost is a reasonable $7 for adults, $3.50 for kids 6 to 12, and $1 for little ones 5 and under. The Skyride operates daily (weather permitting) from June 28 to Labor Day, on weekends only in spring and fall. Hours are 11am to 4:30pm. Call 518/263-4223 for further information.

Hunter is also widely known for its **Summer Festivals,** which run the gamut from the German Alps Festival to the National Polka Festival, to the Mountain Eagle Authentic Native American Indian Festival, to the International Celtic Festival, with several stops in between. Program and ticket information can be obtained from Exposition Planners, Bridge Street, Hunter, NY 12442 (tel. 518/263-3800).

Ten or so more miles on N.Y. 23A will bring you to the little village of **Tannersville,** a town of false-fronted Victorian buildings with an almost Western look. After the age of the tanneries this area became a center of upscale summer development, much of which still exists. Several private residential parks, their roads barred to nonmembers, are clustered around Tannersville. The swellest is **Onteora Park,** a former artists' colony that became almost posh around the turn of the century. Fine mansions still line Onteora Road, north of the Tannersville light. The park itself, centered around a clubhouse, golf links, and a private lake, is filled with picturesque cliff-hanging dwellings designed in rustic mountain style. However, it's not open to the public. Neither is **Twilight Park,** located east of the nearby village of Haines Falls on steep slopes overlooking Kaaterskill Clove. Twilight isn't quite as luxe as Onteora, but some of its houses have wonderful views of **Kaaterskill Falls.** You can't see the falls from the road, even though they're only half a mile from 23A. The access trail joins 23A beside a hairpin curve about a mile east of Haines Falls. It's marked, but first-timers might have trouble finding it.

Instead of hiking you might want to rent a horse. The **Silver Springs Ranch,** on

N.Y. 16, Tannersville (tel. 518/589-5559, or toll free 800/258-2624), can include you on a guided trail ride anytime from 9am to 5pm. The cost is about $18 per hour.

Where to Stay & Eat in the Hunter/Tannersville Area

Best idea for an informal meal in the area is the curiously named **Last Chance Antiques and Cheeze Café,** Main Street (N.Y. 23A), Tannersville (tel. 518/589-6424). They do actually *sell* antiques, and there's not an inch of wall space that isn't covered with some item of Victorian-era bric-a-brac, a gilt-framed picture, a hunk of imported cheese, a barrel of something-or-other, or a package of gourmet food. Like Tannersville itself, this establishment has a faint Western atmosphere, reminiscent of a general store in some 19th-century Colorado boom town. Besides gourmet items, the Last Chance has a varied menu that includes cheese fondue, pot pie, pastrami sandwiches, nachos, French onion soup, yogurt fruit salad, fresh pressed cider, chili, and melted brie on raisin pumpernickel, at reasonable prices. Expect to pay about $5 for a hefty sandwich and up to about $8 for a house specialty. Usually the cheese-cake's terrific. A narrow porch out front is ideal for summer dining. Open daily from 10am until 7pm. All major credit cards accepted.

The nicest spot in the area for dinner, and indeed for staying overnight, is **Redcoat's Return,** Dale Lane (off Platte Clove Road, N.Y. 16), Elka Park, NY 12427 (tel. 518/589-6379). This square four-story clapboard building surrounded by broad porches was built as a rooming house in 1912. The present English owner (hence the name Redcoat's Return) has revamped and redecorated the place into a cozy and comfortable inn/restaurant. The Victorian eclectic lobby is decorated with rich dark colors, a moosehead over the fireplace, a Chinese screen, books aplenty, a piano, and a fish tank. The 14 rooms are small but nicely turned out with painted iron beds and pretty patterned wallpaper. About half have private baths and rent for $95 nightly, including a full breakfast. Skip the private bath and the double-occupancy rate drops to $85. On holiday and winter weekends there's a minimum stay, so inquire in advance. Alternatively, you might make a reservation just for dinner. Roast duckling with orange sauce, broiled sirloin, and poached filet of sole, served in atmospheric surroundings, cost between $15 and $18 à la carte. To find Redcoat's, follow N.Y. 16 south from the Tannersville light for about 4 miles to Dale Lane on your right. You can see the inn from here, sharing its meadowy valley with an aluminum-sided family resort which, once you pull into Redcoat's, becomes magically invisible. All major credit cards accepted.

Another place for old-world (in this case "mittel-European") charm and hearty food is **Deer Mountain Inn,** P.O. Box 443, Route 25, Tannersville, NY 12485 (tel. 518/589-6268). The inn features a panoramic Catskill mountain view and offers seven well-appointed guest rooms, all with private baths and color TVs. Overnight rates (including a full breakfast) run from $75 to $110, double occupancy, the latter for one of the rooms with a fireplace. Dinner, served in the downstairs dining room from 6 to 10pm on Wednesday to Monday, has a set price of $19.95 per person, and it's famous in the area. What's for dinner? Masses of Polish sausage, chicken, lamb chops, pork chops, steak, stroganoff, you name it, plus bouquet platters of fresh vegetables. After one of owner Danielle Gortel's meals, an evening walk is definitely in order. AE, MC, and V accepted.

Also useful to know about in the Hunter/Tannersville area is **Hunter Mountain Lodging Bureau,** on N.Y. 23A, Hunter, NY 12442 (tel. 518/263-4208), a free central booking agency in a small shopping plaza opposite the ski area entrance. The staff can book you into any one of 20 participating area hotels, motels, inns, and condos, plus a collection of private chalets that rent to transients. Expect to pay about $90 to $150 nightly, double occupancy, often with a minimum stay required. Someone's at the phone every day from 10am until 6pm.

AN EXCURSION TO WINDHAM

Everything that is ramshackle in Hunter has been polished and perfected in nearby Windham, a mere 8 miles to the north via Route 296 to Route 23. The major attraction is skiing at the Windham Mountain ski area, formerly a private club supported by the likes of an ex–New York governor, Hugh Carey, and the Kennedys.

Known today as **Ski Windham,** Windham, NY 12496 (tel. 518/734-4300, or toll free 800/729-7549), the facilities and their ambience are among the most modern and upscale on the eastern seaboard. Rental facilities are great; the staff is polite and professional; there are a children's learning center and good beginner areas; and even the food at the new three-story lodge is good. Windham is very much of a family resort; the hotdoggers and party animals are all, with few exceptions, down at Hunter Mountain. Windham is just as pleasant to visit in summer, when you can play golf and/or go horseback riding. Even just passing through and having a meal is a delight.

Where to Stay in Windham

The nicest bed-and-breakfast I've ever been in is here in Windham: **Albergo Allegria** ("inn of happiness"), located on Route 296, Windham, NY 12496 (tel. 518/734-5560; fax 518/734-5570). It is a sprawling wooden Queen Anne/ Victorian affair whose 20 rooms, with modern baths and color cable TVs, are decorated tastefully with period antiques. There's a large and peaceful lobby ideal for reading, plus a second-floor videotape library and VCR. Breakfast, the only meal served (and only to guests), is a magnificent spread of real Belgian waffles, gourmet omelets, and the like that would put most Sunday brunches to shame. Standard rooms, depending on size, season, and location, cost from $45 to $125, with suites from $75 to $175 per night, double occupancy. All major credit cards accepted.

Alternately, there's **Hotel Vienna,** Route 296, P.O. Box 487, Windham, NY 12496 (tel. 518/734-5300), a contemporary bilevel structure that is exceptionally clean and quiet. No drunken college students roaming these halls! Decor consists of textured-plaster walls, modern wooden ceiling beams, imported textiles, lace curtains, and a well-ordered European ambience. Each of the 30 rooms has two queen-size beds, a color TV, and a private bath and costs from $90 to $120 nightly (the latter for a room with a Jacuzzi), double occupancy. AE, MC, and V accepted.

On the eastern outskirts of town is **Point Lookout Mountain Inn,** Route 23, East Windham, NY 12439 (tel. 518/734-3381). As the name implies, there is a view, and a spectacular one at that; I could see five states. There are 15 rooms with private baths and color TVs; as long as you're in an even-numbered room, you'll get a pretty great "valley" view. A "raid-the-refrigerator" breakfast is included in the nightly charge of $65 to $95, double occupancy. All major credit cards accepted.

Where to Eat in Windham

For German-Swiss alpine cuisine, which seems somehow appropriate in these surroundings, try **Chalet Fondue** on Route 296 in Windham (tel. 518/734-4650). The atmospheric decor is highlighted by rough stucco walls, wine barrels, and tiled stoves. Authentic specialties run the gamut from a pair of wieners ($7.50), to Swiss *geschnetzeltes* ($13.50), to a romantic champagne cheese fondue for two ($26). More standard fare is also on the menu, for the less adventurous. Open for dinner only on Wednesday through Monday from 4 to 10pm, from 2pm on Sunday and holidays. All major credit cards accepted.

Traditional American fare can be had at **Chetford's Sir Sirloin Room** on Route 23 in Windham (tel. 518/734-3322). Steak and beef in various permutations, plus broiled seafood, veal, chicken, and pork chops, usually cost from $12 to $20. The dining room has a stone fireplace, stucco walls with dark-wood trim, the occasional wagon wheel, and a pleasant family atmosphere. Open daily for dinner only from 4 to 10pm. AE, MC, and V accepted.

Opposite Albergo Allegria, in a century-old building on Route 296, is **La Grigilia Ristorante** (tel. 518/734-4499). Northern Italian and American classics are the order of the day here, served at tables with mauve cloths beneath stained-glass panels. Pasta, shrimp scampi, and the expected veal and chicken dishes cost between $10 and $18. "Early birds," from 4 to 6pm on Monday through Friday, can order from the same menu for about one-third less. A lavish Sunday brunch is available from 11am to 3pm and costs $14.95 for adults and $7.95 for kids under 10. Regular dinner hours are Sunday to Friday until 9:30pm, until 10:30pm on Saturday. All major credit cards accepted.

FROM THE MOUNTAINS TO THE HUDSON AND ATHENS

Route 23 eastbound leaves Windham and within about 20 or so miles reaches the western bank of the Hudson River. Shortly after passing the junction with the New York State Thruway (I-87) and before crossing the river, take Route 385 northbound to the delicious village of Athens (pop. 1,700).

Located on the west bank of the river directly opposite the city of Hudson, Athens is a place that both progress and gentrification, with their attendant pros and cons, seem to have overlooked entirely. It is a village of wonderful 18th-century stone houses, grand Georgian and Federal riverview mansions, and an intact Victorian commercial center.

Notable among the latter structures is **Stewart House Inn,** 2 N. Water St., Athens, NY 12015 (tel. 518/945-1357). Besides architecture, this inn offers a wonderfully gemütlich atmosphere that captures what is most appealing and romantic about the Hudson River Valley. It is filled with antiques, Oriental rugs, and 19th-century faux-grained walls. You can have Sunday brunch or dinner either in the bar with its great view of the Hudson or in a separate formal dining room. Cuisine is continental American. The bistro menu in the bar doesn't list anything for over $10. In the dining room, main dishes like basil agnolotti or the quail-and-venison game combo run from about $14 to $19. You can eat in the bar on Sunday and Tuesday to Friday from 6pm until midnight (from 5pm on Saturday); dining-room hours are 3:30 to 10pm on Tuesday to Sunday. Upstairs are five delightful antique-filled rooms, with private baths, that cost a maximum of $88 for a double on the weekend, less during the week (negotiate—they're flexible). MC and V accepted.

---

3. The Resorts

South of the Catskill park, near the towns of Monticello (pop. 6,300), Ellenville (pop. 4,400), and Liberty (pop. 4,300), are the famous Catskill resorts. In many minds these huge establishments are synonymous with the very name Catskill. However, they aren't in the Catskill Mountains at all.

To be sure, the terrain around Monticello is hilly and quite beautiful. There was a boarding-house era up here too, at the end of the 19th and in the early 20th centuries. Except that these boarding houses, instead of closing down as the present century progressed, kept growing bigger and bigger. After World War II, they blossomed into modern Miami Beach–style behemoths with private golf courses, private lakes, sometimes a dozen tennis courts, indoor pools, outdoor pools, ice-skating rinks, steamrooms, riding stables, bike trails, ski slopes, health clubs, planned activities for tots, planned activities for teens, and in fact everything else they could think of to attract guests.

Woody Allen's movie *Annie Hall* begins with a great gag about two elderly Jewish ladies at a Catskill resort. "The food is so bad!" complains the first. "And they don't give you enough!" replies the second. This joke, which is actually the exact opposite of the true situation, still serves as an amusing introduction to those specific hallmarks of the Catskill resort experience. The first is the hotel nightclub with the Catskill comedian. Some of these clubs really do feature first-rank talent, names everyone's heard. The second is the hotel dining room where you can (and indeed you are urged to) eat everything that isn't nailed down. Food is something of a preoccupation in this neck of the woods (certainly it's no place to go on a diet). The third is socialization. Hotel blurbs all tout a fairly dizzying array of activities that will keep you, your kids, your parents, and all your friends busy from the instant you set foot on the manicured grounds.

In recent years the big resorts have suffered declining popularity. They are not, I'm sorry to say, particularly beautiful. To many people this makes no difference. As long as the place is well kept and has a ton of facilities, they won't mind. But the national resurgence of interest in historic preservation and finer craftsmanship, plus the development of nearby Atlantic City, NJ, into a casino center, has left many of the Catskill resorts in the wrong court. Some have turned themselves into part-time "conference centers," others have begun developing bits of their land into vacation condominiums, while still others have turned into religious or meditation centers, and many have just gone belly-up.

It still remains possible, however, to enjoy a traditional Catskill resort holiday, complete with more food than you dreamed you could eat, daytimes filled with poolside lounging and planned activities, and nighttimes spent in a glitzy nightclub chortling over Borscht Belt gags. It's estimated that there are still 198 holes of golf in the immediate environs of Monticello, plus 32 pools (of the immense Olympic variety) and 154 tennis courts.

Since the last edition of this book, several resorts have fallen by the way. Most hotels that remain are still managed by the families that founded them. These hotels (with their toll-free telephone numbers) are the **Concord** (800/431-3850), **Nevele Hotel** (800/647-6000), **Kutsher's Country Club,** (800/431-1273), **Fallsview Resort and Country Club** (800/822-8439), **Raleigh Resort and Country Club** (800/446-4003), **Villa Roma Resort and Country Club** (800/533-6767), **The New Brown's Hotel** (800/3-BROWNS), and **Pines Resort Hotel** (800/36-PINES). The Concord is probably the most elaborate of the bunch. Typical daily rates, including three full meals, range between $85 and $120 per person, with significant discounts for five-night or weekly stays. These rates are discounted by another 10% to 20% during autumn, winter, and spring.

If this all sounds interesting, I suggest that you phone one or more of the above establishments and request individual brochures and rate sheets.

THE CAPITAL DISTRICT

1. GREATER ALBANY
2. TROY
3. SARATOGA SPRINGS
4. THE ROAD WEST—COOPERSTOWN & CAZENOVIA

New York City may not be the "real" New York. But Albany most certainly is. Besides containing the Capitol itself, the Capital District boasts fine shopping; many historic sightseeing attractions; and exotic Saratoga Springs, cash-rich home of racing touts and dancing tutus.

1. Greater Albany

Henry Hudson never made it to China, but in the fall of 1609 he did reach Albany. Today's charming little city holds the distinction of being both the capital of New York State and the oldest permanent settlement in the 13 colonies. From its early days as an important trading post, Albany has evolved into a major regional financial center as well as the eye of New York's hurricanes of political power and influence.

Twenty years ago Albany had fallen pretty low. The story is a familiar one of post-war population shifts, boom development in adjoining suburban areas, and destructive downtown "urban renewal." But if ever a city has had magic dust sprinkled on it, that city is Albany. It seems like three-quarters of the downtown area, blocks rich with 19th-century architectural fabric, is now protected by local landmark laws. I've never seen so much restoration under way in one place. The result is an exceedingly attractive and livable urban setting, graced with magnificent architecture and considerable amenities. The city isn't expensive, doesn't sprawl, and is fun and easy to explore.

ORIENTATION
Albany is disproportionately sophisticated for its size, a fact best illustrated by the skyline of the **Governor Nelson A. Rockefeller Empire State Plaza.** This immense complex of 1960s marble-clad government buildings is clearly visible from many miles away. You'd never expect anything so big in a city of 102,000 people.

The Empire State Plaza and the **State Capitol** sit right at the heart of the town. **State Street** runs about half a dozen blocks from the Capitol steps to the Hudson. On State and adjacent cross streets is where you'll find the biggest and finest con

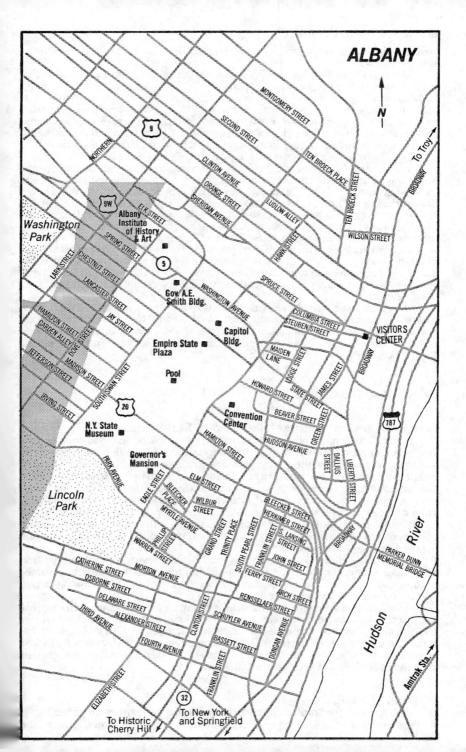

mercial buildings, as well as the local Hilton hotel and the heart of the downtown business district.

Albany is situated on the west bank of the Hudson River and connected to the other shore by a free bridge, which is part of I-90. A spur of the Interstate system, **I-787** runs right along the Hudson shoreline, depriving the city of its waterfront but delivering traffic from I-90 in the north and I-87 (New York State Thruway) in the south to the very center of town with amazing efficiency. There is ample parking underneath the Empire State Plaza. As a matter of fact, there is free street parking all over the city, including angle parking ıght on State Street. Driving a car around is actually a cinch, at least when the state legislature isn't in session.

Immediately bordering the business center are tree-lined residential streets consisting of small-scale 19th-century brick and brownstone rowhouses. There are six separate historic districts adjoining downtown, about which I'll say more later. Behind the Capitol itself, located on an extension of State Street, are the finest of the in-town mansions. Then comes **Washington Park,** an 84-acre preserve designed by the ubiquitous Frederick Law Olmsted. Beyond the park the city becomes more architecturally modest and soon tapers off into suburbs.

Today's elite live north of I-90 in neighboring **Loudonville.** The huge discount shopping malls for which Albany is famous are located in the environs of **Wolf Road,** a few miles west of town at the intersection of I-90 and I-87. Interesting restaurants and bars are scattered all over the city. The roster of interesting hotels, alas, is not extensive.

I loved the street names in Albany. For roadways running north and south they went in big for birds: Quail, Partridge, Lark, Dove, Swan. The east-west streets today bear the names of Founding Fathers (Jefferson, Washington, Hamilton, Madison, Jay), but before the Revolution they bore names like Mink, Otter, Snipe, Lion, and Tiger. Elk Street is about the only one left.

SIGHTS & ATTRACTIONS

Governor Nelson A. Rockefeller Empire State Plaza

It cost $1 billion (in the 1960s) to construct this multibuilding office plaza situated smack in the center of town. The first impression is of blinding light, a result of acre upon acre of pure-white marble gleaming in the sun. The plaza has an outdoor pedestrian concourse that extends a full quarter mile south from the side of the State Capitol. Lining it is a series of stylistically unified white-marble office buildings, dazzling reflecting pools, trees clipped into cubes, occasional outdoor art, and nice views of the city and the forests beyond. Actually it looks a lot like the capital of some Third World country determined to prove its worth in the modern world. The architecture may be a little sterile, especially in contrast to the older stone confections nearby, but it sure is impressive.

The tallest building on the plaza is the **Corning Tower,** notable for its free 42nd-floor **observation deck.** Below grade is the **Indoor Concourse,** an awesomely long enclosed mall lined with striking modern art of the 50-foot-long-canvas school and numerous shops and offices.

A walk up and down the plaza is an absolute must for all visitors. A free map of the place, with detailed descriptions of the buildings and all that goes on within them, may be obtained at the **Visitor Assistance Office** (tel. 518/474-2418), located at the north end of the main Underground Concourse (which is actually just across the street from the State Capitol Building). Among the buildings descʳıbed in the Empire State Plaza Guide are the following:

ESIPA at the Egg

ESIPA stands for **Empire State Institute for the Performing Arts;** the Egg is that peculiar sort-of-egg-shaped concrete structure next to the Corning Tower. The

Egg has been acclaimed as the most accessible theater in the United States. Which means, I suppose, that the programming appeals to a broad spectrum of the population. Inside its curvaceous concrete walls is a 900-seat auditorium where anyone from the Alvin Ailey dance company to Chuck Mangione, from Wynton Marsalis to the Boys Choir of Harlem, from Bobby Short to the cast of *Les Misérables,* is likely to be performing. Ticket prices vary but are quite reasonable by Manhattan standards. For information on current productions, call the Visitor Assistance Office at 518/ 474-2418.

New York State Museum

The days of museum corridors lined with cases full of historic "artifacts" are over, at least here. The New York State Museum is more of an entertainment experience than anything else. Located in a self-consciously modern building covered with marble louvers and located at the south end of the Empire State Plaza, it consists of two very large halls devoted respectively to the "Adirondack Wilderness" and the "New York Metropolis." A third hall is dedicated to New York's "Native People."

This is a very slick installation indeed, one consisting of artifacts, photos, dioramas, scale reconstructions, and filmclips. Visitors advance through the huge darkened exhibition halls like Hansel and Gretel in the forest. Around every corner there's another exhibit bathed in dramatic light, augmented as often as not with sound effects from bird calls to clanking subway trains. A life-size diorama depicts a logjam in a mountain stream, right down to real water. Over on the New York City side is an astonishing cutaway scale model of Grand Central Terminal, a 1925 Fifth Avenue bus, an entire subway car with nearby monitors that show a video called *Working the A Train,* and a collection of antique fire engines.

The museum has additional exhibits, but these are the highlights. It's open daily from 10am to 5pm, and admission is free. For further information, call 518/474-5877. The main entrance is on Madison Avenue, which is one floor below the open-air concourse at the south end of the Empire State Plaza. Plenty of parking is available in the museum's adjacent lot.

State Capitol

This fantastical pink-granite monster was started in 1867 and completed in 1899. It then burned in 1911 but was restored by 1914 to even greater grandeur. It sits at the head of State Street, the apotheosis of everything that's wrong but still lovable about Victorian architecture. After years of neglect and abuse, it's undergoing a piecemeal restoration.

The State Capitol has more types of arches and columns and pilasters than you can name. Its interior is the definition of Edwardian opulence, especially the restored **Senate Chamber,** the faintly Byzantine **Assembly Chamber,** and the famous **"Million Dollar Staircase."** This latter feature is located on the western side of the building and is a perfect maze of intricately carved granite stairs and landings. They crisscross their way upward in a most leisurely fashion inside a splendid interior space lit by sinuous old bronze fixtures.

Free tours of the Capitol leave daily on the hour from 9am until 4pm from the **tour reception area** located on the east side of the main floor. Alternatively, you can pick up a tour leaving from the Visitor Assistance Office at the north end of the Empire State Plaza's Main Underground Concourse. You can also just poke around by yourself. For more information, call Visitor Assistance at 518/474-2418.

Walking Around Downtown

The year 1986 was Albany's tricentennial, an event celebrated among other things by publication of an excellent small guidebook titled *Albany, Still Making History, 1686-1986.* If you can't find a copy in bookstores (it was a promotional piece without traditional bookstore distribution), you might try the aforementioned Visitor Assistance Office in the Empire State Plaza Main Concourse or the "I Love New York" office (tel. 518/474-4116) on the mezzanine of One Commerce Plaza (a modern office building adjacent to the State Capitol on the corner of Washington and Swan).

The point of having this guide is its excellent walking tours. The chapter by Judith Botch of the Historic Albany Foundation divides downtown Albany into three tours: State Street Hill, Capitol Hill, and Residential State Street. They're informative, easy to follow, and lots of fun. If you are unable to locate a copy of *Albany, Still Making History,* you can still stroll down State Street and admire its provincial grandeur. Perhaps most grandiose after the Capitol itself is the Flemish palace at the foot of the hill at State and Broadway. It's now the Central Administration Building of the State University of New York but it was built as the central office of the Delaware and Hudson Railroad. Its picturesque tower is one of Albany's most appealing landmarks. Immediately to the north of the Capitol building, radiating from the intersection of Eagle and Elk Streets, is **Capitol Hill.** This area abounds with fine 19th-century row houses and public buildings. Elk between Eagle and Hawk is particularly interesting. The 1883 **Albany City Hall** on the corner of Eagle and Pine is architect Henry Hobson Richardson at his "most Romanesque." It sports yet another of Albany's famous towers.

You should also take a stroll along the three-block stretch of **Upper State Street** between Swan and Northern Boulevard. This is an upper-class late-Victorian district of attached town houses. Not many are used as private houses anymore, but the streetscape is wonderfully intact and gives a good sense of the texture of upscale provincial life a century ago.

Albany Institute of History and Art

Set back on a lawn two blocks from the Capitol, this elegant old-fashioned museum eschews the glitz and showmanship of new-style display "environments." What it offers instead is a jewellike collection of local portraits, silver, furniture, and the like, served up in an atmosphere of patrician calm. There is some really exquisite stuff in here, from Dutch period chests and chairs to pictures of the imperious old aristocrats who owned them. It's quite interesting to look at the faces of all the Ten Broecks, Schuylers, Van Rensselaers, Wendells, and so forth who ran the world hereabouts in centuries past. Total gallery area isn't too big, but lovers of beautiful things can spend many hours in this justly famous local institution at 125 Washington Ave. (tel. 518/463-4478). Hours are Tuesday through Friday from 10am to 5pm and Saturday and Sunday from noon to 5pm. Admission is free.

Albany Urban Cultural Park Visitors Center

This ambitious orientation center is really an Albany city family album. It's a photo museum of what Albany used to look like, and if you've enjoyed exploring today's city and already gotten the feel of it, then you'll doubtless get a kick out of this collection of old maps and photos. There are great shots of the old D&H Building, the State Street banks during the 1920s, Union Station as it looked when trains still stopped there (current rail service to Albany terminates on the other side of the Hudson in Rensselaer), Richardson's City Hall upon completion in 1883, plus the current renewal districts as they looked before they needed renewal. The display is cleverly mounted complete with moving parts that visitors can operate. But, for me, it was the old pictures that really made it fun.

The Urban Cultural Park and its new **Henry Hudson Planetarium** are located in Quackenbush Square, the rather grand name of a cluster of restored commercial buildings located on Broadway immediately north of the exit ramp from I-787. The closest city cross street is Clinton Avenue. The museum is free and open weekdays from 10am until 4pm, and also weekends in summer. For information, call 518/434-5132.

Four Historic Mansions

The first is the **Schuyler Mansion,** called originally the Pastures and built in 1761 by the aristocratic Philip Schuyler. Alexander Hamilton married a Schuyler daughter in this house; Gen. John ("Gentleman Johnny") Burgoyne was a houseguest-cum-prisoner after the British debacle at Saratoga; Washington and Franklin were guests in their time, as were most of the prominent people who passed through Albany. The Georgian house is beautifully restored, filled with original furnishings, and owned by the State of New York. Admission is free. Hours are Wednesday through Saturday from 10am to 5pm and Sunday from 1 to 5pm; open weekends only during January, February, and March. The location is in a rather shabby district south of the downtown area at 32 Catherine St. (tel. 518/434-0834), on the corner of Clinton Street (not to be confused with Clinton Avenue on the other side of town).

Less than a dozen blocks to the south is **Historic Cherry Hill,** a capacious old clapboard house with a gambrel roof and an interior full of beautiful furniture, silver, crystal, and paintings. Built in 1787 by Philip Van Rensselaer, this comfortable country seat remained in the hands of family descendants until 1963. It was once the hub of a 900-acre farm; today its pretty grounds are surrounded by featureless industrial and residential suburbs in the lee of I-787. Cherry Hill is at 523½ S. Pearl St. (tel. 518/434-4791). Hours are Tuesday through Saturday from 10am to 3pm and Sunday from 1 to 3pm; closed January.

The **Ten Broeck Mansion** is a patrician brick mansion in the Federal style, built in 1798 by one Gen. Abraham Ten Broeck. It was once called Arbour Hill, a name that now applies to the gentrifying neighborhood that surrounds it. The house is screened from the neighborhood (not all of which is so very wonderful) by a dense leafy park. It was donated to the Albany County Historical Association in 1947 by the Olcott family, various members of which had occupied it for a century. A trip up here is a good excuse to take a look around Arbor Hill. You'll find the entrance to the grounds at 9 Ten Broeck Place, a one-way lane that runs perpendicular to Ten Broeck Street (tel. 518/436-9826). To get on it going in the right direction you'll have to drive up Clinton Avenue to North Swan Street, then turn right down Ten Broeck Place toward Ten Broeck Street. Open March through December on Wednesday through Friday from 2 to 4pm and on Saturday and Sunday from 1 to 4pm.

The **New York State Executive Mansion** is a fairly enormous old Victorian mansion set well back from Eagle Street behind a stone wall topped with an iron fence. It was built in 1856 as a private house and has been enlarged and altered by successive governors on an almost-continuous basis ever since. Teddy Roosevelt installed a gym; FDR put in a pool; Al Smith had a zoo; Nelson Rockefeller built a nuclear fallout shelter. The mansion is open to the public only on Thursday, and then only by reservation at least two weeks in advance. The address is 138 Eagle St., just south of the big ramp that connects I-787 with the Empire State Plaza garage, and the phone number for tour reservations is 518/474-2418.

Hudson & Mohawk River Cruises

An outfit called **Dutch Apple River Cruises** (P.O. Box 395, Albany, 12201) operates excursion boats on the Hudson from the foot of Broadway and Quay Streets (near the old D&H Building). As we went to press, the daily two-hour sightseeing cruises were priced at $8.50 for adults, $7 for seniors, and $5 for children 5 to 12. Also available were daily Sunset Dinner Cruises for about $28 for adults and $12 for kids, the price including a full buffet; Saturday lunch and Sunday brunch cruises ($17 for adults, $9 for kids); and weekend Moonlight Cruises (adults pay $10) with a cash bar and a live band. The new excursions include the Erie Canal Lock Cruise, the Albany to Kingston Cruise, and the four-day Burlington (Vt.) to New York City Cruise through the Champlain Barge Canal. Call 518/463-0220 for current prices and schedules.

Across the Hudson River is the **Capt. JP Cruise Line,** 278 River St., Troy (tel. 518/270-1901). The 600-passenger *Capt. JP* operates daily from May through October 15, with 2-, 3-, and 4-hour cruises priced from $6 for the Port of Albany Cocktail Cruise to $28 for the Prime Rib Dinner Cruise. Call for more information.

For those interested in a three-day excursion on the old Erie Canal from Albany to Syracuse (or the other way), contact the **Mid-Lakes Navigation Co. Ltd.** (tel. toll free 800/545-4318). Or, for a weeklong adventure on the Champlain or Erie Canal systems, consider the **Collar City Charters** at 427 River St., Troy, NY 12180 (tel. 518/272-5341). You might, for example, charter their 41-foot canal boat *Van Rensselaer* for as little as $200 per person (based on six-person occupancy) and be your own captain for an entire week. The charter season runs from early May until mid-November.

An Architectural Side Trip to Schenectady

Albany occupies the southern point of a triangular metropolitan district that includes the industrial cities of Troy and Schenectady. Schenectady (pop. 68,000), on the western extremity of the tri-city area, is a General Electric company town that is by most measures a fairly modest place. It does contain a sensational restored movie palace called **Proctor's,** now the scene of concerts and theatricals, about which I'll say more later. For sightseers interested in architecture and history, Schenectady also contains two intriguing in-city neighborhoods.

The first is called the **Stockade,** a reference to an actual wall that protected (albeit none too successfully) 17th-century settlers from Indian attack. Today's Stockade is an unbelievably quaint district encompassing perhaps 12 or so downtown blocks between the Mohawk River, Washington Avenue, and State Street. It has all the charm of Georgetown, together with the same wonderful inventory of 18th-century buildings. The streets are narrow and crooked, overarched with trees, and lined with delicious restored houses. It's literally a world apart, and quite a treat for those interested in this sort of thing. You can take a self-guided walking tour of the Stockade aided by one of the blue circulars printed and distributed by the **Schenectady Historical Society.** The society maintains quarters in a suitably picturesque building in the Stockade at 32 Washington Ave. It's open Tuesday through Friday from noon to 5pm and Saturday from 9am to 1pm (tel. 518/374-0263). Also useful to know about, depending on your plans and interests, is the annual "Walkabout" in the Stockade, which is held on the last Saturday in September. For $8, you can see the interiors of six of these wonderful houses, plus four of the neighborhood's beautiful churches. An alternative source of information on the Stockade is the **Schenectady Chamber of Commerce,** 240 Canal Square, at the corner of Smith and Broadway, near the back wall of Proctor's (tel. toll free 800/962-8007).

Schenectady's other district of architectural note bears the amusing name of **The Plot.** More correctly it's the G.E. Plot, a parcel of land developed by General Electric in the early years of the 20th century for upper-level Schenectady executives. The Plot adjoins the campus of Union College and is only a few minutes' drive, first up Union Street and then Union Avenue, from the Stockade. The main streets in The Plot are Lenox, Wendell, Stratford, and Lowell, lying between Nott and Rugby Road. It's a perfectly wonderful collection of big old houses in practically every style imaginable, from Queen Anne to Mediterranean to Georgian. This is good-quality stuff too, set on spacious grounds, along quiet roads lined with mature trees. Most people would probably call them mansions. The Plot is still a neighborhood of beautifully kept private houses whose residents have a high regard for what they've got.

The fastest way to Schenectady from Albany is via I-90 to I-890, the latter road being a spur that cuts through Schenectady's downtown. It's about a 20-minute drive. To get to the Stockade, take the Washington Avenue exit off I-890, proceed to the end of the ramp, cut straight across State Street onto narrow Washington Avenue, and then you'll be in the middle of it. Better ask directions to get to The Plot. But it's not far via Union Street, which traverses the middle of the Stockade.

A GOOD MEAL IN SCHENECTADY Back in the 1970s, Schenectady's old Van Curler Hotel was converted into a community college. Today its most successful program is the Hotel, Culinary Arts and Tourism Department.

Move over Culinary Institute of America! The Schenectady County Community College has just opened **The Casola Dining Room** in Elston Hall, at the corner of State Street and Washington Avenue (tel. 518/346-6211, ext. 125). Lunch is served in a formal setting on Monday, Tuesday, Thursday, and Friday at noon; dinner is available on Wednesday only at 7pm. A beef, chicken, fish, or pasta dinner, plus salad, bread, and something tempting from the dessert trolley, costs but $11.50 per person. The students do everything themselves; reservations are a must; bring your own wine.

The **Glen Sanders Mansion,** housed in an adapted 1670–1713 historic stone riverside mansion located across the Mohawk River from Schenectady at 1 Glen Ave., Scotia (tel. 518/374-7262), is a definite must for regional dining. The restaurant sports original Dutch doors, fireplace mantels, wide-plank floors, smoothly planed 18-inch-thick beams, chair rails, and low doorways giving it the feel of a real old-world country inn. The staff is dressed in black tie and works three separate dining rooms in the historic section of the complex, as well as the large and tastefully decorated Riverside Ballroom (for banquets). The dining rooms are comfortable and elegant, furnished with Oriental rugs, flowering plants, and reproduction Queen Anne furniture and lighting fixtures. Lunch is served Monday through Friday from 11:30am to 2pm; expect to pay from $6 for sandwiches and burgers to about $12 for hot specials. Dinner is available Wednesday through Saturday from 5 to 10pm (3 to 7pm on Sunday) and features main courses like steak au poivre, scallops with pesto cream, and lobster pie (my favorite), all priced from $12 to $23. All major credit cards accepted.

WHERE TO STAY IN GREATER ALBANY

Though an appealing city to visit, Albany suffers from a real shortage of interesting hotels. What follows is a selection, from deluxe to moderate in cost, chosen from the best of what there is.

Here as elsewhere it's possible to find accommodations with a bit more character in the booming world of **bed-and-breakfasts.** As this cottage industry matures, however, it grows more expensive: $75 to $85 for a double in somebody's house is not my idea of budget lodgings. Even if you're more likely to find doubles priced at $50 to $60, you have to be willing to make somebody else's household at least a limited part of your vacation. Some travelers find this an appealing idea; others definitely do not. The efforts of bed-and-breakfast hosts to be completely unobtrusive are rather poignant, as it's an impossible task.

Nevertheless, those unafflicted by a compulsion for total privacy might well find a bed-and-breakfast an enjoyable alternative to familiar hotels and motels. The **American Country Collection,** operated by Arthur Copeland, acts as a sort of central booking agency for B&Bs all around the Capital District. The address is American Country Collection, The Willows, 4 Greenwood Lane, Delmar, NY 12054 (tel. 518/439-7001). Although Mr. Copeland prefers three weeks' notice and a deposit, last-minute reservations are sometimes accepted when possible.

Note: Many hotels here in Albany, as in other cities, offer **reduced-rate packages,** especially during slack weekends. Sometimes package rates require advance reservations. Sometimes "advance" means nothing more than asking at the desk when you check in or possibly phoning ahead. Wherever you go, it never hurts to ask whether any package rates are in effect. They won't tell you unless you ask. Here now are recommended hotels, ranging downward in price from deluxe to moderate:

An alternative to the standard hotels is **Mansion Hill Inn,** near the Governor's Mansion, at 115 Phillip St. (at the corner of Park Avenue), Albany, NY 12202 (tel. 518/465-2038, or 518/434-2334). This urban inn is my favorite downtown accommodation and offers a collection of interesting rooms and suites housed in a complex of historic buildings. The larger accommodations each include a living room, den, full kitchen, master bedroom, bath, and even balcony with views of the Hudson and the Helderberg Mountains. Each standard room has two queen-size beds, a private bath, a TV with free HBO, and a phone. There's plenty of off-street parking for everybody. Also on the premises is a stylish bistro, which is recommended below. Rooms start at $95 nightly; suites go up to $145. All major credit cards accepted.

Best hotel downtown is **Omni Albany,** State and Lodge Streets, Albany, NY 12207 (tel. 518/462-6611, or toll free 800/445-8667; fax 518/462-2901). This is a modern affair of brown brick and smoked glass with an ideal downtown location in the middle of all that makes Albany so unique. This former Hilton has lush modern lobbies, atmospheric restaurants full of plants and brass and rattan chairs, an indoor pool, and free parking for guests. The rooms are big, exceedingly comfortable, and full of burled furniture and thick rugs. It's all very new, clean, and modern. Single-room rates range from $120 to $140; doubles run $135 to $155—the different prices depend on where your room is located, and a bit on the state of the market. All rooms, whether they have a high-floor view or not, are the same. All major credit cards accepted.

Albany Marriott, 189 Wolf Rd., Albany, NY 12205 (tel. 518/458-8444, or toll free 800/228-9290; fax 518/458-7365), is the newest hotel complex in the Capital District. This facility boasts over 300 rooms, 11 multipurpose parlors, 10 banquet rooms, a grand ballroom, 2 restaurants, a bar, a nightclub, a health club, an indoor and an outdoor pool. The coordinated maroon-and-tan rooms are outfitted with king-size and double beds, climate control, AM/FM radios, and color TVs with free HBO and pay movies. For formal dining, try Ashley's, appointed with brass and mirrors, or the more casual Market, open from 6am to 11pm daily. Kick's, a tropical-theme nightclub, features bands six nights a week and is a local hot spot. Room prices vary according to one's government, military, or corporate affiliation. But if you're a writer with no associations, expect to pay $129 for a single and $141 for a double—or only $99 for either one on weekends. All major credit cards accepted.

The best hotel in town is the **Desmond,** 660 Albany Shaker Rd., Albany, NY 12211 (tel. 518/869-8100; fax 518/869-7659), located near the north end of Wolf Road, close by the airport and within sight of I-87 (this part of which is called the Northway). From the outside it appears to be an agglomeration of Colonial houses mashed together into a sort of condensed village. Inside it's terrifically handsome, full of first-class Colonial revival decor, hardwood oak floors, beautiful moldings, brass chandeliers, and wing chairs. About half the 322 guest rooms face into a pair of roofed interior courtyards, one of which contains a free-form pool. A typical room will have thick rust-colored carpeting, Colonial-style wood furniture, mirrored closet doors, a phone in the bathroom, and a corduroy wing chair. Rates for these very handsome rooms are about $119 single and $131 for a double. To get here from downtown (about a 10-minute drive), take I-90 westbound to I-87 (the Northway) and get off at exit 4. The ramp will deposit you on Albany Shaker Road and the hotel is to your left on the other side of the Northway. This hotel contains an excellent restaurant called Scrimshaw, described below. All major credit cards accepted.

Early each February, the Desmond also hosts the nationally famous **"American Wine Festival."** This food-and-wine extravaganza is a major industry event that attracts over a hundred winery exhibitors from all over New York State. It consists of daily wine tastings, an elaborate Friday-night dinner dance, wine auctions, a Saturday-night buffet, plus a series of Sunday lectures. It's a fun weekend that's not to be missed if you're planning to be in the area. Call the hotel for details and reservations.

Holiday Inn–Turf on Wolf Road, 205 Wolf Rd., Albany, NY 12205 (tel. 518/458-7250, or toll free 800/HOLIDAY; fax 518/458-7377), is the old Turf Inn recently bought and renovated by the Holiday folks. This upgraded facility now features 300-plus rooms, a great indoor pool, an outdoor pool with a café, tennis courts, a Holidome recreation center (family amusement area), two restaurants, and a 1950s theme nightclub. On-site restaurants include the Turfhouse Grill, which serves full meals from 5:30am to 11pm, and Playfields, a sports bar laden with etched glass and brass, featuring light fare. A nightclub called Fenders is an oldie dance club decorated with 50s paraphernalia. It has a DJ seven nights a week. The rooms, all redecorated with new queen-size beds, cost $91 for a single and $99 for a double. Rooms with Jacuzzis are available for $113 nightly. All major credit cards accepted.

All the familiar chains are well represented in Albany. Ramada and TraveLodge, for example, are just down Western Avenue from the Tom Sawyer. Others are over on Wolf Road, among them **Days Inn,** 16 Wolf Rd., Albany, NY 12205 (tel. 518/459-3600, or toll free 800/325-2525; fax 518/459-1246). This establishment stands at the start of the Wolf Road shopping strip for which Albany is so well known. It's a flat-roofed modern construction surrounded by new and immaculate lawns and landscaping. Inside it are 168 brand-new rooms each decorated with beige textured-vinyl wallcoverings, brown wall-to-wall carpeting, a color TV, a chair, a desk, perhaps a framed picture of a partridge, and a clean functional bath. It has a mass-market look but is nonetheless comfortable for that. And rates are very low: $57 for singles, $61 for doubles—except during August, when rooms cost up to $66 nightly, single or double. All major credit cards accepted.

Cheaper yet, but quite attractive in spite of its low prices, is **Red Roof Inn,** 188 Wolf Rd. (next to the Sheraton Airport Inn), Albany, NY 12205 (tel. 518/459-1971, or toll free 800/848-7878; fax ext. 444). All Red Roofs have a Colorado-ski-lodge look and a huge swooping red roof over the lobby. This one has 116 immaculate rooms with patterned spreads, burgundy-brown-cream color schemes, color TVs, patterned wallpaper, and nice modern baths. Single-room rates range from $43 to $63; doubles cost only $46 to $71. No pool or restaurant. In fact, Red Roof Inns across New York State offer some of the best travel bargains I've seen. You might want to call the toll-free number above and request a copy of their national directory. Or you could write to Red Roof Inns, Inc., 4355 Davidson Rd., Hilliard, OH 43026. All major credit cards accepted.

And I'm afraid to say that that, unfortunately, with the exception of Mansion Hill Inn, is about as much variety as you're going to find in Albany. Unless you're willing to undertake an 11-mile drive east across the Hudson to the village of Averill Park and try **Gregory House,** Averill Park, NY 12081 (tel. 518/674-3774). This is a little complex of dark-brown buildings surrounded by pretty flower gardens and sporting an attractive pool. The restaurant, described below, is in a 150-year-old house. The 12 inn rooms are in a new compatible structure adjacent. These rooms have dark floors, private baths with flowery shower curtains, random antiques, hooked rugs, and a most attractive, well-kept air. The place definitely has style, and the presence of the excellent restaurant is further inducement to stay here. Double-occupancy room rates fall mostly between $65 and $80 nightly, including continental breakfast. Averill Park straddles N.Y. 43, reached via exit 7 (Washington Avenue) from I-90. I've timed the drive; it's 15 easy minutes from I-787 in downtown Albany. All major credit cards accepted.

WHERE TO EAT IN GREATER ALBANY

The city has quite a sophisticated assortment of restaurants. First we'll tackle those in the downtown area, starting with the upper bracket and moving down. After that we'll move to the fringes of town.

Downtown Restaurants

La Serre, 14 Green St. (tel. 518/463-6056), is an elegant oasis located just off downtown State Street. A greenhouse overlooks little Green Street from behind trees and a tall iron fence. Inside are several exceedingly elegant rooms, alternately paneled in rich mahogany or mirrors. There are sprays of gorgeous flowers, immaculate white and pink linen, and the tinkle of laughter and piano music. Cuisine is French continental and quite reasonable at lunch, when main courses like veal meunière, the crêpe du jour, and seafood fettuccine cost $8 to $11. At dinner expect to pay $18 to $23 for an à la carte selection like veal Oscar, steak bordelaise, bouillabaisse marseillaise, or duckling au poivre. Open daily from 11:30am until 2:30pm for lunch, and 5:30 to 9:30pm for dinner. It's a beautiful place and the food is famous. All major credit cards accepted.

Within walking distance of both the Empire State Plaza and the Governor's Mansion is the aforementioned restaurant at **Mansion Hill Inn,** 115 Phillip St., at Park Avenue (tel. 518/465-2038, or 434-2334). The restored brick building was originally constructed by an Albany brush maker. Today, the former commercial space has been converted to a delightful sunny restaurant, with Laura Ashley wallpaper, frosted glass wall sconces, sea-green wainscoting, and cast-iron pillars. It has a stylish late 20th-century urban look to it. Lunch, a $10 undertaking, served Wednesday through Friday from noon to 2pm, attracts as many locals as guests. Dinner attracts a stylish crowd from all over the city. It is served Monday through Saturday from 5 to 10pm, and the à la carte menu stretches from a vegetable arcobolino at $11.25 to rack of lamb for $18.55. All major credit cards accepted.

Jack's, 42 State St. (tel. 518/465-8854), is a horse of a different color. Opened in 1913, it's a seafood-and-oyster house with unpretentious decor and a reputation for good food and a unique old-time Albany atmosphere. The lofty-ceilinged dining room is an institution, filled with red-leatherette chairs, gilt-framed pictures of Albany, and boisterous crowds. Huge sandwiches (available only at lunch) cost around $4 to $7, ditto for clams and oysters of almost every description. Seafood selections like fresh swordfish filet, Boston bluefish, and combination seafood grill run about $12 to $20; chopped sirloin, chef's salad, and omelets are about half that. Open daily from 11:30am until 10pm. Very typical of Albany. The food is great, so try and include a meal here if you can. All major credit cards accepted.

Ogden's, Howard and Lodge Streets (tel. 518/463-6605), is a stylish new restaurant in a former Edwardian-era telephone building. Besides the attractive high-ceilinged dining room there's a wonderful outdoor terrace with a yellow-and-white awning, hanging plants, and crisp white linen. The lunch menu offers things like ginger chicken, filet of sole, giant combination sandwiches, sophisticated salads, and so on for around $5 to $15. At dinner you might order a New York–strip steak, tournedos Rossini, veal japonaise, chicken française, Dover sole, free range chicken, or other faintly nouvelle geographic specials priced mostly from $15 to $24. Ogden's serves lunch Monday through Friday only from 11:30am to 2:30pm; dinner is available Monday through Saturday from 5:30 to 10pm. All major credit cards accepted.

Yono's, 239 Hamilton St. on Robinson Square (tel. 518/436-7747), is a favorite with Albany's political types. The restaurant occupies a historic 1840s brick town house that contains some glorious interior spaces. The grandest is a second-floor dining room with a 24-foot ceiling and a view of the Empire State Plaza across the street. Cuisine here is continental with an Indonesian accent. Dinner, the only meal served, is offered on Monday to Saturday between 5:30 and 10pm; most things cost between $11 and $20. Yono himself, incidentally, is a recent recipient of the American Culinary Federation's Chef of the Year Award. All major credit cards accepted.

Quintessence, 11 New Scotland Ave. (tel. 518/434-8186), occupies a 1930s stainless-steel diner that has been renovated with a unique art deco and neon motif. The clientele of this diner, located one block south of the park, is as lively as the decor. Food is served from 8am to 2am daily. My last supper there consisted of an appetizer of alligator with papaya glaze ($3.95) and a main course of sautéed scallops in vodka-tarragon cream sauce on black squid-ink pasta, also called scallops negro ($8.95). Breakfast, lunch, dinner (with nightly themes), and brunches are priced very moderately. There are a DJ and dancing Wednesday through Saturday, plus a band on Sunday night. All major credit cards accepted.

I'm a particular fan of neighborhood tavern/restaurants, especially if good food is combined with a lot of character. Three very excellent Albany establishments fit this description. The first is **Lombardo's,** 121 Madison Ave. (tel. 518/462-9180), which is complete with vintage neon sign, white-tile floors, booths, and a separate bar room with the original 1919 liquor license. Nobody decorated this place to look old, it just does. Cuisine is Italian—eggplant parmigiana, homemade sausage, lasagne, ravioli, stuffed shells, all sorts of pastas with all sorts of sauces—and prices are moderate. Getting out of here for $10 a head is eminently do-able; open Monday to Saturday from 11am to 11pm. The location is just off the intersection of Madison and South Pearl, quite near the Pastures. All major credit cards accepted.

Several blocks away is **Pastures Tavern,** 147 S. Pearl St. (tel. 518/463-7222), which is a new tavern adjacent to the newly restored Pastures Historic District. It has a natural-wood facade with small-pane tavern windows, a long skinny natural-wood bar inside, plus lofty ceilings, terra-cotta floors, butcher-block tables, and exposed-brick walls. There is rock and roll on the jukebox, and the crowd is attractive and young-looking. Hot sandwiches, burgers, plus things like chicken wings, onion soup, and taco salad, are served daily from 11:30am until midnight. The atmosphere is great, and everything costs less than $6. All major credit cards accepted.

Hurley's is located on the other side of town on gentrifying (working at it, but not there yet) Clinton Avenue, at the corner of Quail Street (tel. 518/434-6854). This is an old corner tavern, modernized unpretentiously and filled at most hours with a young exuberant crowd watching TV at the bar up front or putting away sandwiches and chicken wings at tables in the back. Nothing fancy here, but great burgers and sandwiches for usually less than $5. Open Monday through Saturday from 11:30am to 4am and Sunday from noon until 4am (food served until 3am). All major credit cards accepted.

Hungry sightseers looking for cafeteria-style sandwich shops in the downtown area should know about **Bruegger's Bagel Bakery,** a chain whose various locations feature high-tech pipe rails, blond-wood café chairs, and all sorts of sandwiches from $3 to $4. There's a convenient Bruegger's near the Omni on North Pearl Street at the corner of Maiden Lane. Practically next door on Maiden Lane is **Sandwiches to Go,** which is bright, clean, and attractive, offering almost any sandwich you can think of for about $3. Both places are packed at lunch with downtown office workers.

Good Suggestions Farther Afield

Stone Ends Restaurant, located a mile south of Thruway exit 23 on U.S. 9W in Glenmont (tel. 518/465-3178), is only five minutes from downtown Albany and is well worth the trip. Owner/chef Dale Miller is a Culinary Institute of America graduate whose restaurant has received the Escoffier Award of Honor and the Travel-Holiday Award. The building is a modern 1950s Frank Lloyd Wright sort of a place with blue-stone gable walls and floors. The decor is accented with art nouveau light fixtures and leaded glass. The waiters are in black tie, and the music is soft and classical. As for the food, it is progressive American with a distinct European influence. Main dishes include prime rib of (Provime) veal, steak (black Angus) Diane, and salmon with seafood sausage (mousse), and they cost $16 to $26. Stone Ends is open for dinner only from 4:30 to 10pm on Monday through Thursday and from 4:30 to 11pm on Friday and Saturday. On Friday and Saturday there's live piano music in the dining room and bar. All major credit cards accepted.

An authentic Indian restaurant called **Sitar,** 1929 Central Ave. (tel. 518/456-6670), is only five minutes west of downtown Albany. The owners have been delighting the community on Central Avenue for over 15 years and have a very loyal following. A large wood carving at the front door consists of two parts: The top is Kalimata, the goddess of darkness; the bottom is the awe-inspiring Shiva, god of regeneration of goodness. The Sitar's Oriental arches and stuccoed walls are decorated with inlaid wood and ivory. The kebab and tandoori dishes are skewered and charcoal-broiled in clay ovens. The Indian bread called *nan* is baked by means of fastening the dough to the under lip of a large clay-pot oven, then watching until it falls. The chef catches the nan before it hits the red-hot coals. This operation can be witnessed through a 4- by 8-foot window opening onto the kitchen from the bar. Lunch is served Tuesday through Friday from 11:30am to 2pm and costs $6 to $7. The Sunday buffet, served from noon to 3pm, costs $10. Dinner is available from 5 to 10pm Tuesday to Sunday and is priced between $8 and $17. All major credit cards accepted.

Scrimshaw is located in the Desmond Hotel, at exit 4 on the Northway/I-87. The address again is 660 Albany Shaker Rd. (tel. 518/869-8100). Here the staff is in colonial costume, and the atmosphere suggests prosperous New England. As a matter of fact, new though it may be, the Scrimshaw is singularly attractive in a high traditional manner. There are numerous dining rooms, all decorated with formal swagged curtains, Queen Anne armchairs, brass wall sconces, and framed paintings of ships. You might have a drink before dinner in the handsome bar with its beams and leather furniture. The luncheon menu offers omelets, seafood, various grills and broils, plus all manner of salads, priced mostly from $5 to $10. At dinner you'll pay more like $14 to $26 for selections such as grilled swordfish, breast of duck, sole *en* *papillote,* or roast prime rib. Open for lunch on weekdays only from noon to 2pm; dinner is served Monday through Saturday from 5 to 10pm. All major credit cards accepted.

Located about equidistant from downtown in the exact opposite direction from the Desmond is the restaurant at **Gregory House** in Averill Park (tel. 518/674-3774). Dinner here truly is a treat, taken in one of several intimate dining rooms by candlelight under beamed ceilings. The place has a very nice old-fashioned country inn atmosphere and features Swiss/northern Italian dinner main courses priced mostly from $11 to $24. Open for dinner only on Tuesday to Saturday from 5pm until people go home (from 4pm on Sunday). For directions, see the description of Gregory House under the hotel listings, above. All major credit cards accepted.

Back in Albany's western suburbs, in the Stuyvesant Plaza, at Western Avenue and Fuller, is **T.G.I. Friday's** (tel. 518/489-1661). That it looks identical to every other Friday's in the land detracts not one whit from its considerable appeal. Outside are red-and-white awnings to distinguish it from everything else in the plaza. Inside is the familiar raised bar, Tiffany-style colored-glass lamps, brass rails, hanging ferns, etched glass, and crowds of satisfied patrons. Every day from 11:30am to 1am you can order things like pasta salads, gourmet burgers, oversize sandwiches, sweet-and-sour chicken, enchiladas, or more elaborate fare like a mixed seafood plate or chicken piccata, mostly priced between $5 and $12. The bar, open daily until 2am, is always busy. All major credit cards accepted.

Grandma's, 1273 Central Ave. (tel. 518/459-4585), isn't far from the other end of Fuller Road. The owner studied fast-food techniques and combined it with a family-run atmosphere—the result is Grandma's, a local family-style, fast-food restaurant. It looks rather like a suburban diner, its clean and functional interior softened by Victorianish lighting fixtures. It's famous for its pies and baked goods, as well as for its reasonable lunches and dinners. Expect to pay between $5 and $10 for triple-decker sandwiches, barbecued chicken, and special omelets. They're big on breakfasts here too, especially Belgian waffles (under $5). Open daily from 6am to midnight. All major credit cards accepted.

ALBANY AFTER DARK

Drinking & Dancing

The newest, wildest downtown party place is **QE2** at 13 Central Ave. (tel. 518/434-2023). Lights, heavy metal, jolly drinkers . . . you get the picture. A "yuppier" crowd frequents **Parc V Café,** out in Colonie, close by the Desmond Americana, on Albany Shaker Road and the Northway (tel. 518/869-9976).

As long as you're in the area, the newest and possibly the hottest night spot in town is **Kick's,** at the Albany Marriott, 189 Wolf Rd. (tel. 518/458-8444). Bands, DJs, and laser light shows line 'em up on weekends. Another good idea, just up the road at the Holiday Inn–Turf, is the 1950s-theme nightclub **Fenders** (tel. 518/458-7250).

Theater

Shakespeare in the Park is a regular summer occurrence in Albany's Washington Park, as it is in Manhattan's Central Park. Most shows are mounted in July at an outdoor theater adjoining the lake house. The best way to find out whether shows are planned during your stay is call the Albany Arts Office: 518/434-2032.

A broad range of theatricals is staged between September and May at the **Egg** that curiously aerodynamic-looking thingummy that sits midway down the Empire State Plaza. The Empire State Institute for the Performing Arts (ESIPA) is the genius behind the productions; the box office number is 518/473-3750.

Proctor's, the extravagantly elegant restored movie palace in nearby Schenectady, is almost worth a trip just for a glimpse of its Hollywood imperial interiors. This great architectural treasure now features an eclectic calendar of shows and concerts from contemporary drama to opera, to punk rock, to ballet, to musicals, to symphony orchestras. Call the box office between 10am and 6pm on Monday through Saturday at 518/346-6204 or 382-1083. It's only about a 20-minute drive from downtown Albany, via super-expressway (I-90 and I-890) virtually all the way.

SHOPPING

Albany is famous for its megamalls, many of which are lined up along Wolf Road to the west of town near the intersection of the Northway (I-87 and I-90). There are so many of these malls, not just on Wolf Road but throughout the area, that it's not practical to try and describe them all. Highlights include these:

Cohoes Specialty Stores, 43 Mohawk St., in the nearby city of Cohoes (tel. 518/237-0524), is perhaps best known for its premium-quality and designer clothing for men and women at discount prices. In many ways it's a sort of upstate Loehmann's.

The newest mall in town is **Crossgates,** out on Western Avenue (N.Y. 20) near the start of the Northway. Jordan Marsh, Filene's, and J. C. Penney are the anchors. Also worth a look is the new Macy's at **Colonie Shopping Mall** (tel. 518/459-1950). **Off-Price Center/Northway Mall,** on Central Avenue (N.Y. 5) between Wolf Road and Fuller Road, sells women's clothing, men's clothing, shoes, electronic equipment, linens, children's wear, you name it, at fairly fabulous discounts. Open daily; the phone number is 518/459-5320.

My favorite place to shop in Albany is **Stuyvesant Plaza,** where the Northway begins (tel. 518/482-8986). It has an exquisite collection of 62 specialty stores and restaurants. Definitely worth a shopping stroll in atmospheric downtown Albany is **Lark Street** in the 100 to 300 blocks. Here you'll find a small-scale potpourri of boutiques, antiques shops, cafés, bars, jewelry stores, and the like, each with its own unique flavor.

---

2. Troy

The old industrial city of Troy (pop. 56,600) is located at the navigable headwaters of the Hudson River at its junction with the Erie and the Champlain canal systems. Troy played a major role in the American industrial revolution due to the efforts of local inventors like Henry Burden, who began developing the city's iron industry in 1822. The Burden works manufactured the first mass-produced horseshoes and nails in the United States. Other important residents included educators Amos Eaton and Emma Willard. Willard, a pioneer in liberal education for women, founded a school in Troy (which still exists) in 1821. Due to the public interest aroused by Amos Eaton's mechanical and scientific genius, the **Rensselaer Polytechnic Institute** (RPI) was established here in 1824.

The great 19th-century ferment of industrial and educational activity made Troy a city of free-thinking laborers. The first female labor union was founded here, as was the largest men's local in the country. The labor movement brought the benefits of better living standards, but also the problems of riots and strikes. Even today, Troy takes its politics very seriously.

During the 1960s, the city decided to demolish major sections of Fifth Avenue and the old downtown district. For 20 years, bulldozed lots remained unbuilt and whole streets of vintage town houses stood abandoned while local politicians dithered. In the meantime, local preservationists aggressively condemned the city's demolition of its outstanding Victorian structures. Fortunately for Troy, the demolition was stopped, and much that is of value here today was thus saved.

A new generation of more enlightened city leaders came to power in the 1980s.

The open space along the river was transformed into a park, and the empty buildings downtown were restored. Troy today is an appealing blend of a few modern buildings and an opulent treasure of Victoriana. The 19th-century burlesque houses, breweries, bordellos of the great madames, and the factories billowing black smoke may be gone, but a sense of the past still remains on the streets of Troy.

WHAT TO SEE & DO

Your first stop should be the new **Riverspark Visitor Center** next to the city hall at 251 River St., Troy, NY 12180 (tel. 518/270-8667). This is the best and most exciting visitors' center I've ever seen. It's worth the trip to Troy all by itself.

The center provides a multimedia introduction to the Riverspark Urban Cultural Park, which covers Troy and 6 adjacent communities along a 28-mile heritage trail with over 70 cultural and historically significant attractions. It is open Wednesday through Saturday from noon to 5pm and Sunday from 1 to 5pm; closed major holidays. Admission is free.

Two blocks away is the **Rensselaer County Historical Society,** 59 Second St., Troy, NY 12180 (tel. 518/272-7232). Housed in the old Hart-Cluett mansion and carriage house, the historical society has a well-organized library on local history and a vast selection of exhibits including Troy-built stoves, fine arts, 19th-century furniture, and Currier and Ives prints. Open Tuesday through Saturday from 10am to 4pm; admission is $2 for adults and $1 for kids.

The grandest vintage building in town is the famous **Troy Savings Bank Music Hall,** at the corner of Second and State Streets (box office at 88 4th St., Troy, NY 12180; tel. 518/273-0038). Constructed between 1871 and 1875, the building was designed by George Browne Post, the architect who built the famous Cornelius Vanderbilt mansion at 1 West 57th St. in Manhattan. The music hall is considered by many critics and performers to have the best acoustics in the world.

During the late 19th century it was traditional for banks to incorporate a public space, like a music hall or a theatre, into the design of their buildings as evidence of community spirit. Unfortunately, few of these have survived. The spirit that gave rise to them is not always so evident among our financial institutions today either. The Troy Savings Bank is a vivid exception, as are its efforts to restore downtown Troy. The restored Victorian music hall is a major draw for the community and attracts internationally famous performers.

If you're traveling with kids, you all might enjoy **The Rensselaer County Junior Museum,** 282 Fifth Ave., Troy, NY (tel. 518/235-2120). Animals, puppet shows, folksinging, arts and crafts, outdoor summer programs, a planetarium—get the picture? Open Wednesday through Sunday from 1 to 5pm; admission is $3 for adults and $2 for kids.

Those interested in a more thorough introduction to Troy's industrial past might want to contact the **Hudson-Mohawk Industrial Gateway** at the Burden Iron Works Office Building, foot of Polk Street, Troy, NY 12180 (tel. 518/274-5267). The Gateway presents guided tours and cruises that interpret the industrial and architectural history of this historically important region. Call them for schedules and fees.

WHERE TO STAY & EAT IN & AROUND TROY

Besides the standard downtown accommodations described below, you should consider **Gregory House,** a country inn in nearby (8 miles away) Averill. See the Albany hotel section above for a complete description.

The best deal in downtown Troy is the new **Troy Super 8 Motel** right on the river at 1 4th St., Troy, NY 12180 (tel. 518/274-8800; fax 518/274-0427). It is a standard budget-style Super 8, with 77 units priced from $43 to $48. Local phone calls and movie rentals are included in the rates, and all rooms have remote-control TVs and king-size beds. There is no restaurant, but plenty of good ones are located within easy walking distance. All major credit cards accepted.

The Cape House Restaurant, 254 Broadway (tel. 518/274-0167), specializes in fine seafood—including a raw bar—and great steaks and chops. The decor is a tasteful combination of antiques and stylish decorator touches like the modified balloon curtains in the front windows. The dining room has Windsor chairs, oversize shaker peg boards with hanging dried herbs, and ceiling fans. Lunch is served from 11:30am to 3pm on Monday through Saturday, and most things cost between $3 and $9. Dinner is available on Monday to Thursday from 5 to 10pm (until 11pm on Friday and Saturday) and from 3 to 8pm on Sunday. Expect to pay from about $9 (for chicken madrilene) to $18 (for center-cut loin lamb chops). All major credit cards accepted.

A popular spot for pre- and aprés-theater dining is **Capriccio Allegro,** opposite the Troy Music Hall, at 33 Second St. (tel. 518/271-1942). The restaurant has two sections: One is informal and provides a view of the open kitchen and the chef at work; the other is more formal and decorated with classical guitars on the wall, track lighting, black-and-white-checkered tablecloths, and fresh flowers. The bistro fare is an eclectic mix of Mediterranean influences, with a heavy French and northern Italian accent. Lunch is served on Monday through Friday from 11:30am to 2pm and costs around $4 to $8 per main course. Dinner, available on Monday through Thursday from 5 to 9pm and until 11pm on Friday and Saturday, is chosen from a new menu daily; most main courses cost between $7 and $19; the prix-fixe dinner is $20. Open Sunday from 4pm. MC and V accepted.

For a great meal with a Hudson River view, try **River Street Café,** 429 River St. (tel. 518/273-2740). The café has two levels, is open for dinner only from Tuesday through Saturday (5:30 to 10pm), and features an American bistro menu with things like chicken with sweet red-pepper sauce for $14 and a veal rib chop for $19. The decor consists of exposed-brick walls, a fine mahogany service bar on the second floor, fresh flowers, and the aforementioned view. No liquor, alas; only wine and beer, and a good selection of both despite the fact that there are no New York State wines! No credit cards accepted.

Also bear in mind the restaurant at the recommended **Gregory House** in nearby Averill Park (see "Good Suggestions Farther Afield" under "Where to Eat in Greater Albany" for a description).

---

3. Saratoga Springs

How to convey the vintage luxury and atmosphere of this old resort in a few short paragraphs? Saratoga Springs (pop. 23,900), 44 miles north of Albany on the Adirondack Northway (I-87), is a place graced with a famous racetrack at which millions are won and lost by high-rolling gamblers. The season is only some five short weeks in August. But during those weeks the restored Victorian streets are clogged with fancy cars and definite urban types (socialites to "dese-dem-an-dose" guys). The restaurants are packed, and hotel prices triple. The swell mansions along North Broadway and Union Street ring to the sound of laughter and popping champagne corks. In the words of Heywood Hale Broun, August in Saratoga is a time when "hopes begin to seem like expectations, where fantasies look like investment opportunities."

What started it all is a series of natural mineral springs that bubble to the earth in various locations around town. Usually they are sheltered beneath open-air pavilions and described on adjacent plaques, and their various-tasting waters are free for the taking (bring your own glass or cup). During the last century "taking the cure" at Saratoga, which is to say dressing up and drinking a lot of water, fit nicely with betting heavily at the track, gambling at one of the swank casinos, and eating oneself almost insensate at the opulent restaurants and hotel dining rooms of the day.

The controversial Madame Jumel, once the wife of Aaron Burr (subject of wonderful descriptive passages in Gore Vidal's novel *Burr*), was an early summer resident. Her house on Circular Street still stands. Diamond Jim Brady and Lillian Russell were big fans of Saratoga summers too. So was a fellow named John Morrissey, founder in 1863 of the local thoroughbred racing track (also president of a New York City gang called the Dead Rabbits). Numerous other colorful types inhabit the pages of Saratoga's past. But Jumel, Brady, Russell, and Morrissey epitomize the tone of the place, a heady brew of illicit luxury, fast money, and lots of fun. Interestingly enough, for all the changes wrought by the 120-plus years since the founding of Morrissey's Horse Haven Race Track, for all the wars and upheavals and social changes this country has undergone, August in Saratoga is approximately the same as it always has been.

The famous springs, or at least most of them, are now preserved within the confines of a New York state park. Built in the 1930s and occupying 2,000 manicured acres, it's a world of classical pavilions and serene outdoor pools, all very much in the European spa tradition. Culture has also come to Saratoga with a capital "C" in the form of the Saratoga Performing Arts Center (SPAC), which is a huge open-air shell on the grounds of the Spa State Park.

Notwithstanding all that, the horse remains the object of greatest interest, be it on the thoroughbred track or the harness-racing track, or on the auction block at the famous annual Fasig-Tipton Yearling Sales, or on the field of the Saratoga Polo Association, or on the minds of all the Rolls-Royce and Seville drivers of August.

WHAT TO SEE & DO

The town slows down during the depths of winter. But there's lots to do in spring, summer, and fall, whether or not you're a particular fancier of horseflesh. First thing to note is the address and phone number of the extremely helpful **Saratoga County Chamber of Commerce,** at 494 Broadway (U.S. 9), Saratoga Springs, NY 12866, just south of the Sheraton Hotel (tel. 518/584-3255). The chamber is the source of maps, up-to-the-minute information on what's going on around town, advice on hotels and restaurants, and so on. The staff couldn't be nicer or more readily prepared with good advice for visitors. Alternately, they staff a well-stocked **tourist information booth** open during the summer, located in the middle of town on Broadway at the entrance to Congress Park, as well as the **Urban Cultural Park Visitors Center** across the street at Drink Hall, 297 Broadway, Saratoga Springs, NY 12866 (tel. 518/587-3241).

Saratoga Spa

Saratoga's naturally carbonated mineral springs were discovered by Europeans in 1771. Friendly Native Americans brought Sir William Johnson up here in a litter, as this worthy agent of the king was too gouty to walk on his own two feet. By 1803, Saratoga had already become sufficiently famous to warrant the erection, by Gideon Putnam, of a hotel strictly for visitors taking "the cure." Fashion smiled on Saratoga throughout the 19th century. But while palatial hotels, restaurants, casinos, and tracks were carefully cultivated, the springs were ironically neglected.

By the beginning of this century, Saratoga's booming industry based on extraction of carbon dioxide from the naturally carbonated springs threatened to pump the place dry. A hue and cry was raised in time, the result being a New York State Reservation, created in 1909 and charged with protecting the springs from rapacious commercial development. In 1927, Gov. Franklin D. Roosevelt appointed a further commission to study the possibility of transforming Saratoga Springs into a European-style health spa. The result of that commission's efforts was the erection of an elegant series of buildings that constitute today's state park. Designed by one Joseph Henry Freedlander in a chaste Georgian/Classical revival style, the new complex was opened to the public on July 26, 1935.

The reservation didn't actually become a state park until 1962, when an 18-hole golf course and an additional pool were added. Today's spa encompasses 2,000 acres, hosts 1½ million visitors each year, includes about 10 different natural springs welling up in various locations, plus the deluxe Gideon Putnam Hotel, the outdoor SPAC shell, pools, and pavilions, and bathhouses. Despite its heavy use, it's quite a beautiful place.

The Spa State Park is located on the southern edge of Saratoga Springs, bordering U.S. 9 (South Broadway) and N.Y. 50 (Ballston Avenue). The main entrance is on U.S. 9 next door to the Lincoln Baths Building. Probably the best place to get a map of the spa is at the chamber of commerce, 494 Broadway (tel. 518/584-3255). Within hours of your arrival at Saratoga the chances are you'll hear about something called the **ninety-minute relaxer.** This is a popular treatment at the spa consisting of a soak in a private tub of fizzy mineral water, followed by a professional massage, and topped off by a wrap in warm sheets. It's fairly heavenly and costs only around $30. Reservations are required for this and other bath treatments. The Roosevelt Baths (tel. 518/584-2011) are open all year from Wednesday through Sunday; the Lincoln Baths (tel. 518/584-2010) operate only during summer.

You can sample the various **spring waters** just by driving up to them and taking a drink. A visitors' pamphlet titled "The Springs of Saratoga" locates them all and gives a bit of history about each. (The best tasting in town, in my opinion, is the Hathorn No. 1, which isn't in the spa at all but on the northern edge of Congress Park.) The famous **Saratoga Mineral Water,** whose stylish-looking bottles are available in supermarkets everywhere, is bottled in the park itself in a plant on N.Y. 50. On the grounds of the spa itself, next door to the former bottling plant, is one of the state park's more interesting springs. Identified as Geyser Well No. 7, it contains enough radium to warrant a sign warning drinkers against more than one glass a week.

Besides baths, springs, picnic areas, and golf courses, the state park sports two beautiful outdoor pools. My favorite is the **Victoria Pool,** an immense and architecturally gorgeous facility surrounded by classical pavilions, comfortable chaises, a snackbar, and changing rooms. Adults can laze away a sunny summer day for a modest $4 (for kids 6 to 12, $2). Towel rental is but 50¢ additional.

Besides everything mentioned above, the state park has tennis courts, ice-skating rinks, jogging courses, picnic areas, and of course the aforementioned golf course. For up-to-the-minute information on fees and so forth, call the Spa Park Office at 518/584-2000.

An interesting alternative to the park baths is the **Crystal Spa,** 92 South Broadway (tel. 518/584-2556). A mineral bath here will cost $12, a massage $24, and a sauna $5.

SPAC

The **Saratoga Performing Arts Center** (SPAC) is quite an ornament to the city of Saratoga. Located on the grounds of the Spa State Park (entrance on N.Y. 50, Ballston Avenue), it's the summer home of both the New York City Ballet in July *and* the Philadelphia Orchestra during August. Besides its resident companies, SPAC stages shows by the likes of Willie Nelson, Bob Seger, Manhattan Transfer, George Benson, Twyla Tharp, Bob Dylan, Tom Petty and the Heartbreakers, the Temptations, and the New York City Opera. Lawn seating is available in addition to seats in the covered shell, which occupies a sort of natural amphitheatric hollow. Sight lines and general ambience are wonderful.

For ticket and program information, call the box office at 518/587-3330 between the hours of 10am and 5pm during the summer only. The adjacent **Hall of Springs,** an immense Classical revival interior dripping with 1930s elegance, serves a dinner buffet on concert nights. You can call them at 518/584-9330 or 587-8000 for information and reservations.

Landmarks Around Town

The **Saratoga County Chamber of Commerce,** 494 Broadway (tel. 518/584-3255); the tourist information booth at Congress Park; and the new **Urban Cultural Park Visitors Center,** at 297 Broadway in the old Drink Hall (tel. 518/587-3241)—all carry a useful brochure titled "Saratoga Springs Urban Cultural Park." For those who want to get to know the city and its wonderful 19th-century architecture, this brochure is a must. It will lead you knowledgeably around and among the porticoed and turreted mansions, public gardens, and old hotels.

Saratoga isn't a big place; you can easily get the feel of it in an afternoon. Not to be missed are **Congress Park,** a little enclave filled with splashing fountains, froufrou pavilions, and elaborate beds of brightly colored flowers; the **Casino,** a restored Victorian memento of the days of high-stakes gaming and high-cost dining; **Circular Street,** notable for various mansions, among them the amazing Batcheller House at the corner of Whitney Place; **North Broadway,** five concentrated blocks, between the middle of town and the campus of Skidmore College, lined with huge trees and great mansions; and **Union Avenue,** location of the famous Race Course and similar to North Broadway, but with a lot more traffic and fewer fine houses.

Saratoga's **Broadway** was once the site of three enormous Victorian-era hotels: the United States Hotel, on the corner of Division; the Congress Hall, between Spring and Congress Streets; and the Grand Union, between Washington and Congress. These palatial old joints were famous for their pillared balconies stretching hundreds of feet along Broadway and rising to a height of four or five full floors. Alas, all three are gone, replaced with the most mundane shopping malls imaginable. The rest of Broadway still retains its classy old brick buildings, most of which have been sensitively restored in recent years, plus handsome shops and restaurants.

Horse Racing

Saratoga has three tracks. **Saratoga Race Course,** oldest active thoroughbred racetrack in the United States, is the most famous of them all. Dating from 1864, it's a world of striped awnings, gilded cupolas, grassy paddocks, fancy cars, beautiful women, fevered betting, rich owners, and the fastest horses in America. It's open only in late July and August; post time is 1pm, and there are races every day but Tuesday. Traditional here during race weeks is the "Sunrise Breakfast," available trackside from 7am. You can watch the horses being walked out, even attend a handicap seminar in the Paddock Club. Be advised, the track is formal. No shorts or T-shirts; and in the clubhouse dining rooms you'll need a jacket and tie. Outdoor food concessions, however, abound.

For further information, call the Race Course General Information number at 518/584-6200 or the Saratoga County Chamber of Commerce at 518/584-3255. Gates open at 11am; admission to the grandstand is $2; to the clubhouse it's $5. Go early—it's mobbed. You'll find the track on the eastern edge of town on Union Avenue about half a dozen blocks from Congress Park.

Saratoga Harness Raceway is the standardbred track, where trotters and sulkies replace the more aristocratic thoroughbreds. The trotters run 10 months a year. Grandstand admission is $1.75; to the clubhouse it's $3. Post time is typically 7:45pm. This establishment recently changed hands, so call 518/584-2110 (or the chamber of commerce at 518/584-3255) for up-to-date information.

The third track, visible on all the maps of town, provokes the curiosity of numerous visitors. It's located just the other side of Union Avenue from the famous Race Course, is called **Oklahoma Track** and is used only for training and therefore not open to the public.

Interesting to know about, while I'm on the subject of horse racing, is the annual **Fasig-Tipton Yearling Sale,** which usually takes place around the second week in August. The scene is the Humphrey Finney Pavilion, located on East Avenue (tel. 518/587-2070). Buyers from around the world watch a tuxedo-clad John Finney conduct auctions where prices for untried horses can go into the millions. Potential bidders might be readers of this book, but you don't have to be to attend the auction. The atmosphere is definitely big league and seating is limited, so call ahead.

Saratoga Polo Association

Besides thoroughbred racing, the month of August now also witnesses a full schedule of exciting polo matches. For $5 a head, you can join the crowd at the field out Seward Avenue on the western edge of town. Call the Saratoga County Chamber of Commerce at 518/584-3255 or 584-8108 for current match schedules.

National Museum of Racing & Hall of Fame

Located across Union Avenue from the Saratoga Race Course is a state-of-the-art museum dedicated to American thoroughbred horse racing. The exhibits are almost as exciting as the track itself. Upon entering the building you will sense the tension of the track with the sounds of jockeys yelling, horses being handled, and the starting gates flying open. Elsewhere you can trace the history of thoroughbred racing from 17th-century New York and Virginia to the present day. The actual hall of fame is much more than a fascinating collection of memorabilia; it is a high-tech multimedia center where one can actually select and watch any historic race film with the aid of a computer. A wide-screen theater room features a great 20-minute film that is guaranteed to move the most dispassionate tourist. The museum is open all year Tuesday through Saturday from 10am to 4:30pm. Admission is $3 for adults (the best bet you'll ever make) and $2 for students and senior citizens.

National Museum of Dance

Opened in 1986 in a former spa building (the Washington Baths) on South Broadway (U.S. 9), this establishment has the distinction of being the only dance museum in America. Exhibits and demonstrations record the history and development of modern dance. There are photo essays, costume exhibits, and a library/resource center that features lectures and video presentations. Special events are held throughout the season. The museum is presently open from late May through September on Tuesday through Sunday from 10am to 6pm. Closed holidays. Beginning in September, the museum will be open Thursday through Saturday from 10am to 5pm and Sunday from noon to 4pm. Admission for adults is $3; students and seniors pay $2; kids are a buck. For additional information, call 518/584-2225.

Yaddo

The former Saratoga estate of industrialist Spencer Trask and his wife, Katrina, has been operated as a retreat for writers and artists since the 1920s. The mansion itself is off-limits to visitors, but the lovely gardens are open free to the public during daylight hours. Yaddo (tel. 518/584-0746) is a world of velvety lawns, marble statues, and somber 80-foot-tall pine trees presided over by a majestic (to say the least) stone mansion with a five-story central tower. At the foot of the rose garden is a statue of *Christalan,* dated 1900 and dedicated "to the children of this house" (all four of the Trasks' children perished in a smallpox epidemic). Be sure to see the moody and mysterious woodland garden on the hillside behind the rose garden. Yaddo is located on Union Avenue, past the Race Course and just before the intersection with the Northway.

Antiques

An outfit called **Regent Street Antiques Center,** 153 Regent St. (tel. 518/584-0107), contains not just a collection of more stoneware crockery than you've ever seen but also the shops of approximately 30 dealers. Merchandise runs the gamut from rugs and oil paintings to books and silver, dishes and framed pictures, and more. It's a good browse; open daily from 10am to 5pm.

Saratoga National Historical Park

The Battle of Saratoga was one of Britain's pivotal defeats during the American War of Independence. Two American heroes emerged from the battle: Benedict Arnold, later of West Point infamy; and Col. Daniel Morgan, forever of Green Mountain Boys fame. Saratoga foiled the British plan to split the colonies in two along the line of the Hudson Valley. And temporarily anyway, it established Arnold as a national figure of great promise.

One looks in vain for the old town of Saratoga on the map these days. That's because it's now called Schuylerville, in honor of the aristocratic Schuyler family whose country seat is part of the Saratoga National Historical Park, P.O. Box 648, Rte. 32, Stillwater, NY 12170 (tel. 518/664-9821). Interestingly, General Schuyler had been relieved of command of the Continental troops hereabouts just prior to the battle. To add injury to insult, the retreating Gen. John Burgoyne burned Schuyler's country house to the ground in the course of his retreat. Schuyler's personal loss did not, however, prevent him from later treating the vanquished "Gentleman Johnny" with every courtesy. Subsequent to the debacle at Saratoga, Burgoyne was confined to the Pastures, Schuyler's town residence near Albany, as a combination prisoner/houseguest.

Schuylerville and the Saratoga National Historical Park are located about 14 miles due east of Saratoga Springs via N.Y. 29. The bulk of the park consists of the actual terrain, still rural and undeveloped, on which the famous battle occurred.

Students of the Revolution are going to love this place. Besides an informative **visitor center** full of audiovisual exhibits and enlightening brochures, there is a paved one-way loop, 9 miles long, at which key points in the course of the battle can be visited much like stations of the cross. If anything, there might be rather more here than is possible to absorb in a single day. One does feel a twinge of guilt skipping the odd site along the way. There now exists, unfortunately, a $3 per car fee. Should you be on a bike or on foot they expect a payment of $1 per person.

On the southern edge of Schuylerville, on today's U.S. 4, is **Schuyler House** (tel. 518/695-3664), a restored Colonial manse built in 30 days on the ruins of the house burned by Burgoyne. All the nails and hardware were salvaged from the ashes of the former house. It's quite a pretty old place, immaculately restored, rather smaller than it looks from the outside, partially furnished with 18th-century pieces and open daily June to Labor Day from 9am to 5pm. No charge.

The other site of interest is the **Saratoga Monument,** a Victorian-era obelisk that can be climbed for a breathtaking view of the surrounding mountains. On a clear day the panorama stretches from the Catskills to the Berkshires to the Adirondacks. Fitness buffs won't want to miss this staircase. Like the Schuyler House, the monument is open daily June to Labor Day from 9am to 5pm. The monument is on Burgoyne Street, atop a hill overlooking the center of Schuylerville.

WHERE TO STAY

Instead of starting with the most expensive place in town, I'm starting with the one I think is hands down the best. **Adelphi Hotel,** 365 Broadway, Saratoga Springs, NY 12866 (tel. 518/587-4688), has three-story Victorian columns supporting a porch overlooking the middle of Broadway. Erected in 1877, it has an intricate brown-and-yellow paint job that oozes period charm. Inside is a lobby loaded with Victorian frou-frou furniture, a stenciled ceiling, rococo revival sofas, and fringed draperies. A skylit staircase leads to 35 perfectly wonderful rooms, all unique and decorated with antique rugs and furniture, pictures on silk cords, swagged curtains, bordello color schemes, perhaps crystal drips on the bedside lights or involved chandeliers. All have high ceilings and private baths. An upstairs lounge packed with potted plants and appealing Victorian clutter leads to a wicker-filled porch beyond whose blossom-laden flowerboxes lies the panorama of Saratoga's famous Broadway. What a place for breakfast. Downstairs is an atmospheric café/bar for drinks and light meals and an outdoor garden with tables and chairs near the new pool. Open only May through October; off-season rates (May, June, September, and October), single or double, range from $80 to $135 nightly for the smallest room to the biggest suite. Add another $40 for stays during Skidmore graduation, holiday, and foliage weekends; add about $50 for each night of a July weekend (and figure a two-night minimum too). And during August (gulp), the nightly rate range leaps to $170 to $290, with a two-day weekend minimum. MC and V accepted.

All the rate structures in Saratoga are similarly complicated. And like all hotel charges, they're quite likely to change. The above description is meant to give you a feel for the local vagaries in price. This is, after all, a seasonal resort. Wherever you decide to stay, phone ahead for precise rates. The Adelphi, though not the costliest place in town, is the most atmospheric and my particular favorite.

The grand **Gideon Putnam Hotel,** Saratoga Spa State Park, P.O. Box 476, Saratoga Springs, NY 12866 (tel. 518/584-3000; fax 518/584-1354), is a big 132-room Georgian Colonial affair right in the middle of the state park. Built with the rest of the spa in the 1930s (and still owned by the State of New York), it has an elegant sweeping driveway, lofty white columns, a marble-floored lobby with lots of potted plants and a suave beige color scheme, plus lots of restaurants and bars. The hotel has been recently renovated, and all rooms are furnished with appropriate-looking Georgian Colonial pieces, along with new bedding, carpeting, and drapes. The old Roosevelt Bath House is presently being upgraded in association with the hotel. In addition to traditional mineral baths, massages are available. Open year-round. The Gideon Putnam basks, with good reason, in its reputation of being the *ne plus ultra* of racing week addresses. There's no question that it's the most famous hotel in town. In the winter (November through April) a standard double room here will cost you about $94 nightly; in the shoulder seasons (May through mid-June and September through October) that same room will be $114; the upward spiral culminates during racing weeks, when double-occupancy rates start at about $239 nightly.

Since the hotel is located within the boundaries of the state park, there is easy access to myriad summer activities. These include 18-hole golf, six tennis courts (three clay), an Olympic-size pool, and the performing arts center. A favorite combination in winter is cross-country skiing followed by a mineral bath and a fine meal at the hotel. Speaking of food, the Gideon has three dining rooms turning out breakfast (7:30 to 10am), lunch (noon to 2pm), and dinner (6 to 9pm) daily under the direction of a European-trained master chef. The Sunday brunch (11am to 2pm; $15 or $18 with unlimited mimosas or bloody marys) is a particular draw. Lunch might be one of the sandwiches starting at $5 or a dish like moussaka or seafood crêpes for about $8. At dinner, you can choose from things like veal scallops for $17, filet mignon, and stuffed shrimp for $20. All major credit cards accepted.

The **Saratoga Springs Sheraton,** 534 Broadway, Saratoga Springs, NY 12866 (tel. 518/584-4000, or toll free 800/325-3535; fax 518/584-7430), sits right in the middle of town contiguous to, and indeed a part of, Saratoga's new convention center. This place has everything—a fancy restaurant called the Sandalwood, an indoor pool, game rooms, exercise rooms, meeting rooms, you name it. It's relatively new (built in 1983), huge (190 rooms, which seems huge in Saratoga), modern (brown-brick, squared-off, no-frills architecture), and open all year. Essentially it's just a sexy motel with a lot of facilities and a vast lobby filled with Colonial furniture and oil paintings beneath acres of acoustic ceiling. The rooms are examples of state-of-the-art motel luxury. They typically have plush rose carpeting, wing chairs, baths equipped with hairdryers and telephones, framed pictures of horses, color TVs, and good-quality fabrics and furnishings. Indeed this place attracts a fair share of comfort and money-oriented sale and racing week heavies. During the off-season (November through April) a room for two costs $86 a night; during the shoulder seasons (May through July and September through October) doubles cost about $120 nightly. In August a double will run you between about $235 a night, and up to $450 for what they call a "king-alcove" (essentially an oversize room with a kitchenette and some living room furniture). All major credit cards accepted.

Inn at Saratoga, 231 Broadway, Saratoga Springs, NY 12866 (tel. 518/583-1890; fax 518/583-2543), is a brand-new hotel in a fully renovated old gabled wooden building. Its tiny lobby is decorated with tasteful striped paper, oak floors, gilt-framed mirrors, and period pictures on the walls. What was once the porch is now the Ascot Lounge for drinks; a former sitting room is now the hotel dining room. Everything in this place is perfect and new and salmon and beige. There is gracious Muzak in the halls, thick patterned rugs, and a definite plush look to things. The rooms feature great old-fashioned wallpapers, wing chairs, floral comforters, swagged curtains, brand-new baths, 25-inch TVs, full-length mirrors, and turn-down service. Nightly rates are your typical Saratoga tangle of dates and categories. The place is open all year and double-occupancy rates vary from about $70 to $90 in winter to $190 to $250 or so during August racing weeks. Suites, of course, cost more. As always, phone ahead to confirm the exact prices. All major credit cards accepted.

Holiday Inn, Broadway at Circular Street, Saratoga Springs, NY 12866 (tel. 518/584-4550; fax 518/584-4417), looks just the way you'd expect a Holiday Inn to look. The building adjoins Congress Park, and unlike the Victorian concoctions in the neighborhood, it has your basic flat roof, brick walls with random "used" bricks, panels of glass, and neatly clipped shrubs. There's a quite attractive outdoor pool, as well as 150 rooms available year-round. The place has been kept up very nicely and renovated regularly. Accommodations are spacious, equipped with two queen-size beds, thick rugs, nice pictures, textured wallcoverings, phones, and color TVs. Adjacent to the lobby is a closet full of gurgling video games as well as a bright restaurant serving breakfast, lunch, and dinner and doubling as a nightclub. Management provided me with two solid pages of single-spaced rate categories. Basically, doubles seem to hit a winter low of about $60, climb to shoulder highs of about

$75, before rocketing into the August racing weeks' stratosphere of $185 a night. All major credit cards accepted.

The Washington Inn is located just north of the Spa State Park at 1 South Broadway, Saratoga Springs, NY 12866 (tel. 518/584-9807). Consisting of two large turn-of-the-century boarding houses, the inn offers travelers a budget option for the hectic summer season. Open June through September only, the Washington offers 19 rooms with private baths, TVs, and phones. The July rate is $60 for a double and $70 for a twin. August rates are $90 and $99, respectively. Reservations are suggested. MC and V accepted.

Numerous motels line Broadway shoulder to shoulder south of Congress Park and the Holiday Inn. Most are 30-odd years old and have rate structures that reflect the extreme bell curve of the Saratoga racing season.

Also in this price range is **Downtowner Motel,** 413 Broadway, Saratoga Springs, NY 12866 (tel. 518/584-6160; fax 518/584-2907), located in the middle of Saratoga's central shopping, dining, and people-watching district. Downtowner is a middle-aged motel, albeit well kept and architecturally updated. All 42 rooms overlook a 42-foot-long lap pool housed in a two-story atrium. Accommodations have cable color TVs, phones, private baths, and air conditioning. During racing season expect to pay from $99 to $125, double occupancy; off-season rates drop as low as $45. All major credit cards accepted.

WHERE TO EAT

Deluxe

Ye Olde Wishing Well, on U.S. 9 about 4 miles north of town (tel. 518/584-7640), is definitely worth the trip. This is the sort of place where rich daddies take their little girls to dinner on Skidmore parents' weekends and where stable owners toast one another over a winning season. Only dinner is served, from 5 to 10pm on Tuesday to Friday and Sunday (to 11pm on Saturday), and the place is closed for three weeks in January. When it's open, it's packed. Diners are distributed in a collection of rustic/elegant old rooms of the stone-fireplace-and-exposed-beam variety. I had the biggest lamb chop I've ever had at the Wishing Well. Also available are king crabmeat au gratin, hot seafood platter, sirloin steak, filet mignon, and roasted fresh turkey, all of which come with salad and potato and cost between about $11 and $23 per à la carte selection. All major credit cards accepted.

Five miles south of Saratoga is a gourmet northern Italian and seafood restaurant called **The Elms,** 2721 U.S. 9, Malta (tel. 518/587-2277). In 1959, Filomena Viggiani, at 58, opened her first restaurant. Today it's become an institution, run with the help of daughter/hostess Esther and son/chef Michael. Chances are, if you've had a fine pasta plate anywhere in this neck of the woods, it was made in this kitchen. Distributed in eastern New York State, the Viggianis' pastas come in an ever-growing variety of flavors, including egg, spinach, tomato, artichoke, beet, carrot, tomato-basil, tomato-rosemary, lemon–white pepper, egg–black pepper, garlic–white pepper, fennel-lemon, saffron, even chocolate and squid ink. The decor of The Elms, unlike that of so many Saratoga restaurants, has no Victorian frills, antiques, or other gimmicks. But during August, when no reservations are accepted, you may find yourself standing in line with a duchess or a member of the American aristocracy or maybe even a movie star. Dinner main courses like shrimp Fra Diavolo, *tagliatelle pescatora* (my favorite), and *linguine al pesto* mostly cost from $9 to $17. Open for dinner only from 5 to 10pm; Sundays from 4 to 9pm; closed Monday in July; open daily in August. The restaurant is closed from Thanksgiving to mid-February and on Monday and Tuesday the rest of the year. All major credit cards accepted.

Eartha's Kitchen, 60 Court St. (tel. 518/583-0602), is famous for mesquite grilling. The location is in a quiet residential area between Union Avenue and Spring Street. Eartha's interior has a crisp country look, decorated with traditional Victorian Saratoga colors of bachelor cream, jumel red, and congress green. The wine bar sports wicker furniture and is a great place to taste Eartha's newest vintage.

The restaurant, which is a local center for wine tasting, is open for dinner from 5pm to 11pm every night during July and August, only Tuesday through Saturday the rest of the year. The menu changes daily and offers a selection of wonderful grilled and sautéed dishes from $15 to $18. All major credit cards accepted.

About a 15-minute drive south of Saratoga on N.Y. 50 and west on Charlton Road, you'll find the **Charlton Tavern,** 746 Charlton Rd., Charlton (tel. 518/399-9951). The tavern was an 18th-century stagecoach inn, now converted to an intimate restaurant with a large open-hearth fireplace, wood-burning stove, exposed hand-hewn beams, and wide-plank floors. The Maloney family has run the restaurant for more than 20 years and its continental/American cuisine is well known in the Capital District. Lunch ($4 to $7) and dinner ($10 to $18) are available from 11am to 9pm on Tuesday through Thursday and to 10pm on Friday and Saturday. All major credit cards accepted.

Moderate

Lillian's, 408 Broadway (tel. 518/587-7766), is a local favorite serving dependable steaks, seafood, and chicken. The restaurant's Victorian decor combines etched glass, stained-glass panels over the bar, mahogany woodwork, brass fixtures, tin ceilings, and Tiffany-style lamps. Antiques, Laura Ashley wallpaper, and a mauve/dark-green interior color scheme create a comfortable dining environment. Lunches are served Monday through Saturday from 11:30am to 4pm. Hot main courses and sandwiches are mostly from $4 to $7. Dinners cost from $14 to $18 and are available Monday through Thursday from 5 to 10pm, to 11pm on Friday and Saturday. All major credit cards accepted.

The Wheat Fields, 440 Broadway (tel. 518/587-0534), true to its name, specializes in pasta, made before your eyes in the front window where homemade breads are also baked and elaborate desserts displayed. You may not have realized so many different types of pasta existed. Enjoy platters of it, topped with inventive and/or traditional sauces, in either the appealing sidewalk café or one of the two clean and summery dining rooms. Lunch sandwiches and other light main courses are priced mostly from $4 to $10; dinner main courses like ravioli *con funghi* and *bistecca alla* Tuscany typically cost from about $10 to $17. Hours are 11:30am to 10pm on Monday through Thursday, until 11pm on Friday and Saturday, and from 4:30 to 9pm on Sunday. No reservations are taken; all major credit cards are accepted.

Around the corner at 40–42 Lake Ave. is **The Parting Glass** (tel. 518/583-1916), a large and authentic-looking Irish public house. It's actually more of a complex complete with a dark-oak bar surrounded by cozy booths and featuring 140 different beers, an enormous dining room upon whose stage nearly every Irish singer of merit has appeared at one time or another, and the Dub Lin Dart Hall consisting of 10 boards and even a pro shop. Open daily from 9am until 3am in summer, the Parting Glass serves a huge Irish breakfast buffet for $7.95, lunchtime burgers and hot sandwiches for about $5 to $8, and dinner main courses ranging from pasta to strip steak priced at about $7 to $12. Off-season hours are 11am to 2am on Sunday to Thursday and until 3am on Friday and Saturday. All major credit cards accepted.

The Olde Bryan Inn, 123 Maple Ave. (tel. 518/587-2990), which is just off U.S. 9 a block north of the Sheraton parking lot, looks from the outside like it might be a luxury restaurant. It occupies a restored stone house dating from 1832, the oldest in Saratoga. The interior is decorated with working fireplaces (three of them), exposed-stone walls, church pews, exposed beams, wide-plank floors, hanging ferns, and wooden tables. There is rock and roll on the jukebox, and the ambience is great. A single menu is available all day and features all manner of hearty sandwiches (corned beef reuben to BLT club to Canadian grill) priced at about $5 each; "light" items (chili, vegetable wrap, seafood salad, pasta primavera) ranging from around $4 to $8; and "hearty" selections (such as Cajun blackened steak, seafood kebab, prime rib, Jamaican shrimp sauté), most of which cost between $10 and $17. Open daily all year from 11:30am until midnight. All major credit cards accepted.

Sperry's, 30½ Caroline St. (tel. 518/584-9618), is a cute casual café with a great old mahogany bar. Located in a late two-story 19th-century brick building, the restaurant is decorated with resort memorabilia, including a mural depicting stagecoach scenes. Lunch is served between 10:30am and 5pm on Tuesday through Sunday; Sperry's famous jambalaya costs but $3.50, and the sliced London broil is a buy at $6.50. Dinners are available on the same days, from 5 to 10pm, and feature dishes like jambalaya with shrimp, sautéed veal, and so on, for about $11 to $18. All major credit cards accepted.

Professor Moriarty's, 430 Broadway (tel. 518/587-5981), is at the absolute center of Saratoga Springs. It's in essence a classy bar and burger joint, with a diminutive outdoor terrace on Broadway and a very busy interior decorated with saloon tile floors, brick walls, Victorian woodwork, antique light fixtures, oak tables, café chairs with brown-leather seats, and racing paintings. At lunch a burger and fries will run you around $4.50, a Moriarty burger is about $5, and various deli sandwiches run between $4 and $6. At dinner an amusing menu divides courses into the "Plot" (appetizers), the "Crime" (main courses), and the "Verdict" (dessert). Puns abound, chief among them being a dessert called "Death by Chocolate." Most main courses (such as chicken Moriarty, bay scallops, prime rib) cost between $10 and $18. Open daily, year-round, from 11:30am to 5pm for lunch and 5 to 11pm for dinner. The bar is very lively at night and stays open much later. All major credit cards accepted.

Budget

And don't forget **Bruegger's Bagel Bakery,** 451 Broadway, between Caroline and Lake Streets (tel. 518/584-4372), where all manner of sandwiches on all manner of bagels cost but $2 to $4. It's bright, clean, modern, cafeteria style—even has an outdoor terrace in the summer. The same outfit operates similarly attractive locations in Albany. Open Monday to Saturday from 7am to 7pm (to 5pm on Sunday). No credit cards accepted.

---

4. The Road West—Cooperstown & Cazenovia

Though somewhat geographically isolated, Cooperstown and Cazenovia are two aristocratic upstate towns with more than luxury real estate to recommend them. They both lie along the natural route between the Capital District and the Finger Lakes that I call "The Road West."

COOPERSTOWN

Only 70 miles west of Albany, at the foot of Otsego Lake, lies Cooperstown (pop. 2,300). This attractive village was founded by 1786 by William Cooper, father of the famous American novelist James Fenimore Cooper. Besides having important literary associations, Cooperstown is where Abner Doubleday is reputed to have invented the game of baseball in 1839. (Actually, a compelling historical case can be made for Hoboken, NJ, and 1846 as the correct place and date, but I won't go into that in a section on Cooperstown.) Regardless of where the game originated, Cooperstown is where the Baseball Hall of Fame is today located. Baseball and Cooper —what could be more American?

For the benefit of those who've never actually read anything by James Fenimore Cooper, here is Mark Twain on the subject of Cooper's literary style: "The conversations in the Cooper books have a curious sound in our modern ears. To believe that such talk really came out of people's mouths would be to believe that there was a time when time was of no value to a person who thought he had something to say when it was the custom to spread a two-minute remark out to ten; when a man's mouth was a rolling-mill, and busied itself all day long in turning four-foot pigs of thought into thirty-foot bars of conversational railroad iron by attenuation." This is from an 1897 essay titled "Fenimore Cooper's Literary Offenses."

Here is Louis C. Jones, author of *Cooperstown,* an informative publication of the New York State Historical Association (headquartered in Cooperstown): "It is easy enough to criticize Cooper's tortuous style, his unrealistic conversations, his fatuous 'females,' his endless descriptions, but he remains one of our literary giants and as much a pioneer in our literature as his father was in the wilderness. More than any other writer until the advent of Mark Twain, Cooper gave Europeans their most convincing picture of our country."

And Cooperstown is a delightful place to explore. It's situated at the foot of a beautiful lake and its physical plant has benefited from generations of attention from one rich and interested family. Its rural elegance is enhanced by a sumptuous lakefront resort hotel called the Otesaga, which has been operating here in an essentially unchanged manner since 1909. Filled with huge shade trees, beautiful old houses, a charming late 19th-century business district, good inns and restaurants, and lots of fascinating museums, Cooperstown is an excellent place to explore while en route across upstate New York.

If there is a fly in this otherwise pleasant ointment, it is the old bugaboo of commercialism. Baseball as a theme has taken such a vigorous hold on Cooperstown's business district as to devour nearly every bit of retail space. The natives have been heard of late to mutter darkly that the way things are going, they'll soon have to drive to Albany to buy a pair of shoes. Of course, if baseball memorabilia and/or paraphernalia is your thing, you'll be in heaven. This town is becoming to baseball what Manhattan's diamond district is to diamonds—namely, there is nothing else to buy.

Sights of Cooperstown

The village has three important museums, whose existence is due in large part to the generosity of the Clark family (of Singer Sewing Machine fame): the Baseball Hall of Fame, the Fenimore House Museum, and the Farmers' Museum.

Former "Tonight Show" host Johnny Carson pointed out in a monologue one night that the last two words of America's National Anthem are "Play Ball!" The **Baseball Hall of Fame** is a Georgian brick shrine to those of our fellow countrymen who have most excelled in this most American of pastimes. Superfans won't be disappointed by the collection here. There is a "Great Moments Room" with 9-foot blowups; a collection of over 1,000 artifacts (bats, balls, gloves) tracing the evolution of the game; the "All-Star Game Display," which is a clever mounting of clippings, programs, and pictures from the past; the "Ballparks Room," memorializing famous parks (complete with old turnstiles, benches, and seats); the "Hall of Fame Gallery," where 200 immortals are fittingly represented by bronze plaques; plus lots more, much of it dealing with players and games of the recent past. Museum admission is $8 for adults, $3 for "juniors" (7 to 12). Summer hours are 9am to 9pm daily from May through October; during the rest of the year the museum closes at 5pm. The museum is located on the corner of Main and Fair Streets, adjacent to the middle of the village (tel. 607/547-9988).

If you elect to visit more than one of the Cooperstown museums, you'll be entitled to a discount combination ticket, available at any one of the three museums. Tuck that bit of knowledge away; I'll return to it shortly.

Fenimore House is the former Georgian Revival mansion of Edward Severin Clark, grandson of Singer partner Edward Clark. Edward S. Clark was the "Squire" of Cooperstown in his day. His white-columned stone mansion was completed in 1932, the year before he died. His heirs saw to its (gentle and tasteful) conversion to a museum, which today contains an important collection of American folk art. Fenimore House's splendid rooms display woodcarvings, paintings, duck decoys, weather vanes, and tavern signs. Usually there's an interesting interpretive display mounted at any given time. When I was there the one on deck was called "A Shifting Wind" and demonstrated the different meaning folk art has had to the house's various custodians over the passage of years. Fenimore House, which stands on the site of the original Cooper farm, is also the headquarters of the New York State Historical Association. The folk art museum charges $6 for adults and $2.50 for juniors and is open daily from 9am to 6pm from May until the end of October. Winter hours vary; call before you go at 607/547-2533.

Farmers' Museum is adjacent to a reconstructed **Village Crossroads.** These installations occupy the former stable complex and adjacent grounds of the old Clark estate. Endangered buildings from hither and yon have been salvaged, moved to the spot of the Crossroads, and painstakingly restored. Nowadays all manner of colonial and early republican domestic business goes on here—shoeing horses, baking bread, spinning thread, printing broadsides, and the like. Besides the demonstrations are all manner of exhibitions and shows held at various times each summer. It's a most attractive and carefully researched (if prettified) view of life on the edge of the frontier. It certainly demonstrates pioneer American ingenuity. Open daily May through October from 9am to 6pm; during April, November, and December, open Tuesday through Sunday from 10am to 4pm; closed January through March. Admission is $8 for adults and $3 for juniors (7 to 15); the phone number is 607/547-2593.

As for those reduced-rate tickets: put briefly, you can save about 20% off the individual prices of two and 25% off the per-museum price of all three.

Other things to do in Cooperstown would include **walking around town** and admiring the prosperous Victorian streetfronts along Main Street and the leafy byways of Pine Boulevard, Lake Street, and Chestnut Street between Main and Lake. The center of the village is at Chestnut (also designated as N.Y. 80 and 28) and Main; more than six or seven blocks in any direction will put you out in the country. You can really get to know the village by taking a self-guided **walking tour of Cooperstown,** directions for which are printed by the New York State Historical Association and available free at both the Fenimore House and the Farmers' Museum.

Perhaps you'd enjoy a **cruise on Lake Otsego,** the famous Glimmerglass of James Fenimore Cooper. The *Chief Uncas* is a vintage lake boat operated during the summer by **Lake Otsego Boat Tours.** For sailing times and prices, call 607/547-9710.

Culture in Cooperstown doesn't stop at just museums. Would anyone have guessed that it's also the home of a flourishing opera company? The **Glimmerglass Opera** celebrated its 15th-anniversary season in 1989, and the third season in the company's new home. The **Alice Busch Opera Theatre** is a 900-seat, partially open-air theater a few miles north of Cooperstown on N.Y. 80. What's more, the performances are all in English. For summer program and ticket information, contact Glimmerglass Opera, P.O. Box 191, Cooperstown, NY 13326, or phone the box office at 607/547-2255 or 547-5704.

Finally, you might like to know about the new **Alfred Corning Clark Gymnasium** on Susquehana Avenue (tel. 607/547-2800). This is a fitness, recreation, and "adventure" facility with an Olympic-size pool, high diving boards, a state-of-the-art Nautilus center, an aerobics studio, bowling alleys, an indoor running track, a basketball court, and even climbing walls. The only thing missing, believe it or not, is a baseball diamond. Open Monday through Friday from 6:30am to 10pm, until 9pm on Saturday, and Sunday from 9am to 6pm. Adults over 21 pay $6 daily for unlimited use of the facilities; for those under 21 the cost is a mere $3; to combine aerobics classes with facility use costs $11 daily.

Actually you could spend quite a few happy days here, unwinding to be sure. A more romantic and out-of-the-way spot is hard to imagine.

Where to Stay in Cooperstown

The places I like best usually are small, old, and charming. **Cooper Inn,** Lake Street at Chestnut Street (P.O. Box 311), Cooperstown, NY 13326 (tel. 607/547-2567), is all of that and more. It's a handsome early Italianate house with white shutters and elaborate brackets under the eaves, sitting amid parklike grounds in the middle of town. Inside is a fine central hall with a graceful staircase and assorted lounge rooms filled with lovely antiques and an air of patrician calm. The 15 rooms are located upstairs, some with black-marble fireplaces, others with elaborate ceiling rosettes, all with private baths and old-fashioned furnishings, cable color TVs, and tons of charm. And guests here can use the plush facilities down the block at the Otesaga. Double-occupancy rates at the Cooper range from about $115 to $130 during the July to Labor Day season. They're about $80 during the rest of the year. All major credit cards accepted.

Right across the street, with its own deep lawn and immense maples, is the satisfyingly Victorian facade of **Inn at Cooperstown,** 16 Chestnut St., Cooperstown, NY 13326 (tel. 607/547-5756). The inn is a three-story mansard-roofed Second Empire confection whose inviting front porch is filled with rocking chairs. Inside everything has been restored to a level of perfection that one soon comes to expect in Cooperstown. The atmosphere is most appealing, if slightly less gentrified than over at the Cooper Inn. Downstairs is a small lounge with a TV, adjacent to which is a breakfast room. All the floors are refinished; all the paint is crisp; every Victorian antique gleams. Each of the 17 newly decorated rooms has a private bath, thick wall-to-wall carpeting, table lamps with pleated shades, gauzy curtains on tie-backs, and dark-stained Colonial-reproduction furniture. Double-occupancy rates include a continental breakfast and range from about $80 to $90 nightly, with reduced winter packages available. All major credit cards accepted.

One of the architectural and psychological anchors of Cooperstown is the aforementioned **Otesaga Hotel,** Lake Street (P.O. Box 311), Cooperstown, NY 13326 (tel. 607/547-9931; fax 607/547-9675). This huge (125 rooms) Georgian palace sits right on the lake amid velvety lawns and specimen trees, a block or two from the center of town. There is a formal columned portico (and a formal dress code in the evening), beyond which lie vast traditional public rooms decorated with pale colors, gleaming brass, lots of floral prints, and sweeping lake views. It's a very fine 1909 building in very fine condition, with not a tacky addition in sight. Besides the lake frontage, there are a big outdoor pool, a bar, a lounge, an adjacent golf course, and an old-fashioned main-floor dining room worth a visit for lunch or dinner whether or not you stay here. Room decor is more chaste than the Edwardian architecture of the place might suggest. But the rooms are big and the furnishings all seem to be pretty new and of high quality. All rooms have TVs and private baths and are spanking clean. The Otesaga is open only from May until the end of October, during which time the per-person Modified American Plan (breakfast and dinner included) rate per day per person ranges from about $110 to $145, double occupancy, depending on the size and location of the room. *Note:* This is a resort hotel and as such offers accommodations on the MAP basis only.

Also good to know about is the string of immaculate little mom-and-pop motels that dot N.Y. 80 along the northern half of Otsego Lake. Prototypical of these is the **Lake View Motel,** on N.Y. 80 (R.D. 2, Box 932), Cooperstown, NY 13326 (tel. 607/547-9740), whose 14 units have thick rugs, cable color TVs with HBO, AM/FM radios, direct-dial phones, vaguely traditional-looking furnishings, and gleaming private baths. It was built over 25 years ago but looks brand-new. The location is right across the road from a lakefront landing at which you can swim or rent a boat or a canoe. From late June until Labor Day double-occupancy rates range from $90 to $95 nightly; there's a $20 drop in prices during the rest of the year. A number of other motels in the vicinity are just as nice; this one appealed to me the most. MC and V accepted.

Where to Eat in Cooperstown

A meal at **Otesaga,** on Lake Street (tel. 607/547-9931), should be a part of any visit because it's such a part of the town. The hotel dining room is only slightly smaller than a football field—or perhaps more appropriately, a baseball diamond—and features lofty ceilings, lots of moldings, and (if you're lucky) a good view of the water. Lunch and dinner are both sumptuous buffets at which you can have as much as you want of anything you see. The price, which includes tip and tax, is a surprisingly affordable $8 for breakfast, $12.50 at lunch, $27 at dinner, and $15 for Sunday brunch. The dining room is open every day during the hotel's season (May through October) from 7:30 to 9am for breakfast, noon to 2pm for lunch, and 6:30 to 8:30pm for dinner. MC and V accepted.

Right in the village is an atmospheric tavern/restaurant called **Bold Dragoon,** 49 Pioneer St. (tel. 607/547-9800). Half of it's a bar with a regular clientele; the other half is a cozy narrow dining room with pine-paneled booths, dim lighting, and rock and roll on the jukebox. Expect to pay well under $4 for sandwiches and burgers at lunch, and around $6 to $10 for dinners like chicken parmesan, pork chop, broiled scallops, and roast beef, all of which include soup or salad, potato, and vegetable. They even have "light" dinner items (honey-dipped chicken, chef's salad) for $4 to $5. Open daily all year long: 11:30am to 2:30pm for lunch and 5 to 9pm for dinner. No credit cards accepted.

The **Doubleday Café,** at 93 Main St. (tel. 607/547-5468), has oak wainscoting, baseball paintings on the exposed-brick walls, lofty ceilings, and the occasional hanging fern. Breakfast, lunch, and dinner are served every day from a menu that lists nothing over $7. Greek and Mexican burgers are a reasonable $3.75, an omelet with toast a mere $2. MC, DC, and V accepted.

Located in the basement of the Tunnicliff Inn, at 34–36 Pioneer St., is a terrific pub called **The Pit** (tel. 607/547-4063). It's open all year for lunch and dinner, with afternoon sandwiches and burgers costing $3 to $6 and traditional evening platters of fish, meat, and poultry priced from about $11 to $16. The atmosphere is fun and boisterous. If you'd like your meal in more sedate surroundings, there's a chandelier-lit dining room upstairs, complete with a fireplace and crisp white linen. All major credit cards accepted.

Locals love **Lake Front,** overlooking Otsego Lake at the foot of Fair Street (tel. 607/547-8188). The decor is modern and pleasant (murals, picture windows, acoustic ceilings with iron chandeliers). The extensive and sophisticated lunch menu has elaborate sandwiches (teriyaki turkey, Cooper Special, barbecued beef on a kaiser), plus interesting dishes (marinated chicken breast, "spreads" consisting of cold sandwiches served with a grilled stuffed tomato, omelets of all sorts) almost all of which are priced below $7. At dinner you might have something like filet mignon chasseur, broiled lamb chops, chicken au gratin, sautéed scallops, or duck à l'orange, which will likely cost you somewhere between $10 and $17. The chef studied at the famous Culinary Institute of America in Hyde Park. Between Easter and late October, lunch and dinner are served daily from 11am to 5pm and 5 to 9pm, respectively. During the off-season, lunch hours are 11am to 2pm. MC and V accepted.

For deli sandwiches, homemade salads, fresh breads, pâtés, imported cheese, and beverages to go, try **Danny's Main Street Market,** 92 Main St. (tel. 607/547-4053). This colorful 19th-century market, complete with tile floor and stamped-tin ceiling, offers five daily varieties of freshly ground coffee, tasty chili and homemade soup by the cup, all manner of cold salads (macaroni at $2.40 per pound to artichoke at $5.89 per pound), and overstuffed sandwiches priced reasonably from about $3 to $5. An excellent place to pick up picnic provisions.

CAZENOVIA

About 100 miles west of Albany on N.Y. 20 is Cazenovia (pop. 2,600). This delectable upstate village has wonderful inns, a picturesque lake, an abundance of handsome early 19th-century architecture, and a beautiful and historic mansion bequeathed to the State of New York in 1968. The mansion is called Lorenzo and has been, in its ups and downs, a bellwether of the fortunes of Cazenovia itself. There are other fine estates in the nearby rolling countryside and along the shores of Cazenovia Lake. But Lorenzo is the soul of the town.

Cazenovia was founded in 1793 by one John Lincklaen. The founding of the town and the sale of lots were a part of but one of many speculative land subdivisions taking place across upstate New York in those days. Lincklaen was the agent of an outfit called the Holland Land Company, and he named his new town after Theophile Cazenove, a sort of T. Boone Pickens of his day and Lincklaen's boss.

For about 20 years both Lincklaen and Cazenovia prospered. Trouble started when it became known that the Erie Canal was going to bypass Cazenovia. The Holland Land Company decided to liquidate its area holdings immediately. In order to protect the value of his own lands Lincklaen felt compelled to buy *all* the company's unsold land in the Cazenovia vicinity. Construction had hardly started on the Erie Canal in 1817 when land prices in Cazenovia, not unexpectedly, crashed. Lincklaen died in 1822, deep in debt. The following year his widow sold Lorenzo, at that time one of the finest estates in America, for $100. She retained only the right to live in the house until she died.

But that was not the end of the Lincklaens. Through judicious marriages and adoptions, Mrs. Linklaen and her family managed to preserve and indeed enhance their position in Cazenovia. Their name was Fairchild during the late 19th and early 20th centuries. They still ruled at Lorenzo when other mansions, this time for summer people, began rising all around them. They were Remingtons until the 1950s, and Ledyards at the end, when George S. Ledyard, as much of an "aristocrat" as this country is ever likely to produce, died at Lorenzo in October 1967.

Today's visitors to the village can savor its elegant traditions in various ways. You can, for instance, stay at one of its **charming inns,** about which I'll say more below. If you fancy Colonial, patrician Federal, Greek Revival, and mid-Victorian architecture, you can spend many pleasurable hours on do-it-yourself **walking tours** and **driving tours.** The village is full of elegantly columned Greek Revival houses shaded by huge trees. It's truly a treat to walk around. The Cazenovia Preservation Foundation, Inc., P.O. Box 266, Cazenovia, NY 13035, publishes two pamphlets titled, respectively, "5 Walks in the Village of Cazenovia," and "5 Drives, Town of Cazenovia." These brochures cost 50¢ each and are usually available at the Lincklaen House Hotel, the Town Office, local bookstores and drugstores, or in advance by mail from the Preservation Foundation, Box 627, Cazenovia, NY 13035.

It's worth noting that Cazenovia didn't survive in quite so handsome a condition all on its own. The local preservation foundation has been working for over 25 years urging merchants to take down ugly signs and storefronts, and encouraging owners to restore buildings aesthetically. The result is a village without unsightly signage, where the gas stations that do exist actually still wash your windows.

The brick Federal mansion of **Lorenzo** is, of course, the principal attraction in town. It's not huge as mansions go, but it has a fine position looking up the length of Cazenovia Lake, and the lands around it are still rural and bucolic. Inside it looks just like the lived-in house of some rich old family. All the original stuff is still here —paintings, fabulous upholstered furniture, crystal chandeliers, silver, dishes, photographs in silver frames, the lot. Behind the house is a lovely garden bordered by lines of ancient evergreens called the Dark Aisle. Planted in the 1850s to screen the gardens from the surrounding fields, they contain romantically gloomy paths. Lorenzo (tel. 315/655-3200) overlooks the lake and N.Y. 20, but the entrance is on N.Y. 13 going toward DeRuyter. The house is open May to Labor Day on Monday to Saturday from 10am until 5pm (from 1pm on Sunday). The grounds are open all year on Wednesday to Monday from 8am until sunset. Admission is free.

Aside from touring Lorenzo, soaking up the ambience in the streets, and enjoying good meals and atmospheric lodgings, there isn't a lot else to do in Cazenovia. There is, however, the annual **Lorenzo Driving Competition.** This is an exposition of horse-drawn vehicles that takes place on the third weekend in July. There is also **Christmas at Lorenzo,** an annual holiday celebration in the old house. You might consider writing to the Cazenovia Business Association, P.O. Box 66, Cazenovia, NY 13035, to inquire whether other special events might be taking place at the time of your visit.

Where to Stay & Eat in Cazenovia

I love **Lincklaen House,** 79 Albany St., N.Y. 20, Cazenovia, NY 13035 (tel. 315/655-3461). In fact, my wife and I spent a night there during our honeymoon. It's a three-story brick building in the middle of town, not too big, with small white-columned porches and dark-green shutters. The lobbies and public rooms on the main floor have a gracious and dignified air. There is old painted paneling, red-leather furniture, Oriental rugs, big fireplaces, a graceful old staircase, and a lovely old dining room with painted paneled columns. There are only 21 rooms, all with private baths. They're absolutely immaculate and decorated with pretty wall stencils, chenille spreads, new TVs, tons of fluffy towels, and comfortable armchairs. Double-occupancy room rates vary from about $70 nightly for a small room with a double bed to $130 for larger accommodations and suites. Befitting its status as a local institution (it's been a hotel since 1835), the Linklaen House is open all year long. MC and V accepted.

Brewster Inn, N.Y. 20 on Cazenovia Lake, Cazenovia, NY 13035 (tel. 315/655-9232), is a fine shingled manse with velvety lawns that sweep down to the water's edge. Built as a summer home in the late 1880s for a railroad man and sometime Rockefeller partner named Benjamin Brewster, it contains lots of handsome woodwork; a gorgeous three-story staircase; gilt mirrors; Empire antiques; gleaming floors; thick rugs; and nine guest rooms, each with a private bath. Some of the rooms have features like Jacuzzis mounted adjacent to king-size brass beds. Others look like nice old-fashioned guest rooms in your rich grandmother's house. The furnishings are of no precise period, but the effect is certainly good. And the rooms, with their tall ceilings and old moldings, are inherently elegant. Two people will pay anywhere from about $65 to $225 nightly, depending on whether or not they want the Jacuzzi and the fantasy-provoking bed. Five of the nine rooms cost under $100. MC and V accepted.

Brae Loch Inn, on N.Y. 20 at the corner of Forman Street (tel. 315/655-3431; fax 315/655-2787), has 15 great rooms and offers wonderful Scottish hospitality. The Barr family has brought to Cazenovia not just a good inn and restaurant but also the largest Scottish gift shop in New York State. Rooms here are very comfortable; filled with antiques; and have private baths, color TVs, and air conditioning. Prices range from $80 for a room with a double bed to $125 for a room with a queen/king canopied bed (bridal suite). Brae Loch is a Victorian barn of a place with modern additions. Best accommodations, in my opinion, are in the old part. All major credit cards accepted.

For meals too, **Brewster Inn** (tel. 315/655-9232) is hard to beat. The original lake-view porch has been enclosed, furnished with tables and chairs, and converted into a singularly smooth operation that dispenses dinner only from 5 until about 9pm, seven days a week. Sample menu items include blackened sea bass, poached salmon, roasted duckling, London broil, cape scallops, and roast beef and cost between about $13 and $16 à la carte. MC, DC, CB, and V accepted.

Lincklaen House, 79 Albany St. (tel. 315/655-3461), serves both lunch and dinner in its charming white-painted paneled dining room or, if the weather is nice, on a terrace in the back. Lunch is typically a $5 to $10 affair, chosen from selections that include omelets, club sandwiches, and inventive salad plates. At dinner you might try country inn chicken, sirloin steak, broiled scallops, or baked ham with port wine sauce, priced from about $10 to $18. Lunch hours are 11:30am to 2pm; dinner is served from 5:30 to 9pm; open daily. MC and V accepted.

The restaurant at the aforementioned **Brae Loch,** at the corner of Albany and Forman Streets (tel. 315/655-3431), is rather posh-looking, with a rich darkwood staircase and crimson wallcoverings. Most people eat in the low-ceilinged atmospheric basement, which is a warren of brick-walled, candlelit rooms, all very dim and red. Only dinner is served Monday to Friday from 5 to 9pm (to 10pm on weekends). The menu features things like lamb chops, Rock Cornish hen, filet mignon, lobster tail, crabmeat au gratin, and mixed grill for prices between $12 and $18 per à la carte selections. All major credit cards accepted.

For something simpler, try **Alberts,** 52 Albany St. (N.Y. 20) just east of the Square (tel. 315/655-2222). This little old gray-and-white building contains a pair of simple rooms, one with a bar, the other with booths and tables with paper placemats. It's a local spot for sandwich and burger lunches for $4 or less as well as dinners that rarely top $10. Breaded veal, deep-fried sea scallops, open steak sandwich, stuffed flounder, chicken in the basket, and spaghetti dishes are typical evening alternatives. Open daily from 11am until 11pm. All major credit cards accepted.

THE MUSICAL MUSEUM AT DEANSBORO

About midway between Cooperstown and Cazenovia, some 7 miles north of N.Y. 20, is the village of Deansboro. This otherwise anonymous hamlet is worth a detour for the sake of the Musical Museum, N.Y. 12B, Deansboro (tel. 315/841-8774). Operated by the Sanders family since 1948, this is a delightful and unusual display of antique music boxes, melodions, wildly elaborate player pianos, grind organs, mechanical violin players, band organs, automatic singing birds (real skins on wooden forms!), calliopes, and vintage phonographs. There are 17 rooms full of the stuff, much of which you can crank up, switch on, pump up, or trigger yourself. The Sanderses take special pride in their "hands on" policy, which has allowed almost two generations of visitors to touch and activate some of the most amazing musical gizmos you're ever likely to see. Also on the premises is a shop specializing in old lamps and a gift shop. Open daily from 10am until 4pm, April through December. Definitely a one-of-a-kind place. Admission is $5 for adults and $4 for children.

THE ADIRONDACKS

Fully one-sixth of New York State lies within the so-called Blue Line of Adirondack State Park. That's six *million* acres of land (much of it forested), with more than 40 mountain peaks over 4,000 feet in height and around 2,000 lakes.

Actually, only about half this acreage is owned by the state and protected by the "forever wild" provisions of the state constitution. The rest of it belongs to folks like you and me and contains houses and motels, shops and estates (called "great camps" in this neck of the woods), filling stations, car dealerships, and ski areas. Of course, none of this development is too closely spaced. The Adirondacks are sparsely populated to say the least. Many private holdings up here number in the tens (sometimes hundreds) of thousands of acres.

The Indians avoided the Adirondacks, at least in the winter. It was the white man's lust for timber and fur that led to the first real settlements. By the late 19th century, the charms of the mountain wilderness began to attract the attention of America's bursting crop of industrial millionaires. Clever hoteliers like the legendary Paul Smith, as well as inspired developers like William West Durant, managed to put the stamp of fashion on the place. It was said of Smith, in his 1912 obituary, that "When he went to the Adirondacks many years ago the woods were full of Indians; when he died they were full of millionaires." In 1896, it is interesting to note, undeveloped land around fashionable Upper St. Regis Lake (which is really in the middle of nowhere) was selling for $4,000 an acre.

William West Durant, son of a railroad millionaire, devoted most of his life to promoting the development of the Adirondacks as a vacation preserve for the rich. The rustic/elegant school of architecture and furniture design that we call the "Adirondack style" and is today an important part of our national cultural heritage exists largely because of Durant and his tireless promotional efforts. W. W. Durant strove for effect, for opulence in the midst of untamed wilderness, for the "improbable, if not the impossible." People with names like Vanderbilt, Webb, Morgan, Woodruff, Bache, Rockefeller, Lewisohn, Garvan, and Stokes were captivated by the Adirondack style. The name referred not just to massive, rustic architecture, but to an image as well. The Adirondacks were a place where one might see a woman in full evening dress, dripping with diamonds, being paddled to dinner in a canoe by a man in a boiled shirt and tails; where one's dinner might be served in a room with a ceiling of hand-rubbed logs and walls covered with antique French damask; where the "camp" of one's host might contain 60-odd buildings, employ a permanent staff of 80-odd locals, and be visited but 3 weeks a year.

Besides the great camps were the great hotels, long-vanished wooden palaces where city dudes dropped $20 tips and drank champagne on the piazzas, society women waltzed to the music of imported orchestras, and grizzled mountain men found new careers as "guides." Of course, intrepid types were hiking into the mountains and roughing it for real even while the great camp era was at its peak. The development of the Adirondacks as an outdoor playground for the masses, however, has been a relatively new phenomenon. The state park dates from the late 19th century, but its use by other than millionaires, occasional Teddy Roosevelt types, and lumber companies is a development not much more than 30 years old.

1. Deciding Where to Go

I suspect that many people leave the Adirondacks feeling cheated and disappointed because they didn't find the type of experience that would have satisfied their expectations. Therefore, I've divided the balance of this chapter into four sections, each corresponding to a distinctly different type of Adirondack vacation.

To start with I'll describe a representative sampling of the most interesting **vacation resorts and retreats.** These establishments are destinations unto themselves, where your meals and activities are part of the total package and the ambience of the surroundings—mountains, lakes, crystal-clear atmosphere—is the point of the whole trip. The selection ranges from a famous hotel on the shores of Lake George, to a great camp on Upper Saranac Lake that takes in guests, to a couple of old-fashioned family hotels and secluded retreats in the mountains, to a gaggle of dude ranches where the daily emphasis is on Western-style horseback riding.

After that I'll talk about the most famous of the **resort towns,** notably Lake Placid and Lake George Village. These towns are attractions in and of themselves, and each has its own complement of accommodations in various price ranges.

Next I'll discuss the **wilderness experience:** hiking, boating, hunting, camping, that sort of thing. This book is not a wilderness guide, but at least this section will point those interested in the right direction for more detailed information.

The last section suggests scenic routes, interesting stops, and famous attractions for people who, while en route somewhere else, don't want to miss a taste of New York State's famous upstate wilderness. Together with the section on resort towns, this material will enable you to plan an enjoyable itinerary on your own.

2. Vacation Resorts & Retreats

I'll start with the most impressive of them all, the **Sagamore,** on Lake George at Bolton Landing, NY 12814 (tel. 518/644-9400, or toll free 800/THE-OMNI; fax 518/644-2604). The hamlet of Bolton Landing is about 10 miles due north of Lake George Village on N.Y. Route 9N. There's a turnoff in the center of town, clearly marked with Sagamore signs. A short drive takes you to a bridge leading to the Sagamore's private island. Beyond this are a gatehouse and a separate building for guest registration.

The historic core of the Sagamore complex is an enormous green-shuttered white clapboard inn dating from the 1920s. It's surrounded by painstakingly precise formal plantings, sweeping drives, views of the "Queen of American Lakes" (that's Lake George), surmounted by an elaborate white cupola, and listed on the National Register of Historic Places. The hotel was renovated to the tune of some $65 million and reopened in 1985.

Some 53 rooms and 47 suites are contained in the original hotel building. Another 120 rooms and 120 suites occupy 7 modern "cottage" complexes distributed around the island. The cottages are quite luxurious, but to my taste the old hotel is more appealing. I could go on for pages describing the Sagamore. It contains beautiful restaurants; a marina with lake swimming; a private launch called the *Morgan* (which can seat 88 for dinner); a nightclub; a health club and spa; indoor and outdoor tennis courts; an indoor pool; a nearby golf course; a shopping promenade; and beautifully decorated rooms with thick rugs, remote-control TVs, handsome traditional furniture, and the look and feel of real luxury.

The hotel has a splendid view of Lake George, whose shoreline looks almost uninhabited from this vantage point. I can't think of more aesthetically appealing surroundings for a summer vacation in the mountains. I hasten to note, however, that the Sagamore is open all year long and offers numerous packages (Golf, Fall Foliage, Spa, Classic Romance, Murder Mystery, Easter Weekend) during cool and colder months.

In the height of summer (July through August) there's a three-night minimum stay at prices that vary from about $150 to $390 per person per night. Breakfast and dinner are available for an additional $42 per person. Those prices remain the same in May, $150 to $390 June, September, and October, but management drops the three-night minimum. From November through April the rate range descends to between $79 and $149 per person per night. No minimum stay is required in winter, except on certain special weekends. The package plans mentioned above offer considerably reduced rates throughout the year, except June, July, and August. All major credit cards accepted. This memorable place is without question the nicest in the mountains.

A few miles south of the Sagamore is **Canoe Island Lodge,** on N.Y. 9N (P.O. Box 144), Diamond Point, NY 12824 (tel. 518/668-5592; fax 518/668-2012). Though a considerably less pretentious affair than the Sagamore, it has a great deal of charm and a nice warm atmosphere. The 56 units are distributed among a collection of little log cabins and shingled lodges hugging a steep hillside overlooking Lake George. At the center of the complex is an attractive old-fashioned lodge with peeled-beam ceilings, hooked rugs, burlap-shaded lamps, a huge stone fireplace, and a great woodsy-family atmosphere. During July and August management requires a three-day minimum stay. During other months, they don't encourage overnighters, but if you present yourself at the door and they have the space, of course they'll take you in.

Rates include breakfast and dinner and range from about $76 to $140 per person per night. Stay for a week and you'll get a slightly better rate. Stay during the shoulder months (May, June, September, October) and they'll toss in lunch for no extra charge. Meals are taken in a huge log-walled dining room overlooking the lake. There isn't a pool, but there are 600 feet of private lakefront—plus a dock with all manner of boats—and a private island just offshore. Accommodations are modern, comfortable, and sparkling clean. Closed November through April.

About 15 miles northwest of Lake George Village, via U.S. 9 and N.Y. 28, is Friends Lake and **Balsam House,** Friends Lake, Chestertown, NY 12817 (tel. 518/494-2828; fax 518/494-4431). The Balsam is a rambling Victorian clapboard affair with a mansarded tower, a big porch, 20 guest rooms, and a famous restaurant. There are a private beach and boathouse on Friends Lake, a three-minute walk down a gravelly path. The place has been completely renovated and redecorated in plummy Victorian tones with lots of upholstered furniture and swagged curtains. The rooms have private baths and phones, pastel carpeting, wicker headboards, and occasional antiques. They're smallish but very nice. The best part of the place is its congenial and hospitable atmosphere. And, of course, its excellent country French restaurant. During weekends and holidays two people will pay $135, Modified American Plan (MAP; breakfast and dinner included), nightly for a room. During the week that rate drops to $115 nightly. Bed and breakfast only costs $50 less. The restaurant is a big, comfortable, thickly carpeted, dimly lit room with a copper-topped island in the middle. The crystal and silver glisten, the linen is immaculate, and food is excellent. Cuisine is French country and includes stuffed chicken breast, duck à l'orange, baby lamb, poached turbot, fried shrimp in sweet mustard sauce, and steak au poivre. Only dinner is served, and most selections cost between $12 and $22. Daily dinner hours are 6 to 9 pm (until 8pm in winter); also on the premises is a very congenial lounge. All major credit cards accepted.

Also in Chestertown, but on the other side of Friends Lake, is **Friends Lake Inn,** Friends Lake, Chestertown, NY 12817 (tel. 518/494-4751; fax 518/494-7423). This stylish country inn offers romantic candlelit dining and 17 comfortable rooms decorated with antiques and reproductions, equipped with private baths, plus a few Jacuzzis. There is a library on the first floor, as well as a game and TV room complete with videotapes. Besides the parlor and dining room is an enclosed porch with views of the lake. The dining room is quiet and countrified, with a pressed-tin ceiling, chestnut woodwork, and a large brick fireplace. A number of patrons drive all the way from Albany (90 minutes) for an intimate dinner "à deux," priced from about $11 to $20 per à la carte main course. In winter, guests downhill ski at nearby Gore or go cross country on 15 miles of nearby cross-country trails. In summer, there's a dock on Friends Lake for lolling in the sun, taking a dip, launching a canoe, or going out windsurfing. Double-occupancy room rates range from $65 midweek, including full country breakfast, to $160 on weekends for a room with Jaccuzi, breakfast, and dinner. Special weekend ski and white-water rafting packages are available as well. MC and V accepted.

Thirty-two miles northwest of Warrensburg, overlooking Thirteenth Lake, is a vintage inn called **Garnet Hill Lodge,** 13th Lake Road, North River, NY 12856 (tel. 518/251-2821). Built in 1936, this rustic 22-room log lodge has an atmospheric living/dining room of varnished knotty pine and offers close proximity to such traditional Adirondack pastimes as hiking, fishing (particularly for landlocked salmon and brook trout), and canoeing. In fall and spring, there is also white-water rafting, and during the snow season there are nearly 35 miles of adjacent cross-country ski trails (plus rentable equipment on premises). MAP rates (including breakfast and dinner) are $58 to $80 per person in summer, and $60 to $90 during winter. Closed for two weeks in November. No credit cards accepted.

Those who care to get up, and I mean up, and away should consider **The Highwinds Inn,** Barton Mines Road, North River, NY 12856 (tel. 518/251-3760). The road climbs 2,400 feet in 5 miles from the banks of the upper Hudson River. During my last trip, I arrived at the old Barton Garnet Mines for a late dinner in the midst of a snowstorm. I was certain that my wife and I would have the inn to ourselves, but to our amazement the dining room was filled with a crowd of local diners and overnight guests. Our hostess, making no reference to the howling storm outside, said only that we had missed a wonderful sunset. The next morning we took a tour of the mines and admired what must be one of the most spectacular views in New York State. The secluded Highwinds Inn offers four overnight rooms with baths, plus several wilderness cabins. The dining room has a bistro/French country menu that changes frequently. Pasta primavera costs $11, while a filet mignon is $18. Dinner hours are daily from 5 to 9pm. Those who decide to stay the night can tour the mine area, cross-country ski, go out on a trail bike, swim, play tennis, or visit the Gore Mountain Mineral Shop on the premises. Overnight per person rates, including breakfast and dinner, are $75 on weekends (with a two-night minimum) and $60 during the week. Closed in November and April. MC and V accepted.

Secluded within a 12,000-acre private forest on Elk Lake, described by National Geographic as "the jewel of the Adirondacks," is **Elk Lake Lodge,** North Hudson, NY 12855 (tel. 518/532-7616). The main lodge, built in 1904, is the protypical rustic-yet-luxurious Adirondack "camp," complete with huge fieldstone fireplace and Adirondack craft-movement furnishings. There are six twin-bedded rooms with private baths in the main lodge, plus seven adjacent cottages with living rooms, modern baths, and occasionally kitchens and fireplaces. Meals are served in the main lodge beside the fireplace, overlooking the lake and the high peaks of Boreas, Colvin, Nippletop, Dix, and Macomb. Guests have the use of the inn's canoes and boats; the Elk Lake area is also a favorite destination for fishermen. The lodge is open from early May to mid-November only; expect to pay between about $95 to $120 per day per person for room and meals. No credit cards accepted.

Some 10 miles east of Lake Placid, deep in the middle of the woods, is **Bark Eater Inn,** Alstead Mill Road, Keene, NY 12942 (tel. 518/576-2221; fax 518/

576-2071), which is a haven for those who seek a gracious sort of simplicity. Originally a stagecoach stop, the inn has stone fireplaces, wide-board floors, antique furnishings, and lots of 19th-century charm. There are several rooms in the 150-year-old main building, none with private bath. Four private-bath accommodations are located in a renovated carriage house and a log cabin in the woods. Besides a stable with horses for trail riding, you'll find a restaurant whose excellent north country breakfasts are included in the room rates. Expect to pay from $45 to $55 per person for bed and breakfast; add another $24 per person for a complete gourmet dinner. AE, MC, and V accepted.

Guests at Marjorie Merriweather Post's famous Camp Topridge used to fly up to the mountains on her private prop-jet, be driven by limo to the shores of Upper St. Regis Lake, transfer to Mrs. Post's private boat to cross the water, land at her wonderfully posh Adirondack-style boathouse, walk to the private funicular for the ride up the side of the ridge, and emerge at last on the threshold of a luxurious living room 60 feet long by 70 feet wide. Now that was luxury!

The other great camps were almost as luxurious, among them William Rockefeller's Camp Wonundra. Today Wonundra has been renamed **The Point,** Saranac Lake, NY 12983 (tel. 518/891-5674; fax 518/891-1152), and is open to paying guests. Staying here is about the closest you can come to the Adirondack millionaire experience. It's a beautiful place, complete with Adirondack-style main lodge; ancillary buildings; and a boathouse replete with vintage speedboats, canoes, and sailboats (use of which is gratis to guests). Each of the 11 rooms has a name and a distinct character. My favorites are the four in the main lodge—Mohawk, Morningside, Algonquin, and Iroquois. Meals are taken houseparty style in the great hall, a grand interior space with natural-wood walls, zebra rugs, stuffed animal heads, and the obligatory stone fireplace. One of the highlights of my short life was waterskiing on Upper Saranac Lake at what seemed like 50 mph behind a Mastercraft speedboat belonging to The Point.

Rates here include the use of all facilities, plus all meals, and drinks as and when you want them from serve-yourself bars located around the house. A couple will pay between $675 and $825 nightly for this historic luxury. Closed in April; reservations are a must. AE accepted.

Some 40-odd miles south of Upper Saranac Lake is Blue Mountain Lake, a mountain crossroads that is home to several crafts shops, the famous Adirondack Museum (see "Lake George to Blue Mountain Lake," below), as well as two perfectly wonderful camp-style Adirondack hotels. Now don't forget that around here "camp" means a lot more than a pup tent in a clearing. **The Hedges,** Blue Mountain Lake, NY 12812 (tel. 518/352-7325), was built originally for Brigadier Gen. Hiram B. Duryea. It's a picturesque product of the 1880s, a complex of charmingly asymmetrical log, shingle, and stone buildings on the edge of beautiful Blue Mountain Lake. There are 14 separate cottages, plus another 14 rooms in the main building and an adjacent stone lodge built about 1886 for Duryea's son. The interiors have that great old-fashioned camp look, a product of much stained tongue-and-groove paneling, old photos, gray-blue wicker furniture, big fireplaces, stamped-tin ceilings, and stuffed animal heads. Rooms and cottages are simple but all have private baths and lots of rustic character. I liked the accommodations in the stone lodge best, as they're the most formal.

The Hedges is a place to relax, swim, lie in the sun, take out the canoe, hike, visit the nearby Adirondack Museum, enjoy big family-style meals in the hotel dining room, and generally unwind. Most people stay for at least a couple of days, but overnight guests are always welcome, even in July and August. MAP rates start at about $60 per person and top out at about $80. All rooms require occupancy by at least two persons. Open from about mid-June to mid-October. No credit cards accepted

On the other side of the lake is **Hemlock Hall,** Blue Mountain Lake, NY 12812 (tel. 518/352-7706), another wonderful old shingled Victorian house, this time set up on a hillside and enjoying a perfect Adirondack view of lake and mountains. The main house has stone fireplaces; wood paneling; lots of books; a wicker-filled porch; and a boathouse with a sandy beach and a full complement of canoes, row boats, and sailboats. The woods adjacent to the house are filled with really pretty little cottages, most with fine water views and private baths. Accommodations in the main house share baths. As at Hedges and elsewhere, two meals are included in the room rate. The public rooms are transformed twice daily into dining halls where everyone sits down together, resort style. The atmosphere is friendly and informal; there are usually lots of kids. Between mid-June and the end of September, the MAP daily rate for double occupancy is about $100 in the main house and about $120 in the cottages with private baths. These rates drop about 10% in the shoulder seasons. Open mid-May to mid-October. Both Hemlock and Hedges are refreshingly unspoiled. No credit cards accepted.

Near the southern edge of the Adirondack State Park, close to Lake George Village, is the little town of Lake Luzerne, noted for dude ranches. The most elaborate of these is **Roaring Brook Ranch,** Lake George, NY 12845 (tel. 518/668-5767; fax 518/668-4019), whose sign on N.Y. 9N proclaims it to be a "tennis and ranch resort." The property is a large modern campus composed of dark-stained wood-sided buildings set on steep hillsides. There are tennis courts, velvety lawns, pools, gardens, fountains, 600 acres, and some 38 horses. While not elegant, it certainly is nice. The 134 accommodations resemble units in a good-quality motel. They have two double beds, TVs, phones, full tile baths, and nice modern furniture. MAP rates also include a free tennis clinic and riding once a day. From late June until Labor Day you'll pay between about $88 or so per person per day. Deduct about $12 daily if you don't care to ride. Spring and fall rates are $10 less. The main lodge contains an immense catering-hall-style dining room, a coffeeshop, a bar, and a lobby with barn siding and wagon-wheel chandeliers. There's plenty of family-style entertainment in the evening. Open all year. MC and V accepted.

---

3. Lake George to Blue Mountain Lake

LAKE GEORGE VILLAGE

Don't judge Lake George by Lake George Village (pop. 1,050). The "Queen of American Lakes" really deserves the title. It is crystal clear, entirely spring-fed, surrounded by magnificent mountain scenery, and an altogether appealing place. But Lake George Village, situated at its southern end, is not going to appeal to everybody.

Father Isaac Jogues named it Lac du Saint-Sacrement during an expedition in 1646. Sir William Johnson, royal agent for Indian affairs and an important man in these parts, renamed it in 1755 after King George II. It's typical of the lack of vengefulness in the American spirit that it was never renamed.

Lake George was enormously strategic during colonial and Revolutionary days, as it formed an important part of the water of the water route composed of lakes and rivers connecting Canada with New York City. In 1755, Fort William Henry was erected here by the British with an eye to protecting this route. And herein lies a particularly gruesome tale.

In March 1757, during the French and Indian War, the fort was attacked by 1,600 French soldiers under the command of General Montcalm. The French had convinced 3,000 Indians from 33 different tribes to make common cause with them against the English. By August it was clear to the English commander, Monro, that even if the fort itself was safe, the people within it (including many women and children from the surrounding settlement) were going to starve. Montcalm arranged a peaceful surrender. The Indians, however, disregarded Montcalm and fell upon the unarmed English. They then proceeded to butcher and scalp each and every one of them, culminating the proceedings by a ritual drinking of blood. Montcalm's horrified Frenchmen, outnumbered two to one by their allies, were unable to stop the massacre. When the Indians withdrew to the forest, the French piled the mutilated victims inside the fort and set fire to it all. This true tale is the basis of James Fenimore Cooper's *The Last of the Mohicans.*

By 1810, a peaceful village named Caldwell occupied lands adjacent to the old

Fort William Henry. By 1900, the Delaware and Hudson Railroad was depositing summer visitors at an elegant station practically on top of the former earthworks. There is no more railroad, even though the old station still stands alongside the reconstructed fort on Beach Road. Nor is there much of anything else that is "elegant" in Lake George Village.

What to See & Do in Lake George & Vicinity

Useful to know is the location of the **tourist information booth,** where all manner of brochures and helpful advice can be had for the asking. It's on the south side of town, just above the intersection of N.Y. 9N and 9L (near exit 22 of I-87) and at the south end of the village on U.S. 9 opposite Prospect Mountain.

The village itself is today a diminutive strip of tourist trinket shops, T-shirt emporia, and motels that comes alive for the summer season and slumbers the rest of the year. It is Coney Island in the mountains, albeit a very clean and family-oriented Coney Island. The main drag is U.S. 9, also called Canada Street, and in August there is so much traffic on the four blocks that form the heart of Lake George Village that white-gloved traffic cops are required on almost every corner. The lakefront is lined with restaurants; souvenir shops; and docks where you can rent speedboats, aquabikes, wetbikes, minihawks, or paddleboats and arrange parasail excursions. There's also a small beach in **Shepard Park,** which is right in the middle of all this, with a sandy shoreline, a lifeguard, and a pier.

Every inch of downtown Canada Street is devoted to souvenirs, amusement arcades, and establishments like the **House of Frankenstein** (tel. 518/668-3377), where giggling preteens can be seen on the sidewalk getting their picture taken with the bolt-necked one himself. On the southern edge of town are more elaborate amusement parks like **Water Slide World** (tel. 518/668-4407), with a pool featuring four-foot artificial waves, plus bumper boats and hot tubs. A few miles south of town on U.S. 9 is the biggest of them all, **Great Escape Fun Park** (tel. 518/792-6568), which bills itself as New York's largest theme park. Its 100 different rides have names like Desperado Plunge Flume, Sea Dragon, Screamer, and Steamin' Demon. There are additionally all manner of shows, attractions, and facilities. Great Escape costs $19 for adults and $16 for kids from 3 to 11.

Lake George Beach State Park (tel. 518/668-3352), a short hop from the village on Beach Road, is a world away from all this. Administered by the State of New York, it's a long strand of clean white sand, called the Million Dollar Beach, at the middle of which is a bathhouse. Parking in the adjacent lots costs $3 daily; it's another $1 to get onto the beach; a locker and use of the showers will run you another buck. The view up the length of Lake George is superb.

Lake George Steamboat Company, at the Steel Pier on Beach Road (tel. 518/668-5777), has been carrying passengers on Lake George since 1817. These days it operates three different boats: the *Mohican,* the *Minne-Ha-Ha,* and the *Lac du Saint-Sacrement.* All manner of cruises are available, from the basic one-hour shoreline cruise (for about $7.50 for adults and $3.50 for kids), to the Minne-Ha-Ha Dixieland Moonlight Cruise (about $12.50 and $6), to various other dinner and island and jazz-band varieties. Call them for further information and departure times. A competing outfit, **Lake George Shoreline Cruise Boats** (tel. 518/668-4644), docks nearby on Beach Road and offers similar services.

The reconstructed **Fort William Henry,** on the grounds of the Fort William Henry Motor Inn between Canada Street and Beach Road (tel. 518/668-5471), is a painstaking reconstruction surrounded by neat lawns and clipped bushes, and containing a museum complete with a costumed acting company. Daily tours and stage shows take place from May 1 to mid-October. Admission is $8. Besides blasting muskets, booming cannons, grenadier demonstrations, and musketball molding, you can also catch a slightly edited version of Randolph Scott and Binnie Barnes in the 1936 film version of *The Last of the Mohicans* right here in the fort.

Immediately south of Lake George Village, practically opposite the tourist information office, is the entrance to **Prospect Mountain,** known as **"The 100-Mile View."** This 5½-mile scenic road ascends to the 2,030-foot summit of Prospect

Mountain, from which a glorious view can be had. It's open from 9am until 6:30pm every day from May until October. There's a $4-per-car charge at the gatehouse.

Other things to do in Lake George might include taking in dinner and a Broadway show at the **Lake George Dinner Theater,** in the Holiday Inn on U.S. 9 (tel. 518/668-5781). There's a new production every summer, with nightly performances (except Monday) between late June and mid-October. The price is under $40 per person in the evening and about $28 for the Wednesday lunch matinee.

The **Warren County Tourism Dept.,** Municipal Center, Lake George, NY 12845 (tel. 518/761-6366), and the **Lake George Chamber of Commerce,** P.O. Box 272, Lake George, NY 12845 (tel. 518/668-5755), publish calendars of events and festivals in the Lake George area and can also provide you with a copy of the *I Love New York Warren County Travel Guide.* So if you need to know any more, you can direct your questions to them.

Where to Stay in Lake George & Vicinity

The **Sagamore** is the place to stay on Lake George; it is described above in "Vacation Resorts & Retreats," above. In the village itself, my favorite is **Fort William Henry Motor Inn,** U.S. 9/Canada Street, Lake George, NY 12845 (tel. 518/668-3081; fax ext. 325). This place stands in the middle of an 18-acre campus that includes the reconstruction of historic Fort William Henry, several restaurants, various shops, a sometime summer theater, and a pair of motel buildings with 99 rooms between them. There's a big parking lot full of late-model American sedans, an absolutely huge free-form outdoor pool (the largest in the Adirondacks) surrounded with big cement terraces and lots of chairs, acres of rolling lawn, an indoor pool, the Olde Tankard Taverne, and a pair of miniature golf courses. Rooms are divided between the new building and the old, but as a practical matter there's not much difference between them. They are spacious and contain color TVs, telephones, nice modern baths, two double beds; about half have views of Lake George. Double-occupancy rates depend on time of year and view and range from a low of under $48 to a high of close to $240 nightly. This nice, informal, family-oriented resort motel has the best location in Lake George. All major credit cards accepted.

Mass-produced it may be, but the **Holiday Inn,** U.S. 9/Canada Street (P.O. Box 231), Lake George, NY 12845 (tel. 518/668-5781, or toll free 800/356-5625; fax 518/668-9213), is still the most aesthetic hotel in town. The location is south of town, adjacent to U.S. 9, atop a little plateau with quite a splendid view of the lake and the nearby village. It's your traditional long, low, flat-roofed, modern-looking Holiday Inn, with lots of terraces and sliding doors and walls accented with used bricks. Inside the lobby the decor is quasi-Colonial, with lots of leather furniture, a TV permanently on, even a fireplace. There are a coffeeshop, a lounge, a restaurant, an indoor pool that's actually big enough to swim in, a very nice outdoor pool, laundry facilities, and superlatively nice rooms. Accommodations have thick rugs, color TVs, usually a pair of double beds, Colonial-reproduction furniture, and sometimes a truly gorgeous view of Lake George. In the high season (late June to the end of August) a double will cost between about $95 and $185 nightly; the rest of the year that range drops to $58 to $85. All major credit cards accepted.

On U.S. 9 immediately north of Lake George Village center is an unbroken line of "resort-type" lakefront motels. I'll be honest: They didn't make a big impression on me. An exception is **Lake Crest,** 366 Canada St., Lake George, NY 12845 (tel. 518/668-3374), which is sort of cute and cabin-y and has a courtyard/parking lot with leafy trees instead of glaring unadorned pavement, a coffeeshop, and 40 attractive motel-style units. The decor consists of shiny varnished pine walls, emerald-green rugs, nice baths, venetian blinds, and color TVs. The property, like all its neighbors, is long and skinny. At the lake end are seven rooms with water view, as well as a pool and a small private beach. Family operated since 1947, Lake Crest is open only from April until October. High-season (end of June to Labor Day) double-occupancy room rates vary from $86 to $135 nightly; the rest of the year the same rooms cost $49 to $98. MC and V accepted.

There are a zillion other motels in Lake George, but I'm hard-pressed to find much difference among them. Fortunately, other accommodation options exist nearby. The honky-tonk atmosphere stops abruptly as one leaves the village heading north on N.Y. 9N. The road winds through a deep forest dotted with pretty vacation houses and the occasional startlingly grand mansion. The surroundings are considerably more in keeping with the image of Adirondack beauty.

There are a number of attractive motels along 9N between Lake George Village and Bolton Landing, among them **Melody Manor**, N.Y. 9N, Bolton Landing, NY 12814 (tel. 518/644-9750). This place has a long black macadam drive running down the middle of a velvety lawn, a big pool with a chain-link fence around it, a collection of neat-as-a-pin buildings in motel-Bavarian style, a tennis court, a restaurant/lounge, and a private lakefront with dock and rowboats. The 40 rooms are pretty big, and each is nicely decorated with tables and chairs, usually a pair of double beds, a color TV, and sometimes a view of the famous Sagamore glittering in the distance across Lake George. Open only from May to November, the Melody Manor requires a three-night minimum stay during the months of July and August. The high-season tariff for two ranges from about $90 to $115 nightly; the rest of the season doubles are available for about $67 to $75 a night. The name, incidentally, commemorates the steam organ in a vanished mansion that once occupied the site. All major credit cards accepted.

Where to Eat in Lake George & Vicinity

Lucille's, across from Shepard Park at 259 Canada St. (tel. 518/668-9224), is an altogether appealing double-level seafood restaurant with a neon lobster out front and rope rails on the terraces. This is a big, convivial place with an antique nickelodeon; piano music on the weekends; a convivial bar; and dining rooms with varnished-wood tables, nautical motif paintings, and views of Lake George. At lunch you can buy steamers, lobster rolls, chowders, chili, and fried oysters, plus "onshore" sandwiches, for between about $7 and $10. Dinner selections include lobster salad, broiled halibut, shrimp marinara, sautéed brook trout, softshell crabs, plus lamb chops, porterhouse steaks, and veal and pasta specialties. Most dinner choices cost between about $10 and $20, with some as much as $30. Open from mid-May to the end of October; lunch and light items are served from noon until the midnight closing on the upper level; the downstairs dining room opens at 5pm. All major credit cards accepted.

The Shoreline Restaurant and Marina, Kurosaka Lane (tel. 518/668-2875), features enclosed and deck dining overlooking a modest fleet of five tour boats (tel. 518/668-4644). The restaurant offers American and continental cooking with an accent on mesquite-grilled specialties. The dining area is on different levels so as to afford everyone a view of the lake. The decor includes light-wood diagonal pine paneling accented by mirrors and lots of glass. Dinners, accompanied by live piano, range from $11 to $25 for things like chicken teriyaki, Cajun jambalaya, and veal de Champlain, served from 5 to 11pm daily. Breakfast, from 8 to 11am, includes the usual fare; lunch, served from 11:30am to 4pm and consisting of creative sandwiches and variations on the dinner menu, costs from $5 to $10. Sunday buffet brunch is available from 10:30am to 2pm for $11 for adults and $6 for children. The Shoreline is closed January and November. All major credit cards accepted.

Mario's is on the north side of town, opposite motel row at 469 Canada St. (tel. 518/668-2665). It's a cheerful, busy, well-kept family-style Italian restaurant. An extensive breakfast, available only July and August, is served daily from 8am to 1pm and includes real maple syrup on grilled french toast ($2.95) and old-fashioned hot cakes ($2.50). At dinner, served daily from 3:30 to 11pm, there's a full complement of pastas, seafood, cacciatores, parmigianas, marinaras, plus veal, steaks, and several chicken dishes. Typical dinner choices cost about $10 to $16. The children's menu informs us that "for over 35 years Mario's has been providing the younger set with their own menu. We've also had the pleasure of seeing some of these youngsters returning with children of their own. It was a pleasure then, and it still is." Closed November and the first half of December. All major credit cards accepted.

Boardwalk, at the lake end of Amhearst Street, facing Shepard Park (tel. 518/668-3242), is a natural wooden waterside-looking sort of place. The downstairs din ing room has a big bar, red-and-white-clothed tables, beams everywhere, and water views from every table. Upstairs is an outdoor deck overlooking Lake George where light meals are served during the day and Top 40 dance music is played at night. Outside is a dock where you can rent speedboats, paddleboats, and jet skis. The lunch menu features burgers and all manner of hot and cold sandwiches, priced from about $5 to $8. At dinner you can choose from the catch of the day, king crab legs, New York sirloin, spareribs, seafood platter, or shore dinner in a basket, priced from around $10 to $20. Open daily from mid-May until October: Lunch is served from 11:30am to 4:30pm; dinner starts at 5pm and continues until about 11pm. Open in the winter too, but not every day. All major credit cards accepted.

Other good places are located in areas near, but not in, Lake George Village. For example, **East Cove**, N.Y. 9L and Beach Road (tel. 518/668-5265), is all of a two-minute drive from the center of town down Beach Road past the state beach. It's a log-cabin affair with a wonderful Adirondack-style dining room complete with shiny log walls, thick rugs, and mustard-colored tablecloths. Dinner selections like center-cut pork chops, prime rib, seafood Newburg, Cornish game hen, and New York sirloin are priced from about $12 to $18. Light meals (burgers, half a chicken, fish and chips) cost about half that. Open daily for dinner only from 5 to 10pm; Sunday brunch is served from 11am until 3pm; closed Tuesday during the rest of the year and for most of November.

A couple of good restaurants are up N.Y. 9N in Bolton Landing, among them **The Algonquin,** Bolton Landing (tel. 518/644-9442). This is a sleek and attractive place with gray wash siding, an outdoor terrace with yellow umbrellas, and two dining floors decorated with pine paneling and beamed ceilings and affording fine lake views from large picture windows. Handsome lunches consisting of elaborate sandwiches (Monte Cristo, French dip, seafood salad), burgers of every stripe, omelets, and salads cost between about $5 and $8. Most dinner choices are $12 to $20. Open daily, May through October, from noon until 10pm; closed Tuesday and Wednesday the rest of the year. All major credit cards accepted.

THROUGH WARRENSBURG & FRIENDS LAKE TO NORTH CREEK

If you're a nut for antiques, you might enjoy a trip up to the village of **Warrensburg,** about 4 miles north of Lake George Village on U.S. 9. There are over a dozen different shops on the south side of the town, most right on U.S. 9. An atmospheric old inn called **Merrill Magee House** (tel. 518/623-2449) is located in the middle of town, is open all year, and serves dinner main dishes like beef Wellington, veal Oscar, and roast beef suprême (with melted brie) between 5 and 11pm daily in the $13 to $19 range. Lunches are available from 11am to 3pm for about $5 to $7. There are 10 great rooms upstairs as well, furnished with a romantic mixture of antiques, lace, linen, fireplaces, and private baths. Expect to pay from $85 to $95; check for special weekend packages. Closed in March. All major credit cards accepted.

If you continue north on Route 9 for several miles, you'll soon intersect with Route 28. Turn onto 28 in the direction of **North Creek.** In about 4 miles you'll pass Potter Brook Road on your right (the turn off for the Balsam House and the Friends Lake Inn, described in "Vacation Resorts & Retreats," above). In another 15 miles you'll arrive at the community of North Creek. This village has become a major destination in the southern Adirondacks by virtue of the presence of **Gore Mountain Ski Area,** North Creek, NY (tel. 518/251-2411 for special programs, 518/251-2523 for ski conditions, toll free 800/342-1234 for general information within New York State). Gore is owned by the state but operated by the Olympic Regional Development Authority, which also runs Whiteface Mountain in Lake Placid. Gore has New York's only gondola lift plus 41 downhill trails (totaling 17½ miles), of which about 90% are at the intermediate level.

Besides being a mecca for downhill skiers, North Creek is one of the top ten white-water rafting areas in the nation. A 15-mile stretch of rapids along the upper Hudson just north of town offers even seasoned adventurers the opportunity to experience major adrenaline rushes. **The Hudson River Rafting Company,** North Creek, NY 12853 (tel. 518/251-3215, or toll free 800/888-RAFT) first began taking groups over these rapids more than 20 years ago. Excursions go out every spring (April and May) and fall (September and October) and cost $75 per person, plus $15 to rent the wetsuit.

A mark of the coming of age of little North Creek is the recent arrival of the luxurious **Copperfield Inn,** 224 Main St., P.O. Box 28, North Creek, NY 12825 (tel. 518/251-2500, or toll free 800/424-9910; fax 518/251-4143). This is a world-class hotel, complete with a uniformed bell staff, an elegant dining room, and quantities of polished green marble and brass. There is nothing in the least "Adirondack rustic" about the place, but it is certainly handsome and up-to-date. Rooms feature marble baths with oversized roman tubs, color TVs with VCRs and HBO, phones, and double queen or single king beds. The bar does a busy après-ski business and has live music on Friday nights; and the restaurant serves breakfast, lunch, and dinner at prices more moderate than one might expect. Double-occupancy room rates range from $110 to $170 during winter and summer seasons declining to between $100 and $140 in spring and fall. All major credit cards accepted.

Bear in mind that North Creek is also the location of two previously recommended retreats, the **Highwinds Inn** and the **Garnet Hill Lodge** (see "Vacation Resorts & Retreats," above).

ON TO BLUE MOUNTAIN & RAQUETTE LAKES

Some 20 miles west of North Creek, on Route 28, is the intersection with Route 30. Unlikely as it seems, this lonely-looking spot with its combination gas station/general store is a major crossroads in the central Adirondacks. Immediately adjacent to it is the hamlet of **Blue Mountain Lake.**

Here is where two recommended resort hotels are located, Hemlock Hall and The Hedges. It's also the hometown of the famous **Adirondack Museum,** "the best of its kind in the world," according to *The New York Times*. The museum houses a fascinating collection that depicts regional history and art. It's set on a sprawling campus, in 25 different buildings, with fine water and mountain views. The collection includes all manner of artifacts and memorabilia, such as the famous locomotive that operated from 1900 to 1929 on the three-quarter-mile carry on Raquette Lake (it was the shortest railroad in the world). There are also all manner of freshwater boats, including a rigged sailboat bobbing under a huge glass dome, numerous reconstructed historic buildings and shops, and an important collection of paintings. Over two million people have visited this museum since 1957. The average visitor spends three hours here and comes away raving about the place. Open daily from Memorial Day weekend to mid-October from 9:30am until 5:30pm. Admission is $10 for adults, $8.50 for seniors, and $6 for kids. Call 518/352-7311 for information.

Some 14 miles west of Blue Mountain Lake on N.Y. 28 is Raquette Lake, a center of Adirondack great camp development. One of the most famous of them all is **Camp Sagamore,** conceived by William West Durant in 1896 as a year-round home in the heart of the wilderness. By 1901, Durant was forced to sell Sagamore at a terrible loss to Alfred G. Vanderbilt. Vanderbilt went down on the *Lusitania* in 1915, but his widow continued to spend summers here until her death in 1954. After a period of ownership by Syracuse University, Sagamore was saved from destruction at the proverbial 11th hour by an alliance of local preservationists. Since 1975 it has been the scene of all manner of creative programs, plus a meticulous ongoing restoration.

Sagamore is currently a conference center whose varied programs include historic tours, personal and professional development workshops, and recreational programs. It is also open daily from July 4th through Labor Day and weekends in the fall for tours. It consists of 29 buildings that constitute some of the best examples of Adirondack-style architecture extant. Although the original furniture was auctioned off in 1975 and the current institutional use is not quite as opulent as intended by former owners, Sagamore is still a fascinating and beautiful place. Its current guardians love it dearly too—all 46 bedrooms and 26 stone fireplaces of it.

Daily summer tours leave at 10am and 1:30pm and cost $6 for adults and $3 for kids. If you'd like information on the many programs offered here, contact Sagamore Lodge and Conference Center, Sagamore Road, Raquette Lake, NY 13436 (tel. 315/354-5311).

4. Lake Placid & the Northern Frontier

The adjacent communities of Lake Placid and Saranac Lake are 9 miles apart on a 55-mph highway. **Lake Placid** (pop. 2,500) is unquestionably the more important of the two. It's a bustling, prosperous resort village with big-time hotels (there's a Hilton smack in the center of the place), lots of good restaurants, and a full range of year-round resort facilities. Lake Placid was the site of two Winter Olympics, in 1932 and 1980. For many people it remains today primarily a ski resort, the slopes being on nearby Whiteface Mountain. Winter is perhaps more of a high season than summer. However, there are plenty of things to see and do in Lake Placid all year long. **Saranac Lake** (pop. 5,600) has far fewer facilities and attractions. It does have a great hotel, however, and a couple of very interesting restaurants, about which I'll say more later.

Lake Placid was settled by Mohawk Indians and then by non-Indian miners and lumbermen. Alas, the local ore proved inferior and the winter weather (notably 1816, known as the "year without a summer") too intimidating. In 1845, Lake Placid became the focus of a social experiment conducted by one Gerrit Smith. Free land was given to any free black man who cared to come up here and work it. This was a daunting challenge to say the least, and one that ultimately failed. But not before it attracted John Brown, who came to teach efficient farming techniques to newly arrived African-American settlers. Lake Placid was the town from which Brown departed in 1859, bound for the U.S. Arsenal at Harpers Ferry, VA. His intention was to arm southern slaves with arsenal weapons and lead them in an insurrection. Here was where his body was returned after his execution by the Commonwealth of Virginia. His farm and gravesite, a few miles south of town, are now a state historic site (see below).

Another of Lake Placid's famous residents was Dr. Melvil Dewey, originator of the Dewey Decimal System used in libraries and founder of the old Lake Placid Club. This once-exclusive organization (it no longer exists as a private club) is credited with introducing America to winter sports. In the process it had a major impact on the village of Lake Placid. After two Winter Olympics the village now has a highly developed infrastructure geared to everything from tobogganing to bobsledding, to skijumping, to snowmobiling, to alpine skiing, to something called the luge (which is a feet-first plunge down a refrigerated bobsled course). In summer you can hike, swim, boat, listen to outdoor concerts in the village park, and visit the various Olympic sites, one of which is an auto route to the top of Whiteface Mountain. Also during summer are the prestigious **Lake Placid Horse Show** and the **I Love New York Horse Show,** both of which take place in July.

As mentioned earlier, less is going on over at Saranac Lake. The town has a nice old-fashioned business district, in the middle of which is the Hotel Saranac, run by the students of nearby Paul Smith College and recommended below. Every winter during the second week in February, Saranac Lake hosts a **Winter Carnival,** the oldest in the United States. There are skating races, a hockey tournament, cross-country ski races, and torchlight skiing, wrapped up on Sunday night with the "storming of the ice palace," a big fireworks display. The last weekend in January in Saranac Lake witnesses the **International Sled Dog Championships,** sponsored by the manufacturers of Alpo dog food. This features events like the six-dog, the weight-pull eliminations, the Mushers' Ball, and culminates with a big dance and an awards ceremony.

Both Lake Placid and Saranac have very helpful and efficient visitor information organizations. In Lake Placid you should take your questions to the **Lake Placid Visitors Bureau,** Olympic Arena, Lake Placid, NY 12946 (tel. 518/523-2445). In Saranac Lake, inquiries should be directed to the **Saranac Lake Area Chamber of Commerce,** 30 Main St., Saranac Lake, NY 12983 (tel. 518/891-1990).

WHAT TO SEE & DO IN THE LAKE PLACID AREA

There's a lot going on at any given time. Every month the **Lake Placid Visitors Bureau** mimeographs a sheet for tourists called "Action in Lake Placid," which lists it all. Best place to pick up a copy is either at your hotel or the "I Love New York" office at 90 Main St.

Skiing on Whiteface Mountain is the town's premier attraction. This is a big installation, located a few miles east of Lake Placid on N.Y. 86. All sorts of lift, lesson, and hotel packages are available. Additionally there are competition events of various sorts taking place at the Olympic facilities throughout each winter. Skiers desiring fuller information on Whiteface Mountain can either call Whiteface Information at 518/946-2223, or write to the Lake Placid Visitors Bureau (see above). The bureau can send you fee schedules, a description of the mountain, a listing of fall and winter events, and the like.

For thrills, you might consider taking a ride on the **Olympic bobsled run** down Mount Van Hoevenberg (tel. 518/523-4436). Believe me, this is an experience you'll never forget. The bobsledding season runs from late December until mid-March, and you can do it Tuesday through Sunday from 1 to 3pm. It's well worth the $25 fee. The same facility also offers a **luge run,** which might be described as shooting down an ice run on your back in your own personal bobsled. You can do this on Saturday and Sunday from 1 to 3pm, during the same season.

During summer and fall, visitors can take something called the **Olympic Tour,** which is a self-guided visit to the various sites of former Olympic Games. These include the Olympic Ski Jump Complex (where you can ride to the top of an amazing pair of giant slides looming over the forest), Mount Van Hoevenberg (with bobsled and luge tracks, plus video displays), the Whiteface Memorial Highway (tough on the transmission and the brakes, but an awesome view and a nifty "castle" on top), and the Whiteface Mountain Chair Lift (like the drive, but minus the car). Each of these attractions can be visited separately for between $3 and $5 per adult and $2 and $4 per child. Or you can buy a combination ticket to all four for $12 per adult and $7 per child. Tickets are available at the individual facilities; a descriptive "Olympic Tour" brochure, with a map and a rate schedule, sits in stacks on most hotel desks.

Summer visitors might also like to have a look at **John Brown Farm,** a New York State Historic Site, on John Brown Road, off N.Y. 73 just south of Lake Placid (tel. 518/523-3900). This is a modest place but evocative of great events. You can take a self-guided tour of the farmhouse, the 244-acre farm, and the adjacent grave of the famous abolitionist Wednesday through Saturday from late May until late October. The hours are 10am to 5pm (from 1pm on Sunday). There is no admission fee.

Over in Saranac Lake is the **Robert Louis Stevenson Cottage,** where the author of *Treasure Island* took up residence in 1887. Stevenson buffs are going to love this place, which is in totally original condition and contains the largest collection of Stevenson mementos in America. There are old photos, ice skates, a lock of the great man's hair, items of clothing, even cigarette burns on the mantelpiece courtesy of Stevenson's own cigarettes. Open from July 1 until September 15; admission is $1 for adults and 50¢ for kids. Call 518/891-1990 for further information.

Also pleasant in the summer are **Lake Placid Boat Rides,** an hour-long, 16-mile excursion on an enclosed tour boat that wends its way past islands and private estates to the base of Whiteface Mountain. Boats leave the Lake Placid Marina (not far from Mirror Lake Inn) between two and four times daily from late May until mid-October. The fare is $6 for adults and $4 for kids; call 518/523-9704 for departure times.

Also good to know about are the free weekly **Cushion Concerts** performed in Lake Placid's Main Street Park by the Lake Placid Sinfonietta. Ask "I Love New York" (tel. 518/523-2412) when the next one's scheduled. The Sinfonietta, by the way, was started by the famous Lake Placid Club back in 1919 and offers a full summer musical program in the Lake Placid Center for the Arts.

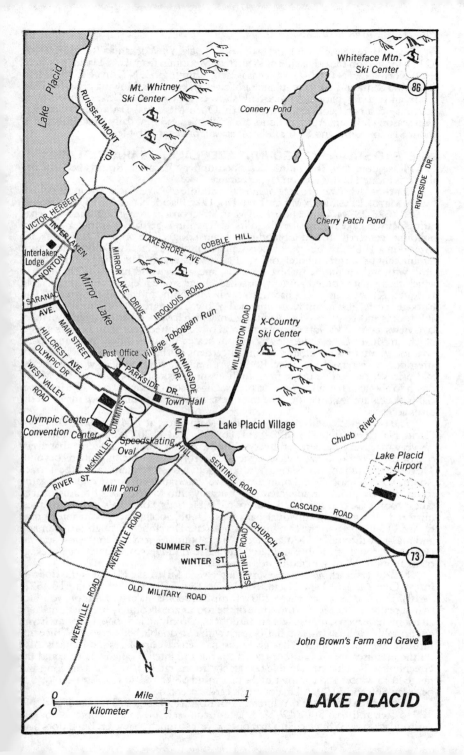

Lake Placid

Mt. Whitney Ski Center

Whiteface Mtn. Ski Center

86

Connery Pond

RUISSEAUMONT RD.

Cherry Patch Pond

RIVERSIDE DR.

VICTOR HERBERT

INTERLAKEN

Interlaken Lodge

NORTON

LAKESHORE AVE.

COBBLE HILL

SARANAC AVE.

MAIN STREET

MIRROR LAKE DRIVE

Mirror Lake

IROQUOIS ROAD

WILMINGTON ROAD

X-Country Ski Center

HILLCREST AVE.

OLYMPIC DR

Post Office

PARKSIDE DR.

Village Toboggan Run

MORNINGSIDE DR.

WEST VALLEY ROAD

Town Hall

Olympic Center Convention Center

Speedskating Oval

MILL HILL

Lake Placid Village

Chubb River

Lake Placid Airport

RIVER ST.

McKINLEY

CUMMINS

Mill Pond

SENTINEL ROAD

CASCADE ROAD

AVERYVILLE ROAD

AVERYVILLE ROAD

SUMMER ST.

WINTER ST.

SENTINEL ROAD

CHURCH ST.

73

OLD MILITARY ROAD

N

John Brown's Farm and Grave

0   Mile   1

0   Kilometer   1

LAKE PLACID

If you're traveling with kids, take note of **Santa's Workshop** (tel. 518/946-2211), located on the other side of Whiteface Mountain from Lake Placid in (where else?) North Pole, NY (true!), which is west of Wilmington, NY, on N.Y. 431. Here you'll find Santa and a full complement of elves making toys, blowing glass, cooking candy, and carving plastic. A twice-daily show called *Christmas Capers* features puppets, magic, a band concert, and so forth. Open Memorial Day to mid-October; high-season (July and August) hours are 9:30am to 4:30pm daily and admission is about $10 for adults and $7 for kids; off-season prices are a bit less.

WHERE TO STAY & EAT AROUND LAKE PLACID & SARANAC LAKE

Please note that **The Point**, described under "Vacation Resorts & Retreats," above, is located in this area on Upper Saranac Lake.

For those who want to stay right in the middle of Lake Placid, the most deluxe spot is **Mirror Lake Inn**, 5 Mirror Lake Dr., Lake Placid, NY (tel. 518/523-2544; fax 518/523-2871), a short hop from Main Street on a narrow isthmus of land separating Mirror Lake from Lake Placid itself. The inn is actually a complex of seven buildings centered around a brand-new Main Lodge. The original lodge was destroyed in a 1988 fire, but the owners replaced it with a graceful Colonial structure reminiscent of the grand hotels of Lake Placid's yesteryear. The living room is beautiful, with walnut floors, mahogany walls, and a rosewood fireplace. The library, which teems with stuffed animals, also has a huge stone fireplace and comfortable antiques. A cozy lounge is adjacent to the living room, and across the street is The Cottage, a café/restaurant recommended below. There are 100 extremely comfortable rooms and 16 suites or minisuites, all of which have two-person whirlpool tubs, lake views, color TVs, lots of character, and often a lofted bedroom. Besides a sand beach on Mirror Lake, there are an outdoor heated pool, an indoor pool and spa, a boathouse, a tennis court, and beautiful gardens in the summer. Complimentary afternoon tea is served every day. Rooms are available either with or without meals, and prices for a double range from high-season peaks of $105 per person, MAP, down to about $70 double without meals. Off-season rates are about 30% less; special packages are available too. The main restaurant here is famous. All major credit cards accepted.

The **Lake Placid Hilton**, at the head of Main Street at 1 Mirror Lake Dr., Lake Placid, NY 12946 (tel. 518/523-4411; fax 518/523-1120), is no grand hotel, but it's very nice, very modern, and very Hiltony. Also it's well planned so that every one of the 176 rooms has a view, either of Mirror Lake or the mountains beyond. There are two indoor pools, two outdoor pools, a big restaurant called the Terrace Room, the Dancing Bear Lounge with live entertainment most nights, a game room, and reciprocal arrangements at a nearby club for the use of tennis courts. Guest rooms are big, furnished with two double beds, color TVs, private phones, mirrored closets, and individual balconies. Double-occupancy room rates range from $115 to $145 in the two high seasons (late December through early January and mid-July through mid-August), down to about $68 to $108 in the low seasons (January through mid-June and late October to mid-December); reduced package plans abound. All major credit cards accepted.

Nearby (everything is near everything else in little Lake Placid) is the **Holiday Inn**, 1 Olympic Dr., Lake Placid, NY 12946 (tel. 518/523-2556; fax 518/523-9410). This is a vast place whose 200 refurbished rooms make it look more youthful than it really is. The views from some of the rooms are absolutely breathtaking. Not all rooms have views, nor is there an outdoor pool (only an indoor). All rooms have a comfortable Holiday Inn familiarity, each with two double beds, color TV, nice furniture, and plenty of space. The newest rooms even have fireplaces and Jacuzzis. Also on the premises are six outdoor tennis courts, a nightclub called Cristy's, and the Greenhouse Restaurant. Double-occupancy room rates change all year long but range from winter and summer highs of around $80 to $190 to off-season lows of between $60 and $100. All major credit cards accepted.

Whiteface Inn Resort, Whiteface Inn Road (P.O. Box 231), Lake Placid, NY 12946 (tel. toll free 800/422-6757), unfortunately no longer contains the old Adirondack-style Whiteface Inn that once gave it so much character. But it does have its own 18-hole championship golf course, a spectacular outdoor heated pool, tennis courts, a boathouse, 1,200 feet of lakefront, a restaurant called the Adirondack Room, and an interesting variety of accommodations. The rooms overlooking the pool resemble comfortable motel units; the cottages vary in size from one room to eight bedrooms and are painted brown and dotted around the wooded slopes above the pool; the lodge colony is a collection of vintage log cabins right on the lakeshore —the most desirable by my lights. Rates are quoted per unit, not per person. They are so complicated as to defy simple categorization. To give you an idea, one of those great log cabins with a fireplace, a separate bedroom, a TV, a couple of rocking chairs, and a view of the lake can cost as little as $55 on a winter weekday, as much as $120 on a summer weekend. The motel units cost $90 in summer and about $70 in winter. Groups of skiers frequent this place because you can get so many people into the larger cottages. It's a good deal. All major credit cards accepted.

Located next to the Whiteface Inn Resort is **Lake Placid Manor,** Whiteface Inn Road (P.O. Box 870), Lake Placid, NY 12946 (tel. 518/523-2573; fax 518/523-1124). The Manor, built in 1882, has glorious views of the lake and Whiteface, as well as a rustic opulence associated with the great camps of the Adirondacks. The gourmet restaurant is open daily for breakfast, lunch, and dinner. Breakfast includes things like creative omelets and pancakes with real maple syrup and costs $3 to $8; lunch is $5 to $15; and a dinner of perhaps poached monkfish or sauté of veal might cost $16 to $22. There are 34 rooms tucked away in various buildings on the property. The decor is Adirondack rustic and includes private baths, phones, and TVs. Rates are from $55 to $150 a night per person. All major credit cards accepted.

Hotel Saranac, 101 Main St., Saranac Lake, NY 12983 (tel. 518/891-2200; fax 518/891-5664), is a big, square, circa-1930 brick building right in the middle of Saranac Lake. One of its distinctions is that it's run by students of nearby Paul Smith's College, School of Hotel Management. Don't think for a moment that this is an amateurish operation. The place has several excellent restaurants and 92 extremely nice rooms, decorated with shag rugs, big beds with wooden headboards, cheerful wallpaper, spotless private baths with stacks of fresh towels, color TVs, and phones. The rooms are incredibly cheap. "Bed-and-breakfast" minipackages (any two nights) are available for about $42 to $70 per person, complete. They have all sorts of other package deals as well. The ambience is wonderful, and the place couldn't be more comfortable. All major credit cards accepted.

Of the many motels in and around Lake Placid and Saranac, my favorite was **Schulte's Motor Inn,** on N.Y. 73, Lake Placid, NY 12946 (tel. 518/523-3532). This place has a very Bavarian look, highlighted by painted woodwork, cuckoo clocks, and cutout wooden balconies, all extremely immaculate and carefully tended. There are 15 motel units and 15 little cottages, the latter bearing names like Spruce, Birch, Beech, and Tamarack. In the center of this complex is a very nice outdoor pool. Accommodations all have color TVs, private baths, and very pleasant modern decor. The motel units have velour bedspreads; the little cottages have miniature kitchenettes and are the definition of the word *cute.* In summer and winter two people will pay from $45 to about $85 for one of the motel rooms, and from $45 for a cottage for two, up to about $85 for a cottage that will accommodate six. Off-season rates are about 20% less.

You can also rent a whole house, for a night or a week, from Lisa Barrie at **Merrill L. Thomas Real Estate,** 65 Main St., Lake Placid, NY 12946 (tel. 518/523-2519; fax 518/523-2796). Some of the listings available as we went to press included an authentic Adirondack-style eight-bedroom house on Lake Placid for $800 per night; a five-bedroom house on Mirror Lake for $300 nightly; and assorted one-bedroom condos on the golf course for $90 to $150, depending on season. Some good deals are available here, and, of course, all are fully furnished.

Last but certainly not least is **Stagecoach Inn,** Old Military Road, Lake Placid, NY 12946 (tel. 518/523-9474). This wonderful old green wooden building has a long wicker-filled porch, hanging pots of plants, and a country location just outside Lake Placid. It was built as an inn during stagecoach days, and indeed it was the first hotel in Lake Placid. Today it's a sleepy little bed-and-breakfast filled with tongue-and-groove wood paneling, antique furniture, lace curtains, a vintage organ, fireplaces and wood stoves, and nine extremely charming bedrooms. The most expensive rooms have fireplaces and private baths and cost $90 nightly for two, including breakfast. For $65 to $85 nightly you'll get a room without a fireplace but with a private bath. Another four rooms share two baths and cost $65 nightly. Open almost (but not quite) all year. No credit cards accepted.

Do plan one meal in the **Averil Conwell Room** at Mirror Lake Inn, 5 Mirror Lake Dr. (tel. 518/523-2544). The dining room is bilevel and provides excellent views of Mirror Lake from all areas. A floral burgundy carpet accents mahogany walls decorated with hanging plants and a series of restored murals by Averil Conwell depicting Lake Placid's history. At least two nights a week there is piano music in the adjacent living room of the inn. Typical à la carte dinners include home-smoked trout, smoked shrimp, or smoked salmon appetizers; rack of lamb; Adirondack mixed grill; stuffed shrimp with crabmeat mousse; and many daily chef's features. A special low-fat menu is available too. Prices range from $12 to $25. Open daily for breakfast from 7 to 10am and for dinner from 6 to 10pm. Reservations suggested. All major credit cards accepted.

The Woodshed, opposite the Olympic Speed Skating Oval at 237 Main St. (tel. 518/523-9470), has a couple of intimate dining rooms and an inventive menu. In the front they serve things like broiled haddock, stuffed pork chops, lasagne, chicken Dennison, spaghetti, and burgers, priced at around $8 to $17. In the back, called Lindsay's, the fare consists of steak au poivre, rack of lamb, veal chalet, scampi in a cream sauce, and poached salmon, which cost between about $11 and $22 à la carte. Open daily for dinner only from 5pm to midnight in the front room (where a "light" menu is also available) and from 6 to 10pm in the romantic back room. All major credit cards accepted.

Also across from the Olympic Speed Skating Oval is **Fireside Steak House,** 229 Main St. (tel. 518/523-2682). Don't be misled by the name; this local favorite offers not only beef but chicken and seafood as well, all at moderate prices. The restaurant has two sections: the Sidewalk Café, with greenhouse, flowering plants, and fireplace; and the Firehouse Steak Room upstairs, with an open-pit charcoal fire, cathedral ceilings, a balcony overlooking the street, and prices between $5 and $25 per main course. The Firehouse is open daily for dinner only from 5 to 11pm. All major credit cards accepted.

Interlaken, located behind the Mirror Lake Inn at 15 Interlaken Ave. (tel. 518/523-3180), is an old Victorian house with a pleasant dining room paneled in dark oak, with burgundy linens and rugs. The food is great—veal with peaches, pork in mustard sauce, steak au poivre—at a fixed price of $25 per person Thursday through Monday; seating is between 6 and 8pm. A number of period guest rooms with private baths are also available here and cost from $80 to $160 per couple, including dinner. All major credit cards accepted.

On the other side of town is **Villa Vespa,** 85 Saranac Ave. (tel. 518/523-9959), on the road to Saranac Lake. This is an attractive Italian restaurant with stuccoed walls, a beamed ceiling, red-leatherette booths, and a statue of a Cupid. Try one of the assorted pastas (priced mostly between $8 and $10) or veal piccata, shrimp marinara, breast of capon, or fried calamari (which cost anywhere from about $11 to $16). Open daily for dinner only from 5 to 10pm, with mandolin music every evening; closed Tuesday in slow seasons. All major credit cards accepted.

Less expensive fare (and lunch, which isn't served at any of the above) can be had in the middle of Lake Placid at three excellent establishments. **The Cottage** opposite (and owned by) the Mirror Lake Inn, Mirror Lake Drive (tel. 518/523-2544), is a lively bar, right on the water, with an adjacent deck for warm-weather dining. Inside is a cathedral ceiling, a wall of pictures of regular patrons, a jukebox full of rock and roll, assorted tables, and good-looking bartenders. Sandwiches with names like the Cottage Club Reuben and South of the Border cost around $5. There are also chili, salads, quiche, and homemade soup. All major credit cards accepted. **Jimmy's** is across from the Hilton at 21 Main St. (tel. 518/523-2353). There's a bar up front and a diminutive lake-view dining room with diagonal oak paneling in the back. It's small and very informal and serves up all manner of sandwiches (club, grilled cheese, burgers), plus salad platters and omelets, for around $4 to $10.

Lunch is served Tuesday to Sunday from 11:30am until 5pm; dinner is Tuesday to Sunday from 5 to 9:30pm; closed Monday, plus other nights too in the off-season. MC and V accepted. Finally, there's **Artist's Café**, 1 Main St. (tel. 518/523-9493), an intimate little tavern/restaurant with wood paneling and inviting cushioned booths. Lunch omelets, burgers, and sandwiches run about $4 to $9; dinner specials like a 16- to 24-ounce T-bone steak, steamed shrimp, seafood platter, and king crab legs cost $6 to $19. Open daily all year, for lunch from 11:30am until 3:30pm and for dinner from 5 to 10pm. All major credit cards accepted.

Lydia's, at Hotel Saranac, 101 Main St. in Saranac Lake (tel. 518/891-2200), is definitely worth a visit for lunch or dinner. The students of Paul Smith's College, who run both the hotel and the restaurant, do a crackerjack job, and prices are most reasonable. Lunch selections include a full range of sandwiches, omelets, burgers, and crêpes, skillfully cooked and professionally presented. Boy, do they try hard to please! Prices are all under $4. At dinner you might try buttermilk chicken, pork cutlet Dijon, salmon steak, tournedos Rossini, or sea scallops, priced from $8 to $14. Periodically the Regis Room assumes new identities and menus when a graduating class works up a cuisine and a set of meals all its own. The modern, thickly carpeted, and romantically lit room looks like a lavish coffeeshop. Upstairs in the grand ballroom is a Thursday-night buffet, also designed and cooked by students, priced at about $11.50 for adults and $6.50 for kids. It was an elaborate French affair at the time of my visit. Whatever it is when you get there, I'm sure it'll be good. Breakfast and lunch are served daily in the Regis Room from 7:30am until 2pm; dinner (including the Thursday-night buffet in the ballroom) starts at 5 and runs until 9pm. All major credit cards accepted.

Near the south end of Upper Saranac Lake, maybe 15 minutes southwest via N.Y. 3 from the town of Saranac Lake itself, is **Wawbeek** (tel. 518/359-2656). This Adirondack-style lakefront restaurant deep in its own private forest is about the most atmospheric place imaginable. Built as a private camp in the late 19th century, it has lofty ceilings, old wood paneling, a romantic porch overlooking the lake, and an upstairs bar with old leather and wicker furniture. Only dinner is served, from a menu featuring filet mignon, medallions of lobster, sautéed sea scallops, rack of lamb for two, swordfish steak, and shrimp in cognac. A la carte prices are mostly from $12 to $21. Open from May through September, daily from 5 to 11pm. MC and V accepted.

---

5. The Wilderness Experience

The **New York State Department of Environmental Conservation,** Albany, NY 12233 (tel. 518/457-3521), publishes maps and descriptions of trails throughout Adirondack State Park. These publications are usually single sheets folded in four and are necessarily brief. The DEC also publishes booklets like "Tips for Using State Lands," "Use of New York State's Public Forest Land," and "Adirondack Canoe Routes." Write and ask for a free selection.

Various Adirondack-area chambers of commerce will also send literature that can help do-it-yourself types experience the wilderness. For example, **Saranac Lake Area Chamber of Commerce,** 30 Main St., Saranac Lake, NY 12983 (tel. 518/891-1990), has a number of interesting folders describing easily accessible parts of the wilderness. These can enable you to savor ancient forests, fern groves, bogs, and silent lakes, all located short distances from public parking areas. Write and it'll send you what it's got. Other helpful chambers of commerce are located in Indian Lake, NY 12842 (tel. 518/648-5112); North Creek, NY 12583 (tel. 518/251-2612); Lake Placid, NY 12946 (tel. 518/523-2445); as well as in other north country communities.

Besides local chambers of commerce and the Department of Environmental Conservation publications, there exists a considerable body of other literature on the Adirondack wilderness. Among the most thorough, readable, interesting, and *useable* works are those by Barbara McMartin, who is a recognized expert on the area. McMartin has published three books that include good maps (better than those in DEC publications), photos, careful trail descriptions, and historical notes. *Fifty Hikes in the Adirondacks*, published in 1980 by the New Hampshire Publishing Co., Somersworth, NH, contains detailed directions to the best sights the Adirondack wilderness has to offer. Some of these treks are relatively easy; others aren't. *Discover the Adirondacks, 1* and *Discover the Adirondacks, 2* are companion volumes, also by McMartin, that describe everything from swimming holes to wilderness fishing grounds, picnic and camping sites to waterfalls and gorges. These books, also published by the New Hampshire Publishing Co., are copyrighted 1974 and 1979, respectively. Taken together, these works detail an exceptionally full range of outdoor wilderness activities for people at all levels of competence.

Fishing is one of the most time-honored of reasons for an Adirondack vacation. In the clear waters of Lake George, as well as in many smaller lakes and rivers through Warren County, are fish of all descriptions, from landlocked salmon to largemouth bass, brook trout to northern pike. **Warren County Tourism Dept.,** Municipal Center, Lake George, NY 12845 (tel. 518/761-6366), publishes a most informative booklet titled "Grand Slam Fishing," which covers everything from license requirements to the names and addresses of licensed outfitters.

All sorts of other outfitters and guide services exist throughout the Adirondack Park. They can design and arrange hunting trips, canoe trips, bike trips, and trekker trips to virtually any destination, and/or for any length of time. Lists of reputable guides and outfitters are usually available through local chambers of commerce (see the list above). Two good ones are **Raquette River Canoe Outfitters,** P.O. Box 653, Tupper Lake, NY 12986 (tel. 518/359-3228), and **St. Regis Canoe Outfitters,** P.O. Box 20, Lake Clear, NY 12945 (tel. 518/891-1838). They'll be glad to send you literature on the sorts of services they provide.

6. More Attractions in Adirondack State Park

Those traveling to or between the resorts and towns described above will doubtless want to know about additional attractions within Adirondack State Park. This last section will therefore be a sort of "mopping up" operation and/or a reference guide for others who are in transit elsewhere but still want an interesting route.

THE ROAD TO FORT TICONDEROGA
Let it be said from the outset that the **Northway** (I-87), which runs up the eastern flank of Adirondack State Park, is a very beautiful road. I know that interstate highways can be dull. But scenically speaking, this is not the case with the Northway.

An alternative route northward from Lake George Village is N.Y. 9N, which is joined by N.Y. 22 at Ticonderoga on Lake Champlain. The virtue of 9N is that it parallels beautiful Lake George and traverses some fine woodlands. And it's also the road to historic **Fort Ticonderoga,** a restored 18th-century military complex including the fort, a museum, a uniformed fife-and-drum corps, and daily July and August cannon-firing demonstrations.

The restoration lies 2 miles east of the town of Ticonderoga (pop. 2,900), a sleepy place on the LaChute River, and overlooks the strategic outlet from Lake George to Lake Champlain. The former importance of this modest aquatic connection—it was once called "the key to a continent"—is a little hard to grasp in our day of airplanes and superhighways. But two centuries ago considerable blood was let by French, English, and American soldiers so that their masters might control it. It was to Fort Ticonderoga that Montcalm retired after the butchery at Fort William Henry. It was at Ticonderoga, too, that Benedict Arnold demonstrated the bravery and brilliance that would lead him to another and greater victory at Saratoga.

The fort complex is quite an installation, located at the end of a long tree shaded approach. It has been preserved due to the efforts of the Pell family, various of whose members began purchasing and protecting the lands here as early as 1820. Admission to three separate sites—the fort, Mount Defiance, and Mount Independence (across Lake Champlain on the Vermont side)—is included in the charge: $7 for adults, $5 for kids 10 to 13, free for kids under 10. The fort is open daily mid-May until late October from 9am until 5pm (until 6pm in July and August). Parking is free and abundant, and there's a lunchroom on the premises.

To provide a water-level point of view on the great stone fortress and its dependencies, they now offer an optional **hour-and-a-half cruise on the M/V Carillon,** connecting Fort Ticonderoga, Mount Independence, Hand's Cove (from which Ethan Allen and the Green Mountain Boys departed for their fateful raid of May 10, 1775), and Shoreham, Vermont. Four narrated tours a day depart from each location on this all-new replica of a 1920s Thousand Islands cruise boat. Tickets are $7.50 for adults and $4.50 for children. Weather permitting. For more information, call 518/585-2821.

Students of 18th-century military history might also like to take a look at **Crown Point State Historic Site,** which is a dozen or so miles north of Ticonderoga, east of N.Y. 9N on the road to the Lake Champlain Bridge. Crown Point is a ruin, and there are no costumed fife-and-drum corps here. But there is an informative visitor center that describes the various battles that once raged in this now-silent place, and the admission is free. The French started the place in 1734, the British took it over subsequently, and the Americans overran it in 1775. Open June through October on Wednesday through Saturday from 10am to 5pm and on Sunday from 1 to 5pm. Call 518/597-3666 for further information.

Travelers heading north on N.Y. 9N/22 may wonder about that strange cutout monster by the road outside **Port Henry.** He's green, wears a large grin, and has a scaly back. Too cute for comfort, perhaps, but this is supposed to be "Champ," the monster of Lake Champlain. Indeed a body of literature (serious or not, I can't tell) exists that cites the various sightings of this supposed creature. Not much else is doing in Port Henry, so criticism of the Champ phenomenon is, if nothing else, uncharitable.

A PAUSE AT WESTPORT

Ten miles north of Port Henry is the very pleasant village of Westport (pop. 600). Established in the 19th century as a very low-profile resort, this lakefront settlement has manicured summer estates on its southern fringes, capacious Victorian and elegant Greek Revival houses on its streets, lovely lake views, a pretty village green with a shingled clock tower and a nice inn, and a summer-stock theater. It's unhurried, uncrowded, and unspectacular. But while there isn't much to do here, it's an awfully nice place to pass through, and perhaps stay for the night.

If you decide on this latter course, try the **Inn on the Library Lawn,** Westport, NY 12993 (tel. 518/962-8666). This is a pretty Victorian commercial building, painted yellow, situated in the center of the hamlet, equipped with a false front above the second floor, and offering 10 rooms. All accommodations have private baths, and some have views of the glittering waters of Lake Champlain at the foot of the hill. Interior decor is quite simple and clearly the result of late 1970s structural alterations. But the rooms have big windows, Victorian-pattern wallpaper, the odd antique, and a comfy unpretentious charm. Between mid-May and mid-October a double room costs $65 to $90 a night; the rest of the year it's $45 to $65. All major credit cards accepted.

For a meal in Westport, try the **Westport Yacht Club,** an Old Arsenal Road (tel. 518/962-8777). This is a very fresh and attractive-looking place located right on the water. It's at the foot of a dirt road that cuts off N.Y. 9N/22 just before the Inn on the Library Lawn. The dining room is furnished with oak captain's chairs, tables with crisp white linens, and wide windows overlooking Lake Champlain and the mountains beyond. The lunch menu has quiche, club sandwiches, burgers, tacos, and various salads, priced from about $3 to $8. Dinner selections include swordfish steak, filet mignon, broiled scallops, trout amandine, and chicken Calvados and cost between $11 and $18. Luncheon hours are 11:30am to 3pm; dinner is served from 5:30 to 10pm; open daily from mid-May until the end of September. All major credit cards accepted.

And if you do decide to stay over, be sure to check out **Depot Theater,** located on the north end of town in the former D&H Railroad Station (tel. 518/962-4449). Past summers have seen classic film series in June as well as summer-stock productions in July and August. Tickets are a modest $10 a seat.

THE THOUSAND ISLANDS

The Thousand Islands is the name of an archipelago of small (often downright tiny) islands located near the mouth of the St. Lawrence River, at the outflow of Lake Ontario. Native American legend has it that the Master of Life, temporarily away from his shining Sky-lodge, created the islands by accident. He had promised all the peoples of the world an earthly paradise (the tale here parallels the Garden of Eden story pretty closely), if only they would stop quarreling. They promised; he delivered the garden; they broke the promise; he picked the garden up in a blanket and started to carry it back. But just as he parted the Sky-curtain en route home, the blanket broke and the garden tumbled into the St. Lawrence River, breaking into a thousand pieces. And there it is today, the Thousand Islands.

Evidently the garden contained lots of fish. For legendary fishing is what first attracted summer visitors to the region. Originally these were campers who roughed it in an untamed and quite beautiful river wilderness. But by the end of the 19th century, newly rich men with names like Pullman, Browning, Emery, and, above all, George C. Boldt, began covering the little islands with high-Victorian summer "cottages." The grandest of them all was a Rhenish castle built by Boldt, president of the Waldorf-Astoria Hotel Corporation in New York, founder of the Thousand Islands Club, and the man most responsible for establishing the Thousand Islands as a fashionable resort.

By the turn of the century, Alexandria Bay possessed two fairly spectacular summer hotels. Crossmon House and Thousand Island House had huge porches, elaborate towers, and steeply mansarded roofs from which giant American flags whipped in the wind. The little islands sported literally dozens of elaborate stone-and-shingle vacation houses, mansions really, set on tiny manicured watergirt fiefdoms and accessible only by boat. A large depot at Clayton served New York Central Railroad passengers, who could walk across the platform directly onto elaborate steamers or private yachts.

Today the great hotels are gone, replaced by motels and vacation resorts that for all their facilities have none of the old pizzazz. Alexandria Bay and Clayton are pleasant, small, unpretentious summer-resort towns that cater about equally to the summer people in their island mansions, the seasonal fishermen, and the tourists passing through. You couldn't really call the Thousand Islands an American Venice. But it does have a similar dependence on water transportation. In fact, if you don't get out on a boat at least once during your visit, you haven't really seen the place.

The season is short in the Thousand Islands—and sometimes a bit cool. Alexandria Bay and Clayton bustle in high summer, but by late October almost everything closes down. By January it's 40° below zero, and those great old houses out there in the river are frozen solid. About the only things moving are the giant supertankers, gliding majestically up and down the St. Lawrence Seaway, between islands one-fifth their size.

Can't leave this introduction without a word about the famous salad dressing, can I? Yes, Thousand Islands dressing was invented here (supposedly, anyway). The story goes that George Boldt's steward aboard his yacht whipped it up one day during a luncheon party. Boldt was so pleased that he promoted the man to the kitchens of the Waldorf-Astoria. From there that man rose to fame, ultimately to become known as Oscar of the Waldorf.

1. Alexandria Bay

Affectionately abbreviated Alex Bay, this is a rather pretty, very unpretentious upstate summer resort (pop. 1,300) consisting of old buildings on a maze of tree-lined streets. You couldn't call Alex Bay gentrified in any sense. But there are attractive shingled churches, pleasant old houses, handsome 19th-century commercial buildings, and a leisurely uncrowded air. There is also a touch of honky-tonk along James Street in the form of amusement arcades, nightclubs, and souvenir shops. But it's nothing compared to, say, Lake George Village. Many of the people who come to Alex Bay in summer are modest folk up for a fishing vacation. The waterfront is very active, crowded with motels, marinas, and incongruous glimpses of those supertankers creeping in and out of sight behind the islands offshore.

WHAT TO SEE & DO IN ALEXANDRIA BAY

A good source of advance information, as well as helpful on-the-scene advice, is **Thousand Islands International Council**, P.O. Box 400, Alexandria Bay, NY 13607 (tel. toll free 800/8-ISLAND in the U.S. and Canada; from other areas, call 315/482-2520 collect). This agency is devoted to promoting tourism on the St. Lawrence River for the Jefferson County and East Ontario region and is oriented equally toward visiting Canadians and Americans. The office is located between Alex Bay and Clayton adjacent to Thousand Island Bridge.

Fishing

The principal attraction of the Thousand Islands remains the excellent fishing, and Thousand Islands International Council is a good source of advance fishing information. All manner of booklets listing fishing guides, charterers, marinas, trailer sites, groceries, tackle shops, and more exist, and the council will be glad to send them to you. Other sources of information for fishermen include **Alexandria Bay Chamber of Commerce**, Alexandria Bay, NY 13607 (tel. 315/482-9531, or toll free 800/541-2110); **Clayton 1000 Islands Chamber of Commerce**, Riverside Drive, Clayton, NY 13624 (tel. 315/686-3771 or toll free 800/252-9806); and **Cape Vincent Chamber of Commerce**, James Street, (P.O. Box 482), Cape Vincent, NY 13618 (tel. 315/654-2481). New York State's "I Love New York" campaign is responsible for magazine-size travel guides to regions throughout the state. The *I Love New York Seaway Guide*, subtitled the *Chautauqua/Allegheny Travel Guide*, covers a good many more places than the Thousand Islands. But it does have a fat central "fishing section," consisting of about half the guide and devoted entirely to fishing and fishermen. You can get a copy free of charge by writing to Chautauqua/Allegheny Travel Guide, Dept. SNI, Mayville, NY 14757.

Boldt Castle

This 120-room stone mansion is a melancholy place with a peculiar history. It was started in 1900 by hotel magnate George C. Boldt, and millions were spent on its construction until work was summarily halted in the beginning of 1904 because of the death of Mrs. Boldt. Her husband was too emotionally upset either to have the house completed or to ever again set foot on the island on which it stood.

It was allowed to moulder for three-quarters of a century. During that time, one suspects, a good many of the island houses on "millionaire's row" opposite Alex Bay were either outfitted or at least augmented with architectural fabric from the place. From a distance its complex roofline and multiple towers are picturesque in the extreme. Inside, despite a decade of "stabilization" by the Thousand Islands Bridge Authority (the present owner), the place is a shell. Shreds of original paneling and plaster remain here and there. Mostly it looks like an immense basement.

Visitors to the island must come either on one of the boat tours (see below) or by water taxi from either the upper or the lower docks on James Street in Alex Bay. Besides the castle, the island includes a five-story stone playhouse, called the Alster Tower, and a triumphal stone water gate intended for arriving yachts. Across a channel on nearby Wellesley Island is a fabulous old shingled boathouse, built by Boldt for his boats and yachts and listed on the National Register of Historic Places. Every year between mid-May and the beginning of October, about 180,000 people make the trip from Alex to Heart Island to have a look at Boldt Castle. It certainly is a moody place, evocative of considerable grandeur. A slide show in one of the unfinished rooms helps give one the idea of what the place was, or might have been. Admission is $3 for adults, $2 for kids. For further information, call the Thousand Islands International Council at toll free 800/8-ISLAND.

Boat Tours
James Street, the main business drag of Alex Bay, is all of four blocks long and anchored at either end by a pair of docks. **Empire Boat Tours,** whose parking lot is entered via Church or Fuller Streets (tel. 315/482-5254), operates U.S. Coast Guard–inspected boats from the Upper Dock, at the western end of James Street. In the words of their brochure, the boat tours "make every trip a complete Island tour, showing you the magnificent homes of many of the social and business leaders of the United States and Canada, the undeveloped sections of the Island region which still remain in their primeval state, as well as many hidden bays and channels." Boats will ferry you over to Boldt Castle for about $7 for adults, $3 for kids; take you on a one-hour Sun Set Cruise for around $8, $4 for kids; or take you on a two-hour Two-Nation Tour for about $12 and $5.50, respectively. You might also inquire about the Island Mansion Tour, costing $14 for adults and $8 for kids, to **Cherry Island,** a typical islet in millionaire's row with a pair of fabulous old mansions.

Empire's competition is called **Uncle Sam Boat Tours,** which operates from the dock at the lower (eastern) end of James Street (tel. 315/482-2611 or 482-9611, or toll free 800/ALEX BAY). The Uncle Sam boats are a little larger, and from what I can make out the tours seem to be a bit longer (and at least in some cases a bit more expensive too). There are regular departures from May through October, plus ferry service to Boldt Castle.

Excursion to Ogdensburg & the Frederic Remington Art Museum
About 35 miles northeast of Alex Bay, via N.Y. 12 and N.Y. 37 (the so-called Seaway Trail), is the town of Ogdensburg (pop. 12,400). This was the childhood home of Frederic Remington, one of the most famous artists and sculptors of America's Western frontiers and mountain wildernesses. Remington died in 1909 of a botched appendectomy at the age of 48 (a major malpractice suit would no doubt have ensued had it occurred today), after which his widow returned to Ogdensburg. She rented a fine mansion at the corner of Washington and State Streets, a house that would in time become a museum of her husband's art.

The **Frederic Remington Art Museum** contains marvelous bronzes, oils, watercolors, and pen-and-ink sketches depicting Remington's buckskin-clad frontiersmen, covered wagons, Native Americans in war paint, birchbark canoes on storm-tossed lakes, and cowboys on bucking broncos. There is even a faithful re-creation of his last studio, plus a good gift shop.

In summer (May through October) the museum is open Monday to Saturday from 10am to 5pm (from 1pm on Sunday); the rest of the year it's open only Tuesday through Saturday from 10am to 5pm. Admission is $3 for adults and $2 for seniors and youths (13 to 16). The address is 303 Washington St., Ogdensburg (tel. 315/393-2425).

WHERE TO STAY IN ALEXANDRIA BAY

A brand-new four-story brick **Riveredge Resort Hotel,** Holland Street, Alexandria Bay, NY 13607 (tel. 315/482-9917 or toll free 800/ENJOY-US; fax 315/482-5010), has risen from the ashes of a devastating 1988 fire. No expense has been spared in the construction of this state-of-the-art 125-room resort hotel, crowned with 28 split-level suites on the top floor. With majestic views of the St. Lawrence River and Boldt Castle from all the rooms, this year-round hotel also features private balconies, Jacuzzis, cable TVs, boat accommodation up to 250 feet, a health spa, a sauna, an exercise room, two restaurants—even indoor and outdoor pools with hot tubs. They even have a separate building for boaters in transit, with baths, showers, laundry, vending machines, water, electric, phone, and TV. Room and suite rates range between $80 and $225 from May to mid-June; $100 to $250 to Labor Day; $80 to $170 to early November, when winter rates decline to $60 and $130 (highest rates denote Jacuzzi or duplex suites). All major credit cards accepted.

The biggest and most elaborate resort in the Thousand Islands is **Bonnie Castle,** Alexandria Bay, NY 13607 (tel. 315/482-4511, or toll free 800/955-4511; fax 315/482-9600). At the heart of this huge place, engulfed by new construction, is a house built by a 19th-century author referred to as the "great" J. G. Holland (ever heard of him? me neither). The 120 modern guest rooms are really Hilton quality, with their thick rugs, modern tiled baths, good-quality furniture, wet bars, cable color TVs with free HBO, and direct-dial phones. Some have fantasy bathtubs and mirrored ceilings. Across several acres of blacktopped parking lot is Bonnie Castle Manor, consisting of the old house and its huge new additions. "The Home of the Stars" says the sign outside. Inside is a glittery/glamorous nightclub that holds 700 and books acts like the Inkspots, the Platters, and Al Martino. "Name" or not, there's always somebody there, as management assures me there is entertainment every night of the year. Adjacent is a lush restaurant with lots of picture windows and water views, featuring lunch and dinner service every day year-round. Double-occupancy room rates at the peak of the summer season (late May to Labor Day) range from $120 or so to around $235 nightly, the latter rate for a room with a king-size bed and a Jacuzzi. Rates decline in stages to a deep winter low of about $60 to $150 a night. Also on the premises are an immense outdoor pool, an indoor pool, and several tennis courts. All major credit cards accepted.

Of the bunch of other big resorts in town, my favorite is **Edgewood,** Alexandria Bay, NY 13607 (tel. 315/482-9922; fax 315/482-5210). Founded by a group of Cleveland businessmen as a private club in the 1880s, Edgewood is today a complete modern resort on a beautifully landscaped property immediately west of downtown Alex Bay. In the middle of things is a big old clapboard summer hotel left over from the old days and unused except for special functions. Today's accommodations are located in modern motel buildings that hug the shoreline. Rooms have beamed ceilings (many of them do, anyway), decks overlooking the water, color TVs, phones, and a nice 1960s contemporary look. There are 160 of them, plus a big outdoor pool, an attractive beach and dock, three lounges, and a resort-type restaurant whose adjacent Gazebo Room offers nightly entertainment. Open year-round with double-occupancy rates ranging from a high of $60 to $150 nightly (mid-May to Labor Day) to a low of $30 to $99. All major credit cards accepted.

Capt. Thomson's Resort, P.O. Box 68, Alexandria Bay, NY 13607 (tel. 315/482-9961, or toll free 800/253-9229 in New York State; fax 315/482-2611), is located at the lower end of James Street, adjacent to the Uncle Sam Boat Dock. This is a complex of two-story, redwood-stained, motel-type buildings built on the perimeter of a little point extending out into the river. There's a nice pool, and the 117 reasonably priced units have color TVs and pleasant motel-modern furniture. The most expensive room for two at the peak of summer (July and August) is $160 a night; other doubles can be had during that same period for about $86. Prices in the "early" and "off" seasons range from about $75 to $90 nightly. All major credit cards accepted.

Popular with fishermen for its location and its good rates is **Fisherman's Wharf Motel,** 15 Sisson St., Alexandria Bay, NY 13607 (tel. 315/482-2230). This diminutive establishment has but 24 units, all of which overlook the upper harbor and the marina. Rooms are simple but quite pleasant, each with cable TV, a little refrigerator, and two double beds. If you come with a boat that's less than 25 feet long, you can even tie it up for free right outside your door. Simple, but the ambience is very authentic. Double-occupancy room rates vary from about $60 to $85 during the late June to Labor Day high season. Before and after that you can stay here for about $45 to $70 double. Closed from November to May. All major credit cards accepted.

WHERE TO EAT IN ALEXANDRIA BAY

Bonnie Castle and Riveredge, described above, both have interesting restaurants for either lunch or dinner. The best-known upscale independent restaurant in town is **Cavallario's Steak and Seafood House,** on Church Street near James (tel. 315/482-9867). You can't miss its false-fronted castellated facade. Inside, the castle decor continues with cutout gilded knights mounted on red velvet, crossed lances, wrought iron, and thick rugs. Only dinner is served, on Monday to Saturday from 4 until 10pm (from 3 to 10pm on Sunday), from a menu offering such things as surf and turf, veal Francis, honey-orange duckling, snapper "maison," and chicken Kiev. A la carte prices are mostly from $13 to $18, but go all the way up to $26.50. Open from early May until late October. All major credit cards accepted.

Admiral's Inn, at the corner of James and Market Streets (tel. 315/482-2781), is an old wooden house with a pretty covered porch/café furnished with blue-plastic tablecloths and white chairs. Inside is a neighborhoody bar and several pleasant, small dining rooms with bay windows, plastic-covered chairs, blue tablecloths, and cheerful print curtains. The lunch menu consists of sandwiches, burgers, "tasty tidbits" (which might double as appetizers on a dinner menu), plus soups and salads, priced between $4 and $8. At dinner you can order spaghetti, homemade lasagne, fried chicken, pork chop or turkey dinners, trout, and scallops for about $8 to $12, with a few items going as high as $25. Open April to mid-October; meals served Monday to Thursday from 11am until 10pm (until 11pm on Friday and Saturday). All major credit cards accepted.

There are two other good lunch places in downtown Alex. **A Summer Place,** 24 James St. (tel. 315/482-9805), across the street from the Admiral's Inn, is another informal tavern with a very good lunch menu. All sorts of salads, sandwiches, and burgers are available for around $3 to $6. It's dim, friendly, and very informal —and the food is good. Closed November to May. Alternatively, you might try the little **Dock Side,** 17 Market St. (tel. 315/482-9849), another vintage small-town tavern with a friendly atmosphere and good bar sandwiches for $3 to $4. Open Monday to Saturday all year from 10am until 2am (from noon on Sunday). No credit cards accepted.

2. Clayton

About 11 miles west of Alex Bay, via N.Y. 12, is the riverfront village of Clayton (pop. 1,800). This is a sleepy place, pretty in its own unpretentious way, well known to fishermen who return year after year and to summer people with island homes in the vicinity. The big resorts, most of the bars, the boat tours, and indeed most of the consciousness of the Thousand Islands is centered on Alex Bay. Yet Clayton has a few attractions of note.

First and foremost must be the **fishing.** Clayton is, after all, the home of the Muskie Hall of Fame. As fishing has already been described in some detail under Alex Bay, let me (with due respect to Clayton) refer you to that section above.

In the late 19th century, Clayton was a famous center of freshwater boatbuilding, a tradition still honored today. Every year, for example, there's an **antique boat show** that attracts up to 300 antique boaters every August. There's also the famous **Antique Boat Museum** at 750 Mary St. (tel. 315/686-4104), the largest freshwater maritime museum of its kind in the world. Here you can see everything from dugout canoes to the sleek varnished commuter boats of the old Thousand Islands millionaires. There are also rare periodicals, old photos, and displays of all manner of power and nonpower boats. Open mid-May to mid-October; admission is $5.

WHERE TO STAY & EAT IN CLAYTON

Most of the action is in nearby Alex Bay, but several establishments offer good value in Clayton as well. **Quarterdeck Motel and Restaurant,** east of the village on N.Y. 12, Clayton, NY 13624 (tel. 315/686-5588), is a modest establishment located behind a popular restaurant of the same name. It has but 12 units, with sliding glass doors that lead to little terraces, distant water views, cable color TVs, and very attractive modern decor. They cost only $55 a night double at the height of summer. Winter rates are $35 double. The restaurant is a cozy, family-style pine-paneled affair with an adjoining bar. Open for dinner only with homemade pastas and grilled specials, from $7 to $14. Open Sunday to Thursday from 5 to 9pm (to 10pm on Friday and Saturday). MC and V accepted.

Another pleasant and inexpensive place to stay is **Bertrand's Motel,** 229 James St., Clayton, NY 13624 (tel. 315/686-3641). Located in the heart of downtown Clayton, this is a 1963-vintage two-story motel with 28 rooms and a certain small-town charm. There are pretty gardens outside, as well as rooms with blond furniture, cable color TVs, and a well-kept family-owned air. Double rooms cost about $60 in July and August; that rate drops to about $50 the rest of the season. Closed December through March. All major credit cards accepted.

Out on N.Y. 12 again, just east of Clayton, is the very popular **Clipper Inn** (tel. 315/686-3842). This attractive establishment consists of a collection of cheerful contemporary rooms with lots of wood lattice and a vaguely nautical motif. Only dinner is served, the menu offering such selections as sole Oscar, broiled scallops, frogs' legs, and seafood scampi, plus Italian pasta dishes and assorted steak and chicken dishes. Prices are from $8 to $18. Open for dinner only from 5 to 10pm daily April through December. All major credit cards accepted.

Last, but not least, is **Koffee Kove,** on James Street (tel. 315/686-2472) opposite Bertrand's Motel. This is the sort of small-town sandwich shop for which I have a soft spot in my heart. It's a cheery, pine-paneled, fluorescent-lit, unpretentious place dispensing delicious sandwiches on homemade bread for around $2 to $3. What could be finer than a piece of homemade pie to follow (available for a modest $1.50)? Open daily year-round from 6am to 8pm.

---

3. An Excursion to Sackets Harbor

Thirty-odd miles southwest of Alexandria Bay (via Interstate 81 to Watertown, then east on Route 3 to the shore of Lake Ontario), is the attractive historic village of Sackets Harbor (pop. 1,000). Eleven years after it was settled, in 1801, as a frontier farming hamlet, Sackets Harbor became the focus of the world.

On July 19, 1812, five British battleships sailed into Black River Bay and confronted a single American warship, the *Oneida,* anchored in Sackets Harbor. Local farmers joined the fray, wrapping 24-pound cannon balls with old carpet so that they would fit into the sole 32-pound cannon they possessed. It was "Old Sow," as that cannon was familiarly known, that fired the first shot of the War of 1812. Outnumbered but ever resourceful, our forebears retrieved as many British cannonballs as they could, loaded them back into Old Sow, and used them for return fire. In fact, it was a recycled British 32-pounder that, when shot from the mouth of Old Sow, ripped the mast off the British flagship *Royal George.*

During and after the War of 1812, Sackets Harbor developed as an important center for ship building and naval operations. In 1815, the famous **Madison Barracks** were constructed. This elaborate military complex, consisting of stone buildings and a parade ground on a scenic site overlooking Lake Ontario, continued to expand until the 1920s. It is today the finest collection of period military architecture in New York State. What's more, it is complemented by wonderful 19th-century commercial and residential buildings in the adjacent village as well as the historic Sackets Harbor Battlefield immediately to the west.

WHAT TO SEE & DO IN SACKETS HARBOR

Walking around town, exploring the historic sites, and soaking up the wonderful scenery and atmosphere constitute the principal occupation hereabouts. An excellent orientation booklet entitled "Harbor Walk, a Guide to the History and Architecture of Sackets Harbor" is available for $2 at **Urban Cultural Park and Visitors Center,** in the Sacket Mansion, P.O. Box 17, Main St., Sackets Harbor, NY 13685 (tel. 315/646-1700). You can get the same booklet from **Seaway Trail, Inc.,** 109 Barracks Dr., Sackets Harbor, NY 13685 (tel. 315/646-1000).

The nearby **Sackets Harbor Battlefield** and **Union Hotel Historic Site** are administered by the New York State Office of Parks, Recreation and Historic Preservation. They are fascinating places, especially to students of American history. An onsite interpretive center is open from late May until late September on Wednesday through Saturday from 10am to 5pm and on Sunday from 1 to 5pm, including holidays. The grounds are open all year from 8am until sunset.

You can also take a self-guided walking tour of the **Madison Barracks** with the aid of an orientation map and history guide that describes all 38 historic buildings in the complex. The map is available at the Barracks' information office (tel. 315/646-3374), open on Monday through Friday from 9am to 5pm.

If you're in town between Thursday and Sunday, you can leaven all this historical experience with stand-up comedy at **Lake Ontario Playhouse,** 103 West Main St., Sackets Harbor, NY 13685 (tel. 315/646-2305). Showtime is nightly at 9pm, and admission is a reasonable $5.

WHERE TO STAY & EAT IN SACKETS HARBOR

Old Stone Row Country Inn, 85 Worth Rd., Sackets Harbor, NY 13685 (tel. 315/646-1234; fax 315/646-1235), offers a variety of modern rooms scattered throughout the old Barracks buildings. Originally designed as small apartments, these accommodations are all different. Typically they have knotty-pine Colonial furniture, cable TVs with HBO, phones, microwaves, and small refrigerators. Prices range from a weeknight low of $50 for a small studio to a weekend high of $95 for a "luxury suite." AE, MC, and V accepted.

Dockside in the center of the village is **Ontario Place Hotel,** 103 General Smith Dr., Sackets Harbor, NY 13685 (tel. 315/646-8000; fax 315/646-2506), the owners of which have turned a pair of vintage waterfront buildings into a single 39-room hotel. All accommodations have phones, modern private baths, cable TVs, and air conditioning at prices that start at $55 nightly in the winter and $69 during the summer high season (May 15 through October 15). All major credit cards accepted.

For a creative bite to eat, try **Old Stone Row Restaurant,** 336 Brady Rd. (tel. 315/646-2923). The airy high-ceilinged dining room has exposed-brick and stone walls, lazy ceiling fans, and a fine view of the historic parade grounds and Lake Ontario. Dinner main dishes like Moroccan lamb kebabs and Sicilian tortellini Syracuse style cost mostly between $9 and $13. Open Monday to Saturday from 5:30pm all year long; lunch is served during July and August only. AE, MC, and V accepted.

Also in the waterfront area is **The 1812 Steak and Seafood Company,** 212 West Main St. (tel. 315/646-2041). This is one of those places where you can look your lobster straight in the eye before choosing him or her from a tank. The decor employs exposed brick, plus lace curtains, crisp linen tablecloths, candlelight, and a cosy bar. Steaks (London broil to filet mignon) can cost from $11 to $15; shrimp, chicken, and various fresh seafood platters are priced a bit lower; the big Sunday buffet is only $5.95. On Wednesday through Monday dinner hours are 4 to 10pm; order before 6pm, and you can have the $7.95 early-bird special. The Sunday buffet is served from 9am to 1pm only, after which the regular menu is in effect until early closing at 4pm. All major credit cards accepted.

XVII

THE FINGER LAKES DISTRICT

1. WHAT THE FINGER LAKES ARE LIKE
2. SYRACUSE
3. NORTHERN TIER
4. ROCHESTER
5. SOUTHERN TIER

The operative word here is *rural*. The Finger Lakes District lies south of Lake Ontario at the very heart of New York State. It's a region of rolling hills, big views, and long valleys, many of which contain deep, narrow lakes. Seneca Lake, for example, is 650 feet deep, its bottom being 250 feet below sea level.

1. What the Finger Lakes Are Like

On the map the Finger Lakes look like the splayed fingers of a multidigited hand. On the ground the area has an agricultural look. Fields and farms and vineyards dominate the landscape between the various towns and cities. There are forests too, but the hand of man lies clearly on the area (appropriate, considering its name) and there's no sense of wilderness. There are, however, quite a few deep ravines and waterfalls in this part of the world. Many are rather impressive and are preserved on the grounds of state parks we'll visit later.

A great deal of wine is made in the Finger Lakes District—more wine, in fact, than in any other part of America outside California. If you're so inclined you can spend a considerable amount of time vineyard hopping. The countryside is wide and lovely, and the 50-some vineyards themselves, sited on gentle sloping hills overlooking panoramas of lake and hillside, are often quite beautiful. The wine too is coming of age. At last we're seeing New York State wines included (deservedly) on lists in some of the best restaurants in America.

A great deal of interesting and informative (not to mention opulently designed and illustrated) free promotional literature is available on New York State wines these days. You can request it by contacting the New York Wine and Grape Foundation, 350 Elm St., Penn Yan, NY 14527 (tel. 315/536-7442).

A BIT OF HISTORY

Until the time of the American Revolution the Finger Lakes were a stronghold of the Iroquois Confederation. After a few particularly bloody raids against white settlers, in which British complicity was suspected, Washington dispatched Gen.

John Sullivan on an expedition to "chastise and humble the Six Nations," as the Indians hereabouts were known. In 1779, Sullivan's men swept through the Finger Lakes, killed just about every Indian there, and utterly destroyed all their settlements. Numerous historic markers commemorate the more bloodcurdling of his successes. Sullivan received the official thanks of Congress in October 1779, despite angry criticism of the campaign. Few people in the area today seem to have any idea who he was or what he did.

The Finger Lakes prospered with the advent of the Erie Canal, and much of the fine Greek Revival architecture of that period remains. So do a lot of classical place names. Cities, villages, and townships alike bear the most distinguished names imaginable. Your map will reveal not just Ithaca, but Syracuse, Ovid, Pompey, Romulus, Homer, Ulysses, Scipio, and even Brutus.

The agricultural and light industrial economy of the area today is quite able to support the population without the help of tourists. Yet the rural charms and tranquility of the Finger Lakes draw a steady stream of visitors every year. In summer, there are the vineyards and the country roads, the pretty towns, and deep, clear lakes. There's also grand-prix racing at Watkins Glen and thoroughbred horse racing at the Finger Lakes Track near Canandaigua. In fall there's the changing foliage. And any time of year there are attractive and romantic places to eat and stay a night or two. Then there is Rochester, a great little city that's definitely worth a visit.

USEFUL INFORMATION

Although not every town or city in the region is included in this chapter, I have tried to hit the high spots. Surely you'll find enough in the pages ahead to give you what the local tourist organization calls "The Finger Lakes Feeling." That organization, by the way, is called the **Finger Lakes Association,** 309 Lake St., Penn Yan, NY 14527 (tel. 315/536-7488, or toll free 800/548-4386), and has been in business since 1919. It will send you a copy of the encyclopedic *I Love New York Finger Lakes Travel Guide,* if you like, for $2. It can also provide all manner of other information that might be helpful in planning your trip.

And for an extensive listing of bed-and-breakfast establishments in the Finger Lakes region you can contact either the Finger Lakes Association or the **Finger Lakes Bed & Breakfast Association** at 309 Lake St., Penn Yan, NY 14527 (tel. 315/536-7488). Its guidebook costs $3.

---

2. Syracuse

Charles Dickens visited Syracuse in 1869 and wrote the following.

I am here in a most wonderful out-of-the-world place, which looks as if it had begun to be built yesterday, and were going to be imperfectly knocked together with a nail or two the day after tomorrow. I am here in the worst inn that was ever seen, and outside is a thaw that places the whole country under water. . . . I have tried all the wines in the house and these are only two wines for which you pay six shillings a bottle or 15, according as you feel disposed to change the name of the thing you ask for. (The article never changes.) The bill of fare is in French and the principal article is Paeltie de shay! I asked the Irish waiter what this dish was and he said "it was the name the stewart giv' to oyster patties—the French name." . . . We had an old buffalo for supper and an old pig for breakfast and we are going to have I don't know what for dinner at 6. In the public room downstairs, a number of men (speechless) with their feet against the

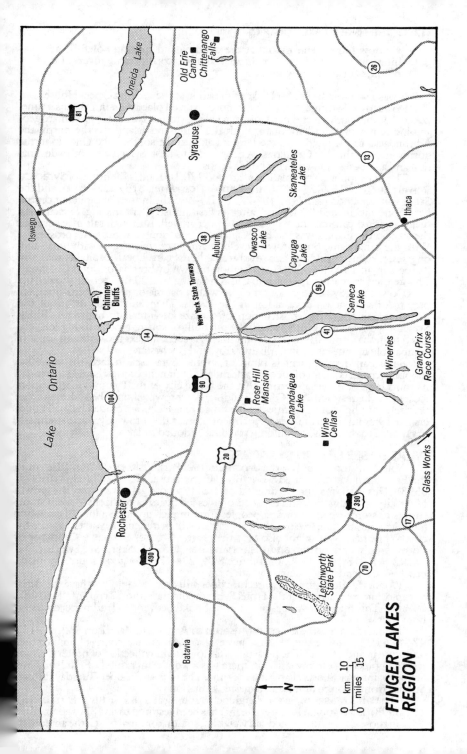

FINGER LAKES REGION

window frames, staring out at the window and spitting dolefully at intervals. . . . And yet we have taken in considerably over 300 pounds for tomorrow night.

It was a sold-out house for Dickens's reading at the Weiting Opera House.

Downtown Syracuse today is a far more civilized place than in Dickens's time. Located at the southern end of Onondaga Lake, Syracuse is at the approximate geographic center of New York State. With the Thousand Islands to the north, the Adirondacks to the northeast, the Finger Lakes to the south, Lake Ontario to the northwest, and the Erie Canal transversing it east to west, Syracuse is both a destination and a logical staging area for holiday trips.

The city supports a population of around 170,100 and is the home of **Syracuse University** (tel. 315/423-1870), the **Carrier Dome** (tel. 315/423-4634), and the **State Fair Grounds** (tel. 315/487-7711). It is also the industrial capital of central New York, nicknamed "Salt City" after its first industry, salt mining. Syracuse is a major regional cultural and recreational center as well. Although salt may have put the city on the map, it was the Erie Canal that contributed most to its prosperity. With the canal came boom-town development—streets clogged with horse-and-buggies, thriving businesses, and rowdy canal-house bars. Local hospitality may have its roots in an 1870 New Year's celebration thrown by beer baron John Greenway. This gentleman roasted a giant ox in Clinton Square, and 20,000 people showed up.

Downtown Syracuse, as was the case with most major northeastern cities, fell prey to urban-renewal devastation in the 1960s. Then, in the 1970s, insult was added to injury by the construction of a maze of Interstate highways. Today, Syracuse's downtown center is a patchwork quilt of square-block parking lots, elevated highways, and islands of tall buildings. As such, it lacks the style and flavor of comparable upstate cities, like Albany, Troy, and Rochester.

Suburban development is rampant around Syracuse. In fact, the suburban shopping center concept of the "miracle mile" or "franchise strip" is said to have had its roots here. It is perhaps fitting that the home city of the Pyramid Corporation, located in the restored Post Office Building downtown, should be suffering from precisely the plight of other cities whose urban retail cores are eroded by mall builders like Pyramid. Even Sibley's Department Store, a downtown Syracuse landmark, has moved to the malls; its building stands abandoned today.

WHAT TO SEE & DO IN SYRACUSE

Your first stop should be the **Urban Cultural Park Visitors Center,** adjacent to the Erie Canal Museum at 318 Erie Blvd. E., Syracuse, NY 13202 (tel. 315/471-0593). This is an imaginative orientation facility whose galleries depict the growth of the city, its industries, and the sorts of lives led by its past citizens—from stonecutters to storekeepers to theater people. You can pick up quite a lot of fascinating historical tidbits, plus free tour brochures that will better enable you to explore the city. While here, you might also visit the nearby **Greater Syracuse Chamber of Commerce's Convention and Visitors Bureau** at 572 S. Salina St., Syracuse, NY 13202 (tel. 315/470-1900, or toll free 800/234-4797), a good source for maps, brochures, calendars of events, and advice.

Wonderful downtown architecture does still exist. Should you have the desire to explore it, you can stop at the Hotel Syracuse and pick up a $2 copy of "Let's Take a Walk." This informative self-guided tour booklet covers 36 landmarks on a one-hour tour.

Included on it is the **Everson Museum of Art,** at 401 Harrison St. (tel. 315/474-6064), an impressive-looking piece of contemporary concrete architectura sculpture in and of itself. The museum is famous for its collection of pottery, ceramics, and porcelain. On my last visit, there was a wonderful exhibit of Hudson Rive School paintings. Shows change all the time. The museum is open Tuesday throug Sunday from noon to 5pm; the suggested donation is $2.

The **Canal Museum,** in the Weighlock Building at 318 Erie Blvd. E. (tel. 315/471-0593), is a National Register site that has been restored to its 1850s appearance Back in those days it functioned as a weighing station for canal boats, the antecedent to today's truck stations along the Interstate highways. Adjacent to the museum is a vintage 65-foot canal boat that you can board to explore and peruse exhibits documenting canal life and the growth of Syracuse. Open Tuesday through Sunday from 10am to 5pm; admission is $1 for adults and 50¢ for kids.

While in town you might also like to catch a show at the **Landmark Theatre,** 362 South Salina St. (tel. 315/475-7979), as much for the sake of its fantastic Indo-Persian movie-palace architecture as for the show itself. The Landmark has a sumptuous lobby, a sweeping staircase, gilded and vaulted ceilings, and a fabulous proscenium arch. Everything from symphony concerts, to popular singers, to Broadway touring companies play the Landmark. Tours of the building are available by appointment.

A few minutes north of Syracuse, off the Onondaga Lake Parkway, is an unusual "living museum" called **Sainte Marie Among the Iroquois,** P.O. Box 146, Liverpool, NY 13088 (tel. 315/453-6767). This is a sort of upstate Indian version of Old Bethpage Village down on Long Island (see Chapter VIII under "Selected Suburban Attractions"). You can observe blacksmiths and carpenters, taste 17th-century foods, and savor the tone and texture of life when French settlers were first meeting and living with the local Indians. Open Tuesday through Sunday from 10am to 5pm; admission is $3 for adults and $1.50 for children 5 to 15.

The largest enclosed shopping mall in America was developed by Syracuse's own Pyramid Corporation and is appropriately located in Syracuse itself. The **Carousel Mall** contains 1.5 *million* square feet of retail shopping space, enough to suck dry the most vigorous of established downtown urban retail cores. Located in the northern section of town on a 50-acre site that formerly housed an industrial scrapyard, this mother of all malls contains 130 specialty stores, 6.5 acres of imported Italian-marble floor tiles, a 12-screen cinema complex, 27 elevators, 34 escalators, myriad fast-food and full-service restaurants, and even 25 adjacent baseball fields. Our Canadian neighbors drive hours to shop here; so does everyone in the region.

WHERE TO STAY IN SYRACUSE

Conventions are a big business hereabout, and almost 4,000 rooms are available for transient overnight accommodations. Right in the middle of downtown is one of the more interesting of these establishments, **The Hotels at Syracuse,** 500 S. Warren St., Syracuse, NY 13292 (tel. 315/422-5121, 315/471-7300, or toll free 800/255-3892). This is actually a complex of two hotels, the stately old Hotel Syracuse and the newer Hilton Towers, connected by an enclosed esplanade. Admittedly, my favorite is the old Syracuse, built in 1924 to the designs of architect George B. Post and one of the few survivors of its kind left in New York State after the 1960s urban-renewal blitzes. It features a grand neoclassical lobby; a fabulous mirrored ballroom on the 10th floor; and charming rooms boasting Stickley furniture, capacious tiled baths with pedestal sinks and huge tubs, and the expected phones and color TVs. The contrasting Hilton is a contemporary tower with typical up-to-date Hilton rooms. There are 725 units all told; a good thing, since a very brisk convention business is done here. All major credit cards accepted.

Over by Syracuse University **Sheraton University Inn and Conference Center,** 801 University Ave. (P.O. Box 801), Syracuse, NY 13210 (tel. 315/475-3000, or toll free 800/325-3535), is an ultramodern affair of steel and tinted glass. *Amenities* is the watchword here, for there's a full gamut of indoor pool, exercise room, whirlpool, and sauna, overlooking the lobby itself through walls of glass. There are two restaurants, plus 232 plush guest rooms priced between $111 and $148 nightly. All major credit cards accepted.

Several blocks to the north is **Genesee Inn,** 1060 East Genesee St., Syracuse, NY 13201 (tel. 315/476-4212), whose plant-filled two-story atrium buzzes with the conversation of diners and loungers. The 98 recently redecorated rooms boast Colonial-style cherrywood furniture manufactured by the local Stickley Furniture Company. Prices range from $52 to $135 nightly, depending on room size and location. All major credit cards accepted.

On the outskirts of town, in the East Syracuse area known as Carrier Circle (at

Exit 35 of the New York State Thruway), is a cluster of over a dozen nationally known chain motor hotels. In my opinion, **Courtyard by Marriott,** 6415 York-town Circle, Syracuse, NY 13057 (tel. 315/432-0300), is the most attractive and offers the best buy. The modern rooms are attractively decorated and come with queen-size beds, color cable TVs, and little private terraces. Additionally, the motel offers a small indoor pool, a whirlpool, a restaurant, and a lounge. Marriott has built this identical building all across America. In Syracuse, it costs between $54 and $76 nightly to stay here. All major credit cards accepted.

Also in the area are a **Holiday Inn** (tel. 315/437-2761, or toll free 800/238-8000); a **Day's Inn** (tel. 315/325-2525); a **Quality Inn** (tel. 315/463-6601, or toll free 800/228-5151); and a **Howard Johnson Motor Lodge** (tel. 315/437-2711, or toll free 800/654-2000)—to name only a few. It's possible to find rooms here-about for as low as $39 nightly.

WHERE TO EAT IN SYRACUSE

My favorite is **Pascale Wine Bar and Restaurant,** 204 W. Fayette St. (tel. 315/471-3040), downtown in the new AT&T Building. The decor has a breezy California look, due in large part to the open kitchen. You can watch the chefs in their whites tending wood-burning pizza ovens and whipping up everything from creative sandwiches (about $5) to the "Pizza from Hell—No Sissies" (about $6). There are also things like wood-grilled herb-marinated hanger steak for $7.50, wood-roasted herb-crusted salmon for $16.50, and wood-grilled black Angus ten-derloin with green-peppercorn sauce for about $18. Lunch is served Monday through Friday from 11:30am to 2pm; dinner hours are Monday through Thursday from 5:30 to 10pm, until 11pm on Friday and Saturday. All major credit cards accepted.

Nikki's Downtown, 201 S. Salina St. (tel. 315/424-1172), is housed in a Na-tional Register–listed building constructed in 1876 in high Victorian Gothic style. The solid-mahogany interior of Nikki's was installed for the original H. J. Howe jewelry store, and the old vaults downstairs are now used for intimate dining. Lunch, served on Monday through Friday from 11:30am to 3:30pm, includes sand-wiches or options like blackened catfish and chicken tchoupitoulas priced from $3.50 to $9. Dinner, which features continental, French, Cajun, and charbroiled items, is available on Monday through Thursday from 5 to 10pm, to 11pm on Fri-day and Saturday, and to 9pm on Sunday. Main courses cost $13 to $22. Sunday brunch ($9.95) is served from 11am to 2:30pm; reservations are suggested. All ma-jor credit cards accepted.

Down the hill from Syracuse University is **Phoebe's Garden Café,** 900 E. Genesee St. (tel. 315/475-5154). This is certainly a charming place, with its en-closed porch, secluded dining room, and terraced atrium all decorated with an-tiques, large plants, brass light fixtures, and bentwood chairs. Midday meal selections include sandwiches, burgers, and main dishes like chicken-and-shrimp jambalaya, costing between $4 and $10. Evening meals are similar and cost between $8 and $13. Open for lunch on Monday through Saturday from 11:30am to 3pm; dinner hours are Monday to Thursday from 5 to 10pm, until 11pm on Friday and Saturday. Closed Sunday. AE, MC, and V accepted.

Back downtown again, a great restaurant for lighter fare is **Pastabilities,** 311 S. Franklin St., next to Armory Square (tel. 315/474-1153). As the name suggests, this place features its own pasta in a variety of hot dishes and cold salads. Music is played in the courtyard in summer as well as inside the restaurant on Saturday night. Lunch is served cafeteria style on Monday through Saturday from 11am to 3pm; table-service dinners from $6 to $16 are available from 5 to 10pm on Monday through Thursday, until midnight on Friday and Saturday. MC, V, and DC accepted.

Housed in a restored 1876 former hotel, the opulent **Crown Bar and Grill,** 307 W. Fayette St. (tel. 315/474-0772), is particularly popular as we go to press. There are an impeccably restored carved mahogany bar, lots of etched-glass dividers, stamped-tin ceilings, ornate old gas chandeliers, and plenty of plush Victorian-style upholstery. Lunch, served on Monday to Saturday from 11:30am to 2:30pm, might be anything from chicken salad croissant for $4.25 to grilled Pacific salmon for $16.25. Dinner selections range from fettucine Alfredo with rock shrimp for $10 to sautéed tournedos for $17.95. Dinner is served on Monday to Thursday from 6 until about 10pm, later on Friday and Saturday. The bar has lots of interesting beers, as well as good wines by the glass. All major credit cards accepted. Closed Sunday.

Located in the elaborately mansarded 1867 Gridley Building is **F. W. Gridley,** 103 E. Water St. (tel. 315/475-4212). The basement vaults of this former bank now contain an excellent restaurant that serves both lunch and dinner. The former might consist of salads or sandwiches from $4 to a petite filet mignon for $9. Dinners of fowl, chops, venison steak, and seafood cost from $10 to $17. Open Monday through Thursday from 11:30am to 10pm, until 11pm on Friday and Saturday. AE, MC, and V accepted.

Good food will at times follow the masses from downtown to the malls. A case in point is **L&N Seafood Restaurant** in the Carousel Mall, 9542 Carousel Center (tel. 315/466-3110). The decor is a carefully contrived mixture of forest green and gray-washed oak, highlighted with burgundy tiles, knot displays, large-scale ship models, and a fascinating collection of 19th-century nautical prints. Food ranges from mesquite-grilled fresh fish to beef and poultry. A reasonably priced ($5 to $9) express lunch menu is available between 11:30am and 4pm; most dinner main courses cost between $8 and $15. L&N is open Sunday to Thursday until 10pm, until 11pm on Friday and Saturday. All major credit cards accepted.

---

3. Northern Tier

The New York State Thruway runs right across the top of the Finger Lakes. But in order to really see anything of the area, U.S. 20 (joined in places by N.Y. 5) will be your principal east-west route across the northern tier. Much of the road traverses vast rural areas. You climb steadily to the top of a ridge, admire an immense vista, descend to the bottom of a valley, and start all over again. The hills, like the lakes, all seem to run roughly north and south, and all seem about the same height.

Parts of U.S. 20 are pretty built-up, especially the stretch between the northern ends of Seneca and Cayuga Lakes. The north-south roads, however, that wend between the various lakes toward the southern tier are almost all extremely rural. Traffic is light, horizons are wide, the sky is big. The land has a solitary, muscular feel to it, rather like the Midwest. And psychologically that's exactly where it is.

We'll begin on the east and work our way toward Rochester.

SKANEATELES

This might well be the prettiest community in the Finger Lakes. It was founded in 1794 and burned to the ground in 1835; many, if not most, of the buildings dating from its reconstruction still stand today.

What to See & Do

The village (pop. 2,800) is situated at the head of Skaneateles Lake, and it's a grove of white-columned Greek temples, elaborate Victorian summer houses, and manicured country estates. The architecturally handsome **business district** is on U.S. 20. **West Lake Road,** which intersects U.S. 20 within sight of the light at the center of town, consists of a fabulous procession of 19th-century summer houses, some quite grand. The surrounding countryside is mostly farmland. The look of the town may be somewhat different, but the atmosphere here is much like that of Cazenovia (described under "The Road West—Cooperstown & Cazenovia" in Chapter XIV).

There was a time when the denizens of Skaneateles did things like mine potash, distill whisky, and grow teazles (a sort of Velcro-like plant used a century ago to raise the nap on woolen cloth). Nowadays they sail on the lake, make prudent investments, and lavish loving attention on their beautiful town.

You can cruise on the lake too, on a handsome boat called the *Judge Ben Wiles* (it looks like an antique, but actually it's new). **Mid-Lakes Navigation Co.** operates the *Judge Ben Wiles* from a dock opposite the Sherwood Inn, in the middle of town. Various cruises are available, from the Mail Cruise (Mid-Lakes has one of the last water-route mail contracts in the U.S., and you can come along for $15 per person) to the Weekend Village Cruise (which takes about an hour and costs about $7), to the Dinner Cruise ($30, including a full meal). For information and reservations, call 315/685-8500 or toll free 800/545-4318; cruises operated only in July and August.

Where to Stay & Eat
Sherwood Inn, 26 W. Genesee St., Skaneateles, NY 13152 (tel. 315/685-3405), is the nicest inn I saw in the whole Finger Lakes District. It's a rambling 19th-century shingled affair with a big screened porch. It's painted blue with black shutters and overlooks the lake, the *Judge Ben Wiles,* and one of the village's beautiful manicured parks. There's a remodeled Colonial look inside, with putty-colored walls, brass chandeliers, wing chairs, and handsome woodwork. To one side of the lobby is a paneled tap room; on the other is an excellent restaurant, about which I'll say more in a moment. Upstairs are 13 very attractive rooms, furnished with brass beds, modern baths, assorted antiques, phones, and tasteful color schemes. No color TVs, but after all, it's a country inn. Open all year. Rates for a double room range from about $69 to $145 a night, depending on room size and location.

Sherwood Inn Restaurant is a really charming and comfortable place, consisting of big, traditional rooms and, in summer, the screened porch. It has crisp linens, attentive service, and good food. Sample items from the lunch menu include grilled chicken breast à l'orange and swordfish kebabs and cost about $5 to $8. The dinner menu features prime rib, crabmeat au gratin, swordfish, New York sirloin, and duckling Cointreau, priced from $12 to $18 à la carte. The lunch menu is available all day in the tap room. Lunch is served daily all year long from 11:30am to 4pm; dinner is Sunday to Friday from 5 to 10pm (to 11pm on Saturday). All major credit cards accepted.

Another famous place in Skaneateles is **Krebs** (named after the family that once ran it as a boarding house), located on U.S. 20 heading west from Sherwood Inn (tel. 315/685-5714 or 685-7001). This is a pretty little white house in the midst of a residential district. Out front is a small porch with rocking chairs and a neon sign reading "1899." Only Sunday brunch and dinner are served, the latter a prix-fixe affair with either five or seven courses composed of solid and delicious American cooking. The price per person is about $26 to $33, depending on which meal you take. The first floor is given over to bright, airy dining rooms with flowers on the tables and white covers on the chairs. Upstairs is a little pine-paneled lounge and a couple of Victorian sitting rooms. Open from early May until late October; dinner is served from 6 to 9pm; Sunday brunch is from 10:30am to 2pm. All major credit cards accepted.

For something quick, tasty, and cheap, try **Doug's Fish Fry,** which dispenses fries, chowder, clam strips, fried scallops and shrimp, gumbo, franks, fish sandwiches, and more from a little storefront on Jordan Street (which intersects U.S. 20 at the light). Most things cost $2 or $3; full dinners run $4 to $6. Most of the business is take-out, but there's a counter against the wall, facing the open kitchen and a new dining room. Doug's is extremely popular; it's open all year, and every day in the summer. Summer hours are Sunday to Friday from 11am to 9pm (to 10pm on Saturday); closed Sunday in winter. No credit cards accepted.

AUBURN
This vigorous little city (pop. 32,500) lies but 7 miles due west of Skaneateles on U.S. 20. Founded as Hardenbergh Corners at the end of the 18th century, it was renamed in 1803 after a line from a poem by Goldsmith, "Auburn, loveliest village of the plain." Much of its historic loveliness has been sacrificed, however, on the alta

of free-flowing traffic. The new "arterials" do carry you around in a hurry, but aesthetically they've done a lot of damage.

What to See & Do

South Street (N.Y. 38) in Auburn is where the former squirearchy built their stately pleasure domes. Architecturally it's much beleaguered, but there are still some great houses along here. A drive down South Street to the city limits is worth it, if only to get Auburn's measure of its own worth in the era when measures were more tangible than they are today.

Also on South Street are two important attractions. **Seward House,** 33 South St. (tel. 315/252-1283), was the home of William Henry Seward, one of America's greatest secretaries of state. Seward was the man whose famous 1850 speech refuted the constitutional "rights" of slaveholders, claiming that there was a "higher law than the Constitution." He was a two-term governor of New York, a founder of the Republican party, and a proponent of the acquisition of Alaska (known as "Seward's Ice Box"). His imposing painted brick house is actually a chaste Federal town house much enlarged. As a matter of fact, it was the first brick house in Auburn. The interior was redecorated with singular lavishness in the mid-Victorian period and it's something to see, especially its sexy staircase and window treatments. The walls of the second-floor hall are covered with pictures of every dignitary Seward ever met (quite a collection). Seward descendants lived here until 1951. Open Tuesday to Saturday from 1 to 4pm; closed January through March. Adult admission is $3; for seniors it's $2.50.

"There are two things I've got a right to, and these are liberty or death. One or the other I mean to have. No one will take me back alive." So said Harriet Tubman during her years in the Underground Railroad. Tubman was a black woman who escaped slavery and returned again and again to the South as a "conductor," one who led other black people north to freedom. She is credited with saving at least 300 souls. Her code name was "Moses," and so famous did she become that a bounty was on her head all over the South. Interestingly, few believed the intrepid Moses was really a woman. William Seward, resident of an Auburn mansion at the north end of South Street, sold Harriet Tubman a far more modest house at the south end of that same thoroughfare. Here in the last days of her life she ran a home for aged black people. The house still stands, a simple two-story frame affair set back from the road right at the city line. The historic plaque out front reads as follows: "Harriet Tubman—Moses of her people—served the underground railroad—frequented this site after the Civil War." Although not open to the public on a regular basis, **Tubman House** can be visited by appointment on Monday through Friday from 11am to 5pm. Those interested should call 315/253-2621 to make arrangements. The exact address is 180 South Rd.

On a lighter note, Auburn also has a **dinner theater,** presented during July and August in the ballroom of the Springside Inn, West Lake Road (N.Y. 38) (tel. 315/252-7247). Productions have included *Evita, Carousel,* and *Fiddler on the Roof.* The total cost for dinner and a show is around $32 on Friday and Saturday and $30 during the rest of the week. The Springside is an excellent restaurant and an ambient inn as well; see the description below.

Where to Stay & Eat

Right in the middle of town is a **Holiday Inn,** 75 North St., Auburn, NY 13021 (tel. 315/253-4531, or toll free 800/HOLIDAY; fax 315/252-5843), with an enclosed atrium that contains a pool and 178 very nice modern rooms distributed on five floors, all with phones, color TVs, immaculate modern baths, and all the traditional Holiday Inn–type comforts. There are a bar/lounge and a big restaurant. Double rates range from $58 to $90 nightly, depending on location and whether you want a king-size bed. All major credit cards accepted.

The aforementioned **Springside Inn,** West Lake Road (N.Y. 38), Auburn, NY

13021 (tel. 315/252-7247), is a many-gabled red Victorian structure that's out of town, but only by about five minutes (these places don't sprawl too much). It's set back on lovely grounds and is of interest equally because of its restaurant and its rooms. First the restaurant: It's big and beamed and possesses a large stone fireplace and a handsome casual atmosphere. Besides Sunday brunch, only dinner is served, from a "Bill of Fare" that includes sautéed veal, lobster tail, filet mignon, and chicken Cordon Bleu, priced from $9 to $15 à la carte. Hours are Monday to Saturday from 5 to 10pm; Sunday brunch ($9.95) runs from 10:30am to 2pm; Sunday dinner is from 1 to 6pm.

The rooms upstairs are totally idiosyncratic, furnished with stray antiques, thrift-shop pieces, old wallpaper, and the occasional acoustic ceiling. The baths have a summer-camp look, and the floors creak. But it's clean, and it does have charm and atmosphere. And at $65 for a double, including breakfast, you can't go wrong. MC and V accepted.

A good place for convivial barroom atmosphere, a youthful crowd, rock and roll on the jukebox, and $4 burgers and sandwiches is **Curley's,** adjacent to one of Auburn's swooping arterials at 96 State St. (tel. 315/252-5224). Besides a great, loud, dimly lit bar is a multilevel dining room with dark-wood paneling, colored-glass hanging lamps, and a quieter atmosphere. Besides the bar menu you can order evening dinners like fried scallops, stuffed pork chops, all manner of pasta dishes, and hot sandwiches, plus steaks and prime rib. Prices for the main courses are from $10 to $13; hot sandwiches and pastas cost $5 to $7. Open for lunch Monday to Saturday from 11am to 2:30pm and dinner from 5 to 9pm. The bar, of course, is open much later. All major credit cards accepted.

SENECA FALLS

This old mill town (pop. 7,500), about 15 miles west of Auburn on N.Y. 5 and U.S. 20, has wide streets, a comfy ungentrified air, and a 19th-century brick-and-stone downtown area that's eloquent of former wealth and power. Seneca Falls is also a truly historic place, being the 1848 site of the first Women's Rights Convention. Two local residents, Elizabeth Cady Stanton and Amelia Bloomer, gained national recognition—and suffered a good deal of abuse—for among other things their work drafting a "Declaration of Sentiments" approved by the convention. Although they ultimately eliminated the demand for the vote, the document contained some pretty strong language anyway: "The history of mankind is a history of repeated injuries and usurpations on the part of man towards woman having in direct object the establishment of an absolute tyranny over her." This tyranny was then itemized in a manner that raised the hackles of almost every Victorian gentleman in the land. The document noted that, "in view of this entire disenfranchisement of one-half of the people of this country . . . we insist that they have immediate admission to all the rights and privileges which belong to them as citizens of these United States."

Today in Seneca Falls is something called the **Women's Rights National Historical Park,** which is dedicated to the memory of these very courageous women. There are plenty of men today who would become violent reading the whole Declaration. One can imagine the courage it took to draft it in 1848. The Women's Rights Historical Park is still in its infancy, and as a practical matter, there's not too much as yet that's open to the public. But there is a very informative and stirring **visitors' center** at 136 Fall St., between the Gould Hotel and the site of the Weslyan Methodist Chapel (until recently a launderette), where the convention of 1848 was held, plus several other historic sites scattered between Seneca Falls and the nearby town of Waterloo (pop. 5,300). The visitors' center is open from 9am to 5pm daily. The **Elizabeth Cady Stanton House,** at 32 Washington St., Seneca Falls, certainly merits a visit. The hours are daily from 9am to 5pm from June to September, and from noon to 4pm during the rest of the year. In Waterloo is the restored **McClintock House** (same hours), where the Declaration of Sentiments was drafted. The park is administered by the National Park Service, whose local address is P.O. Box 70, Seneca Falls, NY 13148 (tel. 315/568-2991). All the sites are free.

Also in Seneca Falls is a converted bank building that is now the home of the

National Women's Hall of Fame, 76 Fall St. (tel. 315/568-2936). This too is a modest attraction, notwithstanding the importance of its mission. So far 38 women have been elected to the Hall of Fame, individuals ranging from Amelia Earhart to Emily Dickinson, from Abigail Adams to Harriet Tubman, and from Eleanor Roosevelt to Elizabeth Cady Stanton. Photos and descriptive text tell the story of each woman honored. Some of these tales are truly amazing. Open Monday through Saturday in winter from noon to 4pm; on Sunday too in May through October from 9:30 to 5pm. Admission is free. During my fieldwork I didn't find a single local person who had visited either this or the Women's Rights Historical Park. Too bad—I thought they were very impressive.

Where to Eat

The **Gould,** at the corner of Fall and State Streets, Seneca Falls, NY 13148 (tel. 315/568-5801), is an old brick building in the center of town right next door to the visitors' center of the Women's Rights National Park. It has an opulent late-Victorian look inside, a function of chandeliers with tinted-glass shades, potted palms, pictures in heavy gilt frames, and rich woodwork. Lunch might be a Monte Cristo, eggs Benedict, fettuccine carbonara, an energy salad, or a Gould burger, priced from about $5 to $8. At dinner there is breast of chicken, broiled sea scallops, pork chops, filet mignon, and veal chasseur, costing between $10 and $22. Lunch is served on weekdays only from 11:30am until 2pm; dinner is a daily affair from 4 to about 9pm (on Sunday a brunch for $9.95 is served from 11am to 2pm). AE, MC, and V accepted.

GENEVA

Geneva, at the head of Seneca Lake, is among other things the "Lake Trout Capital of the World." It's a moderate-size upstate town (pop. 15,100) with a lakefront boulevard (N.Y. 5 and U.S. 20) behind which lies an elderly downtown business district. **Castle Street** is the main drag, off of which radiate several architecturally interesting side streets. Those who like to explore old towns should peruse both **North and South Main streets,** and **Genesee Street.** Despite ill-considered modernizations here and there, the place retains a vintage upstate charm. It certainly has a lot of churches too.

South Main Street bends around the top of Seneca Lake, and shortly after crossing a viaduct over N.Y. 5/U.S. 20, comes to **Hobart and William Smith Colleges.** The combined campuses of this pair of liberal arts institutions (one for men, the other for women) constitute a dignified and leafy enclave. South Main hereabouts is lined with elegant houses, many of which belong to the local fraternities and sororities. N.Y. 5/U.S. 20 west of town is lined with shopping centers, a factor in the current condition of Castle Street.

On the east side of Geneva is a splendid restored Greek Revival mansion that's the pride of the entire region. This is **Rose Hill,** on N.Y. 96A a mile south of N.Y. 5/U.S. 20 (tel. 315/789-3848). Dating from the 1840s, the house was once the center of a large model farm. Its magnificent pillared portico overlooks Seneca Lake and is a landmark visible from Geneva. The entire house has been painstakingly restored and furnished through the generosity of an anonymous donor. Wallpapers, chandeliers, silver, and Empire antiques, are all of museum quality. Tours start with a slide show that tells the tale of Rose Hill's ups and downs (like many such estates, it once teetered on the edge of demolition). Outside is an exquisite formal garden. Surely one of the most beautiful sites in the Finger Lakes, Rose Hill is open May through October on Monday through Saturday from 10am to 4pm and on Sunday from 1 to 5pm. Admission is $2 for adults and $1 for kids.

This town is graced with not one but two exceedingly splendid former mansions now operating as true country inns. The first is **Geneva on the Lake,** N.Y. 14 (an extension of South Main Street), P.O. Box 929, Geneva, NY 14456 (tel. toll free 800/3GENEVA; fax 315/789-0322). This place was an absolutely first-class private house in its day. It was completed in 1914 for one Byron M. Nester, to plans drawn by Lewis Albro and the famous Harrie T. Lindeberg. In 1949, the Roman Catholic church, which then owned the property, added a pair of modern flanking wings to the central section, which Albro and Lindeberg had closely modeled on an Italian Renaissance palace.

The present owners, the Schickel family, at first altered the building into luxury apartments, each with a full kitchen and usually one or two bedrooms. They later decided to operate it as a resort hotel wherein the original apartments would become luxurious suites. Those in the Catholic wings are quite lush and modern, but those in the old house have sumptuous architectural details. They all have first-class traditional reproduction furniture, color TVs, and private phones. Between the house and the lakefront are elaborate gardens with clipped ornamental hedges and a knockout of a pool, and down by the lake itself is a private boathouse. There's no big lobby or restaurant, but throughout the year dinner is served on Friday, Saturday, and Sunday evenings in what was formerly the main hall and is now called the Villa Lancellotti Dining Room, to the accompaniment of live musical entertainment. Also served is the master chef's magnificent Sunday brunch, as well as breakfast each morning throughout the year. Typical main courses cost between $20 and $32. Double-occupancy rates depend on size and location of the various rooms and range from about $140 to $399 between June and the end of November and from $92 to $273 during the rest of the year. My favorite rooms are in the original house, but I hasten to add that every unit really is beautiful, and the Schickel family brings a new meaning to the word *hospitality*. All major credit cards accepted.

A bit farther south on N.Y. 14 is **Belhurst Castle,** P.O. Box 609, Geneva, NY 14456 (tel. 315/781-0201; fax 315/789-0359), a perfectly immense stone Victorian mansion with ivy-clad walls and a huge slate roof. It sits brooding in the middle of a park of mature trees overlooking Seneca Lake. Built in 1885, it is the very definition of the term *white elephant*. And yet it's also quite wonderful and mercifully unspoiled. Inside are lots of dark shiny paneling, immense fireplaces, and ornate light fixtures. This place is as satisfyingly elaborate as one could wish. The entire downstairs—conservatory, porches, drawing rooms, dining room, the lot—is now a huge atmospheric restaurant. Lunch will cost from $5 to $9. Dinner is à la carte, chosen from a menu that contains such things as veal Oscar, scallops au gratin, poached salmon, lobster thermidor, duck à l'orange, prime rib, and filet mignon. Prices are $13 to $24 for main courses.

Upstairs are 12 great old-fashioned mansion bedrooms, each with a modern private bath, most with natural woodwork, some with ornate mantelpieces, all with lofty ceilings and oodles of atmosphere. Among other things, this place was once a casino operated by a high-roller called "Red" Dwyer. Today on the second-floor landing it still has a gravity-fed spigot that dispenses gratis glasses of wine. The Belhurst is open all year and charges between $80 and $115 a night for two people, depending on the room. A few elaborate suites are available for $175 to $275 double. The restaurant is open daily for lunch from 11am to 2pm and for dinner from 5 to 9:30pm. Sunday brunch ($11.95) is served from 11am to 2pm. MC and V accepted.

For more moderate fare in modern appealing surroundings, try **Crow's Nest,** located on the lake beside a small marina off N.Y. 96A (tel. 315/781-0600). Take the first right turn on 96A below N.Y. 5/U.S. 20, cross the tracks, and turn immediately right again. This trim little gray-shingled place has a pretty water-view terrace shaded by locust trees and an airy dining room with gray industrial carpeting and white walls. Lunch (or "launch," as the menu terms it) might be something like an open steak sandwich, crabmeat salad plate, chicken in the nest, or beer-broiled cold shrimp, which might cost from $4 to $8. Sample dinner selections include broiled scallops, broiled haddock, veal parmigiana, baked chicken, fantail shrimp, plus steak and duckling, priced mostly between $8 and $18. Lighter items are also available at dinner. Open daily year-round: Lunch is served from 11am to 4pm; dinner is on Monday to Friday from 4 to 9pm (to 10pm on Friday and Saturday). All major credit cards accepted.

CANANDAIGUA

Although settled in the late 18th century, Canandaigua has a late-Victorian look. Main Street, a broad four-lane thoroughfare, runs perpendicular to the shore of Canandaigua Lake, gradually ascending a gentle hill and (oddly) becoming more handsome the farther it gets from the water. Rising above the center of Main Street and dominating the entire skyline is the dome of the Ontario County Courthouse. Everything is very straight and orderly in this town: Even the land is fairly flat. Canandaigua (pop. 10,400) has the decided look and feel of the Midwest.

What to See & Do

The name Canandaigua is a corruption of the Native American term for "chosen place." In 1863, a New York City banker named Frederick Ferris Thompson chose it for the site of an elaborate Victorian country estate called **Sonnenberg** ("Sunny Hill" in German). After Thompson's death in 1902, his wife, Mary Clark Thompson, proceeded to create a great garden in his memory. The Smithsonian calls Sonnenberg "one of the most magnificent late Victorian gardens ever created in America." And this is no understatement.

After 40 years of neglect under U.S. government ownership, Sonnenberg was purchased by a preservation-oriented foundation that has undertaken the restoration of the Versailles-like gardens, plus the task of restoring and refurnishing the main house. The estate sits on a 50-acre superblock in the middle of Canandaigua. It feels like you're off in the country, but really you aren't. The mansion, designed by one Francis Allen, is a great big gloomy Queen Anne–Victorian monster, its roof spikey with towers and pinnacles and chimneys, and its interior a bit vast and cold.

The gardens, however, are beautiful and elaborate almost beyond belief. There are shaped yews, formal axes, geometric beds of annuals, marble fountains, statues of lions, putti, goddesses, magnificent retaining walls, a rose garden with elaborate semicircular beds, a Japanese Garden with a teahouse and tumbling brook; a colonial garden with a quarter mile of boxwood hedge and a formal aviary, even an outdoor Roman bath (the as-yet-unrestored estate pool). And this is just a partial list. Also on the premises is a lunchroom, located in a wing of the greenhouse complex and called the Peach House. You can get sandwiches and salads here for between $5 and $7 every day that Sonnenberg is open.

Admission is $6 for adults, $5 for seniors, and $2 for kids. Open daily in mid-May until mid-October from 9:30am to 5:30pm. It's truly something to see. There are signs on Main Street directing you to the main gate of Sonnenberg. If you need any further information, call them at 716/394-4922, or write to Sonnenberg Gardens, 151 Charlotte St., Canandaigua, NY 14424.

If you're not up to your gills yet with historic houses, have a look at **Granger Homestead** and its adjacent **Carriage Museum,** 295 N. Main St. (tel. 716/394-1472). Gideon Granger (1767–1822) was both a founder of Canandaigua and a United States postmaster for Presidents Jefferson and Madison. When completed in 1816, his elegant three-story Federal mansion was, in his own words, "unrivaled in all the Nation." After Sonnenberg, it's almost simple. Yet this is a magnificent example of early American architecture, one that would look quite at home on some patrician street in Salem or Providence. The adjacent Carriage Museum has sleighs and surreys and buckboards and barouches and introduces visitors to the use of horse-drawn vehicles in Victorian society.

The charge to visit both the house and the carriage museum is $3 for adults and $1 for kids. The Granger House is open May through October, Tuesday through Sunday from 1 to 5pm.

About 6 miles from Canandaigua, off Exit 44 of the New York State Thruway, is the **Finger Lakes Race Track,** home of the $150,000 New York State Breeders' Futurity. There's space for 4,000 cars, and you can wager on daily doubles, exactas, and trifectas. Post time is 1:30pm from April through November. General admission is $2; call 716/924-3232 for further information.

The newest attraction in the area is the **Finger Lakes Performing Arts Center** at the Community College of the Finger Lakes (tel. 716/454-2620), which is now the summer home of the **Rochester Philharmonic Orchestra** (tel. 716/222-5000). The center features outdoor classical, pops, and superstar concerts from June to September. Call for schedules and prices.

To appreciate the Finger Lakes one has to get out on the water, so try **Captain**

Gray's Boat Tours (tel. 716/394-5270). These one-hour lecture tours of Canandaigua Lake originate at the Sheraton Inn dock at the foot of Main Street at 2, 4, 6, and 8pm daily between June and September.

Where to Eat & Stay

For atmospheric dining, you might consider **Canandaigua Lady,** P.O. Box 856, Canandaigua, NY 14424 (tel. 716/398-3110), which is a boat that offers dinner and moonlight cruises. Also try **Lincoln Hill Inn,** 3365 E. Lake Rd. (tel. 716/394-8254), located in an old brick farmhouse on the outskirts of town. Lincoln Hill consists of a pleasant collection of rooms on two levels, decorated with exposed-brick walls, crisp linens, deep-burgundy accents, and lots of candlelight. At dinner you can choose from a list that includes chicken, prime rib, tournedos, pork chops, pasta primavera, and coquilles St. Jacques and costs between $10 and $18. Dinner is served daily from 5 to 10pm. Open all year. All major credit cards accepted.

The best place to stay in town is the lakeside **Thendara Inn and Restaurant,** which is actually 5 miles south of U.S. 20 at 4356 East Lake Rd., Canandaigua, NY 14424 (tel. 716/394-4868). The restaurant is elegantly detailed with breathtaking lake views. Dinner only is served on Monday through Saturday from 5 to 10pm and on Sunday from 4 to 8pm. These gourmet meals cost from $12 to $19; lighter fare is available at the **Boathouse** on the lake every day in the summer (May to October) from 11am to midnight. Burgers and fish fries cost from $2 to $6. The inn has five rooms, all with private baths and one with a skylit Jacuzzi, priced from $90 to $135 a night, including a continental breakfast. Closed from January to mid-March. All major credit cards accepted.

Budget accommodations abound along the N.Y. 5/U.S. 20 strip east of town. Alternatively, you might try **Canandaigua Inn on the Lake,** 770 S. Main St., Canandaigua, NY 14424 (tel. 716/394-7800; fax 716/394-5003). This is a deluxe lakefront motel at the end of a long landscaped drive. Low wings flare this way and that and a big illuminated "S" graces the side of a dramatic stone wall. There are 147 rooms, a big beautiful outdoor pool, a restaurant, bar, lakefront gardens, and a busy resort atmosphere. The entire place has undergone a recent refurbishment/redecoration. Accommodations all have color TVs, private phones, and nice furnishings. Rates vary according to season and view. Doubles will cost anywhere from a summertime high of about $90 to $135 nightly to a midwinter low of around $60 to $105. All major credit cards accepted.

You can save money and stay in very comfortable and attractive surroundings at **Budget Lodge,** N.Y. 5/U.S. 20, Canandaigua, NY 14424 (tel. 716/394-6170, or toll free 800/727-2775; fax 716/396-5550). This little motel, situated opposite Wal-Mart, contains but two dozen immaculately clean rooms, each with a cable color TV, shiny black built-in furniture, 1960s-moderne lamps, and a private bath. The double rate is between $38 and $56, and that's a bargain. No pool, no private phones in the rooms, no restaurant. But so what? All major credit cards accepted. Or there's an **Econo Lodge,** Canandaigua, NY 14424 (tel. 716/394-9000, or toll free 800/446-6900; fax 716/396-2560), just down the road. This establishment offers quite nice modern rooms, each with a private bath, wall-to-wall carpeting, a color TV with HBO, a phone, plus a lobby full of vending machines. Double-occupancy rates for the 65 rooms range between about $47 and $57 in summer and $39 and $47 in winter, the higher rates for a room with a king-size bed. All major credit cards accepted.

Kellogg's Pan-Tree Inn, 130 Lake Shore Dr., Canandaigua, NY 14424 (tel. 716/394-3909), is a modest, modernish motel/restaurant opposite Canandaigua's lakefront park. Lunch sandwiches and salads are $3 to $7 mostly; dinner selections like chicken pie, fish fry, ham steak, and french-fried shrimp cost about $7 to $12. Hours are 7am to 7:30pm daily. Behind the bright 1950s-looking restaurant is a collection of little flat-roofed buildings, each of which contains a trio of motel units. Rooms have twin double beds, cable color TVs, color-tiled baths, and an appealing vintage motel look. They're cheap too: $45 to $49 nightly per double in the late-June to Labor Day peak, $38 to $40 the rest of the open season. The entire establishment closes from late October until the beginning of May. MC and V accepted.

---

4. Rochester

Everybody told me I'd like Rochester—and they were right. This appealing old city of about 241,700 inhabitants has lots of architecturally important neighborhoods to explore, plenty of exciting and unusual restaurants, places to stay with character, and a number of unique and interesting sightseeing attractions. There are even a lively nightlife and abundant good shopping.

Rochester straddles the Genesee River, which fact is not immediately apparent. You can zip back and forth across the many downtown bridges without even noticing that you're on top of dramatic rapids and adjacent to a waterfall with a 100-foot drop. The power of this falling water fueled early sawmills and nurtured later industries that would eventually become international giants. Rochester was the cradle of Eastman Kodak, Bausch and Lomb, Sybron, and even Xerox. It's a city whose native industrialists have poured millions upon millions of dollars into local philanthropies. Paramount among them was George Eastman, the bachelor industrialist whose dry plate and film company founded in 1882 now employs 40,000 people here. Eastman donated the money for the University of Rochester, the famous Eastman School of Music, the Rochester Philharmonic, even for the construction of a number of local parks.

Rochester is also the town where Western Union was founded, where the escaped slave Frederick Douglass printed his famous newspaper *The North Star,* where the famous anarchist Emma Goldman took her first American factory job at the age of 17, and where Susan B. Anthony was arrested while trying to vote. So much milling was once done within the city limits that Rochester was called for a time the "Flour City." Nurseries and horticultural establishments eventually became so prevalent that the nickname was changed to the "Flower City."

Of course, everything has not been roses in Rochester's past. Urban decline, riots in the early 1960s, flight to the suburbs, the growth of the Sunbelt—all took their toll hereabouts. But the city today is active, vital, livable, and terribly efficient. There is a downtown core of glass high-rises, looped and relooped by a perhaps overly efficient system of expressways. There is a high consciousness of the value of old buildings, and these are being restored and refurbished all over town. It's an easy place to get around too, and parking is convenient.

WHAT TO SEE & DO IN ROCHESTER

Be advised of the existence of the very helpful **Greater Rochester Visitors Association,** 126 Andrews St., Rochester, NY 14604 (tel. 716/546-3070, or toll free 800/677-7282). The office is staffed by trained professionals who are not only anxious but also able to help visitors with all sorts of suggestions and advice. It is a source for maps, brochures on historic walking tours (see below), and all manner of additional touristic publications. They maintain a 24-hour telephone number too, with a recorded message listing current events and activities around town. Called the **Events Line,** the number is 716/546-6810.

GeVa, which is institutionalized shorthand for the Genesee Valley Arts Association, is a residential professional theater in Rochester. It mounts between six and eight Broadway-type productions every year. The theater, in a restored brick-and-limestone building at the corner of Woodbury and Clinton Avenues, has a wonderful period interior. For ticket and program information you can write in advance to GeVa, 75 Woodbury Blvd., Rochester, NY 14607, or call 716/232-1363.

On the south side of Rochester, down Mount Hope Avenue, is **Highland Park,** the scene each May of the annual Festival of Lilacs. Laid out in 1888 by a pioneer local nurseryman named Ellwanger, Highland Park's 20 acres of nothing but lilacs (not counting the 10,000 hand-planted pansies and the 15,000 tulip bulbs in the borders) are something to see. There are 1,200 bushes and 500 varieties, plus festival events under a big tent. Lots of fun, and the aroma of all those lilacs is unforgettable.

The **George Eastman House,** on Rochester's millionaires' row at 900 East Avenue (tel. 716/271-3361), has been carefully preserved and is open to the public. It is a very big and elaborate mansion, in a Colonial Revival style, with imposing fluted Corinthian columns overlooking East Avenue. Inside is a unique museum divided into displays showing the evolution of cameras and photography and a collection of famous photographs by past and present masters of the art. In the rear section of the building are huge galleries filled with zillions of cameras, plus curious contraptions like a zoetrope (a spinning slitted drum with pictures mounted on the inside) and a mutoscope (crank it and it flips a pack of cards) that were the forerunners of motion pictures. Eastman's house is something to see as well. In 1932, Eastman himself, having contracted a degenerative disease and already in his 70s, put all his affairs in order, went up to his room one evening, and shot himself. He left a note which read, "I have done all I set out to do. Why wait any longer?" The Eastman House is open Tuesday through Saturday from 10am to 4:30pm (from 1pm on Sunday); admission is $5 for adults, and $3.50 for students.

Another important Rochester philanthropist was Margaret Woodbury Strong, whose gift to Rochester was the **Strong Museum,** One Manhattan Square (actually Woodbury Avenue; tel. 716/263-2700). Opened in 1982, this is a low-slung ultramodern downtown installation with great expanses of smoked glass and cast concrete, set among clipped lawns dotted with overscale modern sculpture. The setting is ironic, since the collection itself consists of domestic artifacts from the 19th and early 20th centuries that taken together illustrate changes in American traditions, styles, and pastimes from a middle-class living room point of view. There really is a lot of nifty stuff here, organized in changing displays with names like "Light of the Home: Middle Class Women, 1870 to 1910," "Changing Patterns: Household Furnishings, 1820 to 1929," and "The Great Transformation." The permanent collection contains something like 20,000 dolls, plus all manner of textiles, furniture, ceramics, and old toys. Open Monday through Saturday from 10am to 5pm and Sunday from 1 to 5pm. Admission is $3 for adults, $2.25 for seniors and students, and $1 for kids.

Looking around town is a source of considerable pleasure in Rochester. Indeed, this town has more buildings listed on the National Register of Historic Places than any other municipality of equivalent size. For an informative strolling tour of downtown, go to the Visitors Information Center at 126 Andrews St. and ask for the brochure titled "Main Street Historic Markers." Even if you don't tour the downtown pavements on foot, try and have a look at **city hall,** 30 Church St., a superb late-1880s Romanesque structure with a vintage three-story interior atrium. The building is open to the public on weekdays from 9am to 5pm. And while you're in the area, be sure to look up at the wings on top of the **Times Square Building,** off Main and State—very Flash Gordon.

On the northern edge of the downtown business district is one of the great wonders of Rochester, the **High Falls of the Genesee River.** If these falls were sitting in the middle of the countryside, they would doubtless be the centerpiece of a state park. Yet this 100-foot cataract has been overlooked for decades, rendered invisible by industrial development and road improvements. However, all that has now changed.

Today at the falls there is an urban cultural park orientation facility called, not surprisingly, **Center at High Falls,** 60 Brown's Race (tel. 716/325-2030, or 716/232-3362 for the recorded events schedule). Exhibits trace both the geologic and the industrial evolution of the falls area, and a viewing platform provides excellent vantage points from which to appreciate what was heretofore Rochester's least known attraction. On certain summer evenings there is also a laser light and sound show, projected onto a 500-foot section of the gorge wall and entitled "River of Light: A Celebration of Rochester and the Genessee." The show traces the city's sto

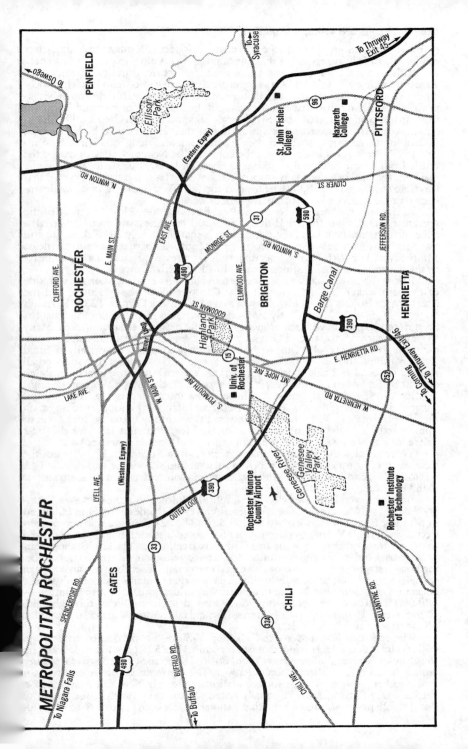

ry from its beginnings right into the 21st century. It's actually quite inspiring. Better call for schedule information, as this sort of program is vulnerable to funding cuts.

Although the High Falls have languished in obscurity during our times, they were once well known. In 1829, a swaggering daredevil named Sam Patch hit Rochester with a trained bear in tow. Patch purported to have jumped off the top of Niagara Falls. Wandering from bar to bar one night, he bragged that it would be no big thing to jump off the top of Rochester's High Falls and survive. Over 1,000 onlookers subsequently gathered and saw him do just that. Emboldened by his success, Patch announced that he would make a second leap, on Friday the 13th of November, 1829. Perhaps his undoing was the cold on that November day or maybe the bottle from which Patch was drinking so liberally. In any case, halfway across the platform that had been specially suspended above the falls, and before a crowd that this time numbered over 8,000, he tripped and fell. They found his body far downstream on St. Patrick's Day, frozen in a cake of ice.

Rochester's millionaire's row was along **East Avenue.** Although most of the great mansions built in the late 19th and early 20th centuries have been converted to either apartments or offices, the good news is that practically all of them are still standing. East Avenue very much preserves its original air of opulence and privilege. Almost every late-Victorian architectural style is represented, culminating in the restrained magnificence of Eastman House. Be sure to drive down it.

Before the era of East Avenue, Rochester's elite were ensconced on the west side of town in what's called Corn Hill. The **Campbell-Whittlesey House** and the **Hout-Potter House,** now jointly known as the **Landmark Center,** 123 S. Fitzhugh St. (tel. 716/546-7029), are early 19th-century veterans of a neighborhood that has been rioted, expresswayed, abandoned, and finally reclaimed and gentrified. Many wonderful early-Victorian and Greek Revival houses exist hereabouts, and a meander through its streets will be just to the taste of architecturally/historically oriented travelers. The Campbell-Whittlesey House is one of those places that survived all manner of social and neighborhood upheavals, original furniture intact. Although modest by East Avenue standards, it's still chock-a-block with polychrome ceilings, gold cornices, and great period furniture. Most interesting is a set of "musical glasses," in their original box, made to be played by rubbing a moistened finger on their respective rims. You can tour the house Friday through Sunday from noon to 4pm, March through December. Admission is $2 for adults and 25¢ for kids. (P.S.: Take a look at nearby Atkinson Street for other good Corn Hill houses.)

There are all sorts of other things to ferret out in Rochester. If you've got the time, ask the Visitors Center for a copy of their tabloid-size visitor's guide called "A Visitor's Guide to Rochester," which goes into far more detail on local attractions than I can here.

But before you leave the field, you should also know about the **Genesee Country Village and Museum,** about 20 miles southwest of Rochester on Flint Hill Road in Mumford, off Thruway exit 46 (tel. 716/538-6822). This is a midwestern version of Sturbridge Village, a collection of 55 restored historical buildings, all moved to the site from other parts of the area. There are farmhouses, blacksmith shops, carriages, barns, old stores, and costumed denizens cooking soup, throwing pots, shoeing horses, staging parades, and organizing country fairs. There's also a carriage barn with 40 horse-drawn vehicles, as well as a gallery that contains the nation's largest collection of wildlife art. It's quite a place, very educational and very beautiful— 120,000 visitors come here every year. Open daily in mid-May through mid-October from 10am to 5pm (to 4pm in spring and fall). Admission is $10 for adults, $8 for seniors, and $5 for kids.

The **Spirit of Rochester** (tel. 716/865-4930) is a triple-decked cruise ship, 150 feet long and 30 feet wide, that can accommodate 525 passengers. Docked on the Genesee River at the **Riverview Yacht Basin,** 18 Petten St., the *Spirit of Rochester* cruises Lake Ontario May through October. The ship's decks can be enclosed for foul weather, so it is popular for celebration cruises on New Year's Eve and St. Patrick's Day. This vessel is regionally noted for the daily lunch cruise (noon to 2pm) at $28 per person and for the chef's choice dinner buffet cruises (6 to 9pm) for $45.

The more intimately scaled *Sam Patch* is a 54-foot powered reproduction of an Erie Canal boat. It is named after the unfortunate soul who in 1829 fell from the top of the Genessee High Falls to his death below. His namesake carries 49 passengers on three daily one-hour trips between Corn Hill on the Genesee River and the Erie Canal crossing in Genesee Valley Park, and back. Morning and afternoon weekday cruises leave at 10am and 2:30pm and cost $8; the lunch cruise at noon is priced at $15; weekend and dinner cruises are also available. Contact *Sam Patch*, Coral Hill Navigation, 140 Troop St., Rochester, N.Y. 14608 (tel. 716/288-2340).

WHERE TO STAY IN ROCHESTER

This is a sizable town with many places to stay. Be reminded that the following suggestions constitute a much-abbreviated list, ranging from deluxe to moderate.

In the middle of the downtown shopping district, near the convention center, is the new **Hyatt Regency Rochester**, 125 E. Main St., Rochester, NY 14604 (tel. 716/546-6777), described by its architect as a "27-story metal-paneled guest-room tower." The Hyatt was designed first and foremost as a businessperson's hotel, and it contains all manner of business-related technology. It is certainly handsome, however, and tourists should consider it as well. You'll find easy auto access; a cavernous marble lobby; and extremely comfortable rooms, some with breathtaking city views. All have luxurious baths, color TVs, and the expected amenities. There are also a "junior Olympic" pool (45 feet long), a health club, and a quite good northern Italian restaurant called Palladio. The Hyatt's basic double-occupancy room rate is $135; corporate rates are $119; on weekends you can get a special rate of $89 (remember always to ask if there are special rates being offered when inquiring about room rates). All major credit cards accepted.

Also in the heart of downtown is **Rochester Plaza**, 70 State St., Rochester, NY 14614 (tel. 716/546-3450, or toll free 800/468-3571; fax 716/546-8714). This rose-colored high-tech box is set on square columns and contains 364 luxurious rooms. The lobby level has lots of smoked glass and vaguely art deco detailing. There are brass bands set into the buff-colored walls, dramatic floral arrangements, tailored contemporary furniture, and an air of low-key, big-city prosperity. The center of the ultramodern building is an open courtyard with a beautiful pool overlooked by mirrored walls. Rooms are very blond, pale buff, and rose, all with cable color TVs, phones, clocks, thick rugs, plush headboards, upholstered armchairs, and an overall first-class look. Downstairs are all manner of bars and restaurants, appealingly decorated and not cheap. Room rates are a bit of a tangle and depend entirely on supply and demand. The basic double rate seems to be about $128 nightly. But if you reserve a room in advance at the "supersaver" rate, you'll pay $89 for a double during the week and as low as $79 nightly on weekends. All manner of packages exist as well and basically boil down to reduced room rates plus a few extras in return for advance reservations. The key to all of this is to call in advance. There's a slight surcharge for pool-view rooms, but city views are usually just as nice.

On the outskirts of town, off Route 96 near Exit 45 of the New York State Thruway, is a glamorous hotel/resort called **The Lodge at Woodcliff**, Woodcliff Drive, Box 22850, Rochester, NY 14692 (tel. 716/381-4000, or toll free 800/365-3065; fax 716/381-2673). This modern brick-and-glass complex enjoys fine views of Rochester, from both the rooms and the excellent Horizons restaurant. The Lodge has its own nine-hole golf course, an indoor/outdoor heated pool, tennis courts, a fitness club, and a whirlpool and saunas. The standard double-room rate is $110 during the week and $99 on weekends. All major credit cards accepted.

There are hot and cold running Holiday Inns all over Rochester, but **Holiday Inn Rochester South**, 1111 Jefferson Rd., Rochester, NY 14623 (tel. 716/475-1510; fax 716/427-8673), is surely the state-of-the-art example. The location is on the southern, suburban edge of Rochester, on a private triangular island completely surrounded by expressways. There are 250 rooms contained on six floors of brown brick. The place is turned in upon itself and focuses on an elaborate indoor atrium, a sort of Hanging Gardens of Babylon revisited, complete with pool, kiddy playground, and palm trees in planters. It looks quite good and certainly dramatic. So do the guest rooms, which are decorated in fashionably pale shades of buff and blue and contain color TVs, thick rugs, and plush furniture. Most doubles cost between $85 and $95 nightly; there are much better deals on weekend packages, some of which require as little as one night's stay. All major credit cards accepted.

Wellesey Inn, East Henrietta Road, N.Y. 15E (adjacent to I-390 exit 16), Rochester, NY 14623 (tel. 716/427-0130, or toll free 800/654-2000; fax 716/427-0903), has neither a pool nor a restaurant. But it does have rooms so new and so nice that you'll wonder how other places can charge so much for such similar accommodations. Rooms with king-size beds, color TVs, free parking, and very attractive tweedy/tailored furniture cost but $45 to $55 nightly. Next door is an outpost of the ubiquitous T.G.I. Friday's chain of bar/restaurants. All major credit cards accepted.

An interesting suburban alternative to downtown accommodations is **Oliver Loud's Inn** at 1474 Marsh Rd., Pittsford, NY 14534 (tel. 716/248-5200), near Thruway exit 45. The inn, located directly on the Erie Canal, features eight handsomely appointed rooms, decorated with Oriental rugs, antiques, and antique reproductions and equipped with phones and private baths. In the common room downstairs you can take afternoon tea, sherry, or champagne by the roaring fire. This establishment is part of a complex developed by Vivienne Tellier and her husband, Andrew Wolfe. Back in 1985, Oliver Loud's Inn was located 5 miles away in the township of Egypt and slated for demolition. A year later it had been moved to its present site and restored. Today it stands next door to Tellier and Wolfe's **Richardson Canal House** restaurant (recommended below), in combination with which it comprises one of the most picturesque settings in upstate New York. The double-occupancy room rate at the inn is $135.

WHERE TO EAT IN ROCHESTER

The old Gothic-style city hall of Rochester, built in 1873, now houses in its former jail cells **Chapel's,** 30 W. Broad St. (tel. 716/232-2300), one of New York State's best French restaurants. The elegant conversion of these old prison cells into three distinct dining areas makes "doing time" nowadays an absolute culinary delight. Award-winning chef/owner Greg Broman and his wife/manager, Colleen, present *cuisine du marche* (food of the market) in superb French nouvelle style. The restaurant is decorated with a number of Margaret Strong's antiques (see Strong Museum) and also has a 19th-century lounge area. A really great bargain and treat is lunch, available from 11:30am to 2pm on Tuesday through Friday and priced from $4 to $11. A true dining experience is the five-course dinner, perhaps starting with oyster stew, after which one might choose the *escargots aux nouilles fraîches,* move on to the salad with hazelnut vinaigrette, then to the main course, possibly a feuillette of quail with spinach salpicon and two sauces, and wind up with a dessert made daily by the pastry chef. Dinner is served from 5:30 to 9pm on Tuesday through Friday, to 10pm on Saturday. The cost of à la carte selections is between $15 and $24. All major credit cards accepted.

Another luxury choice with a wholly different atmosphere is **Edward's,** just off Main Street at 13 S. Fitzhugh St. (tel. 716/423-0140). Considered by many to be the best restaurant in town, it occupies a rich Edwardian-accented suite of rooms in the basement of the 1873 Academy Building. Inside, all is dim and lush, with faux marbre and mirrored accents, black flowered-chintz pillows, walls covered with books and pictures, the tinkle of piano music, and the low music of cultivated laughter and clinking crystal. Lunch might be tournedos with wild rice, fresh pasta primavera in cream, poached chicken, or vegetable quiche, costing between $5 and $11. Dinners change daily but might include à la carte selections like coquilles St. Jacques, medallions of veal, sautéed chicken breast, and tournedos, priced between $13 and $24. Open Monday to Thursday for lunch from 11:30am to 2pm and for dinner from 5:30 to about 9pm (until 10pm on Friday and Saturday).

You might not expect to find a good restaurant inside a museum, but **Gallery Café,** in the lobby of Rochester's Memorial Art Gallery, 500 University Ave. (tel. 716/473-6380), is precisely that. The dining areas have grand Georgian Revival architecture, pale-yellow walls hung with art, and intriguing views of modern sculpture. Reasonably priced luncheons ($4 to $9) can be had from 11:30am to 2pm on

Tuesday through Saturday; dinner, like mushroom ravioli or filet of beef, is served from 5 to 9pm on the same days and costs between $12 and $19. There's also a Sunday brunch from 11am to 2pm. All major credit cards accepted.

Park Avenue, especially in those blocks near the intersection of Berkeley and Park, is a particularly appealing neighborhood about 20-odd blocks from downtown. It's an old residential area, a block away from the architectural glories of East Avenue, but possessing a distinct charm of its own. Park Avenue is a fine place to browse through little shops, stroll the tree-shaded streets on summer evenings, and catch a bite to eat at any of numerous inexpensive restaurants. A neighborhood standby is **Hogan's Hideaway,** which is located behind 197 Park Ave. (tel. 716/442-4293). This place is a local favorite and offers a great light menu with daily specials like quiches, omelets, and a vegetarian stirfry. Hogan's features a small bar/lounge, a greenhouse, and a café dining room, all of which are open on Monday through Saturday from 11:30am to 11pm. All major credit cards accepted.

Nearby is **Charlie's Frog Pond,** 652 Park Ave. (tel. 716/271-1970). This place is cute, cheap, and decorated with frog motifs, plus booths, brass rails, and a jukebox full of rock and roll. Menu placemats list all manner of hot and cold sandwiches, eggs, omelets, homemade soups, and salads, most of which cost between $2 and $5. Open Monday through Friday from 7am to 9pm, Saturday from 8am to 7pm, and Sunday from 9am to 3pm. No credit cards accepted.

Between Park and East Avenues is another restaurant row. There are lots of attractive places along here for moderately priced meals. For one of life's kinder experiences, try **Crème de la Crème,** located in an old Victorian town house at 295 Alexander St. (tel. 716/263-3580). After entering the canopied doorway and passing the stairway to several second-floor dining rooms, you'll be confronted with gigantic glass display cases filled with the most sinful selection of tortes, tarts, trifles, and truffles, to say nothing of the éclairs, mousses, napoleons, baklava, cheesecakes, pies, and cakes. If this doesn't have your tastebuds screaming for satisfaction, try a quiche or a seafood pita with cappuccino or perhaps champagne. Open Monday through Saturday from 11am to 1am for light dining and Sunday from 9am to midnight. An English afternoon tea is served daily from 2 to 6pm, and a champagne brunch is offered on Sunday until 3pm. All the desserts are priced at $3.75, with sandwiches and hot main courses from $5 to $8. All major credit cards accepted.

A popular place for those still young at heart is the plumber's dream theme restaurant **J. Wellington's Waterworks,** located "down-under" 315 Alexander St. (tel. 716/546-5770). This basement eatery is decorated with two-inch copper plumbing fixtures incorporated into the railings, coatracks, partitions, and the circular staircase to the bathrooms. Noted for its pizzas, hamburgers, potato skins, and ("for fowl food fanciers") chicken wings, the Waterworks is truly an American experience. The last time I dropped in, one could not help but notice a local businessman entertaining an entire table of Japanese dignitaries, who, despite obvious culture shock, were all having fun. With the exception of pizza, the individual menu prices are between $1.75 and $8.29. The restaurant is open daily: from 11:30am to midnight on Monday through Friday, from 5pm to 2am on Saturday, and from 5pm to midnight on Sunday. MC and V accepted.

La Petite Maison, 54 Park Ave. (tel. 716/256-0390), serves French country cuisine—*croque monsieur* (ham and melted Swiss), *salade de confit de canard* (sliced duck over spinach), grilled lamb chop, chicken fricassee, and the like—in a cute little town house decorated with fleur-de-lis wallpaper and sporting an appealing outdoor porch for summertime dining. Open Monday to Saturday from 11am to 11pm; luncheon prices are generally from $4 to $8, while dinner main courses cost about $12 to $16. All major credit cards accepted.

Perhaps the best moderately priced restaurant in Rochester is **Kopper Kettle,** 976 Chili Ave. (tel. 716/235-8060). Chili Avenue is a major artery that runs west from the downtown area. The Kettle is large; modern; family run; and nicely decorated with wood paneling, stained-glass accents, thick rugs, and hanging plants. At the counter area or in the spacious dining room you can enjoy the usual gamut of salad-and-sandwich lunches, plus full meals like broiled pork chops, chicken croquettes, New York–strip steak, grilled liver, shrimp and ham jambalaya, and broiled rainbow trout, priced from $7 to $12. There are new specials almost every day. And on Tuesday there's even piano music in the dining room. Open Monday to Friday for lunch ($4 to $5) from 11:30am to 2pm and for dinner from 4:30 to 8:30pm. All major credit cards accepted.

The Filling Station, 30 Mount Hope Ave. (tel. 716/325-4856), is an innovative café converted from an old-time automobile service station. The menu reflects the environment: "starters & tune ups" (appetizers), "fuels" (drinks), "lubricants" (salad dressings), "T-bird" sandwiches, and "customized" burgers. Decorated with a neon car motif and old automobile posters, the café has an airy California feel. The Filling Station is open from 7am to 10pm on Monday through Thursday, to 11pm on Friday, from 9am to 11pm on Saturday, and from 9am to 8pm on Sunday. The Filling Station is known for its sandwiches, light dinners, and desserts. Breakfast costs between $2 and $5; lunch is $4 to $7.50; dinner will cost from $7.50 to $15. All major credit cards accepted.

On several occasions during trips to Rochester we've had great late-night dinners at **Bangkok Restaurant,** opposite the Rochester Plaza at 155 State St. (tel. 716/325-3517). One orders by the stars at the Bangkok: One star is hot, two tastes good, three tastes great, four leads to numbness at the top of the head, and five is nuclear. The service is warm (no pun intended), helpful, and humorous, and the waiter will typically ask other customers to give testimonials. The storefront dining room, decorated with a mauve/rose Laura Ashley wallpaper and pink tablecloths, is a favorite with downtown office workers. It's open Monday through Thursday from 11am to 10pm, until 11pm on Friday and Saturday. Lunch combos are priced under $5; dinner ranges from $6 to $15. MC and V accepted.

Oscars, 470 Monroe Ave. (tel. 716/244-7077), is an authentic New York–style deli, decorated with Hollywood posters and signed photographs. This local favorite offers all manner of deli items, plus complete dinners from $6 to $18. It's a comfortable, friendly, neighborhood type of place, with an outdoor patio for al fresco dining in good weather. Open Sunday to Wednesday from 11:30am to midnight, until 1am Thursday through Saturday. All major credit cards accepted.

On Rochester's eastern outskirts, not far from Thruway exit 45, is the aforementioned **Richardson Canal House,** at 1474 Marsh Rd., in suburban Pittsford (tel. 716/248-5000). This former tavern was built in 1818 on the banks of the still active Erie Canal and has survived with virtually all of its original architectural detail intact. The building was meticulously restored in 1980 by Vivienne Tellier and her husband, Andrew Wolfe, and is now part of an Erie Canal complex that includes four other period buildings including **Oliver Loud's Inn** (see above). The interior is a maze of well-appointed dining rooms on two separate floors. The decor includes period antiques, original paint colors, stenciling, wall murals, and a working fireplace in the tap room. Only dinner is served—a $32 five-course affair on Monday to Saturday from 6 to 10pm. All major credit cards accepted.

Rochester's suburban ring is full of good restaurants. One of the most unusual is **Red Creek Inn,** 300 Jefferson Rd. (tel. 716/424-1080), a barn-sided roadhouse in shopping-center land whose sign proclaims "Fine Food—Music—Drink—Friends." It's pretty big inside, filled with tables in the greenhouse room, a big bar with a color TV, and lots of room for late-night dancing and entertainment. This might be anything from untried comedians to bands like the Skycoasters ("the partying-est band in town"), to Duke Robillart and the Pleasure Kings, to midweek DJ dance nights. A very extensive menu includes lunches like the incredible burrito, mucho macho nacho, chicken wings, hot pastrami, mozzarella burger, and grilled cheese ("what can we say . . . it's very nice"), most of which cost between $4 and $6. The "Cajun Cookin'" menu offers dinners like blackened chicken, red snapper with pecan butter sauce, blackened sirloin steak, and barbecued shrimp, priced around $8 to $12. The kitchen is open Monday through Thursday from 11am to midnight, on Friday and Saturday to 1:30am, and on Sunday from 3pm to midnight. All major credit cards accepted.

About 10 expressway minutes east of downtown Rochester is **Daisy Flour Mill,** 1880 Blossom Rd. (tel. 716/381-1880). This is a real mill, although it looks considerably more glamorous today than it did when Rochester was known as the

"Flour City" and a succession of millers kept it running 24 hours a day. The dir multileveled interior is still equipped with a dizzying array of huge belts, silent machines, beams, and catwalks. There are exposed-stone walls, a basement lounge called the Mill Race Bar, and all manner of atmospheric nooks and crannies furnished with tables and chairs. Dinner might be chicken Louisiana, veal piccata, prime rib, veal Rochester, and Long Island duck, the majority of which are priced between $10 to $18 à la carte. Weekday dinners are served from 5:30 to 10pm; hours on Friday and Saturday are 5 to 11pm; Sunday hours are 2 to 9pm. Open year-round. There is no lunch service available. To get there, take the Blossom Road exit eastbound from I-590. All major credit cards accepted.

ROCHESTER MISCELLANY

There's an abundance of good **bars** in town, an unusual one being **Blades**, 1290 University Ave. (tel. 716/442-6979), in a former sawblade factory on the south side of town. It's a particularly popular and atmospheric spot, as is **Law's**, 689 South Ave. (tel. 716/461-0310), which features Victorian ambience and dancing at night. Other good places to dance include the aforementioned **Red Creek Inn**, 300 Jefferson Rd. (tel. 716/424-1080); **Shnozz'z**, in the Village Gate Square complex at 302 N. Goodman St. (tel. 716/271-8334); and a glittery disco called the **Glass Onion**, 81 Marshall St. (tel. 716/454-4538). And for laughs, try your luck at **Zinger's Comedy Café**, 150 Andrews St., near St. Paul Street (tel. 716/325-9857), whose Thursday-, Friday-, and Saturday-night shows features three comedians apiece.

Rochester naturally has its complement of big **shopping malls,** most of which aren't particularly different from their counterparts elsewhere. With two exceptions. The first is **Midtown Plaza,** a stone's throw from the Strong Museum in downtown Rochester (tel. 716/454-2070). Despite its up-to-date look, this was the very first enclosed downtown shopping plaza in the United States and is now something like 25 years old. There are about 100 shops and services here, plus parking for 2,000 cars in adjacent underground lots. Also worth a visit is the converted factory building on the near east side, now called the **Village Gate Square,** 274 N. Goodman St. (tel. 716/442-9168). Lots of unpretentious antiques/secondhand stores in here, plus Schnozz'z (a bar described above), plus haircutters, ice cream stands, booksellers, basket stores, and a courtyard with all manner of outdoor summertime activities.

A SIDE TRIP TO LETCHWORTH STATE PARK

Approximately 30 miles south of Rochester on I-890 is New York's own Grand Canyon: **Letchworth State Park,** Castile, NY 14427 (tel. 716/493-2611 or 716/493-3600). Letchworth preserves a 17-mile stretch of the Genessee River where the waters have carved a canyon 600 feet deep in some places. The sandstone walls have been fantastically sculpted over the millennia into almost Grecian flutings and Gothic buttresses. With the exception of Niagara Falls, no other natural feature on the eastern seaboard is quite so awe inspiring.

Every year Letchworth attracts some 700,000 visitors, who motor slowly from one overlook to the next, and/or explore the dozens of scenic trails that lead to the riverbank or the dramatic falls. Open daily from 6am until 11pm; a $3-per-car fee is collected between 9am and 5pm during the mid-May to mid-October high season.

There are interesting places to stay in Letchworth. Unbeknownst to most visitors, the state maintains 80 **woodland cabins** tucked away in the park's 14,350 acres. They cost as little as $94 to $250 per week but must be reserved at least 90 days in advance by calling 716/493-3600.

More accessible is **Glen Iris Inn,** 7 Letchworth State Park, Castile, NY 14427 (tel. 716/439-2622; fax 716/439-5803), which occupies the wooden Victorian mansion of William Pryor Letchworth. The former 1,000-acre private estate of this Buffalo industrialist turned philanthropist formed the core of today's state park. The Inn, which is within earshot of the 107-foot **Middle Falls,** has 14 charming rooms with all the modern conveniences, plus a fairly huge country-style restaurant that serves breakfast, lunch, and dinner at moderate prices all year long. Rooms in the Inn cost between $65 and $125 nightly; seven additional kitchenette units located behind the main house in the Pinewood Lodge can be had for $60 a night. All major credit cards accepted.

Next door to the inn is **William Pryor Letchworth Museum** (tel. 716/493-3617), with an interesting collection of Indian and pioneer artifacts. Open daily in summer from 10am to 5pm, Saturday and Sunday only in spring and fall; admission is free. Behind the museum are a pair of log cabins. The **Seneca Long House,** built circa 1700 and moved to this site in 1871 from nearby Canada, NY, is considered the oldest-surviving example of log architecture in America. The **Nancy Jemison Cabin,** circa 1800, was built by the daughter of a woman kidnapped by Indians in 1755 at the age of 13. Mary Jemison outlived two Indian husbands and five of her eight children. She died in 1833 at the age of 91.

A short distance north of the inn is **Inspiration Point,** from which there is a superb view of the 71-foot **Upper Falls** and a 240-foot-high railroad bridge spanning the river chasm. You can gaze to the north from here and see for almost 10 miles up the gorge. The subtle effects of changing sunlight on the canyon walls are quite beautiful.

---

5. Southern Tier

ITHACA

Referred to variously in the past as Storm Country, The Pit, and Sodom, this attractive small city was eventually named Ithaca in the late 18th century by Simeon DeWitt, surveyor-general of New York State. It sits on the southernmost shore of 38-mile-long Cayuga Lake, in a region of steep hills and picturesque chasms. There are about 28,700 full-time residents, plus about 25,000 college students who attend either Cornell University or the much-smaller Ithaca College.

In 1779, a colonel on the staff of Gen. John Sullivan named Henry Dearborn swept through the Ithaca area. The Continental Army's mission, as mentioned earlier, was to eliminate the threat of pro-British Native Americans, a task they accomplished with sobering thoroughness. But once the Indians were gone, Ithaca flourished. It was a mill and manufacturing town throughout the 19th century. In 1912, the movies arrived. In 1913, Essenay Studios released its first Ithaca production, *The Hermit of Lonely Gulch,* starring Francis X. Bushman. Serials like *The Exploits of Elaine* (not to be confused with *The Perils of Pauline*) were filmed here throughout the 1910s. Some still remember Irene Castle's arrival in town to work on a serial titled *Patria.* She is supposed to have arrived with 2 servants, 20 trunks, and a pet monkey.

The movies were a short-lived phenomenon, petering out by the end of the 1920s. The business of education, however, has grown to become Ithaca's mainstay. Cornell was founded in 1868; what is today's Ithaca College started in 1892. These institutions dominate the town and give it a great deal of its vitality and dimension.

The old 19th-century city center has been restored and rediscovered of late. Two blocks of downtown State Street have been closed to traffic, planted with trees, and transformed into a pedestrian shopping mall called **Ithaca Commons.** This might well be the most successful and aesthetically appealing project of this sort in New York State. Ithaca Commons is not an isolated island amid a wasteland of parking lots. Instead it's part of the fabric of downtown, surrounded by other streets with shops and cars and plenty of on-street parking.

Looming to the east over the compact downtown is a steep hill crowned by the campus of **Cornell University.** The streets are so steep on the uphill slope that the second floor at one end of a house is at ground level at the other. This area, with its late 19th-century architecture, looks a great deal like a miniature San Francisco. To the north of town is a separate municipality called **Cayuga Heights,** a densely wooded bedroom community to adjoining Ithaca. Immediately south of down town is another hill, atop which is the modern campus of **Ithaca College.** The cᴖ pus isn't much architecturally, but the view up Cayuga Lake is memorable.

What to See & Do

Known as the "Little Apple," Ithaca and the surrounding area have all the cultural, recreational, and culinary resources worthy of this nickname. Well worth a visit or a call is the Ithaca/Tompkins County Convention and Visitors Bureau, 904 East Shore Dr., Ithaca, NY 14850 (tel. 607/272-1313, or toll free 800/28-IHACA), at the foot of Cayuga Lake. The staff is very enthusiastic and even showed a jaded old-time Ithaca visitor like myself many new and exciting sites.

Ithaca has a businesslike air. There's nothing unduly sumptuous or ornate about its architectural heritage, and yet as 19th-century American cities go it's an appealing specimen. At the heart of the downtown area, on the corner of Cayuga and Seneca Streets, is **Clinton House,** formerly a hotel and the center of civic life. Its rescue and restoration constituted the first and perhaps most important effort of an organization called Historic Ithaca. This pioneering local preservation organization maintains an office in the corner of the old Clinton House, at which you can pick up a **walking-tour brochure** titled "Circle Greenway Walk Ithaca." Upstairs on Clinton House's former lobby floor is a museum dedicated to local history, which, depending on your interests, might well be worth a stop. Whether you're into walking tours or not, do take a drive through the **East Hill Historic District.** The main drag is Buffalo Street, uphill toward Cornell, between Parker and Quarry.

There are abundant **waterfalls** around Ithaca, including Cascadilla Creek, which is practically downtown. Cascadilla tumbles picturesquely from the heights of the Cornell campus to within four blocks of Ithaca Commons. The entrance to the footpath up the gorge is adjacent to the intersection of Court and Linn Streets.

Just outside town are two really lovely natural attractions. Just south of town is **Buttermilk Falls State Park,** on N.Y. 13 (tel. 607/273-5761), a series of cascades and rapids with 10 waterfalls, 2 glens, and a natural pool. Eight miles to the north of Ithaca is **Taughannock Falls State Park,** on N.Y. 89 in Trumansburg (tel. 607/387-6739), with both a swimming beach on Cayuga Lake and a 215-foot waterfall, the highest fall east of the Rockies. Very impressive, especially the steep-walled gorge down which Taughannock Creek rushes toward Cayuga Lake. Both parks are open all year.

Other things to do in Ithaca? What about a dinner cruise aboard the historic 60-foot **M-V Manhattan** (tel. 607/272-4868)? This attractive Port of New York cruiser was built in Manhattan in 1917. For about $30 per person, you can enjoy a full dinner with the panoramic view of Cayuga Lake outside. There are daily 6pm departures between May and September. The dock is at the **Old Port Harbor** restaurant (see below). Call for information and reservations.

You might also like to take a spin through the campus of **Cornell University,** located on the heights overlooking the city from the east. You can pick up a copy of the "Cornell Campus Guide" at the Ithaca Chamber of Commerce Tourist Information Office, near N.Y. 13 in Stewart Park on the shore of Cayuga Lake. Among other things on campus are **Cornell Plantations** (tel. 607/255-3020), a pretty theme garden in a bosky dell, and **Herbert F. Johnson Museum of Art** (tel. 607/255-6464), an ultramodern and architecturally arresting building with a famous collection and a great view of the lake. The museum is open Tuesday to Sunday from 10am to 5pm. Like the Cornell Plantations, it's free. If you're an explorer like me, you'll at least want to have a quick look at **Ithaca College** too. Its square gray towers, located south on N.Y. 96B, are clearly visible from downtown. Better to be up here looking at Ithaca than the other way around.

And there's **Ithaca Commons,** the downtown pedestrian shopping mall composed of restored 19th-century buildings and occupying two blocks of State Street. Besides being an attractive place to stroll and browse, summer visitors might also enjoy the free Thursday-night concerts held here. The Ithaca Concert Band is the backbone of this annual series, which also includes jazz, soul, and country groups.

Remember too that Ithaca is in the heart of wine country. A useful brochure titled **"Cayuga Wine Trail"** is available at the Convention and Visitors Bureau (tel. 315/272-1313), or you can request a copy by writing to P.O. Box 123, Fayette, NY 13065. The tour covers eight wineries, among the most interesting of which are **Knapp Vineyards** (tel. 607/869-9271) and **Swedish Hill Vineyards** (tel. 315/549-8326).

Where to Stay In & Around Ithaca

Statler Hotel, Cornell University, Ithaca, NY 14853 (tel. 607/257-2500, or toll free 800/541-2501; fax 607/257-6432), is a new hotel facility located right in the center of Cornell University. The nine-story complex of 150 deluxe rooms with panoramic views of the campus and Cayuga Lake is accented with a first-rate restaurant, Banfi's. From the valet parking to classic rooms equipped with dual-line phones for PC hookups, TVs with VCR hookups, refrigerators, and minibars, the Statler offers a full-service hotel experience and then some. The hotel is also a functional classroom for Cornell's world-renowned Hotel Administration School. Accommodations cost about $100 for a standard room with a queen-sized bed, up to $150 for a suite. All major credit cards accepted.

Located in the heart of downtown Ithaca is **Ithaca Holiday Inn,** 222 S. Cayuga St., Ithaca, NY 14850 (tel. 607/272-1000; fax 607/277-1275). This establishment combines the inn with a newer 10-story tower containing 55 luxury rooms with great views of Ithaca and the surrounding countryside. There are 175 rooms plus an indoor pool and the Gazebo Restaurant. Standard rooms cost $80; tower rooms cost from $90. All major credit cards accepted.

N.Y. 13 north of Ithaca is an expressway that curves up and over the top of Cayuga Heights. At the intersection of Triphammer Road is a concentration of suburban culture that includes major chain-motel installations, huge shopping malls, and so on. The **Sheraton Inn,** Triphammer Road and Hwy. 13, Ithaca, NY 14850 (tel. 607/257-2000, or toll free 800/257-6992; fax 607/257-3990), is by far the nicest of this group. There are 106 rather posh rooms, decorated with tweedy sofas, brass moldings, rice-paper-like vinyl wallcoverings, luxurious baths, private phones, color TVs, and subtle color schemes. On premises is an indoor pool of proper proportions (it used to be an outdoor pool before they enclosed it), a restaurant, and a lounge. Doubles run between about $69 to $97 nightly. All major credit cards accepted.

In the immediate vicinity are a huge Ramada Inn and a Howard Johnson Motor Lodge, both offering similar, if not quite as attractive, accommodations for about $10 or so less per night.

Next to Cornell is an excellent-value family-run motel called **Collegetown Motor Lodge,** 312 College Ave., Ithaca, NY 14850 (tel. 607/273-3542, or toll free 800/745-3542; fax 607/272-3542). This place contains 41 units, was built in 1960, and is located in an alpine section of town whose streets are full of college kids. Inside, it's very spiffy indeed. There is no pool or restaurant and only a tiny lobby (with reddish marble desk nonetheless, plus track lights and potted plants). But rooms are of a quality that normally costs much more. They have thick rugs, oak furniture, color TVs with HBO, clock radios, stacks of oversize towels, even little baskets of bathroom amenities. Doubles pay between $63 and $95 nightly, depending on room size and location. All major credit cards accepted.

For an alternative to downtown accommodations, you might want to try **La Tourelle,** 1150 Danby Rd. (south of town on N.Y. 96B), Ithaca, NY 14850 (tel. 607/273-2734, or toll free 800/765-1492; fax 607/273-4821). Located behind L'Auberge du Cochon Rouge (see "Where to Eat in Ithaca," below), this country inn is a fanciful version of a European alpine auberge. It's new, nicely detailed, decorated with bleached French-influenced furniture and heavier Mexican carved pieces. The views from the western rooms are spectacular, overlooking the valley and Lake Cayuga. An all-year tennis facility is on the property. Tasteful fireplace suites are available, as are tower suites with bright-red interiors, 10-foot-diameter circular beds, Jacuzzis (small), mirrored ceilings, color TVs with VCRs (videotapes available at front desk), and nonisolated bathroom fixtures. The per-room tariff is $75 to $95 for a room with one queen- or king-size bed, $95 to $110 if you need two queen-o king-size beds, and $100 to $125 for the fireplace and tower suites. All major credit cards accepted.

Eight miles north of Ithaca, adjacent to the famous Taughannock Falls State Park, is a handsome Victorian manse called **Taughannock Farms Inn,** N.Y. 89, Trumansburg, NY 14886 (tel. 607/387-7711). This is a great big cream-colored clapboard establishment with a lantern on top and spacious porches on the bottom, plus sweeping views of the lake from within. The interior is filled with beautiful painted woodwork, crystal sconces, and Victorian wallpapers. Much of the main floor is given over to a handsome and popular restaurant. Upstairs are five elegant, perfectly restored guest rooms, graced with lofty molded ceilings, splendid lake views from big windows, and good-looking antiques. The rooms have private baths and rent for $85 to $125 double, including a continental breakfast. Its adjacent guesthouse costs $125 for two or $145 for four. The restaurant overlooks Cayuga Lake and offers full dinners between $17 and $28. This is a good-looking place. All major credit cards accepted.

About an equal distance from town, but this time on the eastern side of Cayuga, is **Rose Inn,** N.Y. 34 (P.O. Box 6576), Ithaca, NY 14851 (tel. 607/533-7905). This terribly elegant place occupies a fine early Italianate mansion set amid farm country with distant views to the hills beyond Cayuga Lake. There are a country kitchen where breakfast is prepared, a handsome dining room where gourmet feasts are served on china and crystal (for $50 per person), and a really terrific circular staircase that climbs up to a cupola. This is one of those truly unique establishments where the new rooms are actually just as nice as the old ones. They're all very luxurious, furnished with thick carpets, good antiques, handsome woodwork, and lamps and wallpapers. No phone, TV, or pool, but lots of country elegance. Double rates for bed and breakfast vary from $100 to $150 for doubles and $175 to $250 for suites. Of the 14 rooms, all have private baths, and large Jacuzzis are featured in the suites. No credit cards accepted.

Twenty or so miles north of Ithaca is the pristine village of **Aurora** (pop. 900), in the center of which is **Aurora Inn,** Main Street, Route 90, Aurora, NY 13026 (tel. 315/364-8842). The inn was built in 1833 on the scenic eastern shore of Cayuga Lake. Newly renovated, it features 14 guest rooms (all with private baths, phones, and TVs), large public rooms on the first floor, expansive porches on both floors, a bar and dining room, and wonderful views of the lake. The inn has lots of quiet country charm and a helpful innkeeper named Ann Cosentino, who makes you feel at home and dispenses useful advice. Guests can also use the facilities at nearby Wells College, which include a pool, a library, tennis courts, and a nine-hole golf course. Aurora is a lovely village to explore by foot. There are several small mansions on the lake, numerous interesting mid-Victorian buildings in town, and 5 miles of walking trails along the lake shore. The inn also serves meals; lunch is available daily from 11:30am to 2pm (in the $4 to $9 range); dinner is served on Sunday to Thursday usually from 5 to 9pm (to 10pm on Friday and Saturday) and costs about $11 to $20 for dishes like grilled breast of chicken and Oriental tuna steak. MC, V, CB accepted.

Where to Eat in Ithaca

The best place in town is the quaint and charming **Auberge du Cochon Rouge,** south of town past Ithaca College on N.Y. 96B (tel. 607/273-3464). Auberge is housed in a diminutive yellow farmhouse whose numerous little rooms have wide-plank floors, beamed ceilings, and elaborate place settings. Cuisine is classical and country French and divine: pasta with lobster and smoked salmon, filet mignon with béarnaise sauce, rack of lamb, confit of duck with Cassis sauce, and stuffed quails cost around $17 to $23 à la carte. Open daily for dinner only from 6 to 10pm; Sunday brunch is served from 11am to 2pm. All major credit cards accepted.

The new toast of the town is **Thai Cuisine,** 501 S. Meadow St. (tel. 607/273-2031), where a polite and formal atmosphere reigns. Decor includes dazzling white table linens and curtains, handsome brass bent-back chairs, track lighting, and contemporary art. Sunday brunch is a special treat, wherein diners have the choice of over 30 appetizer-size dishes priced at $2 apiece. This is a good introduction to the

66 main courses on the menu, no two of which taste the same. Thai cuisine employs a lot of coconut, pineapple, curry, and hot pepper and has a very distinct flavor. The restaurant is open Tuesday through Sunday for lunch from 11:30am to 2pm; dinner is Tuesday to Thursday and Sunday between 5 and 9:30pm (until 10pm on Friday and Saturday). The average lunch dish costs between $5 and $7; dinner selections, like half a roast duck topped with jumbo shrimp, scallops, clams, and crabmeat, are priced between about $7 and $20. All major credit cards accepted.

Ithaca is also the home of famous, collectively owned **Moosewood Restaurant,** located in the Dewitt Building at Cayuga and Seneca Streets (tel. 607/273-9610). Founded in 1973, the Moosewood has become synonymous with creative cooking techniques and ethnic cuisine with a vegetarian emphasis. Much of its fame stems from the Moosewood cookbooks, which have to date sold over 1½ million copies. There are eighteen owners, who all work in the restaurant and participate equally in all decisions. Despite the business clientele, one has a sense that the 1960s are still alive and well hereabouts. Lunch is served Monday through Saturday from 11:30am to 2pm; most dishes cost about $5. The dinner hours are Monday to Thursday from 5:30 to 8:30pm (to 9pm on Friday and Saturday); the menu changes daily, but you should expect to pay about $9 for vegetarian dishes to $11 for fresh fish. No credit cards accepted.

Something of a secret in town is **Banfi's,** in the Statler Hotel (tel. 607/257-2500). Staffed by both industry professionals and hotel-school students from Cornell, the food and service here are exceptional. Lunch is available Monday through Friday between 11:30am and 2:30pm; sandwiches run about $5, and main courses go as high as $8. A lunch buffet is also available for $5.50. Dinner is served Monday through Saturday from 5:30 to 9pm and ranges from about $9 for pasta to $17 for a roast rack of lamb with minted tarragon glaze and onion marmalade. All major credit cards accepted.

Also in the Statler is **Terrace Restaurant** (tel. 607/257-2500), which by day is a faculty lounge and by night becomes a student-run theme restaurant, where the cuisine varies from Tex-Mex to Japanese and dinner may be accompanied by a theatrical production. Open September through May on Monday to Friday from 5:30 to 8:30pm. Call for programs and prices. All major credit cards accepted.

Joe's Restaurant, 602 W. Buffalo St. (tel. 607/273-2693), has been recently restored to its original 1930s look: neon, a Wurlitzer jukebox, a monitor-top refrigerator, and an old Coke machine. The atmosphere is set for fine Italian dining. The veal is organic, homemade sauces accompany all pasta dishes, and fresh seafood is offered daily; dinner fare runs between $7 and $16. Open for dinner only from 4 to 10pm on Sunday through Thursday, to 11pm on Friday and Saturday. All major credit cards accepted.

On the Cayuga Lake Inlet is **Old Port Harbour,** 702 W. Buffalo St. (tel. 607/272-4868), which bills itself as "a little piece of Europe" on the water. Decorated in a nautical theme with lots of glass overlooking the canal, the restaurant, featuring cuisine ranging from Cajun to continental, serves lunch Monday to Saturday from 11:30am to 2pm (Sunday brunch from 11am to 3pm with music) and dinner daily from 5:30 to 10pm. Lunch will cost between $5 and $8, with the dinner fare from $12 to $19. All major credit cards accepted.

Five minutes south of Ithaca on N.Y. 13 is a flamboyantly Gothic house with steep gables and painted bargeboard. This is **Turback's,** N.Y. 13 (tel. 607/272-6484), a Victorian setting for New York State cuisine. In its various dining rooms, amid plants, a book-lined bar, hanging forests of Tiffany-glass shades, and racks of wine, you can enjoy things like Empire apple chicken, Long Island duckling, Cornell barbecued chicken, pasta primavera, and Dutchess County ham steak, which cost around $10 to $19. Only dinner is served, daily from 4:30 to 9:30pm. All major credit cards accepted.

Ithaca's downtown **restaurant row** is located adjacent to Ithaca Commons on North Aurora Street, between State and Seneca Streets. On this single block are half a dozen different restaurants, ranging from **Hal's Deli** (deli sandwiches; tel. 607/273-7765), to **Plums'** (brass fixtures and mahogany, serving hamburgers and hot main courses; tel. 607/273-8422), to **Simeons on the Common** (plush sand

wiches and evening entertainment; tel. 607/273-2212), to **Ragmann's** (ba
ers with atmosphere; tel. 607/273-5236), to the **Fisherman** (brick walls, blo
niture, and very fresh seafood; tel. 607/273-9108), plus numerous
Everything's moderately priced, and they're never all closed at once.

Last but not least is **"Just a Taste" Wine and Tapas Bar,** 116 N. Aurora St. (tel.
607/277-WINE). Tapas are a Spanish tradition, a series of "little dishes" of various
types of food. It's more a style of eating than a type of cuisine. The tapas here represent cooking from around the world and range from $3 to $5 each. The menu also
lists traditional dishes priced at $8 for pasta with pesto to about $12 for beef tenderloin. The main attraction at "Just a Taste," however, is the huge selection of wine by
the glass via the largest Cruvinet nitrogen unit I've ever seen. If you wish, you can
buy a "flight," which is an opportunity to taste up to five different wines for one
modest price, then record your reactions to each on a formated paper place mat.
Open Sunday to Wednesday from 11:30am to 10pm; until midnight Thursday
through Saturday. All major credit cards accepted.

CORNING

This tidy industrial town (pop. 13,000) houses one of the largest tourist attractions in New York State: the **Corning Glass Center.** This well-designed series of exhibits, all pertaining to glass and its unusual history, is housed in a glittering
museum with sensually sculpted reflective walls. It's easy to find, fun to visit, intellectually exciting, and really something that no visitor to this part of the world
should miss. Most don't—half a million people went through the Corning Glass
Center last year alone.

It's divided into three parts, connected in sequence and tourable at your own
speed. The first, called the "Corning Museum of Glass," contains unbelievably fabulous and precious objects made of glass that are arranged chronologically. I remember particularly a solid-glass banquet table, made in 1878, surmounted by a cut-
glass-and-ormolu punchbowl the size of my wife. The "Hall of Science and Industry" is full of pushbutton exhibits and screening rooms where formerly inexplicable
things like binary coding and fiber optics suddenly become quite clear and simple.
Don't think for one moment that it's either too complex or too intellectually demanding. It isn't. You could easily wander around here all day with an expression of
uncritical wonder on your face. Last is the "Steuben Factory," presumably named
after Baron von Steuben and Steuben County. This is an actual working factory, a
place full of glowing ovens and glass in every condition, from molten blob to etched
vase. You can watch the entire process from grandstand seats and from along a glass-
walled corridor. Beyond are gift shops, where glass is for sale.

The Corning Glass Center is open daily from 9am to 5pm. Admission is $5 for
adults and $3 for youths 6 to 17. The average visit lasts two hours, but you could
easily spend a day. For further information, call 607/974-8271.

Corning itself is kind of an interesting place. "The Crystal City," as it has been
styled, is obviously a company town, and just as obviously the company cares what it
looks like. In 1972, the Cheming River rose above its banks and made a total wreck
of **Market Street,** Corning's busy main business thoroughfare. The event was
seized upon by the powers-that-be as an opportunity to "restore" the entire downtown with an eye to re-creating its brick Victorian charm.

As a result, Corning doesn't look like many other places. It has many brick sidewalks and lots and lots of planted locust trees. There are hardly any commercial signs
that stick out. The original 19th-century streetscape was probably a lot less smooth,
filled as it must have been with signs, clocks, sheds, railings, and all the other necessary furniture of a busy sidewalk. The present-day Corning is also probably prettier,
whatever its historic veracity.

Market Street, which is listed on the National Register of Historic Places, is a
fun place to browse and stroll. It's full of shops and cars and people, anchored at its
very center by **Baron Steuben Place.** This is a six-story brick hotel from the 1920s
that closed down in 1974 and has been renovated into a complex of boutiques and
galleries that includes a gourmet snackbar and a restaurant.

Also in Corning is the largest collection of Western art (that's cowboys and Indians I'm talking) in the East. The **Rockwell American Museum**, Denison Parkway (N.Y. 17) and Cedar Street (tel. 607/937-5386), occupies Corning's former city hall, now (naturally) restored. The excellent collection includes works by New York's own Frederic Remington, Albert Bierstadt, W. R. Leigh, and many others. Good gift shop too. During July and August the museum is open weekdays from 9am to 7pm, to 5pm on Saturday, and from noon to 5pm on Sunday. During the rest of the year hours are 9am to 5pm on Monday to Saturday (from noon on Sunday).

Hotels In & Around Corning

There are some interesting ones at least, if no great bargains. **Corning Hilton Inn,** Denison Parkway/N.Y. 17, Corning, NY 14830 (tel. 607/962-5000; fax 607/962-4166), is a sleek, low-slung channeled cement-block affair surrounded with landscaped parking lots full of shady locust trees. Inside is a hushed modern lobby with an indoor atrium complete with fountain, multiple levels, leather furniture, contemporary tapestries, and an adjacent atmospheric restaurant called the Garden Court. The 180 rooms are just like you'd hope they'd be in an upstate Hilton. Those in the new wing truly exemplify up-to-the-minute luxury in terms of equipment and pastel color schemes. Besides color TVs, private phones, and marble sinktops, guests at the Hilton enjoy an on-premises health club and an indoor pool. A double room costs about $72 to $138 nightly. All major credit cards accepted.

A few miles west of Corning via N.Y. 17 is a small neighboring community called Painted Post. Several hotels are located here, the best being **Best Western Lodge on the Green,** P.O. Box 150, Painted Post, NY 14870 (tel. 607/962-2456; fax 607/962-1769). This is a luxurious motel in excellent repair that's well on its way to becoming a high-1960s period piece. There are 135 units, housed in low modern buildings on a manicured campus of lawns and trees and flower beds. Outside the lobby is a covered porte cochere with slim steel columns; inside are cathedral ceilings and two-story glass walls. The big rooms come equipped with thick carpets, padded headboards, cable color TVs, digital clocks, radios, direct-dial phones, and good-quality furniture. A large number have views across a grassy inner lawn toward a handsome outdoor pool. Minimum-rate rooms face a parking lot, but otherwise they're just as nice. From May through October, a double room will cost between $79 to $89 nightly; the rest of the year those same rooms cost $60 to $65. Also on the premises are a lounge and a restaurant. The lodge is located adjacent to N.Y. 17 and U.S. 15. Take the Gang Mills exit off U.S. 15; you'll see it from the ramp. All major credit cards accepted.

Where to Eat in Corning

Baron Steuben Place, the restored gallery/boutique/restaurant complex in the middle of Corning at Market Street and the Centerway, contains two eating establishments of note. **Ice Cream Works** (tel. 607/962-8481) has marble-topped tables, a white-tile floor, an old-fashioned carved-wood bar with a marble-topped counter, fans on the ceilings, and an overall 19th-century ice cream parlor look. You can get sandwiches of every description here, plus burgers, soups, salads, melts, sundaes, and fancy sundaes, priced mostly between $2 and $10 and available all day long. All major credit cards accepted. Open daily in the summer from 10am to 10pm; winter hours are 11am to 5pm. Under the same roof is **Epicurean Café** (tel. 607/962-6553), which offers high-class sandwiches with names like Classic, All American Kid, and Elite, plus Savory Entrée Croissants and other inventive fare. Most prices are under $5. Open all year on Monday to Saturday from 8am to 6pm. All major credit cards accepted.

For something a little different, try **Upstate Tuna Co.,** 73–75 Historical E. Main St. (tel. 607/936-TUNA). There is an air of excitement here, and it's not the pop and jazz background music or the fact the place offers over 50 varieties of beer at the Italian granite bar. You will be greeted by a hostess, presented with drinks by your waitress, then informed that you will have to cook your own food over a large gas charcoal grill in the corner of the dining room. The waitress will take your side orders, but it's up to you to head for the meat and fish counter, make your selection, and belly up to the grill, where you can meet and mix with the other guests. Armed with spatula and marinades, you too can pretend to be an expert chef. All in all, it's good fun and a great way to meet people. Main courses run from about $7 to $17. Open daily from 5 to 10pm; the bar stays open until 1am. AE, MC, and V accepted.

On Bridge Street off the western end of Market is **Rojo's**, 36 Bridge St. (tel. 607/936-9683), is a dim and atmospheric tavern with a central bar; green-shaded hanging lights; lots of dark woodwork; dark-green walls covered with pictures, street signs; a greenhouse; and old photos. Burgers, big combination sandwiches, quiches, all manner of snacks, plus hot dishes and even pizza, cost between about $5 and $8 each, or $9 to $17 for dinners. Anything on the menu is available Monday through Saturday from 11am to 10pm (to 1am in summer). All major credit cards accepted.

For dependable family-style Italian cuisine at moderate prices, try **Sorge's**, 66–68 W. Market St. (tel. 607/937-5422). This brightly lit modern establishment has a long counter along one wall and an adjoining dining room filled with tables. Sorge's has all manner of sandwich, egg, and salad lunches, plus a full range of Italian dishes, children's portions, and daily specials. Even the full-course dinners rarely exceed $12; lunch looks like about a $4 ticket. Open daily from 7am to 11pm. All major credit cards accepted.

About 10 miles east of Corning is one of New York State's most famous "destination restaurants," **Pierce's 1894 Restaurant**, 14th Street and Oakwood Avenue, Elmira Heights, NY 14903 (tel. 607/734-2022). Pierce's has been managed by the same family since 1894. During this time it has evolved from a corner bar to a complex of six individually styled dining areas whose themes range from a Victorian parlor to the wine cellar in a Tudor castle. This place can serve in excess of 400 patrons at a shot, and they all get exceptional food and service. I have to say that not only in New York, but in New England and Pennsylvania as well, I find people constantly asking me about Pierce's. In addition to the food, Pierce's has become a mecca for wine connoisseurs. In fact, *Wine Spectator* calls Pierce's the "wine treasure trove of upstate New York." Open for dinner only on Tuesday through Saturday from 5 to 10pm and on Sunday from noon to 9pm. Meals range from Welsh rarebit at $10 to a melt-in-your-mouth broiled filet mignon for $20.50. Reservations a must. All major credit cards accepted.

WATKINS GLEN

This unassuming village (pop. 2,400), founded in 1863, sits at the southernmost tip of Seneca Lake. It's famous for two not-very-compatible attractions: international auto racing and a silent and spectacular natural glen.

In 1986, after a hiatus of several years, **Watkins Glen International** resumed a full schedule of summer auto races. The track is about 4 miles from the village. At least once a month it hosts a major racing weekend, filling the country air with the scream and whine of high-speed engines. Everything—from stockcars to factory prototypes, from GTOs to vintage cars, from "pony cars" to sports cars—races here, sometimes for big money. The approximately 3½-mile-long track is adjoined by campsites, club areas, and a new spectator/photo stand. For ticket and program information, contact Watkins Glen International, P.O. Box 500, Watkins Glen, NY 14891 (tel. 607/535-2481).

Adjoining the village itself is **Watkins Glen State Park** (tel. 607/535-4511), whose centerpiece is a 1½-mile-long gorge filled with waterfalls, grottos, and caverns. It's very deep and accessible by unobtrusive stone paths and staircases. There must be approximately one stair for every year nature took to form this place. Watkins Glen is no Grand Canyon, but it is very beautiful and very sensitively accessed and protected. Elsewhere on the park's 1,000 acres are campsites, toilets, parking fields ($4 daily per car), and a splendid big outdoor pool. The park itself is free. Open daily from 8am to dusk; the Gorge Trail is open only from mid-May to late October.

Also in the state park is a jazzy outdoor sound-and-light show called **Timespell,** which takes place in the gorge every night from May through October. Lots of eerie music, artificial rushing winds, and vivid lights and images projected on the walls of the gorge. The whole thing takes about half an hour and costs $5. For program and ticket information, call Timespell at 607/535-4960.

Vineyards and wineries abound hereabouts as well. If you'd like to visit them, a good suggestion is to stop first at the **Schuyler County Chamber of Commerce,** across from the park in Watkins Glen at 1000 N. Franklin St. (tel. 607/535-4300), and ask for a copy of **"The Wines and Wineries of Seneca Lake."** Published by the **Seneca Lake Winery Association,** P.O. Box 91, Hector, NY 14841, this pamphlet will direct you to 16 wineries, most of which are adjacent to the southern half of Seneca Lake. Some are boutique wineries; others have interesting restaurants; a few produce internationally famous wines.

If you have time to visit only one or two, my first choice would be **Hermann J. Wiemer Vineyard,** Route 14, Dundee, NY 14837 (tel. 607/243-7971). Hermann Wiemer is presently on the cutting edge of advanced quality New York State wine, based on the grafting of European vinifera grape vines to native American root stock. Wiemer, who traces his heritage back over 300 years of German winemakers, was greatly influenced by the success of Dr. Konstantin Frank, the father of the North American vinifera grapes. A large part of the vineyard operation consists of grafted vine sales to other vineyards from the Niagara Frontier to Long Island. Open Monday to Saturday from 10am to 5pm and Sunday from 11am to 5pm. There is no charge for tastings or for the self-guided tour.

If you've time for only one other vineyard, I'd stop by **Wagner Vineyards** on the other side of Seneca Lake on Route 414, Lodi, NY 14860 (tel. 607/582-6450). This is a large and well-established facility noted for its success with both vinifera and native American hybrids. Tastings are free, and the modern octagonal winery is most interesting. Open daily for free tours from 10am to 4pm. Next door is **Ginny Lee Café** (tel. 607/582-6574), which serves good lunch with a views of the lake. The café is open mid-May through mid-October on Monday to Saturday from 11:30am to 4pm and on Sunday from 10am to 4:30pm. MC and V accepted.

Where to Stay & Eat

Glen Motor Inn, N.Y. 14 (P.O. Box 44), Watkins Glen, NY 14891 (tel. 607/535-2706; fax 607/535-7635), sits on a hillside north of town, overlooking Seneca Lake. It has a restaurant and bar at the top of the hill and 40 units plus an outdoor pool on the lower slopes. Rooms have color TVs, tiled bathrooms, nice-quality furniture, and fine lake views. The charge for a double room is about $65 to $85 nightly, the latter price the one you're most likely to encounter. It's simple but comfortable. Open April 1 to the beginning of November. All major credit cards accepted.

A variety of light snacks are available in the village, at a restored brick factory building now called **Seneca Market.** Snack counters with names like Clam Shack and Sen Fu Chan dispense varying cuisines. You eat at picnic tables on a gravel court overlooking the lake. An adjacent building is filled with boutiques and souvenir stands. Open May through October.

Alternatively, you might try a meal at **Seneca Lodge,** at the south end of Watkins Glen State Park (tel. 607/535-2014). The dining room here is in a big Adirondack-type building with log walls, heavy beams, a stone fireplace, and flocks of green-clothed tables with paper placemats. At lunch (daily from 11:30am to 2pm), salads and sandwiches run from $2 to $6. Dinner selections like broiled scallops, rainbow trout amandine, pork chops, chicken Kiev, T-bone steak, and London broil cost between $8 and $18 (most being right in the middle) and is served daily from 6 to 9pm. Open May through November. Look for the sign on N.Y. 14 just south of the main entrance to the Watkins Glen State Park. All major credit cards accepted.

Wildflower Café, 301 Franklin St., (tel. 607/535-9797), has a sort of a San Francisco accent by virtue of lots of stained glass, a blue pressed-tin ceiling, exposed brick walls, bentwood chairs, and an elaborately detailed oak bar. Lunch might be burgers or gourmet pizza ($3 to $6); dinner choices range from chicken pie to veal Cordon Bleu (about $10 to $16). Open daily from 11:30am to 4pm for lunch and 4 to 10pm on weekends only for dinner. All major credit cards accepted.

There are also dinner cruises on Seneca Lake, offered by **Captain Bill's** from the foot of Franklin Street, Watkins Glen, NY 14891 (tel. 607/535-4541 or 4680). The *Stroller IV* is a 50-foot, enclosed 49-passenger vessel that offers a narrated 50-minute sightseeing cruise. You can have the cruise and dinner too aboard the 65-foot, 150-passenger *Columbia*, which will take you out for three hours. Sightseeing cruises cost $6.50 for adults and $3 for children under 12; dinner cruises range from $17 to $29.95 for adults and $10 to $19 for the kids.

HAMMONDSPORT

The village square here could have been painted by Norman Rockwell. It has a little gazebo and mature shade trees and is overlooked by stolid two-story 19th-century commercial buildings, many in the throes of restoration. Hammondsport (pop. 1,100), on the southern shore of Keuka Lake, has a decidedly somnolent air, notwithstanding numerous interesting shops along Sheather Street and a few comfortable smalltown restaurants and taverns overlooking the square.

The biggest attraction in town is the local **wine**. The industry started near Hammondsport in 1860 in what is today the Taylor/Great Western/Gold Seal complex in nearby Pleasant Valley. Today there are 34 different wineries in the Finger Lakes region, all but four of which are adjacent to Keuka, Seneca, and Cayuga Lakes. The wineries are grouped in three associations: the Keuka Lake Winery Association, the Seneca Lake Winery Association, and the Cayuga Wine Trail. Brochures exist with maps locating various member wineries. The idea is to tour around the region at your own speed, stopping at whichever winery you've either heard of or that simply catches your attention along the road.

The facilities at the different wineries vary considerably. The big ones, notably Taylor (described below), have visitor centers, gift shops, bus tours, and all sorts of glitz. The little ones are just vineyards where someone will appear from behind a barn, show you around, and offer you a glass of wine before you leave. None charges admission, and all take a great deal of pride in their product. To get a copy of the brochure titled "Keuka Lake Winery Route," write the **Keuka Lake Winery Association,** R.D. 1, Box 45, Hammondsport, NY 14840. This will direct you through 43 miles of vineyards surrounding Keuka Lake.

My own favorite in the region is **Dr. Frank's Vinifera Wine Cellars,** 9749 Middle Rd., Hammondsport, NY 14840 (tel. 607/868-4884). Dr. Konstantin Frank was a wine pioneer who proved that European grapes could not only survive the cold climate of upstate New York but flourish here as well. It is he who was truly responsible for the development of New York's wine industry, and his work is being carried on to this day by his descendants. I am a great fan of his champagne. Free tastings are available Monday through Saturday from 9am to 5pm and Sunday from 1 to 5pm.

Tours of the **Taylor Wine Company** (not to be confused with an unrelated operation called the Wine Museum of Greyton H. Taylor) constitute the second-largest tourist attraction in the area after the Corning Glass Center. The Taylor Wine Company (tel. 607/569-2111) operates daily tours from 10am to 4pm between May and the end of October (the rest of the year it closes at 3pm and all day Sunday). The winery is a large modern complex set amid cornfields and vineyards just west of N.Y. 54 in Pleasant Valley. There's a big modern visitor center filled with displays pertaining to wine-making and Taylor's various products. A 35,000-gallon former wine tank has been converted to a theater for wine industry films, and a horseshoe bar dispenses gratis samples to whoever bellies up. The free tour takes about an hour, covers the entire process of wine-making, and ends up in a gift shop.

Also in Hammondsport is the **Curtiss Museum** (tel. 607/569-2160), half a mile south of town on N.Y. Route 54. Curtiss was an aviation pioneer, credited with, among other things, founding naval aviation. The museum's new facility on Route

54 is less picturesque than the old one on Lake and Main Streets back in the village, but it contains a larger display area, plus a restoration shop, increased library and archive space, a museum shop, and a 100-seat theater. There are some wild-looking antique planes in this place. In 1907, these things were puddle-jumping 1,000 feet or so at a time. By 1908, Curtiss kept the *June Bug* off the ground for a whole mile. Already by 1910, he was demonstrating the feasibility of aerial bombing. And in 1911, he performed the historic act of taking off and landing from the deck of the U.S.S. *Pennsylvania*. He became rich during World War I and was a major local employer. By 1919, he was able to cross the Atlantic via Nova Scotia and the Azores in a flying boat. In 1930, at the age of 52, he died during a routine appendectomy in Buffalo.

The museum also has collections of toys, china dolls, quilts, bicycles, even military uniforms. From May through October, it is open Monday to Saturday from 9am to 5pm and Sunday from 11am to 5pm; between November and April, the hours are Monday to Saturday from 10am to 4pm and Sunday from noon to 5pm. Admission is $4 for adults, $3 for seniors, and $2 for kids.

Finally, if you'd like to get out on Lake Keuka, you might book a cruise on the triple-deck, 500-passenger, air-conditioned (and heated) *Keuka Maid,* Box 648, Hammondsport, NY 14840 (tel. 607/569-BOAT), which offers lunch, brunch, and dinner-dance cruises from May through October. Call the number above for rates and schedules.

Where to Stay & Eat Near Hammondsport

The area is not strong on accommodations. The best I found (from the standpoint of comfort and value) was **Days Inn at Bath,** 330 W. Morris St., Bath, NY 14810 (tel. 607/776-7644; fax 607/776-7650). This five-story modern motor inn has variously been a Ramada Inn, a Quality Inn, an independent operation, and now a Days Inn. There are a restaurant with moderately priced daily specials; a bar with a happy hour; and bright, pleasant modern rooms furnished with thick rugs, white-vinyl swivel chairs, color TVs, textured wallcoverings, and direct-dial phones. The atmosphere is like a modest Holiday Inn. Doubles cost between $55 and $65 a night depending on whether the room has a queen-size, two doubles, or a king-size bed. All major credit cards accepted.

Village Tavern, overlooking Hammondsport's village square at the corner of Mechanic and Pulteney Streets (tel. 607/569-2528), has booths, a bar filled with locals, and a nice friendly atmosphere. Sandwiches, burgers, and super sandwiches go for about $3 to $6 at lunch. In the evening dinners include broiled haddock, fried clam strips, lasagne, chicken parmesan, and shrimp in a basket for between $6 and $15. On Saturday night there's even piano music. Open daily for lunch from 11am to 3pm and for dinner from 5 to 9pm. The bar, of course, stays open longer. MC and V accepted.

Across the square is **Crooked Lake Ice Cream** on Sheather Street (tel. 607/569-2751), which serves sandwiches and luncheon specials in the $2 to $5 range, plus a broad selection of ice cream concoctions, every day of the year. This is a small-town luncheonette; no dinner is served.

Just down the street is **Park Inn Hotel** on the Village Square, Hammondsport, NY 14840 (tel. 607/569-9387). In operation since 1861, it has recently been redecorated and now offers two-room suites with private baths, priced from $55 to $85. Lunch is served in the dining room on Monday through Saturday from 11am to 2pm and costs about $3 to $5. Dinner is available on the same days, from 5 to 10pm, and is priced from about $7 for the locally famous fish fry to $15 for the beef and reef. MC and V available.

The nicest restaurant in the area is **Pleasant Valley Inn,** on N.Y. 54 (Bath-Hammondsport Road; tel. 607/569-2282), located in a pink-and-white Victorian house quite near the Taylor Wine Co. The inn is divided into a series of very pretty rooms decorated with involved period wallpapers, lofty ceilings, crystal chandeliers, spotless white linens, and elaborate curtains. There's also an informal bar with low ceiling beams and a congenial older crowd. Luncheons like seafood Newburg, liver and onions, omelets, and various sandwiches cost from about $5 to $8. Dinner selections such as New York sirloin, broiled sole, tenderloin tips marsala, veal à la crème, and duckling are priced from about $13 to $30 à la carte. Open daily during summer from 11:30am to 3pm for lunch and from 5 to 9pm for dinner (to 10pm on Friday and Saturday). During the cooler seasons it's closed on Monday. All major credit cards accepted.

XVIII

THE NIAGARA FRONTIER

1. BUFFALO
2. NIAGARA FALLS, NY, AND CANADA
3. CHAUTAUQUA

The western extremity of New York State is best known for Niagara Falls, a mighty cataract on the Niagara River connecting Lakes Erie and Ontario. But there are other attractions hereabouts, notably the somewhat battered but still magnificent city of Buffalo and a cultural institution whose name has entered into the language itself, Chautauqua.

1. Buffalo

New York State's second-largest city (pop. 357,900) is a blue-collar town that amassed considerable wealth and power before hard times began in the 1960s. Today, having passed through the Valley of the Shadow of Suburban Flight and Urban Renewal, it has emerged unexpectedly as a boom town of the Northeast. The cause of this is a bilateral Free Trade agreement established in January of 1989 that will ultimately phase out all tariffs between the United States and Canada. Suddenly, Buffalo has become a major trading center exhibiting all manner of new civic and commercial vitality.

Buffalo is filled with 19th- and 20th-century architectural treasures. If some are still boarded up or hemmed in by the incredible number of downtown parking lots, many others are in gorgeous shape. Since the adoption of the 1975 Buffalo Landmark and Preservation Code, there's been a great new awareness of the local architectural resources. Things are being renovated everywhere.

Buffalo is well along on an ambitious plan to rejuvenate its downtown core around Niagara and Lafayette squares. Main Street, for example, has been converted to a combination pedestrial mall/streetcar route. The "streetcar" is a sleek new surface train called the **Metro,** whose fare is gratis throughout the downtown area. The route isn't long but the idea is good. And it's bringing renewed life and activity back to the city's core.

Buffalo grew rich on trade between the Midwest and the East. It was a terminus of the Erie Canal, a fact whose impact is hard for many of us to really understand

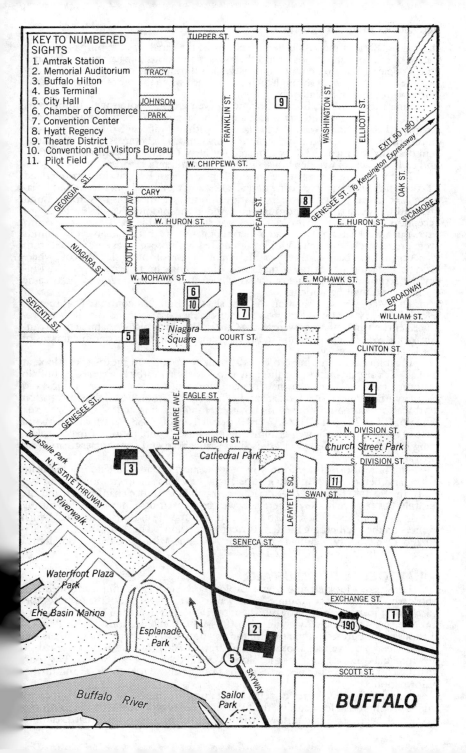

KEY TO NUMBERED SIGHTS
1. Amtrak Station
2. Memorial Auditorium
3. Buffalo Hilton
4. Bus Terminal
5. City Hall
6. Chamber of Commerce
7. Convention Center
8. Hyatt Regency
9. Theatre District
10. Convention and Visitors Bureau
11. Pilot Field

BUFFALO

these days. Back in the 1820s, before railroads, the canal was the only practicable means of transporting goods. It had the most tremendous impact on trade imaginable. People in Buffalo became immensely rich through the commerce of that day because everything went through their town. Then when the age of rails arrived, the tracks went through Buffalo too.

After the Civil War, Buffalo became an even greater boom town. Immigrants poured in. Smokestack industries rose along the lakefront and the southern edge of town. By 1901, Buffalo was a world-class city with magnificent banks, office towers, municipal buildings, splendid mansions along famous Delaware Avenue, a park system designed by Frederick Law Olmsted (of New York City's Central Park fame), and endless tracts of wooden houses filled with immigrant laborers.

That was also the year of the famous Pan-American Exposition, a wonderland of columned white temples, ornamental lakes, and triumphal ways erected in Delaware Park. The exposition brought exotic exhibits and famous visitors from around the world. It was a truly glamorous event. And in the middle of it, while attending a reception, President William McKinley was shot. At first it was thought he'd survive. But a week later he was dead, a victim of gangrene that set in after his wounds were prematurely sewed up. Vice President Teddy Roosevelt was summoned from the Adirondacks back to the Delaware Avenue mansion of Ansley Wilcox, where he'd been staying at the time of the attack. After paying his respects to Mrs. McKinley, he returned to the Wilcox house, where after a short ceremony he became America's youngest president.

The McKinley assassination did not shadow Buffalo's continued prosperity. Heavy industry continued to grow. The great Pierce-Arrow automobile was produced entirely in Buffalo, as were all the Curtiss Wright airplanes manufactured during World War II. Plenty of big industries remain, despite the economic travails of the last quarter century.

If exploring interesting old cities appeals to you, by all means take a look at Buffalo. It's also an interesting alternative to staying in nearby Niagara Falls. Buffalo is not at all a typical tourist town, of course. Most visitors come here on business and depart without much of a look around. The helpful **Greater Buffalo Convention and Visitors Bureau,** in the former Statler Hotel building at 107 Delaware Ave., Buffalo, NY 14202 (tel. 716/852-0510, or toll free 800/283-3256), will give you a map of the downtown as well as numerous other useful publications. Anybody planning to explore Buffalo is well advised to write ahead and/or contact them upon arrival.

The bureau can also inform you of local sports events. Buffalo is a big team town, and between the **Buffalo Bisons** at the new Pilot Field (minor-league baseball), the **Buffalo Bills** (1991 American Football Conference champions), and the **Buffalo Sabres** (ice hockey), there may well be an exciting game scheduled during the time of your visit. There's also a vigorous cultural life in Buffalo, much of which centers on the re-emerging theater district (more below). The Arts Council in Buffalo and Erie County maintains a 24-hour **ARTSline** with information on all area events. The number is 716/847-1444.

WHAT TO SEE & DO IN BUFFALO

Let's take a look around town. Exploring the city is a definite adventure for those who like that sort of thing. A good way to do this is on one of the **Architectural Walking Tours** sponsored by the Theodore Roosevelt Inaugural National Historical Site, 641 Delaware Ave. (tel. 716/884-0095). "Reflections of the Past . . . Visions of the Future" is their title for the downtown tour. There are also excursions down Delaware Avenue, another in and around Allentown (a well-preserved intown neighborhood), and another along Main and North Pearl Streets. The tours usually cost about $5 per person. Call the number above for schedules and further information.

Admittedly, this degree of detail is not going to interest all visitors. But casual sightseers should at least admire the following: **Lafayette Hotel** (on the southwest corner of Lafayette Square; now closed; designed by Louise Blanchard, the first woman architect in the United States); the **Old Post Office** (a fantastic stone Victorian concoction on Ellicott and Swan Streets, which is now the downtown campus of Erie Community College); the **Prudential Building** (Louis Sullivan's wondrous 1896 office tower covered entirely with sculpted terracotta); **Buffalo City Hall** (a 1932-vintage art deco opus that out–Radio City's Radio City Music Hall); **Buffalo Savings Bank** (a lavish expression of the aesthetic that gave rise to the Pan-American Exposition, located at the confluence of Main, Huron, Genesee, and Washington Streets and now called the Goldome Center); **Delaware Avenue** (the former millionaires' mile, now bereft of its elm trees and most of its mansions; some palatial Newport-type survivors still stand in the blocks immediately north of North Street); and the **Elmwood Strip** (a stretch of Elmwood Avenue, between Bidwell Parkway and Forest Avenue, noted for trendy bars and interesting shops and restaurants). This is a very minimal itinerary but one that will give a quick idea of what's here.

The **Theater District** occupies a short stretch of Main Street (the present Metro route) just north of the Hyatt Regency Buffalo Hotel. It's a surprised-looking group of old buildings (surprised because, unlike most of the surrounding blocks, they haven't been bulldozed), containing almost half a dozen legitimate theaters, plus shops and restaurants. The restoration of the Theater District is just completed at this writing and there's clearly a future here. There are lots of pink-granite paving blocks and newly planted trees. Shops are opening up, and fine old buildings have been restored. People clearly care.

Centerpiece of the Theater District is **Shea's Buffalo Theater,** one of the last intact vaudeville house/movie palaces in the country. Shea's is a satisfyingly baroque confection from 1926. It's full of Italian marble, gilded moldings, Czech crystal, and opulent murals. George Burns and Gracie Allen, Bob Hope, the Marx Brothers, Red Skelton, Duke Ellington, Benny Goodman—the list of famous names who have appeared here goes on indefinitely. In 1975, after failing to get even an upset bid of $100,000, the city decided to tear the place down for yet another parking lot. Volunteers barricaded the doors. Nonprofit organizations went to work. The entire theater was restored, and today it boasts a full calendar of Broadway shows, top-name entertainers, rock concerts, and more. Call ARTSline at 716/847-1444 to see what's playing here or at the other district theaters. Tours of the interior are available by appointment only; call 716/847-0850 for information.

Buffalo and Erie County Naval and Servicemen's Park is a long name for a small park containing three famous navy ships. The official address is 1 Naval Park Cove (tel. 716/847-1773), a waterfront area that has been separated from downtown by the elevated lanes of the New York State Thruway. The road that takes you there (and to the nearby Erie Basin Marina) is located two blocks south of the Hilton Hotel. U.S.S. *Croaker* (one of 17 World War II submarines), U.S.S. *The Sullivans,* and U.S.S. *Little Rock* are on loan from the U.S. Navy and open to visitors daily from April through November. *The Sullivans* was named in memory of five young Sullivan brothers, all of whom died on November 13, 1942, aboard the cruiser *Juneau* in the Solomon Islands. Admission is $6 for adults and $3.50 for seniors and kids.

The aforementioned **Theodore Roosevelt Inaugural National Historic Site (Wilcox Mansion)** occupies a big old house at 641 Delaware Ave., at North Street (tel. 716/884-0095). It's modest by later Delaware Avenue standards, and its location, hemmed by new commercial buildings and across the street from a Howard Johnson, exaggerates this modesty. Parts of the house were originally the officers' quarters for the Buffalo Barracks, erected in 1838 during the so-called Patriots' War in Canada. After that died down the property passed into private hands and became a part of the march of fashion up Delaware Avenue. Ansley Wilcox mansionized the place, and he and his wife continued to live there until the early 1930s. Concerned citizens saved the house from demolition in the late '60s, and in 1971 it was opened as a historic site administered by the U.S. Department of the Interior. You can prowl its elegant halls and get the whole McKinley/Roosevelt inaugural tale on Monday to Friday from 10am to 5pm (from noon on Saturday and Sunday). Parking is around back on Franklin Street.

Naturally a big city like Buffalo has its share of museums. But particularly interesting is **Albright-Knox Art Gallery,** 1285 Elmwood Ave. (tel. 716/882-8700). The gallery is perhaps best known for its outstanding collection of art of the last 40 or so years. Pop, op, conceptualism, kinetic art and color field, minimalism, and various trends of the late 1970s and '80s are represented by the works of Clyfford Still, Frank Stella, Jackson Pollock, Jean Dubuffet, Roy Lichtenstein, and others. Other historical periods, from antiquity to impressionism, are represented as well. And the collection is housed in a splendid Greek temple adjacent to the site of the 1901 Pan-American Exposition. Open from 11am to 5pm on Tuesday through Saturday, from noon to 5pm on Sunday. Admission fee is $4 for adults and $3 for students and seniors.

Buffalo and Erie County Historical Society, 25 Nottingham Ave. (tel. 716/873-9644), is a museum and research library documenting over 125 years of the Niagara Frontier history and heritage. Exhibits cover American Indians, the building of the Erie Canal, and the Pan-American Exhibition. The museum is housed in the only structure remaining from the 1901 Exposition, built of Vermont marble and inspired by the Parthenon. The historical society is open Tuesday through Saturday from 10am to 5pm and Sunday from noon to 5pm.

Buffalo Museum of Science, Humbolt Parkway (tel. 716/896-5200), features exhibits on anthropology, geology, zoology, astronomy, and botany. The **Kellogg Observatory** is great for the stargazer, and the dinosaur room will fascinate kids. The museum is open Tuesday through Sunday from 10am to 5pm. The admission is $3 for adults and $1.50 for children.

For the kid in all of us go to the zoo. **Buffalo Zoological Gardens** are situated in Delaware Park (tel. 716/837-3900) and are part of the original 1875 Frederick Law Olmsted design. The zoo contains sculptured landscapes and fascinating animal collections in both indoor and outdoor interpretive areas. Open all year from 10am to 5pm daily. Admission is $5 for adults and $3 for kids.

It's also possible to cruise around Lake Erie, taking in the sights of Buffalo from one of the **Miss Buffalo Cruise Boats.** Afternoon sightseeing cruises leave daily in July and August, and on weekends in June and September. The fare is $10 for adults and $7 for kids. On summer evenings additional cruises combine sightseeing with dinner, Dixieland, or "'50s to '60s." For sailing times and reservations, contact **Buffalo Charters, Inc.** (tel. 716/856-6696).

For a three-day Erie Canal cruise, contact **Mid-Lakes Navigation Co. Ltd.** (tel. 800/545-4318) for a trip between Buffalo and Syracuse on the cruise boat *Emita II.* This lazy jaunt on the Erie Canal includes bus transportation, all meals, and two nights in hotels for around $450 per person.

WHERE TO STAY IN BUFFALO

Staying here provides an opportunity to combine an exciting hotel experience with easy accessibility to both Niagara Falls and the charms of old Buffalo itself. That aforesaid "hotel experience" is **Hyatt Regency Buffalo,** Two Fountain Plaza (the corner of Main and West Huron Streets), Buffalo, NY 14202 (tel. 716/856-1234, or toll free 800/228-9000; fax 716/852-6157). The Hyatt occupies the 16-story Genesee Building, a brick-and-limestone office tower built in 1923 and converted to a hotel in 1984. It's a gorgeous place with an attached sun garden whose many levels are filled with fountains, potted trees, and restaurants. Rooms are particularly luxurious, with tall ceilings, buff and beige palettes, pleated shades, thick rugs, marble baths, padded headboards, cable color TVs, direct-dial phones, and deluxe-looking modern furniture. Standard double-room rates vary from about $99 to $145 nightly, which is a bargain for what you're getting. There are three restaurants on the premises, plus an indoor pool on a high floor with a great view, plus a health club plus the Genesee Sports Bar, accessible from the atrium lobby on Main Street via the Genesee Building's original marble-framed doorway. Parking is extra at a park/lock across the street. All major credit cards accepted.

Good value accommodations in luxurious surroundings can also be had at the **Buffalo Hilton,** 120 Church St., Buffalo, NY 14202 (tel. 716/845-5100; fax 716/845-5377). This cast-concrete behemoth at the edge of the downtown core wa built in 1980 and played an important early role in local redevelopment efforts. It's connected to an immense brick sports complex, which includes six indoor tennis courts. The lobby is a vast marble-floored atrium where buffet lunches are served amid ficus trees. Standard rooms have vaguely French provincial–looking furniture, marble-topped sinks, thick rugs, cable color TVs, and direct-dial phones; they cost mostly between $115 and $154 a night, double occupancy. Actually, 95% of available rooms are likely to be at the low end of that range, making this a superlative bargain. And guests also have the use of an indoor pool, plus the tennis, squash, and racquetball facilities next door. In addition to the Atrium, there is another pair of on-site restaurants, plus a couple of atmospheric hotel bars. All major credit cards accepted.

There's a new **Journey's End Suite Hotel** located in the center of the downtown Theater District at 601 Main St. (at the corner of Chippewa), Buffalo, NY 14203 (tel. 716/854-5500, or toll free 800/668-4200; fax 716/854-5500, ext. 103). Each of the 146 units is a comfortably furnished suite complete with a sofa bed in the living room, king-size beds in the bedroom, two TVs, a wet bar with coffeemaker and small refrigerator, two phones (free local calls!), and an attractive contemporary decor. All this costs about $60 on the weekend and a bit under $90 during the week, double occupancy. An excellent deal. All major credit cards accepted.

For something completely different, there's **Hotel Lenox,** 140 North St., Buffalo, NY 14201 (tel. 716/884-1700, or toll free 800/82-LENOX; fax 716/885-8636). This early 20th-century structure, in the heart of the historic district, is making its way back more by dint of charm than capital input. When I inquired about climate control, for example, the bellman quickly threw open the window. I later learned that air-conditioning units were available, even though I didn't actually see one. Some rooms are quite large, and some have nifty old-fashioned baths. The price per night ranges from a very reasonable $59 up to about $89; it's $8 extra for a room with a full kitchen. Lots of personality. All major credit cards accepted.

Sheraton Inn Buffalo Airport, 2040 Walden Ave. (exit 52E off I-90), Buffalo, NY 14225 (tel. 716/681-2400, or toll free 800/325-3535; fax 716/681-8067), is a theme hotel located adjacent to the new 1½ million square foot **Galleria Mall.** It boasts 300 deluxe Miami Beach–type rooms, most of which have balconies overlooking a lush tropical courtyard complete with gazebos and a pool. The courtyard is covered by an atrium roof in the winter and open to the sky above in good weather. The spacious guest rooms have queen-size beds, thick carpeting, AM/FM clock radios, and the usual TVs and phones. Complimentary coffee and wake-up calls in the morning, a dessert and cordial cart in the evening, plus nightly turndown service and a pass to the Preferred Travelers Club, are all included in the rates. Facilities include the Gazebo Bar, the Courtyard Deli, the Garden Park Café, and Twigs Lounge. Room rates range from $95 to $135 double. All major credit cards accepted.

Located in the eastern suburb of Clarence is a quaint inn called **Asa Ransom House,** 10529 Main St., Clarence, NY 14031 (tel. 716/759-2315). Innkeepers Robert and Judy Lenz have established a regional reputation both for their restaurant and for the charming overnight accommodations upstairs. The original house was built in 1853 and tastefully enlarged in 1975 to accommodate the new dining room. The restaurant has a cozy country feel to it with wood wainscoting, blue print curtains with white tassels, rush seated chairs, oil lamps on the tables, and exposed beams. The food is a Yankee/English collection of dishes like apple-cheddar chicken, steak-and-kidney pie, assorted vegetarian and light dishes, and filet mignon, priced from $10 to $20 à la carte. Dinner is available Sunday through Thursday from 4 to 8:30pm; lunch is served only on Wednesday, from 11:30am to 2:30pm. Each of the nine guest rooms has private bath and antique decorations; seven have fireplaces. Double-occupancy room rates are $90 and $145 nightly. The inn is closed completely on Friday and Saturday. MC, V, and DC accepted.

There are all sorts of other hotels in Buffalo, but these six make staying here a particular pleasure. A recommended budget alternative on the edge of the expressway loop that rings Buffalo is either of the two area **Red Roof Inns.** The first is adjacent to New York State Thruway Exit 49, Bowmansville, NY 14026 (tel. 716/633-1100 [fax, ext. 444] or toll free 800/843-7663). The second is at the Millersport Highway exit of I-290, which is a beltway through the northeast quadrant of greater Buffalo. Both interchanges are equally convenient for travelers heading either into Buffalo or north to Niagara Falls. They each have gaggles of motels located nearby. The Red Roofs belong to a chain I've recommended elsewhere. They are brand-new and very attractive, offering 109 rooms (the same at each location) each decorated with wall-to-wall carpeting, a table with chairs, a color TV, vinyl textured wallcoverings, and a direct-dial phone. There are no pools, no restaurants, and no fancy lobbies. But for $35 to $60 a night double, who's complaining? Mass production and volume marketing have served the Red Roof well—it's a great buy for the money. For a copy of the Red Roof Inns directory, write to them at 4355 Davidson Rd., Hilliard, OH 43026 (tel. 614/876-3200). All major credit cards accepted.

WHERE TO EAT IN BUFFALO

Here are a dozen or so suggestions culled from a long roster of good local places. In the downtown area, just west of the Convention Center, is **Café Jordan,** 166 Franklin St. (tel. 716/854-1955). Owner Don Woods is the star of numerous instruction videos produced by San Francisco's California Culinary Academy and titled "Cooking at the Academy." His Buffalo restaurant is light and airy, with bentwood chairs, potted plants, and french doors separating the tap room from the dining area. A "creative American" meal costs $6 to $8 for lunch and $14 to $22 for dinner. Lunch is served Tuesday to Friday from 11am to 3pm; dinner is served Wednesday to Saturday from 5 to 9:30pm. Major credit cards accepted.

Over on the pedestrian mall in the Theater District is **Bijou Grill,** 643 Main St. (tel. 716/847-1512). The grill has an art deco feel with neon clocks, hanging Saturn glass lamps, stage-set lighting, and salmon-and-turquoise color scheme. Nouvelle cuisine delights like Florentine burger, grilled souvlaki, quattro formaggio pizza, and spinach salad giambotta are priced from $4 to $6. The restaurant has a summer sidewalk café and is open from 11:30am to midnight Sunday through Thursday, to 2am on Friday and Saturday; Sunday brunch is served until 3pm. All major credit cards accepted.

Across the street next to Shea's Theater is **Beau Fleuve,** 150 Theater Place (tel. 716/855-3029), a quaint-looking northern Italian restaurant decorated with light-blue paisley wallpaper, a black-marble bar, and framed steel engravings depicting historic scenes of Buffalo and Niagara Falls. The cuisine has a California flair, and the wine list is extremely extensive. Lunch, served Monday to Friday between 11:30am and 3pm, typically costs between $4 and $7. Dinner is available daily from 5 to 10pm with the most expensive main courses priced at about $15. What's to eat? Things like marinated steak pita, voodoo pasta with shrimp, and scallops and Louisiana andouille sausage. All major credit cards accepted.

Lord Chumley's, located in the Allen Street area at 481 Delaware Ave., near Virginia Place (tel. 716/886-2220 or 716/884-8414) is probably the most architecturally opulent restaurant in upstate New York. Designed by an interior designer back in 1926, the restaurant's lush period rooms run the gamut from Regency to Louis XV. At lunch, there are burgers, open-face steak sandwiches, and the like for between $5 and $12; dinner main courses like angel-hair pasta with pesto and pinenuts and veal Oscar generally cost between $9 and $19. Open Monday through Thursday from 11:30am to 10:30pm, until 11pm on Friday and Saturday, and from 4 to 9:30pm on Sunday. All major credit cards accepted.

On the water at the downtown Seaway Piers Marina is **The Pier,** 325 Furhmann Blvd. (tel. 716/853-4000). This is a pretty big place, with a duplex dining room that seats 250 people, all of whom are guaranteed water views. Basically it's a steak, chicken, and fish place with a menu that lists $4 to $9 appetizers as "first a-pier-ance," $15 to $23 steaks as "here's steerin' at you," salads as "garden of eatin'," and desserts as "pier pressure." All major credit cards accepted.

Back in the Allen Street Historic District is a Mediterranean bistro called **Biac's,**

581 Delaware Ave. (tel. 716/884-6595). Housed in a 19th-century town house, Biac's serves lunch and dinner daily (no lunch on Sunday) in a collection of appealing brick-walled, wooden-floored rooms. Pizzas, pastas, salads, and focaccia sandwiches with smoked salmon or grilled tuna cost between $4 and $6.50 at lunch. During dinner, you can order chicken with artichokes, a French veal chop, or a small pizza for anywhere between $6 and $18. Lunch is served Monday through Saturday from 11:30am to 4pm; dinner runs Monday to Friday from 5:30 until 11pm, until 1am on Saturday; Sunday hours are 2 to 10pm. All major credit cards accepted.

The best French restaurant in town is **Rue Franklin**, 341 Franklin St. (tel. 716/852-4416), a quaint place with balloon curtains in the garden room (overlooking a small rock garden) and a full bar covered with marble. With over 75 choices of wine, the menu ranges from pheasant and duck foie gras pâté at $6.50 up to roast filet of lamb with stewed vegetables at $19.50. The restaurant serves dinner only on Tuesday through Saturday from 5:30 to 10pm; dessert is available until midnight. All major credit cards accepted.

My favorite lunch and light dinner spot is **Preservation Hall,** 752 Elmwood Ave. (tel. 716/884-4242). This vegetarian restaurant serves pita sandwiches, pasta and grain salads, fruit salads, hot and cold soups, and an endless array of daily specials. This very comfortable place, decorated with antiques, possesses a homey feeling. Since it's located not far from the park and zoo, you might try ordering a basket lunch and enjoying some of Frederick Law Olmsted's fine work. The standard menu items are from $3 to $4, with dinner specials from $5 to $6. MC and V accepted.

Crawdaddy's, 2 Templeton Terrace (tel. 716/856-9191), is a big new place out by the Erie Basin Marina, near the Sailors and Servicemen's Park. Pieces of driftwood and wooden pilings out front set a nautical mood. Inside are numerous atmospheric dining rooms decorated with acres of weathered barn siding, plush flowered rugs, paisley-upholstered booths, and Tiffany-style colored-glass shades. A lower-level bar has a sunken dance floor presided over by a screen showing rock videos. In the separate dining rooms you may well have a view of the marina and the skyline beyond. Lunch consists of club sandwiches, chef's salad, fruit plates, steak sandwiches, omelets, burgers, and broiled fish. The main courses cost about $6 to $9. At dinner you get a huge full meal with main courses like filet mignon, prime rib, pork tenderloin, seafood linguine, fresh brook trout, and lobster tails. And that will cost you anywhere from $13 to $25. Open for lunch Monday through Saturday from 11am to 3pm; dinner is Monday to Thursday from 4:30 to 11pm, until midnight Friday and Saturday; on Sunday they serve a brunch from 9:30am to 2:30pm, then dinner from 5 to 11pm. All major credit cards accepted.

Sports fans might want to know about **Pettibones Grille** (tel. 716/846-2100), the elegant restaurant atop the grandstands at Pilot Field Baseball Stadium. Pettibones, decorated with modern mahogany furniture, green-marble flooring, 10-foot arched windows surrounded by modern brass light fixtures, and huge silkscreen prints on the walls, is no mere sports bar. Lunch, served Monday through Friday from 11:30am to 3pm, features a great selection from the tuna salad melt (about $5) to an open-faced New York–strip steak sandwich (for about $8). Dinner is available Tuesday to Sunday from 4:30 to 8pm if there's a game; Tuesday to Saturday from 5 to 9pm if there isn't. The evening menu includes things like tortellini à la Bolognese and mixed grill, priced between $10 and $22 à la carte. A game ticket is required to eat at game time. All major credit cards accepted.

For great family southern Italian dining try **Chefs,** 291 Seneca St. (tel. 716/856-9187), a family-operated favorite that offers oversized helpings at moderate prices. Open Monday to Saturday from 11:45am to 9pm; the most expensive item on the menu is spaghetti and veal for $9. All major credit cards accepted.

Anchor Bar, 1047 Main St., at the corner of North (tel. 716/886-8920), is reputed to be where Buffalo-style chicken wings were invented. It's a very friendly family-style Italian restaurant, with a dimly lit bar full of regulars and a comfortable modern dining room adjacent. There are all sorts of special lunches, like the Greek salad, hot dog and a cup of soup, beef buckshots, vegetarian lasagne, plus omelets, sandwiches, meatballs, spaghetti, not forgetting the famous chicken wings (in strengths up to "suicidal if you're daring") for between about $4 and $6. At dinner you'll choose from chicken cacciatore, homemade ravioli, various pasta dishes, barbecued ribs, or chicken livers, plus many lunch items (not forgetting the famous chicken wings) for prices ranging from about $4 (at the sandwich end) to $14 (at the specialties-of-the-house end). Open daily for lunch from 10:30am to 3pm and for dinner from 3pm to 12:30am. All major credit cards accepted.

The Elmwood Avenue strip has lots of interesting places to eat, plus a collegiate/yuppie atmosphere that one encounters in certain parts of many cities these days. Two good places with lots of atmosphere and reasonably priced food (plenty of things between $5 and $10, cheaper at lunch) are **Cole's**, just south of Forest Avenue at 1104 Elmwood (tel. 716/886-1449), and **Jimmy Mac's** at 555 Elmwood on the corner of Anderson Street (tel. 716/886-9112). Both are open daily and serve food from 11am to 11pm.

A LITTLE NIGHTLIFE

Buffalo is a party town where the bars are open until 4am. I have personally seen traffic jams on the international bridges to Canada at 5am. These people haven't been out shopping either. The following is a short list of suggestions:

Marquee at the Traft, 100 Theatre Place (tel. 716/852-0522), offers live jazz, folk, and blues; typical showtime is 8pm. **Impaxx,** 652 S. Ogden St. (tel. 716/824-0752), books country, rock, and occasionally blues bands on Tuesday through Saturday.

Nietzsche's, 248 Allen St. (tel. 716/886-8539), features live rock, blues, and/or jazz every night. **Lafayette Tap Room,** 391 Washington St. (tel. 716/855-8800), is known for blues and rock bands. **The Continental,** 212 Franklin St. (tel. 716/842-1292), is for punk rock and heavy metal.

The Calumet Arts Café, 54 W. Chippewa St. (tel. 716/882-4537), presents all sorts of stuff and should definitely be checked out if you're planning a night on the town.

2. Niagara Falls, NY, and Canada

Oscar Wilde said he'd have been more impressed if the falls plunged uphill. Surely the drive through the dreary industrial outskirts of the city of Niagara Falls, NY, is not much encouragement. The falls themselves, however, are certainly impressive, and New York State's well-designed **Niagara Reservation State Park/Visitor Center** (tel. 726/278-1796) is worthy of a visit.

It should be noted from the outset that the best views of the falls, and by far the most appealing hotels and restaurants, all lie on the other side of the Niagara River in the better-positioned city of Niagara Falls, Canada. So why is Niagara Falls, NY, such a boom town? The answer to that is the aforementioned bilateral U.S.-Canadian Free Trade Agreement, which brings Canadians across the border in droves to shop for better priced and more lightly taxed consumer goods. It's hard to exaggerate the degree of this commerce; you have to see it to believe it. Whether such an artificial situation will continue to enrich Buffalo and Niagara Falls for any length of time is moot. For now business is, shall we say, better than just good.

There is a scenic route between Buffalo and Niagara Falls, but it entails leaving the United States via the Peace Bridge to Canada. I'd suggest you do exactly that and take the Niagara Parkway for the 20 miles between Fort Erie and Niagara Falls, Canada. Alternately, you can drive to Niagara Falls, NY (the two cities face each other on either side of the falls), via Interstate 90 north out of Buffalo. Take the first exit after the toll bridge that crosses the east branch of the Niagara River and get right onto the **Robert Moses Parkway.** This four-lane expressway, at the moment, leads right to the center of Niagara Falls, although other sections might be in service by the time

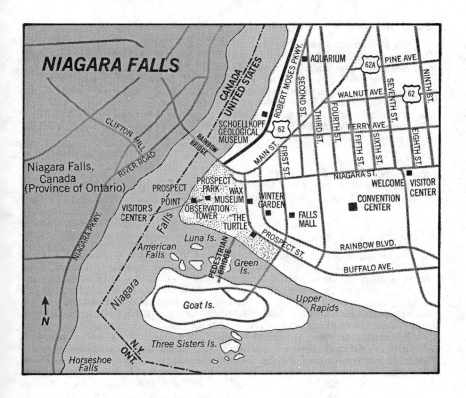

you read this. Even if they are, just follow the signs that say "Tourist Information and Convention Center."

For the tourist, the city is quite compact. Your first stop should be at the tourist information office. Look for the huge Quonset-hut roof of the modernistic **Convention Center.** This place does extra duty as a bus station too, and as a nesting place for innumerable birds.

A two-block-long pedestrian mall, **Falls Mall,** connects the Convention Center with the **Wintergarden.** This is a 10-story greenhouse that's angular in shape; totally glazed; supported by fat cement columns; and filled with exotic plantings, stone-bordered pools, full-size trees, and a restaurant. Niagara Falls has the same democratic atmosphere you'll find in places like Lake George Village, except that there's a real city attached. Built in 1978, the Wintergarden is the focus of Niagara Falls' annual winter **Festival of Light.** For 44 days, between the end of November and the first week in January, the city is decorated with millions of lights, the Convention Center is filled with animated displays, and the Wintergarden looks like an immense multicolored jewel. Many private businesses along the Convention Center/ Wintergarden axis join in the spirit. The effect, on a winter's night, is quite wondrous. Besides decorations, there's a daily schedule of free events and music in and around the Wintergarden, plus performances in the Convention Center by the likes of Bill Cosby and Judy Collins. A free daily calendar of events is available throughout the festival area during festival time.

Adjacent to the Convention Center, you will find the **Niagara Falls Convention and Visitors Bureau,** 345 Third St., Niagara Falls, NY 14303 (tel. 716/285-2400, or toll free 800/421-5223; fax 716/285-0809).

The falls themselves are only about as distant from the Wintergarden as the Wintergarden is from the Convention Center. The problem is, we Americans seem to be awkwardly positioned right on top of them, while our Canadian friends across the river have the fine unobstructed view. It's quite possible, let me hasten to say, to get great views of Niagara Falls from the American side. But it does take more doing.

In pursuit of the ideal view, plus general orientation, you might also try the new **Niagara Falls Official Information Center,** Fourth and Niagara Streets (tel. 716/284-2000), or **Niagara County Tourism,** 139 Niagara St., Lockport, NY 14094 (toll free 800/338-7890).

SEEING NIAGARA FALLS, NY

There are a number of worthy attractions in the vicinity of the falls themselves. But we'll start, of course, with the purpose of the trip.

The Falls

A bit of orientation first. The Niagara River is flowing northward at this point, and its course is not direct. There are two cities of Niagara Falls, one on the Canadian side of the river and one on the eastern, American, side. Because of vagaries in the course of the river, the falls are immediately adjacent to, and somehow on the same side of the river as, the American city. We've done all sorts of things to crane our collective neck over the edge for a better view. The most successful was the erection of the **Prospect Park Observation Tower,** which stands perhaps 100 feet away from the cliffs, thus permitting an excellent view of the falls.

Just as there are two cities called Niagara Falls, so there are two cataracts as well, with a bit of parkland called Goat Island in between. **Horseshoe Falls** (called also **Canadian Falls**) joins the Canadian city on one side and Goat Island on the other. It's shaped in a horseshoe curve, hence the name. **American Falls** are comparatively straight and join Goat Island on one end and the American city on the other. Goat Island is nearer to the American side, which is perhaps the reason it belongs to us.

The falls themselves, plus a certain amount of shoreline on both sides, are public parks. Niagara Falls State Park (created in 1885, and the first park of its kind at the time) is on our side, and Queen Elizabeth Park is on theirs. There's a considerable skyline on the Canadian side, obviously devoted to the resort industry. The American city is smaller because our hotels don't have views of the falls.

There's a simple, do-it-yourself sequence for seeing the best of the falls from the American side.

First: Take the car to **Goat Island.** The road over the bridge starts at the former Niagara Hotel, which is now Days Inn, on Rainbow Boulevard. From Goat Island you can see the river rapids as the water approaches the lip of the falls. There's parking at the upstream end, and a path to the **Three Sisters Islands,** mere rocks in the torrent hurtling toward the lip of the Horseshoe Falls.

Second: Drive the car to the lot ($3 charge) at the other end of the island, adjacent to the Top of the Falls cafeteria restaurant (tel. 716/285-3316). Then proceed on foot to the respective tops of **Horseshoe Falls** and **American Falls.** It's a pleasant and easy walk of only a few minutes' duration. All that thundering water is fairly intimidating. Everything's safe, of course, but it seems as if you could reach out and touch the water. There was a time when Goat Island and all the land along the shore was privately owned. High fences were erected and people paid for the right to squint through peepholes.

Third: Visit **Cave of the Winds,** if you're so inclined. An elevator on Goat Island will take you to within 25 feet of the foot of the American Falls. Admission is $4 for adults and $3 for kids. The loan of a thick yellow slicker comes with the deal.

Fourth: Drive the car back across the Goat Island Bridge and park in the Rainbow Shopping Center lot adjacent to the Wintergarden. At the end of the Falls Mall in line from the Convention Center through the middle of the Wintergarden, is the **Niagara Reservation Information Center** (tel. 716/278-1770) and the **Prospec**

Park Observation Tower. A footbridge (25¢ at the turnstile) connects the tower with the clifftop itself. It contains an elevator (free) that will take you either up or down. The upper-level observation decks belie the notion that there's no good view from the American side. The panorama is awesome, and it's also the best available on this side. At night you can admire colored lights trained on the thundering waters from the Canadian side, as well as the brilliantly lit hotels and amusement parks of Niagara Falls, Canada.

Fifth: Take the Prospect elevator down to the *Maid of the Mist* (office tel. 716/284-8897; dock phone 716/284-4233). This boat ride to the base of the falls is Niagara Falls' No. 1 tourist attraction, and has been since 1846. It's an exciting (albeit a wet) affair, consisting of being clad in a yellow slicker, crowded onto an open boat, and piloted apparently toward destruction until the boat turns around just short of the falls. The trip takes about half an hour, operates from mid-May to October, and costs about $7 for adults and half as much for kids. Niagara Falls often seems like a lion in a zoo—no longer dangerous. Being right at the base of it reminds us what it once was.

Sixth: Have a look at the new visitors center run by the Niagara Reservation State Park.

Seventh: Stroll the short distance from the Observation Tower to **Prospect Point,** where a ring of American flags commemorates the ordeal of the Iranian hostages. Here you can meditate on the surging white froth that spills over the adjacent top of the American Falls. Here, too, despite the coin-operated viewers, the lawn-bordered paths, and the nearby high-rises, one still has a sense of nature untrammeled. Interesting to note: If the respective local power companies together drew all the water they could out of the Niagara River, the falls would dry up.

Eighth: Take the **Rainbow Bridge** (tel. 416/354-6043) to Canada, where the view of the falls is significantly more spectacular and—that historically being so—the accommodations are of a higher standard. To cross into Canada, make sure you bring proof of American citizenship such as birth or baptismal certificate, voters registration card, state firearm permit, FAA or FCC license, draft card with birthplace, citizenship card, or papers. Should you be from a foreign country, have a passport available. To see the falls from Canada is well worth this paperwork, and the likelihood is that the authorities won't request any papers. For information on the Canadian side of Niagara Falls, contact the **Niagara Falls/Canada Visitors and Convention Bureau,** 4673 Ontario Ave., Suite 202, Niagara Falls, Ontario, L2E 3R1 (tel. 416/358-3221), or the **Ontario Travel Information Center,** 5355 Stanley Ave., Niagara Falls, Ontario, L2E 7C2 (tel. 416/356-6061). The trip to Canada is well worth it.

Niagara Falls is **illuminated** every night, all year long, at different times depending on the season. For scheduled hours, call the Convention and Visitors Bureau at 716/285-2400, or toll free 800/421-5223.

Niagara Power Project

Located a few minutes north of Niagara Falls at 5777 Lewiston Rd., in Lewiston (tel. 716/285-3211, ext. 6660), this is one of the largest electric power projects in the world. About 17% of all the electricity used in New York State is produced here. The water that turns the 13 immense waterwheels is drawn (carefully) from the river, upstream from the falls, then delivered here to the plant via 4 miles of underground tunnels. The **visitor center** consists of all sorts of play-with-'em displays, plus historical museums and a grand view of the Niagara Gorge. Open all year, and admission is free; call for exact hours.

Aquarium of Niagara Falls

Located just north of downtown at 701 Whirlpool St. (tel. 716/285-3575 or 716/692-2665), the aquarium is a major tourist attraction as well as an important research and educational facility. Here, for example, was where artificial seawater was developed. It's lots of fun. There are hourly trained-dolphin shows, plus all sorts of changing exhibits (on endangered species, different habitats in the sea, birds of prey). It's not too erudite but very enlightening. Open daily from 9am to 7pm (to 5pm in winter); admission is $6 for adults and $4 for kids.

Native American Center (The Turtle)

This unusual organization occupies quarters that are shaped like a giant turtle, a reference to Native American legends concerning the origin of the world. It's more of a center for Native American culture than a tourist attraction per se. But it's so interesting that visitors flock here. The central round body of the turtle is a big arena for dancing exhibitions, shows, and theatrical productions. Adjoining this are galleries devoted to Indian history, culture, and art, plus an excellent craft-cum-gift shop. Hours are 9am to 6pm daily summer and 9am to 5pm on Tuesday to Friday (noon to 5pm on Saturday and Sunday) in winter. Admission is $3 for adults, $2.50 for seniors, and $1.50 for kids.

Excursion to Artpark in Lewiston

About 7 miles north of Niagara Falls, on the banks of the Niagara River, is the village of **Lewiston.** This is a pleasant suburb with old stone and wood buildings facing a very wide main street, plus subdivisions in the background.

Every summer Lewiston hosts a sort of Saratoga West called **Artpark,** centered around a 2,400-seat auditorium at which ballet, musicals, concerts, children's theater, and symphony are staged. All manner of arts and crafts, offered for sale by the artists themselves, are available as well. For current or upcoming schedules, you can contact Artpark at P.O. Box 371, Lewiston, NY 14092 (tel. 716/754-9001).

Hungry in Lewiston? Try **Apple Granny,** 433 Center St. (tel. 716/754-8037), which is in an old historic-looking building in the middle of the village. There are a bar on one side and a family-style dining room on the other. The menu features ribs, sandwiches, burgers, seafood, and charbroiled chicken, plus late-night snacks, for about $5 to $13 in the main. Open daily from 11:30am until 1:30am. There's even dancing, nightly after 10pm. All major credit cards accepted.

Old Fort Niagara

Another 7 miles north of Lewiston is historic Old Fort Niagara. And if reconstructed forts with military reenactments, fife-and-drum corps, tent camps, archeological digs, and the lot are your cup of tea, here's another one. Old Fort Niagara overlooks Lake Ontario from the mouth of the Niagara River. It was enormously strategic in earlier centuries, and an ocean of French, British, Colonial, and Native American blood was shed in order to control it. The present buildings date from the early 18th century and are in a fine state of preservation. Open daily from 9am to 7:30pm all year; admission is $6 for adults, $5 for seniors, and $3.50 for kids between 6 and 12. In this age of uncertain state budgets, you'd better call for exact hours: Old Fort Niagara Assn., Inc., P.O. Box 169, Youngstown, NY 14174 (tel 716/745-7611).

WHERE TO STAY IN NIAGARA FALLS, NY

If I were to stay on the American side, my preference would be one of the luxurious new rooms and suites above my favorite restaurant in town, **The Red Coach Inn,** 2 Buffalo Ave., Niagara Falls, NY 14303 (tel. 716/282-1459; fax 716/282-2650). These accommodations are decorated with antique Victorian cherry furniture and Old English canopy beds; some of the suites have fireplaces, kitchens, an Jacuzzis. Prices range from $75 for individual rooms to $175 for the two-bedroom suites in high summer. All major credit cards accepted.

The most appealing full-service hotel in town is the **Radisson Hotel Niagara Falls,** Third and Old Falls, Niagara Falls, NY 14303 (tel. 716/285-3361; fax 716

285-3900). There are 400 rooms, contained in a modern brown-brick building with rounded edges. Inside you'll find the requisite complement of restaurants, bars, and lounges, plus an indoor pool. Accommodations have color TVs, plus furniture and lots of space, and cost between $89 to $99 nightly for a double in summer (mid-May to mid-September) and about $52 to $62 in winter. The hotel is connected to the Convention Center and to the huge ultramodern Rainbow Shopping Mall by an all-weather walkway. All major credit cards accepted.

The classic standby with the best American views of the falls is the former Niagara Hotel, now called **Niagara Falls–Days Inn,** 201 Rainbow Blvd., Niagara Falls, NY 14303 (tel. 716/285-9321). With the exception of the marquee, this landmark hotel is still recognizable with its grand lobby, notable mezzanine, dining room, and ballroom. If the building and lobby were really restored, it would put American side accommodations back in style and revitalize the tradition of honeymooning at the falls. For those of you who experienced the Niagara Hotel in its heyday, I'm sure the memories and the fact that it still stands will at least be reassuring. The rooms have been redecorated with modern mauve and gray furniture. The White Parrot cocktail lounge has an all-new sound and light system, with a DJ on weekends. The Portofino Restaurant serves from 6:30am to 10pm. The double-occupancy room rates are $49 to $99 from June to September and $39 the rest of the year. All major credit cards accepted.

All the chains are in town, and they all offer essentially the same good motel-quality accommodations at similar prices. **Holiday Inn,** 114 Buffalo Ave., Niagara Falls, NY 14303 (tel. 716/285-2521); **Quality Inn,** 443 Main St., Niagara Falls, NY 14303 (tel. 716/284-8801); and **Ramada Inn,** 401 Buffalo Ave., Niagara Falls, NY 14303 (tel. 716/285-2541), all have pools. **Howard Johnson Motor Lodge Downtown,** 454 Main St., Niagara Falls, NY 14303 (tel. 716/285-5261); and **TraveLodge,** 200 Rainbow Blvd., Niagara Falls, NY 14303 (tel. 716/285-7316), do not. Room rates collectively are higher in summer and range from about $65 to $110 or so for two persons. All take all major credit cards.

Double rooms at **Best Western Red Jacket Inn,** five Moses-expressway minutes east of the Convention Center at 7001 Buffalo Ave., Niagara Falls, NY 14303 (tel. 716/283-7612; fax 716/283-7631), are as nice as many of those in town, and a bit cheaper. This place has a nice big outdoor pool overlooking the I-190 toll bridge across the Niagara River, plus a bar and a reasonably priced restaurant. From mid-May until the end of September, doubles cost $99 to $109 nightly; the rest of the year, you'll pay $72 to $78 for the same room.

For something different, investigate a bed-and-breakfast through **Rainbow Hospitality,** 466 Amherst St., Buffalo, NY 14207 (tel. 716/874-8787).

WHERE TO EAT IN NIAGARA FALLS, NY

Starting at the top, there's **Red Coach Inn,** next to the Turtle at 2 Buffalo Ave. (tel. 716/282-1459). This is a 1920s Tudor building with leaded windows, iron chandeliers, stone fireplaces, oak tables, comfortable armchairs, and costumed waiters and waitresses. Lunch consists of omelets; salads; and main courses like London broil, baked scrod, fish and chips, and eggs Benedict. The cost for most of these is between $5 and $9. At dinner you can choose from prime rib, broiled haddock, crisp glazed duckling, and chopped tenderloin, to name only a few, priced from $10 to $20. In summer, open Monday to Thursday for lunch from 11:30am to 4pm and for dinner from 4 to 10pm (until 11pm on Friday and Saturday and only for dinner from 5 to 9pm on Sunday). Winter hours are a little shorter. All major credit cards accepted.

The Como, 2220 Pine Ave., near 22nd Street (tel. 716/285-9341), is a local Italian restaurant with thick rugs, mirrored walls, Mediterranean stucco arches, white cloths, and huge portions. Almost every pasta, veal, and chicken dish imaginable is available, plus low-priced luncheon specials, meatball sandwiches, and traditional selections like lamb chops, roast beef, and Porterhouse steak. Typical lunch selections cost about $5; at dinner the range is from about $6 to $14. Open on Monday through Saturday for lunch from 11:30am to 2:30pm and for dinner on Monday to Thursday from 2:30pm until midnight (to 1am on Friday and Saturday); Sunday hours are noon to midnight. All major credit cards accepted.

Last, but not least, is a combination restaurant/country-western nightclub called **Dallas Alley,** 3004 Niagara St., at 30th Street (tel. 716/282-9498). The restaurant consists of a multilevel dining room decorated with mooseheads, artificial hanging plants, quilted tablecloths, and an overall atmospheric clutter. The adjoining bar is dim and glittery. The restaurant serves full dinners only, chosen from a menu featuring grilled meats and seafood, for about $5 to $14. Open Monday to Saturday from 4 to 10pm (from 2pm on Sunday); live music every weekend until 3am. All major credit cards accepted.

SEEING NIAGARA FALLS, CANADA

To see Niagara Falls properly, you must cross the Rainbow Bridge to the Canadian side. From this vantage point, on the north side of the Niagara River, the falls are an awesome and memorable spectacle. The Canadian riverfront, in total contrast to that on the American side, has always been controlled by a **Niagara Parks Commission.** As such it has been historically groomed and protected with public (not private) interests in mind. The result is a manicured park, 35 miles in length, running from Fort Erie to Niagara-on-the-Lake and encompassing some 3,100 acres, the Niagara Parkway, bike trails, walking paths, and the beautiful 154-acre Queen Victoria Park that overlooks the falls themselves.

The **Niagara Parks Commission,** P.O. Box 150, Niagara Falls, Ontario, L2E 6T2 (tel. 416/356-2241), is a totally self-sustaining entity that obtains revenues from its own restaurants, souvenir shops, golf courses, marina, campgrounds, botanical gardens, greenhouses, and tourist attractions like Table Rock Scenic Tunnel and the Niagara Spanish Aero Car.

This splendid park system admittedly is flanked in places (specifically along Clifton Hill) by a circuslike midway with garish halls of horror, museums of the unmentionable, and myriad T-shirt and souvenir shops more typical of the American side. The Canadian park also lacks the sort of sophisticated visitors center that is increasingly a hallmark of American parks, including Niagara Falls. Helpful information booths are set up each summer, and approximately 2 miles from the falls is the **Niagara Falls Canadian Visitor & Convention Bureau,** 4673 Ontario Ave., Suite 202, Niagara Falls, Ontario, L2E 3R1 (tel. 416/356-6061). Another option for information is the **Niagara Parks Commission,** P.O. Box 150, Niagara Falls, Ontario, L2E 6T2 (tel. 416/356-2241, or toll free 800/263-2558), which hopes to establish a visitors center in the falls area at some point in the future.

Just standing on the balustraded riverbank and gazing at the unobstructed panorama of thundering water is enough for most visitors. You can do that one better, however, via a hair-raising helicopter ride right over the falls themselves. During my last visit, a Frenchman professed that visiting Niagara without going up in a helicopter was "like going to Paris without seeing the Eiffel Tower."

Well, I "flew the falls" and lived to tell about it, thanks to **Niagara Helicopters Limited,** 3731 Victoria Ave., Niagara Falls, Ontario, L2E 6V5 (tel. 416/357-5672). This was a thrill I'll never forget. Our party boarded a four-passenger jet ranger, the smallest in their fleet, put on headphones for a recorded narration, and roared off toward the whirlpool. Then it was up the rapids to the Rainbow Bridge, over Queen Victoria Park, until we arrived directly above the Horseshoe and American Falls. Here we circled in ever decreasing concentric rings while I took pictures and the helicopter banked completely on its side.

What a show! Blue sky, brilliant sunshine, gorgeous rainbows, incredible perspective on the falls, giddying levels of adrenalin pumping through my system; it was worth every penny of the $96 U.S. per couple for the 15-minute ride. Children under 11, should they dare to come along, are charged a mere $15. Flights depart daily from 9am to dusk, weather permitting. All major credit cards accepted.

Canada's Niagara Park Commission also owns and operates a number of note worthy attractions. The first of these is the **Table Rock Scenic Tunnel,** which takes you down 125 feet behind Horseshoe Falls to an observation deck where you can practically reach out of your protective slicker and touch the tonnage of falling water. There are 650 feet of tunnels down here, including an additional observation platform midway down the side. The tunnels are open from 9am until dusk and cost $5.50 for adults and $2.25 for kids.

The elevator at the **Great Gorge Adventure,** located just below the Whirlpool Rapids Bridge, brings you to the very edge of the treacherous Whirlpool Rapids. A scenic interpretive trail will tell you all about the geological history of the area and the daredevils who risked their lives trying to conquer the rapids of the lower Niagara gorge. Great Gorge Adventure is open daily from 9am to dusk and charges $4.50 for adults and $2 for children.

The **Niagara Spanish Aero Car** is a cable-car ride with an unparalleled view of the swirling waters of the whirlpool. The car travels across the Niagara River between two points in Canada. You get off in the middle, marvel at the whirlpool, get back on, and return. It's open daily from 9am until dusk; the admission is $5 for adults and $2.50 for kids.

Money Tips

For best-value money exchange, use the **duty-free shops** at either end of the Rainbow Bridge or the **exchange locations administered by the Niagara Parks Commission.** The banks in Niagara Falls, NY, and the private exchange booths on the Canadian side will scalp from 2% to 4% of the exchange rate each way (that's a total loss of 4% to 8% on every converted American dollar). You should also check with your credit card company and be sure your Canadian charges are posted at correct American dollar market rates. Be certain that your American dollar purchases at Canadian Niagara Parks Commission restaurants and shops are calculated at correct market exchange rates too.

Be advised that at 7% Canadian Goods and Services Tax (GST) and an 8% Provincial Services Tax (PST) are both applicable to all purchases in Canada. *But,* both taxes are *refundable to nonresidents!* Get receipts and save them. The refunds do not apply to meals, gas, tobacco, or alcoholic beverages, but the 7% GST on total receipts over $100 (including hotel rooms) will be refunded immediately at any duty-free shop, where applications can also be obtained for mail-in refunds for the 8% PST. If you have questions about any of this, call the **Visitors Rebate Program** in Canada, at toll free 800/66VISIT, or in the States call 613/991-3346.

WHERE TO STAY & EAT IN NIAGARA FALLS, CANADA

The newest and most spectacular hotel in town is the 20-story **Sheraton Fallsview Hotel,** 6755 Oakes Dr., Niagara Falls, Ontario, L2G 3W7 (tel. 416/374-1077, or toll free 800/325-3535; fax 416/374-6224). This glass-walled establishment is atop a bluff, meaning that the majority of its oversized rooms have extraordinary direct views of Horseshoe Falls. You'll feel as if you're right on top of the water, even from the whirlpool tubs in the baths. Even the hallways by the elevator banks have astonishing views. This well-organized complex features rooms with terraces; an indoor pool with a whirlpool and sauna; an exercise room; a gourmet restaurant called (not surprisingly) the Fallsview; an informal bistro dubbed La Piazza; and Stanley's Lounge, which is a lot of fun. Between late June and late September, double-occupancy room prices run from $175 to $230 (to $350 for suites); the rest of the year, expect about a $60-per-unit reduction. All major credit cards accepted.

I've always had a weakness for grand old hotels, and that is an apt description of **Skyline Brock Hotel,** 5685 Falls Ave., Niagara Falls, Ontario, 12E 6W7 (tel. 416/374-4444, or toll free 800/263-7135; fax 416/357-9550). Built in 1929 of dressed white limestone, it has 12 stories overlooking the falls, Oaks Gardens, and Rainbow Bridge. Notable guests have included everyone from Elizabeth II and the Duke of Edinburgh (before her coronation) to Marilyn Monroe. The lobby—with sweeping, dual brown-marble stairways and crystal chandeliers—connects stylish street-level shops with an elegant lounge and ballroom. In warm weather, guests have the use of the rooftop pool at the adjacent Skyline Foxhead Hotel. On the ninth floor of the Brock is the handsome Rainbow Dining Room with unobstructed views of the falls. Rooms are priced according to view and season: From late May to late September, expect to pay somewhere between $99 and $169; those rates fall to between $59 and $129 during the rest of the year. All major credit cards accepted.

Adjacent to the Brock is its more modern sister hotel, the **Skyline Foxhead Hotel,** 5875 Falls Ave., Niagara Falls, Ontario, L2E 6W7 (tel. 416/357-3090, or toll free 800/648-7200; fax 416/357-9550). Built in the 1960s, this 14-story, 395-room establishment has balconies on the falls side and larger rooms than the Brock. However, it lacks the older building's character. The lobby has been redone in light buff marble and is flanked with street-level retail shops. Facilities include the Penthouse Restaurant and Lounge and the aforementioned rooftop pool with its spectacular views of the falls and city. The room rates depend on the view and range from $79 to $155 in late October through late May, rising to between $125 and $190 during summer. All major credit cards accepted.

Closer to the falls, but without a view, is a combination hotel/restaurant called **Old Stone Inn,** 5425 Robinson St., Niagara Falls, Ontario, 62G 7L6 (tel. 416/357-1234, or toll free 800/663-1144). This former 1904 flour mill has been redesigned into a cozy, countrified restaurant with an alpinelike three-story addition containing 114 upscale rooms. There are an atrium area with health club, sauna, and whirlpool; a heated outdoor pool; a stone-walled lounge called the Rendez-Vous; plus a lobby with a large fireplace, leather wingchairs, and a handsome men's-club atmosphere. Located in the stone section of the complex is **The Millers Bistro** dining room with its wood-burning fireplace, brass chandeliers, wine racks, bookcases, and cathedral-style ceilings. The menu here is prepared by European-trained chefs, and dinners are accompanied by a resident harpist. Lunch is served from 11:30am to 2:30pm on Monday through Saturday and costs between $3 and $10 for salads to the teriyaki steak. Dinners are served between 5 and 10pm on Sunday through Thursday, until 11pm on Friday and Saturday. Expect to pay about $13 to $20 per à la carte main course. Between May and mid-September, a room at the inn will cost $120 for a double; expect to pay from $55 to $85 the rest of the year.

Over near city hall, about two blocks from the Whirlpool Rapids Bridge, is a gourmet Chinese restaurant called **Jasmine Garden,** 4624 Erie Ave. (tel. 416/354-1291). Housed in a two-story 1880s commercial brick building, Jasmine Garden specializes in Cantonese/Szechuan cooking and is both a local favorite and a major destination for Americans from the other side of the river. There are two dining areas: the Garden Room with its planted atrium as well as the old storefront area with rose-and-white linen tablecloths, black-lacquer chairs, and shell screens. On Friday, Saturday, and holiday evenings, there is an ornate buffet, complete with sugar sculptures, a 20-pound white-chocolate goat (the year of our research was the year of the goat), a vast array of food, and a decadent dessert display—all offered for $13.28 per person. Lunch is served Monday through Friday between 11:30am and 2:30pm; the excellent $5 lunch special changes daily. Dinner is available every night from 5pm to 10pm; dishes cost between $7 and $19. All major credit cards accepted.

Located in the Maple Leaf Village next to Brock Skyline Hotel is **Shaboom 50's Restaurant and Night Club,** on the third level of 5785 Falls Ave. (tel. 416/354-3838). This 1950s-theme restaurant/diner was inspired by the Crew Cuts' 1954 hit, "Sha-Boom." The walls of the double-height dining room are practically encrusted with memorabilia, including Technicolor posters for *Jail House Rock, The Attack of the 50-Foot Woman,* and, of course, *Niagara,* starring Marilyn Monroe. The bar is decorated with the front end of a 1965 Chevy (complete with painted flames), which appears to have crashed through the brick wall, pinning a roller-skating waitress mannequin to the floor beneath it. The soda bar offers period-piece shakes, floats, and sodas, as well as the liquor, beer, or wine of your choice. As to the "cuisine," there's "The Hand Jive," "My Only Sin," "Rebel Without a Cause," and such, all of which are standard diner fare. Prices are reasonable ($2 to $16, the latter for a steak called "Ben Cartwright Cut"); the kitchen is open daily from 11:30am to midnight; dancing with a disc jockey starts at 9pm. All major credit cards accepted.

3. Chautauqua

About 65 miles southwest of Buffalo is the lakeside village of Chautauqua (pop. 4,600), famous since 1874 as the home of the **Chautauqua Institution.** Dedicated to the pursuit of culture and the arts, Chautauqua sent bands of performers and artists into rural America throughout the late 19th and early 20th centuries. As a result, the word *chautauqua* came to mean a summer series of lectures, concerts, or performances.

But the institution's focus was ever on the village itself, where every July and August there is a full schedule of lectures on pertinent topics, instruction in arts and languages, concerts, opera, and other musical performances. A typical season might include appearances by the likes of Jeb Magruder, Dinah Shore, Albert Shanker, and Neil Sedaka. In addition to the rich cultural fare, the village offers sailing and swimming on Chautauqua Lake, golf, tennis, instruction in dance, music, or theater, plus the pleasure of being in a near idyllic village setting.

Cars are restricted in Chautauqua, which is filled with leafy trees, narrow streets, and delightful Victorian buildings. Although it's a real village, complete with hotels, restaurants, a post office, shops, and all the expected services, it's also a preserve with a gate that bars all but holders of valid passes. These are available on a daily basis at the gate for between $10 and $20 for adults. The price depends on the day of the week you come and on who's appearing that night (the pass entitles you to attend whatever's scheduled).

Although it is possible to visit Chautauqua for a day trip, most people plan longer stays. All manner of packages—from "Weekend Getaways," to periods of seven nights or longer—are available. They include passes plus accommodations in all price categories. The hotels are overwhelmingly Victorian and good-looking and range from the deluxe **Athenaeum** (tel. 716/357-4444), which charges $120 per person and up, including all meals, to an array of inns and guesthouses where two can stay for $250 a week or less.

You can request full particulars of current or upcoming seasons by writing to the Chautauqua Institution, Chautauqua, NY 14722 (tel. 716/357-6200, or toll free, 800/836-ARTS). "Certainly the best 'Whole Package' you'll find anywhere," says *Smithsonian* magazine. "An unusual blend of intellectual stimulation and summertime fun," adds *The New York Times.* And it's one of the ornaments of New York State, add I.

THE ROAD BACK TO BUFFALO

Between May and September, a 100-foot-long reproduction sternwheeler called **Chautauqua Belle** plies the waters of Chautauqua Lake on a daily basis, weather permitting. She docks near Route 394 in Mayville (tel. 716/753-2403), which is just a few miles north of Chautauqua. Departure times are 11am, 1:15pm, and 3pm daily, and the fare is $12 for adults and $6 for children under 12.

If you resist the temptations of *Chautauqua Belle,* you may instead succumb to those of **William Seward Inn,** S. Portage Road, Westfield, NY 14787 (tel. 716/346-4151). Westfield (pop. 3,400) is on the shore of Lake Erie about 6 miles from Mayville. The Greek Revival inn sits atop a knoll with a fine prospect of the surrounding area. It was once the country home of William Seward, U.S. Senator and Secretary of State under Presidents Lincoln and Andrew Johnson. Seward is best remembered as the most passionate proponent of the purchase of Alaska, once dubbed "Seward's Folly." He is less well known for having survived a vicious knife attack by a co-conspirator of John Wilkes Booth in the theater where Lincoln was assassinated. Today his upstate New York country home offers travelers the choice of 14 antique-filled rooms, all with private baths, plus another 4 in the nearby carriage house. Double-occupancy overnight rates include a full gourmet breakfast and run from $80 to $125; a five-course dinner is available to inn guests only on Thursday through Sunday at 7pm. The cost is $36 per person; bring your own wine. All major credit cards accepted.

About 16 miles northeast of Westfield on scenic Route 20 is the town of Fredonia (pop. 11,100). **The White Inn,** 52 Main St., Fredonia, NY 14063 (tel. 716/672-2103; fax 716/672-2107), is a white-pillared mansion with a 100-foot veranda overlooking Main Street. It offers 13 bedrooms and 10 suites, all with a private bath, a phone, air conditioning, and antique or period reproduction furniture. A full breakfast is included in the room rates, which top out at $149 a night. Downstairs are a cozy pub with an atmospheric fireplace as well as a busy restaurant that serves lunch and dinner. Major credit cards accepted.

INDEX

GENERAL INFORMATION

DESTINATIONS

Now Save Money on All Your Travels by Joining
FROMMER'S ™ TRAVEL BOOK CLUB
The World's Best Travel Guides at Membership Prices

FROMMER'S TRAVEL BOOK CLUB is your ticket to successful travel! Open up a world of travel information and simplify your travel planning when you join ranks with thousands of value-conscious travelers who are members of the FROMMER'S TRAVEL BOOK CLUB. Join today and you'll be entitled to all the privileges that come from belonging to the club that offers you travel guides for less to more than 100 destinations worldwide. Annual membership is only $25 (U.S.) or $35 (Canada and foreign).

The Advantages of Membership

1. Your choice of three FREE travel guides. You can select any **two** FROMMER'S COMPREHENSIVE GUIDES, FROMMER'S $-A-DAY GUIDES, *or* FROMMER'S FAMILY GUIDES—plus **one** FROMMER'S CITY GUIDE *or* FROMMER'S CITY $-A-DAY GUIDE.
2. Your own subscription to **TRIPS AND TRAVEL** quarterly newsletter.
3. You're entitled to a **30% discount** on your order of any additional books offered by FROMMER'S TRAVEL BOOK CLUB.
4. You're offered (at a small additional fee of $6.50) our **Domestic Trip-Routing Kits.**

Our quarterly newsletter **TRIPS AND TRAVEL** offers practical information on the best buys in travel, the "hottest" vacation spots, the latest travel trends, world-class events and much, much more.

Our **Domestic Trip-Routing Kits** are available for any North American destination. We'll send you a detailed map highlighting the best route to take to your destination—you can request direct or scenic routes.

Here's all you have to do to join:

Send in your membership fee of $25 ($35 Canada and foreign) with your name and address on the form below along with your selections as part of your membership package to **FROMMER'S TRAVEL BOOK CLUB, P.O. Box 473, Mt. Morris, IL 61054-0473.** Remember to select any **two** FROMMER'S COMPREHENSIVE GUIDES, FROMMER'S $-A-DAY GUIDES, *or* FROMMER'S FAMILY GUIDES—plus **one** FROMMER'S CITY GUIDE *or* FROMMER'S CITY $-A-DAY GUIDE.

If you would like to order additional books, please select the books you would like and send a check for the total amount (please add sales tax in the states noted below), plus $2 per book for shipping and handling ($3 per book for all foreign orders) to:

FROMMER'S TRAVEL BOOK CLUB
P.O. Box 473
Mt. Morris, IL 61054-0473
(815) 734-1104

[ ] **YES.** I want to take advantage of this opportunity to join FROMMER'S TRAVEL BOOK CLUB.
[ ] **My check is enclosed.** Dollar amount enclosed_____*

Name_____
Address_____
City_____ State_____ Zip_____

To ensure that all orders are processed efficiently, please apply sales tax in the following areas: CA, CT, FL, IL, NJ, NY, TN, WA and CANADA.

*With membership, shipping and handling will be paid by FROMMER'S TRAVEL BOOK CLUB for the three free books you select as part of your membership. Please add $2 per book for shipping and handling for any additional books purchased ($3 per book for foreign orders).

Allow 4–6 weeks for delivery. Prices of books, membership fee, and publication dates are subject to change without notice.

Please Send Me the Books Checked Below:

FROMMER'S COMPREHENSIVE GUIDES
(Guides listing facilities from budget to deluxe,
with emphasis on the medium-priced)

	Retail Price	Code		Retail Price	Code
☐ Acapulco/Ixtapa/Taxco 1993–94	$15.00	C120	☐ Jamaica/Barbados 1993–94	$15.00	C105
☐ Alaska 1994–95	$17.00	C130	☐ Japan 1992–93	$19.00	C020
☐ Arizona 1993–94	$18.00	C101	☐ Morocco 1992–93	$18.00	C021
☐ Australia 1992–93	$18.00	C002	☐ Nepal 1994–95	$18.00	C126
☐ Austria 1993–94	$19.00	C119	☐ New England 1993	$17.00	C114
☐ Belgium/Holland/ Luxembourg 1993–94	$18.00	C106	☐ New Mexico 1993–94	$15.00	C117
☐ Bahamas 1994–95	$17.00	C121	☐ New York State 1994–95	$19.00	C132
☐ Bermuda 1994–95	$15.00	C122	☐ Northwest 1991–92	$17.00	C026
☐ Brazil 1993–94	$20.00	C111	☐ Portugal 1992–93	$16.00	C027
☐ California 1993	$18.00	C112	☐ Puerto Rico 1993–94	$15.00	C103
☐ Canada 1992–93	$18.00	C009	☐ Puerto Vallarta/Manzanillo/ Guadalajara 1992–93	$14.00	C028
☐ Caribbean 1994	$18.00	C123	☐ Scandinavia 1993–94	$19.00	C118
☐ Carolinas/Georgia 1994–95	$17.00	C128	☐ Scotland 1992–93	$16.00	C040
☐ Colorado 1993–94	$16.00	C100	☐ Skiing Europe 1989–90	$15.00	C030
☐ Cruises 1993–94	$19.00	C107	☐ South Pacific 1992–93	$20.00	C031
☐ DE/MD/PA & NJ Shore 1992–93	$19.00	C012	☐ Spain 1993–94	$19.00	C115
☐ Egypt 1990–91	$17.00	C013	☐ Switzerland/Liechtenstein 1992–93	$19.00	C032
☐ England 1994	$18.00	C129	☐ Thailand 1992–93	$20.00	C033
☐ Florida 1994	$18.00	C124	☐ U.S.A. 1993–94	$19.00	C116
☐ France 1994–95	$20.00	C131	☐ Virgin Islands 1994–95	$13.00	C127
☐ Germany 1994	$19.00	C125	☐ Virginia 1992–93	$14.00	C037
☐ Italy 1994	$19.00	C130	☐ Yucatán 1993–94	$18.00	C110

FROMMER'S $-A-DAY GUIDES
(Guides to low-cost tourist accommodations and facilities)

	Retail Price	Code		Retail Price	Code
☐ Australia on $45 1993–94	$18.00	D102	☐ Mexico on $45 1994	$19.00	D116
☐ Costa Rica/Guatemala/ Belize on $35 1993–94	$17.00	D108	☐ New York on $70 1992–93	$16.00	D016
☐ Eastern Europe on $30 1993–94	$18.00	D110	☐ New Zealand on $45 1993–94	$18.00	D103
☐ England on $60 1994	$18.00	D112	☐ Scotland/Wales on $50 1992–93	$18.00	D019
☐ Europe on $50 1994	$19.00	D115	☐ South America on $40 1993–94	$19.00	D109
☐ Greece on $45 1993–94	$19.00	D100	☐ Turkey on $40 1992–93	$22.00	D023
☐ Hawaii on $75 1994	$19.00	D113	☐ Washington, D.C. on $40 1992–93	$17.00	D024
☐ India on $40 1992–93	$20.00	D010			
☐ Ireland on $40 1992–93	$17.00	D011			
☐ Israel on $45 1993–94	$18.00	D101			

FROMMER'S CITY $-A-DAY GUIDES
(Pocket-size guides with an emphasis on low-cost tourist accommodations and facilities)

	Retail Price	Code		Retail Price	Code
☐ Berlin on $40 1994–95	$12.00	D111	☐ Madrid on $50 1992–93	$13.00	D014
☐ Copenhagen on $50 1992–93	$12.00	D003	☐ Paris on $45 1994–95	$12.00	D117
☐ London on $45 1994–95	$12.00	D114	☐ Stockholm on $50 1992–93	$13.00	D022

FROMMER'S WALKING TOURS
(With routes and detailed maps, these companion guides point out
the places and pleasures that make a city unique)

	Retail Price	Code		Retail Price	Code
☐ Berlin	$12.00	W100	☐ Paris	$12.00	W103
☐ London	$12.00	W101	☐ San Francisco	$12.00	W104
☐ New York	$12.00	W102	☐ Washington, D.C.	$12.00	W105

FROMMER'S TOURING GUIDES
(Color-illustrated guides that include walking tours, cultural and historic
sites, and practical information)

	Retail Price	Code		Retail Price	Code
☐ Amsterdam	$11.00	T001	☐ New York	$11.00	T008
☐ Barcelona	$14.00	T015	☐ Rome	$11.00	T010
☐ Brazil	$11.00	T003	☐ Scotland	$10.00	T011
☐ Florence	$ 9.00	T005	☐ Sicily	$15.00	T017
☐ Hong Kong/Singapore/			☐ Tokyo	$15.00	T016
Macau	$11.00	T006	☐ Turkey	$11.00	T013
☐ Kenya	$14.00	T018	☐ Venice	$ 9.00	T014
☐ London	$13.00	T007			

FROMMER'S FAMILY GUIDES

	Retail Price	Code		Retail Price	Code
☐ California with Kids	$18.00	F100	☐ San Francisco with Kids	$17.00	F004
☐ Los Angeles with Kids	$17.00	F002	☐ Washington, D.C. with Kids	$17.00	F005
☐ New York City with Kids	$18.00	F003			

FROMMER'S CITY GUIDES
(Pocket-size guides to sightseeing and tourist accommodations and
facilities in all price ranges)

	Retail Price	Code		Retail Price	Code
☐ Amsterdam 1993–94	$13.00	S110	☐ Montreál/Québec		
☐ Athens 1993–94	$13.00	S114	City 1993–94	$13.00	S125
☐ Atlanta 1993–94	$13.00	S112	☐ New Orleans 1993–94	$13.00	S103
☐ Atlantic City/Cape			☐ New York 1993	$13.00	S120
May 1993–94	$13.00	S130	☐ Orlando 1994	$13.00	S135
☐ Bangkok 1992–93	$13.00	S005	☐ Paris 1993–94	$13.00	S109
☐ Barcelona/Majorca/			☐ Philadelphia 1993–94	$13.00	S113
Minorca/Ibiza 1993–94	$13.00	S115	☐ Rio 1991–92	$ 9.00	S029
☐ Berlin 1993–94	$13.00	S116	☐ Rome 1993–94	$13.00	S111
☐ Boston 1993–94	$13.00	S117	☐ Salt Lake City 1991–92	$ 9.00	S031
☐ Cancún/Cozumel 1991–			☐ San Diego 1993–94	$13.00	S107
92	$ 9.00	S010	☐ San Francisco 1994	$13.00	S133
☐ Chicago 1993–94	$13.00	S122	☐ Santa Fe/Taos/		
☐ Denver/Boulder/Colorado			Albuquerque 1993–94	$13.00	S108
Springs 1993–94	$13.00	S131	☐ Seattle/Portland 1992–93	$12.00	S035
☐ Dublin 1993–94	$13.00	S128	☐ St. Louis/Kansas		
☐ Hawaii 1992	$12.00	S014	City 1993–94	$13.00	S127
☐ Hong Kong 1992–93	$12.00	S015	☐ Sydney 1993–94	$13.00	S129
☐ Honolulu/Oahu 1994	$13.00	S134	☐ Tampa/St.		
☐ Las Vegas 1993–94	$13.00	S121	Petersburg 1993–94	$13.00	S105
☐ London 1994	$13.00	S132	☐ Tokyo 1992–93	$13.00	S039
☐ Los Angeles 1993–94	$13.00	S123	☐ Toronto 1993–94	$13.00	S126
☐ Madrid/Costa del			☐ Vancouver/Victoria 1990–		
Sol 1993–94	$13.00	S124	91	$ 8.00	S041
☐ Miami 1993–94	$13.00	S118	☐ Washington, D.C. 1993	$13.00	S102
☐ Minneapolis/St.					
Paul 1993–94	$13.00	S119			

Other Titles Available at Membership Prices

SPECIAL EDITIONS

	Retail Price	Code		Retail Price	Code
☐ Bed & Breakfast North America	$15.00	P002	☐ Marilyn Wood's Wonderful Weekends (within a 250-mile radius of NYC)	$12.00	P017
☐ Bed & Breakfast Southwest	$16.00	P100	☐ National Park Guide 1993	$15.00	P101
☐ Caribbean Hideaways	$16.00	P103	☐ Where to Stay U.S.A.	$15.00	P102

GAULT MILLAU'S "BEST OF" GUIDES
(The only guides that distinguish the truly superlative from the merely overrated)

	Retail Price	Code		Retail Price	Code
☐ Chicago	$16.00	G002	☐ New England	$16.00	G010
☐ Florida	$17.00	G003	☐ New Orleans	$17.00	G011
☐ France	$17.00	G004	☐ New York	$17.00	G012
☐ Germany	$18.00	G018	☐ Paris	$17.00	G013
☐ Hawaii	$17.00	G006	☐ San Francisco	$17.00	G014
☐ Hong Kong	$17.00	G007	☐ Thailand	$18.00	G019
☐ London	$17.00	G009	☐ Toronto	$17.00	G020
☐ Los Angeles	$17.00	G005	☐ Washington, D.C.	$17.00	G017

THE REAL GUIDES
(Opinionated, politically aware guides for youthful budget-minded travelers)

	Retail Price	Code		Retail Price	Code
☐ Able to Travel	$20.00	R112	☐ Kenya	$12.95	R015
☐ Amsterdam	$13.00	R100	☐ Mexico	$11.95	R128
☐ Barcelona	$13.00	R101	☐ Morocco	$14.00	R129
☐ Belgium/Holland/ Luxembourg	$16.00	R031	☐ Nepal	$14.00	R018
☐ Berlin	$13.00	R123	☐ New York	$13.00	R019
☐ Brazil	$13.95	R003	☐ Paris	$13.00	R130
☐ California & the West Coast	$17.00	R121	☐ Peru	$12.95	R021
☐ Canada	$15.00	R103	☐ Poland	$13.95	R131
☐ Czechoslovakia	$15.00	R124	☐ Portugal	$16.00	R126
☐ Egypt	$19.00	R105	☐ Prague	$15.00	R113
☐ Europe	$18.00	R122	☐ San Francisco & the Bay Area	$11.95	R024
☐ Florida	$14.00	R006	☐ Scandinavia	$14.95	R025
☐ France	$18.00	R106	☐ Spain	$16.00	R026
☐ Germany	$18.00	R107	☐ Thailand	$17.00	R119
☐ Greece	$18.00	R108	☐ Tunisia	$17.00	R115
☐ Guatemala/Belize	$14.00	R127	☐ Turkey	$13.95	R027
☐ Hong Kong/Macau	$11.95	R011	☐ U.S.A.	$18.00	R117
☐ Hungary	$14.95	R118	☐ Venice	$11.95	R028
☐ Ireland	$17.00	R120	☐ Women Travel	$12.95	R029
☐ Italy	$18.00	R125	☐ Yugoslavia	$12.95	R030